D1563117

Constitutional Problems Under Lincoln

Constitutional Problems Under Lincoln

Revised Edition

by J. G. Randall

Professor of History Emeritus

THE UNIVERSITY OF ILLINOIS

GLOUCESTER, MASS.

PETER SMITH

1963

Reprinted, 1963
By Permission of
UNIVERSITY OF ILLINOIS PRESS

TO

Ruth Painter Randall

CONTENTS

FOREWORD TO THE REVISED EDITION

This book was published in 1926, but for a number of years it has been out of print. To make it once more available is the chief motive of the present republication, but the opportunity has been used to correct errors found in the original, to bring the bibliography up to date, to do considerable revision, to take account of Civil War material newly come to light, and, in a few instances, to indicate recent action and opinion concerning questions similar to those arising under Lincoln.

The volume was, and remains, a study based on sources. Treatises and secondary accounts have been examined so far as they exist, but the method of the book has been that of breaking new ground in an extensive searching of first-hand material for the Civil War period. The present treatment is of considerable length, but a number of other volumes could be produced without exhausting the theme. This could be illustrated in a score of ways. For example, let the student take the subject of the legal status of those who resided within the area of the seceded states. Were they all "rebels" merely because they inhabited so-called "rebel" territory? Then let him take that voluminous congressional document, *House Report No. 262*, 43 Congress, 1 session, in which the pronouncements of United States authorities on this topic are elaborately summarized. Having done this, let him ask himself what it all "adds up to." What did it mean, in Union legal interpretation, to be a "rebel"? By technical legal pronouncement it was understood that all who inhabited "insurrectionary" territory were "rebels." (*House Report* above cited, p. 6 ff.) But this signified very little in actuality. Men were not in fact prosecuted and punished for what was considered the crime of rebellion or treason. The complications and ramifications of this one topic would fill weighty tomes, yet this is but one of dozens of elaborate constitutional questions of the period. In view of the records, rules, reports, debates, investigations, briefs, decisions, dissents, orders, and learned polemics which the subject embraces, the present book may be regarded as a selection and a condensation. As was said in the preface of the original edition, many things have been left in the inkpot.

Conditions and techniques of research have undergone considerable "modernization" since the author's student days. Extensive use of photostats and microfilms, the development of archival administration together with superb archives buildings for state and nation, the availability of grants in aid, the processing of manuscripts, the preparation of archival guides and manuscript calendars, the expansion of government agencies with their own research staffs—all such things have served greatly to facilitate the procedures of historical study in America. When the author first used the papers of the attorney general's office, they were casually housed in an old-fashioned building in Washington, rented by the government; it was obvious that they had not been previously used for historical purposes. In that period documents pertaining to confiscation and captured property were found (after sifting the haystack) in what was correctly called the "miscellaneous division" of the treasury department. It was a kind of Old Curiosity Shop, where, as compensation for the labor, the student could at least have complete assurance that no one else in historical study had been over that mess of material before. (Contrary to the usual impression, such hard-to-find records are not always dry as dust. They contain significant human-interest material. The combing and searching of archives still remains to a large extent an undeveloped resource for historical investigation.)

The question of the Constitution in working adjustment with national life, and in relation to social, economic, and political motives, briefly sketched in the first chapter, has been examined more fully by the author elsewhere. ("The Interrelation of Social and Constitutional History," *Amer. Hist. Rev.*, XXV, 1-13, Oct., 1929). Constitutional history is more than a legal study. The historian must search the human factors that surround a "case." With the use of a variety of material, much of it in manuscript, he must penetrate beneath the formal pages of judicial decisions to discover, in terms of the personal equation and the contemporary setting, why a judge's mind inclines as it does, and why a President selects as he does (and has throughout American history) when he appoints judges.

Pronouncements of courts are not merely a matter for the legal fraternity or for books in a law library. Courts have not only great power over legislation; they exert far reaching control over economic forces; they are of large importance in the executive field. It was only by one vote, and only with the support of justices of his own choosing, that Lincoln escaped a most embarrassing rebuke of his use of the war power. In the five-to-four decision in the *Prize Cases* Lincoln's presidential acts early in the war were held valid, but only against a powerful minority which included Chief Justice Taney along with Nelson, Catron, and Clifford. Every one of the five who sustained Lincoln (Grier, Swayne, Davis, Miller, and Wayne) was, of course, indispensable in order to constitute a majority. Three of them—Swayne, Miller, and Davis—were of Lincoln's own choosing, while another—Wayne of Georgia—was of the deep South. A study of the case shows how slender was the thread on which this famous decision hung.

The effectiveness of the Constitution is a matter of democracy at work. An alert and well disposed public is essential if "equal justice under the law" is to be honored in the observance. The Constitution prohibits Congress from abridging freedom of speech and press; but (leaving aside the fact that, according to some authorities, this prohibition has been violated by Congress in 1798, in 1918, and later) the question whether we actually have liberty of spoken and written opinion rests with the community. Intolerance as to a certain type of opinion, or as to the rights of minorities, may be more of a controlling factor than constitutional pronouncements by robed justices. The extent to which the Supreme Court has come to the rescue when freedom of opinion and other civil rights of human beings have been abridged by Congress, has been exaggerated (See Henry W. Edgerton, in *Cornell Law Quarterly*, 1937), and in any case the effectiveness of what both Congress and the courts have said depends in the last analysis upon the determined will of the American people to make constitutionally protected rights a continuing reality. In a true sense the people have the power of superior appeal.

When this is remembered, one of the impressive things in American history is the high degree of prestige of the Supreme Court, whose decisions as a rule are observed and obeyed without the necessity or even the suggestion of punitive action by the Court itself, through its marshal. Though in some respects the American people have a tendency toward lawlessness, as Lincoln sadly noted in his address to the Young Men's Lyceum,[1] they have for the most part shown a great respect for their highest tribunal. Where the opposite is true, the fact is highly exceptional. The power and effectiveness of the Court depend not so much upon physical force as upon the basic purpose, public awareness, and fair-minded attitude of the people. All this serves to emphasize the obligation of the Court to keep step with the times, and to remember that its far reaching power must be wielded in adaptation to the social and economic needs of a complex world. The Court may make mistakes, but public opinion is brought to bear by free discussion, and there is always the chance of ultimate reversal.

Where a democracy faces a tremendous war challenge there are two conflicting problems that necessarily arise. (1) There is the question of preserving civil rights, remembering that opponents at home, and also the enemy, have rights. (2) There is at the same time the necessity of getting ahead with the wartime task, and not allowing dissent at home to go so far as to force the nation down to destruction. Opposition is useful while matters are being discussed in order to decide how the national effort shall be focused. When that focusing has been fixed, and the nation is committed to a policy, or when it is engaged in a life-and-death struggle, there may yet be value in some opposition, but not in the kind

[1] J. G. Nicolay and John Hay, eds., *Complete Works of Abraham Lincoln*, I, 35-50. Where Lincoln's words are quoted, the reference (unless otherwise stated) is to the twelve-volume edition of Nicolay and Hay. Hereafter in the foreword, citations to this work will be merely to volume and page. The date of Lincoln's notable address before the Young Men's Lyceum (incorrectly given by Nicolay and Hay as 1837) was January 27, 1838.

that is no better than partisanship, or negative obstructionism, or irresponsible accusation, or maneuvers to embarrass or block the existing administration. Yet this latter type of opposition can hardly be suppressed in a democracy. That is another way of saying that if the people themselves fall short, then democracy to that extent fails. Faith in the people, and intelligent response by the people to justify that faith, are democratic prerequisites. Yet this is not all: governmental safeguards should be so devised as to give effect to genuine popular mandates, and men in public trust should never forget their duty to discover, understand, and not distort, the people's will.

Many people seem to think that it is only a despotism or dictatorship that accomplishes results or "gets things done." The record is far otherwise. The War of 1914 was not won by the undemocratic Central Powers. Wilson's message, even within the boundaries of those powers, was a tremendous force in that war. Except for partisan obstructionism in the Senate, the Wilsonian democratic message could have been of tremendous importance in world peace. Nor was the Axis War of 1939-1945 won by the tyrannical despotisms of the Nazis and Fascists. Not all the horrors of Buchenwald, torture chambers, the gestapo, slave labor, master-race ideology, genocide, anti-Semitism, Lidice, and Himmlerism could bring victory to the Axis.

In broad periods of peace, and in the fearful debacle of war, it is the democracies that have proved the more "efficient," though war-making performance is not the main argument for democracy; that argument is set in a frame of sanity, and of life in its regular course, not of war. Its success in war is rather offered as proof that despotisms fail even at those points where they are supposed to have special advantages or talents. The failure of authoritarian or tyrannical powers in peace is evidenced by the constant terrorism of a pervasive state police to bolster up their artificial regimes. The fact that they have stupidly started, and ultimately lost, great wars, while also failing in peace, is one of the unforgettable lessons of modern times. The failure of democracies has been in not binding together the strength of peace-minded nations in effective cooperation for the purpose of preventing war. These nations simply did not use the commanding power for order and peace that they potentially had in the decades from 1919 to 1939.

When the true validity of democracy is more widely recognized in a sick and deranged world, men abroad will understand the significance of the American constitutional example, and Americans at home will remember that the strength of the nation lies in the force and integrity of the democratic principle; they will realize the folly of imitating the cynical and unfair tactics of totalitarian regimes.

To develop this type of understanding it is important to know the whole record of American constitutional development. In that national story the period of Lincoln is but one of many chapters, but it is a chapter deserving of study and restudy. Some of the measures seemed drastic, such as the use of martial law and arbitrary arrests, but the Lincoln administration, after all, conducted the conflict *in vinculis*. Stanton's secret police was deplorable, but it was exceedingly mild by "modern" standards. The Union government did not go to the limit of the war power, nor descend to the low level of barbarity shown in recent examples. Smearing and character assassination were not Lincolnian devices. (The nearest approach to that was in the congressional committee on the conduct of the war, which became an unfair instrument of radical inquisition. See *The Civil War and Reconstruction*, 367-370; also bibliography under W. W. Pierson and T. Harry Williams.)

It should be remembered that the Lincoln administration planned ahead, looked to a continuing nation, and gave thought to the coming period of peace. Not only in conducting war should the Lincoln regime be remembered, but also in emancipation, in state-and-federal adjustment, in railroad promotion, homesteads, land-grant colleges, agricultural advance, freedom of the press (departures from that freedom being untypical), freedom of opinion, and promotion of liberal causes. If the present volume is occupied with war problems, the period should be viewed in the broader setting of the nation's purpose and destiny, of which Lincoln was ever conscious.

Lincoln did not play up the "glories" of war. In 1848 he referred to Polk's uneasy conscience: "he feels the blood of this [Mexican] war, like the blood of Abel, is crying to Heaven against him." With scathing bitterness he then spoke of "the exceeding brightness of military glory,—that attractive rainbow that arises in showers of blood." (I, 341.) As to war's by-products he wrote in 1863: "Thought is forced from old channels into confustion . . . Confidence dies and universal suspicion reigns. . . . Every foul bird comes abroad and every dirty reptile rises up." (IX, 157.) He did not believe that war was "inevitable." In his first inaugural he said he would act "with a view and a hope of a peaceful solution of the national troubles." (VI, 176.) The present writer is not impressed with the argument that such statements constituted a trick or maneuver, that Lincoln had cryptic and hidden purposes, that his motives were "provocative," and that his solemn declarations were a kind of deception. On this controversial subject one line of interpretation is given in the article by Charles W. Ramsdell, "Lincoln and Fort Sumter," *Jour. of So. Hist.*, III, 259-288 (1937). Ramsdell's argument is that Lincoln deliberately maneuvered to have the South "fire the first shot"—i.e., that Lincoln really intended to bring on war. The present author does not agree, as a matter of historical fact, with this representation of Lincoln's motives. (See *Lincoln the Liberal Statesman*, chap. iv; see also Kenneth M. Stampp, *And the War Came: The North and the Secession Crisis* [1950].)

In the treatment of this subject, reliable clues have been overlooked, while stock phrases which misrepresent Lincoln's purpose are tiresomely repeated. One should remember Lincoln's statement to Mrs. Gurney in September 1862: "If I had had my way, this war would never have been commenced." (VIII, 51.) To brush this statement aside as insincere is a kind of dodge; accusations of insincerity should never be raised unless proved. To take bodies of evidence showing Lincoln's peaceful appeals and efforts and wave them aside by the too-easy assertion that the President did not mean what he was saying, or intend what he was doing, is simply to color the whole treatment by an author's interpretations and conjectures.

If one thinks of Lincoln's statesmanship only as strategy, he misses the main point. Lincoln sensed the significance of an enduring world problem. In his keen awareness of the evils of society, and the social abuses that needed correction, he did not believe that war was the civilized answer. He said in that first inaugural, which needs constantly to be restudied and quoted: "My countrymen, one and all, think calmly and well upon this whole subject. Nothing valuable can be lost by taking time. . . . Intelligence, patriotism, Christianity, and a firm reliance on Him who has never forsaken this favored land, are still competent to adjust in the best way all our present difficulty." (VI, 184.)

There is also the statement in his second inaugural which bears upon the subject of 1861 intent. Recalling his inaugural of four years before, he mentioned that it was "devoted altogether to saving the Union without war." (XI, 44-45.) There is a certain Lincolnian verity and sanity in the comment of Bonar Law: "There is no such thing as inevitable war. If war comes it will be from failure of human wisdom." (Burton Stevenson, ed., *The Home Book of Quotations*, 5th edition, p. 2108. For similar but not identical words by Bonar Law, see *Parliamentary Debates*, Ser. 5, Vol. LXV, p. 2084.)

Nor did Lincoln believe in "preventive war." In his letter to Herndon of February 15, 1848, he denounced the idea that the President could order an invasion on the supposition that this was necessary in order to "repel" an "expected" invasion. (II, 2.) War is sometimes called an "instrument of national policy," but Lincoln did not consider it so. "Suppose you go to war [he said], you cannot fight always; and when, after much loss on both sides, and no gain on either, you cease fighting, the identical old questions . . . are again upon you." (VI, 181-182.)

Lincoln did not favor retaliation in the sense of using vengeful and brutal methods on the understanding—or report— that such methods had been used by the other side. His attitude in this matter was shown in a number of cases—e.g., in connection with the affair at Fort Pillow, Tennessee (April 12, 1864), when Confederates under General N. B. Forrest attacked Negro troops and killed hundreds of them instead of taking them prisoners. (It was alleged and believed at the North, but denied by Forrest, that this amounted to a massacre of men of color who had surrendered.) There was considerable agitation about this incident, which was of precisely the sort to stir up the war mind. Lincoln avoided retaliation after a very careful study of the subject in consultation with his cabinet, whose opinions he requested in writing. (R. T. Lincoln Collection, Libr. of Cong., nos. 32780-32920.) In a letter to the Secretary of War which has recently come to light (May 17, 1864) he used the significant expression, "blood can not restore blood, and government should not act for revenge." (Not in Lincoln's *Works;* photostat in files of Abraham Lincoln Association; and see *Indianapolis Star, Dec. 12, 1948.*) A conflict with "no weapons barred" was not his policy.

This subject offers another example of difficulty arising from a study of history based on proclamations, orders, and other public documents without a full examination of the setting, circumstances, and sequel of such orders. On July 30, 1863, Lincoln issued an order of retaliation proclaiming that "for every soldier of the United States killed in violation of the laws of war, a rebel soldier shall be executed." Such execution of Confederate prisoners, however, did not take place, and it would be a mistake to interpret the order as indicating that the purpose of the President was to have these executions. The purpose was, by showing firmness and threatening retaliation, to insure that rules of warfare as to the protection of prisoners, and as to non-discrimination because of race, would be observed. The pith and substance of the order is in the words: "The law of nations, and the usages and customs of war, as carried on by civilized powers, permit no distinction as to color in the treatment of prisoners of war . . . ." This matter of retaliation was one of the ugliest subjects of the war, in which Confederate declarations were angry and menacing, but the record is clear that Lincoln's main object was not actually to exercise retribution, but to make it unnecessary.

In this connection one must consider with great caution the familiar principle, or slogan, of "military necessity." (See below, pp. 26 ff., 512.) It is a tricky principle, having a conceivable element of truth, but being subject to great abuse and misapplication. There are times when public safety may require the use of otherwise illegal force. But procedures under martial law or military government are a matter of degree, of discretion, and of means chosen. Penalties and severity should be part and parcel of the emergency. They should not pass beyond what the situation actually demands.

In thinking of "military necessity," one should ask: Necessity for what? If the necessity is for an aggressive attack as upon Belgium in 1914, or for beginning a needless war, the "justification" becomes a self-condemnation. To uphold extreme and unlawful conduct on the ground that "necessity knows no law," a commander should be required to show that the main object is justified, that the case is desperate, that the public urgency is imperative, that the means chosen are without a reasonable alternative, and that these means are conducive to an honorable result. If wrongly applied, military necessity may be a fraud. Order itself should not be bought at too high, or too brutal, a price. No reputable commander will do a deeply dishonorable thing. Even at its best the invoking of "military necessity" is an admission that something wrongful or at least irregular is being done. One does not plead military necessity for an act of unquestionable validity or of normal legality. This applies to the whole subject of war including combat between armed forces, which has been the subject of repeated international regulation; but, for our purpose, it is especially applicable to matters of military government in its civil relationships.

Among the fundamentals announced in George Mason's eloquent document of 1776, the Virginia Declaration of Rights, is the statement that "the military should be under strict subordination to, and governed by, the civil power." There is no principle in the American system that is more important. Allow the military to "take over," and the way is opened for a *coup d'état*, for the flouting of a constitution, for the suppression of civil guarantees, and for armed force as the basis of setting up and overthrowing governments. The *coup d'état* is fortunately not an American custom. Military revolutions have not superseded elections. Even when a man of long-standing army service, and notable chiefly for that, has become President (a practice whose wisdom is rather doubtful), he is expected to function as a constitutional President, not as a military strong man.

The conduct of Lincoln in recognition of this principle is of great interest. He gave orders for the governing of the army, but that meant, among other things, that he could *overrule* generals. The main significance of having the President serve as Commander in Chief is to make sure that ultimate control of the army belongs to the civil power. This principle was stated on July 5, 1861, by Edward Bates, attorney general under Lincoln: "He [the President] is the chief civil magistrate of the nation and being such *and because he is such* [author's italics] he is the constitutional Commander in Chief of the Army and Navy, and thus within the limits of the Constitution he rules in peace and commands in war . . . ." (*War of the Rebellion: Official Records*, ser. II, vol. II, 29.)

Lincoln was not in uniform. He was not in the armed services, 1861-65. He was nevertheless Commander in Chief. One should not be misled by this title. A word may have more than one meaning. The army was under military "command," but under civilian direction. The military arm was the *instrument* of the government. To suppose the opposite—that the government should be the football or creature of the army—would be a complete negation of the American democratic concept.

Lincoln issued the emancipation proclamation of January 1, 1863, as "an act of justice, warranted by the Constitution upon military necessity," but the invoking of "military necessity" for emancipation was for a humanitarian purpose; it involved no army abuse. Over and over Lincoln insisted that military measures be employed with the utmost discretion and caution. Numerous examples of this are revealed in the records of his presidency. He rebuked one of the minor generals (J. G. Blunt) for "sending a military order . . . outside of your lines . . . to take men charged with no offense against the military, out of the hands of the courts, to be turned over to a mob to be hanged." Such action, said Lincoln, "can find no precedent or principle to justify it." (IX, 88.) In another case Lincoln wrote to General Butler warning against a military clash with the civil government of restored Virginia headed by Governor Pierpoint. He particularly objected to Butler's contemplated plan of conducting a vote of the people on a matter of wartime administration. A function of civil government, such as holding an election, ought not, in Lincoln's view, to be usurped by the military power. He added that this instruction did not cover "the case when the military commander, finding no friendly civil government existing, may, under the sanction or direction of the President, give assistance to the people to inaugurate one." (X, 321-323; and see *Lincoln and the South*, 121-123.)

Lincoln differed fundamentally from those Republican radicals of his day who wished to use the war for reducing the inhabitants of the Southern states to an inferior status. He repudiated the idea of carpetbag rule, disliked the confiscation acts, intended to veto the act of 1862 though he finally signed it, and in freeing the slaves proposed that slaveholders be compensated at the expense of the general government. He did this without wavering in his basic conviction that slavery was an evil and a shameful social abuse.

Democracy was Lincoln's lodestar in basic ethics, formal procedures, working relations, and human attitudes. Among the American fathers Jefferson was his guide; to none other of the early leaders did he owe so much. Though it has often been stated that the Constitution did not provide full democracy and did not re-enact the Declaration of Independence, this was not a talking point with Lincoln. The great Declaration was for him the subject of eloquent eulogy. He identified the Constitution with democracy, believing that the people of the nation were "the rightful masters of both congresses and courts, not to overthrow the Constitution, but to overthrow the men who pervert the Constitution." (V, 232.) In his speech at Kalamazoo, Michigan, August 27, 1856, he declared that the Constitution "must be maintained, for it is the only safeguard of our liberties." (Roy P. Basler, ed., *Abraham Lincoln: His Speeches and Writings*, 345; Thomas I. Starr, ed., *Lincoln's Kalamazoo Address Against Extending Slavery*.)

Lincoln was vigorous and eloquent in insisting on respect for law. This was the main theme of his address to the Young Men's Lyceum of Springfield in 1838 (sometimes misdated 1837), when he said: "As the patriots of seventy-six did to the support of the Declaration of Independence, so to the support of the Constitution and laws let every American pledge his life, his property, and his sacred honor. . . . Let reverence for the laws be breathed by every American mother to the lisping babe . . . .; let it be taught in schools, in seminaries, and in colleges; let it be written in primers, spelling-books, and in almanacs; let it be preached from the pulpit, proclaimed in legislative halls, and enforced in courts of justice. And, in short, let it become the political religion of the nation . . . ." (I, 43.)

Lincoln avoided the negative approach. He believed in purposeful government. He cautioned against that policy which is expressed in the words: "Do nothing at all, lest you do something wrong." (II, 31.) "Government," he said, "is a combination of the people of a country to effect certain objects by joint effort. . . . The legitimate object of government is 'to do for the people what needs to be done, but which they can not, by individual effort, do at all, or do so well, for themselves.' There are many such things . . . ." (II, 182-183.) Lincoln's idea that the government should serve the welfare of the people was implemented during his rule in emancipation, the homestead act, the creation of the department of agriculture, the land-grant-college measure, the national banking system, scientific support, government aid in the transcontinental railroad, and other measures. As a young man in the Illinois legislature in the 1830's he had gone "all out" for internal improvements at huge government expense.

The Federal Constitution, in Lincoln's view, was for the Federal union. It did not envisage the destruction of that union. Secession in his view was "void." Violence against the authority of the United States was "insurrectionary or revolutionary, according to circumstances." (VI, 175.) To adopt secession, he thought, was to go all the way to revolution; it was not to act within the Constitution. Southerners, of course, affirmed the opposite doctrine. Lincoln himself recognized that devotion to the Constitution was "equally great on both sides of the [Ohio] river." (VI, 123.) This subject is treated in the first chapter.

In applying the Constitution to changing conditions, Lincoln favored a policy of reasonable adaptation. To this end he opposed a stultifying interpretation that would cause the nation to be hung up on excessive verbalisms or dialetic. It was his view that "nothing should ever be implied as law which leads to unjust or absurd consequences." (VI, 317.) Remembering the saying, "the devil takes care of his own," he added: "Much more should a good spirit—the spirit of the Constitution and the Union—take care of its own. I think it cannot do less and live." (VIII, 158-159.) On March 4, 1861, he said: "I take the official oath to-day with no mental reservations, and with no purpose to construe the Constitution or laws by any hypercritical rules." (VI, 172-173.)

Lincoln had a high respect for the Supreme Court, but he had doubts as to the pontifical infallibility or the finality of its pronouncements. He protested against the notorious Dred Scott decision, not in any irreverent or factious sense, but simply as a refusal to consider the constitutional question closed by a decision which he regarded as undemocratic in effect and erroneous in legal doctrine. He uttered thousands of words on this subject. (Archer H. Shaw, *The Lincoln Encyclopedia*, 87-92.) He considered the decision wrongful, objected to its becoming a precedent, and expected its reversal. In his first inaugural he made an interesting distinction which is significant because Lincoln offered it, though the legal profession would probably not accept it. He did not deny that a constitutional decision by the Supreme Court "must be binding . . . upon the parties to a suit, as to the object of that suit," but he protested against a situation in which "the policy of the government, upon vital questions affecting the whole people, is to be irrevocably fixed by decisions of the Supreme Court . . . in ordinary litigation . . . ." If that should happen, he said, "the people will have ceased to be their own rulers, having to that extent practically resigned their government into the hands of that eminent tribunal." (VI, 179-180.)

The need for correlation of President, Congress, and Court, and of all these branches with the people, was well illustrated in the Lincoln administration. With all his other burdens pressing upon him, Lincoln had to consider how to choose justices with regard to fitness and at the same time recognize such a factor as geographical location, how to leave the way open for recognition of the South in the membership of a tribunal that would survive the temporary shattering of the Union, how to arrange the circuits among the nine justices, some of whom were very old, how to bring the Far West into the pattern of judicial organization, and how to deal with the tangled and complicated litigation arising in California with regard to mineral and land titles holding over from the Mexican regime.

Lincoln made five appointments of justices: Miller, Davis, Swayne, Field (for his understanding of California land questions), and Chase. There was a story with regard to each of these appointments, though they cannot be discussed here, and also with regard to the whole panel of possibilities that the President had to consider in narrowing each choice to one man. In addition, two important steps were taken by Lincoln which had a bearing upon the structural organization of the Court: circuit reorganization, and increase in membership. The law for the reorganization of the circuits (after discussion as to where to put Kentucky, whether to join Indiana with Ohio or with Illinois, how to equalize population, *et cetera*) became law on July 15, 1862. After this, Congress made an all-time record as to the number of justices on the supreme bench. The law of March 3, 1863, provided that the Court should consist of ten justices, a tenth circuit being added to the existing nine, in order to provide for California and Oregon. After much pulling and hauling during the reconstruction period in the matter of legislation concerning the Court, the number of justices was again set at nine in 1869 and has remained so ever since. (On these matters the author has had the use of the manuscript doctoral dissertation, "The Supreme Court during the Civil War," by David M. Silver, University of Illinois, 1940. It is Dr. Silver's intention to publish a book on this subject.)

Lincoln did not favor a weak executive. He was a strong President. If one looks back over American history he will find that practically all the Presidents regarded as outstanding or great were strong executives who asserted their influence as leaders of opinion and guardians of the nation's welfare. Lincoln did not consider that strength and influence in the executive was inconsistent with democracy. As the Civil War was *sui generis*, so Lincoln's strength was unique. It was not, as with Wilson, a matter of effective leadership in legislation and cooperation with Congress. Congress usually went its way; Lincoln, his. It was rare for Congress to pass a major law because Lincoln sponsored or urged it, and there were very few instances in which Lincoln used the veto. The most famous case was that of the Wade-Davis reconstruction bill in 1864. The general situation under Lincoln, not a very favorable one, was that of a President and a Congress who did not precisely pull together and yet who avoided an upheaval or an open clash.

There were times, it is true, when such a clash was narrowly averted. More than once Congress was in the mood to censure and thwart the President. The cabinet crisis of December 1862 was an example. (*Lincoln the President*, II, 241-249.) The manifesto by Wade and Davis in the summer of 1864 was not a congressional act, but it was a stinging denunciation of the President by two of the most influential leaders of the dominant element in Congress. Such a thing as a vote of confidence in the executive by the national legislature is foreign to the American practice. This presents an interesting speculation. If those who assail a chief of state must face up to the necessity of taking sides on a vote of confidence, and if, after carrying a vote in the negative, they are required to take over the responsibility of administration, as is true in the parliamentary type of government, that may clear the air, for it serves as an inhibition or sobering influence upon intemperate opponents and critics. Such, however, is not the American system.

That Lincoln was a strong executive does not, of course, signify that he was a dictator. Elections went forward during war, in striking contrast to European practice. Under Lincoln the Constitution was not set aside. He submitted in 1864 to the free choice of the people and stood ready to relinquish his position without protest to a rival if the people so voted. His famous memorandum of August 23, 1864, indicated that at that time he expected to lose the election, and was studying what his policy should be between election and inauguration in the event of such defeat. A democracy accepts risks, and one of them was the chance—a strong chance it seemed in the summer of 1864—that horses would actually be changed crossing the stream. No dictator would have tolerated such a possibility. But one should not belabor a point which is obvious. Since the word "dictator" suggests a Hitler or other totalitarian rulers, the contrast between their hideous methods and those of Lincoln is so evident that it needs no comment.

It is not argued that Lincoln's administration was without fault, and it does no harm in the appraisal of American democracy to remember that there have been improvements since then, just as there are further improvements yet overdue. Where praise is fulsome, uninformed, and uncritical, it is historically unconvincing. Eulogy is of greatest value when tied down to reality, and a favorable verdict carries more weight if both sides are heard. There were irregularities under Lincoln which have not become sound precedents, procedures which have not set the pattern for later executives. It would be idle to deny that mistakes occurred in the legislative, administrative, and military fields. Measures of that day would hardly be cited as models in such matters as cabinet government, relations between the Executive and Congress, State government in relation to the Federal, the formation of army units, the use of bounties in recruiting, or the Civil War type of conscription, whether considered from the standpoint of reasonable method or of results. There was fraud, profiteering, graft, and corruption. Lincoln was honest, but the same cannot be said of some who were concerned with army contracts, bounty brokerage, cotton manipulation, trading with the enemy, and the like.

There were heartaches and disappointments under Lincoln. He was the target of savage, sarcastic, and belittling criticism. No President has suffered more abuse, much of it from his own party. It was a tragic time. He did not prevent war, and it was not his peace that was carried out. Failure to prevent war, however, was not his fault, and as to the pattern of peace he did not fail in planning, while the dominant radicals of Congress, "successful" in the sense that they had their way, did fail both in planning and in execution.

Against these factors, however, which can be ignored only if one is giving a superficial treatment, one must remember Lincoln's spokesmanship for democracy, his craftsmanship in the human art of government, his manner of meeting and answering criticism instead of eliminating dissenters, his steps toward the elevation of the Negro race, his avoidance of dictatorial excess, his development of new governmental resources, his support of welfare measures, his sense of balance, self control, skill of management, breadth of outlook, and concentration on the main issue. Not everyone can wear Lincoln's hat, nor should others try it, but no leader could fail to profit by a study of his spirit, his principles, and his method.

That Lincoln's "stretching" of the Constitution did not cause the people to lose their liberties was due to a number of factors which will appear in later pages. Especially there was Lincoln's dislike of arbitrary rule, his reasonableness in practical adjustment, and his disinclination toward military excess. Severity of wartime control was tempered, clemency was readily bestowed, practice was milder than theory, and certain orders of army officers were overruled.

One must avoid the mistake of supposing that every principle asserted for the sake of legal consistency, or of prestige abroad, was made effective, or that every harsh measure of Congress was carried into practical execution. The confiscation act of 1862, which should not be thought of as if intended to allot lands to Negroes (that was not the provision), occasioned a prodigious amount of congressional oratory, but it was not enforced by the tiny staff of Edward Bates, attorney general. Some of the district attorneys tried to enforce it, but the total result was very small. This non-enforcement of the act applied both to property in the usual sense, and to slaves of "persons . . . in rebellion." Such slaves were pronounced "free," but this was by a loose legislative phrasing which did not amount to a legal divesting of title, nor a provision as to just how title should be divested in a situation where it was clear that not all slaves were included. In consequence, this feature of the law was not carried out; it amounted to little more than a paper declaration. (See below, pp. 362-363.) Nor should one place too much stress on the fact that the Confederacy was not "recognized." It was not, to be sure, conceded to have international standing as an established nation, and it should be noted that no foreign country gave recognition of such standing. It was, of course, not admitted that the Richmond government had supplanted or superseded the government of the United States for the South—i.e., that the Union was permanently broken. Human beings, however, were not made to suffer for such lack of recognition. Belligerent rights were "conceded," usages of war were applied to Southern armies, and Grant's terms to Lee in April 1865 included an important guarantee that men and officers would not be prosecuted.

In the problem of subversive activity Lincoln did not forget that government through law is one of the fundamental American values. He understood the importance of effective loyalty tests instead of name calling, of fair-minded procedures in place of an irresponsible witch hunt. Referring to lawless outrages in his day, he warned against "the growing disposition to substitute the wild and furious passions in lieu of the sober judgment of courts, and the worse than savage mobs for the executive ministers of justice." (I, 37.) If persons were accused of disloyalty, he believed that they ought "not to be punished without regular trials in our duly constituted courts under the forms and all the substantial provisions of law and of the Constitution . . . ." (VII, 281.) Even in time of war he was "slow to adopt" extreme measures. (VIII, 303.) He realized that if "innocent persons" were arrested, the resulting "clamor" would be "of some service to the insurgent cause" (*ibid.*). He favored an oath of loyalty as a genuine pledge (a very simple one), and of course he recognized that a man could be prosecuted for what he had done in the past if criminal or illegal, but he wrote: "On principle I dislike an oath which requires a man to swear he has not done wrong. It rejects the Christian principle of forgiveness on terms of repentance. I think it is enough if the man does no wrong hereafter." (IX, 303.)

In the case of Vallandigham, the most prominent and forceful of Northern agitators against the Union war effort, Lincoln avoided suppressive measures. The Supreme Court did not overrule the action of the military commission in this case, but Lincoln set aside the sentence of imprisonment and promptly substituted exile within the Confederate lines. Vallandigham soon reappeared in the North, bursting with anti-Lincoln propaganda, but in this later phase Lincoln simply let him alone. Under this silent treatment the agitator's degree of influence depended upon events and upon popular reaction to his attacks. That reaction was favorable to Lincoln, as was shown in the Ohio election for governor in 1863, when Vallandigham was defeated by a strong Unionist (John Brough), and in the presidential election of 1864, when Democratic defeat was due in part to a "peace platform" (deemed pro-Confederate) adopted with the influence of the Vallandigham element in the Chicago convention. The whole episode showed that in permitting vigorous expression of dissent in war time, and in allowing opposition newspapers to operate (suppressions being exceptional), the Lincoln government showed a high regard for citizens' rights under the most trying conditions.

It is in keeping with Lincoln's view to hold that loyalty is not enforced conformity. "It is allegiance to the traditions that have guided our greatest statesmen and inspired our most eloquent poets—the traditions of freedom, equality, democracy, tolerance . . . . It is a realization that America was born of revolt, flourished on dissent, became great through experimentation." (Henry Steele Commager, "Who Is Loyal to America?" *Harper's Magazine*, Sep. 1947, p. 198.) After mentioning the "fast-failing efforts of our present totalitarian enemies," the Supreme Court of the United States, in the Barnette case, declared: "Those who begin coercive elimination of dissent soon find themselves exterminating dissenters. Compulsory unification of opinion achieves only the unanimity of the graveyard." (319 U.S. 624; quoted by Commager in the article just cited.) In a period of terrific wartime agitation in Missouri Lincoln advised General Schofield to be cautious as to armed coercion and "to use it [the military establishment] as far as practicable to compel the excited people there to leave one another alone." (IX, 147-148.) The word "compel" in that passage is of special interest. It suggests the compulsion of democracy, of self control, of discipline, of give-and-take, of restraint among men whose opinions differ but who nevertheless have a common stake in the right to live and in the maintenance of public safety. It was in this connection that Lincoln gave his significant instruction against the use of suppressive measures in the realm of opinion. (See below, p. 508.)

It has been well said of Lincoln: "He made effective weapons of truths as old as mankind, and as ever new as tomorrow morning. . . . Neither time nor circumstance alters them." (Archer H. Shaw, ed., *The Lincoln Encyclopedia*, x.) Times change, but Lincoln's words are timeless, Often they have the quality of proverbs, but not as superficial truisms. Stereotypes, catchwords, or repetitious phrases of political cant were not his stock in trade. There has been, however, no intention to develop the lessons and parallels of Lincoln's problems for the decades that followed 1865. (See bibliography, below, under C. Herman Pritchett.) Problems under Wilson have been very briefly mentioned, but the tremendous issues of "World War II," and beyond, have not been canvassed. That is because they do not lie within the scope of this book. The midpoint of the "so-called twentieth century" can, of course, learn much from the past, and from Lincoln. Thoughts of present issues—occupation of enemy lands, peace making on a world basis, war-crime trials, and the colossal stupidity of war in an atomic age—come before us, and it is firmly believed that in the best of American political traditions, and in the United Nations, one may find the answer, but the tasks are so challenging and far reaching that facile treatment or superficial analogies would be a disservice.

Military treatment of our mounting problems, and legal treatment, are not enough. Never before in American history has there been such a vast expansion of the armed forces in time of peace as since 1945. As Lincoln said, "we cannot escape history." (VIII, 131.) The dilemma of our time is to remember that weakness may invite war in a predatory world, but also to be ever alert so that preparations for possible war, and constant talk of such preparations, may not tend actually to touch off the explosion. Blame for war is not to be shifted or diffused into thin air by setting up the orders of a "state," or a chief of state, as a shield for criminality; and by present standards—belatedly asserted in the Nuremberg trials—aggressive war is itself a crime. In the charter of the United Nations and elsewhere the United States is solemnly pledged not to commit that crime. It will be well to remember the spirit of Lincoln as we face a great moral issue: super-weapons on an incredible scale are constantly developed, but their true service for civilization is in terms of their not being used. It is said often, and it cannot for a moment be overlooked, that they are useful in the genuine American sense only as a deterrent. Their purpose is primarily to deter an aggressive nation from making an attack; their legitimate object would certainly not be to start a "preventive war."

To read "the laws and customs of war" is a disheartening business. Not so long ago students of international law learned of established rules on a variety of subjects—the manner of beginning hostilities, treatment of prisoners, the sparing of non-combatants, denying wholesale deportation, avoiding the bombardment of cities, guaranteeing neutral territory, and so on—but now the mere mention of such rules seems curiously dated, and if poison gas has been but little used in recent warfare, the main reason is not a sense of civilized restraint, but a fear of retaliation, and, more especially, the danger of poisoning the air for the nation's own troops. Hague conventions and their successors have not solved the ironic problem of mitigating the conduct of war.

The idea that any nation may legitimately begin a war, but that methods of slaughter may be softened, is hopeless. The solution must be found elsewhere. The only hope of free nations—not merely as a matter of "ideals," but of survival—lies in the prevention of war. One may deride the idea of "One World," but it is more evident now than ever that all peoples belong to the world fraternity; their concern as to the necessity of peace is universal. The United States foolishly wasted one of its greatest resources—the principle and program of Wilson for international order. Had the United States used its potent leadership thirty years ago through the League of Nations to maintain a united front of peace-minded countries, the overwhelming strength of those countries could have been asserted without an unreasonably large armament, the doom of a despotic aggressor could have been made certain in advance, and Hitler could have been stopped without war. Thus the untold confusion since 1939, and since 1945, would not have resulted.

Wilson's great difficulty, as Lincoln's in planning for peace, was division at home. (*Lincoln the Liberal Statesman*, chap. vii.) Lincoln and Wilson to the contrary notwithstanding, wars that could have been averted have been allowed to come, and each new war makes the problems of continued peace—or even of inaugurating a state of peace—more confused and difficult.

It is a great irony that the wholesome sanity of the vast majority of nations and governments which might have been rallied to prevent the Axis War is now faced by the tragically overgrown power of a madly aggressive few who could plunge the world into another debacle of war, to be followed by another unpredictable postwar muddle.

The President who was re-inaugurated in 1865 was not merely using beautiful words when he advised "a just and lasting peace among ourselves, and with all nations." (XI, 47.) In 1861 he had said: "this issue embraces more than the fate of these United States." (VI, 304.) His views, including his ideas of peace and war, and of constitutional democracy, are not to be discussed as if they had validity only for his country, or only for the 1860's. As the problems of each new era unfold, we recur, and never without profit, to fundamental principles as stated by Lincoln.

June 20, 1950 J. G. R.

ACKNOWLEDGMENTS

In remembering those who have given guidance, comment, and help in specific research the writer realizes the deficiency of any acknowledgment. Friends who have given service cannot be adequately thanked, and some of them are no longer with us. Yet the author must record his debt to C. H. Van Tyne, A. C. McLaughlin, William E. Dodd, Helen Nicolay, Avery Craven, A. J. Harno, C. A. Berdahl, W. S. Robertson, T. C. Pease, H. J. Eckenrode, and Earl G. Swem. Of great value has been the assistance of the Library of Congress (divisions of law, legislative reference, bibliography, and manuscripts); the National Archives; the attorney general's office; and various agencies of the University of Illinois—the Library, the Research Board, and the Graduate College. Recent work pertaining to republication has been greatly assisted by Frank Freidel, especially with reference to Lieber; and by Charles M. Kneier with reference to military government. Special mention must be made of the capable work of Wayne Temple, graduate student and research assistant at Illinois.

CONSTITUTIONAL PROBLEMS UNDER LINCOLN

CHAPTER I

INTRODUCTION

I. The relation of constitutional questions to social motives and forces
II. Growth and adaptation of the American Constitution to meet the needs of a developing nation
III. Conditions and influences affecting judicial decisions
IV. Constitutional phases of the question of secession: Possibility of regarding the question as extra-constitutional

I

The purpose of this volume is to examine those measures of the Lincoln Government which involved significant constitutional issues. The American Civil War began with an elaborate constitutional discussion over the right of a State to secede from the Union, and as the great struggle progressed, a notable succession of legal problems demanded attention. Never before or since has the Government of the United States been subjected to such a severe test. While Lincoln spoke of the cause for which he contended as no less than the maintenance of democracy in the world, such a man as Wendell Phillips denounced Lincoln's government as a "fearful peril to democratic institutions" and characterized the President as an "unlimited despot."[1] In the

[1]As quoted by John Hay, Lincoln said: "I consider the central idea pervading this struggle is the necessity . . . of proving that popular

doubtful struggle to preserve the Union, the war Congress and the war Cabinet had many a hard choice to make when measures out of harmony with American notions of civil liberty seemed the only alternative to defeat and disintegration. "Must a government, of necessity, be too strong for the liberties of its own people, or too weak to maintain its own existence?"[2] was the question Lincoln propounded when making one of his difficult decisions, and this question embodied a real dilemma which his government continually confronted. To study in some detail, both historically and legally, the manner in which these constitutional problems of the Civil War presented themselves, to note the measures taken in solving them, and to offer such an appraisal of these measures as historical research may justify, is our task. In approaching this task, some introductory comment upon constitutional interpretation may be of profit.

Whether any great question is primarily "constitutional" is doubtful. Laws and constitutions have importance not in themselves, but because of the social purposes which they embody. The question of nullification, for instance, was first of all social and economic; only in a secondary sense was it constitutional. In South Carolina there were certain conditions of society which

---

government is not an absurdity." *Diaries of John Hay*, Dennett, ed., 19. On the eve of the Civil War W. H. Russell wrote to John Bigelow: "Every friend of despotism rejoices at your misfortune; . . . it is assuredly a grave and serious obstacle to the march of constitutional liberty." (Russell to Bigelow, London, Feb. 4, 1861: Bigelow, *Retrospections of an Active Life*, I, 346.) For Phillips' views see his speeches; also, Nicolay and Hay, *Abraham Lincoln: A History*, IX, 37, and J. F. Rhodes, *History of the United States from the Compromise of 1850 to the Final Restoration of Home Rule at the South in 1877*, III, 558. Joel Parker of the Harvard Law School referred to Lincoln as a government in himself, "an absolute, . . . uncontrollable government; a perfect military despotism." (*Ibid.*, IV, 169.)

[2]Nicolay and Hay, *Complete Works of Abraham Lincoln* VI, 304.

the political leaders of the State deemed important; and the State-rights view, with the nullification theory as a corollary, was urged not for its own sake, but as an essential means of defending and preserving these conditions. The motives that produced the nullification principle, the real springs of action, were social and economic; the arguments were constitutional. Economic factors connected with secession cause scholars to regard it as more than a movement for constitutional rights.[3] For the Constitution itself there is the "economic interpretation,"[4] and for Jeffersonian principles an economic basis has been argued.[5] The desire to protect property interests, as a stabilizing social force, may in large part account for the constitutional views of Hamilton and his followers, and even of Washington himself; but if the constitutional opinions of these men be studied for their own sake, these underlying motives might well

[3]The theme that the South was the great producing section while the North was the wealth-accumulating section was eloquently though rather unscientifically developed by T. P. Kettell in *Southern Wealth and Northern Profits*, published on the eve of the Civil War. He set forth elaborate figures to show how the North kept the South in comparative poverty and economic dependence through its control of manufacturing, shipping, banking, and international trade. There are many articles along the same line in the pages of *DeBow's Review* for the fifties.

[4]"The members of the [constitutional] Convention were, with a few exceptions, . . . personally interested in . . . the establishment of the new system. The Constitution was essentially an economic document. . . . [It] was ratified by a vote of probably not more than one-sixth of the adult males. . . . The leaders who supported the Constitution in the ratifying conventions represented the same economic groups as the members of the Philadelphia convention. . . . In the ratification, it became manifest that the line of cleavage for and against the Constitution was between substantial personalty interests . . . and the small farming and debtor interests. . . . The Constitution . . . was the work of a consolidated group whose interests knew no State boundaries and were truly national in their scope." (Charles A. Beard, *An Economic Interpretation of the Constitution of the United States*, 324-325.)

[5]Charles A. Beard, *Economic Origins of Jeffersonian Democracy.*

escape notice. What Hamilton said about implied powers should always be read in the light of the fact that Hamilton wanted a national bank, and that, in general, he wanted a strong government for the stabilization of the particular economic system to which he was devoted. Not always do the words of a speech reveal the speaker's motive. True historical insight must penetrate through the statements, writings, and arguments of political leaders to the broad human purposes which they were seeking to accomplish.[6] Viewed in this light, constitutional history becomes a part, and an important part, of social history.

A familiar example showing how social motives control constitutional interpretation appears in connection with the tendency toward "rebuilding the nation on interstate commerce." As a social observer has written with some exaggeration, "Once . . . we had need of a Constitution with many sections . . . and clauses: . . . now one is sufficient . . . the power to regulate interstate commerce."[7] The suppression of rebates and discriminating charges by railroads, the inspection of foodstuffs, the restriction of vice, the prevention of accidents—all these great social purposes have, so to speak, surged against the constitutional barriers until they have broken through; and the interstate commerce clause is the breach through which they have passed.

This social utilization of the Constitution, so familiar in our own time, is not a new thing; and in the treatment of former periods of our history it is well to seek out the social motives constituting the reality of which constitutional arguments are but the reflection. Only

---

[6]The development of political theories to meet political needs runs as a central theme through the pages of C. L. Becker, *The Declaration of Independence.*

[7]Shailer Mathews, *The Making of Tomorrow*, 180.

so may we preserve the important study of constitutional history, and yet retain a due sense of proportion toward those influences of social development which are the great factors of human progress.

II

It will profit the student of history and politics to broaden his view and definition of the Constitution. As Woodrow Wilson said, the Constitution "cannot be regarded as a legal document." It must be "a vehicle of life."[8] Wholly apart from the matter of amendment, the Constitution is more than the instrument of 1787. Just as the word "constitution" in England denotes the whole body of law covering fundamentals of government which successive generations of Englishmen have built up, so in America the Constitution is a matter of growth, development, and interpretation. Constitutional history is not the study of a document, but rather of a social process—the process by which a community re-expresses from time to time its will concerning its government, refitting, reinterpreting and expanding its fundamental law so as to keep abreast of new issues. In this process the Constitution is gradually being molded to fit the nation as a garment is shaped to fit the wearer. It is the nation wearing the Constitution, so to speak, and breathing and acting within it, that we should have in view; and it is only because the American Constitution is fortunately not a strait-jacket that the growing nation has been able substantially to preserve it.[9]

---

[8]Woodrow Wilson, *Constitutional Government in the United States*, 192.

[9]"The effort to continue uninterruptedly in accord with a federal Constitution . . . made at a time . . before the railroad, before the telegraph, before the thousand and one changes that have broken

One of the Civil War writers, Whiting, has given us an excellent statement of the adaptability of our Constitution. The narrow constructionists, he says, "have supposed it incapable of adaptation to our changing conditions, as if it were a form of clay, which the slightest jar would shatter; or an iron chain girdling a living tree which could have no further growth unless by bursting its rigid ligature. But sounder judges believe that it more resembles the tree itself, native to the soil that bore it, waxing strong in sunshine and in storm, putting forth branches, leaves, and roots, according to the laws of its own growth. . . . Our Constitution, like that of England, contains all that is required to adapt itself to the present and future changes and wants of a free and advancing people."[10]

Where a constitution has this quality of adaptability, it becomes especially important to distinguish between the constitution on paper and the constitution in reality. The practical application of any document prescribing a fundamental law necessarily proceeds by a sort of "trial and error" system, and while certain clauses of the constitution are enormously expanded in their application, others are not put into practical effect. A stranger to our institutions would, in fact, obtain only an incorrect and artificial conception of our government if he confined his attention to the Constitution itself. He would have to be told that certain features of the Constitution are never carried out in practice, while some of the most fundamental powers of our government are exercised without any definite constitutional

---

down State barriers in fact and welded us in reality, if not in law, into one mass in many . . . particulars . . . has . . . demanded numerous adjustments. These adjustments have been made easy in part by the general terms in which the Constitution . . . is framed." (A. C. McLaughlin, *The Courts, the Constitution, and Parties*, 283-284.)

[10] Whiting, *War Powers under the Constitution*, 9.

authorization. He would have to learn that the President is not in reality chosen by the electoral college; that his power to adjourn Congress has never been exercised; that taxes have rarely been apportioned according to population, and that certain reconstruction amendments have not been enforced; while the power of the courts to declare laws invalid, together with many other governmental powers, have no constitutional basis beyond more or less reasonable inference.[11]

One of the frequent faults of constitutional discussion is an excessive reliance upon the political wisdom of a by-gone generation. In this attitude of mind one is apt to attach a particular sanctity to debates contemporaneous with the generation which established the Constitution, as for instance the discussion that took place during Jefferson's administration concerning the suspension of the *habeas corpus* privilege. It cannot be denied that in the minds of judges, closeness to the time of the constitutional convention is often regarded as giving special weight to a debate or an opinion. Nor is this tendency peculiar to conservatives, for the spectacle of radicals appealing to "the Fathers" is by no means unusual. It is an old trick of reformers to preach a return to the purer and higher principles of the past.

But is this backward look wholesome? Is there, after all, anything "sacred" about the Constitution? Time has amply attested the wisdom and even the remarkable

[11]A. C. McLaughlin finds ample basis in the "natural right" philosophy, in the principle of separation of powers, and in American experience prior to 1787, for the notion that the courts may declare a law unconstitutional. E. S. Corwin points out that "judicial review was rested by the framers . . . upon certain general principles which in their estimation made specific provisions for it unnecessary." (A. C. McLaughlin, *The Courts, the Constitution, and Parties*, 3-107; E. S. Corwin, *The Doctrine of Judicial Review*, 17.) See also C. G. Haines, *The American Doctrine of Judicial Supremacy*, and C. A. Beard, *The Supreme Court and the Constitution.*

power of divination of the statesmen of 1787, but that is not to say that the product of their labor has a right to outlive its practical usefulness. To accept the sanctity of a document as one of the postulates of constitutional law would obviously be a cramping and paralyzing procedure. Our best tribute to the makers of the Constitution is not to preserve the work of their hands unchanged, but to emulate their efforts in bringing the best thought of the age to bear upon problems of political development.

III

There are special precautions to be observed in the use of court decisions for historical purposes. One must of course take into view the circumstances and conditions controlling a judge in the formation of his judicial conclusions. His opinion is conditioned by his own capability, his prejudices, the influence of his colleagues, the traditions and body of principles which have become a part of him.[12] Constitutional orthodoxy, if we may

[12]Attorney General Bates's inner thoughts on the Supreme Court during the Civil War may be noted here. "Every day I am pained," he wrote, "at witnessing the proceedings in this highest of all courts—both the substance and the mode. Heretofore the maxim *stare decisis* was almost ostentatiously announced; but now, it looks as if cases were determined on grounds of policy only, and upon local and transient reasons." After referring to the California land cases and the Fossatt case, he continued: "The great and now comic error which has well nigh destroyed the dignity . . . of the court is the extreme looseness . . . of the courts below, allowed and encouraged here [so that] no man—not the Chief Justice—knows what is the *true record* of the court below." Bates also commented on the extreme age of the justices, remarking that five members were "failing": Taney, Wayne, Catron, Grier, and Nelson. At that time retiring justices of the Supreme Court received no pensions. (MS. Diary of Edward Bates, April 10, 11, 1864.) After Chief Justice Taney's death Justice R. C. Grier wrote to Stanton as follows: "I think the President owes it to you that you should be suffered to retire in this honorable position." (Grier to Stanton, Oct. 13, 1864: Stanton

use the expression, is always of great force in shaping judicial views. The distinction between orthodoxy and heresy in matters of constitutional law is of such importance that it is not easy for a judge to escape the orthodox opinion. The liberal interpretation regarding "implied powers," for instance, is orthodox, while the strict-constructionist view that would treat the phrase "powers not delegated" as if it read "powers not expressly delegated," is heresy. It would take a most unusual mental effort for a judge in our own time to accept the Jeffersonian point of view on this question.

This element of orthodoxy in constitutional interpretation is given added force by the ingrained judicial habit of citing precedent.[13] Decisions of former courts, though never conceded to be unalterable, are usually welcome; and if a former decision in an analogous case can be found, the court will often cease further inquiry.

A recent legal writer speaks of "the old bogey man standing astride the road to . . . progress in the law of the land . . . that is, the custom of the courts expressed in the old phrase *stare decisis et non quieta movere*—stand by precedents and do not disturb points settled by adjudications." "This," he says, "is to allow the dead hand of the primitive past to guide the progressive present," and he adds that it is mere custom, grow-

Papers [MSS., Library of Congress], No. 55720.) In December, 1861, Congress considered a radical reorganization of the Supreme Court. Forfeiture of respect for the court seemed to be implied in the whole debate.

[13] "The law is progressive . . ., adapting itself to new relations . . . which are constantly springing up in the progress of society. But this progress must be by analogy to what is already settled." (Greene, C. J., in 1 R. I. 356.) "It was admitted . . . that the application . . . is without precedent. . . . The fact that no such application was ever before made in any case indicates the general judgment of the profession that no such application should be entertained." (Mississippi *vs.* Johnson, 4 Wall. 475. This was an application to enjoin President Johnson against enforcing the Reconstruction Acts.)

ing out of the fact that judges are human, tending to follow beaten paths and to take the line of least resistance.[14]

Of course it is also true that the courts are constantly developing the law along new lines, but it is much easier for a given doctrine to succeed if the precedents are with it than if they are against it. Nor should we deny that this conservation of existing judicial doctrine has its good side.

Another important factor that must be borne in mind in seeking to evaluate judicial decisions is the unwillingness of a court to pass judgment upon a political question. Sometimes the line of distinction between political and justiciable questions may be difficult to draw; but when a given subject is understood to be political, the court will withhold judgment.

On this subject Justice Nelson, announcing the Supreme Court's decision in *Georgia* vs. *Stanton*, said:

> The judicial power is vested in one supreme court, and in such inferior courts as Congress may ordain and establish; the political power of the government in the other two departments. The distinction between judicial and political power is so generally acknowledged in the jurisprudence both of England and of this country, that we need do no more than refer to some of the authorities on the subject. They are all in one direction. . . . [Quoting from Justice Thompson in *Cherokee Nation* vs. *Georgia*] "I certainly do not claim, as belonging to the judiciary, the exercise of political power. That belongs to another branch of the government. . . . It is only where the rights of persons or property are involved, and when such rights can be presented under some judicial form of proceedings, that courts of justice can interpose relief."[15]

---

[14] James M. Kerr, "Uniform State Laws and the Rule of Stare Decisis," *Am. Law Rev.*, LVI, 497.

[15] 6 Wall. 50, 71, 75. (See also Luther *vs.* Borden, 7 How. 1)

This, it should be remembered, is a real limitation upon the judicial department. Where a policy of government has been carried through and completed by Congress and the executive, so long as the question involved is primarily political, the court has no choice but to accept it as an accomplished fact. The judicial department may assume the adjustment of details involving personal or property rights, but as to the main policy, the judges are necessarily silent and acquiescent. In a constitutional study of great periods of stress and strain, such as the Civil War, there are many topics, as for instance the creation of West Virginia, concerning which the Supreme Court would attempt no independent decision.

It is also worth remembering that the "war mind" affects even judicial decisions. The historian who has read many of the judicial utterances of the Civil War period cannot fail to be struck by this fact. Judges are human and the heat of war inevitably affects their thinking. When, for instance, a bitter partisan warfare was being waged in Indiana and the anti-war Democrats were seeking to force upon Governor Morton a special session of the legislature so that they might thwart his measures, the Supreme Court of the State was used as the tool of these scheming politicians.[16]

The decision in *Kneedler* vs. *Lane*, declaring the conscription law unconstitutional, when examined with reference to the circumstances attending its issuance, appears to be merely an incident of a better partisan warfare. The Democratic party of Pennsylvania at this time was bitterly opposed to the Lincoln administration, and the Democratic judges denounced the law, while the

[16]W. D. Foulke, *Life of Oliver P. Morton,* I, Ch. XXII. See also W. H. H. Terrell, *Report of the Adjutant General of Indiana,* I, 289 *et seq.*, for the effect of war prejudices upon court decisions.

administration judges upheld it. Judge Woodward's adverse decision was so popular with his party that they nominated him for governor; but the ballots of pro-Lincoln men defeated him, and finally, after this Union triumph, the newly chosen Chief Justice Agnew, brought about a reversal of the Court's former position, which he referred to as having been "made in a one-sided hearing . . . in a preliminary way, during a time of high excitement, when partisan rage was furiously assailing the law."[17]

In districts where, during the Civil War, ill will against the Lincoln administration was keen, such disaffection frequently found expression in court decisions which sought to obstruct essential processes of conducting the war, as for instance, decisions seeking to release by *habeas corpus* writ in a State court, men who had been drafted into the United States army. Though the high ideal of an impartial judiciary is one that has been closely approximated in this country, yet the historian cannot fail to note occasional lapses into partisanship, even on the part of our judges.

IV

In surveying the legal aspects of the Civil War, one of the first points to claim attention is the elaborate discussion concerning the constitutional merits of secession. It was not as a constitutional problem, however, that this question was settled, but rather as a practical political issue of the highest importance. As the present study is primarily devoted to constitutional prob-

---

[17]Nicolay and Hay, *Abraham Lincoln: A History*, VII, 375; 45 Pa. 310. The New York *Tribune* referred to Woodward's decision as a "partisan harangue." (New York semi-weekly *Tribune*, Nov. 13, 1863, p. 4.)

lems which the prosecution of the war engendered, a strict definition of our field of inquiry might seem to exclude secession, which, from the writer's viewpoint, is an extra-constitutional matter. In view of the importance of the issue, however, and the fact that the Supreme Court made some notable pronouncements regarding the constitutionality of secession, some comment on the subject may be appropriate.

The proposition that secession might be grounded on fundamental principles as a basic popular right, received less attention than it deserved, while voluminous arguments were poured forth to show that secession was a lawful procedure within the Constitution. And in reading the able arguments of such men as Stephens and Davis one is impressed with the thought that their statement of the case for secession as a constitutional right was so strong that (for their purpose) the other grounds of justification, while not ignored, could be permitted to remain in the background.

The States, as these Southerners contended, did not part with their sovereignty when they voluntarily entered the Union. Sovereignty is not a quality pertaining to government—that is the old feudal, monarchical view—in a democracy it is a quality inherent in the people. So State sovereignty does not mean sovereignty of State governments, but rather of the people of the States. Sovereignty cannot be surrendered by mere implication. A grant of any sort to be legally valid must be in express terms, and this is especially true in the case of a grant covering such an important matter as sovereignty.

The Constitution, according to this view, was made by the States. The phrase "We the people of the United States" means the people of the States, for the "United States" is not a distinct people, but a union of several peoples. The "supreme law clause" of the Constitution is no infringement upon State rights. There is a distinction between "supreme law" and "paramount authority." Supreme law is exercised by the government, but paramount authority resides with the people. To supreme law we owe obedience, but to paramount authority we owe something higher, namely, allegiance. The exercise of supreme power is by delegation from sovereign authority, and in the case of the powers of the United States Government they are supreme only so long as the authority delegating them continues the trust. The "supreme law clause," it was urged, did not make the United States Government sovereign over the States. It was not a proposal of the nationalizing element within the constitutional convention, but a substitute measure presented by the State-rights party in order to avoid the nationalists' proposal for a negative on State laws.

The people, they said, may bestow supreme power where they will, and what they bestow they may recall. Thus the people of the States, possessing the right to bestow supreme governmental power as they should see fit, conferred such power upon a general government as their agent, limiting, to that extent, their State *governments*, but not limiting their own sovereignty. According to this interpretation, the "supreme law clause" involved no diminution, much less a final surrender, of that sovereignty which resides in the people of the States, and the Articles of Confederation were as truly the Supreme law of the land as the Constitution.

The ratification of the Constitution, according to the Southern argument, was by the States; and the instrument was binding only upon "the States so ratifying the same." Nine States might have formed the new union under the Constitution, leaving the other four out; and as a matter of fact eleven did "secede" from the old union under the Articles of Confederation, and established the Constitution, leaving two of the States, North Carolina and Rhode Island, outside. Thus the Constitution itself originated by an act of secession! But not only was the Constitution ratified and established by States; its operation depends upon the States. The election of Senators, the choice of President and Vice President, and other important features of the Federal machinery, operate "by States."

Some of the States, so the argument ran, reserved the right of withdrawal in their acts of ratification.[18] Vir-

[18]Such was the argument of A. H. Stephens in his *Constitutional View of the War between the States.* A close study of the ratifying ordinance reveals a distinction between the phrase "people of Virginia" and the phrase "people of the United States." The wording was as follows: "We the Delegates of the People of Virginia . . . now met in Convention. . . . Do in the name and in behalf of the People of Virginia declare . . . that the powers granted under the Constitution being derived from the people of the United States may be resumed by them whensoever the same shall be perverted to their injury or oppression." The New York convention declared that "all power is originally vested in and consequently derived from the people," and that "the powers of government may be reassumed by the people, whensoever it shall become necessary to their happiness." The Rhode Island act of ratification (dated May 29, 1790) made known "That there are certain natural Rights of which Men, when they form a social compact, cannot deprive or divest their Posterity, among which are the Enjoyment of Life and Liberty, with the means of acquiring, possessing and protecting Property and pursuing and obtaining Happiness and Safety. That all power is naturally vested in and consequently derived from the People; that Magistrates, therefore, are . . . at all Times amenable to them. That the Powers of Government may be resumed by the People, whensoever it shall become necessary to their Happiness." In both Rhode Island and New York numerous reservations were inserted covering, in general, such points as were later embodied in the "bill of rights"—i.e., the first ten amendments. Massachusetts, New Hampshire, and Virginia accompanied their acts of ratification with the recommendation of various amendments. South Carolina declared, following the formula of ratification, that the right to prescribe the manner of holding the elections to the Federal legislature should be "forever inseparably annexed to the sovereignty of the several States." Pennsylvania, New Jersey, Connecticut, Georgia, and Maryland made no reservations. The North Carolina convention on August 1, 1788, issued a "Declara-

ginia, it was said, stated in her ratifying ordinance that the powers granted under the Constitution, "being derived from the people of the United States may be resumed by them, whensoever the same shall be perverted to their injury or oppression." New York and Rhode Island made similar "reservations" and the other States, in accepting such ratification, assented to the principle that the right of withdrawal was retained. Besides, the Constitution being a "compact" between the States, if any of the confederated parties failed to live up to the terms of the compact, the other confederates were relieved of any further obligations.[19]

On the Union side, the binding effect of the Constitution upon the States, and the impossibility of seces-

---

tion of Rights" as a suggestion for amending the Constitution, "previous to . . . Ratification on the part of . . . North Carolina." The actual ratification by North Carolina on December 21, 1789, was without reservation. The writer's study of this subject has led him to the conclusion that none of the commonwealths formally and explicitly reserved in its resolution of ratification the right of State withdrawal, though several of them put on record the right of the people of the United States to resume governmental powers granted in the Constitution. There still remains, however, the belief of many historical scholars that the majority of the American people assumed at the time of ratification that State withdrawal was possible if the Union should prove unsatisfactory. This view is by no means confined to Southern writers. (MacDonald, *Jacksonian Democracy* [The American Nation: A History, Vol. 15] 105 *et seq,*; *Ratification of the Constitution* [MS. in Libr. of Cong.], *passim*; *Documentary History of the Constitution* [published by the State Department,] Vol. II.) For the historical background in the discussion of State rights one should read the article on "Sovereignty in the American Revolution: An Historical Study," by C. H. Van Tyne, in the *Am. Hist. Rev.*, XII, 529-545.

[19]These arguments supporting secession are chiefly to be found in Alexander H. Stephens, *A Constitutional View of the War between the States*, and Jefferson Davis, *Rise and Fall of the Confederate States of America*. For Davis' works, see *Jefferson Davis, Constitutionalist: His Letters, Papers and Speeches*, ed. by Dunbar Rowland. Stephens' replies to his critics are to be found in A. H. Stephens, *The Reviewers Reviewed: A Supplement to the "War between the States."* Documents on both sides are collected in Allen Johnson, *Readings in American Constitutional History, 1776-1876*, 454-463.

sion as a right within the Constitution, were vigorously argued. Though there were many able champions of this view, the arguments most worth quoting were, perhaps, that of President Lincoln in his message to the special session of Congress on the fourth of July, 1861, and Motley's able "Letter to the London *Times*," published in 1861.

> What is "sovereignty" in the political sense of the term? [asked President Lincoln.] Would it be far wrong to define it "a political community without a political superior"? Tested by this, no one of our States, except Texas, ever was a sovereignty. And even Texas gave up the character on coming into the Union. . . . The States have their status in the Union, and they have no other legal status. If they break from this, they can only do so against law and by revolution. . . . The Union is older than any of the States, and, in fact it created them as States. . . . Unquestionably the States have the power and rights reserved to them in and by the National Constitution; but among these surely are not included all conceivable powers, however mischievous or destructive, but, at most, such only as were known in the world at the time as governmental powers; and certainly a power to destroy the government itself had never been known as a governmental . . . power. . . . Whatever concerns the whole should be confided to the whole—to the General Government; while whatever concerns only the State should be left exclusively to the State. . . . Whether the National Constitution in defining boundaries between the two has applied the principle with exact accuracy is not to be questioned. We are all bound by that defining. . . . What is now combated is the position that secession is consistent with the Constitution—is lawful and peaceful. . . . The prinicple . . . is one of disintegration, and upon which no government can possibly endure.[20]

[20]Nicolay and Hay, *Complete Works of Abraham Lincoln* (Gettysburg Edition), VI, 315-318. The portions quoted above give but a minor part of Lincoln's argument concerning the legal merits of secession. The historical argument that "the Union is much older

Writing to an English audience, which found much in the Southern position to awaken sympathy and which applauded the aspirations of the Confederacy toward independence in much the same way that public opinion in the World War period applauded the efforts of various European peoples for "self-determination," John Lothrop Motley set forth the reasons why the United States Government was under the necessity of forcibly resisting secession. His argument against the constitutional validity of secession is one of the ablest statements of the Union point of view. Motley stated that before 1787 we were a "league of petty sovereignties" and that in the few years of the league's existence we sank into a condition of impotence so that life and property were insecure, laws could not be enforced, and we were unable either to guarantee the fulfillment of our part of the treaty with England or to obtain England's fulfillment of her obligations. But the sagacious men of that time, having "had enough of a confederacy," made a truly national government, one that its opponents called a "consolidated" government. As the chief concern of the men of the time was to cure the defects of the old confederacy, they made a government which operated not

---

than the Constitution" was developed in his first inaugural; and the theme that the Union is older than the States was elaborated in a letter to A. H. Stephens which appears in Tracy, *Uncollected Letters of Abraham Lincoln*, 124-128. Lincoln also argued that no organic law had a provision for its own termination; that the Union is perpetual; and that "secession is the essence of anarchy." In the July message to Congress he further contended that no State was ever a "State out of the Union"; that large national sums spent for Florida and Texas created obligations that should not be escaped; that secession takes no account of the obligation to pay the national debt; that the Confederate Government itself faced disintegration if unlimited secession should be permitted; and that for all the States but one to drive that one out would be as justifiable as secession. See also Lincoln to the *North American Review*, January 16, 1864, in Nicolay and Hay, *Works*, IX, 284.

through the States, but directly upon every individual in the country, exercising supreme powers, while the States were "prohibited . . . from exercising any of the great functions of sovereignty." He continued:[21]

The right of revolution is indisputable. . . . There can be nothing plainer . . . than the American right of revolution. But then it should be called revolution. "Secession, as a revolutionary right," said Daniel Webster . . . "is intelligible. As a right to be proclaimed *in the midst of civil commotions*, and *asserted at the head of armies*, I can understand it. But as a practical right, existing under the Constitution, . . . it seems to be nothing but an absurdity, for it supposes resistance to Government under the authority of Government itself; it supposes dismemberment without violating the principles of Union; it supposes opposition to law without crime; . . . it supposes the total overthrow of Government without revolution."

Having noted the important clauses of the Constitution by which the States were shorn of the attributes of sovereignty, being denied the power to coin money, maintain armies, make compacts, and the like, Motley proceeded thus:

Could language be more Imperial? Could the claim to State "sovereignty" be more completely disposed of at a word? How can that be sovereign . . . which has voluntarily accepted a supreme law from something which it acknowledges as superior?

The Constitution is perpetual, not provisional or temporary. It is made for all time—"for ourselves and our posterity." It is absolute within its sphere. "This Constitution [. . .] shall be the supreme law of the land, anything in the Constitution or laws of any State to the contrary notwithstanding." Of

---

[21] "J. L. M.," in London *Times*, May 23-24, 1861. (The text of Motley's letter as above given has been checked by comparison with the original in the *Times*.)

what value, then, is a law of a State declaring its connexion with the Union dissolved? The Constitution remains supreme, and is bound to assert its supremacy till overpowered by force. . . .

But it is sometimes asked why the Constitution did not make a special provision against the right of secession. . . . It would have been puerile for the Constitution to say formally to each State, "Thou shalt not secede." . . . This Constitution is supreme, *whatever laws a State may enact*, says the organic law. Was it necessary to add, "and no State shall enact a law of secession"? To add to a great statute . . . a phrase such as "and be it further enacted that the said law shall not be violated," would scarcely seem to strengthen the statute.

. . .

It is strange that Englishmen should find difficulty in understanding that the United States Government is a nation among the nations of the earth. . . . The "United States" happens to be a plural title, but the Commonwealth thus designated, is a unit, "*e pluribus unum*."

. . .

The terms of the treaty between England and Scotland were perpetual, and so is the Constitution of the United States. The United Empire may be destroyed by revolution and war, and so may the United States; but a peaceful and legal dismemberment without the consent of the majority of the whole people is an impossibility.

. . .

That great law [the Constitution] . . . was ratified by the people of all the land. . . . It was promulgated in the name of the people. "We, the people of the United States . . . do ordain and establish this Constitution." It was ratified by the people—*not by the States* acting through their Governments, . . . but by the people electing especial delegates within each State; and . . . in none of these ratifying Conventions was any reserve made of a State's right to repeal the Union or to secede.[22]

---

[22]See note 18 of this chapter.

> And thus, when the ratifications had been made, a new Commonwealth took its place among the nations of the earth. The effects of the new Constitution were almost magical. Order sprang out of chaos. Law resumed its reign, debts were collected, life and property became secure, the national debt was funded and . . . paid. . . . At last we were a nation.
>
> . .
>
> Neither the opponents nor friends of the new Government in the first generation after its establishment held the doctrine of secession. . . . Each party continued to favor or to oppose a strict construction of the instrument; but the doctrine of nullification and secession was a plant of later growth. It was an accepted fact that the United States was not a confederacy.

Such, in brief outline, were the strongest arguments on both sides of this historic debate. To arbitrate the controversy is not the historian's function, but it is essential that both points of view be appreciated. It is recognized that the principle of State sovereignty permeated the old form of government under the Articles of Confederation. The wording was "Each State retains its sovereignty, freedom, and independence." The Constitution is usually set off in contrast to the Articles and regarded as the product of the nationalizing party which is supposed to have "triumphed" in the convention, as if the State-rights party had accepted defeat. But the outcome of the convention was not the complete "victory" of one party over the other so much as a compromise accepted by both sides, for the Constitution could not have been adopted without the votes of the State-rights element.

It should not be forgotten that there was a national "side" to the purposes of the State-rights party. Men of this party were ready to make concessions in order to provide a more adequate government; but, if we accept their own interpretation of their acts, they did not knowingly yield State sovereignty. Webster and Marshall argued with convincing logic that the people, in forming the Constitution, consciously abandoned their sovereignty as State communities in favor of an all-inclusive national sovereignty; but is it not possible that the logic of Webster and Marshall was better than their history, and that they may have been reading back into the thought of that earlier time a view which was not after all the prevailing sentiment of "the Fathers"? It is an historic fact that the South did not accept the Webster-Marshall doctrine; and if historical continuity be made the test, it could be urged that the advocates of State rights fully believed in an unbroken continuity which linked their views with those of the architects of our government. Honesty and sincerity certainly characterized this point of view, and shall we not say that it had a certain historical validity? At least we should understand it if we are to make a study of the war of secession.

Viewed after the lapse of more than half a century, the arguments for the "constitutionality" of secession hardly seem, on either side, to go to the core of the subject. The Southerners, in the broader sense, did not strike for State secession *per se*; they struck for the larger object of a new union in which all the neighbors would be harmonious and congenial. Furthermore, instead of thinking merely of the constitutional justification for their movement, they were virtually appealing to the court of world opinion on the basis of fundamental rights; for whatever motives would justify secession would also justify an appeal to the right of revolution. The people of the North, on the other hand, gave freely of life and treasure not merely because they believed secession unconstitutional, but because the majority of them were devoted to the Union and believed that only by maintaining its integrity as one people could the United States realize its highest destiny. On each side the feeling for or against the desirability of secession was a stronger factor than the attitude regarding its constitutionality.

Even Lincoln's arguments on this subject should not be regarded as mere matters of legal reasoning, for Lincoln's constitutional interpretation rested upon motives; and the significant fact which gave force to his leadership was not so much his belief in the unconstitutionality of secession as it was his fundamental conviction that the Union was bound up with the welfare of the country.

The fact that so much was made of the constitutional argument may be attributed in part to the law-abiding instincts of the American people. The South, no less than the North, revered the Constitution, and to both sides it seemed a shocking thing to cast aside the restraints of the time-honored instrument; while in a less stable country the thought of revolution would have been readily accepted without any backward look of regret at the shattered fragments of the fundamental law. It need not be considered a reflection upon the earnestness of the contemporary arguments if the historian of the present should treat the whole subject of secession as extra-constitutional.

It was but natural that the effects of Union triumph should be registered in our constitutional interpretation. The orthodox view which emerged from the Civil War was stated by the Supreme Court in the following words:[23]

> The Constitution . . . looks to an indestructible Union composed of indestructible States. When, therefore, Texas became one of the United States, she entered into an indissolu-

[23] Texas *vs.* White, 7 Wall. 724-726.

ble relation. . . . Considered . . . as transactions under the Constitution, the ordinance of secession . . . and all the acts of [the] legislature intended to give effect to that ordinance, were absolutely null. They were utterly without operation in law.

In the settlement of that famous query "Can the Federal Government coerce a State?" the emphasis was shifted, and the question "Can a State constitutionally withdraw from the Union?" was answered in the negative.[24]

In the practical and vital sense the most serious question in 1860-61 was not the constitutionality, but the wisdom of secession. To affirm that secession was constitutionally possible was not the same as believing that it was prudent or desirable. It was futile to present to the Southern mind the idea that secession was constitutionally invalid. Southerners (including Unionists) believed that "their national citizenship . . . came through their state citizenship. When their state seceded they lost their national citizenship, and not to go along with their state made them traitors or men without a country."[25]

---

[24]For further study of secession in its legal aspects the following points may be noted. The Constitution forbids a State from entering "into any . . . confederation," and from "entering into any agreement or compact with another State" without the consent of Congress. (Art. I, sec. 10, cl. 1 and cl. 3.) This section has been interpreted as rendering the Confederate States' Government illegal. (Williams *vs.* Bruffy, 96 U. S. 183; Lamar *vs.* Micou, 112 U. S. 476.) The answer of the South to this contention was that these prohibitions applied only so long as the States remained in the Union, and that they did not preclude withdrawal. In Dodge *vs.* Woolsey, 18 How. 331, 351, the Supreme Court declared that the States are not independent of each other in respect to the powers ceded to the United States; and it has been declared in various decisions that the States have but a qualified sovereignty. (See, for instance, Fletcher *vs.* Peck, 6 Cranch 136; U. S. *vs.* Rauscher, 119 U. S. 412.) For a full citation of cases on this subject, see *Sen. Doc. No. 96*, 67 Cong., 2 sess., pp. 261 *et seq.* and pp. 361 *et seq.* An elaborate report covering both sides is given in *House Rep. No. 31*, 36 Cong., 2 sess., and the debates of the Thirty-Sixth Congress should also be studied.

[25]E. Merton Coulter, *The Confederate States of America, 1861-1865*, 17.

CHAPTER II

THE CONSTITUTION AND THE WAR POWERS

I

Concerning governmental powers in time of war, there is a striking contrast between the view which prevailed in imperial Germany (to take an example of a militaristic nation) and that which holds in England or the United States. There is in English-speaking jurisdictions, for instance, nothing which corresponds to the German *Kriegzustand*. Under the old German system, it was within the competence of the Kaiser to proclaim a "state of war" throughout Germany, and thus to inaugurate a sweeping military régime under which the ordinary laws and the authority of the civil courts were superseded by the orders of the generals commanding the various districts into which the country was divided.

This military régime, be it noticed, was launched purely by executive action, and covered the whole country. It was universal martial law, not limited martial law based on the fact of invasion, or actual defiance of authority in particular parts of the country. It applied everywhere, and rested merely on the Emperor's proclamation of the state of war. Under it the commanders could make seizures and arrests without warrant, imprison without judicial process, suppress newspapers, prevent political meetings, and do many similar things with entire disregard to the restraints of the civil law.[1]

Such a condition actually existed in Germany throughout World War I and it may serve for us as a starting point to illustrate what is meant by the "war power" when carried to the extreme.

In contrast to this expansion of executive action during war, the Anglo-Saxon tendency has been always to emphasize the "rule of law," and to regard the military power as subordinate to the civil. In England, and also in the United States, martial law, which has been described as "no law at all," has been very sparingly used; and any general order, subjecting the whole nation to military rule for the duration of the war, regardless of any insurrection or threat of invasion, would be most unlikely. This disposition to hold the government at all times within the law, and this wariness in the exercise of military power over civilians, are fundamental postulates in any discussion of war powers in the United States.[2]

The inevitable appeal from law to necessity was, of course, frequently presented during the Civil War. "Ne-

---

[1]The legal basis for martial law in Germany was Article 68 of the German Imperial Constitution. Walter F. Dodd, *Modern Constitutions*, I, 348; Burt E. Howard, *The German Empire*, 46. Certain phases of this subject are discussed in the writer's article, "Germany's Censorship and News Control," in the *North American Review*, July, 1918.

[2]The subject of martial law as it is regarded in England and the United States is treated below in Chapter VII, and the citation of authorities is given in note 7 of that chapter.

cessity knows no law"—"*inter arma silent leges,*" were the oft-repeated slogans. Yet there are at least three ways in which military authority should be restrained (by law) in time of war:

1. By treaty obligations, except those which war terminates. Often treaty provisions are made for the special case of war. It is only in that sense that such treaties have significance.

2. By the so-called "laws of civilized warfare."[3] For the Civil War the United States issued a comprehensive code which had a significant history. Those chiefly active in its preparation were Francis Lieber, noted German-American authority on public law, and Henry W. Halleck, general in chief of the Union armies.

3. By a due regard for citizens' rights, both in con-

---

[3]In this work Lieber's service, and his initial impulse, were of primary importance. With three sons in the army (one in Confederate service) he knew the agony of scanning casualty lists; one of his sons was killed and another severely wounded. He noted that usages of war were inadequately systematized and that many points required clarification: runaway slaves, pillage, espionage, the penalty for spies, retaliation, flags of truce, treatment of prisoners, stealing, burning of homes, attitudes toward non-combatants, seizure and destruction of private property, and newly arising questions of Nebro emancipation. Coming up through Lieber's elaborate study and his voluminous correspondence with Halleck, the military code took shape with the assistance of a special army board headed by General E. A. Hitchcock, and was issued in May 1863. It appeared as "General Orders No. 100: Instructions for the Government of the Armies of the United States in the Field."[It was made binding upon all Union armies and enforceable through courts-martial. Though the making of "Rules for . . . the land and naval Forces" is a constitutional function of Congress, and though Congress has set up "Articles of War," these have traditionally been supplemented by army regulations promulgated as an executive function; it is in the latter category that the "Lieber code" belongs. *War of the Rebellion: Official Records of the Union and Confederate Armies* [hereafter cited as "O.R."], ser. II, vol. 5, pp. 671-682; ser. III, vol. 3, pp. 148-164. Correspondence between Halleck and Lieber is to be found in the Lieber MSS., Huntington Library, San Marino, California. On this subject the writer acknowledges the valuable counsel and assistance of Dr. Frank Freidel of the University of Illinois. His article in the *Miss. Vall. Hist. Rev.* for March 1946 is the best brief discussion of this involved subject. See also his book, *Francis Lieber: Nineteenth Century Liberal*. The Supreme Court has held that international law "is part of our law." (Hilton *vs.* Guyot, 159 U. S. 113, 163.)

quered territory and at home. Even during war the personal and property rights of the citizen, according to the Anglo-Saxon viewpoint, must be preserved. Unless there is actual invasion or insurrection, the laws are not to be suspended by a military régime at home; and in the case of occupied enemy territory, the ordinary administration of the laws by the local authorities is supposed to continue, subject only to the intervention of military force in the case of a serious unlawful outbreak.

To ignore these three restraints is simply to conduct war in an uncivilized manner. War, properly conducted, is not anarchy; and, though the maxim contains perhaps a kernel of truth, it is not in keeping with the American view to repeat that "necessity knows no law."

II

We may now ask: How far are the "war powers" consistent with the American Constitution?[4] The pertinent provisions of the Constitution are the following:

> The Congress shall have power . . . to declare war; . . . to raise and support armies, but no appropriation of money to that use shall be for a longer term than two years; to provide and maintain a navy; to make rules for the government and regulation of the land and naval forces; to provide for calling forth the militia to execute the laws of the Union, suppress insurrections and repel invasions; to provide for organizing, arming, and disciplining the militia, and for governing such part of them as may be employed in the service of the United States, reserving to the States . . . the appointment of the officers, and the authority of training the militia according to the discipline prescribed by Congress; . . . [and] to make all laws which shall be necessary and proper for carrying into

[4]Some treatment of the "war powers" in the United States is given in *House Rep. No. 262*, 43 Cong., 1 sess., pp. 10-11.

execution the foregoing powers, and all other powers vested . . . in the Government of the United States.

In addition to these specific provisions, it should be mentioned that the executive power is vested in the President, that he takes oath "faithfully [to] execute the office of President," and to "preserve, protect and defend the Constitution of the United States," and that he is "Commander-in-Chief of the army and navy," and of the militia when in Federal service.

These are provisions that relate directly to the subject of war. But there are other provisions of a limiting sort, which seem inconsistent with the full exercise of the war power. There is the limitation which prohibits any law abridging freedom of speech or of the press, or the right of assembly; and in the fourth, fifth, and sixth amendments there are important guarantees covering security from unreasonable searches or unwarranted arrests, freedom from criminal punishment except upon indictment and trial, immunity of persons and property from interference without due process of law, and protection of the accused by the use of those devices which tend to insure complete judicial determination of every fact, and absolute impartiality in the conduct of trials. These devices include speedy trial by an impartial jury, the right of the accused to be informed of the nature of the accusation, the right to summon witnesses in his behalf as well as to confront contrary witnesses, and the right of counsel. In the various discussions concerning the "war powers" during the Civil War, the first, fourth, fifth, and sixth amendments, and the *habeas corpus* clause were more particularly held in mind than any other parts of the Constitution. The reserved power theory, and the fact that the Constitution as a whole was a grant of power to Congress, while such power as was not granted was withheld, were also frequently emphasized.

Apart from particular provisions, the pacific, non-aggressive spirit of the Constitution was stressed. The Supreme Court itself has pointed out that the Constitution-makers wanted to make war difficult, and that the sentiment of opposition to wars of conquest or of aggression had much to do in shaping the provisions which relate to war. The convention definitely intended to preclude an aggressive war.[5] Instead of conferring upon Congress the power "to make war," the power to "declare war" was substituted; and while it is generally conceded that Congress also has the power to "wage war," to "carry on war," or to "prosecute war,"[6] still such power is to be derived rather by implication than by express mention.

In attacking the problem of the war powers under the Constitution, the men of Civil War time were, in general, divided among three different opinions:

1. Opponents of the Lincoln administration held that the Government should stick to the Constitution even in war; that a strict interpretation of the instrument should be adopted which would disallow many of the measures taken by the Government, and that these measures should therefore be abandoned.

2. Extreme advocates of the war power held that the Constitution is not operative during such a crisis as the Civil War presented. This was the view of Thaddeus Stevens, who said he "would not stultify" himself by supposing that a certain measure was constitutional, but he went ahead and voted for it regardless of its uncon-

---

[5]Fleming *vs.* Page, 9 How. 603; Chambrun, A. de, *Le Pouvoir Executif aux Etats Unis*, Ch. v.

[6]See *infra*, p. 42, n. 26.

stitutionality.[7] Senator Sumner agreed with this view. "War," he declared, "cannot be conducted *in vinculis*. In seeking to fasten upon it the restraints of the Constitution, you repeat the ancient tyranny which compelled its victims to fight in chains. Glorious as it is that the citizen is surrounded by the safeguards of the Constitution, yet this rule is superseded by war which brings into being other rights which know no master."[8] In such a view there is a quality of forthrightness and frankness which most statesmen of the time did not exhibit. Many there were who found everything legal which they desired to do. Such an attitude has been associated with the term "Jesuit ethics" and its motto has been thus stated: "Fix your mind and attention upon one object which you think a lawful one, and then all the means are lawful."[9]

3. A third position was to admit that the Constitution is binding during war and yet to maintain that it sanctions extraordinary powers. Those supporting this view differed from the first group in adopting a liberal interpretation which would justify severe measures as lawful within the Constitution.

On this broad issue the Supreme Court spoke as follows in the Milligan case: "The Constitution of the United States is a law for rulers and people, equally in war and in peace, and covers . . . all classes. . . . No doctrine involving more pernicious consequences was ever invented by the wit of man than that any of its provisions can be suspended during any of the great exigencies of government. Such a doctrine leads directly

---

[7]*Cong. Globe*, 37 Cong., 3 sess., pp. 50-51.

[8]*Ibid.*, 37 Cong., 2 sess., p. 2196.

[9]*Ann. Cyc.*, 1863, p. 289. Much thinking is mere rationalizing: "finding arguments for going on believing as we already do." (J. H. Robinson, *Mind in the Making*, 41.)

to anarchy or despotism, but the theory of necessity on which it is based is false; for the government, within the Constitution, has all the powers granted to it which are necessary to preserve its existence."[10]

A like opinion was expressed by Mr. Hughes, former justice of the Supreme Court, in 1917. "While we are at war," he said, "we are not in revolution. We are making war as a nation organized under the Constitution, from which the established national authorities derive all their powers either in war or in peace. The Constitution is as effective to-day as it ever was and the oath to support it is just as binding. But the framers of the Constitution did not contrive an imposing spectacle of impotency. One of the objects of a 'more perfect Union' was 'to provide for the common defense.' A nation which could not fight would be powerless to secure 'the Blessings of Liberty to Ourselves and our Posterity.' Self-preservation is the first law of national life and the Constitution itself provides the necessary powers in order to defend and preserve the United States. Otherwise, as Mr. Justice Story said, 'the country would be in danger of losing both its liberty and its sovereignty from its dread of investing the public councils with the power of defending it.' "[11]

There is a passage in the opinion of Justice Agnew, of Pennsylvania, concerning the constitutionality of the draft, which is worth quoting in this connection. It announces what might be called the principle of the supremacy of a general power for vital purposes. The

---

[10] 71 U. S. 2. One of the great doctrines of the Milligan case was that Congress is restrained by the Constitution even during war. See Chafee, *Freedom of Speech*, 33.

[11] "War Powers under the Constitution," an address of Charles E. Hughes before the American Bar Association, Saratoga, N. Y., Sept., 1917. *Sen. Doc. No. 105*, 65 Cong., 1 sess., p. 3.

judge said: "Where a general power is vested in plain and absolute language, without exception or proviso, for high, vital, and imperative purposes, which will be crippled by interpolating a limitation, the advocate of the restriction must be able to point out somewhere in the Constitution a clause which declares the restriction, or a higher purpose which demands it."[12]

It would be safe to sum up the prevailing views of our judges by saying that the war powers are entirely consistent with the Constitution, and that these war powers include all that is essential to the nation's preservation.

III

One of the questions that was much discussed during the period of the Civil War was that of the duration of the war powers, and on this point there was no little confusion of thought. Holding that war powers last only during war, many insisted that, once the conflict was concluded, the validity of rights acquired under wartime measures ceased.

But it is a mistake to suppose that war powers include only those acts which have effect during war. Rights under the laws of war must, of course, *be exercised* only during war, but it does not follow that acts performed under such rights lose their effect and validity when the war ends. There are various things, such as the forfeiture of contraband goods and the seizure of enemy private property on enemy ships, which may be done *once for all* under the laws of war. If measures of this nature should be undone after the war, such a course would be unusual, not regular, and would be based most probably upon some special treaty provision. There are

[12] 45 Pa. 238.

various things which a belligerent may lawfully do with permanent legal effect. Peace does not normally undo such acts.

Many measures, of course, are in their very nature temporary. Such would be the occupation of private houses for billeting soldiers, the use of public buildings, the holding of prisoners, and the like. These measures are originally taken in the consciousness that they are limited to the duration of the war. But other measures, quite as clearly within the laws of war, do outlast the conflict.

There was much doubt and argument as to the post-war validity of various acts performed as "war measures" during the Civil War, but in cases where such doubts were reasonable the measures in question were, to begin with, of doubtful validity, as, for instance, the President's proclamation emancipating the slaves. If the permanent emancipation of enemies' slaves had been as universally recognized under the laws of war as the permanent confiscation of contraband goods, there would have been less question as to the post-bellum effect of the proclamation. As a rule those who doubted the permanent validity of this edict of emancipation doubted its immediate law-worthiness as well. In general, those acts taken with an intention of permanency which fell within the category of proper war measures, were of lasting validity.

IV

In the next place we are led to inquire: What were the "war powers" during the Civil War? This is a subject which will be elaborated in succeeding chapters, but a few general matters may be noted at this point.

The Government had, of course, the power to use its

army and navy against the army and navy of the enemy, but this use of military force against military force is not what is ordinarily meant by the "war power." The term usually relates to the use of governmental authority outside the usual and normal sphere. It is this extraordinary reach of the Government's strong arm, bearing upon civilians, that we usually have in mind when we speak of the "war power"; for the use of military methods in dealing with military situations is too obvious to excite comment.

It may be well to note first the war power of the President, and then consider that of the legislature. There is a certain looseness in the constitutional grant of executive power which is in sharp contrast to the specification of the powers of Congress. It is the "legislative powers *herein granted*" that are bestowed upon Congress, but it is simply the "executive power" that is vested in the President. In consequence of the meager enumeration of presidential powers in the Constitution, this branch of our law has undergone a process of development by practice and by judicial decision.

Some of the main lines of this development may be noted. The President, like every other officer, is under the law. "There is no undefined residuum of power which he can exercise because it seems to him to be in the public interest." The President's sources of power must be found in the Constitution or in some act of Congress.[13] Yet the President has large discretionary power—a power which assumes great importance in times of emergency. If not authorized to assume the role of dictator, he is at least clothed with latent powers which in time of war are capable of wide expansion. It seems to have been the definite intention of the Con-

[13]W. H. Taft, *Our Chief Magistrate and His Powers*, 139-140.

stitution-makers that the power to repel sudden attacks should be lodged in the President, and it is reasonably maintained that he has authority to wage a defensive war without direct authorization from Congress. The President controls the army and navy and may order them where he thinks best. In addition to his authority over military persons, he has great power over the rights of civilians, a power especially related to the declaration of martial law and the establishment of military commissions. "Powers of police control" have been assumed by various presidents and this sometimes involves the withholding of certain individual rights normally guaranteed, as when aliens are held under surveillance, dangerous citizens summarily arrested, or censorship imposed in the interest of public safety.[14]

As interpreted by President Lincoln, the war power specifically included the right to determine the existence of "rebellion" and call forth the militia to suppress it; the right to increase the regular army by calling for volunteers beyond the authorized total; the right to suspend the *habeas corpus* privilege; the right to proclaim martial law; the right to place persons under arrest without warrant and without judicially showing the cause of detention; the right to seize citizens' property if such seizure should become indispensable to the successful prosecution of the war; the right to spend money from the treasury of the United States without congressional appropriation;[15] the right to suppress news-

---

[14]For an able and comprehensive discussion of this whole subject, see C. A. Berdahl, *War Powers of the Executive in the United States* (*Univ. of Ill. Studies in the Social Sciences*, Vol. IX).

[15]In reporting to Congress various measures taken to meet the national emergency, Lincoln stated that early in the war he gave large powers to certain trusted citizens who were to make arrangements for transporting troops and supplies and otherwise providing for the public defense. Doubting the loyalty of certain persons in the government departments, he directed the Secretary of the Treasury to

papers; and the right to do unusual things by proclamation, expecially to proclaim freedom to the slaves of those in arms against the Government. These were some of the conspicuous powers which President Lincoln exercised, and in the exercise of which he was as a rule, though not without exception, sustained in the courts.

Analyzing the President's war power further, we find that besides the executive power, which during the war expanded enormously, there was a considerable amount of "presidential legislation" (for in many cases it virtually amounted to that), and there were also notable instances of presidential justice.

The subject of presidential legislation is difficult, because the President's power of issuing regulations and executive orders shades almost imperceptibly into the exercise of the legislative function itself. President Lincoln issued "regulations" for the enforcement of the Militia Act of 1862 which established conscription for the first time during the war. The act itself did not specifically authorize conscription at all, and so far as the draft was used in 1862 (in Indiana, Wisconsin, and other States) it rested upon these executive regulations. What is more, these regulations permitted State governors to devise for their States compulsory systems of raising the militia if they preferred not to follow the plan included within the President's regulations. In

---

advance two million dollars of public money without security to John A. Dix, George Opdyke, and Richard H. Blatchford, of New York, to pay the expenses of certain "military and naval measures necessary for the defense and support of the Government." This would seem to have been in violation of that clause of the Constitution (Art. I, sec. 9, par. 7) which provides that "no money shall be drawn from the Treasury but in consequence of appropriations made by law." Lincoln confessed the irregularity of this procedure when he said, "I am not aware that a dollar of the public funds thus confided without authority of law to unofficial persons was either lost or wasted." (Lincoln's message to Congress, May 26, 1862: Nicolay and Hay, *Works*, VII, 189-194.)

another chapter this subject will be more fully discussed,[16] but for our present purpose it is important to notice that the President was accused of usurping the legislative power in promulgating such far-reaching regulations.

Other instances of presidential action resembling legislation were not lacking. On May 3, 1861, the President enlarged the army of the United States by his call for volunteers,[17] an act which is to be carefully distinguished from the earlier call, on April 15, for 75,000 militia. The May call was of the sort that usually follows congressional action authorizing the increase of the army. It was made *in anticipation* of congressional authority, which was later given in the short special session of '61. A still more striking instance, which was widely regarded as executive assumption of legislative power, was the proclamation of December 8, 1863, in which Lincoln promulgated a comprehensive plan of reconstruction, outlining in detail the method by which the States of the South were to be restored to the Union.[18]

One more example of presidential legislation may be noted. In issuing a "general order" embodying the rules of war applicable to armies in the field, Lincoln was promulgating a whole code of laws. It could be argued with good reason that in so doing he was performing that function which the Constitution gives to Congress of making "rules for the government and regulation of the land and naval forces."[19] In England such rules are established by Parliament, as in the

---

[16]Chapter XI.

[17]"I never met anyone who claimed that the President could, by proclamation, increase the regular army." (John Sherman in letter to Cincinnati *Gazette*, Aug. 12, 1861, New York *Tribune*, Aug. 23, 1861, p. 7.)

[18]Nicolay and Hay, *Works*, IX, 218.

[19]*U. S. Constitution*, Art. I, sec. 8, par. 14.

Mutiny Act, while at various times our own Congress has put forth a military code in its "Articles of War." Though the code was derived from existing international law, its promulgation was none the less a truly legislative function.

Though the President did not hesitate to act if necessary without congressional authorization, it is also to be noted that, in part, the President's war power is derived from Congress. This fact is well expressed by Mr. Hughes in the following words:

> It is . . . to be observed that the power exercised by the President in time of war is greatly augmented outside of his functions as Commander-in-Chief through legislation of Congress increasing his administrative authority. War demands . . . efficient organization, and Congress in the nature of things cannot prescribe many important details as it legislates for the purpose of meeting the exigencies of war. Never is adaptation of legislation to practical ends so urgently required, and hence Congress naturally in very large measure confers upon the President the authority to ascertain and determine various states of fact to which legislative measures are addressed. . . . We thus . . . find . . . a vast increase of administrative authority through legislative action springing from the necessities of war.[20]

As to presidential justice, we should note in the first place that the separation of the executive and judicial branches is not as complete as is often supposed. Not only does the President have the power of pardon, which may undo any punishment decreed by a Federal court; he has also, through his Attorney General and the district attorneys, the important function of initiating and conducting prosecutions. The extent to which cases shall be prosecuted judicially is a matter resting with

[20]Charles E. Hughes, *op. cit.*, p. 9.

the President. He may favor a vigorous enforcement, or he may let the laws be violated with impunity. Even while a case is pending, the Government's attorney may bring about a dismissal of the proceeding by a *nolle prosequi*, which terminates the case as effectively as if a decree for the defendant had been pronounced by the court. This, of course, is a normal, regular function of the executive; but its special importance in war, when unusual penal statutes are to be carried out, will be readily recognized.

The President is the fountainhead of military justice, and as such has the power of review over the decisions of military courts. Through the declaration of martial law, and the establishment of military commissions to try civilians, the authority of the military courts is greatly expanded, and the ordinary civil courts are for the time superseded. That this can all be accomplished in war time by the President is but another way of saying that presidential justice during war is an important factor. It was the view of the Supreme Court that this expansion of the executive power was carried too far under Lincoln's administration, and that exceptional tribunals in districts not affected by actual insurrection were illegal.[21]

As a further illustration of presidential justice, it may be noticed that various "special war courts" were created by the authority of President Lincoln. The military power in conquered territory was interpreted as conferring the right to create civil and criminal courts to handle the sorts of cases that are normally handled by the ordinary State courts. Department commanders had the right to create such courts under the authority of the President. The provost court of the United

[21] *Ex parte* Milligan, 4 Wall. 106.

States army for the city of New Orleans had a general criminal jurisdiction (not confined to military cases), and the more important "provisional court of Louisiana," created by President Lincoln in December, 1862, had an almost unlimited jurisdiction, its powers being confined only "by the limits of human acts and transactions capable of becoming subjects of judicial investigation."[22] Dealing with matters that ordinarily fall within State jurisdiction it enforced Federal laws as well.

In addition to these cases of judicial authority exerted by the President, there were various acts of Congress which conferred judicial, or quasi-judicial, functions upon executive officers. The Freedmen's Bureau, for instance, had its own courts, whose authority overbore that of the State tribunals; and the Secretary of the Treasury, as a consequence of his administration of the act concerning captured and abandoned property, exercised, for a while, the judicial function of determining individual cases where claims were made for the restoration of property on the basis of loyalty. Taking it all together then, it will be seen that President Lincoln's acts and the acts of those under his authority, extended far beyond the executive sphere, and trenched upon the domain of Congress and of the courts.

V

When we turn to the war power of Congress, we encounter a subject which has been widely debated. It was contended by Senator Sumner in 1862 that the war powers of the national legislature were virtually without

[22]Judge Charles A. Peabody, "United States Provisional Court for . . . Louisiana, 1862-1865," *Amer. Hist. Ass. Ann. Rep.* 1892, pp. 199-210; *Ann. Cyc.*, 1864, pp. 480 *et seq.*

limit. "There is not one of the rights of war," said he, "which Congress may not exercise; there is not a weapon in its terrible arsenal that Congress may not grasp."[23] Sumner's contention was that whatever powers are to be found within belligerent rights may be assumed by Congress during war. This matter was threshed out in a notable debate between Sumner and Browning of Illinois in the Senate on June 25, 1862.[24] Browning's contention was that rights of war were not legislative, but executive; and that, by their very nature, questions of military necessity were to be decided by the military commanders acting under the authority of the Commander-in-Chief of the army. Browning agreed that the Government of the United States was clothed with full belligerent powers during war, but he insisted that these powers were confided in the President, who was answerable to the people, whereas, if Congress usurped power, the citizens, he maintained, were without a remedy. Browning even went so far as to "defy . . . any man to point to one single word . . . in the Constitution which confers upon Congress any power to do any act in the exigency of war which it cannot do in times of peace."[25]

The judicial interpretation of this question lends support to the Sumner, rather than the Browning, view. Full powers of sovereignty in the conduct of war have been conceded by the courts to belong to the national legislature. Congress has the power to provide for the conduct of war, as well as to declare war.[26] When it comes to measures to be taken against the enemy, the

---

[23]*Cong. Globe*, 37 Cong., 2 sess., p. 2918.

[24]*Ibid.*, pp. 2917 *et seq.*

[25]*Ibid.*, p. 2923.

[26]"Of course the power to declare war involves the power to prosecute it . . . in any manner in which war may be legitimately prosecuted." (Miller *vs.* U. S., 78 U. S. 305.)

limit of the authority of Congress is to be found only in the definition of "belligerent powers." It has been held by the Supreme Court that in the use of the belligerent powers, Congress is not bound by the Fifth and Sixth Amendments of the Constitution; in other words, constitutional guarantees do not extend to the enemy. In this connection, a distinction has been drawn between "municipal regulations," meaning acts relating to the nation's own citizens, and measures taken against the enemy.[27]

Only with regard to the former have constitutional guarantees been held to apply. When we consider, therefore, the powers of Congress over citizens in loyal, peaceful communities at home, we have the Supreme Court's authority for the statement that the limitations of the Constitution are in full force here.[28] If the extraordinary war power is to be extended over citizens in territory outside the war area it must be through the power of Congress to suspend the *habeas corpus* privilege, and to institute martial law. These are questions of such great dispute that they will require a careful and detailed treatment later; but in passing we may note that the decision in the Milligan case, denying these extraordinary powers over districts distant from the war, was pronounced with a certain hesitation and tendency to waver, and that four of the justices declared that, if Congress had deemed it expedient to set up military rule in such territory on the ground of imminent public danger (even though actual threat of invasion might be wanting), it would have been perfectly competent to do so.

If we should seek to enumerate the war powers exercised by Congress during the sectional struggle, we

[27] *Ibid.*, pp. 304-305.
[28] *Ex parte* Milligan, 4 Wall. 106.

would find that they included the confiscation of property; the creation of special war crimes, such as rebellion, conspiracy, and obstructing the draft; the raising of an armed force by conscription, including even aliens who had declared their intention of becoming citizens; the admission of the newly formed state of West Virginia in spite of widespread doubt as to the constitutionality of such a procedure; the approval of the President's suspension of the *habeas corpus* privilege, as well as many other executive acts savoring of legislation; the taxation of the enemy by the use of an unusual kind of "direct tax" which enabled particular pieces of real estate to be virtually confiscated by the United States; the protection of officers committing wrongs by extending immunity for acts performed under the President's orders; the extension of the jurisdiction of Federal courts so as to permit cases involving official immunity to be transferred from State to Federal tribunals; the issuance of paper money with the legal tender quality; the authorization of the President to take possession of the railroads and telegraph lines when the public safety should require it, and numerous other unusual and extraordinary measures. In addition to all this, Congress broke over into the executive field through its "Committee on the Conduct of the War" and sought to exercise control even over military operations.

In this enumeration we have omitted those powers which Congress assumed during the reconstruction period, since that falls outside the scope of this book. If we chose to examine these reconstruction measures, we would find perhaps the most far-reaching powers that Congress ever assumed, including the creation of a military régime in the South by which the functions of the State governments were superseded.

VI

In the actual use of the war powers, great circumspection and leniency were manifested by President Lincoln's administration, and the Government showed a wholesome regard for individual liberty. There was, for instance, no such invasion of private rights as was involved in England's Defense of the Realm Act of 1914,[29] while the comparison with military government within Germany during the World War makes the Union administration seem mild indeed. It is true that dangerous possibilities lurked in the executive "suspension of the writ"; that civilians were made prisoners of state by the thousand without judicial process; that some of the Union military officers out of touch with Lincoln's spirit had the erroneous notion that war breaks down the rule of law and substitutes the rule of force; and that as a consequence of imperfect central control over subordinate officers many frivolous arrests were made and unwarranted orders executed. The alarm raised by such an agitator as Vallandigham and his "peace party" may even have had, here and there, some justification. Yet, in the main, the limitations of governmental power were carefully heeded, so carefully that at times it did seem that war was actually being conducted *in vinculis*, which may, after all, be the best way for it to be conducted.

The extreme caution regarding emancipation may serve as an illustration. Not only was scrupulous care exercised to place the whole policy frankly on the basis of the war power—i.e., the authority appropriate to the military occupation of conquered territory—but even

---

[29] Thomas Baty and J. H. Morgan, *War: Its Conduct and Legal Results* (London, 1915).

the power so restricted was not fully used, several important sections then held by Union arms being specifically exempted from the proclamation. The long delay in adopting emancipation and the Government's offer of compensation in the case of slaves freed by voluntary State action, show a disposition to proceed cautiously and legally, as well as a recognition of the vested interests involved.

In other fields also, the Government's action showed great restraint. Though disloyal newspapers, such as the Columbus (Ohio) *Crisis*, the New York *Daily News*, the New York *World*, and many others, were very outspoken in their denunciation not only of the Government but of the whole Union cause, yet respect for the "freedom" of the press was shown. The harmful activity of many disaffected journalists was tolerated, and instances of suppression were not sufficiently numerous to argue a general repressive policy.[30]

The treatment of political prisoners was mild, and such hardships as they suffered were attributable to the prevailing customs in prison discipline, some of which still exist. Often the release of individual prisoners was so freely ordered as to seem almost capricious, and early in 1862 all prisoners of state were released from military custody by a sweeping order, an oath of loyalty and a recognizance being the only terms exacted. Lincoln's intention, it must be remembered, was often milder than that of his officers. In the case of Vallandigham, for instance, there is good evidence that he would not have sanctioned the original order for the arrest had the matter been referred to him.

In the punishment of those who committed what might be called "war crimes," being guilty under the law

---

[30]This subject is treated in Chapter XIX.

of "treason," "conspiracy," "obstructing the draft," and the like, action was decidedly lax. The severer measures were not carried into practical execution. The Treason Act, for example, was not enforced, even though the penalty for this crime had been softened from death to fine and imprisonment. Another severe measure, the confiscation of property, was but lightly applied.

Everywhere during the war one finds this tempering of severe rules. Deserters were somehow saved from death; orders against disloyal persons were enforced with discretion; extenuating circumstances were given weight; escape from penalties was made possible by taking the oath of allegiance; ignorance of the law was often accepted as an excuse; first offenses were passed over; and spies even were released on the acceptance of stipulated terms. The Government, moreover, took the people into its confidence; the motives back of war measures were frankly avowed, and Lincoln often argued with great care to justify the use of unusual powers. On the whole, the prosecution of this grim war revealed a democratic regard for human feeling and a wholesome respect for individual liberty. When one reflects how much further the administration could have gone with popular and congressional support, and when one recalls the serious proportions of Northern disaffection, executive restraint in the use of the war power will be considered more worthy of comment than individual instances of harshness.

If Lincoln was a dictator, it must be admitted that he was a benevolent dictator. Yet in a democracy it is a serious question how far even a benevolent dictatorship should be encouraged.

CHAPTER III

THE LEGAL NATURE OF THE CIVIL WAR

I. Legal determination of the dates for the beginning and ending of the war
II. Controversy concerning the presidential "dictatorship"
III. The insurrectionary theory of the war
IV. The concession of belligerent rights to the Confederacy
V. The dual character of the war

I

In its legal characteristics, the war of the States presents various unique features. Unlike a foreign war, it began without a declaration or "breach of relations," and it closed without a treaty. Conflicting notions existed as to its legal nature, and no single theory of the war was exclusively maintained by the Union Government. The subject will be somewhat enlightened if the reader will bear in mind that war brings its civil consequences, and that a "state of war" on the civil side may be discussed apart from the military phases of the struggle. Being a domestic conflict, yet with all the proportions of a foreign war, the struggle naturally engendered legal complications which would be confusing to an outside observer. As in the Revolution, where it was remarked that the colonists "took up arms against a preamble," much attention was devoted to matters of form, and many things were done, or said, for mere theory's sake. As a consequence, the laws and the debates usually sounded extreme and harsh, whereas the actual conduct of the war and the enforcement of the laws was greatly tempered by practical and humane considerations. The fact that certain rights were *claimed*, does not signify that they were *exercised*, and is is necessary to distinguish between the rights that were made legally available, and those that were enforced.

Concerning the date of its beginning, the war presented certain legal difficulties. Neither side chose to issue a declaration of war; for, according to the Southern, State-sovereignty view, secession was a peaceable act, while by the Northern theory such secession was a pretended right having no legal effect and was best resisted by the maintenance of a waiting attitude, with a readiness to strike back in case any overt act of resistance to national authority should be committed. When one remembers, however, the legal importance of the distinction between a state of war and a state of peace, not only in domestic but also in international aspects, the necessity of fixing some legal date for the opening of of the war will be recognized. War and peace being antagonistic legal conditions which cannot coexist, some definite point of time had to be selected which would mark the termination of the one and the beginning of the other.

The actual fixing of such a time rested with the President and Congress, but the judicial department found the matter of such importance in the determination of controversies that it was necessarily called upon to *define* the period of the war.[1] In its search for some public act to mark the legal opening of the war, the court selected the President's two proclamations of

[1]Phillips *vs.* Hatch, 1 Dillon 571; U. S. *vs.* Anderson, 9 Wall. 56, 71.

blockade (that of the 19th of April, 1861, applying to South Carolina, Georgia, Alabama, Florida, Mississippi, Louisiana and Texas; and that of April 27th applying to Virginia and North Carolina) and declared that these were the dates at which the legal state of war began for the States concerned.

Two presidential proclamations were also held to have determined the legal close of the war: the proclamation of April 2, 1866, declaring the insurrection to be at an end in every State except Texas, and the final proclamation of August 20, 1866, declaring the insurrection to have ceased in every State. It will thus be seen that the legal termination of the war followed about a year after its effective termination through the military surrenders of Lee and Johnston.[2]

---

[2]The decision as to both the beginning and the end of the war was made in the case of the Protector, 12 Wall. 700. The question at issue was whether an appeal from a decree of the United States Circuit Court for Louisiana should be allowed, a motion having been brought from the United States Circuit Court for the southern district of Alabama that the appeal be dismissed. As the law stood, appeals had to be brought within five years from the time of the decree complained of. The decree in this case was rendered April 5, 1861, and the appeal taken on May 17, 1871. Since the statute of limitations did not run during the "rebellion," it was necessary for the court to ascertain the exact duration of the war in order to determine the period to be deducted in calculating the amount of time that had elapsed. The court decided that the war began in Alabama on April 19, 1861, and ended April 2, 1866. It was thus found that, disregarding the war, more than five years had elapsed, and the appeal was therefore denied. Several points in this decision are worth noting: (1) The court chose the proclamations of blockade rather than the proclamation calling out the militia as the opening date. (2) It was the President's act, rather than any act of Congress, that was selected. The minority of the court, however, in the Prize Cases, thought that the war legally began on July 13, 1861, when Congress recognized the insurrection. (3) The war was held to have begun in different States at different times. Neither of the above-mentioned proclamations of blockade applied to Tennessee or Arkansas. It would appear that the first proclamation declaring an insurrection in those two States was that of August 16, 1861, in which all the eleven States of the Confederacy were declared in insurrection and commercial intercourse

II

In studying the legal nature of the war, one must distinguish two elements of the problem. There is first the controversy concerning the manner of its beginning,—whether this was not so irregular as to invalidate the "state of war" as a legal condition. Secondly, a vast amount of discussion centered upon the question whether the conflict was a public war or a mere domestic insurrection.

Taking up the first of these problems we find that the conflict began during a recess of Congress and that for nearly three months all the necessary measures of resistance were executive acts, performed in the absence of legislative authorization. To that extent it was a "presidential war." Between the firing at Sumter, April 12, 1861, and the assembling of Congress on July 4, all the measures taken to protect the national cause and prosecute the war against the Confederacy were taken by or upon the authority of the President. Some of these measures, such as the call for the militia, were not likely to be seriously questioned as a part of the Presi-

---

with them prohibited. (4) While holding that the President's proclamation of blockade served to mark the legal beginning of the war, the court held elsewhere (in the Prize Cases) that the President, in proclaiming the blockade and doing other things to meet the emergency, was not creating a war, but was merely taking measures to protect the United States in a war that was thrust upon the Government. The few days between the firing of Confederate guns on Fort Sumter and the President's proclamation of blockade were disregarded by the Supreme Court in judicially defining the opening date; and yet in the Treaty of Washington (concerning wartime claims against Great Britain) the commencement of the war was fixed at April 13, 1861. For a legal discussion of the beginning and ending of the war, see *House Rep. No. 262*, 43 Cong., 1 sess., pp. 2-3. This document gives schedules of proclamations by Presidents Lincoln and Johnson concerning the condition of the insurgent States at various times from 1861 to 1866.

dent's proper functions, but certainly the enlargement of the army and navy and the suspension of the *habeas corpus* privilege were open to grave doubts, while the proclamations of blockade were widely regarded as unwarranted. In referring to his proclamation of May 4, 1861, calling for enlistments in the regular army far beyond the existing legal limits, Lincoln himself frankly admitted that he had overstepped his authority.[3] It was such acts as these that gave rise to the charge of "military dictatorship," and this charge seemed to gain weight from the President's deliberate postponement of the special session of Congress until July 4, though the call for such session was issued on April 15.

The alleged "unconstitutionality" of this conduct of President Lincoln was urged as a leading argument by those who contended that the whole process by which the "war" began was illegal. This matter was elaborately threshed out before the Supreme Court in the *Prize Cases.*[4] Certain ships had been captured for violating the President's blockade proclamations of April 19 and 27 and in the contentions as to the lawfulness of these prizes the whole issue of the legality of the war in its early stages was drawn into controversy.[5] War, it

---

[3]Nicolay and Hay, *Works*, VI, 308.

[4]67 U. S. 635.

[5]Charles Warren, the able historian of the Supreme Court, emphasizes the far-reaching political importance of the decision in the Prize Cases. In this connection he quotes R. H. Dana, Jr., who privately wrote in 1863: "In all States but ours . . . the function of the judiciary is to interpret the acts of the Government. In ours it is to decide their legality. . . . Contemplate . . . the possibility of a Supreme Court deciding that this blockade is illegal! . . . It would end the war, and how it would leave us with neutral powers, it is fearful to contemplate! . . . The . . . contemplation of such a possibility makes us pause in our boastful assertion that our written Constitution is clearly the best adapted to all exigencies, the last, best gift to man." (Charles Warren, *The Supreme Court in United States History*, III, 104.) Dana was overstating it. See below, pp. 54, 55.

was argued, must begin with a declaration; Congress alone has the power of declaring war; the President's power of suppressing an insurrection is not tantamount to the war power; and his right to promulgate a blockade order becomes valid only after war has become a legal fact through a congressional declaration. War, therefore, did not lawfully exist, it was said, when these early captures were made; hence there could be no valid blockade and no prize jurisdiction in the Federal courts.

As was naturally to be expected, these arguments were brushed aside, and the court upheld the legality of the war from the time of the President's blockade orders, sustaining fully the executive acts taken during the legislative recess.

> A civil war [said the court] is never solemnly declared; it becomes such by its accidents—the number, power, and organization of the persons who originate and carry it on. When the party in rebellion occupy and hold in a hostile manner a certain portion of territory; have declared their independence; have cast off their allegiance; have organized armies; have commenced hostilities against their former sovereign, the world acknowledges them as belligerents and the contest is *war*. *They* claim to be in arms to establish their liberty and independence in order to become a sovereign state, while the sovereign party treats them as insurgents and rebels who owe allegiance and should be punished with death for their treason. . . . As a civil war is never publicly proclaimed *eo nomine* against insurgents, its actual existence is a fact in our domestic history which the court is bound to notice and to know.

Turning to the President's acts, Justice Grier, speaking for the majority of the court, declared that while the President does not initiate war, he must resist force by force. Domestic rebellion may be war, and war may be unilateral. Here he quoted Lord Stowell that "war may exist without a declaration on either side.[6] . . . A declaration of war by one country alone is not a mere challenge to be accepted or refused at pleasure by the other." The President, Grier maintained, was bound to meet the war in the shape it presented itself "without waiting for Congress to baptize it with a name." Foreign powers, he pointed out, had recognized the struggle to be war, and it was unreasonable to ask the court "to affect a technical ignorance of a war which all the world acknowledges to be the greatest civil war known in all the history of the human race." On the basis of this reasoning the court held that a state of war legally existed at the time of the President's blockade orders in April, 1861, and that such blockade orders were valid.

It is a significant fact that four judges out of nine, including the Chief Justice, dissented from this opinion. The grounds of their dissent were that the legal change from peace to war profoundly affects private relations; that a declaration is necessary; that a civil war must be *recognized* by the war-making power within the Government; that the President's power to deal with an insurrection (being an exercise of power under the municipal laws of the country, not under the law of nations) is by no means equivalent to the war power, and that Congress alone has the power of declaring, or legally recognizing, war. According to the dissenting view, the act of Congress of July 13, 1861, which recognized a state of war as between the Government of the United States and that of the Confederate States, was the legal beginning of the war, and captures before that date were invalid.

It will be noticed that the point on which the court divided was as to the existence of a legal state of war

[6] 1 Dodson 247.

between April and July. The whole court agreed that from July 13, 1861, when Congress officially recognized a state of war, the President became invested with the war power, and the legal concomitants of a state of war were in force. They divided, with the Chief Justice in the minority, on the question of the President's power and of the legality of the war before that time.

One of the fundamental points covered in this important decision was the legal effect of the action of Congress approving the President's war measures. The language of the act in which Congress ratified the President's acts is as follows:[7]

> . . . be it . . . enacted, That all the acts, proclamations, and orders of the President . . . [after March 4, 1861] respecting the army and navy of the United States, and calling out or relating to the militia or volunteers from the States, are hereby approved and in all respects legalized and made valid . . . as if they had been issued and done under the previous express authority and direction of the Congress of the United States.

What was the force of this subsequent ratification of acts which many claimed to be unconstitutional? Having held that the President's course in meeting the emergency with warlike measures was entirely legal in itself, the court was under the necessity of proceeding circumspectly in dealing with a legislative provision which seemed to imply some defect in the measures taken by the executive,[8] and which was denounced as

[7]Act of Aug. 6, 1861 "to increase the Pay of the Privates in the Regular Army and . . . Volunteers in the Service of the United States, and for other Purposes," sec. 3. (*U. S. Stat. at Large*, XII, 326.)

[8]Senator Sherman, while vindicating the President, assumed that his acts were illegal. "I am going to vote," he said, "for the resolution [to approve and confirm the President's acts], and I am going to vote for it upon the assumption that the different acts of the Administration recited in this preamble were illegal. . . . I am willing to

creating a war "*ex post facto*." The counsel for the claimants of the vessels refused to recognize the principle of a retroactive legalization of the presidential proclamation of blockade. Such a principle they declared to be entirely out of harmony with the theory of our government; for it would make the President the "impersonation of the country," would erect a dictatorship, and would put constitutional government at an end whenever the President should think that the life of the nation was in danger.

The Supreme Court upheld this ratifying measure, but at the same time prudently refused to admit that it was necessary. "If it were necessary to the technical existence of a war that it should have a legislative sanction," said the court, "we find it in almost every act passed at the extraordinary session of . . . 1861 . . . and finally, . . . we find Congress . . . passing an act 'approving, legalizing and making valid all the acts . . . of the President, as if they had been *issued and done . . . under the previous express authority* and direction of the Congress.' "[9] The position of the court was that there was no defect in the action of the President, but that, if such a defect had existed, this subsequent legislation of Congress would have sufficed to cure it.

It would perhaps be a mistake to spin out an academic discussion of all that seems to be implied in this portion of the decision in the *Prize Cases*. Had there been a defect in the measures adopted by the President, said the court, the later action of Congress would have cured it. This would seem to mean that the President may do

---

make them as legal and valid as if they had the previous sanction of Congress." (Quoted in Upton, *Military Policy of the United States*, 231.)

[9] 67 U. S. 670-671. (In the text of the decision the italics are used as above, but the quotation marks are employed loosely.)

illegal things, things quite beyond the scope of his power; and yet, in case these acts are within the legislative power, Congress is competent to cover them with the mantle of legality. The decision does not quite imply all this. The significant thing is that the court did not consider that the President had exceeded his power. Had they so decided, and then proceeded to interpret the subsequent ratification of Congress as curing all illegality, the decision would have had a very far-reaching effect indeed, and would have seemed to legitimize a dictatorship analogous to that of Bismarck from 1862 to 1866, when parliamentary life in Prussia was suspended and an army budget was carried through by the king and the upper house against the opposition of the popular branch of the legislature. It should be noted that, according to the court's view, President Lincoln had not initiated a war, but had taken measures to resist a war that was thrust upon the Government, and that it was his duty to do so. In evaluating the significance of a court decision, the fair method is to note above all *what the court holds*, and not to place undue stress upon what may be implied in the secondary arguments by which the court amplifies its opinion. What the Supreme Court held in the *Prize Cases* was that war legally existed in spite of the fact that Congress had not acted, and that the blockade was legal. The decision should be interpreted in view of these pronouncements; and any form of refined comment which would elaborate all the asides and parentheses of the decision is likely to lead to mistaken conclusions. To say that the decision upheld the principle of presidential dictatorship would be incorrect.

This question of the dictatorship, however, should not be passed over lightly, and some of Lincoln's arguments in his own defense may have gone beyond the limits which sound legal reasoning would recognize. Lincoln's defense was two-fold: *first*, that the national safety imperatively demanded that these vigorous measures be taken; and *second* (and here is the doubtful part), that as he had not exceeded the power of Congress, he supposed that all would be made right by subsequent legislative approval.[10] Lincoln's course was undoubtedly patriotic, capable, and forceful, for which reasons it has been generally applauded; and yet it argues a curious commingling of legislative and executive functions for a President to perform an act which he adjudges to be within the competence of Congress and then, when the measure has been irrevocably taken, to present Congress with an accomplished fact for its subsequent sanction. For not only is there the well-known principle that a legislature may not delegate legislative powers, but the possession of a constitutional power implies the right to withhold as well as the right to perform it. In other words, when a certain branch of the Government is given an optional, not a mandatory, power, it is thereby given full discretion to decide whether or not the power shall be used; and if the decision is in the affirmative it has discretion as to the circumstances, the extent, and the method of its use. This much of legislative discretion is entirely denied when Congress is confronted with an accomplished fact for its approval.

Though Lincoln's acts have not generally been regarded as an abuse of power, yet jurists would probably agree that the exercise of legislative power by an executive officer in anticipation of subsequent ratifica-

---

[10] "These measures, whether strictly legal or not, were ventured upon, under what appeared to be a popular demand and a public necessity; trusting . . . that Congress would readily ratify them. It is believed that nothing has been done beyond the constitutional competency of Congress." (Lincoln, in message to Congress in special session, July 4, 1861: Nicolay and Hay, *Works*, VI, 308.)

tion of his acts is a bad practice. A President is often reluctant to have a Congress "on his hands" in time of grave emergency, and for this very reason it might be dangerous to our democratic institutions to attach too much weight to the Lincoln precedent of 1861. The whole proceeding savors too much of "forcing the hand" of the legislature, and the fact that President Lincoln could adopt this irregular course in such a way as to avoid offense, does not argue that this sort of conduct is essentially sound. The matter becomes even more serious when it is remembered that in such cases the Supreme Court is hardly an effective barrier against executive usurpation. Questions of this sort are political and by their very nature they create a situation in which the attitude of the court is necessarily that of acquiescence.

III

Having noted the controversy concerning the executive measures taken at the outset of the war, we are now led to inquire into the legal character of the conflict itself. Was it a domestic uprising by mere insurgents who owed allegiance to the sovereign power whose authority they were endeavoring to overthrow, or was it a public war between recognized belligerents? In other words, was the struggle a clash *between governments*, or was it a conflict waged by a combination of individuals against their government?

The legal bearings of this problem were far-reaching. Upon its solution depended the Government's official attitude toward the Confederate States. The decision as to whether belligerent powers should be accorded to the Southern Government was involved, and this would inevitably engender foreign difficulties in case other nations should adopt a theory of the war at variance with the theory of the Washington Government. The propriety of various acts of the President would be involved also, for the President's powers and duties in case of insurrection are different from those which obtain in time of recognized war. Many other questions would be involved: the treatment of captured "insurgents" as criminals instead of prisoners of war; the possible punishment of such "insurgents" as traitors, and the confiscation of their property; the use of the municipal power over the territory claimed by the insurgents when such territory should be captured; the legality of Confederate captures at sea, and the disposition to be made of the crews of Confederate warships and privateers. The decision of these and other important issues depended upon the fundamental principle that should be adopted as to what the existing conflict was in its legal character.

Insurrection, it will be readily recognized, is not the same as war. There are varying degrees of disturbances with which a government may be confronted: riot; insurrection; rebellion; civil war. A *riot* is a minor disturbance of the peace which is perpetrated by a mob. An *insurrection* is an organized armed uprising which seriously threatens the stability of government and endangers social order. An insurgent has been defined as "one who in combination with others takes part in active and forcible opposition to the constituted authorities, where there has been no recognition of belligerency."[11] *Insurrection* is distinguished from *rebellion* in that it is less extensive and its political and military organization

[11]Bouvier, *Law Dictionary*. See also U. S. *vs*. Fries, 9 Fed. Cas. 826; Prize Cases, 67 U. S. 635; U. S. *vs*. Smith, 27 Fed. Cas. 1134; Charge to Grand Jury, 30 Fed. Cas. 997; U. S. *vs*. 100 Barrels of Cement, 27 Fed. Cas. 292; 65 Ky. 296.

is less highly developed. The term *insurrection* would be appropriate for a movement directed against the enforcement of particular laws, while the word *rebellion* denotes an attempt to overthrow the government itself, at least in a particular part of the country. *War*, by the legal theory of the 1860's, was a conflict between recognized belligerents; it was "that state in which a nation prosecutes its right by force."[12] It was not in the legal sense a coercion of individuals, but a condition in which individuals are relieved from responsibility for acts that would otherwise be criminal—a condition in which force is exerted either between established nations or between organized groups whose character as belligerent powers is conceded. A nation does not claim the *municipal* power over its enemies in a public war, but it does assert that claim in the case of insurrection or rebellion.

Not only must this distinction between insurrection and war *in general* be recognized, but certain factors should be noted which are incidental to insurrection as it has come to be treated in the United States. Insurrection in this country constitutes treason. It is true that insurrection, strictly speaking, is not war; but our courts have, in connection with the question of treason, expanded the phrase "levying war" to include organized, forcible resistance to the Government.[13] It should also be remembered that the American President has certain peculiar and specific powers which come into being at the time of an insurrection. The President may not declare war, but he may proclaim the existence of a rebellion or insurrection, and in doing so he determines, entirely on his own discretion, whether an insurrection

---

[12]Grier, in Prize Cases, 67 U. S. 635, 666.

[13]U. S. *vs*. Vigol, U. S. *vs*. Mitchell, 2 Dall. 346, 348. See *infra*, p. 76.

exists. He creates the legal state of insurrection, and when he has declared the insurrection to exist, the courts will accept his action in the matter as conclusive and binding upon them.[14] When the existence of rebellion or insurrection has thus been established, the President has the constitutional authority to call out the militia for its suppression. He then becomes the Commander-in-Chief of the militia thus summoned. Moreover, it has been strongly urged that, in case of rebellion, the President may suspend the *habeas corpus* privilege. This suspension carries with it very sweeping powers over the districts in which the suspension applies, for officials acting under the authority of the President may then make arrests without warrant for offenses undefined in the laws, without having to answer for such acts before the regular courts.

It was therefore a matter of considerable legal significance that, from the standpoint of the Government at Washington, the Civil War began as an "insurrection." The execution of the laws, as Lincoln proclaimed, was obstructed "by combinations too powerful to be suppressed by the ordinary course of judicial proceedings."[15] This was the administration theory in a nutshell. The Government had to deal not with an independent power, not even with States, but with unauthorized individuals who had combined to resist the laws. Nor did the tremendous proportions of the war dislodge this theory from the minds of those in direction of affairs; for long after the guns at Sumter had united the South in solid array, the administration still spoke of the Southern

---

[14] *U. S. Constitution*, Art. IV, sec. 4; Act of Feb. 28, 1795, *U. S. Stat. at Large*, I, 424; Act of Mar. 3, 1807, *ibid.*, II, 443; Luther *vs.* Borden *et al.*, 7 How. 1.

[15] Proclamation of Apr. 15, 1861: Richardson, *Messages . . . of the Presidents*, VI, 13.

movement as an "insurrection," a "rebellion," or a "private combination of persons." This theory of the war as an insurrection was thus stated by the Supreme Court: "The rebellion out of which the war grew was without any legal sanction. In the eye of the law, it had the same properties as if it had been the insurrection of a county or smaller municipal territory against the State to which it belonged. The proportions and duration of the struggle did not affect its character."[16]

As a further illustration of the insurrection theory, the meticulous care on the part of the Union Government to avoid any act remotely suggestive of a recognition of the "Confederate States of America," will be recalled. When the commissioners appointed by the Confederate President in conformity with a resolution of the Confederate Congress, sought audience with Secretary Seward in March, 1861, in order to settle "all matters between the States forming the Confederacy and their other late confederates of the United States in relation to the public property and the public debt," they were neither received in person nor officially recognized by the Secretary of State (not even as representatives of a *de facto* government), and the intercourse which took place between them and the administration consisted of memoranda placed "on file" for their perusal, or of indirect and misleading interchanges through unauthorized go-betweens.[17] A wholly unreasonable resentment was felt against England at the time of the Queen's proclamation of neutrality, because the view prevailed at Washington that foreign powers ought to

[16]Hickman *vs.* Jones *et al.*, 9 Wall, 197, 200.

[17]Justice J. A. Campbell's memorandum entitled "Facts of History" is a source concerning these unofficial communications. (H. G. Connor, *John Archibald Campbell*, 122 *et seq.*; *Jefferson Davis, Constitutionalist*, ed. by Dunbar Rowland, V, 85 *et seq.*)

regard the struggle as merely domestic and the Southern "insurgents" should not be given the dignity of belligerents.[18] When Napoleon III of France formally proposed "mediation" between the United States and the Confederate States, Secretary Seward uttered an indignant though respectful protest,[19] while Congress echoed his sentiments in a resolution which denounced such mediation as foreign "interference," and declared that any further attempt in the same direction would be deemed "an unfriendly act."[20] Concerning the exchange of prisoners, as in all matters suggesting official relations with the Confederate States, there was an excessive wariness on the part of the Union Government which left this important question in an unsatisfactory shape. On those occasions during the war when the question of negotiating for terms of peace with the Southern Government presented itself, President Lincoln, while manifesting generosity on collateral points, carefully avoided any recognition of the Confederacy and invariably imposed a condition which amounted to surrender—i.e., the complete reunion of the warring States with the North. It was for this reason that these attempted negotiations, notably the Hampton Roads Conference, ended in failure. Thus throughout the war, all recognition of authority was denied to the Confederacy, and in the Northern official view it remained the

[18] Seward to C. F. Adams, June 3, 1861: *Dipl. Corr.*, 1861, p. 97.

[19] "The United States cannot . . . allow the French government to rest under the delusive belief that they will be content to have the Confederate States recognized as a belligerent power. . . . No mediation could modify in the least degree the convictions . . . under which this government is acting." Seward to Dayton, May 30, 1861. (*Dipl. Corr.*, 1861, p. 215; *The Diplomatic History of the War for the Union*, being the Fifth Volume of the Works of W. H. Seward, ed. by G. E. Baker, 259. For later dispatches on the same subject, see *ibid.*, pp. 359 *et seq.;* 376-381.)

[20] *Cong. Globe,* Mar. 3, 1863, 37 Cong., 3 sess., p. 1360.

"pretended government" of the "so-called Confederate States of America."

IV

To leave the discussion here, however, would give a misleading idea as to the actual treatment given to the Confederacy. It was not contemplated that the full consequences of the insurrectionary theory should be carried out, and side by side with this theory one finds a working attitude which allowed belligerent rights to the Southern Government.

The practical and humanitarian aspects of the question were of primary importance here. As Justice Clifford declared, "Should the sovereign conceive that he has a right to hang up his prisoners as rebels, the opposite party will make reprisals. . . . Should he burn and ravage, they will follow his example, and the war will become cruel, horrible, and in every way more destructive to the nation."[21]

An attempt was made early in the war, before the policy of the Government had matured, to treat Confederate naval officers and seamen as pirates, and this of course involved the death penalty. President Lincoln's proclamation of April 19, 1861, declared the crews and officers of Confederate naval vessels, and of vessels operating under letters of marque issued by the Confederacy, to be guilty of piracy; and, in protesting against the British proclamation of neutrality, one of the points strongly urged by Secretary Seward was that the recognition of belligerency would preclude attaching the piratical character to Confederate ships.

But from every standpoint it was found impolitic and indeed impossible to carry out this policy of punishing

[21]Clifford, in Ford *vs.* Surget, 97 U. S. 613.

for piracy those who were in the Confederate service. It is thoroughly recognized in international law that those who operate at sea under the authority of an organized responsible government observing the rules of war may not be treated as pirates.[22] Internationally, the Confederacy was a recognized belligerent, and to have its ships deemed piratical under the *jus gentium* was entirely out of the question. To treat them as pirates under the municipal law was practically equivalent to treating them as traitors, and, as we shall see when we come to discuss the subject of treason, the Union Government never carried its treason theory into actual practice as against those acting under the official authority of the Confederacy. Besides, when it became known that Southern privateersmen were being held for piracy, retaliation was at once threatened, and certain Union captives were selected as hostages, on whom the Richmond Government intended to retaliate in case the Federals should actually prosecute the piracy charge.

The practical alternatives as to captured crews were either to treat them as prisoners of war or to release them. Usually they were released. In this matter the belligerency of the South was virtually conceded, and this concession of belligerent rights was naturally extended to other matters connected with the prosecution of the war.

The refusal of the Union Government formally to acknowledge Confederate belligerency thus appears to be hardly more than a stickling for theory. In matters relating to the conduct of armies in accordance with the laws of war, the American struggle was not distinguish-

---

[22]President Jefferson Davis protested against the proposal to treat the crew of the *Savannah*, a Confederate privateer captured off Charleston, as pirates. (Davis to Lincoln, July 9, 1861: Rowland, *Davis*, V, 109.)

able from a conflict between independent, civilized nations, for the formalities of war were observed on both sides. The Union Government *treated* the Confederate forces as belligerents even though it did not intentionally *recognize* their belligerency in any direct, formal manner.

This allowance of belligerent rights to the Confederacy was thus stated by the Supreme Court: "To the Confederate army [were] conceded, in the interest of humanity . . . such belligerent rights as belonged under the laws of nations, to the armies of independent governments engaged in war against each other. . . . The Confederate States were belligerents in the sense attached to that word by the law of nations."[23]

The fully matured attitude of the Washington Government toward the Government of the Confederacy may be summarized as follows: According to the Washington view secession was a nullity and the whole Southern movement illegal. Those who took part in it were insurgents warring against their rightful government. They were technically traitors and were amenable to the municipal power for crimes in the same sense that the Whiskey insurgents in Washington's administration were amenable. But besides this, they were enemies in the same sense in which the word "enemy" is used in a public war. The district declared by the constituted authorities to be in insurrection was "enemies' territory" and all persons residing in it were liable to be treated by the United States as "enemies."[24] With regard to these enemies the National Government could exercise both

[23]Opinion of Harlan in Ford *vs.* Surget, 97 U. S. 605, 612.

[24]The harsh rule that all persons residing in the eleven "insurrectionary States" were enemies during the Civil War was held to include even foreigners and those who were in fact loyal to the flag. For citations and arguments on this subject, see *House Rep. No. 262*, 43 Cong., 1 sess., pp. 6 *et seq.*

belligerent and sovereign rights. It could employ the belligerent power of blockading Southern ports, and the sovereign power of prosecuting Southerners for treason. The Confederate States' Government could make no valid law against the United States, but this government was to be regarded simply as the military representative of the insurrection against the Federal authority. To avoid cruelties and inhuman practices, however, belligerent rights were "conceded" to the Confederate armed forces, and this concession placed the soldiers and officers of the "rebel army," as to all matters directly connected with the "mode of prosecuting the war," "on the footing of those engaged in lawful war." For legitimate acts of war, therefore, Confederate officers and soldiers were relieved from individual civil responsibility. This relief from responsibility was based not upon the validity of Confederate legislation, but upon the fact that rights arising from the usages of war were "conceded" by the United States to the Confederate army.

One of the distinguished justices of the Supreme Court went so far as to refer to the Confederate States as a *de facto* government.[25] This contention is borne out by certain decisions involving the liability of marine insurance companies to pay losses in the case of captures made by Confederate cruisers and privateers. If the authority of the Confederacy were utterly null and its government wholly irresponsible, then its ships were piratical and were not entitled to the belligerent right of capture, and in that case the insurers would not be liable. But the courts have held that seizures by a *de facto* government constitute captures to the extent that insurers become liable, and this was the rule applied in

---

[25] Clifford, in Ford *vs.* Surget, 97 U. S. 620, 623.

regard to Confederate captures.[26] As has been often pointed out, the blockade of Southern ports was tantamount to a recognition of belligerency, for the simultaneous attempt to stigmatize Confederate cruisers and privateers as pirates was promptly abandoned. One would not go far wrong in saying that the *de facto* character which was fully recognized by other nations as belonging to the Confederacy, was *in effect* conceded by the Government at Washington, though to admit this *in principle* was more than the political branches of the Washington Government were willing to grant.

V

It thus appears that from one angle the adherents of the Confederacy were regarded as insurgents and traitors, while from another angle they were considered belligerents and public enemies. These two possible views toward the Southern movement were fully developed in the voluminous debate in Congress on the Confiscation Acts. Forfeiture of property was urged on the one hand as a punishment for crime—the crime of participating in a domestic rebellion. Those in revolt were deemed to be citizens of the country against whose government they were revolting; this revolt was therefore treason, and confiscation was appropriate as a penalty against persons, and as a punishment of their guilt. The manner in which the bald principle of "traitor status" was confidently advanced by some of the more radical speakers may be illustrated by a few quotations. Senator Howard of Michigan made a sharp distinction between the existing rebellion and a national war. "We are not waging it," said he, "against public or foreign enemies, . . . but

[26]Fifield *vs*. Ins. Co. of Pa., 47 Pa. 166, cited in 97 U. S. 620.

against persons who owe obedience to this government and are rightfully subject to it. . . . In rebellions the lawful government is not restricted to the instrumentalities prescribed to independent nations. It may not, it is true, violate the laws of humanity, . . . but it may on account of their violated allegiance . . . impose upon [the rebels] such restraining or punitive burdens as the government may think best fitted to repel their violence, to subdue their rebellion, and restore peace and order."[27] And this fiery outbreak from Elliot in the House of Representatives was but typical of many: "Are not these rebels, red-handed and black-hearted, as bad as pirates?"[28] "When this rebellion shall have ceased," he declared, "the parties guilty as chief traitors will be punished."[29]

In contrast with these expressions denouncing the "rebels" as traitors we find certain supporters of confiscation who were quite willing to treat the conflict as a public war instead of a domestic uprising. Said Blair of Pennsylvania: "What are our relations to these rebellious people? They are at war with us, having an organized government in the cabinet and an organized army in the field, and I hold that in the conduct and management of the war on our part we are compelled to act in most respects toward them as if they were a foreign government of a thousand years' existence, between whom and us hostilities have broken out."[30]

Even those, therefore, who were voting together in favor of confiscation failed to concur as to the principle upon which they justified the measure. After following speech upon speech in which attempts were made to rest

[27]*Cong. Globe*, 37 Cong., 2 sess., p. 1717.
[28]*Ibid.*, p. 2235.
[29]*Ibid.*, p. 2234.
[30]*Ibid.*, p. 2299.

the confiscation policy upon some theory or other as to the nature of the war or the standing of the "rebels," one is likely to doubt the value of extended deliberation upon points of legal theory and to reach an attitude of mind in which the avowal of any theory at all—since theory in such cases usually lags so far behind practical intention—seems almost superfluous.

In such an attitude of mind the "double status" theory seems the least objectionable, since it represents a desire to rise above the restraints of rigid consistency and allow a flexible and adaptable line of policy. This principle was well presented by Blair in the same speech from which we have already quoted. To him it did not in the slightest degree affect our "belligerent relations" with the Confederates "that those of them actively engaged in the . . . war are at the same time traitors who, when reduced to our subjection, are amenable to the civil authorities for the crime of treason. Indeed, it is because . . . they are belligerents that they become traitors."[31]

The conflict was thus conceived both as a war and as a rebellion; the Southerners were "rebels," yet belligerents; the legal relations might be at once international and municipal. "Our case is double," said Sumner, "and you may call it rebellion or war as you please, or you may call it both." The war was "mixed." To use Grotius' classification it was at the same time a "private" and a "public" war.[32]

This "double status" principle was not only the basis of Union policy; it was fully affirmed by the Supreme Court. Justice Grier in the *Prize Cases* thus stated the view of the majority of the court:

> The law of nations . . . contains no such anomalous doctrine as that which this Court [is] now for the first time de-

[31]*Ibid.*, p. 2299.
[32]*Ibid.*, p. 2189.

sired to pronounce, to wit: That insurgents who have risen in rebellion against their sovereign, expelled her courts, established a revolutionary government, organized armies, and commenced hostilities, are not *enemies* because they are *traitors;* and a war levied on the Government by traitors, in order to dismember and destroy it, is not a *war* because it is an "*insurrection.*"[33]

In the case of *Miller* vs. *United States*, this doctrine was reaffirmed in the following words:

It is . . . to be observed that when the [confiscation] acts were passed, there was a state of war . . . between the United States and the rebellious portions of the country. . . . War existing, the United States were invested with belligerent rights in addition to the sovereign powers previously held. . . . In the *Amy Warwick* and in the *Prize Cases*, it was decided that in the war of the rebellion the United States sustained the double character of a belligerent and a sovereign, and had the rights of both.[34]

In studying the legal character of the war, therefore, we must recognize its double nature as a basic fact.[35] It remains to inquire what was the real purport of this dual principle. Did it properly mean, as Sumner once said, that the United States might claim belligerent rights for itself while denying them to the Confederate States?[36] This suggests loose oratorical expression rather than sound reasoning. A truer statement would

---

[33] 67 U. S. 670.

[34] 78 U. S. 306-307.

[35] The following additional citations bearing upon the legal nature of the Civil War may be noted: U. S. *vs.* 1500 Bales of Cotton, 27 *Fed. Cas.* 325; *Diary of Gideon Welles*, I, 414; 22 *Cyc.*, 1452; Dole *vs.* New Eng. Mutual Marine Ins. Co., 6 Allen (Mass.) 373; Planters' Bank *vs.* Union Bank, 16 Wall. 495; Leathers *vs.* Commer. Ins. Co., 2 Bush, 296; The Venice, 2 Wall. 277; Cross *vs.* Harrison, 16 How. 189; Rose *vs.* Himely, 4 Cranch 272; Whiting, *War Powers*, 44 *et seq.*, 215, n.

[36] *Cong. Globe*, 37 Cong., 2 sess., p. 2190.

be that the Government all along upheld its claim to the allegiance of the South, and that all the obligations and liabilities of this allegiance were technically held to be in force, while for practical purposes in the actual conduct of the war, the implications of violated allegiance were overlooked, and the Confederacy was accorded belligerent standing. Certainly Sumner's expression is unsound if it means that the rights of a belligerent could be claimed and on the very same point the obligations of a belligerent be repudiated, or reciprocal rights denied on the other side.

Rightly to understand this dual status theory of the war, it should be remembered that, so far as consummated policy was concerned, the traitor-status argument was of slight importance. The treason theory was a familiar matter for argument, but it was the belligerent theory that was acted upon. The Southerners were, in fact, treated as belligerents, however much the inappropriate term "traitor" might be repeated in legislative halls or in the press. The Government's action was never so severe as the words of the radical statesmen. In a problem containing so many involvements it is not remarkable that the Government should choose a middle course, steering between too open and evident a recognition of the Confederacy on the one hand, and too serious a denial of substantial belligerent rights on the other.

CHAPTER IV

THE LAW OF TREASON

I. The general law of treason at the outbreak of the war
II. Legislation regarding treason, conspiracy and rebellion during the war
III. Slight enforcement of the treason statutes
IV. Lenient attitude of the Lincoln Government

I

The one crime which the Constitution of the United States undertakes to define is that of treason. The constitutional provision reads as follows:

> Treason against the United States shall consist only in levying war against them, or in adhering to their enemies, giving them aid and comfort.

Having thus defined the crime, the Constitution-makers proceeded to specify the nature of the proof which should be necessary to conviction, and to introduce a limitation upon the punishment:

> No person shall be convicted of treason unless on the testimony of two witnesses to the same overt act, or on confession in open court. The Congress shall have power to declare the punishment of treason, but no attainder of treason shall work corruption of blood, or forfeiture except during the life of the person attainted.

Elsewhere the Constitution expressly prohibits bills of attainder, which are also inferentially prohibited as to treason in the section just quoted, so the one possible method of procedure against traitors is by judicial conviction under statutes against treason which are passed by Congress. The words "attainder of treason" in the above-quoted clause relate, therefore, to attainder connected with a judicial sentence for treason, and not to attainder by legislative act. It is this judicial attainder which must not "work corruption of blood, or forfeiture except during the life of the person attainted." While Congress, through its delegated powers, is enabled to define various crimes against the United States and provide for their punishment, these specific constitutional limitations touching the particular crime of treason must not be overstepped.

The historical reasons for these constitutional restrictions are familiar. The "bill of attainder"—i.e., an act of a legislature without the safeguards of a judicial hearing, decreeing death and corruption of blood against a particular person for a crime already committed— was regarded as an atrocious thing, wholly out of keeping with American ideas of jurisprudence. Since it had been used in England and in the colonies, the convention felt that it should be prohibited in the Constitution.

In 1790 Congress passed the law against treason which held without modification until the Civil War. In this law the penalty of death was provided for this highest of crimes.[1]

By judicial interpretation a fairly definite body of principles came gradually to be built up around the general subject of treason. "Constructive treason" was eliminated. There must be an actual levying of war. A mere plotting, gathering of arms, or assemblage of men is not treason. The overt act of treason must be

[1] *U. S. Stat. at Large*, I, 112.

proved before collateral testimony can be admitted tending to connect a particular person with such treasonable activity.[2]

The "levying war" includes not only formal or declared war, but also any combination to interfere by force with the execution of any law of the United States. An insurrection to obstruct the execution of an act of Congress is treason, since it amounts to levying war. Enlisting, or procuring enlistment in the enemy's service, is treason; though persuading men to enlist is not, unless consummated by actual enlistment. The mere uttering of words bearing a treasonable import does not constitute the crime. Mere expressions of sympathy with the enemy, although sufficient to justify the suspicion that one is at heart a traitor, are not sufficient to warrant conviction for treason.

Treason differs from other crimes in that there are no accessories. All are principals, including those who aid, abet, counsel, or countenance the act; or who, though absent, take part in the conspiracy which eventuates in treason. This doctrine—that all are principals—is not inconsistent with that other doctrine of American law which excludes "constructive treason." To admit "constructive treason" is to hold a man as traitor for advising treason when no levying of war has actually taken place. If such a levying of war has occurred, however, then those who were distant from the scene, but who gave assistance, are principals in the perpetration of the crime.

Adhering to the enemies of the United States, giving them aid and comfort, constitutes treason in the full sense. This consists in furnishing military supplies, food, clothing, harbor, or concealment; communicating

---

[2]This was the point of law which saved the life of Aaron Burr.

information; building, manning, and fitting out vessels; sending arms; contributing funds; and doing other similar things. The principle is that a man levies war when he acts with those who have set it on foot.

In the case of acts which do fall short of treason they may come within other statutes of Congress for the punishment of lesser, but related, crimes. "Conspiracy," for instance, is the crime of conspiring to overthrow the government or resist the laws; while "misprision of treason" is the offense of those who have knowledge of the commission of acts of treason but do not disclose the fact.[3]

II

Such were the established legal principles concerning treason in 1861. The general law regarding treason, however, was of slight importance during the war. It was there in the background, and, according to the views held by the Union administration and the courts, it was technically applicable to the existing struggle; but it was not pressed as a legal weapon either against disloyal men in the North, or against the adherents of the Confederacy.

Instead, special legislation was passed to shape the law for the emergency. The first instance of such

---

[3]On the general subject of treason in the United States, see: Druecker *vs.* Salomon, 21 Wis. 626; U. S. *vs.* Burr, 25 Fed. Cas. 1, 25; U. S. *vs.* Fries, 9 Fed. Cas. 826, 3 Dall. 515; *In re* Charge to Jury, 30 Fed. Cas. 1015, 1 Sprague 593; McLaughlin and Hart, *Cyclopedia of American Government*, III, 559; Whiting, *War Powers under the Constitution*, 84 *et seq.*; Beveridge, *Life of John Marshall*, III, 403 *et seq.*; Cotton, *Constitutional Decisions of John Marshall*, I, 96 *et seq.*; Hare, *American Constitutional Law*, II, 1127 *et seq.*; *Ann. Cyc.*, 1861, p. 359; S. A. Hackett, in 38 *Cyc. of Law and Procedure*, 951-960.

special legislation is the Conspiracies Act of July 31, 1861.[4]

The purpose of this measure was to deal with offenses involving defiance of the Government, offenses which needed punishment, but for which the treason law would have been unsuitable. The law decreed fine and imprisonment for those who conspired "to overthrow the government of the United States or to levy war against them, or to oppose by force the authority of the government," and provided a similar penalty for conspiring to impede Federal officials or to seize Federal property.

The supporters of this measure felt that it was necessary in order to deal with offenses which did not amount to full treason, but the minority opposed it as a violation of the constitutional provision whose primary purpose was "to restrict the power of Congress in the creation of a political crime kindred to treason."[5] The measure was criticized as affording the utmost latitude to prosecution based upon personal enmity and political animosity. It was, however, regarded with favor by the principal law officers of the Government, whose duty it was to press indictments and to deal with actual prosecutions. These men felt that their activities in bringing offenders to justice for acts of a semi-treasonable character would be greatly embarrassed if their choice were limited to the use of an unnecessarily severe weapon. There were many indictments drawn on the basis of this law, but the cases were not pushed to conviction, since the usual way of dealing with "political criminals" was by summary arrest and detention rather than by judicial proceedings.

---

[4]*U. S. Stat. at Large*, XII, 284. This Conspiracies Act and other criminal laws of the Civil War have remained on the statute books and were used to punish disloyal acts during World War I (Chafee, *Freedom of Speech*, 40-41).

[5]*Cong. Globe*, 37 Cong., 1 sess., p. 233.

Having dealt with conspiracies in 1861, Congress proceeded much farther in 1862 by introducing major modifications in the law of treason itself.

The treason law of 1862 is generally referred to as the "second Confiscation Act," but its title reads: "*An Act to Suppress Insurrection; to punish Treason and Rebellion, to seize and confiscate the Property of Rebels, and for other purposes.*"

Aside from confiscation, the purpose of the law was to bring the statutory provisions concerning treason into harmony with the existing emergency and to soften the penalty for that offense.

As the law then stood, the only possible punishment for treason was death. The act of 1790 was still in force and it provided: "If any person owing allegiance to the United States of America shall levy war against them or shall adhere to their enemies, giving them aid and comfort, . . . such person shall be guilty of treason and shall suffer death." In case of conviction the only alternative by which the offender's life could be saved was pardon.

Since hundreds of thousands of men, most of them youths, were guilty of this grave offense according to the Government's oft-repeated interpretation of the war, the death penalty made the existing law of treason unworkable for the emergency. A few, it is true, favored the retention of the extreme penalty. "If an individual should be convicted of treason against this government," said Senator Trumbull, "I would execute him. . . . I do not believe that this is the time to mitigate the punishment for treason."[6] The prevailing sentiment, however, was more nearly in accord with the view of the Judiciary

[6]Statement of Senator Trumbull, *Cong. Globe,* 37 Cong., 2 sess., p. 2170.

Committee of the Senate. The Committee felt that there should be some differentiation in the punishment.[7] In some cases, they thought death might be justified, but in other cases it would be too severe. They wanted to provide the court with an alternative and a power of discrimination as between the weightier and the lesser cases.

For this reason Section 1 of the Treason Act of 1862 declared:

> Every person who shall hereafter commit the crime of treason against the United States, and shall be adjudged guilty thereof, shall suffer death . . . or, at the discretion of the court, he shall be imprisoned for not less than five years, and fined not less than ten thousand dollars.[8]

This lightening of the penalty for treason was accompanied by another provision more particularly designed for the existing emergency. The second section of the same measure reads as follows:

> If any person shall hereafter incite, set on foot, assist, or engage in any rebellion or insurrection against the authority of the United States, or the laws thereof, or shall give aid or comfort thereto, or shall engage in, or give aid and comfort to, any existing rebellion or insurrection, and be convicted thereof, such person shall be punished by imprisonment for a period not exceeding ten years, or by a fine not exceeding ten thousand dollars, and by the liberation of all his slaves, if any he have; or by both of said punishments, at the discretion of the court.[9]

It will be noted that in this section the death penalty is not authorized at all, and that in fixing the extent of

---

[7]Statement of Senator Clark, *ibid.*, p. 2166.

[8]*U. S. Stat. at Large*, XII, 589. In addition, the offender's slaves were to be set free, and he was to be disqualified from holding office.

[9]Interpreted in *Opins. Attys. Gen.*, X, 513.

the fine and imprisonment, a maximum, rather than a minimum, is set. Though the word "treason" is not used, yet the wording of this section is so comprehensive as to cover the whole case of the Confederates and their adherents, so that the previous section, which does relate to treason, might possibly have been interpreted as inapplicable to them.

Engaging in rebellion was thus declared to be distinct for the crime of treason, while even the graver crime was to be punished by a far ligher penalty than that which previously existed.

Besides the Conspiracies Act of 1861 and the Treason Act of 1862 there was another measure which dealt with disloyal practices. In sections 24 and 25 of the Conscription Act of March 3, 1863, special provision was made for "resisting the draft." Summary arrest with delivery to the civil authorities, followed by fine and imprisonment in case of conviction, was made the penalty for enticing to desert, harboring or aiding the escape of deserters, resisting the draft or counseling such resistance, obstructing draft officers, or dissuading from military duty.[10] The proceeding was to begin with "summary arrest by the provost marshal." This feature of the act was denounced by Davis of Kentucky who declared that arrest by warrant upon affidavit of some person charging an offense against the law was the only legal method.

III

These, then, were the special measures passed during the war for the purpose of dealing with disloyalty. "Treason," "conspiracy," "rebellion," "giving aid and comfort," "resisting the draft"—if broadly interpreted

---

[10] *U. S. Stat. at Large,* XII, 731, secs. 24, 25.

these terms would seem to cover every case which the authorities might wish to prosecute. The legal arsenal seemed to be full. If not, Congress would doubtless supply any deficiency. It rested with the administration, the district attorneys, the juries, and the courts, to determine how far these weapons were to be applied. It is this phase of the problem that deserves particular attention. Having noted the devices that were ready at hand for dealing with disloyalty, we must now turn to the more laborious task of discovering in what spirit and to what extent these devices were actually employed.

The public prosecutors were the Attorney General at Washington and the various district attorneys. It was the function of the Attorney General, a member of the Cabinet, reflecting the views of the President and the administration, to direct the policy of the district attorneys and other law officers of the Government. In each locality these district attorneys must represent the United States in the capacity of prosecutor, obtaining arrests, collecting evidence, fitting the charge to the offense, calling special grand juries, framing indictments, arguing the cases when they came to trial, obtaining additional counsel where necessary, moving the dismissal of prosecutions where conviction was not desired and, in general, doing everything in their power to enforce the various war measures in so far as the Government wished them to be enforced.

Their difficulty was not to discover violators of the law. There were few localities in which disloyalty was absent, while in many districts it reached staggering proportions. Lincoln's political enemies found sufficient support in Indiana to control the legislature, making it necessary for Governor Morton to obtain funds by unofficial means, while the "Copperhead" legislature of Illinois adopted an attitude of such defiance that it was prorogued by Governor Yates. Anti-war societies such as the Knights of the Golden Circle, the Order of American Knights, the Order of the Star, and the Sons of Liberty numbered hundreds of thousands of members. In communication with the enemy, these conspirators sought to promote Union defeat and to overthrow the Government at Washington. Though their activities were confined in the main to such petty things as aiding desertion, discouraging enlistment, recruiting for the enemy, resisting arrests, destroying enrollment lists, demolishing government property and circulating disloyal literature, yet their secret plottings involved more serious schemes. Arms and ammunition were widely distributed so that "rebel" raids into the North might be aided from the rear; and there were plans for the detachment of the region beyond the Ohio in a great "Northwest Confederacy" which was to unite with the South and, by splitting the North, contribute substantially to Confederate success. Assassination of Union officers and release of Confederate prisoners were included within the schemes of these societies. The use of Canadian soil for the hatching of their conspiracies caused impatient generals to insist upon the "right of hot pursuit" (which, however, Lincoln overruled), and international complications were thus threatened. Their most grandiose plots were fantastic, but some of their deeds amounted to aiding an enemy in arms.[11]

In the midst of such disloyalty, however, the tribunals of civil justice failed, in the large sense, to function as

[11]On the subject of disloyalty in the North, see Nicolay and Hay, *Lincoln*, VIII, Ch. i; *Report of the Judge-Advocate-General on the Order of American Knights* (Wash., 1864), Foulke, *Life of Oliver P. Morton*, I, Ch. xxx; *O. R.*, Ser. II, Vol. 2, pp. 240 *et seq.;* Vol. 7, pp. 740 *et seq.;* Rhodes, *History of the United States*, V, 317 *et seq.;* Wood Gray, *The Hidden Civil War;* George Fort Milton, *Abraham Lincoln and the Fifth Column;* Kenneth M. Stampp, *Indiana Politics during the Civil War*.

agencies for the suppression and punishment of treason. Often there was uncertainty as to what treason was. Federal courts were not harmonious on the subject of treason and conspiracy against the United States, and this disagreement proved perplexing to attorneys, commissioners, and marshals. Disloyal acts or conversations which did not amount to treason and yet were so flagrant as to call for some notice—such as "drinking the health of Jefferson Davis"—offered an additional embarrassment. In disaffected regions the Government's prosecutors were sometimes at a loss to know how to resist an attempt to rescue a prisoner. Deputy marshals could be appointed, but the hiring and paying of such deputies was hedged about with legal difficulties, while their effectiveness for a real emergency was doubtful. Where the taint of lurking disloyalty was diffused through the mass of the people, it was a difficult matter to select trustworthy law officers for the Government. In such communities the officials always dreaded the outcome of prosecutions, knowing that the juries would naturally reflect the opinion of the community.[12] Since the *habeas corpus* privilege was suspended and military arrests were occurring on all sides, the officials connected with the ordinary administration of justice felt that matters had been somewhat taken out of their hands; and when the Chief Justice of the United States, in a widely published opinion, took direct issue with the President on this question,[13] he placed a choice weapon in the hands of disaffected agitators who were busy in disseminating anti-administration propaganda. It was under such conditions that the laws against disloyalty had to be applied.

---

[12]The examination of a huge mass of unpublished papers in the office of the Attorney General (now in the National Archives), together with Federal court records in various cities, is the basis for this portion of the discussion.

[13]The Merryman case. See *infra*, pp. 120-121.

Strong solicitations were received from loyal men urging the punishment of "traitors," and the civil arrests and indictments for treason and conspiracy were sufficiently numerous to indicate that the marshals and the attorneys were mindful of their duties. The Chief Justice of Colorado, a Federal territory, wrote in November, 1861, of fifty cases of treason and murder, already on the docket, with forty-three prisoners newly apprehended, their crimes being treason, enlisting for the "rebel" service, and conspiracy. A little later he wrote of fifty-four indictments for treason by the grand jury. Some prominent Virginians were included among the true bills returned at Wheeling early in the war, such men as John B. Floyd and Henry A. Wise being indicted for treason along with about eight hundred others. Fifteen indictments for treason were reported at Baltimore in 1863. At Philadelphia all the crew of the Confederate privateer *Petrel* were solemnly indicted for "high treason," and other indictments for the same offense brought the total number in that city to one hundred twenty-five.[14] Conspiracy cases and actions for obstructing the draft were brought in considerable numbers at Indianapolis, and the Federal records at Cleveland, New York, St. Louis and other places show many similar cases.[15]

---

[14]B. F. Hall, Chief Justice of Colorado, to Attorney General Bates, Dec. 13, 1861; E. M. Norton, U. S. Marshall at Wheeling, Va., to Bates, Nov. 20, 1861; N. J. Thayer, Asst. U. S. Dist. Atty. at Baltimore, to Bates, Nov. 3, 1863; J. H. Ashton, Asst. U. S. Dist. Atty. at Philadelphia, to Bates, Oct. 9, 1861: Attorney General's Papers (MSS., National Archives).

[15]One should not be misled, however, by the number of indictments brought; for, in the first place, the number is small in comparison with the amount of disloyalty, which was of startling proportions, and, in the second place, after the indictments were instituted, they were uniformly continued or dismissed instead of being pushed to trial and conviction.

IV

When we come to examine the policy of the Lincoln administration toward prosecutions for treason we find that leniency and expediency were the controlling motives which led to a cautious attitude and a reluctance to convict, while at the same time it was realized that the maintenance of respect for the Government and the inculcation of a wholesome dread of the consequences of disloyalty required that some effort be made in partial enforcement of the laws on the subject.

For the Attorney General it was a pressing question as to how he should advise the district attorneys, who naturally looked to Washington for uniform instructions on this vital question. Is it the policy of the Government to expedite prosecutions for treason or to defer action? Does the Government merely desire indictments or does it wish cases to be pressed to the extremity? What shall be done with the members of the Order of American Knights who have arms deposited in various places? Shall steps be taken judicially against persons found in correspondence with the enemy? Where political offenders are under military arrest and are confined in state prisons, shall they be handed over to the Federal courts for trial for treason or detained as "prisoners of war"? Or again, shall they be merely released on pledge of loyalty? Must the district attorney wait for full evidence of "overt acts," or should he give heed to the strong solicitations of parties who are daily informing against disloyal men?[16]

Such inquiries crowded the Attorney General's mail. Finding their offices flooded with charges against parties accused of treason, the Federal attorneys could not pro-

---

[16]Attorney General's papers, *passim.*

ceed with their official duties at all without instruction as to the wishes of the administration. The mere calling of a grand jury might, of course, have a good moral effect, and the bringing of indictments might do much to clear the air; but beyond that the attorneys felt indisposed to settle for themselves such far-reaching matters of public policy.

In Washington this grave question had to be treated as a whole and viewed in its practical bearings. Hasty or frequent prosecutions were not desired by the administration. Besides the well-known leniency of Lincoln, which was always an important factor, there was a realization that conviction in such a highly technical proceeding as treason would be difficult to obtain, especially in the case of sympathetic juries. To institute a trial and then fail of conviction would weaken the Government; but success might be even worse, for it would render the victim a martyr. A careful reading of French history in the year following the overthrow of Napoleon will show that the Bourbon monarchy made only a half-hearted attempt to apprehend Ney; and, so far as their standing with the people was concerned, the government felt that the marshal had done them more harm by allowing himself to be captured than by his betrayal at the time of Napoleon's return from Elba.

Attorney General Bates reflected the views of the Lincoln Cabinet when he wrote to one of his district attorneys in July, 1861:

> I am . . . of opinion that an excellent moral effect may be produced by prosecution of some of the most "pestilential fellows" among us. But I think also that the most judicious care is necessary to prevent reaction. Better let twenty of the guilty go free . . . than to be defeated in a single case. You do well not to be overborne by the overheated zeal of even good men, on the outside, who are not responsible for results

as we are. . . . Success in the selected cases is very desirable, but a multitude of cases is not only not desired, but feared, as tending to excite popular sympathy and to beget the idea of persecution. I think it very probable that you may find cases short of treason—e.g., conspiracy, violating the mails, and the like. A few convictions for that sort of crime, I think, would help the cause, by rubbing off the varnish from romantic treason and showing the criminals in the homely garb of vulgar felony.[17]

In the administration policy there was a blending of merciful and practical considerations. A clement course was adopted partly because of the feeling that "you cannot indict a whole people," and also because of the absence of a vindictive policy on the part of the men in power, conspicuously, of course, the President. In a highly characteristic though not a widely known document—the message justifying his contemplated veto of the second Confiscation Act of 1862—Lincoln declared that "the severest justice may not always be the best policy," suggested that a "power of remission" should accompany the provision for the forfeiture of property as a consequence of treason, and pointed out that the persons against whom Congress was legislating in this act would be "within the general pardoning power."[18]

The mild temper of this passage is a fair indication of the spirit of executive clemency which is always an important factor in connection with the enforcement of

---

[17]Bates to A. S. Jones, U. S. Dist. Atty. at St. Louis, July 1, 1861: Attorney General's Letter Books. In another letter of similar import Bates wrote: "It is not desirable to try many cases of treason. It is a crime hard to prove, being guarded by a variety of legal [technicalities]. And even conviction makes the convict all the more a martyr in the eyes of his partisans. . . . It would be unfortunate to be defeated in many such cases. It is far better policy . . . to prosecute offenders for vulgar felonies . . . than for romantic and genteel treason." (*O. R.*, Ser. II, Vol. 5, p. 190.)

[18]*Senate Journal*, July 17, 1862, pp. 872-874.

penal statutes, and this attitude of clemency was reënforced by those considerations which appealed to the practical sense. The laws against treason were too terrible to be fully enforced, while a loose and wholesale appeal to the laws accompanied by a failure to follow through to conviction would cause them to become ineffective and to lose their terror. The misuse of the charge of "treason," as for instance against crews of Confederate privateers, tended to cheapen the charge. Balancing all these factors, the administration inevitably chose the lenient course. In fine, the Lincoln Government was both too circumspect and too humane to follow up the implications of the law of treason.

Where enthusiasm for the war was particularly ardent, this lenient attitude of the Union Government failed to satisfy, and not infrequently the zeal of grand juries outran that of the Federal officers. The accounts from West Virginia, for instance, indicate that the attorney there, Benjamin H. Smith, had a grand jury "on his hands" which caused him no small embarrassment. The grand jurors extended their inquiries, he wrote, in spite of all that he and the court could do. He therefore declined a grand jury at the spring term of the court in 1862 and directed that no grand jury be summoned for Clarksburg or Wheeling at the next term. The judge and the attorney inclined to the conservative view and recommended that inquiries be confined to a few prominent men who had taken an active part in secession. The zealous jurors, however, disregarded the recommendations of the court and undertook a comprehensive pursuit of all who had been in the rebellion.[19] In instances of this sort the question of selecting certain cases for prosecution always presented itself. The Attorney Gen-

[19] Benj. H. Smith, U. S. Dist. Atty. for Western Dist., Va., to Bates, May 16 and Aug. 19, 1862: Attorney General's Papers.

eral's office seemed to favor a judicious selection of a few prominent cases for prosecution, and in some cases instructions to this effect were given.[20]

Toward the lighter offenses, which involved something less than full treason, the Government's policy was also mild. By stretching the phrase "giving aid and comfort" and by a vigorous application of the Conspiracies Act and certain parts of the Conscription Law, a great number of petty indictments could have been pushed for such acts as furnishing supplies, giving harbor or concealment, belonging to a disloyal association, enticing to desertion, and obstructing the draft. In such cases, however, a short military detention followed by release on parole was the rule. In Cambria and Clearfield counties, Pennsylvania, thirty-six indictments for "conspiracy" were brought. It was felt that these were poor and ignorant men who were guilty of no overt act, but were merely members of an unlawful association into which they had been drawn by designing leaders. The indictments against them were therefore dismissed.[21]

Those clauses of the Conscription Act which dealt with disloyal practices were not loosely applied, but were narrowly interpreted. According to the principles actually observed by the courts, the utterance of treasonable words would not be "enticing to desert," and the

---

[20]It was after the war that such advice was more likely to be given. Attorney General Speed wrote as follows to the district attorneys in Tennessee in 1866: "I am directed by the President to say . . . that he deems it important, and you are therefore instructed, to prosecute some few persons who have been indicted for high treason in your court. . . . The persons prosecuted must have been prominent, conspicuous and influential in getting up, sustaining and prosecuting the rebellion." (Speed to U. S. Dist. Attys. at Nashville, Memphis and Rogersville, Tenn., and Louisville, Ky., Mar. 19, 1866: Attorney General's letter books.)

[21]Attorney General's Letter Books, June-July, 1865, esp. J. H. Ashton to President Johnson, Jul. 31, 1865.

publishing of a disloyal editorial would not be "resisting the draft," but these charges were pressed only against those who produced desertion by direct influence upon some one in the service or who resisted an officer engaged in enforcing conscription.

It is a striking fact that no life was forfeited and no sentence of fine and imprisonment carried out in any judicial prosecution for treason arising out of the "rebellion." The case of Mumford, executed by sentence of a military commission in New Orleans in 1862 for having torn down the United States flag, was a most unfortunate blunder, but it was exceptional and isolated.[22] Though the existence of martial law at the time the act was committed is in a large sense not a sufficient excuse, yet it takes the case entirely out of the category of constitutional treason, and the incident should be judged in connection with the many hundreds of offenders who were allowed to go about free of punishment.

Practically the whole activity of the officers of justice in the enforcement of the treason statutes consisted in the bringing of indictments and the incomplete prosecution of a few cases. The typical procedure was to continue indictments which the grand jury brought, keeping them on the docket from one term of court to the next and ultimately to enter a *nolle prosequi*—i.e., to dismiss the cases.

"Dismiss all conspiracy cases in Missouri" was the word from the Attorney General's Office in 1866 to the

---

[22]The perpetrator of this act, General Butler, was removed by Lincoln. Nicolay and Hay, *Lincoln*, V, 268, 269, 278. West H. Humphries, United States District Judge in Tennessee, supported the "rebellion" and on impeachment proceedings he was found guilty of charges which included "levying war." He was thus found guilty of treason by the United States Senate, sitting as an impeachment court, but he was not convicted of this crime in any judicial prosecution. (*Cong. Globe*, 37 Cong., 2 sess., p. 2949.)

United States attorney at St. Louis.[23] "You are to suspend proceedings in the indictment against C. C. Clay for treason and conspiracy until further advised" was the instruction sent to Montgomery, Alabama. In another case the instruction read: "You are hereby authorized to dismiss any indictment against any person for a political offense, if in your judgment it is right and proper to do so." These expressions are typical of the answers sent in the great majority of cases when district attorneys requested advice as to indictments. The law officers were constantly reminded that the dismissal of treason cases was within their discretion, and often there was a definite order from the Attorney General directing such dismissal.

Comparatively few of the treason cases ever came up for trial, and when they did, they occasioned a considerable embarrassment to the Government. The unfortunate consequences which accompanied actual attempts to prosecute these cases are well illustrated in the trial of the Confederate privateersmen at Philadelphia in 1861. The *Petrel*, "on a hostile cruise as a pretended privateer under . . . pretended letters of marque and reprisal from one Jefferson Davis," was captured by the U. S. frigate *St. Lawrence*, and the crew of thirty-five men were indicted before the Federal Circuit Court at Philadelphia for treason, their crime being also described as "piracy." Intense popular excitement was manifested as the cases were brought to trial, some of them before Justice Cadwallader, and others before Justice Grier, but the judges did not seem to enjoy the proceeding. Finally, Justice Grier burst out as follows:

[23] M. F. Pleasants, Clerk in Attorney General's office, to C. G. Mauro, U. S. Dist. Atty. at St. Louis, Oct. 17, 1866; same to J. Q. Smith, U. S. Dist. Atty. at Montgomery, Ala., Feb. 21, 1867; Attorney General Speed to U. S. Dist. Atty. at Louisville, Ky., May 31, 1866: Attorney General's Letter Books.

Justice Grier:

I do not intend to try any more of these cases. I shall leave them to my brother Cadwallader. I have other business to attend to, and do not mean to be delayed here from day to day in trying charges against a few unfortunate men here out of half a million that are in arms against the government. Why should this difference be made between men captured on land and on the sea?

Mr. Earle:

These are privateers.

Justice Grier:

But why make a difference between those taken on land and on water? Why not try all those taken on land and hang them? That might do with a mere insurrection; but when it comes to civil war, the laws of war must be observed, or you will lay it open to the most horrid reactions that can possibly be thought of; hundreds of thousands of men will be sacrificed upon mere brutal rage. . . . I will not sit on another case. I am not going to have the whole civil business of the court and private suitors set aside for useless trifling.[24]

This illustrates the attitude of a practical-minded judge toward the efforts which a puzzled and well-meaning district attorney was making to prosecute some of the treason cases.

In four of these cases conviction was obtained, and an interesting correspondence then ensued between the district attorney and Attorney General Bates. The district attorney asked if it were in line with the policy of the Government to proceed further with the cases. Bates replied that there was no need of haste. "The first great end being attained, by the conviction," he continued, "there are indeed some political reasons, very

[24]Report of proceedings in U. S. Circuit Court at Philadelphia, Nov. 4, 1861. Enclosure in J. H. Ashton to Bates, same date: Attorney General's papers.

operative on my mind, although prudently not proper for publication just now, which make it desirable to hold these cases up to await certain important events now in the near future."[25] The Attorney General then referred to the insurgents' vow of vengeance upon captured Unionists in case punishment upon these convictions should take place. The conclusion of the matter was that judgment was suspended in the case of those convicted, and ultimately all the men indicted were released.

In this instance, the Government authorities showed actual embarrassment at the Government's success, and the unwisdom of attempting to execute the judgments was at once recognized. These proceedings at Philadelphia make it easy to understand why the Lincoln Government never cared to prosecute the treason cases. The purpose of the Government was not to convict any individuals for treason. The purpose was to vindicate the laws and protect the nation against disloyalty. The Government's object was precautionary, not punitive. Arrest and detention of dangerous characters was precisely the object which best suited the administration.[26]

---

[25]Bates to J. H. Ashton, Nov. 10, 1861: *ibid.*

[26]The problem of the post-Lincoln indictment of Jefferson Davis, whose case was dropped, is treated below (see pp. 103-117). For eighty years after Lincoln the subject of treason against the United States remained undeveloped by the Supreme Court. Then in 1945 came the pronouncement in the case of Anthony Cramer (Cramer *vs.* U. S., 325 U. S. 1). While the case was pending it was stated in the New York *Times* (Nov. 7, 1944) that the high Court was "taking up the first treason case in its history." Previous proceedings concerning the crime had been in the lower Federal courts, and never before had the Supreme Court "had occasion to review a conviction" (325 U. S., at p. 24).

In the Cramer case the Supreme Court, having been assisted by a special study for that purpose, presented an elaborate historical disquisition on treason: its English and colonial background, revolutionary experience, consideration in the constitutional convention of 1787, and later history. Emphasis was placed on the complete lack of any executions arising from judicial convictions for treason against the United States. There were no such prosecutions because of loyalism in the Revolution; leaders of the Whiskey Rebellion of 1794 "were convicted of treason and then pardoned by the President"; after the Civil War there was "no blood purge" and "No heads rolled." Cramer was accused of having given aid to "two of the German saboteurs who in June 1942 landed on our shores from enemy submarines to disrupt industry in the United States." The majority of the Court found that evidence of any overt act was insufficient to satisfy the "severely restrictive" constitutional provision on this point. The Court therefore reversed the lower court's conviction. It was a five-to-four decision: Jackson, Frankfurter, Murphy, Roberts, and Rutledge constituting the majority; Chief Justice Stone, Douglas, Black, and Reed dissenting. (The opinion was delivered by Jackson, the dissenting opinion by Douglas.) This heavy dissent tended to give the decision a somewhat inconclusive character. Though acquitted of treason, Cramer did not fully escape. He pleaded guilty of violating the trading-with-the-enemy act, and was sentenced to imprisonment for six years.

Not until March 31, 1947, did the Supreme Court uphold a conviction for treason. This was done in the case of Max Haupt (330 U. S. 631), convicted of aiding his son Herbert, one of the German saboteurs executed in 1942. (That execution was obviously not for treason.) The Haupt decision was eight-to-one, Murphy being the lone dissenter. In the mass sedition trial of 1944 (involving Elizabeth Dilling and many others) the labors of the government were prodigious, the court (the Federal district court for the District of Columbia) was worried almost to distraction by obstructionist defense tactics, and the judge, Eicher, died while the case was in progress. After all this effort the prosecution was dropped and never renewed. United States *vs.* McWilliams *et al.*, 54 Fed. Supplement 791. See *Lincoln the Liberal Statesman*, 126-127, 234-235. Later history under the head of treason is not pertinent to this book and is too elaborate for summary here. Prosecutions have been actively pushed by the department of justice, and in a recent memorandum of that department it is stated: "Of the eleven cases [of treason] which have been tried, convictions have been obtained in nine." The most famous cases of successful prosecution for this crime were those of Douglas Chandler, Robert Henry Best, Max Stephan (whose death sentence was commuted to life imprisonment), Mildred E. Gillars ("Axis Sally"), and Iva Toguri D'Acquino ("Toyko Rose"). Recent prosecutions associated in some manner with communism have been under charges other than treason (e.g., perjury, contempt, conspiracy, or espionage). For Supreme Court cases on this subject, see *United States Supreme Court Digest*, vol. XIII, under the title "Treason."

CHAPTER V

THE TREATMENT OF CONFEDERATE LEADERS

I. Policy toward enforcement of the treason statutes at the close of the war

II. The capitulations of surrender in their bearing upon the liability of paroled prisoners of war to trial for treason

III. Davis' imprisonment, and discussion as to the method of his trial

IV. The Government's preparations for the prosecution: The indictment

V. The fourteenth amendment cited in Davis' defense: Dana's doubts concerning the prosecution

VI. Concluding phases of the prosecution: Dismissal of the indictment

I

After the close of the war in April, 1865, a changed situation presented itself with reference to the enforcement of the treason statutes. Lincoln's moderating influence was gone and in its place there came an atmosphere of hysteria and fierce resentment which produced many wild rumors, among which was the story that Confederate leaders were back of the assassination of the President. In some quarters of the South and the border States—notably in Kentucky—returning Confederates took control of matters and made life intolerable for Unionists. President Johnson, after his policy had matured, was as moderate perhaps as Lincoln,[1] but soon the struggle for "reconstruction" brought vindictive radicals to the top, and the influence of such men inevitably appeared in the courts in connection with "treason" cases.

One therefore notices a considerable increase in the number of treason indictments in the years 1865 and 1866. Over nineteen hundred indictments for treason and giving aid and comfort to the enemy were on the docket in Eastern Tennessee in the latter part of 1865,[2] while in Missouri the pending cases included four for treason and one hundred forty-two for conspiracy.[3] In Maryland the docket of the Circuit Court in the same year showed twenty-five indictments.[4] The suggestion had been made that all who left that State to join the "rebel" army should be indicted, and more than four thousand names had been submitted to the grand jury by the military authorities, but the prevailing opinion seems to have been that only the more prominent should be prosecuted.[5] In Kentucky and Virginia many new cases were brought, though not pressed to conviction, in the years '65 and '66.

At Washington there seems to have been no decisive and uniform policy regarding this matter. On one occa-

[1]The close resemblance of Johnson's reconstruction policy to that of Lincoln is especially revealed in connection with Johnson's attempt to bring the Southern States back into the Union in 1865, and in his violent disagreement with Stanton, Sumner, Stevens and, in general, the radicals who favored harsh measures. As to the treatment of Jefferson Davis, Johnson's attitude seems, at least for a time, to have been more vindictive than Lincoln's.

[2]Chicago *Tribune*, Nov. 29, 1865, p. 1.

[3]W. N. Grover, U. S. Dist. Atty. for Mo., to Attorney General Speed, Sept. 13, 1865: Attorney General's papers.

[4]W. I. Jones, U. S. Dist. Atty. for Md., to Attorney General Speed, Nov. 4, 1865: *ibid.*

[5]N. J. Thayer, Asst. U. S. Dist. Atty. for Md., to Attorney General Speed, June 16, 1865: *ibid.*

sion the Attorney General would advise that the Government did not wish "to keep open the sores made in and by the late struggle,"[6] while again in the face of aggravating circumstances he would call for indictments. Attorney General Speed, in writing to Judge Underwood at Alexandria, Virginia, on April 24, 1865, declared that "the rebellious spirit now rampant must be subdued" and referred to the President's "earnest wish" that offenders be brought to justice.[7] A little later disturbances in Kentucky prompted the remark that "indictments against say a dozen of these traitors will cause them all to know and feel that they have a Government with ample and sufficient power to punish the guilty and defend the innocent."[8] It must be remembered, however, that aggravating circumstances, such as the persecution of loyal Union men, made action seem necessary, and that extreme reluctance was always manifested on the part of the Washington authorities in bringing the indictments. Moreover instructions to "dismiss" regularly followed instructions to begin prosecutions, and the President's pardon policy at this time was extremely liberal.

Perhaps the chief reason for the increase of treason indictments after the war was that at this time the treason laws began to be used against adherents of the Confederacy, whereas during the war the efforts toward prosecution were mainly confined to disloyal men within the Northern States. To speak of the supporters of the Confederacy as "traitors" to-day brings a sense of revulsion to the thoughtful American, who realizes that loy-

---

[6]Attorney General Speed to W. N. Grover at St. Louis, Sept. 20, 1865: *ibid.*

[7]*Ibid.*

[8]W. M. Stewart, Chf. Clk., Office of Attorney General, to Cary Cox, Campbellsville, Ky., May 31, 1865: *ibid.*

alty to a sacred cause burned like a pure flame in the South and that patriotism and devotion to home were the high motives which impelled the men of that section to deeds of self-sacrifice and death.

In order properly to understand the history of that unfortunate period, however, one must remember that the Confederates were regarded by the Union authorities as guilty of treason.[9] Though such an attitude was most regrettable, yet it was a fact that according to the laws those who participated in the war on the Confederate side were liable for "treason" and "rebellion" as modified and softened for the emergency, and this traitor status was fully sustained by the Supreme Court.

This idea of the Confederates as traitors produced a vast amount of extreme talk with regard to the punishment of at least the more prominent ones at the close of the war. "When the rebellion is put down in Eastern Virginia," said Senator Trumbull, "it is to be put down by driving into exile, or killing upon the battlefield, or hanging upon the gallows, the traitors who would overrun and oppress Western Virginia."[10] Secretary Welles also favored the execution of the "rebel" leaders for treason. Neither imprisonment nor exile would be lasting he thought. "Parties would form for [the] relief [of the condemned] and [would] ultimately succeed in

[9]In the various arguments concerning the Southerners' liability for treason, little attention seems to have been paid to the second section of the Treason Act of 1862 in which the crime of "rebellion" was defined and a milder penalty than that for treason was fixed. *Supra,* pp. 80-81.

[10]*Cong. Globe,* 37 Cong., 2 sess., p. 3317. Sumner, while urging mildness in general, declared: "But the tallest poppies must drop. For the conspirators, who organized this great crime and let slip the dogs of war, there can be no penalty too great" (*Ibid.,* p. 2196). Trumbull wrote to President Johnson on April 21, 1865: "Any assistance I can render to bring to punishment the leaders of the rebellion . . . will be cheerfully given." (Johnson Papers [MSS., Library of Congress], Vol. 59, No. 2865.)

restoring the worst of them to their homes and . . . priviliges. Death is the proper penalty and atonement, and will be enduringly beneficial in its influence."[11] Speed, Attorney General at the close of the war, thought it was "the plain duty of the President to cause criminal prosecutions to be instituted . . . against some of those who were mainly instrumental in inaugurating and most conspicuous in conducting the late hostilities." He would regard it as a "dire calamity," he said, "if many whom the sword has spared the law would spare also."[12]

Besides many speeches to this effect by various leaders in Washington, there were resolutions of State legislatures, newspaper editorials, and letters from individuals to public men emphasizing the need of trying the more prominent Southerners. Lincoln, of course, did not share these views. He showed clearly in his last Cabinet meeting and on other occasions a disposition to deal kindly with the enemy;[13] but Johnson declared, in April, 1865, that "treason must be made odious" and "traitors must be punished."[14]

Without quoting other expressions of sentiment along the same line, it is sufficient to note that in 1865 the punishment of a few of the Confederate leaders seemed to be a half-formed policy of the administration. Indictment and trial for treason was the method commonly suggested.

---

[11]*Diary of Gideon Welles,* II, 43 (June 1, 1864). In the manuscript of the diary the words "penalty and" bear the appearance of later insertion.

[12]Speed to Johnson, Jan. 4, 1866. Frankfort, (Ky.) *Commonwealth,* Jan. 16, 1866. But at the same time, in particular cases convictions were not definitely sought.

[13]In Lincoln's last Cabinet meeting, says F. W. Seward, all thought that there should be "as few judicial proceedings as possible." "Kindly feelings toward the vanquished . . . pervaded the whole discussion." (F. W. Seward, *Reminiscences of a War-time Statesman and Diplomat,* (254-257.)

[14]Rhodes, *History of the United States,* V, 521.

II

One of the perplexing questions which arose in this connection was whether Confederate prisoners surrendered by Generals Lee and Johnston in the spring of 1865 and released on parole could be arrested and tried for treason. In the terms of surrender allowed by Grant, Lee and his army were permitted to return to their homes, "not to be disturbed by U.S. authority so long as they observe their paroles and the laws in force where they may reside," and when Johnston surrendered to Sherman, this pledge was repeated as to his army.[15] Since General Alexander P. Stewart and various other Confederate officers and soldiers paroled under the terms of the military capitulations, were under indictment, the question as to the legal effect of the terms of surrender attracted widespread attention. In a lengthy and ponderous letter to President Johnson, Benjamin F. Butler argued the criminal liability of Lee's officers and men and urged that they be tried under the municipal law.[16] Such a course, however, met the emphatic disapproval of General Grant. He wrote as follows on June 16, 1865:

> In my opinion the officers and men paroled at Appomattox Court House, and since upon the same terms given to Lee, cannot be tried for treason so long as they observe the terms of their parole. This is my understanding. Good faith, as well as true policy, dictates that we should observe the conditions of that convention. Bad faith on the part of the government or a construction of that convention subjecting officers to trial for treason, would produce a feeling of insecurity in the minds of the paroled officers and men.

In an endorsement dated August 26, 1867, on the

---

[15] *Ibid.*, V, 126, 170.

[16] *Correspondence of B. F. Butler*, V, 602-605.

papers regarding the treason indictment of General Alexander P. Stewart in Tennessee, Grant quoted the foregoing letter and continued:

> The terms granted by me met with the hearty approval of the President at the time, and the country generally. The action of Judge Underwood in Norfolk [in encouraging prosecutions] has already had an injurious effect, and I would ask that he be ordered to quash all indictments found against paroled prisoners of war and to desist from further prosecution of them.[17]

Ordering the judge to quash indictments! This is a rather amusing illustration of the military attitude, but on the main point Grant's position was consistently maintained, and it apparently exerted a controlling influence upon the administration. Directly after the receipt of the aforementioned endorsement, the acting Attorney General wrote to the district attorney in Middle Tennessee: "I have to say in deference to these views of the General of the Army, to which this office takes no legal exception, that you are directed not to press a prosecution for treason against any person in the situation of Mr. Stewart."[18] This advice harmonized with an earlier instruction sent by Attorney General Speed to one of his district attorneys to the effect that no officers or soldiers paroled by the capitulation should be arrested.[19]

---

[17]Enclosure in letter of Acting Attorney General Binckley to U. S. Atty. for Middle Dist., Tenn., Aug. 28, 1867: Attorney General's papers.

[18]*Ibid.* A Federal grand jury at Norfolk in 1865, though indicting Jefferson Davis for treason, refused to proceed against any who had surrendered to commanding generals on parole and had faithfully kept the terms of such parole: Rowland, *Davis*, VII, 142.

[19]Attorney General Speed to L. H. Chandler, U. S. Dist. Atty. at Norfolk, Va., June 20, 1865: Attorney General's papers.

III

Though a few other leaders were placed in confinement, interest naturally centered upon President Jefferson Davis,[20] whose case was not without its sensational features. On May 2, 1865, President Johnson issued a proclamation offering a reward for Davis' arrest. In this proclamation mention was made of Davis' suspected complicity in the assassination of Lincoln, and this groundless suspicion (which was shared by many persons) strongly affected the official attitude toward the Confederate chieftain. When the matter was referred to a committee of the lower house, the investigators, in a long document which included much irrelevant matter, reported "probable cause to believe

---

[20]Among the Confederate leaders imprisoned at the close of the war were Alexander H. Stephens, Clement C. Clay, Jr., John A. Campbell, Z. V. Vance, John H. Reagan, Joseph Wheeler, William Preston Johnston, F. R. Lubbock, S. P. Mallory, and Burton H. Harrison. (For a fuller list, see Oberholtzer, *History of the United States Since the Civil War*, I, 11-14.) After short periods of military imprisonment these men were released. General Robert E. Lee was not imprisoned. Special interest attaches to the case of Alexander H. Stephens, Vice President of the Confederacy. While in custody at Fort Warren, Boston Harbor, Stephens wrote a very long, polite letter to President Johnson, petitioning for release and reviewing his whole political career and creed. He had been brought up, he said, in the "straitest sect of the Crawford-Troup-Jefferson States' rights school of politics," and considered that reserved sovereignty resided with the people of each State. "If my position in the Confederate Government," he added, "was still retained after I clearly saw that the great objects in view by me in accepting it were not likely to be obtained even by the success of the Confederate Arms—after I saw that the Administration of the New Government was pursuing a line of policy leading to directly opposite results to those I was aiming at, . . . it was mainly with the . . . hope that some occasion might arise when my Counsels might be of more avail than they had been." In concluding, he pointed out that the war was inaugurated against his judgment, and that he accepted its results. (Alexander H. Stephens to President Johnson, Ft. Warren, June 8, 1865: Johnson Papers.) The following month Stephens was released.

that he [Davis] was privy to the measures which led to the commission of the deed" [i.e., the murder of the President]. According to this report the testimony "justified the inference that the murder of Mr. Lincoln was procured by the use of money furnished by the Richmond government," but the report was based upon perjured testimony which the witnesses themselves later retracted and declared to be false.[21]

Though killing the President, or conspiracy in connection with such killing, is not treason,[22] yet the determination to prosecute for treason was intensified in the case of Davis by those unsupported rumors which implicated him in the assassination. Davis was captured on May 10, 1865, in Georgia and placed in confinement under military authority at Fortress Monroe. His treatment while in prison, though not inhumane, was not particularly generous. He was far from enjoying the favorable treatment allowed to Aaron Burr, yet the complaints as to his "sufferings," when narrowed down to specific details, refer chiefly to such matters as noise, light in the room at night, and the denial of visitors.[23]

---

[21]Gordon, *Jefferson Davis,* Ch. xx; Rowland, *Davis,* VII, 160; R. F. Nichols, "United States *vs.* Jefferson Davis," *Am. Hist. Rev.,* XXXI, 266.

[22]Hare points out that the safeguards of the Constitution were suspended when the conspirators responsible for Lincoln's assassination were tried by military commission. He then suggests that assault on the President with intent to kill should be declared treason. (Hare, *American Constitutional Law,* II, 1126.) To do this, however, would necessitate amending the Constitution, in which the crime of treason is defined.

[23]For a time no one was permitted to visit Davis, but this rule was later relaxed. After earnest pleadings, addressed to President Johnson and other men of influence, Mrs. Davis was permitted to visit her husband, and he was allowed to confer with his counsel. While the Attorney General claimed to have no jurisdiction over Davis, yet he gave much thought to the question of his detention and trial, and received weekly reports from the military surgeon, George E. Cooper, as to the distinguished prisoner's health. During Davis'

It was for only a short time that he was kept in shackles. In the later stages of his confinement he was allowed considerable freedom within the fortress grounds, and was given airy rooms in Carroll Hall, a building formerly used for officers' quarters.

During this imprisonment, plans were being matured for Davis' trial.[24] When the question was discussed in Johnson's Cabinet, the chief problem for decision was whether the trial should be by military commission or before the ordinary civil tribunals. Seward favored a military trial and had no faith in the civil courts. Welles doubted whether resort to a military commission would be justified, and favored a civil trial.[25] Opinions differed as to what the charge should be, some favoring the charge of treason, and others, murder. As suggestions poured in from many sources it became evident that those who were most eager for the fallen leader's pun-

---

confinement his correspondence went through the office of the Secretary of War. The military imprisonment of the former Confederate President, which covered two years, was, of course, a severe hardship. Had he been under the civil courts, he would have been admitted to bail while awaiting trial.

[24]Among the sources which the writer has used for the Davis trial are the records of the Federal Circuit Court at Richmond (which he examined personally and of which transcripts were made for his use); the papers and letter books of the Attorney General's office; the Johnson papers; the Diary of Orville H. Browning; the Stanton papers; the "Records and Briefs of the United States Supreme Court"; the original docket of that tribunal; and the extensive collection of Davis papers edited by Dunbar Rowland. Turning from sources to historical studies, one finds a useful survey in Armistead C. Gordon, *Jefferson Davis*, Ch. xx, and a definitive treatment in an article entitled "United States *vs.* Jefferson Davis," by Roy F. Nichols in the *Am. Hist. Rev.*, XXXI, 266-284. See also: D. K. Watson, "The Trial of Jefferson Davis: An Interesting Constitutional Question," *Yale Law Jour.*, XXIV, 669-676; H. H Hagan, "United States *vs.* Jefferson Davis," *Sewanee Rev.*, XXV, 220-225; E. P. Oberholtzer, *History of the United States*, Vol. I; *Southern Hist. Soc. Papers*, I, 319-325; John J. Craven, *Prison Life of Jefferson Davis.*

[25]*Diary of Gideon Welles*, II, 335-336.

ishment wanted a military tribunal; while others, who desired a trial but at the same time wished every concession to fair play, favored a civil proceeding. In one of the many letters which the President received on the subject the suggestion was made that the "treason" was committed by the State of Mississippi before Davis "made war"; that in obeying the order of that State he was but obeying his sovereign; and that, having recognized him as a belligerent, the United States could not consistently charge him with treason. The same writer, however, claimed that as belligerent, Davis had committed various atrocities, such as the Fort Pillow massacre, and that for these "crimes" he could be tried by court-martial.[26] The decision as to method of trial was deferred from time to time, and gradually the idea of a military proceeding was abandoned.

The hesitating attitude of the administration was doubtless due in part to serious divergences of opinion throughout the country with regard to the policy toward Davis. Greeley, with his New York *Tribune*, strong in its influence upon certain sections of Northern opinion, favored a generous treatment, and was emphatic in his advocacy of civil over military tribunals in the case of political offenders. The Chicago *Tribune*, on the other hand, voiced radical opinion in urging severe punish-

---

[26]Former Governor E. D. Morgan of New York to President Johnson, May 31, 1865 (referred to Attorney General Speed): Attorney General's Papers. This argument as to the inappropriateness of the treason charge when applied to acts performed by a recognized belligerent government, was also used by Davis' friends. On this subject James M. Mason of Virginia wrote to Davis as follows: "The principle which they [the Federal authorities] can never get round . . . is, that whatever you did in wielding the Army, and whatever others did in counsel, were *acts of war*—immediately and all the time recognized by a power competent in law to conduct War, and entitling those bona fide so acting to all immunities arising from Acts of War. . . ." (Mason to Davis, Ap. 22, 1868: Rowland, *Davis*, VII, 239.)

ment.[27] Among the resolutions of State legislatures in Davis' behalf, those of Kentucky are particularly worth noting. After announcing the principle that a "brave people should ever be generous, and an enlightened nation never know revenge," the legislature resolved that Davis had committed no crime greater than that of thousands who had received pardon, and that his conviction was not necessary "to settle the legal estimate of treason" nor "to determine whether secession be treason or a right."[28]

IV

After many delays, the Government at Washington finally turned its attention to actual preparations for the Davis prosecution. For this purpose the Government was reënforced by an unusual array of legal talent. Stanbery, Attorney General in 1867, finding that his official duties left no time for the details of the prosecution, and desiring to avoid all active connection with it, appointed William M. Evarts as the leading special counsel for the United States, and R. H. Dana, Jr. was made his associate.[29] In addition to these distinguished lawyers, the Government also engaged on its side H. H. Wells, who had been military governor of Virginia, and the work of these men was supplemented by the official activities of S. Ferguson Beach and L. H. Chandler, who served at different times as Federal district attorney at Richmond. When, on July 18, 1868, Evarts himself became Attorney General, the situation was only slightly changed, for in this new capacity he still continued his

[27]Chicago *Tribune*, Oct. 3, 1865, p. 2.

[28]Resolution of Kentucky Legislature, Dec. 8, 1865.

[29]In the earlier stages of the case, J. H. Clifford and L. H. Rousseau acted as special counsel for the Government.

general direction of the prosecution. The appointment of such special counsel, involving a considerable outlay of money, and the frequent conferences and correspondence which took place on the subject, indicate that the trial of Davis was a matter in which the administration took an active interest.

Certain indictments against Davis that were brought at Norfolk and at Washington in 1865 were dropped; but on May 10, 1866, he was again indicted for treason by the grand jury in the United States Circuit Court at Richmond, Virginia. A year ensued before any steps were taken to prosecute this charge, this delay being due to the military rule which prevailed in Virginia, the unwillingness of Chief Justice Chase to take charge of the case, and the uncertainty of policy as to what should be done with the distinguished prisoner.

In order that the Federal Court at Richmond obtain custody of Davis, it was necessary to release him from the military authorities. This was done by *habeas corpus* writ issued by the Federal Circuit Court at Richmond to General Henry S. Burton, in charge of the prisoner.[30] The importance of this great writ is illustrated by the fact that by means of it Davis' imprisonment under executive and military power was terminated through the normal operation of a judicial process.

On May 13, 1867, as the record reads,[31] "the said Jefferson Davis was led to the bar in custody of the marshal, and, the prosecution not being ready for trial, the defendant, through his counsel, . . . moved that he be admitted to bail, and there being no objection on the

[30]The *habeas corpus* writ directing the release of Davis from military custody, and General Burton's return thereto, are given in Rowland, *Davis*, VII, 168, 169. For proceedings in the President's Cabinet on this subject, see "Notes of Col. W. G. Moore," *Am. Hist. Rev.*, XIX, 99.

[31]Records of the Circuit Court of the United States, Richmond, Va.

part of the Government, Mr. Davis gave bond in the sum of $100,000 to appear in court on November 4."[32]

"The prosecution not being ready for trial"—this was always the obstacle in the Davis proceedings.[33] Again in November, 1867, the Government was unready, and the case was "continued." Elaborate plans were by this time on foot for the preparation of a new indictment. According to arrangements made by the Government's lawyers, General Wells and District Attorney Chandler conducted the day-to-day examination of witnesses before the grand jury, and the evidence so collected, in connection with documents drawn from the Confederate archives at Washington, was to be placed before Evarts and Dana, whose task it was to draw the indictment.[34] On March 26, 1868, the grand jury "appeared in court and upon their oaths presented 'A Bill of Indictment against Jefferson Davis for treason, a true bill.'"

In this lengthy and tiresome indictment the charge is treason under the Act of 1790 and the specifications relate to various acts of a military sort and otherwise, connected with the war. It reads in part as follows:

The grand jurors . . . upon their oaths . . . respectively . . . find and present that Jefferson Davis, late of the city of Richmond in the county of Henrico and District of Virginia,

[32]Among the sureties on Davis' bond were Gerrit Smith, Horace Greeley, and Cornelius Vanderbilt.

[33]One reads between the lines of the proceedings considerable embarrassment on the part of the Government when faced with the problem of actually trying Davis on the treason charge. The record of June 5, 1866, in the Circuit Court at Richmond shows the counsel for the defense vigorously pressing the question as to what the gentlemen representing the United States proposed to do with reference to the indictment for treason then pending, while the prosecution replied with excuses for delaying the trial. See Rowland, *Davis*, VII, 152-153.

[34]Evarts to Chandler, Feb. 18, 1868: Attorney General's papers.

Gentleman, being a citizen . . . of . . . the United States . . . and owing allegiance and fidelity to the said United States, not being mindful of his said duty of allegiance, and wickedly devising and intending the peace of the United States to disturb, and to excite and levy war against the said United States, on the first day of June in the year [1861], at Richmond . . . did . . . traitorously collect and assist in collecting great numbers of persons armed, equipped and organized as military forces for the purpose of levying war against the said United States, and did assume the command-in-chief of the said forces, and with said forces did unlawfully and traitorously take forcible possession of the said city of Richmond and the said county of Henrico. . . . That the said Jefferson Davis . . . did maliciously and traitorously levy war against the said United States and did commit the crime of treason against the said United States . . . contrary to the . . . statute . . . approved on the thirteenth day of April, [1790].

That on the first day of August in the year . . . [1862], a great many persons whose names are to the grand jurors unknown, to the number of [100,000] and more, were assembled, armed, . . . equipped and organized as military forces . . . and were maliciously and traitorously engaged in levying war against the said United States in . . . Virginia . . . and in . . . North Carolina, South Carolina, Georgia, Florida, Alabama, Mississippi, Louisiana, Texas, Arkansas, Tennessee, and Missouri. And that the said Jefferson Davis . . . did send to and procure for the said forces munitions of war, provisions, and clothing, and did give to said forces information, counsel, and advice . . . to assist them in the levying of war as aforesaid.[35]

---

[35]This indictment was copied by the writer from the original in the files of the Circuit Court of the United States at Richmond. The whole document is so elaborate and verbose as to be unreadable. It is given in full in Rowland, *Davis*, VII, 179-195. The indictment was found on the testimony of Robert E. Lee, James A. Seddon, John Letcher, George Wythe and others by a grand jury composed of recently emancipated Negroes and whites who could take the "test oath."

The indictment also mentions the first battle of Manassas, and Davis is charged with having traitorously coöperated with Lee, Benjamin, Breckinridge, and other specified Confederate leaders. His address of February 10, 1864, to Confederate soldiers, is further cited in a legalistic and tautological enumeration of matters selected somewhat at random.

It is noteworthy that instead of treason being charged under the act of July 17, 1862, which allowed fine and imprisonment as an alternative to the death penalty, the charge was brought under the Treason Act of 1790; so that if conviction had been obtained the penalty would necessarily have been death. In that case, pardon alone would have saved Davis' life. This fact made conviction less likely.

V

In spite of the gravity of the offense with which he was charged, Davis was again admitted to bail. Being permitted to choose his counsel, he had selected Charles O'Conor, William B. Reed, R. Ould, and James Lyons. These men had singled out one constitutional point above all others as the principal basis for the defense. They took care to have Davis' oath to support the Constitution of the United States (taken in 1845 as a member of the House of Representatives) made a part of the record. Then, in a paper filed with the Court, they declared that the defendant alleged in bar of any proceedings upon the said indictment the penalties and disabilities denounced against him in the third section of the Fourteenth Amendment to the Constitution, "and he insists that any judicial pain, penalty or punishment upon him for such alleged offense is not admissible by the Constitution and laws of the United States."

The Fourteenth Amendment contains the following provision:

No person shall be a Senator or Representative in Congress, or elector of President and Vice President, or hold any office, civil or military, under the United States, or under any State, who, having previously taken an oath, as a member of Congress, or as an officer of the United States, or as a member of any State legislature, or as an executive or judicial officer of any State, to support the Constitution of the United States, shall have engaged in insurrection or rebellion against the same, or given aid or comfort to the enemies thereof. But Congress may by a vote of two-thirds of each House, remove such disability.

It was arguable that the case of such leaders as Davis had already been dealt with in a constitutional amendment which took into view the violation of a Federal oath, and that disability from office-holding was in the nature of a punishment for the offense of violated allegiance. Not death, nor even fine and imprisonment, was indicated as the penalty, but only disability from holding office, and this disability was removable by action of Congress. Any further punishment seemed to be out of harmony with the amendment, and the disabilities named therein would indeed seem absurd if the purpose were to prosecute the offenders for treason under the old act of 1790 and inflict the penalty of death.[36]

[36]The issue hinged upon the question as to whether the disability feature of the Fourteenth Amendment amounted to a punishment. Davis' counsel argued that it did, and that this was the only punishment that could be legally inflicted; for to add to the existing penalty would be an *ex post facto* provision, increasing the punishment of a crime previously committed. Dana replied for the Government that the amendment did not inflict a punishment, but established "a general permanent provision respecting classes of persons entitled to office," and that it did not repeal existing penalties for treason. Though this point was never settled by the Supreme Court, yet Chief Justice Chase put on record his opinion that the indictment should

In contrast to the confident tone on the part of Davis' counsel, one finds a certain weakening among the Government's lawyers. On August 24, 1868, while the prosecution was still pending, Dana wrote to Evarts, then Attorney General, expressing grave misgivings as to the wisdom of proceeding further with the prosecution. Because of the important points of law and policy which he touched upon it may be well to note rather fully the trend of his comments.[37]

Dana began his letter by pointing out how much his mind had been moved from the first by doubts as to the expediency of trying Davis at all. At length, he said, these doubts had ripened into convictions. He could see no good reason why the Government should make any question whether the late Civil War was treason and whether Davis took any part in it, submitting questions of that nature to the decision of a petit jury at Richmond. The only constitutional question seemed to be whether a levying of war which would otherwise be treason was relieved of that character by the fact that it took the form of secession from the Union by State authority—in other words, whether the secession of a State was a constitutional right. That issue, however,

have been quashed and that further proceedings should have been declared to be barred by the amendment. (Rowland, *Davis*, VII, 200-227.) Strangely enough, it has been maintained that this disability feature of the Fourteenth Amendment was not confined to the Civil War, and is still in force. When, during World War I, the Socialist Congressman, Victor L. Berger, was excluded from the House of Representatives, the committee reporting on his case held section 3 of the Fourteenth Amendment to be effective against him. For able comments, see Chafee, *Freedom of Speech*, 322 *et seq*.

[37]This notable letter by Dana is found in the Attorney General's papers, now in the National Archives. A copy was sent to President Johnson, who wrote thereon the following indorsement: "Richard Dana's opinion in ref. to Jeff. Davis' release. This opinion must be filed with care. A. J." (Johnson Papers, Vol. 144, No. 22377.) Dr. Nichols, in his article above cited, shows that Clifford had doubts similar to those of Dana. (*Amer. Hist. Rev.*, XXXI, 274.)

he supposed to be already settled. The Supreme Court in the *Prize Cases* had held that acts of States could not be pleaded as justification for the war and had no legal effect on the character of the war. He regarded it as a matter of history that the law-making and executive departments had treated the secession and the war as treason.

The only question of fact submitted to the jury would be whether Davis took any part in the war. This he did not consider a fact appropriate for the jury to decide. The indictment would be tried in a region formerly within enemy's territory, a region which was not yet restored to the exercise of all its political functions and where the fires were not extinct. It would only require one juror to defeat the Government and give Jefferson Davis and his favorers a triumph. Such a favorer might get upon the jury, or a fear of personal violence or ostracism might be enough to induce at least one juror to withhold assent to a verdict of conviction. This possible result, said Dana, would be most humiliating to the Government, and none the less so from the fact that it would be absurd.

Then, too, the question of the death penalty presented a difficulty. It would be beneath the dignity of the Government and of the issue to inflict a minor punishment; and as to a sentence of death, Dana felt surc that after the lapse of time which had occurred since the war the people would not desire to see it enforced.

By pursuing the trial, Dana urged, the Government could get only a reaffirmation by a circuit court at *nisi prius* of a rule of public law already settled for this country in every way that such a matter could be settled. In the needless pursuit of this object, the Government would be giving to a jury within the region of the "rebellion" a chance to disregard the law when announced. The jury would also have the opportunity to ignore the fact that Davis took any part in the late Civil War. To assume the risk of such an absurd and discreditable issue of a great state trial for the sake of a verdict, which, if obtained, would settle nothing new, either in law or fact, and which would probably never be executed, seemed to Dana extremely unwise.

Attorney General Evarts transmitted Dana's letter to President Johnson,[38] and there seems little doubt that the views so expressed had influence upon the administration in its attitude toward the Davis proceedings.

VI

The later phases of the Davis case may be briefly stated. The defense moved the quashing of the indictment on the ground of its inconsistency with the disability clause of the Fourteenth Amendment, and the Government opposed the motion.[39] On the constitutional point involved in connection with the motion to quash, the court disagreed and certified their disagreement to the Supreme Court of the United States. At last it seemed that this important case, or rather a particular phase of it, was about to be heard by the highest tribunal of the land; but on December 25, 1868, an unconditional pardon of all who had participated in the war was issued by the President, and shortly afterward the

[38] Dr. Nichols points out that this letter was read in Cabinet on November 6, 1868. (*Am. Hist. Rev.*, XXXI, 281.)

[39] These last proceedings on the motion to quash the indictment were presided over by Chief Justice Chase who had, in the earlier stages, refused to preside over the Circuit Court in Virginia because of the military power exercised in that State. It would be unbecoming in the Chief Justice of the United States, he thought, to preside over a quasi-military court. (Rowland, *Davis*, VII, 157.) Some attributed this attitude of Chase to a reluctance to preside at Davis' trial: *ibid.*, 239.

indictment was dismissed by the Circuit Court at Richmond, and the case was also dropped from the docket of the Supreme Court at Washington.[40] Following two years of imprisonment, and nineteen months on bail, Jefferson Davis was at last a free man. His persistent demand, however, that his case be tried, was not complied with.

Looking back over the various phases of this abortive prosecution, one finds it hard to understand why serious efforts should have been made to obtain a conviction of Davis. The usual practice in such cases is amnesty for political offenses, and in fact this policy of amnesty had been proclaimed and adhered to with regard to those who had supported the Confederacy. The proclamations of amnesty prior to December, 1868, had been qualified by certain conditions and exceptions, but thousands of special pardons were granted to those excluded from the general proclamations. Finally, on Christmas day, 1868, came an amnesty proclamation which covered every one. Other indictments for treason were dismissed, and the active promotion of Davis' prosecution up to the time of the proclamation of unconditional amnesty was unusual. If at any time the word had been sent from Washington to move the dismissal of the indictment, it would have been dismissed, but instead the administration continued its efforts toward a prosecution. As Dr. R. F. Nichols[41] has shown in his excellent study of this sub-

[40]On the unpublished docket of the United States Supreme Court, under the date of February 19, 1869, there is this entry: "on motion of the Attorney General, Adjudged to be dismissed." (Case 327, Dec. term, 1868, *Docket 1868*, *Sup. Court of U. S.*)

[41]After having made an independent study of the Davis case from the sources, the author was fortunately able, when on the point of sending his book to the press, to use in the final revision the scholarly and exhaustive article by Dr. Roy Franklin Nichols in the *Am. Hist. Rev.*, XXXI, 266-284. For a full discussion of the subject one should read this article.

ject, the Davis case was entangled in Reconstruction politics; and the influence of the radicals in Congress was a factor which tended to prevent an earlier release. Johnson, however, with certain of his Cabinet supporters, did not hesitate to brook these radicals, and they were mindful of the fact that in various quarters the political effect of universal amnesty would be desirable; while continued efforts to prosecute the case involved the likelihood of an adverse decision by the Supreme Court or an acquittal by a Virginia jury. Governmental success before both court and jury seemed a remote possibility (except, perhaps, to such a man as John C. Underwood[42]); but such success would itself have been most embarrassing, for it would have involved the death penalty for the President of the Confederacy. In the strong probability of presidential pardon, the conviction of Davis, obtained at considerable cost and with great irritation, would have been futile. Release by the dismissal of the indictment seemed the only way out; and as we have seen in our general survey of the treason cases, this was the regular procedure.[43]

---

[42]John C. Underwood, Federal district judge in Virginia, had promoted the indictment against Davis, and had been active in procuring confiscations in Virginia. His attitude seems not to have been characterized by judicial detachment. Had Davis been brought to trial, it would presumably have been before Judge Underwood and Chief Justice Chase in the Circuit Court at Richmond. R. F. Nichols, *op. cit.*, pp. 267, 269.

[43]Even after Johnson's proclamation of full pardon and amnesty, all who had sworn officially to support the Constitution and had later engaged in the "rebellion" were under the disqualification of the Fourteenth Amendment as to State or Federal office-holding. In 1898 Congress removed the existing disability, though the wording of the act seemed to recognize that similar disabilities would apply to a possible future insurrection or rebellion. *U. S. Stat. at Large*, XXX, 432.

CHAPTER VI

THE POWER TO SUSPEND THE HABEAS CORPUS PRIVILEGE

I. Statement of the constitutional problem regarding the suspension of the privilege of the *habeas corpus* writ
II. Principal arguments for and against the President's power of suspension
III. Ambiguous action of Congress
IV. Inconclusive character of the Civil War precedent
V. Present status of the controversy

This chapter and the three following deal with topics that are virtually parts of the same subject. The present chapter has to do with the President's power of suspending the *habeas corpus* privilege as against that of Congress; Chapters VII and VIII will treat the actual measures resulting from the suspension and involving military control over civilians, while the succeeding chapter will be devoted to the protection of officials from judicial liability for acts, otherwise unwarranted, which were committed during the period of suspension.

I

The question as to whether Congress or the President has the authority to suspend the privilege of the writ is one of the most famous and familiar controversies in our constitutional history. Perhaps no other feature of Union policy was more widely criticized nor more strenuously defended, and the whole subject has been elaborately debated by statesmen, editors, jurists, generals, pamphleteers, and historians.

The provision of the Constitution reads as follows:

> The privilege of the writ of *habeas corpus* shall not be suspended, unless when in cases of rebellion or invasion the public safety may require it.[1]

Plainly the intention is that, in the specified emergencies—rebellion or invasion—this vital privilege may, for the preservation of public safety, be suspended. But various questions immediately arise. Who is to judge of the existence of rebellion or invasion within the meaning of the Constitution? Recognizing that the privilege is to be suspended only when its continued maintenance would menace public safety, who is to determine when that point has been reached? Does the silence of the Constitution regarding the authority to suspend signify that the question was left open, or does a fair construction require one to conclude that the power to suspend was understood by the framers to rest with Congress and that an explicit statement was avoided only because this point of law seemed already established beyond a reasonable doubt? If not an exclusive congressional function, could the suspending power be considered "concurrent" as between the President and Congress, so that the President might act in the absence of congressional provision?

Still other questions would arise, assuming that the foregoing had been settled, as, for instance, whether Congress could delegate the power to the President, whether the President could delegate it to his subordinates, and whether a rebellion in one part of the country could justify the suspension in a remote and loyal part. Such, in broad outline, were the main points at issue in this much-discussed problem.

---

[1] *U. S. Constitution,* Art. I, sec. 9, par. 2.

II

In support of the view that the suspending power lies exclusively in Congress, Chief Justice Taney's well-known decision in the Merryman case stands as perhaps the most vigorous exposition.

The details of the case, which are reserved for later consideration, mark it as a typical instance of conflict between the military and judicial authorities.[2] The essential fact was that a general had resisted the execution of the writ of *habeas corpus* and that in so doing he appealed to the President's suspending order. The Chief Justice in "filing" his opinion argued strenuously that the President had no lawful power to issue such an order. English and colonial precedents were adduced to support this contention. The colonists were shown to have been extremely jealous of executive usurpation, while in England no power short of Parliament could authorize the suspension. Invoking the rule of construction according to context, Taney pointed out that the provision regarding *habeas corpus* appears in that portion of the Constitution which pertains to legislative powers. Story was quoted as authority for the view that Congress has the power to suspend as well as the exclusive right to judge of the exigency requiring suspension. Marshall's opinion in the Bollman and Swartwout case was cited to the effect that "if . . . the public safety should require the suspension it is for the legislature to say so."[3] Since the courts were uninterrupted, Taney maintained that any suspected treason should have been reported to the district attorney and dealt with by judicial process. The

---

[2]*Ex parte* Merryman, 17 Fed. Cas. 144. See *infra*, pp. 161-162.

[3]4 Cranch 101.

overriding of such process in loyal parts of the country he denounced as military usurpation. If such usurpation be permitted, he said, "the people of the United States are no longer living under a government of laws; but every citizen holds life, liberty and property at the will and pleasure of the army officer in whose military district he may happen to be found."

Putting the matter solemnly up to the President, he declared that it would "remain for that high officer, in fulfillment of his constitutional obligation to 'take care that the laws be faithfully executed,' to determine what measures he will take to cause the civil process of the United States to be respected and enforced."

The extent to which President Lincoln stood in need of this solemn admonition may best be judged by his attitude at the time the suspension was authorized. As a matter of fact few measures of the Lincoln administration were adopted with more reluctance than this suspension of the citizen's safeguard against arbitrary arrest. This reluctance appears in the fact that only a qualified suspension was ordered in 1861, that the military authorities were enjoined to use the power sparingly, that the action was taken during a recess of Congress, and that an early opportunity was taken to lay the matter before the special session of Congress convened for the emergency in the summer of '61.

Lincoln's secretaries have preserved for us the original autograph draft of his message to this special session, and it is an instructive exercise to compare this draft with the revised and published form of the message. Selected portions of the earlier and later forms of the message are placed in parallel columns below:[4]

---

[4]Nicolay and Hay, *Lincoln,* IV, 176; Richardson, *Messages . . . of the Presidents,* VI, 24.

Original Autograph	*Published Form*
Soon after the first call for militia, *I felt it my duty* to authorize the commanding general, in proper cases . . . to suspend the privilege of the writ of *habeas corpus*. . . .	*it was considered a duty*
At my verbal request, as well as by the general's own inclination, this authority has been exercised but very sparingly. Nevertheless, . . . *I have been reminded from a high quarter* that one who is sworn to "take care that the laws be faithfully executed" should not himself be one to violate them.	*This authority has purposely been exercised . . . sparingly.* *the attention of the country has been called to the proposition, etc.*
Of course *I gave some consideration to the questions of power and propriety before I acted* in this matter.	*. . . some consideration was given . . . before this matter was acted upon.*
The whole of the laws *which I was sworn to* [*execute*] were being resisted . . . in nearly one-third of the States.	*The whole of the laws which were required to be . . . executed.*
Must I have allowed them to finally fail of execution? Are all the laws but one to go unexecuted, and the Government itself go to pieces, lest that one be violated?	*Must they be allowed to finally fail?*
. . . *But . . . I was not, in my own judgment, driven to this ground. In my opinion, I violated no law.* The provision of the Constitution . . . is equivalent to a provision that [the] privilege may be suspended when, in cases of rebellion or invasion, the public safety does require it.	*But it was not believed that this question was presented. It was not believed that any law was violated.*
. . . *I decided* that we have a case of rebellion.	*It was decided*, etc.

In the original autograph one may read, as it were, the President's mental struggling at the time the decision was taken. In this remarkable document may be seen the clearest indication that the appearance of military dictatorship was a matter of deep concern to the nation's war chief and that his action was determined by what he believed to be the imperative demands of the actual situation. His course in this matter was in keeping with other acts, such as the call for troops and the blockade, in which momentous decisions had to be reached during the recess of the legislature.[5]

In justification of his course Lincoln argued his paramount duty as chief executive to preserve the integrity of the Government, a duty on whose performance the life of the whole Constitution rested. In Lincoln's view there was no violation of the Constitution, since the Constitution permits suspension when the public safety requires it during a rebellion and does not specify what branch of the Government is to exercise the suspending power. As the provision was plainly made for an emergency, he argued, the natural inference is that the President should use his discretion, not that the danger should run its course till Congress could be called together. When the public safety does require it, the suspension is constitutional. After mature thought he decided that a rebellion existed and that the public safety did require a qualified suspension. It was therefore authorized.

Such was Lincoln's answer to the opinion of Chief Justice Taney. For a more detailed defense of the Presi-

---

[5]On this point Lincoln's critics would reply that the long recess of the national legislature in 1861 was an unfortunate condition for which the President himself was responsible, since he might have called Congress into session at once on the outbreak of war. While his proclamation convening the extra session of Congress was issued on April 15, 1861, the day set for the opening of the session was July 4. (*U. S. Stat. at Large*, XII, 1258.)

dent's course one may turn to such documents as the opinion of Attorney General Bates and the elaborate pamphlets of Horace Binney. Bates contended[6] that the three great branches of the Government are coordinate and that the executive cannot rightly be subjected to the judiciary, as would be the case if a high executive function should be obstructed by a judicial writ. The President, he maintained, is in a peculiar manner the preserver, protector and defender of the Constitution; and it is particularly his duty to put down a rebellion because the courts are too weak to do so, while all the means of suppression are in his hands. That the President is judge of the exigency and of the manner of discharging his duty has been already held by the Supreme Court, said Bates, in an analogous case.[7] Granted that the power opens the way for possible abuse, it is just as true that a legislature may be factious or a court corrupt. The President cannot be required to appear before a judge to answer for his official acts. A *habeas corpus* hearing is like an appeal, and a judge at chambers cannot entertain an appeal from a decision of the President of the United States, especially in a case purely political. In spite, therefore, of the Chief Justice's decision limiting the right of suspending the *habeas corpus* privilege to the legislature, Bates contended that, as a temporary and exceptional matter in an emergency, the President has the power to order a suspension and is under no obligation to obey a writ of a court after capturing insurgents or spies. For any breach of trust, he said, the President is answerable before the high court of impeachment and before no other tribunal.

In the writings of the contemporary legal pamphleteer,

---

[6]Opinion of Attorney General Bates, July 5, 1861: *O. R.*, Ser. II, Vol. 2, pp. 20-30.

[7]Martin *vs.* Mott, 12 Wheaton 19.

Horace Binney, executive suspension finds learned support.[8] By way of contrast rather than analogy, Binney begins with a discussion of English practice. He shows that, for centuries before 1679 and in spite of the prohibition of *Magna Carta*, arbitrary imprisonment existed in England. For general and unspecified "high treason," imprisonment by executive warrant, without bail or trial, was practiced; and even Coke admits the propriety of such a proceeding. Under the old rule, "there was no danger of state, whether there was rebellion or invasion or not, in which the Crown could not issue a warrant to arrest and imprison a suspected traitor or conspirator of treason and hold him imprisoned with a practical indefiniteness." By the act of 1679 this power was taken away from the monarch and the guardianship of the *habeas corpus* privilege has since rested with Parliament.

But in this respect American and English law are not analogous. The restriction in England is not a general prohibition of the suspension of the writ, but rather a limitation upon the King, since Parliament may suspend at any time, regardless of whether there is rebellion or not. The motive back of the English law was jealousy of the Crown, while in America, Binney argued, there was nothing in the feeble office of the President that could excite jealousy.[9]

It is only by legislative act that the writ may be overruled in England, but in the United States the Constitution itself authorizes the suspension and no further authorization is needed. All that remains is to bring about the suspension in the conditioned case. In this whole matter, continued Binney, the Constitution must be

[8]Horace Binney, *The Privilege of the Writ of Habeas Corpus under the Constitution* (Philadelphia, 1862).

[9]In this portion of his argument Binney quoted Bulwer-Lytton and De Tocqueville to show that the American executive is "feeble."

judged by itself and not by the English constitution or by the powers of Parliament.

In the debates and records of the constitutional convention there seemed to Binney something mysterious about the *habeas corpus* clause. In his opinion there appeared to be a deliberate hushing of the subject, which was concealed as a sort of skeleton in the closet. The silence regarding such matters as executive imprisonment, the period of time during which the suspension might obtain, the nature of the offense for which the privilege might be withdrawn, the authority to suspend, and the process of warrant and arrest to be pursued—all this inexactness seemed to result from a reluctance to dwell upon the subject.

The framers in Binney's view should have been more explicit, for it is a timid horseman who puts a blind upon his horse. The clause as written by Pinckney had provided that the privilege should not be "suspended by the legislature except on the most urgent and pressing conditions and for a limited time not exceeding——— months." (The number of months was left blank.) Later Gouverneur Morris moved the clause practically as it now stands while the powers of the judiciary were under consideration. It was the Committee on Style and Arrangement which grouped it with the clauses concerning Congress. Thus, according to Binney, the word legislature was "struck out" and the clause as it stands is a substitute for Pinckney's wording which would have placed the power with Congress.[10]

In determining which department has the power to

[10]The selection of Morris' wording instead of Pinckney's seems to indicate that the convention consciously and deliberately rejected a phraseology that would have attached the suspending function to the national legislature. (Gaillard Hunt and J. B. Scott, editors, *The Debates in the Federal Convention of 1787 . . . Reported by James Madison, a Delegate from Virginia*, 227, 477.)

suspend, the vital question, as Binney saw it, is as to which department is more particularly charged with care for the public safety. Does it require an act of Congress, he asked, to declare that a rebellion or invasion exists? No, it is the President's power and duty to decide the existence of a rebellion. So far as the calling out of the militia is concerned, this fact has been fully established, as in the Whisky Rebellion, the *Martin* vs. *Mott* decision, and on other occasions. In an actual rebellion or invasion the declaration and proclamation of the fact rest unquestionably with the executive, and no other department could appropriately decide the fact. What is true as regards the calling of the militia is equally true concerning the suspension of the *habeas corpus* privilege, for considering the methods and devices of rebellion, open and covert, the power of suspending is a most reasonable attribution to the executive power. History, it was pointed out, attests the justice of this interpretation, for during the time of the Burr conspiracy the Senate, from motives of partisanship, passed a bill suspending the privilege for three months in the case of men who had committed treason, nothing being said of rebellion or invasion. From this may be argued the unwisdom of leaving such a function to Congress.

It is a mistake, said Binney, to assume that the Constitution authorized only such things as can be carried into effect by statute. In this matter of withdrawing the writ, the Constitution takes the place of the English Parliament. The Constitution itself, by clear implication legalizes the suspension. "The Constitution does not authorize any department of the Government to authorize it. The Constitution itself authorizes it."

III

It is a striking fact that at the time of heated controversy over this subject, when nearly all were doubting, and many flatly denying the President's right, Congress made no declaration indicative of its will. In Dr. Sellery's scholarly monograph[11] the conclusion is reached that this long inaction served as a tacit sanction of the President's right; but many who were supporting Lincoln, as notably Lyman Trumbull, maintained in principle the exclusive power of Congress, and the inaction may just as well have been due to failure to find any formula upon which a majority could unite. In the search for a compromise that would save the face of the President without sanctioning the principle on which he acted, actual legislation was long delayed, and when it was finally accomplished, a non-committal phraseology was adopted.

In all three of the sessions of the thirty-seventh Congress the subject of the suspension was considered in one form or another. In the hurried special session during the summer of 1861 the previous orders of the President were ratified so far as they related to the army and navy and the calling out of the militia.[12]

This bit of legislation has usually been interpreted as a sanction of the President's suspension of the *habeas corpus* privilege. The ratifying clause, however, made no mention of this suspension, and this omission is all the more remarkable in view of the fact that the question of arbitrary arrests had been made a matter of debate. As if still further to emphasize the reticence of Congress on the subject, the provision was irrelevantly

---

[11]George Clark Sellery, "Lincoln's Suspension of Habeas Corpus as Viewed by Congress," *Bull. of Univ. of Wis.*, Hist. Ser., I, No. 3, pp. 213-286.

[12]*U. S. Stat. at Large*, XII, 326; *supra*, p. 55.

tucked away in an act to increase the pay of privates in the army.

Even if this measure could be regarded as a satisfactory ratification of the President's previous acts, it still did not touch the main issue. The question was not merely the President's power to suspend during a recess of Congress, but his assumption of that power even when Congress is in session. Over and above the brief and defective measure of 1861, which covered an emergency, it remained for Congress to formulate some act of legislation that would apply at least as long as the war continued, and would state the way in which, and the basis upon which, the privilege of the writ might be suspended, assuming, of course, that such suspension was to be approved.

In the second session of the thirty-seventh Congress, extending from December, 1861, to July, 1862, there was also a failure to enact any law on this subject. The House passed a bill directing dismissal of all prisoners except those who might be regularly indicted, and declaring further:

> That it is and shall be lawful for the President of the United States, whenever in his judgment by reason of "rebellion or invasion the public safety may require it," to suspend, by proclamation, the privilege of the writ of *habeas corpus* throughout the United States or in any part thereof, and whenever the said writ shall be suspended . . . , it shall be unlawful for any of the judges of the several courts of the United States or of any State, to allow said writ.[13]

This proposed measure was quite inconclusive as to the President's constitutional right. By this bill, said one Senator, "you declare that it is the right of the President already, and shall continue to be his right to suspend the

[13] *Cong. Globe*, July 3, 1862, 37 Cong., 2 sess., p. 3106.

writ of *habeas corpus*. You do not propose to confer that right upon him, but to recognize it as his."[14] And yet, speaking of the very same bill, a member of the House said: "Congress now gives a general power to the President to suspend the writ of *habeas corpus*, and by . . . implication we may thence infer that he does not possess it of his own power or prerogative."[15]

The Senate Judiciary Committee reported the bill favorably, and Senator Trumbull labored hard to push it to a vote, but the Senate adjourned without action. The matter dragged on until the third session, and even then the "Habeas Corpus Act" narrowly escaped defeat. Finally in the early hours of March 3, 1863,[16] after a tiresome all-night session, a bare quorum of an overworked Senate by a piece of sharp practice on the part of the presiding officer outwitted those who were filibustering against the measure and passed Senator Trumbull's conference bill which had been slowly evolved through weary months of wrangling. The act so passed declared in oracular phrase that "during the present rebellion the President of the United States, whenever, in his judgment, the public safety may require it, is authorized to suspend the privilege of the writ of *habeas corpus* in any case throughout the United States or any part thereof."[17]

As has been often pointed out, these words are capable of a double interpretation. Congress, in declaring that the President "is authorized to suspend," might have been recognizing a presidential power or exercising a legislative one. The ambiguous wording, which was

---

[14]Remarks of Senator Howe, July 15, 1862: *Cong. Globe*, 37 Cong., 2 sess., p. 3362.

[15]Remarks of Representative Biddle, July 8, 1862: *Cong. Globe*, 37 Cong., 2 sess., p. 3183.

[16]*Infra*, pp. 190-191.

[17]*U. S. Stat. at Large*, XII, 755.

intentional, stamps the measure as essentially a compromise between divergent views prevailing among supporters of the administration. (The anti-administration members, of course, voted solidly against the act.) The essence of the compromise lay in the fact that the bill could be voted for both by those who favored and by those who opposed the principle of the exclusive power of Congress to suspend. Thus the only measure passed on this subject during the war left matters precisely where they had been before it was placed on the statute book, so far as the main constitutional issue was concerned.[18]

IV

In the light of Civil War experience, it is doubtful whether any clear-cut principle of undisputed legal authority can be said to exist in American jurisprudence with reference to this fundamental point of law. The Supreme Court has never definitely made a conclusive pronouncement upon the central issue as to whether the suspending power rests with the President or with Congress. The Merryman decision was not that of the Supreme Court; but it was an opinion of one member of the Court, Taney, in a case which he heard while on circuit. Furthermore, it was in chambers, not in open court, that the decision was rendered. The decision is not to be found in the reports of cases tried before the Supreme Court, but in those of the circuit courts.[19] At the time it was rendered it was not at all regarded as a settlement of the matter. On this point the evidence is convincing, for, after Taney's opinion had been rendered,

[18]Other features of the Habeas Corpus Act of 1863, bringing into view the whole question of arbitrary arrests, are dealt with in the succeeding chapters.

[19]17 Fed. Cas. 144.

there were various discussions as to an apprehended decision by the Supreme Court on the President's suspending power. A confidential and unpublished communication from Attorney General Bates to Secretary of War Stanton, dated January 31, 1863, has a significant bearing on this point. Having heard that the Secretary contemplated bringing before the Supreme Court for review certain proceedings of the Supreme Court of Wisconsin involving the President's suspending power, Bates advised emphatically against it, urging that a decision of the Court pronouncing the arbitrary arrests illegal would "do more to paralyze the Executive . . . than the worst defeat our armies have yet sustained," and that such an adverse decision was to be anticipated, in view of the "antecedents and present proclivities" of a majority of the court, taken in connection with the expressed opinion of certain of its members.[20]

Again in February of 1865, there was talk in Lincoln's Cabinet of an apprehended decision to be written by Chief Justice Chase which would definitely maintain the exclusive power of Congress. In consultations between President Lincoln and Attorney General Speed the apprehension was expressed that Chief Justice Chase, who had had various differences with the President, would "fail the administration" on this matter. As reported by Secretary Welles, the President was astonished at such a suggestion in view of Chase's previous commitments, but Welles considered that an adroit intriguer could escape these commitments and that Chase would not hesitate to use the bench for ambitious purposes.[21]

---

[20]Letter of Bates to Stanton (marked "Confidential"), Jan. 31, 1863: Stanton Papers, No. 52223. The Wisconsin decision had been given in the Kemp case, which is discussed later in this chapter.

[21]*Diary of Gideon Welles*, II, 242, 245-246. (Feb. 21-22, 1865.) On Feb. 21, 1865, Welles wrote regarding Chase's apprehended decision on the *habeas corpus* question: "Some intimation comes that . . .

If Chase intended to promote any such decision he either failed to find an opportunity or was unable to carry the court with him, for no such decision was issued. In this Cabinet consultation it is possible that the pending Milligan case was referred to, but in this case the question of the President's power of suspension did not arise.[22] These apprehensions regarding possible decisions concerning the President's right show that the question as to where the suspending power lay was regarded as an open one so far as the Supreme Court was concerned.

It is true that Marshall's opinion in the Bollman case has often been cited as a sanctioning by the Supreme Court of the congressional power of suspension. In that opinion Marshall wrote: "If . . . the public safety should require the suspension . . . it is for the legislature to say so."[23] Taney, as we have seen, cited this passage as a precedent and authority in the Merryman case. But, as the whole context shows, Marshall's meaning was: it is not for the court to say so. The question before the court was not the power of suspending the privilege of the writ, but the provision of the Judiciary Act of 1789 giving courts of the United States the power to issue the writ of *habeas corpus*. As to the withholding of the writ, Marshall argued that this was a political, not a judicial function. In other words, it was not within the discretion of the court to withhold the writ under the

---

the Chief Justice intends to make himself felt by the Administration. . . . I shall not be surprised, for he is ambitious and intriguing." The word "intriguing" was then deleted and the word "able" substituted. The manuscript in the Library of Congress reveals many such changes.

[22]As a matter of fact, Chase dissented from the Milligan decision, being unable to concur in the view that Congress had no power to authorise a military commission in Indiana. (Charles Warren, *The Supreme Court in United States History*, III, 148.) *Infra*, p. 182.

[23]4 Cranch 101.

circumstances of the case. It was in this connection that the passage in question occurs, and the whole passage reads as follows:

> If at any time the public safety should require the suspension of the powers vested by this act in the courts of the United States, it is for the legislature to say so. That question depends on political considerations, on which the legislature is to decide. Until the legislative will be expressed, this court can only see its duty, and must obey the laws.

It is obvious, therefore, that neither the facts of the Bollman case nor the oft-quoted passage of Marshall's opinion have any bearing upon the controversy as to whether Congress or the President has the suspending power.

The fact that many able judges of the period placed the power exclusively with Congress is, however, significant of the trend of judicial opinion. In the Kemp case in Wisconsin, where State judges in separate decisions each asserted the exclusive legislative power of suspension,[24] Judge Paine declared that there were other dangers to be looked to besides success of the rebellion—namely, acquisition of extraordinary powers, and the establishment of dangerous precedents.[25] Though a judge's voice may not be heeded, he said, yet he could only decide according to the Constitution and the law. He held that military arrest on the basis of presidential suspension of the writ could be justified only on the assumption that the President may abrogate the Constitution. But, as the judge argued, the President is to execute the laws only by such means as the Constitution gives him, and war does not break down the distinction between the branches of government. Taking issue with

[24] *In re* Kemp, 16 Wis. 382.

[25] *Ibid.*, pp. 402 *et seq.*

Bates' argument that the President has "political powers" with which the court cannot interfere, the Wisconsin judge maintained that the Constitution and the laws do not give to the President, except where the writ is legally suspended, any political discretion to imprison. The Constitution, he said, "knows no political . . . cause of imprisonment. There must be a 'process of law.' "[26]

Some light is thrown on the attitude of Congress with reference to this subject by an act passed in 1871. Because of reconstruction disturbances in South Carolina it was provided that, in case of unlawful combinations against the United States amounting to rebellion, "it shall be lawful for the President, . . . when in his judgment the public safety shall require it, to suspend the privilege of the writ of *habeas corpus* to the end that such rebellion may be overthrown."[27]

Acting on this authority, President Grant suspended the usual operation of the *habeas corpus* process within nine designated counties of South Carolina with respect to all persons arrested by United States marshals or by military authority charged with participation in unlawful combinations. In the wording of the executive proclamation, the act of Congress is mentioned as the source of the President's authority.[28]

From this instance one may conclude that Congress in 1871 believed that a suspension of the privilege might be authorized by the national legislature, though it was to be put into effect by the President. The President's concurrence in this view is shown by his signature of the bill and by the form in which his proclamation was drawn. There is nothing, however, in either the law or

[26] *Ibid.*, p. 420.

[27] Act of Apr. 20, 1871 (sometimes called the "Ku Klux Act"), sec. 4: *U. S. Stat. at Large*, XVII, 14-15.

[28] *Ibid.*, pp. 952, 953.

the proclamation of 1871 which touches the question of the *exclusive* power of Congress to suspend; and the legislation is significant merely as an instance of the exercise of a power without being conclusive as to the constitutional authority involved.

In this whole matter of the right associated with the *habeas corpus* writ, a rather liberal allowance must be made for unreasoning inference. By long tradition the writ has become so closely associated in popular sentiment with the safeguards of liberty that any discharge of a prisoner by means of the writ seems a vindication of justice. The illogical character of this view will be recognized when one reflects that the writ may be misused, and that in many cases the respondent may be well justified in holding the prisoner. There are, of course, cases in which a proper return to the writ would not involve "bringing the body," as for instance where a commander holds a man by virtue of enlistment in the military service of the United States, or where a legally drafted man is held in custody by a provost marshal. For the court to release a prisoner in such a case would be a plain misapplication of judicial power, yet popular opinion would not discriminate between these and justifiable discharges.

V

To reach an over-all judgment on this historic controversy is not a simple matter. Judging by the views of many Congressmen, the flood of pamphlets, the learned words of Taney, and the pronouncements of lower courts, the weight of opinion would seem to incline to the view that Congress has the exclusive suspending power; and many would doubtless insist that this is the accepted American principle. But in a similar crisis the presidential power to suspend would probably be just as much a potential function as during the Civil War. As to the actual precedent of that war, the outstanding fact is that the Chief Executive "suspended the writ," and that, so far as the legal consequences were concerned, he was not restrained in so doing by Congress nor by the courts.[29]

Even where Congress authorizes the suspension, the actual putting into force of such suspension is a presidential function, exercised by proclamation. If the procedure of 1871 were to be followed, the most essential function would still be left with the President, for Congress in that case empowered the President to suspend the privilege "whenever in his judgment the public safety shall require it," thus leaving the actual suspension to the President, with discretion to act within the limits indicated by the statute.

Since the suspension of the privilege is a "condition, not an act," it would also be necessary for the President to declare the restoration of the privilege—in other words, to terminate the suspension. This again would

---

[29]There were certain prouncements of the Supreme Court which suggested a sort of indirect sanctioning of the President's action in suspending the *habeas corpus* privilege. In the Prize Cases the Supreme Court held that the President did not have to wait for congressional authorization in order to perform acts appropriate to war time. Although the suspension was not directly dealt with in this case, yet the decision showed a disposition to uphold the President's hands. In Mitchell *vs.* Clark (110 U. S. 647) the Supreme Court upheld the constitutionality of the indemnity feature of the Habeas Corpus Act of 1863, declaring it to be valid in its retroactive effect. The court thus approved the immunity granted to Federal officials as to acts performed under presidential authority at any time during the "rebellion," and such officials were in this way sustained in doing things which would have been illegal on the assumption that the President's suspension was invalid. (This subject is discussed further in Chapter IX.) As to the Merryman decision, that was not a pronouncement of the Supreme Court; while in the Milligan case the Court did not go to the point of declaring invalid the action of the President in suspending the privilege, but rather declared against the use of military commissions in peaceful districts.

involve an exercise of presidential discretion. In no case, therefore, can the presidential function be entirely ignored; and there would appear to be an essentially executive quality in the whole proceeding. In the case of President Grant, Congress took the initiative, but in many instances—perhaps in the typical ones—the President would necessarily have to take the initiative, and under such circumstances the Lincoln precedent would naturally be invoked.

The silence of the Constitution was perhaps fortunate as the event proved, for in more than a century and a half under the Constitution the only general suspension occurred at a time when the Government was controlled by an administration highly regardful of individual rights and yet forced by circumstances to adopt summary measures. It was Horace Binney's view that the framers erred in making the language indefinite, but one may well ask whether a specific provision on such a point would not have been more of a hindrance than a help. Considering the rareness of the exercise of the power, and the lack of abuse of it, it might seem to many that the constitutional omission was really a case of golden silence, and that the brevity and flexibility of the clause pertaining to *habeas corpus* was an advantage.

After all, the essential question is not who suspends, but whether the emergency actually calls for summary arrest, and whether the rule of necessity is observed in the taking and holding of prisoners. If due restraints are observed during the period of suspension; if it is merely a "suspension" and not a setting aside of guarantees; if the withholding of the writ is not taken as equivalent to the establishment of martial law or as a justification of summary execution, then no serious outrage upon American sensibilities is likely to be threatened. A close study of what is actually involved in the suspension of the writ offers the best guidance with the reference to the controversial issue which we have been considering. In the two succeeding chapters, therefore, we will examine the executive processes that were in operation while the privilege was suspended and consider the use of military authority in the restraint of civilians.

CHAPTER VII

MILITARY RULE AND ARBITRARY ARRESTS

I

The nature and extent of martial law is a problem upon which Anglo-Saxon opinion has always been wary. In harmony with the principle that government is under, not above, the law, there has developed within modern English jurisdictions a disposition to subject military power to civil authority, and a reluctance to sanction any extension of the jurisdiction of military officers and tribunals over civilians. In the words of the United States Supreme Court, "it is an unbending rule of law that the exercise of military power, where the rights of the citizen are concerned, shall never be pushed beyond that which the exigency requires."[1]

Military rule over military persons is a branch of law having its own special history. Originating in special prerogative courts in England[2] in the period when sol-

[1]Raymond *vs.* Thomas, 91 U. S. 712, 716.

[2]Originally the spelling was "marshal law" and the term denoted the law administered by the Court of the Constable and Marshal

diers were regarded as personal retainers of the monarch, and passing thorugh various stages of development in connection with which the Mutiny Act is a legal landmark, the authority of courts-martial over the armed forces has become clearly established. In America, by the Articles of War,[3] based largely on the English Mutiny Act, a strictly limited statutory jurisdiction is given to courts-martial over military persons in time of war or peace—a jurisdiction which is exclusive but which involves only the power to inflict punishments, not the authority to deal with civil actions.

Military rule, then, occupies a field of its own. Its function is exclusive, and the performance of this limited function need not involve the invasion of any other judicial province.[4] Even over military persons the regular courts have jurisdiction in England and America in the case of ordinary civil relationships where no breach

---

which dispensed military justice. (*In re* the petition of D. F. Marais, *Edinburgh Rereiw*, Vol. 195, p. 80; G. B. Davis, *Military Law of the United States*, Introduction.) The archaic spelling is shown in the following quotation: "Please your Maiestie, let his Neck answere for it, if there be any Marshall Law in the World." (Shakespeare, *Henry V*, IV, viii, 46; *Oxford English Dictionary*, *ad. verb.* "martial," par. 3.)

[3]The Mutiny Act of 1689, annually reënacted and superseded in 1881 by the Army Act (also annually reënacted) has, as G. B. Davis points out, brought the ancient system of military jurisprudence within the purview of the English constitution. The Continental Congress based its "Articles of War" of 1775 upon the English Mutiny Act. (*Jour. of Cong.*, I, 90; 435-482.) Similar enactments were made in 1789, in 1806, and in 1916. (*U. S. Stat. at Large*, I, 95; II, 359; XXXIX, 650; Davis, *Military Law of the United States*, Ch. xix; Hare, *American Constitutional Law*, II, Chs. xlii, xliii.)

[4]Civil courts may not review the proceedings of courts-martial except where the latter have no jurisdiction over the subject matter of the charges, or where they inflict punishment beyond the law. A sentence legally given and confirmed by the President is final, pardon being the only escape. (Dynes *vs.* Hoover, 20 How. 78. See also Johnson *vs.* Sayre, 158 U. S. 109.)

of military duty is involved. In such matters the soldier is treated as being also a citizen.[5]

Martial law is a different matter.[6] It applies to civilians and involves the substitution of a military régime and military tribunals in a whole community in place of the ordinary processes of justice. It is claimed by the advocates of martial law that the executive may, upon his own initiative and discretion, determine when an emergency exists justifying summary process; that he may by proclamation establish a military régime to supplant civil procedure; that an armed force acting only under executive orders may then be set in control of the disaffected district; that special military courts with their own peculiar rules and punishments, independent of appeal, may be established; and that all the normal safeguards and guarantees of criminal justice may be ignored.

A power of this sort once established is capable of almost indefinite expansion. Both the occasion of this régime of summary justice and its duration are matters for the executive to determine. New offenses, unknown

---

[5]In commenting upon the twofold character of the soldier in the United States and in England, Hare points out that on the one side he is liable before the military authorities for acts that would be trivial in a citizen; and on the other hand he is, in common with civilians, subject to the liabilities of common and statute law, and cannot rely upon military orders for acts contrary to law. The soldiers who fired on the mob in Boston in 1770 were tried not by court-martial, but by a Boston jury who responded to the confidence reposed by the acquittal of all except two who were branded for manslaughter. (Hare, *American Constitutional Law*, II, Ch. xlii; Van Tyne, *Causes of the War of Independence*, 288; A. L. Lowell, *Government of England*, II, 491.)

[6]"Many people, ignorantly or wantonly, confound *military law* and *martial* [*law*], as if they were one and the same, while in truth they are the exact opposites of each other. Martial law is the will of the military chief. Military law is the ordinary law of the land which relates to military affairs." (MS. Diary of Edward Bates, March 8, 1865.)

to the ordinary law, may be created. There are no warrants in the case of arrests, no hearings of prisoners on *habeas corpus* petitions, and no opportunity to inquire judicially into complaints of arbitrary treatment. The executive chief is the one source of authority. In effect, the same man becomes at once lawgiver, executive, and judge. Seizures and arrests may be made on mere suspicion by military men—men who by expreience and habit of mind are accustomed to the unbending enforcement of orders and are often impatient of the restraints of civil government.

The resort to such an extreme procedure, both in England and America, has been rare. Neither of the Jacobite rebellions in the first half of the eighteenth century occasioned any interruption of usual judicial processes. In the case of the Irish revolutionist, Wolfe Tone, sentenced in 1798 by a military tribunal, the Court of King's Bench at Dublin intervened on the side of individual liberty and ordered a release on *habeas corpus*, on the ground that, while the ordinary courts were functioning and actual war not waging, such court-martial decrees could not be endured. The Gordon riots of 1780 were suppressed without any proclamation of martial law, and ordinary civil process was thought adequate during the Chartist disturbances of 1839 and 1848 as well as during the serious Fenian outrages in 1867. Even in 1817, when the Habeas Corpus Act was suspended by a reactionary Tory government, there were no sentences inflicted by military authority, and so far as Great Britain is concerned there was no proclamation of martial law from 1689 to the period of World War I. In Ireland, it is true, and also in South Africa, a harsher course has prevailed, but the many vigorous protests from eminent legal authorities suggest that such measures are looked upon as usurpations and are wholly out of harmony with the genius and spirit of English institutions.[7]

II

As to America, the processes of civil justice have proved sufficiently resourceful to cope with grave disturbances. During the Whiskey Insurrection Washington rigidly held the army in subjection to the civil power; martial law was not declared; arrests were made by civil officers on warrants, and the authority of the Federal judge of the district was respected by the military commanders.[8] Certain leaders of the insurrection were convicted in the regular courts, sentenced to death for treason, and pardoned by the President. The case was

[7]On the general subject of martial law in England and the United States, the following authorities may be consulted: Dicey, *Law of the Constitution* (1889), 265; Frederic Harrison, "The State of Siege" in *National and Social Problems*, Chap. x; Finlason, *Treatise on Martial Law;* Forsyth, *Cases and Opinions on Constitutional Law;* Unsigned article apropos the Marais Case, in *Edinburgh Review*, Vol. 195, pp. 79-105; Report of Lord Featherstone's commission on the Featherstone riots, in *Parliamentary Papers*, 1893-1894, c. 7234; Grant *vs.* Sir Charles Gould, in 2 Henry Blackstone 69; Lord Chief Justice Cockburn's Charge to Jury (in a case growing out of a negro rebellion in Jamaica in 1865), *Annual Register*, N. S., 1867, 230-234; Mostyn *vs.* Fabrigas (1774), 1 Cowper 161; G. B. Davis, *Military Law of the United States;* J. I. C. Hare, *American Constitutional Law*, II, Chs. xlii, xliii, xliv; Holdsworth, "Martial Law Historically Considered," in *Law Quar. Rev.*, XVIII, 117; H. Earle Richards, "Martial Law," *ibid.*, p. 133; McLaughlin and Hart, *Cyclopedia of American Government*, II, 402; H. W. Ballantine, "Unconstitutional Claims of Military Authority," in *Yale Law Rev.*, XXIV, 189; F. Pollock, "What is Martial Law?", in *Law Quar. Rev.*, XVIII, 152; H. W. Ballantine, "Martial Law," in *Columbia Law Rev.*, XII, 529; Joel Parker, *Habeas Corpus and Martial Law* (Welch, Bigelow and Co., Cambridge, Mass., 1861); Luther *vs.* Borden, 7 Howard 1; Notes thereon in Lawyers' edition of *U. S. Supreme Court Reports*, XII, 581; *In re* Kemp, 16 Wis. 382; Coleman *vs.* Tennessee, 97 U. S. 509; Moyer *vs.* Peabody, 212 U. S. 78; *In re* Moyer, 85 Pacific 190; *Ex parte* Milligan, 71 U. S. 2; In the matter of Samuel Stacy, Jr., 10 Johnson's [N. Y. Supreme Court] Reports 328 (1813); Dynes *vs.* Hoover, 20 How. 65.

[8]McMaster, *History of the People of the United States*, II, 190-203.

analogous to that of the Gordon riots in England in the fact that, though the troops were called out, the trials were before the civil courts. The precedent of the Whiskey Insurrection was followed in the case of the Burr conspiracy of 1805-06.[9]

General Jackson's excessive zeal in imposing military rule over civilians in Louisiana during the War of 1812 led to a result opposite to that intended. He had made a military arrest under martial law, and when served with a writ of *habeas corpus* by the district court he not only disregarded the writ but imprisoned the judge who issued it. As Jackson was subjected to an attachment for contempt and compelled to pay a fine of $1,000, the net result of the episode was a vindication of civil authority.[10]

---

[9]In the case of the Burr conspiracy, the American preference for civil process over military arrests was shown in the release of Wilkinson's prisoners on *habeas corpus* proceedings in the courts, and in the refusal of the House of Representatives to pass the Senate bill for the suspension of the privilege. Aaron Burr's biographers treat Wilkinson's flourishing of the sword and his melodramatic "bellowings" with marked sarcasm. Samuel H. Wandell and Meade Minnegerode, *Aaron Burr*, II, 118-150.

[10]General Jackson was at this time governing by martial law. Louallier, a Frenchman of New Orleans, had written a defiant letter denouncing Jackson's treatment of Frenchmen, and this was published in a city paper. For this he was placed under military arrest by Jackson's order. The Federal district judge, D. A. Hall, caused a writ of *habeas corpus* to be served upon Jackson, whereupon Judge Hall was arrested and kept for some time in prison. When the Federal district attorney applied to a State judge for Hall's release on *habeas corpus*, both the district attorney and the judge were arrested. Louallier's case was brought before a court-martial which decided that it had no jurisdiction over him and held that he must be released from military detention. Jackson set aside the finding of the court-martial, and his prisoners were released only upon receipt of official news of the ratification of the treaty of peace with England. Judge Hall summoned Jackson for contempt of court and fined him $1000 which Jackson paid. On February 16, 1844, Congress remitted the fine with interest. There seems to have been no adequate reason for this remission other than a desire to pay a compliment to General Jackson when on the verge of the grave. (J. S. Bassett, *Life of Jackson*, 224-230, 745.)

In the Dorr rebellion a Rhode Island governor was upheld in establishing martial law,[11] but the emergency was an unquestioned one, as the very government itself was in danger. In certain states, as in West Virginia, Colorado, Montana, and Oklahoma, resort to martial law has become more frequent; but, though the courts have here and there sustained this policy, the tendency of our law may still be considered adverse to such measures.

In contrast with the Continental practice by which martial law is given a definite niche in the constitutional framework, there is in England and America a certain discredit attaching to summary executive process. It is not a separate and clearly defined body of law, such as equity, for instance, but rather the setting aside of law through the substitution of the commander's will. Such a constitutional principle as that which enabled Germany to be governed under martial law during World War I, or such a procedure as the French *état de siège* is unfamiliar to the Anglo-Saxon legal mind.

Some English authorities refuse to recognize martial law altogether, contending that the resources of the common law are adequate to the maintenance of order even in a serious crisis and that every citizen, whether acting as a soldier or not, is bound to use sufficient force to overcome any resistance to public order.[12] Where the courts are open, and where they are unhampered by any threat of *force majeure*, it is contended that their au-

[11]See the facts in Luther *vs.* Borden, 7 How. 1.

[12]". . . it [martial law] is not a law, but something indulged rather than allowed, as a law." (Sir Matthew Hale, *History of the Common Law* (London, 1779), Ch. ii.) "It is totally inaccurate to state martial law as having any place whatever in the realm of Great Britain" (Lord Loughborough in Grant *vs.* Gould, 2 Henry Blackstone 69). And see Dicey, *Law of the Constitution*, 381. For similar expressions concerning martial law in the United States, see H. W. Ballantine, in *Yale Law Rev.*, XXIV, 198.

thority is to be respected. If a commander disregards the usual guarantees, making summary seizures, arrests, and imprisonments, his proceedings may, indeed, ultimately be held justifiable, but he takes a risk. His action is reviewable by the courts, and in case of any infringement upon private rights beyond the point reasonably warranted by the necessities of the situation, he may be held liable in a civil or even in a criminal action. As against the consequences of such an infringement not even the plea of superior orders can operate as a defense, for no protection flows from the command of a superior wrongdoer. Under this interpretation the civil tribunals would be the final judge of the validity of this summary procedure, both as to the circumstances of its inauguration and the acts performed during its continuance.

On the other hand, a series of decisions may be cited sustaining executives who have instituted martial law and declaring that, where the action was *bona fide*, the courts would make no inquiry into the causes thereof.[13] This is not a problem on which the tendency of either English or American law is unwavering. The lack of a clear-cut principle is testimony to the fact that our minds are unused to any military government over civilians, and this should be a warning to executives to act circumspectly in using such a distrusted and questionable weapon.

III

During the Civil War the line of demarcation between military and civil authority was often blurred. Though military oppression in its extreme forms was absent, yet there were many irritating instances of military encroach-

[13]See *In re* Moyer, and cases therein cited. 85 *Pacific* 190.

ment upon the proper field of civil government. General Lew Wallace, commanding in Maryland in 1864, used his detectives and his quartermaster's department to enforce the acts for the confiscation of "rebel" property, forgetting that military seizure was not legalized by these statutes.[14] Military pressure was applied by General B. F. Butler at Norfolk, Virginia, in defiance of the authority of Governor Pierpoint at Alexandria. In Kentucky civil and military conflicts were frequent. When, for instance, General Hugh Ewing, from military headquarters at Louisville, issued an order requiring local county authorities to levy a tax for military purposes, the governor of the State declared that compliance with this order would be a violation of law.[15] The order of a colonel in the Federal army directing the dismissal of indictments pending in a Missouri court elicited from Attorney General Bates the comment that the colonel might tell the judge "who to try and punish and who to set free, and also [might] furnish him with better opinions than his own to be delivered from the bench!"[16]

The power of the sword even invaded the domain of religious worship. In 1863 a provost marshal at St. Louis tried to silence a preacher and transfer the control of a certain church from one set of men to another. On this subject President Lincoln wrote disclaiming any intention of interfering with the churches. Having so written, he was considerably embarrassed to find that, by formal order of the War Department, Bishop Ames had been given control of all the Methodist churches (in certain Southern military departments) whose pastors had not been appointed by loyal bishops, and that military aid

---

[14] *O. R.*, Ser. I, Vol. 33, p. 989; Vol. 37, pt. 1, p. 638; Ser. III, Vol. 4, pp. 407-413.

[15] MS. Diary of Edward Bates, June 25, 1864 and Nov. 22, 1864.

[16] *Ibid.*, Mar. 28, 1865.

was extended for the maintenance of such control.[17] When at the close of the war Sherman brought Johnston's army to surrender, he included the whole subject of political reconstruction in his terms of capitulation. These instances will perhaps suffice to show the lack of a nice distinction between civil and military rule.

It is with these conditions in mind that one must approach the subject of political arrests during the war. In this branch of the public business a slow evolution of policy is discernible. In the early part of the war the withholding of the privilege of the *habeas corpus* writ was restricted to definite localities specified in various presidential proclamations, beginning with that of April 27, 1861, covering the line from Washington to Philadelphia.[18] During this period prisoners taken under military orders were held under the custody of the Department of State. The emergency at this time was exceedingly grave and hundreds of prisoners were apprehended.

Seward's activities in the year 1861, when his department was in charge of these arrests, were conducted on a scale that seems astonishing when we recall that this Cabinet minister was at the same time in charge of our foreign policy and that his official acts frequently trenched upon the proper field of various other department heads and even of the President himself. Seward soon organized a secret service for the purpose of apprehending prisoners, and had his confidential agents placed

---

[17]Letter of Lincoln to Stanton, Feb. 11, 1864: Nicolay and Hay, *Works*, X, 4-5.

[18]This authority was conferred in President Lincoln's communication to General Scott, April 27, 1861, and was in turn delegated by General Scott to various subordinates (*O. R.*, Ser. II, Vol. 2, p. 19; Ser. I, Vol. 51, pt. 1, pp. 337, 409). A similar order of suspension was issued covering the Florida coast on May 10, 1861, and another applying to the vicinity of the military line from New York to Washington on July 2, 1861. The line within which suspension was authorized was extended to Bangor, Maine, on October 14, 1861. (*Ibid.*, p. 497.)

at strategic points, especially at the ports and along the border, in order to prevent the departure and secure the arrest of suspected persons. Passports were required of persons entering or leaving the country and in this way those deemed to be dangerous were intercepted.

Sometimes the arrests were made by Seward's confidential agents, sometimes by the local police on direct order of Seward, and at other times by the military authorities of the United States or by marshals of the Federal courts. The arrests were made on suspicion. Prisoners were not told why they were seized, nor did the authorities investigate the matter sufficiently to substantiate the charges prior to arrest. As Frederic Bancroft shows, in his admirable biography of Seward, the Secretary of State often proceeded without adequate proof, and the department "never made up its case." Obviously the purpose of the whole proccss was temporary military detention, not trial before the courts. The object in view was precautionary, and the chief concern of the Government was to seize spies or other confidential agents of the Confederate Government, rather than to confine men for vague "disloyalty."[19]

As to the treatment of political prisoners, the evidence reveals little if any basis for the sensational account given in Marshall's *American Bastile*,[20] which was writ-

[19]On the subject of arrests as conducted under the Department of State, see Frederic Bancroft, *Life of Seward*, II, Ch. xxiv; *Ann. Cyc.*, 1862, pp. 508 *et seq.; O. R.*, Ser. II, Vols. 1 and 2, *passim*. The Department of State kept a record book entitled "Arrests for Disloyalty," containing memoranda concerning prisoners. This is published in part in *O. R.*, Ser. II, Vol. 2, pp. 290 *et seq*. The writer has examined the "domestic correspondence" and similar papers of the State Department without discovering data of great significance beyond what has been published.

[20]John A. Marshall, *The American Bastile: A History of Illegal Arrests and Imprisonments during the Civil War* (Phila., 1869). The author of this abusive book was the officially appointed historian of an association of prisoners of state.

ten not as an historical study but as an *ex parte* denunciation of the Government. Prisoners were not brutally treated; and, though their prison terms were not pleasant, such hardships as they suffered were due to lack of room and general conditions of prison administration (many of which still exist) rather than to intentional governmental abuse. Comforts were not denied to prisoners and they were allowed to receive articles sent by friends. Under inspection they were permitted to transmit and receive letters and to obtain newspapers. By special permission they could receive visitors. Seward gave personal attention to the comfort of the prisoners, and the officers having them in charge seem in general to have acted in the same spirit.[21]

In February, 1862, two important steps were taken. A sweeping order provided for a wholesale release of political prisoners, and the control of this branch of the public business was transferred from the State to the War Department.[22] In effecting these releases a special commission was appointed which operated under the Secretary of War.[23]

So far the suspension of the *habeas corpus* privilege had been of limited application. The first measure of general scope touching the suspension of this vital guar-

---

[21]*O. R.*, Ser. II, Vol 2, pp. 111, 118.

[22]The executive order transferring the power to make extraordinary arrests from the State to the War Department was issued on February 14, 1862. By the same order the President directed all political prisoners to be released on subscribing to a parole to render no aid or comfort to the enemy, amnesty being granted for past offenses. Spies were not included in this order of release, and others might be excepted at the discretion of the Secretary of War. (Nicolay and Hay, *Works*, VII, 100; *O. R.*, Ser. II, Vol. 2, pp. 221-223.)

[23]This Commission, consisting of Judge Edwards Pierrepont and General John A. Dix, effected many releases in February, 1862, and the succeeding months. For lists of prisoners so released, see *O. R.*, Ser. II, Vol. 2, pp. 261, 277, 285. In the same volume much of the correspondence of the commission is to be found.

antee was taken on September 24, 1862. President Lincoln then proclaimed that during the existing insurrection all rebels and insurgents, all persons discouraging enlistment, resisting the draft, or guilty of any disloyal practice were subject to martial law and liable to trial by courts-martial or military commissions. Regarding such persons, wherever found, the *habeas corpus* privilege was authorized to be suspended.[24]

That all this procedure was arbitrary, that it involved the withholding of constitutional guarantees normally available, is of course evident. Prisoners were not taken on sworn charges, but simply arrested under executive order. They were released without being brought to trial. At the time when arrests were being actively pushed, the prosecuting officers of the Government were quite lax in the bringing of indictments and in promoting the judicial prosecution of those who were actually violating the laws.

It would be a mistake, however, to suppose that all the conditions of summary justice were present. The number of arrests made, though very large, has been commonly exaggerated.[25] There was no "system" by

---

[24]Richardson, *Messages . . . of the Presidents*, VI, 98.

[25]This subject was examined by J. F. Rhodes, for whom a thorough search of the records was made by Col. F. C. Ainsworth, Chief of the Record and Pension Office, War Department. The records of the Commissary General of Prisoners were found to contain the names of 13,535 citizens arrested and confined in military prisons from February, 1862 to the end of the war. To this one would have to add those arrested under authority of the Navy and State Departments and those confined in State prisons and penitentiaries. Even when these allowances are made, however, the number would be much less than 38,000, which was the exaggerated guess of Alexander Johnston in Laylor's Cyclopedia (*ad. verb.* "Habeas Corpus"). (Rhodes, *History of United States*, IV, 230, n. 2.) Through the kindness of the Adjutant General, a further search on this subject was made for the author, but without yielding any important new conclusions. A long communication from the Adjutant General was received, from which the following may be quoted: "Answering your general inquiry as

which men were quickly advanced to the scaffold or to terms of imprisonment. There was no "revolutionary tribunal" such as that by which the guillotine was fed during the terror in France, nothing similar to the "Star Chamber" of the Tudor period in England.

The practice of the Government throughout the war demonstrated the fact that the suspension of the *habeas corpus* privilege does not automatically institute martial law. It is by no means true, as many supposed at the time of Lincoln's proclamation, that the suspension sets aside all law. It merely permits prisoners to be held until it is consistent with the public safety for them to be either tried or released. It is not the writ that is suspended; it is the privilege.[26] The writ may still issue on petition, but there is no compulsion to obey its mandate if the prisoner, as stated in the return, is held by adequate authority. "Suspension" allows summary arrest, permits detention without judicial hearing to show cause, and without indictment on the basis of an offense recognized by the civil law. The prisoners are merely held till the emergency passes, and then they are either released or tried in the civil courts.

Martial law, on the other hand, allows a military trial for offenses unknown to the civil law, and permits the execution of sentences for which the civil law offers no

---

to what can be added to the statement made to Mr. Rhodes, I regret to say that I am not able to furnish you any more definite information as to the approximate aggregate number of such [political] prisoners. . . . Notwithstanding the many mentions of the subject of political or citizen prisoners in the printed *Official Records*, for the reasons stated by General Ainsworth to Mr. Rhodes, and for other reasons that could be added, I do not believe that it will ever be possible for any one to gather from any source an approximately definite estimate of the total number of such prisoners held by Federal authorities during the Civil War." (Letter of Major General Robert C. Davis, Adjutant General of the United States, to the writer, June 26, 1925.)

[26] *Ex parte* Milligan, 71 U. S. 130-131

basis. It is true that mere detention of the prisoner might itself constitute a considerable grievance, and might be so prolonged as to amount to heavy punishment; but this is certainly a milder infringement of liberty than the rapid completion of all the steps of a summary process, including the execution of the sentence.[27] The compensating element in the situation is that while the privilege is being suspended, the "public safety" is being guarded as the Constitution-makers contemplated; and, if the power of arrest be not abused, unavoidable wrong done to a few individuals may perhaps be tolerated in view of the promotion of general security.

Considering the imperative demands of the emergency, a fair amount of restraint was shown in the making of arrests. An examination of the orders issued from Washington and from the various department headquarters reveals a considerable degree of caution. Mere disloyal remarks were to be overlooked, but such violence of word or act as would disturb the peace was to be deemed sufficient cause for arrest.[28] Higher officers sought to check the tendency of subordinates to make vexatious arrests on mere suspicion, and many annoyances of conduct short of actual aid to the enemy were tolerated. In Baltimore in 1862 the order went out that no citizen was to be arrested and confined for disloyalty or treasonable practices except on written charges under oath.[29] Not only the President himself but the chief generals and members of the Cabinet acted as restraining agencies to temper the severity of overzealous officers.

---

[27]It is true that the President's proclamation of September 24, 1862, declared disloyal persons subject to martial law and liable to trial by courts-martial or military commissions; but the fact remains that military detention followed by release on parole was the practice adopted in the great majority of cases.

[28]*O. R.*, Ser. II, Vol. 2, p. 186

[29]*Ibid.*, Ser. II, Vol. 4, p. 368.

In spite of all this caution, frivolous and unwarranted arrests were not infrequently made. In the case of many of the political prisoners no papers could be found stating the charges against them, and it cannot be denied that some individuals suffered unjustly. Subordinates sometimes acted under a misapprehension of the extent of their authority, erroneously supposing that because the "writ was suspended," all forms of law were gone. In disregard of restraining instructions from Washington, prisoners were sometimes taken on trivial charges, such as "being a noisy secessionist," giving sympathy to the "rebels," selling Confederate "mottoes and devices," of "hurrahing for Jeff Davis." An Episcopal minister of Alexandria, Virginia, was arrested for habitually omitting the prayer for the President of the United States as required by the church service.[30]

But as a rule the men confined in the Old Capitol Prison, Fort Lafayette, Fort McHenry, or the other state prisons were there for good reason. They had been acting as Confederate agents, furnishing supplies to the enemy, encouraging desertion from the service of the United States, committing outrages upon Unionists, stealing military supplies, destroying bridges, engaging in bushwhacking, making drawings of fortifications, carrying "treasonable" correspondence, intimidating loyal voters, or otherwise materially assisting the enemy. Many of the prisoners were actual spies.[31] After the

---

[30]*Ibid.*, Ser. II, Vol. 2, pp. 212-213. When three clergymen of New Orleans were arrested for omitting part of the service, A. Oakey Hall, district attorney of the City and County of New York, addressed a letter to Secretary Stanton on November 12, 1862, suggesting their release on the ground that state interference with matters of religious discipline is "foreign to the genius of our institutions." (A. O. Hall to Stanton, Nov. 12, 1862: Stanton Papers, IX, No. 51991.) As we have seen, President Lincoln felt likewise. *Supra*, p. 148.

[31]The elaborate material presented in the second series of the *Official Records* of the war must be examined for a comprehensive view of the

War Department assumed control of these matters arrests were forbidden unless authorized by the proper authority in Washington or by State executives under whose direction provost marshals were in some States directed to act in the early part of the war.[32]

If arrests were often peremptory, there was compensation in the lenient policy regarding releases. One prisoner, who was shown by "abundant evidence" to be a "shrewd and dangerous spy," was released on parole to have no connection with the enemy, supply him no information, and in no way promote resistance to the authority of the United States.[33] Release on taking the oath of allegiance was granted in another case to a man who, with avowed treasonable intent, had conveyed military information to the enemy.[34] Where the apprehension had been merely precautionary, or where no papers were filed giving charges, releases were uniformly granted. The same may be said with regard to arrests made without suitable authority. Failing health or mentality, poverty, or other misfortune, had considerable weight in determining the question of discharge.

In making these releases, appropriate conditions were specified. In addition to the oath of allegiance, definite stipulations, suited to individual cases, were often exacted, the parties agreeing, for example, not to visit any of the "insurgent States," or hold correspondence with any persons residing in them. Some releases, however, were unconditional; and certain persons who objected on scruple to the form of oath asked were permitted to take

---

subject of arbitrary arrests. A table listing briefly the charges against certain prisoners (and thus illustrating the reasons for arrests) is found in *O. R.*, Ser. II, Vol. 2, pp. 277-279.

[32]Report of the Secretary of War, December 1, 1862: *House Ex. Doc. No. 1*, 37 Cong., 3 sess.

[33]Case of Ellie M. Poole: *O. R.*, Ser. II, Vol. 2, p. 306.

[34]Case of Isaac G. Mask: *ibid.*, p. 310.

the oath in a different form.[35] Prisoners were occasionally held as "hostages," and discharge in such cases would be conditional upon a like discharge of Union men in Confederate hands. Charles J. Faulkner, for instance, at one time minister to France, was released from Fort Warren on condition that Alfred Ely, a New York Congressman captured by the Confederates at Bull Run, should be restored to his seat in Congress.[36] Where releases were denied, this was usually due to refusal to take the oath, uncompromising hostility to the Government, proud protestations of "rebel" sympathies, or serious and well substantiated offenses.[37]

IV

As a result of the suspension of constitutional privileges, conflicts were numerous between military and civil authorities. Arrests and seizures made by provost marshals or other military officers were frequently challenged by the courts; but such officers were, as a rule, under orders to disregard judicial mandates and resist the execution of writs. The numerous resulting conflicts were typical of the legal confusion of the times.

Clashes of this sort often occurred in connection with the draft, though this is a field in which the supremacy of the military authorities was to be presumed. By

---

[35]Case of R. H. Alvey: *ibid.*, p. 349.

[36]*Ibid.*, p. 463.

[37]The following bit of correspondence between Lincoln and Stanton throws light on the subject of the release of prisoners. Lincoln wrote the Secretary of War as follows on August 22, 1864: "I very much wish to oblige [H. W.] Beecher by relieving Howard [imprisoned for complicity in the "bogus proclamation" published in the New York *World* on May 18, 1864] but I wish you to be satisfied when it is done. What say you?" Stanton replied, "I have no objection if you think it right and this a proper time," whereupon Lincoln gave the order: "Let Howard . . . be discharged." (Stanton Papers, XXII, No. 54446.)

statute the decisions of the boards of enrollment regarding exemptions were to be final, but the courts claimed jurisdiction both before and after the boards had given their decisions. Injunctions, *habeas corpus* writs, attachments for contempt, and other judicial processes were interposed as obstacles to the enrolling and drafting officers. One judge ordered the records of the board to be brought into court, but the order was not obeyed. At times the obstructive tactics of the courts seemed calculated to defeat the task of raising troops and arresting deserters, either by throwing officers into custody or by keeping them so constantly before the courts as to prevent the performance of their duties.[38] To overcome this obstruction, provost marshals were instructed by the War Department to decline producing prisoners in court in matters clearly within military jurisdiction, and the serving of civil process in camps and forts was resisted.[39] Very often, however, writs issued by Federal courts, as for instance *habeas corpus* writs for the release of minors who had enlisted without their parents' consent, were obeyed by military officers. Disregard of judicial orders, on the other hand, usually had a valid connection with the necessities of military duty.

It is not difficult to understand the reluctance of military officers to subject themselves to judicial process. To obey a judicial writ, a commander would have to abandon his duty, leave his post, and answer the court's mandate. Resistance would, under varying circumstances, make the officer subject to an attachment for contempt, criminally liable for defying the sheriff or marshal, guilty of murder if he should take a life in the exercise of disputed military authority, or subject to action for damages due

[38]Report of Provost Marshal General, November 17, 1863: *House Ex. Doc. No. 1*, 38 Cong., 1 sess., p. 113.

[39]*O. R.*, Ser. III, Vol. 3, pp. 378-380.

to false imprisonment. If the writ were to prevail over the action of a general or provost marshal, then the court could tie the hands of the officer, and (as was said in *Luther* vs. *Borden*) the army or militia would become a "mere parade."

The complexity, delay, and clumsiness of judicial procedure were felt to be unsuited to the effective handling of a threatening situation. To use Stanton's words, the machinery of the courts "seemed . . . designed not to sustain the Government but to embarrass and betray it."[40] Even for such offenses as enticing men to desert or harboring deserters (offenses likely to be engendered by the draft), all the forms of a judicial proceeding would have to be gone through. A true bill must be presented by a slow plodding grand jury; the defendant must be admitted to bail; and after considerable delay a trial must follow with its challenging of jurors, examination of witnesses, and numerous dilatory motions devised by clever counsel. Such cases were outside the usual routine of the Federal courts; they required unusual study on the part of the law officers; and it commonly happened that a mere indisposition to prosecute might cause the ultimate dismissal of cases in which emphatic indictments had been brought. There was many a case in which the defendant who had been admitted to bail failed to appear at the trial, and the court merely ordered the forfeiture of the recognizance, later setting aside even this penalty.

There was, moreover, a basic physical inability of the judicial arm to cope with a situation involving turbulence and widespread violence. Military authorities sincerely believed that they could not leave matters to the ineffectual efforts of the judiciary. Theoretically, per-

[40] *Ibid.*, Ser. II, Vol. 2, p. 222.

haps, there is no defined limit to the expansion of the executory officers of a court, for in case of trouble deputy marshals or deputy sheriffs may be appointed, and if necessary, a *posse comitatus* may be called out. But practically judicial resources of this sort are decidedly limited. In December, 1858, and February, 1859, a Federal marshal in Kansas, when confronted with serious violence on the part of lawless desperadoes, determined to keep a standing posse continuously in the field until the criminals were arrested or driven out. Several hundred men were assembled for this purpose, and it was not until orders were received from Washington that the men were disbanded.

This incident admirably illustrated the marshal's limitation in the forcible execution of judicial processes. Though no statute then defined the powers of marshals to call in the aid of a posse in the performance of their official duties, it was made clear in this case that the marshal is a ministerial officer intrusted with the execution of specific judicial orders or writs, and that he is by no means authorized to maintain a quasi-military force or to keep a large body of men in the field for an indefinite period in order to break up an insurrection. The employment of a posse, it was pointed out, must be temporary and for a specific object, as for instance the arrest of particular criminals. It must not partake of the nature of a military expedition. Suppression of an insurrection is an executive, not a judicial, function.[41]

---

[41]This discussion concerning the conditions justifying the employment of a *posse comitatus* arose in the claim of W. P. Fain, marshal of the territory of Kansas, for reimbursement of expenses incurred in keeping a large posse in the field for a considerable time. The following papers in the files and letterbooks of the Attorney General's office bear upon the subject: Letter of Acting Secretary of the Interior to E. M. Stanton, Attorney General, March 1, 1861; C. B. Smith, Secretary of the Interior to the President, May 10, 1861; J. Hubley Ashton, Acting Attorney General, to J. M. Schofield, Secretary of War, Sep-

Naturally the general or other military officer who was served with a writ which he felt unable to respect, refused to let his hands be tied. He did what, under the circumstances, seemed to him the only thing to do. Relying on the President's "suspension," he disregarded the writ and either made no return or else in making the return cited the President's orders as justification for not bringing the prisoner. The judge who allowed the writ to issue followed it in some cases with an attachment for contempt, while in other cases he merely "filed" an opinion denouncing the usurpation.

The Merryman case is typical of this sort of conflict between civil and military authority, and brings out in clear relief the cardinal fact that while the President's suspension of the *habeas corpus* privilege was being invoked as the source of military control over civilians, many of the judges were denying the validity of this suspension. Merryman, lieutenant of a secessionist drill company, was arrested in Maryland, taken into custody by General Cadwallader, commander of the department, and confined in Fort McHenry.[42] The case was one among hundreds, and a failure to sustain the military power here would have caused the whole system of "political arrests" on executive discretion to break down. Hearing the petition in chambers, Chief Justice Taney caused a writ of *habeas corpus* to be served, directing the general to produce "the body" in court. Cadwallader's instructions were to hold in secure confinement all persons implicated in treasonable practices and to decline for the time to produce prisoners where writs of *habeas corpus* were issued, by whatsoever authority.

---

tember 10, 1868. (The Department of the Interior at this time had to do with the defraying of unusual expenses connected with Federal judicial prosecutions.) These records are in the National Archives.

[42] *O. R.*, Ser. II, Vol. 1, pp. 574-585; 17 Fed. Cas. 144.

In the respectful return to the writ, he stated the cause for which Merryman was apprehended, cited the President's suspension as authority for the detention, and declined to obey the mandate. Taney then issued a writ of attachment for contempt against the general, but the marshal seeking to serve this writ was refused entrance to the fort and would have encountered superior force had he attempted by a *posse comitatus* to compel the general's appearance. The Chief Justice therefore contented himself with filing the famous opinion which we have considered in the preceding chapter. As he had met resistance in pursuance of duty, he put the proceedings, including the opinion, on record with the clerk of the Federal Circuit Court in Maryland and caused a copy to be transmitted to the President, leaving to that "high official" the obligation of causing "the civil process of the United States to be enforced."[43]

A conflict similar to that of the Merryman case occurred in Washington in October, 1861, when Provost Marshal Porter found himself at odds with Judge Dunlop for resisting a *habeas corpus* writ.[44] In this case the deputy marshal refused to serve the writ of attachment

[43]The later features of the Merryman case, following the famous opinion of Chief Justice Taney, are obscure, and, so far as the writer's observation has gone, have been overlooked. Shortly after the delivery of Taney's opinion, Merryman was released from military confinement in Ft. McHenry and transferred to civil authority. An indictment for treason was filed against him in the United States District Court at Baltimore and he entered into a recognizance in the sum of $20,000 for his appearance in the Circuit Court of the United states for the district of Maryland, to which the case was, on November 12, 1861, remitted. The matter went no further, and, after continuance by order of the court, the case was ultimately dropped. This inconclusive termination of such war cases as were brought before the civil courts was almost universal. (*O. R.*, Ser. II, Vol. 2, p. 226; Letter of A. L. Spamer, Clerk of the District Court of the United States at Baltimore, to the writer, February 6, 1924.)

[44]*Ann. Cyc.*, 1861, pp. 365-367; *Letters and Diaries of John Hay*, I, 47 (quoted in Horace White, *Lyman Trumbull*, 190).

for contempt, being informed by Secretary Seward that the President's suspension of the privilege forbade him to serve process upon any officer. (It would have been truer, perhaps, to say that the President's action made compliance with the writ unnecessary, rather than that it forbade serving the writ.)

Taking his cue from Taney, the judge merely "filed" an opinion declaring that the case was without parallel in the judicial history of the United States; that the court, having exhausted every practical remedy to uphold its lawful authority, found itself powerless before superior force; and that the issue rested with the President.[45]

V

It was for the purpose of terminating such conflicts that Congress passed the Habeas Corpus Act of 1863 which attempted a sort of compromise between camp and bench.[46] On the one side the President's authority to "suspend" was recognized, military commanders were relieved from the obligation to answer the writ, and officers subjected to process for arrests or imprisonments

---

[45]Another case of this general sort was that of John G. Mullen, a minor who had enlisted in Maryland without his father's consent. When a deputy marshal of the Federal court tried to serve a writ of *habeas corpus* in the case, the officer to whom the writ was presented handed it back, remarking that he "would see the court and marshal damned before delivering up one of his men." A long communication concerning this case was sent to the Federal district judge by Major W. W. Morris, who declared that United States soldiers were perfidiously attacked and murdered in the streets and that no arrests were made for these crimes, while an illegal State legislature was debating the abrogation of the Federal compact. Under these circumstances, he considered that the *habeas corpus* writ "might depopulate this fortification." (Major W. W. Morris [commanding at Ft. McHenry, Baltimore] to U. S. District Judge W. F. Giles, May 6, 1861: Attorney General's Papers.)

[46]*U. S. Stat. at Large*, XII, 755.

were given both immunity and the protection of Federal courts. On the other side, lists of state prisoners were to be furnished to the circuit and district courts, and if grand juries found no indictments against them they were to be discharged by judicial order upon taking the oath of allegiance and entering into recognizance for good behavior, of which the court was to fix the sum. Where such lists were not furnished, a judge might discharge the prisoner on *habeas corpus* if satisfied as to the allegations of the petition.

Had this law been complied with, the effect would have been to restore the supremacy of the civil power; for the act contained provisions which, if enforced, would have greatly modified the President's control of prisoners. In the early part of the war, both arrests and releases were at the discretion of the President acting through the military officers. It is literally true that the word of the President (or that of a Cabinet secretary whose power originated in the President) was enough to place a man in confinement, and that the acts of generals and provost marshals in whom discretion reposed were constructively the President's own acts. When orders came from Washington they usually emanated from the Secretary of State, or, later, from the Secretary of War; but in law they were the President's orders, and had the President chosen to specify certain persons for arrest, the system in force would have permitted this. In fact, Lincoln himself sometimes gave the order for arrest.[47]

[47] J. F. Rhodes stated that he had not found an instance in which the President himself directed an arrest, though he "permitted them all." Rhodes, *History of United States*, IV, 235. The following order was signed and doubtless dictated by the President: "Executive Mansion, Washington City, June 15, 1864. Whereas it has come to my knowledge that (J. S. C.) of West Virginia is engaged in treasonable . . . correspondence with . . . an agent of the rebels . . . and has invited . . . the said agent . . . to come to the city of Washington to confer with him . . . it is ordered that Colonel Wisewell, Military Governor

Always it was the President's authority that was appealed to when an officer holding a prisoner declined to produce him in court.[48] As to releases, the President assumed full discretion, and his official word was all that was needed to discharge a political prisoner.

The Habeas Corpus Act, however, distributed the authority previously concentrated in the President. Congress now declared the duty of officers having custody of prisoners, making it mandatory for them to obey a judge's order for discharge.[49] The requirement that lists of political prisoners be furnished to the courts applied to future as well as previous arrests, and the way was laid by congressional action for the speedy release of all citizens against whom no violation of Federal law could be charged. Should the prisoners be detained beyond twenty days without the furnishing of such lists, then on petition of any citizen they were to be discharged on the same terms as if the lists had been furnished.

---

of the District of Washington, arrest and take into custody the said [J. S. C.] and hold him in custody until further order. [signed] Abraham Lincoln." (Stanton Papers, No. 54238.)

[48]Not only could the Chief Executive disregard the mandates of the courts; he could deny information to Congress. When the House of Representatives called for papers regarding the arrest of the police commissioners of Baltimore, and again regarding martial law in Kentucky, the President declined the requests on the ground that the giving of such information would be incompatible with the public interest. (Richardson, *Messages . . . of the Presidents*, VI, 33; *Sen. Ex. Doc. No. 51*, 37 Cong., 2 sess., Vol. V.)

[49]The act provided that, while the privilege was suspended, "no military or other officer [should] be compelled" to produce the prisoners in answer to the writ. After grand juries had met, however, and passed upon the cases of the prisoners, those not indicted were to be ordered discharged by the Federal judge, and "every officer . . . having custody of [any] prisoner [was] directed immediately to obey and execute [the] judge's order." In case of delay or refusal to obey such order, the officer was to be subject to indictment for misdemeanor and punished by a fine of at least $500 and imprisonment in the common jail for at least six months. (*U. S. Stat. at Large*, XII, 755, sec. 2.)

As regards military officers, then, it could be said that, by the provisions of the Habeas Corpus Act, their mandates concerning political prisoners were to come from Congress, and it was intended that the legislative branch of the Government should to that extent recover authority from the executive. A like recovery was to be effected by the judicial branch, for prisoners were no longer to be detained by presidential authority, but were to be released by order of a Federal judge unless indicted by a grand jury for offenses against the United States. The act represented, therefore, on paper, a twofold vindication of the civil authority.

Like other wartime statutes, however, the act seems to have had but little practical effect. Though the question of its enforcement is a difficult historical problem, the writer's researches have brought him to the conclusion that the act was not carried out in sufficient degree to make any noticeable difference in the matter of the arrest, confinement, and release of political prisoners.[50]

---

[50] The writer's independent study of this subject has been reënforced by searches made for him by the kindly coöperation of the clerks of various Federal courts. Mr. William P. Kapper, Clerk of the District Court at Indianapolis, writes as follows: "I have personally gone through all of the order books of both the Circuit Court of the United States and the District Court of the United States covering the entire period of the Civil War and I am unable to find that there was ever any list of prisoners filed by the Secretary of War or the Secretary of State, and there appears to be no order of the Court ordering the release of any citizens held by military authority who were not indicted." The Clerk of the District Court at Cleveland, Ohio, Mr. B. C. Miller, writes: "I carefully leafed the journal from the date of the passage of the Act until 1865 and find no record of any orders . . . releasing prisoners under this Act." Similar results were obtained by searching the records of other courts, and a special search in the War Department, made for the purpose of this book, failed to reveal any measures taken in compliance with the act, other than the Judge Advocate General's letter of June 9, 1863 (mentioned in the text above), in which he reported that Stanton's instructions to furnish a list of political prisoners to the courts had been complied with.

When Stanton directed that lists of prisoners of state be furnished to the judges of the district and circuit courts of the United States, Judge Advocate General Holt reported that incomplete lists had been supplied, but proceeded at once to criticize the act, which he considered poorly framed and "extremely difficult of construction."[51] Holt construed the act as not applying to prisoners triable by military tribunals, or under sentence of such tribunals. This was a significant exception, because it left the executive without restraint in all cases where martial law was instituted and where military commissions were used for the trial of citizens. The Habeas Corpus Act offered no effective obstacle in the case of Vallandigham, a citizen placed under military arrest and sentenced by a military tribunal. In the Milligan decision[52] the Supreme Court held that the act should properly have applied to citizens subjected to such arrest and sentence, which was declared illegal in non-military areas; but this decision did not come until after the war, while Holt's interpretation was the governing rule during the war. Numerous arrests were made after March 3, 1863; and, as Professor Dunning has pointed out, persons arrested after that time were released, not by Federal judges, but by authority of the War Department.[53] Since the Act confirmed the President's right to suspend the privilege of the *habeas corpus* writ and afforded immunity to officers acting under the President's orders, a certain security and legal sanction

---

[51]Holt to Stanton, June 9, 1863: *O. R.*, Ser. II, Vol. 5, p. 765.

[52]The Vallandigham and Milligan cases are discussed in the following chapter.

[53]William A. Dunning, in *Am. Hist. Rev.*, XXIV, 628. Dunning says further: "As to the peremptory requirement that political prisoners be referred to the courts, some perfunctory attention was given to the act immediately after its passage, but the War Department soon settled back into its old procedure." (*Ibid.*, p. 627.)

was thus given to a procedure for which the President had been widely criticized, and the executive branch could thereafter proceed with a certain assurance that it had previously lacked.

CHAPTER VIII

MARTIAL LAW AND MILITARY COMMISSIONS

In the arbitrary arrests which were discussed in the previous chapter the application of military power was of a limited sort, and the extension of executive authority stopped short of the establishment of a strictly military régime. In the present chapter our attention will be directed to further degrees of military rule. Martial law, we shall find, was declared over whole States or large districts; and it will be necessary to note the relations subsisting between military and civil authorities while such martial law was in force. In peaceful regions of the North, citizens were condemned by military commissions though the courts were unobstructed, and issues were thus raised which were more serious than the mere detention of political prisoners in military custody. So grave were the questions here involved that, after the war, the Supreme Court declared illegal the use of military tribunals for the trial of citizens in districts unaffected by actual invasion and remote from the presence of armies.

I

The subjection of designated sections of the country to martial law depended upon local circumstances, and the degree differed according to varying conditions. Such action was at times of minor importance, as for instance when Round Valley in Central California was placed under martial law as a protection to the Indians against whom the whites were committing outrages.[1] In some cases this extreme power seems to have been used in an eccentric manner, as when General Thomas Ewing, Jr., declared martial law at Leavenworth, Kansas, because he "could not get along with the mayor."[2] That martial law was not always considered oppressive is shown by the fact that citizens sometimes petitioned for it. Some Philadelphians, for instance, requested the President to declare martial law in their city at the time of Lee's invasion to enable them to put the city in a proper state of defense.[3] Nor should we suppose that the existence of martial law necessarily involved a condition of extensive or continuous military restraint. Beginning with September, 1863, the District of Columbia was subjected to martial law, and this state of affairs continued throughout the war, but it should not be supposed that residents of the capital city were usually conscious of serious curtailment of their liberties.[4] The condition of martial law was here used as a means of military security. That martial law should be declared in areas of actual military operations was, of course, not remarkable. Large districts in Delaware, Maryland, and Pennsylvania

[1] *O. R.*, Ser. I, Vol. 50, pt. 2, pp. 218, 219, 310.
[2] *Ibid.*, Ser. I, Vol. 22, pt. 2, p. 388.
[3] *Ibid.*, Ser. I, Vol. 27, pt. 3, pp. 188, 366.
[4] *House Rep. No. 262*, Mar. 26, 1874, 43 Cong., 1 sess., p. 6.

were placed under martial law because of the actual presence of Confederate forces in the summer of 1863, but this specific application of military power occasioned no serious complaint.[5]

Where, however, a continuing condition of disloyalty or disturbance offered serious menace to the authorities in their preservation of peace and order, the use of martial law for long periods presented a much graver situation. Such conditions existed in Missouri and in Kentucky.

In Missouri, "rebel" forces were very active and the extent to which such forces were secretly assisted by citizens seemed to the Union generals very alarming. Guerrilla bands were reported to be roaming the country as bandits, taking Union men prisoners and robbing them of horses, wagons, and provisions. A cautious policy, however, was adopted by the Union authorities. Frémont's general proclamation of martial law throughout the whole State was overruled, and the Government contented itself with such a declaration in St. Louis and in the vicinity of railroads and telegraph lines.[6]

More drastic action was taken in Kentucky, where conditions were much the same as in Missouri. In the ebb and flow of important military operations, many counties in Kentucky were alternately occupied by Federal and Confederate soldiers, and were so overrun by guerrillas and home guards that courts could not be held and normal authority for the preservation of order and the protection of persons and property could not be exerted. The anomalous condition of the colored people

[5]*O. R.*, Ser. I, Vol. 27, pt. 3, pp. 437-438, 504.

[6]Concerning martial law in Missouri, see Nicolay and Hay, *Works*, IX, 147-149, XI, 33; *O. R.*, Ser. II, Vol. 5, p. 99; *ibid.*, Ser. I, Vol. 3, pp. 442, 466; *ibid.*, Ser. II, Vol. I, p. 155; *ibid.*, Ser. I, Vol. 8, pp. 395, 401, 611, 818.

was an additional factor contributing to the general disturbance of social order. Recruitment of Negroes for the Federal army produced intense dissatisfaction, and the operation of various Union laws giving freedom to slaves in opposition to the statutes of the State which legalized slavery occasioned widespread irritation. The protection of such Negroes as the Federal authority recognized to be free seemed impossible without an extraordinary use of national authority.

This situation was met, in the first place, by the partial application of martial law in specified districts[7] where the disturbance seemed most serious, and later by a proclamation of President Lincoln, dated July 5, 1864, putting the whole State under martial law.[8] On October 12, 1865, the condition of martial law in Kentucky was abolished by President Johnson.[9]

The instances we have noticed are sufficient to give a general notion of the use of martial law in States not in insurrection during the Civil War. A close study of these instances will reveal the fact that interference with the civil authority was reduced to the minimum even during the continuance of martial law, and that the power over citizens which was entrusted to the military authorities was sparingly used. It was made clear with regard to Kentucky that the power under martial law was not to be used to obstruct the proceedings of the rightful legislature, nor to impede the administration of justice in actions not connected with military operations. A careful reading of Lincoln's proclamation of July 5, 1864 (by which, as we have seen, martial law in the State was instituted) shows solicitude on the part of the President that the ordinary course of justice be inter-

[7] *O. R.*, Ser. I, Vol. 52, pt. 1 (suppl.), p. 277.
[8] *Ibid.*, Ser. I, Vol. 39, pt. 2, p. 180.
[9] *Ibid.*, Ser. III, Vol. 5, p. 125.

rupted as little as possible. Only acts demanded by the military emergency were authorized by the proclamation, and the whole document showed reluctance to use arbitrary measures. The special circumstances requiring such measures were recited as justification for the proclamation. For certain specified objects, martial law was thought to be needed; and beyond these specified and limited objects the Government did not intend to go.

This limited use of military power under martial law was illustrated elsewhere. When, for instance, General Schenck, immediately preceding the battle of Gettysburg, proclaimed martial law in Baltimore and the major part of Maryland, he assured the people "that this suspension of the civil government . . . [should] not extend beyond the necessities of the occasion." He then added: "All the courts . . . and political functionaries of State, county and city authority are to continue in the discharge of their duties as in times of peace, only in no way interfering with the exercise of the predominant power assumed . . . by the military authority. . . .When the occasion for this proclamation passes by, no one will be more rejoiced than the commanding general that he can revoke his order and return to the normal condition of a country at peace."[10] As to martial law in St. Louis, General Halleck made the following statement: "It is not intended by this declaration to interfere with the jurisdiction of any civil court which is loyal to the Government of the United States and which will aid the military authorities in enforcing order and punishing crimes."[11]

These are but typical declarations by military officers illustrating the spirit in which military power was ap-

[10] *Ibid.*, Ser. I, Vol. 27, pt. 3, pp. 437-438.

[11] Order of General Halleck at St. Louis, December 26, 1861: *ibid.*, Ser. II, Vol. 1, p. 155.

plied. The question has sometimes been raised as to whether martial law and civil law can coexist. Without entering into the technical phases of this question, we may notice that in fact they did coexist in various cases during the Civil War. In regions placed under martial law a sort of practical *modus vivendi* was adopted under which the civil courts continued to function as far as possible, their province being invaded by the military only in those instances in which, for specified and limited objects, such interference seemed to the commanding general to be indispensable. In advising the generals as to the conduct of their duties, the authorities at Washington were just as careful to counsel restraint as to urge action.

II

We have now to consider another phase of extraordinary executive authority applied during the Civil War —the condemnation of citizens before military commissions. In a section of enemy territory within military occupation, or in a region under martial law, the use of the military commission for the trial of non-military persons who have committed offenses of a military character—such as spying or bushwhacking—is proper. Where there is no martial law, and where the ordinary civil courts are unimpeded, it has been generally recognized that military tribunals have no proper function to perform in the trial of civilians, and certainly not for offenses outside the military code.

In explaining the use of military commissions during the Civil War, Judge Advocate General Holt stated that they originated in the necessities of the rebellion, and were indispensable for the punishment of crimes in regions where the courts ceased to exist and in cases of which the local criminal courts could not take cognizance. Such commissions were powerful, he said, because unencumbered by technicalities and because their process was executed by the military power of the United States.[12]

Perhaps the typical use of military commissions at the time of the Civil War was for the punishment of offenses coming broadly under the military code when committed by civilians in regions hostile to the United States. The presence of Federal armies in Missouri, for example, while driving thousands into the Confederate ranks, also occasioned many kinds of obstructive tactics and acts of violence on the part of those enemies who remained out of uniform. Since martial law was in force in Missouri, especially along railroad and telegraph lines, we find numerous cases in that State where civilians were tried for bridge burning, destruction of railroad and telegraph lines, and the like. Where civilians furnished information to the enemy, or engaged in sniping or bushwhacking, they were triable by military commission for violation of the laws of war. The vast majority of cases brought before such commissions were of this general sort, and have occasioned little adverse comment. The penalties were severe, but no death sentence could be enforced without reference to the President, and Lincoln's clemency saved many a life.[13]

Widespread criticism arose, however, where citizens were subjected to military tribunals in regions remote from military operations and not under martial law. By order of August 8, 1862, United States marshals and

---

[12]Judge Advocate General's report, in *Report of the Secretary of War*, 1865-1866, p. 1005.

[13]Several hundred pages of the *Official Records* are devoted to the military commissions in Missouri: *O. R.*, Ser. II, Vol. 1, pp. 282 *et seq.*

local magistrates were authorized to imprison persons who discouraged enlistments or engaged in disloyal practices. Immediate report of such arrests was to be made to the Judge Advocate General so that the prisoners could be tried by military commission.[14] Generals in command of extensive "departments" in the North were given authority to conduct such arrests and trials. We have here to deal with a twofold extension of military justice beyond its normal sphere: the offenses were beyond the military code; and the trials were to be conducted in areas remote from military operations.

III

The legality of this broader use of military commissions was threshed out in two prominent cases—the Vallandigham case, decided by the Supreme Court in February, 1864, and the Milligan case, decided in 1866. A comparison of these important cases reveals in a striking manner the effect of the war upon judicial decisions; for the court which upheld the authority of a military commission in 1864 declared such a commission to be illegal in an analogous case two years later. In its main effect, the later decision was a reversal of the former.

General Burnside, in command of the "Department of the Ohio," with headquarters at Cincinnati, issued on April 19, 1863, an order known as "General Orders No. 38" declaring that persons committing acts for the benefit of the enemy would be executed as spies or

---

[14] *Cong. Globe,* 37 Cong., 3 sess., p. 1215: Stanton Papers, No. 51811. (Stanton states that this order was issued "by verbal direction of the President.")

traitors.[15] The order declared further that "the habit of declaring sympathies for the enemy will no longer be tolerated. . . . Persons committing such offenses will be at once arrested, with a view to being tried [as spies or traitors] or sent beyond our lines into the lines of their friends."

On May 1, Clement L. Vallandigham, a prominent anti-war agitator, made a speech at Mt. Vernon, Ohio, for which he was arrested under this order. Burnside caused a military commission to be convened, and the prisoner was brought before this court charged with "publicly expressing, in violation of General Orders, No. 38 . . . his sympathies for those in arms against the . . . United States, declaring disloyal . . . opinions with the object . . . of weakening the power of the Government . . . to suppress an unlawful rebellion."

Vallandigham refused to plead, denying the jurisdiction of the court, but the Judge Advocate entered a plea of "not guilty." In the trial Vallandigham was allowed counsel, was permitted personally to cross-examine witnesses, and was given the advantage of compulsory attendance of witnesses in his favor. At the conclusion of the proceedings he read a "protest" declaring that he was not triable by a military commission, but was entitled to all the constitutional guarantees concerning due process of arrest, indictment, and jury trial. The "alleged 'offense,' " he declared, was unknown to the Constitution and the laws.

---

[15]For proceedings in the Vallandigham case, see: 1 Wall. 243; *O. R.*, Ser. II, Vol. 5, pp. 573 *et seq.; Ann. Cyc.*, 1863, pp. 473 *et seq.; Diary of Gideon Welles*, I, 306, 321; Nicolay and Hay, *Lincoln*, VII, 338 *et seq.* In the writer's investigation, use was made also of the full record and arguments as found in the unpublished "Records and Briefs of the United States Supreme Court" in the law division of the Library of Congress, and of a useful paper prepared by C. M. Kneier, of the University of Illinois.

The commission found Vallandigham guilty and he was sentenced to close confinement during the war. He then applied to Judge Leavitt of the United States Circuit Court at Cincinnati, for a writ of *habeas corpus*, and thus the question arose as to a judicial review of these military proceedings.

The course pursued by Judge Leavitt was unusual. Taking the ground that he might refuse the writ if satisfied that the petitioner would not be discharged after a hearing, he notified General Burnside of the application and invited him to present a statement. The usual procedure would have been to issue the writ as "of right" and let the General's statement appear in his return thereto.

Burnside justified his action on the ground that the country was in a "state of civil war," that in such a time great responsibility rests on public men not to "use license and plead that they are exercising liberty," and that his duty required him to stop intemperate discussion which tended to weaken the army. His statement was a sort of stump speech in justification of his "General Orders No. 38" and his treatment of Vallandigham. Judge Leavitt refused the writ and the case was brought up to the Supreme Court of the United States on a motion for *certiorari* to review the sentence of the military commission.

Vallandigham's attorney argued that a military commission has but a special and limited jurisdiction which does not extend to the trial of a citizen unconnected with the land or naval forces. The charge on which the prisoner was tried was unknown to the law, he contended, and the sentence was in excess of jurisdiction. General Burnside had no authority to enlarge the jurisdiction of a military commission; and as a remedy for such unwarranted excess of authority, the Supreme Court of the United States had the power to issue a writ of *certiorari*.

Taking its opinion bodily from the argument of Judge Advocate General Holt, the Supreme Court refused to review the proceedings of the military commission. In stating the grounds of this refusal, the court declared that its authority was derived from the Constitution and the legislation of Congress, its original jurisdiction being specified in the Constitution itself, and its appellate jurisdiction being derived from the Judiciary Act of 1789. A military commission, it was said, is not a court within the meaning of that act, and the Supreme Court "cannot . . . originate a writ of *certiorari* to review . . . the proceedings of a military commission."[16]

IV

Though from the standpoint of the lawyer there were technical differences between the Vallandigham case and the Milligan case, yet it would appear to the layman

[16]Lincoln wrote to Burnside: "All the Cabinet regretted the necessity of arresting for instance Vallandigham—some perhaps doubting that there was a real necessity for it, but being done all are for seeing you through with it." (*O. R.*, Ser. II, Vol. 5, p. 717.) The President commuted Vallandigham's sentence from confinement during the war to removal within the Confederate lines and this removal was effected. (*Ibid.*, pp. 657, 705-706.) Certain citizens of Ohio sent to the President a long paper protesting against this banishment. They considered his "assumption of the right to suspend all the constitutional guarantees of personal liberty, and even of the freedom of speech and of the press" a "startling" thing, and declared that by such a claim to power the dominion of the President would not only be "absolute over the rights of individuals, but equally so over the other departments of the Government." "Surely it is not necessary," they added, "to subvert free government in this country in order to put down the rebellion, and it cannot be done under the pretense of putting down the rebellion. Indeed it is plain that your Administration has been . . . greatly weakened by the assumption of power not delegated in the Constitution." (M. Birchard and others to the President, July 1, 1863: *ibid.*, Ser. II, Vol. 6, pp. 64-68.)

that essentially the same question was involved—namely, the right of civil courts to set aside the sentence of a military commission, and the illegality of such a commission when used for the trial of citizens in a non-military area.[17]

Milligan had been arrested on October 5, 1864, by order of General Hovey, in command at Indianapolis, and, with certain associates, was brought before a military commission and convicted of conspiracy forcibly to release "rebel" prisoners and to march into Kentucky and Missouri in coöperation with the "rebel" forces in an expedition directed against the United States. It was shown that Milligan and his associates were members of the disloyal societies known as the "Order of the American Knights," and the "Sons of Liberty."

The military commission sentenced Milligan to be hanged, and the date of the execution was fixed at May 19, 1865. Milligan petitioned the United States Circuit Court for a writ of *habeas corpus*, and on division of opinion the case was brought up to the Supreme Court. When the case was decided by that tribunal the war had come to a close, and the bearing of this fact upon

---

[17]The writer's sources and authorities for the Milligan case are: 71 U. S. 2 *et seq.;* Hare, *American Constitutional Law*, II, 958 *et seq.;* Records and Briefs of the U. S. Supreme Court (in the law division of the Library of Congress); MS. Diary of Edward Bates; MSS. in the files of the Attorney General's office; the Johnson Papers in the Library of Congress; Charles Warren, *The Supreme Court in United States History*, III, 140 *et seq.;* Charles E. Hughes, "War Powers under the Constitution," *Sen. Ex. Doc. No. 105*, 65 Cong., 1 sess. (Sept. 11, 1917). Concerning this case, ex-Attorney General Bates wrote: "If the Supreme Court should decide that military commissions are *lawful*, I predict that the judges who give opinion that way will go down to posterity with characters as black as that of Lord Chief Justice Saunders, and that their judgment will be more odious to this nation than Saunders's judgment against the chartered rights of the City of London ever was to the English people." (MS. Dairy of Edward Bates, Feb. 16, 1866.)

the attitude of the court appeared in Justice Davis' announcement of the court's opinion, where he said:

> During the late wicked Rebellion, the temper of the times did not allow that calmness in deliberation and discussion so necessary to a correct conclusion of a purely judicial question. *Then*, considerations of safety were mingled with the exercise of power; and feelings . . . prevailed which are happily terminated. *Now* that the public safety is assured, this question, as well as all others, can be discussed and decided without passion or the admixture of any element not required to form a legal judgment.

On the question whether the Supreme Court could review the action of a military commission, the opinion was the opposite of that announced in the Vallandigham case. "If there was law to justify this military trial," said the court, "it is not our province to interfere; if there was not it is our duty to declare the nullity of the whole proceedings." Reviewing the various constitutional safeguards connected with the arrest, trial and punishment of individuals for crimes, the court declared that these guarantees of freedom (which are not to be set aside during war) had been broken. "Martial law," it was held, "cannot arise from a *threatened* invasion. The necessity must be actual and present; the invasion real, such as effectually closes the courts and deposes the civil administration. . . . Martial rule can never exist where the courts are open, and in the proper and unobstructed exercise of their jurisdiction. It is . . . confined to the locality of actual war." Milligan's trial and conviction by a military commission were therefore held to be illegal.

Citing that provision of the Habeas Corpus Act of March 3, 1863, which directed that political prisoners not indicted by the grand jury should be released, the court held that as there was no indictment against Milligan, the Circuit Court must liberate him.

Four of the justices, including Chief Justice Chase, dissented to the Milligan decision, but it was a limited dissent. The minority agreed that the military commission was without jurisdiction and that Milligan should be discharged. The majority, however, had held not only that the commission was unauthorized, but that Congress had no power to authorize it; and to this doctrine the dissenting judges refused to subscribe. The Constitution, they maintained, provides for military as well as civil government; and in military trials, the safeguards of the Fifth and other similar Amendments do not apply. Since Congress has the power to declare war, it necessarily has "many subordinate and auxiliary powers," and hence, said the minority, "Congress had power . . . to provide for the organization of a military commission, and for trial by that commission of persons engaged in this conspiracy." The fact that Congress had not authorized military commissions in Indiana caused the dissenting judges to regard the Milligan trial as illegal, though they affirmed that Congress was constitutionally competent to create such tribunals.

This dissent has produced the impression of a court about to swing from one opinion to another. As a well known commentator has said: "The question whether the principle of Magna Carta as declared in the Petition of Right, vindicated by the Declaration of Independence, and guaranteed by the Constitution . . . shall give place . . . to the methods which have been despotically introduced [in] Europe, arose in *Ex parte Milligan*, where the wavering balance fortunately inclined to the side of freedom, although with a tendency to oscillate which leaves the ultimate result in doubt."[18]

[18] Hare, *American Constitutional Law*, II, 957-958.

This wavering attitude, it may be added, is emphasized by the fact that, as we have seen, the Supreme Court declined to interfere with a military commission in the Vallandigham case while the war was in progress, and the illegality of such commissions was declared only after the return of peace had removed the occasion for them.

V

It may be appropriate to close this chapter with certain conclusions or summarizations concerning extraordinary uses of military authority during the Civil War:

1. The powers which the executive assumed and the prerogatives which he claimed were far-reaching. They seemed, if applied to great excess, to offer the opportunity for dictatorship. All this was out of keeping with the normal tenor of American law.

2. Congress dealt with the problem, after much delay, by a compromise which involved ratification of the President's course but at the same time required prisoners to be released unless indicted in the regular courts. This legislation was ineffective.

3. The prerogatives assumed and announced in proclamations and the like were not, of course, always exercised. Much circumspection and leniency was manifested in the actual use of extraordinary powers.

4. The suspension of the *habeas corpus* privilege did not, of itself, institute martial law. The use of this *dernier ressort* of the executive power was limited; and even where martial law was declared the normal course of justice and the functions of the civil courts were, in the main, uninterrupted.

5. While military commissions were used for the trial of civilians, cases such as those of Vallandigham and Milligan were exceptional. In areas not under martial

law such military commissions were, according to the Supreme Court, illegal.

6. The civil courts did very little in suppressing dangerous and treasonable activities. District attorneys brought few indictments for such crimes as conspiracy and treason, and the number of cases of this sort actually prosecuted to conviction was negligible. On the other hand, disloyalty was widespread. In view of such extensive disloyalty, the number of political arrests is comprehensible.[19]

7. Summary process meant, as a rule, military arrest and detention, not military trial. Though justifiable in the case of spies and agents of the enemy, this detention was indeed a hardship for many of the prisoners. To a certain extent this hardship was mitigated by a liberal policy regarding releases.

8. Finally, after a close study of the subject, the author feels that the arbitrary arrests were unfortunate, that Lincoln's conception of the executive power was too expansive, and that a clearer distinction between military and civil control would have been desirable.[20] If,

---

[19] Concerning the extent and nature of disloyalty in the North, see above, pp. 82-84.

[20] Lincoln's reasons for the suspension of the privilege and the arbitrary arrests were set forth in his letter to Corning, June 12, 1863, which is generally regarded as one of his ablest papers. He urged that the existing crisis was beyond the power of the civil courts which are intended for the trial of individuals in quiet times; that a "clear, flagrant, and gigantic case of rebellion" existed, for which case the suspension was constitutionally authorized; that the purpose of summary process was "preventive" rather than "vindictive"; that if arrests had never been made except for defined crimes, the constitutional provision would have been useless; that Vallandigham's arrest was not for political purposes but because of damage to the army; and that the Constitution itself makes the distinction between measures authorized for normal times and those permissible in time of rebellion or invasion. Jackson's use of martial law was cited approvingly, and it was shown that normal safeguards of liberty were not injured by this extraordinary use of military authority in a crisis. (Nicolay and Hay, *Works*, VIII, 298 *et seq.*)

however, the Government under Lincoln erred in these respects, it erred under great provocation with the best of motives; and its policy may not be justly criticized without a full understanding of the alarming situation which confronted the nation.[21]

---

[21]Lincoln's reluctance to depart from established American principles; his sympathy for the conscientious objector; his generosity in releasing political prisoners, whom he refused to treat as war criminals; and his claim to the title of the "Great Conciliator" as denoting his real place in history more truly than that of the "Great Emancipator," were effectively set forth in a paper entitled "Abraham Lincoln and the Tradition of American Civil Liberty," read by Professor Arthur C. Cole before the Illinois State Historical Society at Springfield, Illinois, May 7, 1926.

CHAPTER IX

THE INDEMNITY ACT OF 1863

I. Problem of the liability of Federal officers for wrongs committed in their official capacity during the Civil War

II. Passage of the Indemnity Act to relieve officers of such liability

III. Suits against Federal officers: State resistance to the Indemnity Act

IV. Legal difficulties presented in the courts in the practical application of the act

V. Constitutionality of the measure considered: Decision of the Supreme Court holding the act to be in violation of the Seventh Amendment

I

Our attention has been called in preceding chapters to summary arrests and other arbitrary acts consequent upon the suspension of the *habeas corpus* privilege. The essential irregularity of such a situation in American law becomes especially conspicuous when one considers its inevitable sequel—namely, the protection of military and civil officers from such prosecution as would normally follow invasion of private rights and actual injury of persons and property. Such protection was afforded by a bill of indemnity passed in 1863; and this law, with its amendment of 1866, forms a significant chapter in our legal history.

By the ordinary application of the principles of American administrative law, officers guilty of trespasses (such as false imprisonment and unwarranted seizures) would stand unprotected, though the trespass might be in strict keeping with executive orders. It is a well-known principle of our law that governmental officers (with the possible exception of judges who are removable by impeachment but otherwise independent) are liable in damages for official conduct which results in private injuries, and are subject to prosecution in case such conduct bears a criminal character.[1] Under American and other Anglo-Saxon jurisdictions any governmental officer who injures private rights, either by omission or commission, is, with but few qualifications, subject to civil or criminal action precisely as an ordinary citizen would be.[2] This liability of governmental agents is but one phase of the Anglo-Saxon principle that governments are not above law, and that an officer of the government is not given a privileged character superior to that of the common man. All this would mean that, unless some special protection were provided for cases arising during the war, many officers would be sued or prosecuted for acts which in the large sense were not theirs at all, but those of the government.

[1]"Every officer, from the highest to the lowest, in our government, is amenable to the laws for an injury done to individuals. . . . It is a fundamental principle in our government that no individual, whether in or out of office, is above the law. . . . There are three grounds on which a public officer may be held responsible to an injured party. (1) Where he refuses to do a ministerial act over which he can exercise no discretion. (2) Where he does an act which is clearly not within his jurisdiction. (3) Where he acts willfully, maliciously and unjustly . . . within his jurisdiction." (U. S. Supreme Court in Kendall *vs.* Stokes *et al*, 44 U. S. 792, 794.)

[2]For an instance in which the President himself was subjected to an action for damages, one may turn to the case of Livingston *vs.* Jefferson. In 1811 an action for trespass was brought before the Circuit Court of Virginia against "Thomas Jefferson, a citizen of Virginia." The fact that Jefferson had been President was not considered a bar to the suit (which pertained to an official act while in the Presidency), though on other grounds the court declined to take jurisdiction. (Fed. Cas. No. 8411; Beveridge, *Life of John Marshall*, IV, 102.)

For these reasons it has long been customary in England to follow up a proclamation of martial law, or a suspension of the *habeas corpus* privilege, with a retroactive statute of indemnity affording judicial protection to those agents of the Government who, though acting in good faith, have been guilty of breaches of private rights. Following the suspension of the Habeas Corpus Act in 1793, Parliament passed in 1801 an act indemnifying and shielding all who had made summary arrests for treason, and relieving them of the responsibility that would usually have followed such arrests.[3] Another bill of indemnity was passed in 1817 to protect officers who had arrested on suspicion, and who had made seizures without legal process.

Before the war had proceeded far in the United States it became evident that Federal officers, even of Cabinet rank, were being attacked in State courts for acts done in the performance of duty. One of the earliest cases of this sort was that of Pierce Butler of Philadelphia against Simon Cameron, Secretary of War. Butler was arrested by order of Cameron in August, 1861, on suspicion of having received a commission from the Confederacy, and was confined for about a month in Fort Lafayette, after which he was released by order of Secretary Seward on giving pledge of loyalty. On Butler's petition the Supreme Court of Pennsylvania issued a writ which was served upon Cameron when he was about to sail as minister to Russia, the charge being assault and battery and false imprisonment. The official concern occasioned by this suit may be judged by the fact that the President adopted the act of the Secretary of War

[3]These English bills of indemnity offered protection only for *bona fide* acts, done of necessity, and not for excesses of authority. *In re* the petition of D. F. Marais: *Edinburgh Review*, Vol. 195, pp. 79 *et seq*. (esp. p. 90); May, *Constitutional History of England*, II, 256-258

as his own, and directed that the suit should "be fully defended as a matter which deeply concerns the public welfare as well as the safety of the individual officers of the Government." To this end the Federal district attorney at Philadelphia was instructed to give particular attention to the defense of Cameron. As a result, the case was dropped in its preliminary stages.[4]

In 1863 Secretary Seward was subjected to a similar action for false imprisonment in a New York court by G. W. Jones, former minister to Bogotá, who was arrested in a New York hotel and kept prisoner in Fort Lafayette for four months.[5] The effort of Governor Seymour and the judicial authorities of New York to prosecute General Dix for his suppression of the New York *World* is an example of the same disposition on the part of local courts to enforce judicial remedies at the expense of highly placed officials.[6] Secretary Stanton is said to have remarked that if such prosecutions held, he would be imprisoned a thousand years, at least.[7] These instances will suffice to show that the need of protection for Federal officers was real.

II

To supply such protection was the purpose of the act of March 3, 1863, which was at once a bill of indemnity and an authorization to suspend the *habeas corpus* privilege.[8] It is only the fourth and subsequent sections that

[4]*O. R.*, Ser. II, Vol. 2, pp. 507-508; *Ann. Cyc.*, 1862, pp. 511-512.

[5]40 Barbour 563; 41 Barbour 269; 3 Grant 431.

[6]*Infra*, pp. 496-499.

[7]*Diary of Gideon Welles*, II, 206.

[8]In using the name "Indemnity Act" to designate the law of March 3, 1863, contemporary usage has been followed. Senator Trumbull and others referred to the measure while under debate as the "Indemnity Bill," and the same designation appeared in the headings of the record, as well as in many other places. (*Cong. Globe*, 37 Cong., 3 sess., pp. 1459, 1479.)

carry the indemnifying feature. The circumstances of the passage of this act were extraordinary. It was considered during the last hours of a crowded session, amid a hectic atmosphere. Its opponents claimed that it was railroaded through; that various attempts to lay it on the table or delay its passage were roughly overridden; "that it was passed within an hour of its first introduction without having been printed, without reference to any committee, and without opportunity for consideration or discussion." It is true that at first there was practically no debate in the lower house, and that the measure was rushed to its passage within an hour. But later the question was reopened by a Senate amendment, whereupon a long and animated debate followed. This discussion, however, shot wide of the mark, and was hardly more than a general debate on the war and on party policy.

In each chamber there was a lively filibuster against the measure. In the House it took the form of continuous excuses for absence in the case of various members on the ground of "sickness," being "unwell," being "indisposed" and the like. Mr. Colfax of Indiana rose to a question of order and his point was objected to because it had been decided that he was absent! To judge by the record the House was in great hilarity when these proceedings were in progress, and the sergeant-at-arms was appealed to in playful mood at various points; but at the same time it was evident that a real contest was on and that the supporters of the bill were displeased at the filibustering tactics of the opposition.[9]

In the Senate a truly remarkable struggle was enacted. A vigorous minority was working desperately to post-

[9]The filibuster in the lower house appears in *Cong. Globe*, 37 Cong., 3 sess., pp. 1357 *et seq.* The bill passed the House March 2, the vote being 99 to 44: *ibid.*, p. 1479.

pone the measure and prevent a vote, while Senator Trumbull and other leaders were equally determined to put the measure through before the session should close. It was agreed that the conference report on the bill, harmonizing the differences between the House and the Senate, should be taken up at seven o'clock of the same day that the first printed copies of the report were distributed. The parliamentary encounter (which could not be deemed a discussion) proceeded throughout the night and early morning of March 2-3, Senators Powell, Bayard and others holding the floor with endless speeches in which Magna Carta, Shakespeare, Cowper, Molière, Marshall, Webster, and other authorities and poets were quoted; while the friends of the bill used all their powers to keep a quorum, prevent adjournment, and acquire the floor for a motion to concur in the conference report. During this "debate" the yeas and nays on adjournment were taken five times.

Finally, at about five o'clock in the morning, the presiding officer unexpectedly put a *viva voce* vote, announced that the bill was passed, denied the floor to opposing Senators who insisted that the measure had not passed, refused to entertain a motion to reconsider, and, against the protest of the filibusterers, declared the Senate adjourned.[10]

The measure so passed was not designed, as Stevens explained, to indemnify everybody who, at the time of the suspension of constitutional guarantees, had committed trespasses in the name of the Government; but it "indemnified the President, Cabinet, and all who in pursuance of their authority [had] made arrests during the period of the suspension."[11] The fourth section of the act reads as follows:

[10]*Cong. Globe*, 37 Cong., 3 sess., p. 1477.
[11]*Ibid.*, p. 22.

> Any order of the President, or under his authority, made at any time during the . . . present rebellion shall be a defense in all courts to any action or prosecution, civil or criminal, pending or to be commenced, for any search, seizure, arrest, or imprisonment . . . under and by virtue of such order, or under color of any law of Congress, and such defense may be made by special plea, or under the general issue.[12]

In the remaining sections provision is made for the removal of suits of this nature from State to Federal courts (except where judgment is in favor of the defendant) and for imposing a two-year limitation after which no such prosecution or litigation could be begun.[13]

It is significant that Stevens, the author of the indemnifying feature of the House bill, was not one of those who held, with the Attorney General, that the President had the right to suspend *habeas corpus* privilege. Some who concurred in the Attorney General's opinion that the President had the full power to suspend,[14] and to delegate such authority to subordinates, argued that no wrongs had been committed, and that no indemnification was necessary. Conversely, the very basis of the bill of indemnity, in the minds of many who voted for it, was an assumption that the President did not constitutionally have this power, or at least a doubt as to the legality

---

[12] *U. S. Stat. at Large*, XII, 756. This section is taken from the senate bill which differed materially from that of the lower house in its mode of protecting Federal officers. In the House bill all proceedings against officers were declared null and void, while in the Senate substitute, the orders of the President, or under his authority, were declared to be a defense in such proceedings. As Senator Trumbull explained: "We do not propose to say that a suit shall be dismissed, that a proceeding is null and void, but we propose that certain facts shall be a defense to an action." (*Cong. Globe*, 37 Cong., 3 sess., p. 1436.)

[13] The first three sections (which have been discussed elsewhere) have to do with the suspension of the *habeas corpus* privilege and the discharge of political prisoners against whom indictments were not lodged.

[14] *O. R.*, Ser. II, Vol. 2, pp. 20-30 (July 5, 1861).

of this presidential suspension and a desire to clear up the matter once for all.

The act was vigorously denounced in a protest signed by thirty-seven Representatives, including Voorhees, Vallandigham, and other anti-administration leaders. These men pointed out that the acts over which the bill cast protection were illegal trespasses against which redress might admittedly be had under the ordinary administration of the law; that the distinction was not made between the zealous officer and the miscreant; that all offenses were condoned and all redress for injuries taken away, and that the measure would encourage lawless violence.[15]

III

When the Indemnity Act came to be applied in the courts, various defects in the measure came to light, and in many quarters serious difficulties arose because of intense opposition to the act on the part of the State courts. As military pressure was lifted at the close of the war, thousands of suits against Union officers were brought in State tribunals in defiance of the act.[16] In Kentucky, particularly, as the Federal troops withdrew and Confederate soldiers returned, an intense feeling developed between the Union and anti-Union elements. The latter soon gained ascendancy and as a result there were as many as three thousand suits pending against

---

[15] *Cong. Globe,* 37 Cong., 3 sess., p. 165.

[16] The fact that there should be, during and after the war, proceedings in the ordinary courts against United States officers for trespass on account of acts done in their official capacity is eloquent proof of the lack of congeniality between summary methods and the American legal genius. Had such methods been congenial to the American mind, a definite system would long ago have been evolved to take care of such cases.

Union officers by September, 1865.[17] Very high damages were claimed in these suits, and numerous criminal actions were instituted, so that men who acted to uphold the Government were in many instances facing complete ruin. This, of course, was the very thing which the Indemnity Act sought to prevent.

It was alleged that these Kentucky cases grew out of a disposition to use the courts as instruments for the prosecution of Union officials in the interest of outraged secessionists. Confederates were permitted to plead superior orders as defense, while such pleas were denied to Union men. The people were instructed by the leaders that the filing of such suits was a patriotic duty, and were urged to bring as many of them as possible.[18]

Many of these suits, in Kentucky and elsewhere, were civil actions to recover damages for false imprisonment. A citizen of Boston, for instance, having been arrested and confined at Fort Lafayette for eight days, brought suit against the United States marshal making the arrest.[19] A Confederate sympathizer in California who had used grossly abusive language regarding President Lincoln and had expressed approval of his assassination, and who, in consequence, was confined for six days at Fort Alcatraz, sued General McDowell, Commander of the Department of the Pacific, on the ground of false imprisonment.[20] In far away Vermont a man of supposed disloyal tendencies, who had been arrested with-

[17]*Cong. Globe*, 39 Cong., 1 sess., pp. 1983, 2021, 2054, 2065; Frankfort (Ky.) *Commonwealth*, Oct. 24 and Oct. 27, 1865.

[18]*Cong. Globe*, 39 Cong., 1 sess., pp. 1425, 1526, 1527. The files of the Frankfort (Ky.) *Commonwealth*, 1865-66, contain many references to suits against Union officers, and the editorial comment is in strong disapprobation of such suits.

[19]Sturtevant *vs.* Allen, in Sup. Ct. of Mass. See Chicago *Tribune*, Dec. 18, 1865, p. 1.

[20]McCall *vs.* McDowell *et al.* Cir. Ct. of Cal., Apr. 25, 1867. Fed. Cas. No. 8673.

out sworn indictment or warrant and kept in prison seven months on the charge of enticing soldiers to desert, brought an action for damages against the United States provost marshal making the arrest.[21] In such actions juries would fix the damages, though, of course, for errors of law the verdicts could be set aside.

In addition to these civil actions, a number of criminal indictments were brought by grand juries against Union officers and often prosecuted to conviction in entire disregard of the protection and the Federal jurisdiction provided by the Indemnity Act. Such, for the most part, were the Kentucky cases, which attracted chief attention at this time. A Federal officer in that State who pressed horses into service in pursuit of a guerrilla band, was indicted for horse stealing;[22] while the taking of horses for the public use in the Confederate Army, "however wrongful in fact," was declared excusable as a lawful exercise of belligerent right.[23] Officers who under Federal military authority gave passes to Negroes were indicted for assisting the escape of slaves.[24] For firing on guerrillas under arrest in order to prevent their escape, a provost marshal's force was indicted for murder.[25] Election troubles intensified the bitterness, and a number of Union officers were fined four thousand dollars apiece

---

[21]Bean *vs.* Beckwith, 18 Wall. 510.

[22]Frankfort (Ky.) *Commonwealth,* Oct. 27, 1865.

[23]The case was a seizure by one of Morgan's men: Price *vs.* Poynter, 1 Bush 387. See also Commonwealth *vs.* Holland, 1 Duvall 182.

[24]2 Bush 570.

[25]Statement of Representative McKee of Kentucky: *Cong. Globe,* 39 Cong., 1 sess., p. 1526. In a similar case a Union soldier, whose company had been ordered to exterminate all bushwhackers, killed an escaping bushwhacker, who had been a Confederate captain. He was convicted for murder in a Tennessee court and imprisoned on a fifteen year sentence in the State penitentiary. On a *habeas corpus* petition to the Federal district court it was held that the killing was not cognizable by the State court, and a release was ordered. (*In re* Hurst, U. S. Dist. Ct., M. D. Tenn., 1879: Fed. Cas. No. 6926.)

for executing a military order which required certain men to be kept away from the polls. In one county, as reported by Representative Smith in Congress, "the grand jury indicted every Union judge, sheriff, and clerk of election, though not a single indictment was made on the basis of evidence brought in by Union men."[26] As a result of these election difficulties, Governor Bramlette himself, a man of Union sympathies, was placed under indictment,[27] and several prosecutions were directed against General Palmer, the Federal commander at Louisville.[28]

Officers who were convicted in such cases were subjected to heavy fines and in many instances they were placed in the penitentiary. If they pleaded the Indemnity Act as a defense and pointed to their official capacity as agents of the Federal Government, they were met with the answer that the act was unconstitutional (as many judges, of course, sincerely believed), and that, no matter who issued the order, even the President, no legal protection was afforded. If they then sought a transfer to Federal jurisdiction, this was denied on the ground that

---

[26]Representative Smith of Kentucky, in *Cong. Globe*, 39 Cong., 1 sess., p. 1527.

[27]Frankfort (Ky.) *Commonwealth*, Sept. 19, 1865.

[28]Criminal indictments were brought against General Palmer for aiding the escape of slaves (by giving passes to Negroes) this being a felony under Kentucky law. In addition, suits for damages were lodged against him by private parties seeking to recover the value of slaves who had escaped. In Commonwealth *vs.* John M. Palmer (2 Bush 570) the highest Kentucky court held that the Federal Government had no constitutional power to abolish slavery in Kentucky and that General Palmer could not protect himself by pleading an order of the Secretary of War. After the adoption of the Thirteenth Amendment, however, the indictment in this case was quashed. In his memoirs Palmer mentions a number of suits and prosecutions against him, which were defended without expense to the Government, the costs being paid from the General's pocket. He adds, however, that the Government later took charge of the suits and indemnified him for the costs. (*Personal Memoirs of J. M. Palmer*, 264-266.)

no Federal question was involved. Thus deprived of judicial protection, former Federal officers sought military aid; and orders were accordingly issued to the various division and department commanders to use troops if necessary in order to protect those who had been in the military service of the United States "from illegal arrest and imprisonment."[29]

To back up the State courts and to promote these suits and prosecutions against Unionists, a particularly defiant act was passed by the Kentucky legislature. By the terms of this measure, enacted February 5, 1866, to take effect at once, it was made unlawful "for any judicial officer in this Commonwealth to dismiss any civil action . . . for the reason that the alleged wrongs or injuries were committed during the existence of martial law or the suspension of the writ of *habeas corpus*."[30] In a later statute it was provided that an appeal might be taken from the decision of any court which authorized the transfer of a case from a State to a Federal tribunal.[31] The plain intention of this law, as its opponents charged, was to override the jurisdiction of the courts of the United States by means of a State legislative enactment.

It will thus be seen that the Indemnity Act was failing

---

[29]"In consequence of the many and repeated applications made to these headquarters for protection against unjust and illegal arrest and imprisonment of citizens . . . who have been in the military service of the United States . . . Department and District commanders will most strictly prohibit and prevent all such action on the part of the civil authority." (Command of Maj. Gen. Thomas, Hdqrs. Mil. Div. of Tenn., to Gen. J. M. Palmer, Louisville: Frankfort (Ky.) *Commonwealth*, Oct. 3, 1865.)

[30]*Laws of Ky.*, 1866, Ch. 372.

[31]"Either party to any suit in any court of this Commonwealth . . . shall have the right of appeal . . . from the order of any such court transferring . . . a cause to any court of the United States, or staying proceedings . . . with a view of transferring a cause to any court of the United States." (Approved Feb. 16, 1866: *Laws of Ky.*, 1866, Ch. 690.)

of its purpose, and that the protection which it sought to apply by judicial process was proving inadequate. The problem of making the act really effective was in part, of course, merely a matter of asserting Federal authority where it was being defied; but in addition, a strengthening of the statute itself was necessary, and for this reason the act was substantially amended by Congress in 1866. Under the original law, as interpreted by the State courts, an order of the President himself had to be produced in court in order to make available the benefits of the act as a defense. This was a serious limitation, for many of the acts complained of had been committed on the authority of department commanders, provost marshals, and other subordinate officials. In the amendment it was therefore provided:

> That any search, seizure, arrest or imprisonment made, . . . by any officer or person . . . by virtue of any order, written or verbal, general or special, issued by the President or Secretary of War, or by any military officer of the United States holding . . . command of the . . . place within which such seizure . . . or imprisonment was made, . . . either by the person or officer to whom the order was addressed . . . or by any other person aiding or assisting him therein, shall be held . . . to come within the purview of the [Indemnity Act] . . . for all the purposes of defense, transfer, appeal, error, or limitation provided therein. [In case the original order or telegram could not be produced, then "secondary evidence" was made admissible.][32]

This sweeping provision would correct one of the defects of the measure by covering cases where authority for the act in question might not be traceable directly to the President, and would even apply to indirect or verbal orders.

---

[32] *U. S. Stat. at Large*, XIV, 46, sec. 1.

Another feature of the act requiring reënforcement was that relating to the transfer of cases from State to Federal courts. Though the original measure was seemingly complete and explicit on this point, it had not in fact served the purpose of actually asserting and maintaining Federal jurisdiction in the face of strong opposition on the part of judicial officers of the States. The amendment, therefore, was equipped with "teeth." After conferring the full right of removal from State courts to circuit courts of the United States, it provided that if a State court should proceed further with a case after such removal, damages and double costs should be enforceable against the judges and other officers involved, and in addition such proceedings should be void.[33]

IV

In its actual operation thus reënforced, the Indemnity Act presented a number of difficult points. One of the grounds of criticism was the extremely wide reach of Federal jurisdiction which the act provided. From various quarters the argument was advanced that the jurisdiction conferred upon Federal courts was excessive, covering as it did, even a case of trespass between two citizens within a State. In a New York decision, the dissenting judge called it an extraordinary statute that would "give Federal jurisdiction in a case where an act no matter how appalling was claimed to have been done under color of authority derived from the President, no matter how frivolous the claim." The judge further complained that in this manner the person, not the subject matter, was made the criterion of jurisdiction, while in reality the case in point did not present an issue

[33] *Ibid.*, sec. 4.

"rising to the dignity and stature of a Federal question," but involved unwarranted incarceration by one citizen of another who was not subject to military law.[34]

Federal jurisdiction was similarly resisted in *Short* vs. *Wilson*, a case arising in Kentucky in 1866. A Federal captain was being sued for the seizure of a horse and it was claimed that he had resigned his commission and was a private citizen when the seizure was made. The court held that the seizure was "an unauthorized, wrongful spoliation without any . . . legal excuse, a mere trespass exclusively cognizable by the State court." Congress, it was maintained, could neither enlarge nor curtail the constitutional sphere of Federal jurisdiction. Beyond the constitutional boundary, said the court, even the President's acts "will be as void as the ultra-constitutional acts of Congress . . . and an action resulting from it is not a case 'arising under the Constitution or laws of the United States.' "[35] The Indemnity Act was held to be law "so far as it applies to cases over which the Constitution confers jurisdiction on the Federal judiciary," but it could not be justly applied beyond this limit. A lower Kentucky court had ordered the case to be removed in keeping with the Indemnity Act to the United States Circuit Court at Louisville; but the State Court of Appeals reversed this decision, holding that the case was not legally transferable to the Federal court.[36]

The answer to be made to such complaints is that in any case a right reasonably claimed under a Federal act may be made the occasion of a transfer to Federal jurisdiction, and that even though the act may eventually

[34]Jones *vs.* Seward, 41 Barbour 269.

[35]This was an approximate quotation of the wording found in Art. III, sec. 2 of the Constitution. For the case of Short *vs.* Wilson, see 1 Bush 350.

[36]In so deciding, the Court of Appeals applied the Kentucky statute of Feb. 16, 1866, elsewhere treated in this chapter (p. 197 n. 31).

be found to be void, yet the question of its soundness, as well as the validity of the claim presented, may be lawfully deferred to the national courts.[37] The intention was to apply the Indemnity Act, with its reënforcing amendment, only over such subject matter as was truly Federal; and if it were found that a mere wanton trespass had been committed, or that the defendant did not have the character of a Federal official, or that his authority for the specific act was defective, then it would be the duty of the Federal court to remand the case and let the State court handle it. The question as to whether Federal jurisdiction exists, is itself a Federal question; and a court of the United States could be properly criticized, not for entertaining the question, but for deciding it wrongly, or for taking over a case on the basis of a flimsy pleading which failed to show the necessary jurisdictional facts.[38] Only in the latter case would there be any trenching upon State jurisdiction. As a matter of fact, the Federal courts seem to have taken due care to avoid applying the Indemnity Act as a shield for a wanton trespass of the sort that State courts alone could take cognizance of.

Another point raised against the act was its retroactive feature. Since the measure extended protection for orders given and acts committed (or omitted) in the past, Senator Edmunds referred to the act as *ex post facto* and held that its benefits could not apply where martial law had not existed. He ventured the assertion that no

---

[37]For a treatment of the removal of cases from State to Federal courts where Federal questions are involved, see *Standard Encyclopedia of Procedure*, Vol. 22, p. 788.

[38]Where a transfer from State to Federal jurisdiction is sought, the plaintiff's pleading must show the necessary jurisdictional facts; and if a plaintiff puts in a Federal question which has not even a color of merit, the court will dismiss the petition. Hughes on *Federal Procedure*, sections 236, 237, 309.

decision of a civilized court could be found upholding an *ex post facto* law declaring that a past transaction should be guilty or guiltless except as fortifying martial law where civil law had broken down.[39] Without dwelling on this point it may be sufficient to note that the term *ex post facto* properly applies to retroactive measures having to do with crimes, such as those which define new offenses or increase the punishment for existing offenses. In accepted legal usage, and in the intention of the Constitution-makers, such a law as the Indemnity Act would therefore not have been regarded as *ex post facto* legislation. Had the act involved a retroactive delegation of legislative authority to the President, this would have been a different matter, and the objection would then have rested not on the retroactive—or, as inaccurately called, the *ex post facto*—feature, but upon the unconstitutional delegation of power.

A very objectionable feature of the Indemnity Act as amended was a clause which provided for the virtual coercion of State judges. After requiring the transfer to Federal courts of all cases in which presidential or congressional authority could be claimed as protection for wrongs committed, the act continued:

> If the State court shall . . . proceed further in said cause or prosecution . . . , all such further proceedings shall be void . . . , and all . . . judges . . . and other persons . . . proceeding thereunder . . . shall be liable in damages . . . by action in a court of the State having . . . jurisdiction, or in a circuit court of the United States, . . . and upon a recovery of damages in either court, the party plaintiff shall be entitled to double costs.[40]

This punishment of State judges for acts done in a judicial capacity was attacked during the congressional

[39] *Cong. Globe*, Apr. 18, 1866, 39 Cong., 1 sess., p. 2019.
[40] *U. S. Stat. at Large*, XIV, 46, sec. 4.

debate as a violation of those well-known principles of jurisprudence which give to the judge an independent, impartial character and protect him from personal consequences as a result of the performance of judicial functions.[41] Here in the very measure which was intended to exempt Federal officers from liability before the State courts we find a clause subjecting State judges to damages for official acts, and permitting the use of Federal courts to enforce such liability.

The few precedents for such a course are of doubtful character. A New York statute then in force subjected a judge to a penalty of $1,000 for refusing to issue a writ of *habeas corpus* legally applied for, but this law was unusually drastic. The corresponding English statute penalized the judge only for such a refusal during vacation time; and Kent, the learned commentator, remarked that this law of his own State presented "the first instance in the history of the English law" in which judges of the highest common law tribunal were "made responsible, in actions by private suitors, for the exercise of their discretion . . . in term time."[42]

That the Supreme Court of the United States opposed such a treatment of judges is shown in the case of *Bradley* vs. *Fisher*, in which it was declared to be a principle of the highest importance that a judicial officer, in exercising the authority vested in him, should be free to act upon his own convictions without apprehension of personal consequences. In that case the court declared: "The principle which exempts judges of courts of general or superior authority from liability in a civil action for acts done . . . in the exercise of their judicial functions, obtains in all countries where there is any well-

[41]*Cong. Globe*, 39 Cong., 1 sess., pp. 2054-2063.

[42]Kent, *Commentaries on American Law* (14th ed., Boston, 1896), II, 29-30.

ordered system of jurisprudence." The court added that such liability would not apply even in case of malicious or corrupt action, and that for such misconduct impeachment was the appropriate remedy.[43]

Such a clear challenge, however, had been presented to the Federal Government by the defiant attitude of some of the State courts that the provision was retained. It was justified by its supporters on the ground that a judge who, with all the removal papers before him, should refuse to stay proceedings, would be remiss in the performance of a merely ministerial act, and would be going beyond the limit of judicial discretion.[44] In cases of this sort American law recognized the principle that judges might be held liable.[45]

Perhaps the most serious objection to the Indemnity Act was its interference with existing judicial remedies for private wrongs. Suits were obstructed for the purpose of protecting Federal officers without any provision being made for the relief of those who had been de-

---

[43]13 Wall. 335. See also Yates *vs.* Lansing, 5 Johnson (N. Y.) 283; and Randall *vs.* Brigham, 7 Wall. 523.

[44]Howard in U. S. Senate: *Cong. Globe*, 39 Cong., 1 sess., p. 2060.

[45]This whole subject of the liability of judges in American law is summarized in *Lawyers' Reports Annotated* (old series) Vol. 14, p. 138. Judges of superior courts are not personally liable for anything done in a judicial capacity, and no action may lie against them for misconduct, however gross, in performance of judicial duties. But many cases are cited in which judges have been held liable, as for unlawful commitment, refusing to perform ministerial duties, or in cases where judges of inferior authority have exceeded their jurisdiction. In *Ex parte* Virginia (100 U. S. 339), a State judge was indicted in a Federal court for excluding certain citizens as jurors on account of color in violation of a law of Congress passed in 1875. The Supreme Court here upheld as constitutional an act of Congress which punished State judges for such action, making the distinction that the selection of jurors is a ministerial, not a judicial, function, and that in excluding colored men because they were colored, the judge departed from the proper limits of his discretion. It would, of course, be consistent with this decision to contend that, for strictly judicial acts, Congress may not inflict punishment or impose liability upon State judges.

spoiled. This failure to preserve remedies for the individual was frequently referred to by the opponents of the act.[46] As one Senator expressed it, "It is not for . . . Congress to declare by one sweeping act that nothing done in the suppression of the rebellion under authority and by virtue of orders shall give to the injured an action for damages."[47] A different course might well have been taken; for the injured party could have been permitted to recover damages, and then the damages could have been assumed by the United States. Thus the officers could have been protected (i.e., they could have been "indemnified" in the true sense, instead of immunized) and at the same time the aggrieved citizen would not have been deprived of the means of judicial relief. Such assumption of damages by the Government would have been broadly analogous to the compensation of owners for goods seized by military authorities while in occupation of enemy territory or to the principle of compensation in connection with the law of eminent domain. The analogy would lie in the recognition of public ends that were served by the spoliation of the citizen and the consequent duty of public compensation.

A provision of this sort seemed the more necessary in view of the general principle that in case of an act of spoliation constituting a trespass on the part of an officer, no liability for compensation would belong to the United States.[48] In cases of this sort, where the United

[46]At first sight it might seem that the provision in section 7 of the Indemnity Act prohibiting suits after a period of two years, implied that within the two years private remedies would exist. Such a supposition would be erroneous. The limitation prevented suits from being brought after the specified two years, while within that period the act itself would serve as an adequate defense against the recovery of damages.

[47]Senator Cowan in *Cong. Globe*, 39 Cong., 1 sess., pp. 2020-2021.

[48]Wiggins *vs.* U. S., 3 Ct. of Cls. Reps. 412; Mitchel *vs.* Harmony, 13 How. 115.

States Government did not see fit to adopt the officer's act as its own, it was customary to hold that the officer alone would be liable; but this sole remaining liability was extinguished by the Indemnity Act.

This proposition of having the United States assume damages was, in fact, considered in Congress and an amendment offered to that effect.[49] It was pointed out that the adoption of this amendment would have been in keeping with the congressional practice of passing special private acts to indemnify such officers as have been subjected to damages while in faithful discharge of duty. When the matter came up for discussion, however, numerous practical objections were raised. It was urged that the plan was too expensive, that juries would commonly grant larger damages in judgments against the United States than in actions against individuals, and that collusion between parties to the suit would result in a lukewarm defense and a prearranged sharing of the amount awarded between the defendant and the plaintiff.[50] For these reasons nothing was done to correct that portion of the act which was widely regarded as its most substantial defect.

V

It remains to consider the broad question of the constitutional validity of this statute of indemnity. The objections above considered were, of course, used as arguments against the constitutionality of the act. The excessive Federal jurisdiction conferred, the denial of private remedies, the invasion of the proper field of the State judiciary in connection with trespass cases, the

[49] *Cong. Globe*, 39 Cong., 1 sess., pp. 2063, 2065.
[50] *Ibid.*, 39 Cong., 1 sess., pp. 2063-2064.

grant of immunity for "wrongs" committed in districts not under martial law, the interference with the enforcement of contracts, and the retroactive feature—all these points were developed to support the frequent contention that the act was unconstitutional.

One of the emphatic decisions denouncing the act was that of *Griffin* vs. *Wilcox*, an Indiana case arising shortly after the act was passed.[51] Wilcox, a provost marshal at Indianapolis, had arrested a civilian, Griffin, for violation of a military order prohibiting the sale of liquor to enlisted men. Out of such a petty case the judge spun an elaborate argument regarding martial law, war powers, free speech, the purpose of the war, and the methods of the Government at Washington. Throughout this decision there ran an undertone of opposition to the Lincoln administration. The immunity feature of the Indemnity Act was denounced as depriving the citizen of all redress for illegal arrests and imprisonments; for it was pointed out that no additional protection was needed for such acts as were legal. There was no forcible resistance to authority by the people of Indianapolis such as would justify establishing military control over civilians; and the use of martial law methods without such justifying cause was held to be in excess of the war powers. Not even the President, it was maintained, could have properly conferred such authority; and the Indemnity Act could not justify such usurpation.

In spite of many judicial utterances in the same tenor, the act was sustained in its essential features by various decisions of the highest tribunal. The leading case for the constitutionality of the act was that of *Mitchell* vs. *Clark*.[52] General Schofield had ordered a general seizure

[51] 21 Indiana 370 (1863).
[52] 110 U. S. 647.

of intangibles at St. Louis, and as a result certain rents were seized and appropriated by the United States, thus preventing the fulfillment of the contractual obligations of a lease between certain citizens of Missouri. From one aspect, therefore, the case involved the enforcement of an ordinary contract,[53] and this, of course, was subject-matter proper to a State court. The fact that the seizure had been made by a Federal officer, however, opened the way for Federal jurisdiction under the Indemnity Act.

Because of a special feature in this case, the court did not undertake to decide whether General Schofield had the authority to seize the debt or whether the payment to him was a legal discharge of the obligation. The controlling fact, according to the court's interpretation, was that the suit had not been brought within two years, and was therefore barred by the statute of limitations[54] which was a part of the act of indemnity. The position adopted by the court was that "wherever a suit can be removed into United States courts, Congress can prescribe for it the law of limitations not only for these courts, but for all courts." It was therefore held that a Federal statute of limitations was good in a State court; and in this way the jurisdiction of the Missouri court was not only defeated, but this was done without any inquiry into the legal justification for the original seizure.

---

[53]The lessor of two storehouses sued for three months' rent which the tenants had been compelled to pay to the military authorities for "public use" while St. Louis was under martial law.

[54]"No suit or prosecution . . . shall be maintained for any arrest or imprisonment made, or other . . . wrongs done . . . or act omitted to be done . . . by virtue of . . . authority derived from . . . the President . . . or . . . any act of Congress, unless the same shall have been commenced within two years . . . after such arrest," etc. (The limitation, however, was not to commence until the passage of the act: *U. S. Stat. at Large,* XII, 757.)

In considering the question of the constitutionality of the Indemnity Act, the court dwelt upon the purpose of the law, pointing out that Federal military officers often had to perform delicate duties among people who, though citizens, might be intensely hostile to the Government, and that acts might be done for which there was no adequate basis at the time. Then the court proceeded to say: "That an act passed after the event which in effect ratifies what has been done and declares that no suit shall be sustained against the party acting under color of authority is valid, so far as Congress could have conferred such authority before, admits of no reasonable doubt. These are ordinary acts of indemnity passed by all governments when the occasion requires it." The court then reaffirmed a former case which sustained that feature of the Indemnity Act which authorized the removal to Federal courts. The reasoning of the court could be summarized about as follows: (1) The Indemnity Act is constitutional; (2) that act authorizes the removal of cases involving acts done by Federal officers to the Federal courts; (3) this is such a case; (4) Congress has the right to establish the period of limitation for such suits and has in fact done so; (5) consequently, since this case was not brought within the prescribed two years, the plaintiff cannot recover or even prosecute the claim in the State court.

Justice Field emphatically dissented to this opinion. He knew of no law to justify a military officer in obstructing the payment of a debt due from one loyal citizen to another, neither of them being in the military service, nor in an "insurrectionary" State where the courts were inoperative. Civil war in one part of the country did not, in his opinion, suspend constitutional guarantees in other parts. "Our system of civil polity," he said, "is not such a rickety and ill-jointed structure that when one part is disturbed the whole is thrown into confusion and jostled to its foundation." Referring to the suspension of the privilege of *habeas corpus*, he urged that the Constitution does not forbid, during such suspension or by reason of it, the institution of suits by despoiled citizens, nor does the Constitution authorize Congress to forbid it. Though admitting that Congress may indemnify those who, in great emergencies, acting under pressing necessities for the public welfare, are unable to avoid invading private rights in support of the government, he held that "between acts of indemnity in such cases and the attempt to deprive the citizen of his right to compensation for wrongs committed against him or his property, or to enforce contract obligations, there is a wide difference which cannot be disregarded without a plain violation of the Constitution." Neither the act of 1863 nor the amendment of 1866, he held, could properly be construed to apply to actions for breach of contract between citizens in loyal States, since such contracts were under State jurisdiction. If such a construction were possible, then he maintained that the legislation would be unconstitutional.

It should be noted that the principal ground of objection to the court's position in *Mitchell* vs. *Clark* was the extreme application of the Indemnity Act (or, more specifically, the statute of limitation included in the act) so that it defeated a private remedy and prevented the enforcement of an ordinary contract such as would normally lie entirely within State jurisdiction. Both the court and the dissenting opinion upheld the validity of the act so far as the protection of Federal officers was concerned; but Field considered the order of General Schofield unwarranted and would not admit the force of the statute of limitations as a bar in the case, while he also insisted that individual rights should have been better protected. Had Congress provided the desired official immunity by some method that would have preserved private remedies, the chief basis of criticism would have been removed.

It will thus be seen that the essential provisions of the Indemnity Act were sustained by the highest tribunal. There was, however, one feature of the act which did not stand the test of constitutionality. This was the provision for a trial *de novo* of the facts as well as the law in a Federal court after a jury had rendered its verdict in a State court.

The Seventh Amendment of the Constitution provides as follows:

> In suits at common law . . . no fact tried by a jury shall be otherwise re-examined in any court of the United States than according to the rules of the common law.

This amendment has been interpreted in a number of judicial decisions. It has been held that the "common law" here alluded to is the common law of England, "the grand reservoir of all our jurisprudence," and that according to its principles the facts once tried by a jury are not to be re-examined unless a new trial is granted in the discretion of the court before which the suit may be pending, or unless the judgment of such court is reversed by a superior tribunal on writ of error and a *venire facias de novo* is awarded. In either case the new trial would be conducted in the same court in which the former defective trial occurred. On this matter the courts have spoken decisively; and it has been referred to as the "invariable usage settled by the decisions of ages."[55]

---

[55]U. S. *vs.* Wonson, 1 Gallison 5; 28 Fed. Cas. 745. Judge Story in delivering this opinion (in the Federal circuit court for Massachusetts) wrote: "We should search in vain in the common law for an

But the fifth section of the Indemnity Act contained the following clause:

> [It shall] be competent for either party . . . after the rendition of a judgment in any such cause [i.e., in prosecutions against officers acting under authority of the President] . . . to remove the same [from the State court] to the circuit court of the United States . . . and the said circuit court shall thereupon proceed to try and determine the facts and the law in such action in the same manner as if the same had been there originally commenced, the judgment in such case notwithstanding.[56]

The only other instance in which Congress has undertaken to authorize a second trial by a jury in a Federal court while a former jury's verdict in the same case had not been set aside, was during the War of 1812. An "act to prohibit intercourse with the enemy," passed on February 4, 1815,[57] had a provision identical with that above quoted from the Indemnity Act.[58] In fact, the Indemnity Act was modeled upon the law of 1815 in this respect. Though the Act of 1815 had been denounced as unconstitutional in a Federal circuit court in Massachusetts, this provision was repeated in the Acts of 1863 and 1866, in spite of the opposition of Senators who called attention to the matter in debate.[59]

It became the duty of the Supreme Court to pass

---

instance of an appellate court retrying the cause by a jury while the former verdict and judgment remained in full force." See also Capital Traction Company *vs.* Hof, 174 U. S. 1.

[56]*U. S. Stat. at Large,* XII, 757. (This section was retained in the amending act of 1866.)

[57]Ratifications of the Treaty of Ghent were exchanged at Washington. February 17, 1815.

[58]*U. S. Stat. at Large,* III, 195, sec. 8. (There are many points of similarity between this measure and the Indemnity Act of 1863.)

[59]Senators Bayard and Browning dealt with these points: *Cong. Globe,* 37 Cong., 3 sess., pp. 538-539.

upon this feature of the Indemnity Act in the case of *The Justices* vs. *Murray*, which came up from New York in 1869.[60] An action for false imprisonment was brought in the State court against Murray, the marshal of the Federal District Court for Southern New York. Murray's defense was an alleged order of the President, which under the Indemnity Act would have served as a protection; but the jury found no evidence in support of this defense, and a verdict for the plaintiff was therefore rendered. When steps were later taken for a complete retrial in the Federal circuit court, the State authorities resisted on the ground that the Indemnity Act, in this respect, was unconstitutional.

The chief point to which the Supreme Court directed its attention was whether the Seventh Amendment applied to a cause tried by a jury in a State court. On this point the court said: "there is nothing in the history of the amendment indicating that it was intended to be confined to cases coming up for revision from the inferior Federal courts, but much is there found to the contrary. Our conclusion is that so much of the fifth section of the [Indemnity Act] as provides for the removal of a judgment in a State court and in which the cause was tried by a jury, to the circuit court of the United States for a retrial of the facts and law, is not in pursuance of the Constitution and is void."

In keeping with this decision the Federal control of cases under the Indemnity Act would have had to be exercised through removal while the case was pending, or through review by the Supreme Court of the United States on writ of error, and not by a trial *de novo* in an inferior Federal court after the State tribunal had pronounced judgment on the basis of a jury's verdict. But such removal and review have, throughout our history,

[60] 9 Wall. 274.

proved to be adequate instruments for the maintenance of Federal judicial supremacy.

In its many unusual features the Indemnity Act bears the unmistakable stamp of war legislation. The wide range of Federal jurisdiction which it afforded, the extraordinary methods of acquiring such jurisdiction, the denial of private remedies for admitted "wrongs," the subjection of State judges to personal damages, the application of a Federal statute of limitations to State causes, and the unconstitutional provision for a re-examination of facts once tried by a jury—all these elements of the law are the abnormal product of war conditions. The law must be judged in the light of the fact that it was originally passed in the very midst of a desperate war, and was amended in the face of State defiance by a Congress whose main interest was the enactment of drastic "reconstruction" measures. Extreme legislation was characteristic of the period, and this unique measure was only typical of the sort of irregularity that creeps into the law during war or other times of great disturbance.

CHAPTER X

THE RÉGIME OF CONQUEST IN OCCUPIED DISTRICTS OF THE SOUTH

I. Military occupation in general

II. Modification of the general rules of military occupation to suit the peculiar conditions of the Civil War

III. Inconsistent treatment of occupied regions as parts of the United States but also as enemy territory

IV. Conditions attending Union rule in the South: supremacy of Federal over local power; maintenance of military government; confusion of authority

V. Administration of justice in occupied districts

VI. Constitutional basis of the governments of occupation: Succession of governmental changes in the South during and after the Civil War

Where portions of Southern territory were brought under Union occupation a situation existed which presented various legal problems. Our consideration of this subject may well begin with a brief review of the general principles of military occupation, after which we may note the special conditions which obtained during the struggle between the States.

I

The powers of an occupying army in the government of conquered territory are recognized belligerent rights resting upon the rules of war. It is sufficient for our present purpose to recall briefly some of the leading features of this branch of international law, for a full discussion of which the reader is referred to the standard treatises. When a nation at war obtains effective possession of a portion of the enemy's territory, the conquering State assumes, during the period of such possession, the governing power over the territory held. The authority of the dispossessed State is for the time suspended; and outside nations are expected to recognize the rights of the occupying State and to deal with such State as the governing power of the district in question. Private citizens within the district owe temporary allegiance to the occupant; and acts of hostility committed by non-combatants, however patriotic in motive, are condemned by the laws of war. If patriotic ardor urges an inhabitant to resist the occupying power by force, the only legitimate method of such resistance is by joining the armed forces of his dispossessed sovereign. If he remains a non-combatant within the occupied lines, he is expected to acquiesce in the occupant's authority.

The government of the occupied region is essentially a military government, and it is to the military chieftain that one looks as the paramount authority. It does not follow, however, that this military rule should be exercised without restraint. Civilized nations prosecute war in accordance with recognized rules and do not permit themselves to use every method which military force makes physically possible. Military occupation is conducted within limitations, and the occupying power has duties as well as rights. Personal and property rights of citizens are to be respected. The belligerent must not plunder the inhabitants. He must not deport them nor force them to fight against their government. It is his duty to maintain order and to offer security to peacefully minded citizens. The chief significance, in fact, of the law of military occupation is the necessity of preserving orderly government; and it is largely for this reason that the invading power succeeds to that governmental control which formerly belonged to the dispossessed enemy. Offenses of a military nature are to be dealt with by courts-martial or military commissions; but ordinary civil and criminal justice is to be disturbed as little as possible.

The administration of the local government should preferably be left in the hands of the existing local officials whose duty it is to support, not to defy, the occupying power. The customs and laws of the locality are to be respected; and the people should be unmolested in their peaceful pursuits.

A distinction should be maintained between military occupation and annexation. Consequently, the occupying State is not justified in imposing its language, customs and manner of life upon the people of the invaded district nor in forcing upon them an alien religion or culture. Title by conquest, obtained by treaty or by completed war, is a matter very different from the temporary occupancy of an invader.

The invading State has primarily two kinds of powers: ordinary governmental powers (inherited from the dispossessed State) and such extraordinary military power as the occasion demands. A military régime may be necessary because of the activity of bandits or guerrillas, or because of the unsettled condition of society, and drastic measures may become imperative for the public health or safety; but such a military régime should be conceived as a protection, not as a means of oppression. "Military necessity" should be strictly interpreted, and should not be construed as giving license to brutality or malice. The line should be carefully drawn between the justifiable severity of military rule and the wanton excesses of cruelty or revenge. If the occupant's authority is abused the citizen has no redress, unless it be in reparation after the war. Hence a civilized government will put restraints upon officers in charge of a government of occupation.[1]

II

The application of these principles of military occupation during the Civil War now claims our attention. The "rebellion" was "attended by the general incidents of a regular war,"[2] according to the decision of the Supreme Court; and the maintenance of government in occupied districts was not only the right but the duty of the National Government. Federal rights of military occupation in the South according to the general usages of war were thus clearly established; and this branch of the law of nations constituted the primary justification for the government of the occupied districts. There were, however, significant modifications owing to the peculiar nature of the war for the Union. Since the United States was not prosecuting a foreign war, but, according to the Government's interpretation, merely seeking to "suppress an insurrection," it did not consider itself on foreign soil when occupying Tennessee or Louisiana. On the contrary, the Government insisted that it was merely reclaiming its own in "restoring" and "repossessing" the places and districts that had been taken by Confederate forces. All previous authority within the occupied regions had been either Federal or State. As to Federal powers, they were naturally resumed so far as the disturbed circumstances permitted.

---

[1]Besides the recognized treatises on international law, one may consult also the following works and documents for a discussion of the rules of military occupation. G. B. Davis, *Military Law; The Military Law of the United States* (War Dept., Office of the Judge Advocate General, 1911); W. E. Birkhimer, *Military Government and Martial Law;* "Instructions for the government of armies . . . in the field" (*O. R.*, Ser. II, Vol. 5, pp. 671 *et seq*).

[2]The Grapeshot, 9 Wall. 129, 132.

When it came to State functions, the controlling factors were the ultimate obligation to restore the State governments in the exercise of their constitutional powers, and the immediate necessity of governing the occupied regions by extraordinary national authority during the transitional period prior to the completion of reconstruction. Thus it may be said that the rights assumed in occupied regions of the South were the recognized rights of military occupation *plus* that authority which the Union Government exerted in the resumption of Federal functions and in the temporary assumption of State functions while awaiting the establishment of "loyal" State governments.

The fact that the conflict was a domestic war thus increased rather than diminished the rights of the United States as conqueror. The United States was not merely prosecuting a war. It was overthrowing a "pretended" government and reasserting what was regarded as its own rightful power, not hesitating to occupy temporarily the domain of State authority.

The inhabitants of New Orleans in 1862 were in a different situation from those of Tampico in 1847. Both, it is true, were under military occupation.[3] The rights and obligations of a conqueror applied to both; and the war power of the President in each case embraced the maintenance of a government of occupation. But the United States in 1847 was not seeking to supplant the Mexican Government. It was merely exerting its will by force against that Government for certain limited objects. American authorities in Tampico looked forward to the ultimate relinquishment of their authority. At any rate the action of the treaty-making power—an

[3]For a discussion of American occupation in Mexico, see Justin H. Smith, "American Rule in Mexico," *Am. Hist. Rev.*, XXIII, 287-302.

international function—would be awaited before such authority could become permanent.

It was not so in the case of New Orleans. No treaty was anticipated. The purpose of the war was not simply to exert pressure against the Confederate Government, but to destroy that Government and reclaim all the territory within its grasp. The subsequent renewal of constitutional relations between Louisiana and Washington would be fundamentally different from the restoration of international relations between Mexico and the United States. An awkward transitional period would ensue before the renewal of constitutional relations could be made complete; but the chief significance of this transitional period would be that, during its continuance, the Union grip on Louisiana would be maintained in such a manner as to comprehend State as well as Federal functions. So far as local administration was concerned, New Orleans would look to the restoration of control under Louisiana law, just as Tampico would anticipate the reëstablishment of Mexican law; but this restoration of local control would be but a fulfillment of the Constitution of the United States, which recognizes State authority in local affairs, and would be subject to such important modifications as might develop during and after the war. During the occupation Congress would legislate for New Orleans in the exercise of its normal functions, treating that city as an American port within the boundaries of the United States, while Tampico was but a foreign port under American occupation.[4]

[4]In Fleming *vs.* Page it was held that Tampico was a foreign, not an American, port during its occupation by American forces. (9 How. 603.) It is true that tariffs were collected by the American authorities in the Mexican ports, but this collection of duties was an executive measure and was interpreted as the levy of a "contribution" for the support of the army. Congress had no part in the fixing of these tariffs. (*House Rep. No. 119*, 30 Cong., 2 sess.)

Allegiance to the United States was demanded of the people of Louisiana; and the oath of loyalty was insisted upon as a sign of this allegiance. From the Mexicans, however, no such oath was exacted, temporary allegiance to the government of occupation being all that was asked.

III

The special circumstances by which military occupation in the South during the Civil War is to be differentiated from military occupation in general become especially prominent when we consider the opposite elements involved in the reassertion of national authority. Two widely different conditions prevailed in the occupied districts. From one angle the resumption of Federal supremacy in the South meant the extension of loyal territory over which the national law applied. But at the same time, Federal rule in the South also meant the exercise of authority over territory "in rebellion." Let us now examine these two inconsistent principles in their actual application.

In various respects, territory in occupation was treated as a part of the United States. In *Texas* vs. *White*, the Supreme Court held that the Union is indissoluble and that, by its ordinance of secession, Texas "did not cease to be a State, nor her citizens to be citizens of the Union."[5] This principle applied to all the seceded States. Yet the pretended secession, since it amounted to rebellion and war, had far-reaching consequences. It made the residents of the "insurrectionary" regions enemies of the United States (according to the *Prize Cases*) and at the same time "rebels."[6] Some attempt was therefore made to introduce a distinction

[5]7 Wall. 700. (The rights of Federal citizenship were suspended.)

[6]Prize Cases, 2 Black 674, 678, 693; Ford *vs.* Surget, 97 U. S. 594, 604-605; *House Rep. No. 262*, 43 Cong., 1 sess., p. 5.

between districts in occupation and districts still in active rebellion. Military occupation, said the Supreme Court in the *Venice* case, "does not, indeed, restore peace, or, in all respects, former relations; but it replaces rebel by national authority, and recognizes, to some extent, the conditions and the responsibilities of national citizenship."[7]

There were certain notable consequences of this return to (or retention of) national citizenship. Tennessee was expected to furnish her "quota" of troops to the Federal army, and much of Governor Johnson's time was devoted to the recruiting of Union regiments.[8] Colored regiments in Tennessee, Louisiana and elsewhere were formed in response to the Federal law for arming the Negroes. When the direct tax of twenty million dollars was apportioned among the States in 1861, quotas were assigned to all of the States of the Confederacy, and the tax was collected upon the resumption of Union authority.[9] The blockade was lifted from such Southern ports as came under Union control, and trade with these ports, subject to contraband restrictions, was renewed.[10] Customs duties were collected upon this renewed trade, and internal revenue duties were also collected under Federal law. The activities of George S. Denison, whom Secretary of the Treasury Chase appointed to assume charge of the collection of customs in Louisiana and who later took over the internal revenue collections, reveal a vigorous enforcement of the Federal revenue laws during the military occupation.[11]

---

[7]2 Wall. 277.

[8]C. R. Hall, *Andrew Johnson, Military Governor of Tennessee,* Ch. x.

[9]Act of Aug. 5, 1861; *U. S. Stat. at Large,* XII, 294, *Infra,* pp. 423-424.

[10]*U. S. Stat. at Large,* XII, 1263; XIII, 750.

[11]"Letters from G. S. Denison to Salmon P. Chase," *Am. Hist. Ass An. Rep.,* 1902, Vol. 2, pp. 297 *et seq.*

On the other hand, territory in occupation was in certain respects treated as if it were enemy territory, or were still territory in rebellion. Certain examples may be presented to illustrate this fact. There were no normal State and Federal relations subsisting between the Government at Washington and the wartime governments of the South,[12] except, perhaps, in Virginia, and even there the Federal recognition of the feeble "restored" government was but partial.[13] Property was taken under the confiscation acts in occupied regions.[14]

[12]Normal relationships would have involved the regular functioning of the executive, legislative and judicial branches of the State government, representation of the State in both houses of Congress, and, in general, the honoring of State authority in its proper field. Even though restored to loyal control, a State would be in an abnormal condition if under Federal military rule, or if its "governor" were appointed by the President and subject to his orders; for a State governor does not take orders from the President. None of the States of the Confederacy except Tennessee and Virginia were represented in the two war Congresses—i.e., the Thirty-Seventh and Thirty-Eighth. The representation of the "restored government" of Virginia was but partial. (*Infra*, pp. 463-466.) In the Thirty-Seventh Congress, Tennessee was represented in the lower house. In the Senate, however, the State had only one Senator from the time of the expulsion of Nicolson in July, 1861, until Johnson's resignation in March, 1862, and after that no Senator at all, as Johnson's seat was left vacant. The State had no members in either house in the Thirty-Eighth Congress. President Lincoln believed that Johnson, as military governor and head of the provisional government of Tennessee, had the power to appoint United States Senators and was in favor of this being done; but no such action was taken. (Horace Maynard to Johnson, Apr. 24, 1862: Johnson Papers, XVIII, 4106.)

[13]At the time that Virginia was conceived to be under the authority of the "restored government" at Alexandria, certain portions of the State under Union occupation were governed largely by the orders of military officers acting directly under the President. (*Infra*, pp. 466-469.)

[14]General Butler "sequestered" estates of certain prominent Southerners, using Twiggs' mansion at New Orleans as his own residence, and carried out a general policy of confiscation by military orders. The seizures and sales of his "sequestration commission" were extensive. A mass of material on this subject in the Attorney General's files and in the archives of the Treasury Department has been examined by the writer. The following published material may be cited: Parton, *Butler at New Orleans*, 467 *et seq.*; *O. R.*, Ser. I, Vol. 15, pp. 571 *et seq.*;

Cotton worth many millions was seized under the Captured Property Act which could have no application except as a penal measure directed against districts in rebellion.[15] The direct tax, which, as we have noted, was apportioned among the "rebellious" as well as the "loyal" States, was applied in the South with a difference; for a heavy penalty was imposed in those regions where Federal authority had been resisted, and a drastic method of direct collection by Federal officials was employed.[16]

It is hardly worth while to attempt to harmonize these diverse policies toward the South, for inconsistency seemed inherent in the situation. We have noted in a previous chapter the "double-status theory"[17] by which the Confederates were held to be within the country but at the same time enemies of the country. Many of the curious anomalies which followed from this double character remained after conquest, and the regions in occupation were at the same time treated as conquered territory subject to belligerent powers and as parts of the United States.

IV

We may now observe more closely some of the special conditions of Union rule in the South. The first problem that presented itself was the substitution of Federal for local authority. Circumstances determined the extent to which local officers were supplanted by new appointees. If the existing city and county officers showed a willingness to coöperate with the occupying

---

House Exec. Doc. No. 102, 40 Cong., 2 sess.; *Correspondence of B. F. Butler*, Vols. I and II, *passim*.

[15] *Infra*, pp. 323-328.

[16] *Infra*, pp. 317-323.

[17] *Supra*, Chapter III.

authorities, they were in some cases allowed to remain; otherwise they were dismissed. New State executive officers for Tennessee, such as Secretary of State, Comptroller, and Attorney General, were installed by Johnson as military governor; and when the mayor and council of Nashville refused the oath of allegiance to the United States, their offices were bestowed upon Johnson's appointees.[18] In New Orleans, General Butler proposed to the mayor and council that they continue in the exercise of their accustomed functions subject to the paramount military authority which the General embodied. Recognizing the conquest as a fact, and desiring to avoid conflict, the municipal officers at first complied and the city government went on as usual. In return, Butler, in one of his less truculent moods, withdrew the Federal troops from the city, thus removing the appearance of military pressure. This situation was of short duration, however, for before the month was out, Butler had the mayor deposed and imprisoned, and Shepley, military commandant of New Orleans, discharged the mayor's functions.[19]

The next fact which claims our notice is that Union occupation in the South meant the inauguration of a military régime. The will of the commander was the law of the occupied region and the civil government was subordinate to, if not directly in charge of, the commander.[20] Often the commander's will expressed itself

[18] C. R. Hall, *op. cit.*, 42-43.

[19] Parton, *Butler at New Orleans*, 291-298, 336.

[20] The proclamation of General Butler on assuming control at New Orleans made it clear that the city was under martial law. In 1864 Butler wrote: "Now, my theory of the law martial is this—that it is a well-known, well-settled, and well-defined part of the common law of this country, received by us from England and recognized in its proper place by the Constitution, and that proper place . . . is in the camp and garrison. Now the best definition of martial law that I have ever heard was that by Sir Arthur Wellesley, afterwards Duke

in severe and sweeping orders. Summary arrests were made;[21] papers were suppressed; land was condemned for sanitary purposes; railroads were taken over; private houses were commandeered; banks were forbidden to give out Confederate money; ministers were apprehended;[22] church services were closed; public assemblages were suppressed; citizens refusing the oath were threatened with deportation; property was seized for confiscation, and many other extraordinary things were

---

of Wellington, while serving in Spain: 'The will of the Comdg. General exercised according to the principles of natural equity.' If this be so . . . , then all civil rights and governments in camp and garrison where martial law obtains must be subservient to it, and therefore permissive only. Thus civil government may well exist in subordination to martial law controlling, restraining and protecting citizens, when it is so constituted that the government is efficient to the end desired. When it cannot do that, that government is, like any other useless thing, to be cast aside." (*Correspondence of B. F. Butler*, I, 436; IV, 579.)

[21]Andrew Johnson, as military governor of Tennessee, ordered the summary arrest of various persons, including Richard B. Cheatham, Mayor of Nashville; Washington Barrow, William G. Harding and John Overton, signers of the military league between Tennessee and the Confederate States, and Joseph C. Guild, who had uttered treasonable language. On May 12, 1862, Johnson sent to Col. Parkhurst, commanding at Murfreesboro, a list of twelve names, authorizing him to arrest all or part of them according to his discretion. They were all arrested, held for a few days as hostages to guard against violent acts on the part of residents of the city, and then released. On other occasions Johnson authorized subordinates to make arrests, as when he wrote to Col. Mundy in command at Pulaski authorizing him to make such arrests as he deemed proper and expedient. (Johnson Papers, XVII, 3848, 3869, 3880, 3889, 3996; XIX, 4362, 4379; XX, 4486, 4493; XXI, 4693.)

[22]Andrew Johnson wrote in July, 1862, to Governor Morton of Indiana, saying: "Some time since about half a dozen rabid secession preachers of this city [Nashville] were arrested by my direction and are now in prison here." He wanted some of them sent to some camp or prison in Indiana. A similar letter was sent to Governor Tod of Ohio, while General Hovey at Memphis was asked to send some of the preachers beyond the Southern lines and General Boyle at Louisville was asked to confine others. Whether the number of clergymen was sufficient to go round does not appear. After brief imprisonment they were released on parole. (Johnson Papers, Vols. XXIII, XXIV, XXVI, *passim*.)

done, more commonly for the preservation of order, but sometimes out of mere caprice or a sense of irritation. The needlessly severe action of General Butler in bringing about the execution of Mumford for tearing down the flag at New Orleans,[23] and the unfortunate "woman order" issued by that general,[24] are examples of the limits to which military power may extend when a commander plays the Avenging Deity among a proud and resisting population. Legally, the importance of these extreme acts lies in the fact that they show what military government involved. They exemplify the extent to which the city of New Orleans was subjected to the eccentric will of General Butler. Even if we concede that, in the main, this will was exerted for salutary purposes[25]—such as the maintenance of order, the reduction of disease and the relief of the poor—yet the occasional acts of harshness showed how real was the military dictatorship under which the people lived.

The legitimacy of this military rule was sustained by the Supreme Court. In *United States* vs. *Diekelman* the court held that martial law prevailed in Louisiana under the Butler régime, that this law was administered by the general of the army and that it was, in fact, his will. Though arbitrary, it had to be obeyed.[26]

Another characteristic feature of Union control in the South was confusion of authority. Taking Louisiana as an example, we find the forces of occupation under Gen-

---

[23]Parton, *Butler at New Orleans*, Ch. xix.

[24]*Ibid.*, Ch. xviii.

[25]James Parton defended Butler's course at New Orleans and described him as a man of brains, practical sense, courage, honesty, humor, faith, humanity, courtesy and patriotism. On the other hand, President Jefferson Davis proclaimed him an outlaw, and he has perhaps been more generally denounced by Southern writers than any other Union general. For a scholarly account, censuring Butler, see J. R. Ficklen, *History of Reconstruction in Louisiana.*

[26]92 U. S. 520, 526.

eral Butler (and later General Banks), the military governorship of Louisiana, the city and county offices, the judicial establishment, the foreign consulates and the customs-house departments confronting each other in their daily activities with imperfect understanding of their respective jurisdictions, and producing not a little friction by the contact.

While Butler was heading his letters "Department of the Gulf," and signing his name "Benj. F. Butler, Major General Commanding," George F. Shepley, of inferior military rank, was made "Military Governor of Louisiana."[27] The line of demarcation between the authority of Butler and that of Shepley seems not to have been clearly drawn.

A sort of dual government existed in Tennessee. As C. R. Hall shows in his study of Johnson's governorship, Rosecrans, with the rank of Major General, was commander of the department and head of an important active army; while Johnson, a Brigadier General, was military governor of the State.[28] It might have been supposed that Rosecrans would wield the paramount military command, leaving Johnson in general charge of the civil administration. Even the civil government, however, was under military control, so that Johnson was as truly in possession of military authority as was Rosecrans; while the latter, being a superior officer, and the general in command of the army, assumed the chief responsibility, and took such control of civil matters as to thwart Johnson's purposes in many respects. Against the complaints of Johnson, Rosecrans maintained a "detective police"[29] whose inquisitorial and summary

[27] *Correspondence of B. F. Butler*, II, 59.

[28] Hall, *Andrew Johnson, Military Governor of Tenn.*, 75 *et seq.* (The writer has drawn largely from this scholarly volume in studying the situation in Tennessee.)

[29] *Ibid.*, pp. 78-83.

methods caused serious protest, and the intervention of General Halleck at Washington became necessary in order to sustain the civil authority under Johnson.

What we have seen in Louisiana and Tennessee was but typical of Union rule in the South.[30] Orders from Washington were never adequate and much was left to the will of individual generals. In the turbulent conditions of the time, with guerrillas to be suppressed, cotton to be seized, Negroes to be controlled under the novel conditions of freedom, disloyal activities to be put down, secret societies to be stamped out, and a hundred other problems to be faced, it was natural that many irregularities would arise. With the breakdown of regular civil government, and the extraordinary extension of the limits of military rule, an orderly conduct of affairs was not to be expected.

V

The administration of justice in the occupied districts presented many complications. A careful examination of the details of this subject shows that in this as in other respects the conquered regions were under the will of the President and the military authorities. In general, the performance of judicial functions in the invaded regions proceeded along the following lines:

1. Owing to the supremacy of the military power, all judicial functions were exercised under executive control.

2. The Federal judicial power was provided for in part by the reopening of United States courts and in part by conferring Federal jurisdiction upon specially created courts. Members of the Federal Supreme Court did not perform circuit duties during military occupation and

[30] An aggravated case of military interference in matters of civil government occurred at Norfolk in 1864. *Infra*, pp. 466-469.

the performance of Federal judicial functions was otherwise abnormal.

3. The army was, of course, subject to the power of the courts-martial. When the Federal forces were in the "enemy's country," the courts-martial had exclusive jurisdiction over offenses of every grade committed by persons in the military service. A soldier of the United States who committed murder in Tennessee while that State was under Federal occupation, was not subject to prosecution by State tribunals.[31]

4. A military régime existed in the occupied regions and this gave great importance to the military commissions. These tribunals had cognizance of a variety of offenses against the military power of which non-combatants might often be guilty, expecially in a district harassed by bandits or bushwhackers. Civilians were tried by these military courts for robbery, theft, arson, murder, and various other crimes.[32]

5. As to ordinary criminal and civil justice, no simple statement suffices. The recognized rule in such cases is to permit the local courts to continue their functions. Local police matters should properly have been left to the civil authorities, while the provost marshal's duties were limited to matters of military police. Sometimes the existing local courts were continued,[33] but there were important cases where "special war courts" were created by military order for the exercise of ordinary civil and criminal jurisdiction. The Supreme Court sustained the military power, and thus, of course, the executive power,

---

[31]Coleman *vs.* Tennessee, 97 U. S. 509.

[32]Hall, *op. cit.*, 45-46; Halleck's instructions to Rosecrans, March 20, 1863: *O. R.*, Ser. III, Vol. 3, pp. 77-78.

[33]In middle Tennessee the local courts were permitted to operate under military protection, and Governor Johnson did not even press the requirement of an oath of loyalty upon the judges. (Hall, *op. cit.*, p. 45.)

in the wide assumption of judicial authority which the maintenance of these special courts involved.

We may now turn to an examination of some of these special war courts. At Memphis three military commissions were set up, each with a different sort of jurisdiction.[34] There was, in the first place, a military commission of the usual sort which dealt with offenses of a military character which were not appropriate to courts-martial. Theft of military stores by a civilian would be an example. In the second place, a military commission was organized to take cognizance of criminal cases of a non-military sort; while still a third commission, called a "civil commission" but military in management and control, had charge of civil cases.

The same principle was illustrated in Louisiana and it was there that the most remarkable of the special war courts existed. Pressed with numerous claims of foreigners in New Orleans, the State Department urged the necessity of creating a tribunal to decide cases that might otherwise produce international complications; and in October, 1862, President Lincoln created a "provisional court for Louisiana."[35] In the executive order creating this court the President assumed far-reaching judicial power. The provisional judge was given authority "to hear, try and determine all causes, civil and criminal, including causes in law, equity, revenue, and admiralty, and particularly all such powers and jurisdiction as belong to the district and circuit courts of the United States"; and his decision was made "final and conclusive." Judge Charles A. Peabody, who was given this

---

[34]Hall, *op. cit.*, pp. 131-133; Birkhimer, *Military Government and Martial Law*, 143 *et seq.*

[35]*Ann. Cyc.*, 1863, pp. 586 *et seq.; Am. Hist. Ass. An. Rep.*, 1892, pp. 199-210; G. B. Davis, *Military Law*, 303 *et seq.;* Birkhimer, *op. cit.*, pp. 146-152.

unique judgeship, declared that the power of his court "would seem to be the unlimited power of determining every question that could be the subject of judicial decision."[36] The court had at its command the entire physical force of the United States within the department, both afloat and ashore, and its process even penetrated the enemy's lines.

When the validity of his court was questioned Judge Peabody issued a decision explaining the basis of its authority. The court, he declared, rested upon the law of nations, its formation being within the rights conceded to a belligerent in conquered territory. The Government of the United States, "having conquered and expelled from . . . Louisiana the power by which the government of it had been theretofore administered, and having established there its own power, was bound by the laws of war, as well as the dictates of humanity, to give to the territory thus bereft a government in the place . . . of the one deposed."[37] The authority of the court, said the judge, was derived from the President who created it. Though it was admitted that in ordinary times the President could not create courts in this manner, his authority to do this in time of war was held to be analogous to the exercise of other belligerent rights by the commander-in-chief.

The power of the President to establish this court in Louisiana was sustained by the Supreme Court in various decisions. The duty of maintaining government and administering justice in occupied territory, was described as "a military duty, to be performed by the President as commander-in-chief, and intrusted as such with the direction of the military force by which

---

[36] *Am. Hist. Ass. An. Rep.*, 1892, p. 204.

[37] U. S. *vs.* Reiter and U. S. *vs.* Louis, reported in *Ann. Cyc.*, 1864, pp. 481-482.

the occupation was held."[38] The executive right of setting up special courts for the trial of civil cases was sustained as "the exercise of the ordinary rights of conquest."[39]

The constitutional provision vesting the judicial power of the United States "in one Supreme Court and in such inferior courts as the Congress may . . . establish"[40] was urged as a prohibition upon special war courts created by executive authority and clothed with civil as well as criminal jurisdiction. That clause of the Constitution, however, was declared to have "no application to the abnormal condition of conquered territory," but to refer "only to the courts of the United States, which military courts are not."[41] Not only was the "provisional court of Louisiana," which was created by the President's order, sustained on this principle, but an earlier court, called the "provost court," brought into existence simply by General Butler's order, was also sustained on the ground that Butler's acts were the acts of the President.

There were those who believed that this presidential justice, which in its actual operation meant in reality "provost-marshal justice" or "military-governor justice," was carried too far. Speaking of certain acts of General Butler in Virginia, infringing upon the judicial power of the "restored" State government, Attorney General Bates said, "I have heretofore forborne too much, to avoid a conflict of jurisdiction, but it only

[38] The Grapeshot, 9 Wall. 129, 132.

[39] "Thus it has been determined that the power to establish by military authority courts for the administration of civil as well as criminal justice in portions of the insurgent States occupied by the National forces, is precisely the same as that which exists when foreign territory has been conquered and is occupied by the conquerors." (Mechanics' Bank *vs.* Union Bank of La., 22 Wall. 276, 296.)

[40] *U. S. Constitution*, Art. III, sec. 1.

[41] 22 Wall. 295.

makes the military usurpers more bold and insolent. Hereafter, in open, gross cases, I will press the matter to issue."[42] When, in 1867, Chief Justice Chase addressed the bar at the time of the reopening of the Federal court in North Carolina, he explained why the members of the Supreme Court had not come into the State sooner in the discharge of their circuit duties. All the courts, he said, had been for a considerable period subordinated to military supremacy, and the military tribunals had enjoyed an unusual extent of jurisdiction. Under such circumstances he thought it would not be fitting that the highest judicial officers of the land should exercise their jurisdiction under the supervision and control of the executive department.[43]

VI

What was the constitutional basis for the abnormal governments of occupation in the South? There were some who would have justified Federal assumption of temporary governmental powers in the occupied States on the basis of the "guarantee clause"—the clause by which the States are guaranteed a republican form of government, and, for the preservation of such a government, are protected against domestic violence and invasion.[44] To afford this protection, Federal power may be used within a State. The people of the South were not aware of their unrepublican tendencies, but the Union authorities considered them to be under a

[42]MS. Diary of Edward Bates, Aug. 20, 1864.

[43]Whiting, *War Powers under the Constitution*, 596-597. On October 13, 1865, Chase wrote to President Johnson advising against the holding of the United States Circuit Court in Virginia until military authority should be superseded by the civil. (Johnson Papers, Vol. 79, No. 7354.)

[44]*U. S. Constitution*, Art. IV, sec. 4.

"pretended government" maintained by a "slave aristocracy.

It is of interest to notice that President Lincoln was explicit in citing the guaranty clause as a justification for the military occupation of Tennessee. Writing in September, 1863, to Governor Andrew Johnson, he said:[45]

> . . . you are hereby authorized to exercise such powers as may be necessary and proper to enable the loyal people of Tennessee to present such a republican form of State government as will entitle the State to the guaranty of the United States therefor, and to be protected under such State government by the United States against invasion and domestic violence, all according to the fourth section of the fourth article of the Constitution of the United States.

Had the occupied districts been deemed to be within the country and under the operation of the Constitution, the guaranty clause might well have been made the basis of Federal intervention in local affairs. The Supreme Court, however, upheld the occupation, not on the basis of the guaranty clause, but on the principle

---

[45]Nicolay and Hay, *Works*, IX, 127; *O. R.*, Ser. III, Vol. 3, pp. 789, 819. Lincoln's statement to Johnson was sent in response to a telegram from the latter asking for such a statement. (Stanton Papers, XIV, No. 52987.) Johnson's appeal of March 18, 1862, to the people of Tennessee was in the same spirit. Referring to the disappearance of State government, the abandonment of the ship of state, the desecration of the archives and the seizure of public property, he declared that, "the Government of the United States could not be unmindful of its high constitutional obligation to guarantee to every State . . . a republican form of Government," adding that his purpose in Tennessee was "as speedily as may be, to restore her government to the same condition as before the existing rebellion." (C. R. Hall, *Andrew Johnson, Military Governor of Tennessee*, 39; Johnson Papers, XVI, No. 3725 a.) Johnson's action as President in appointing provisional governors in the Southern States in 1865 was also based on the guaranty clause. (Richardson, *Messages . . . of the Presidents*, VI, 314.)

of conquest. In *Coleman* vs. *Tennessee* the Court said:[46]

> The doctrine of international law on the effect of military occupation of enemy's territory upon its former laws is well established. Though the late war was not between independent nations, but between different portions of the same nation, yet having taken the proportions of a territorial war, the insurgents having become formidable enough to be recognized as belligerents, the same doctrine must be held to apply. The right to govern the territory of the enemy during its military occupation is one of the incidents of war . . . ; and the character and form of the government to be established depend entirely upon the laws of the conquering State or the orders of its military commander.

This application of the conquest theory, it should be noted, gave the occupied districts of the South a military régime such as the North did not have. In the Milligan case the establishment of a military régime in Indiana was declared illegal; but such a régime existed in Louisiana, Tennessee, Virginia, and other occupied regions. It existed also, it is true, in those districts where martial law was established in the North, as in Kentucky and Missouri.[47] But in these Northern districts military rule was declared to be justified because of the prevalence of bushwhacking, because of invasion, or for other reasons which would make martial law appropriate, while such rule in the South was sustained simply on the ground of conquest. The Supreme Court's decision denouncing the military commission which condemned Milligan did not affect the validity of that under which Mumford was executed; for in such a matter Louisiana was held to be subject to a different law from that prevailing in Indiana.

---

[46] 97 U. S. 509, 517.

[47] *Supra*, Chapter VIII.

This subject of military occupation naturally blends into the subject of reconstruction, which is not treated in this book. Though Lincoln's purpose was to use military occupation as a way of setting up loyal State governments, thus hastening and simplifying the restoration of the "proper practical relation" of the States to the Union,[48] the reversal of his policy by the radicals under such leaders as Sumner, Stanton and Stevens defeated this magnanimous purpose; and, as the event proved, the military occupation was unnecessarily prolonged after the war.

Southern territory, in general, thus passed through a series of governmental stages, and the following conditions of rule may be noted: (1) Normal Federal and State authority existed before the war. (2) Independent State authority prevailed, or was asserted, between the time of secession and entrance into the Confederacy.[49] (3) Confederate and State authority held sway until overthrown by Federal force. The practical validity of the governments of the individual Southern States and even of the "Confederate States of America" in the ordinary control of human relations was upheld, though they were declared incapable of enforcing any right as against the United States.[50] (4) Military occupation,

---

[48]"We all agree that the seceded States, so called, are out of their proper practical relation with the Union, and that the sole object of the Government, civil and military, in regard to those States, is to again get them into that proper practical relation." (President Lincoln's last public address, April 11, 1865: Nicolay and Hay, *Lincoln*, IX, 460.)

[49]This statement refers particularly to those States which seceded prior to the Montgomery convention of February, 1861, in which the Government of the Confederate States was organized.

[50]Insurrection and war do not loosen the bonds of society, and the Supreme Court treated the ordinary acts of the individual Southern States during the war for maintaining police regulations, punishing crime, protecting property, etc., as valid and binding. (Horn *vs.* Lockhart, 17 Wall. 570. See also 6 Wall. 443; 7 Wall. 700; 20 Wall.

on the basis of the laws of war and under the authority of the President, succeeded when the Union forces took possession. (5) During the period of confusion that was called "reconstruction," military government was continued; but in a legal sense this was hardly the same thing as belligerent occupation. It was justified on the basis of a variety of "theories of reconstruction," such as "State suicide," "reversion to territorial status," and the like. (6) After the completion of reconstruction, normal Federal and State authority was resumed on the basis of an amended Constitution, the amendments having been made in the period of confusion.[51]

459; 22 Wall. 99.) In Thorington *vs.* Smith (8 Wall. 1) the Supreme Court declared the Confederate States to be a "government of paramount force" maintaining a supremacy which made obedience to its authority, in civil and local matters, both a necessity and a duty. In this case a contract for the payment of Confederate money was declared enforceable in the courts of the United States.

[51]Governmental obligations of the Confederacy were extinguished by the Fourteenth Amendment of the Constitution of the United States, which provided that "neither the United States nor any State shall assume or pay any debt or obligation incurred in aid of insurrection or rebellion against the United States . . . ; but all such debts [and] obligations . . . shall be held illegal and void." The United States did not assume the rôle of the "successor" of the Confederate States; and it would be inappropriate to discuss the conduct of the Washington Government toward the extinguished Confederacy on the basis of those practices of international law which pertain to "continuity of states," "state-succession," and the like. It is the successor-state that sometimes (though not always) assumes the obligations of its predecessor; and to argue that the United States should have taken over the Confederate debt would be to assume that the Confederate States had existed before the war as an established international person, and had then been conquered and absorbed by the United States. Even then, prevailing international practice would have suggested that Confederate debts incurred for the war itself should not be assumed. Historically, the Confederacy never achieved full international standing; and it was treated by the United States as a rival and contending government which sought unsuccessfully to become, as to the South, the "successor" of the United States. The defeat of such a rival government did not amount to the overthrow or absorption of an existing "state" in the international sense. As to the principle of state-continuity, it was preserved in the fact that the United States was not supplanted in its control over the South.

CHAPTER XI

LEGAL AND CONSTITUTIONAL BEARINGS OF CONSCRIPTION

I. American tradition and American law regarding conscription in 1861
II. Conscription by presidential regulation and through State authority in 1862
III. Conscription Law of 1863
IV. Discretionary power of the President
V. Military custody over drafted men
VI. Use of State militia for suppressing draft troubles
VII. The conscientious objector
VIII. Liability of aliens under the draft
IX. Constitutionality of the Conscription Acts

I

English and American tradition has long opposed military conscription. Back of this opposition there is a mental attitude which has been bluntly characterized as the Briton's insistence on the right to "do what he likes, . . . march where he likes, meet where he likes, . . . hoot as he likes, threaten as he likes, smash as he likes,"[1] but it may perhaps be more favorably viewed

---

[1]Matthew Arnold, in "Culture and Anarchy." (Arnold, *Works* [Macmillan, London, 1903], VI, 50.) In the first Agreement of the People, 1647, a paragraph was devoted to the subject of conscription, which was declared to be outside the powers of Parliament, being "reserved by the represented to themselves." The second paragraph of the Agreement reads as follows: "That the matter of impressing and constraining any of us to serve in the wars is against our freedom; and therefore we do not allow it in our Representatives; the rather, because money (the sinews of war), being always at their disposal, they can never want numbers of men apt enough to engage in any just cause." (T. C. Pease, *The Leveller Movement: A Study in the History and Political Theory of the English Great Civil War,* p. 208.)

as a manifestation of the Anglo-Saxon's sense of the sanctity of the individual, his repugnance to outside coercion, and his preference for the inner compulsion of patriotism as a motive for military service.

Michelet referred to the French as "a nation of barbarians civilized by the conscription,"[2] suggesting by this exaggerated phrase the idea that a conception of national duty and a habit of discipline have been inculcated through military service; but for centuries, until recent times, the typical Anglo-Saxon resisted the claims of compulsory service under arms. It was with difficulty that conscription was adopted in England a year and a half after the opening of World War I; and even then the exclusion of Ireland indicated that the Government preferred not to carry the principle to its logical extreme, while the violent opposition to compulsory service in Canada and the decision of the great Australian commonwealth to rely wholly upon volunteering, emphasized the well-known British tradition. The Selective Service Act of 1917 in the United States stands out as a surprising triumph of the Wilson administration, and as the first example in American history in which the policy of universal military service proved truly successful.

Prior to the Civil War conscription had never been applied by the national law. During the Revolution some of the States filled their Continental quotas by means of the draft,[3] and a conscription law was considered

---

[2]Quoted by Matthew Arnold, *op. cit.*, VI, 49. Arnold adds that during the Crimean War the manager of the Clay Cross Works in Derbyshire informed him "that sooner than submit to a conscription, the population of that district would flock to the mines and lead a sort of Robin Hood life underground." See also, for general comment on this subject, *The Independent*, Jan. 18, 1915.

[3]In North Carolina, for instance, there was passed in May, 1778, "An Act for Raising Men to Complete the Continental Battalions belonging to this State" which provided that the Continental quota for the

during the War of 1812; but the opposition of New England and the failure of the two houses of Congress to agree caused the abandonment of the measure. For the Mexican War the army was fully recruited by voluntary enlistment.

When the Civil War broke out, three forms of military organization had become definitely established by law and precedent: the regular army, the "volunteers," and the State militia. (1) The regular army, recruited by voluntary enlistment, had been kept within narrow bounds as a small, though highly efficient, peace establishment. In the spring of 1861, after many Southerners had withdrawn, it numbered about 13,000 men. This might be called the normal Federal army. (2) In case of war, the recognized method of expanding the national forces was through a system of volunteering for limited periods of service. In contrast to the regular army, which consisted of professional soldiers, these volunteers were merely citizens coming to their country's defense in time of need and expecting to return to civil life after the need had passed. (3) The third branch, the militia, deserves more particular attention in connection with the subject matter of this chapter. In keeping with that peculiar federal system which characterizes the American republic, the militia was at once a State and a Federal organization. The militia forces were created by State law; their officers were appointed under State authority; and their services were at the command of the State governor.

But the "State militia" was at the same time the

State should be raised from the various militia companies by first making a call for volunteers, for whom a liberal bounty was offered; and, if the required number was not raised by this means, the companies were to ballot for the rest, and the men so chosen were compelled to go or provide substitutes. (*N. C. Colonial Records* XIII, 411.)

"uniform militia," and constituted a definite part of the national system of defense. Its organization and discipline were prescribed by Congress; the arms were supplied by the Federal Government; and the President had the constitutional authority to call them out for national purposes. The militia might be described as a reserve force under State control, but invested with a national character and available for extraordinary national uses.

A series of Federal laws had been passed with the intention of making the militia a really effective agency of the Federal Government. The first of these laws was that of May 8, 1792, which provided (indirectly) for the enrollment of "every free able-bodied white male citizen of the respective States"[4] between the ages of eighteen and forty-five, and then proceeded to indicate a plan of organization (which the State legislatures were to carry into effect) and to prescribe the rules of discipline to be observed. Another act of 1792,[5] superseded in 1795,[6] carried important provisions for calling forth the militia for those distinctly Federal purposes which the Constitution contemplated: executing the laws of the Union, suppressing insurrections, and repelling invasions. This act provided that, whenever the laws of the United States should be opposed in any State by "combinations too powerful to be suppressed by the ordinary course of judicial proceedings," the President might use the State militia to put down such combinations. Other laws had been passed[7] which indicate that it was the intention of Congress to make

---

[4] *U. S. Stat. at Large*, I, 271. (A constitutional definition of Federal citizenship did not then exist.)

[5] *Ibid.*, I, 264.

[6] *Ibid.*, I, 424.

[7] *Ibid.*, I, 119, 403, 522, 576; II, 207.

the militia an actual, and not merely a nominal, part of the national forces.

An examination of these laws will present two considerations giving the militia a special significance in 1861. In the first place, it will be noticed that the emergency, as interpreted by the Lincoln administration, was precisely that for which the use of militia had been expressly authorized. To execute the laws, to suppress an insurrection, to put down combinations too powerful for judicial methods—these were the purposes for which the Government needed troops. In the second place, the militia was a universal organization, comprising (roughly) all white males of military age.

Why, then, did not the Government use the militia—an instrument already existing under the law—as the means of expanding the army, instead of calling for volunteers and later resorting to conscription? In part, of course, the answer is that the militia was used. The first appeal for troops, President Lincoln's proclamation of April 15, 1861, called for 75,000 "militia," and the wording of the proclamation conformed to the militia law of 1795 under whose authority the call was made.[8] Approximately 80,000 troops were raised under this call.[9]

In prosecuting a serious war of large proportions, however, the militia system proved inadequate. The fact was that the "militia of the United States" had hardly more than a paper existence in 1861. The actual organization under the uniform law of Congress had been

---

[8]*U. S. Stat. at Large,* XII, 1258. In Lincoln's message to the special session of Congress, July 4, 1861, he referred to all three branches of the military service. "At first," he said, "a call was made for 75,000 militia. . . . Other calls were made for volunteers to serve three years . . . , and also for large additions to the Regular Army." (Richardson, *Messages . . . of the Presidents,* VI, 24.)

[9]Report of the Secretary of War, July 1, 1861: *Sen. Ex. Doc. No. 1,* 37 Cong., 1 sess., p. 21.

left to the States, and they had neglected in many cases to make the militia a living, effective force. The provision for giving the State governors the appointing of officers was unsatisfactory from the national standpoint, while the three months' limitation offered a further difficulty.

In the second call for troops, that of May 3, 1861,[10] the militia was not asked for, but the President requested volunteers for three years together with additions to the regular army and navy. The President admitted that this call was made without authority of law,[11] in the expectation of later ratification by Congress. This ratification was cheerfully given[12] and from this time on, the volunteers made up the major part of the forces which sustained the Union.

II

It might have been supposed that the transition from the militia system to the volunteering system, which was thus made so early by the Lincoln administration, would have eclipsed the militia once for all as a Federal instrument for conducting the war. This, however, was not the case. On July 17, 1862, Congress passed a halting and poorly devised measure which proved to be the basis for conscription as first used during the Civil War.[13] This law "amended" the statute of February 25, 1795, and provided that whenever the President should call the militia into Federal service he might specify the period of such service (not to

[10]Nicolay and Hay, *Works*, VI, 263.

[11]Message to Congress, July 4, 1861: Nicolay and Hay, *Works*, VI, 308.

[12]*Supra*, p. 55.

[13]The "Militia Act of 1862" seems the best designation for this measure: *U S. Stat. at Large*, XII, 597.

exceed nine months) and might issue rules to cover defects in State laws to provide for enrolling the militia and putting the act into execution. All male citizens between the ages of eighteen and forty-five were included, and the apportionment among the States was to be according to population. Volunteers for this service were to be accepted and rewarded with bounties. On August 4, 1862, this act was applied when President Lincoln ordered a "draft" of 300,000 militia, with quotas assigned to the States.[14]

It is interesting as a matter of legal history to ponder the method by which conscription was authorized in 1862. The law of that year did not expressly provide conscription. Compulsory service could be read into the act in only two ways: first, the President's authority to issue regulations could be (and, in fact, was) construed to include the power of ordering a draft; and second, the provision that the militia "shall include all male citizens between the ages of eighteen and forty-five" involved universal military liability. This latter provision, however (at least as far as white citizens were concerned), was included in the Act of 1792 and had long been a part of established law. So far as the militia was concerned, the nominal principle of universal liability already existed, and Congress was merely taking advantage of this fact. It was applying conscription by the line of least resistance. As the national legislature was not ready for a drastic and thorough conscription law, it merely employed the inefficient militia system, instead of creating a purely national army; and, instead of providing a nation-wide method of conscription, reliance was placed upon State laws

[14] *O. R.*, Ser. III, Vol. 2, p. 291. A statement of the method indicated in executive orders for the application of conscription under the Militia Act of 1862 is given below, pp. 252-253.

which were to be supplemented by presidential regulations.

When carried into actual practice, the Militia Act of 1862 developed all the defects that were to be expected from such a measure. Where the States had their own systems for enrolling and drafting the militia, as was usually not the case, these systems were to be employed; but any deficiencies in State law or practice were to be made up by executive regulations from Washington. The system actually in use in any State, then, might have rested on State law, on plans made by the governor, or upon instructions issued by the War Department. In the correspondence on the subject between Governor Morton of Indiana and Secretary Stanton, it appears that in the absence of any State law on the subject Governor Morton devised a complete scheme for enforcing the act, and afterward received "Order No. 99" from Washington, containing conflicting regulations. He was, however, informed by Stanton that the order from Washington was designed only as a guide where no system existed, and that, as Morton's plan was particularly adapted to the local needs, it was to be followed instead of the executive order.[15]

In a military sense this law of 1862 stands condemned because of its inefficiency. Viewed from the constitutional standpoint it is chiefly significant as an applica-

---

[15]Morton's plan involved the appointment of a commissioner in each county and a deputy commissioner in each township, the actual preparation of the lists to be in the hands of the township officials. The decision to appoint special commissioners instead of relying upon county sheriffs was due to the unreliability of many of the latter, for in Indiana disaffection was a serious menace. The county and township officers together were to act as boards for determining exemptions and the actual draft was to be supervised by the county commissioners. On October 6, 1862, a draft was conducted in Indiana on this basis. (Foulke, *Life of Oliver P. Morton*, I, 198; W. H. H. Terrell, *Report of the Adjutant General of Indiana* I, 40 *et seq.*)

tion of conscription on a large scale by the very minimum of statutory provision. In other words, the act demonstrated how little had to be done in American law in 1862 to produce at least one form of conscription—that is, the liability attaching to the "militia."[16] It was a conscription law without a conscription clause. The all-inclusiveness of the militia was the essential principle upon which the law rested, and that principle had existed from the time of Washington's presidency. The law was a transitional step in the direction of more complete national conscription and, as we shall see, it gave rise to difficulties in the courts.[17] The insufficiency of this half-way measure indicates that Congress had not yet arrived at an attitude of assurance and determination in the matter of compulsory service.

III

The drastic act of March 3, 1863, was of quite a different sort.[18] It specifically provided universal liability for service in the national army, no reference being made to the militia, and established complete Federal ma-

[16]The nature and purpose of the Militia Act of 1862 may be inferred from the following statement of Senator Wilson of Massachusetts at the time of its consideration: "This bill contemplates drafting from the body of the militia of the country a force sufficient to support the country. [It] contemplates calling out the militia in case we fail to obtain the number of men required by the present system of volunteering. It provides that the President, if he calls the militia, shall not be limited to the time specified in existing laws, but may fix the time." (*Cong. Globe*, 37 Cong., 2 sess., p. 3202.) This law, says General Emory Upton, "reads like a chapter from the Journals of the Continental Congress during the darkest days of the Revolution," and he adds that in passing the measure Congress was returning to the "impotent and extravagant" policy which had led in the past to serious military disaster. Commenting in general on the military legislation of 1862, he remarks that Congress "exercised the power to support armies, but the power to raise them it conferred on the governors." (Upton, *Military Policy of the United States*, 434, 436.)

[17]*Infra*, pp. 252-256.

[18]*U. S. Stat. at Large*, XII, 731.

chinery of administration. All able-bodied male citizens between twenty and forty-five, and foreigners who had declared their intention to become citizens, were "to constitute the national forces," and were declared liable to military service. Exemptions were carefully defined and married men were placed in a class that would be subject to call only after the unmarried had been taken. For the enforcement of the act the country was to be divided into enrollment districts, in each of which a Federal provost marshal and a Federal board of enrollment were to be established. The districts were subdivided for enrollment purposes and local enrolling officers were to make full lists of eligible citizens. Men so enrolled were subject "to be called into the military service of the United States" during the continuance of the "rebellion," but in no case was their service to exceed three years. Conscripts were to have the same advance pay and the same Federal bounties as three-year volunteers. In conducting the draft, officers were to take into consideration the number already enlisted, so as to equalize the contributions of men from the various States. Those drafted might be excused either by furnishing substitutes or paying $300 commutation money,[19] both of which practices had been allowed in the old militia systems. If any person should fail to respond to notice he was to be deemed a deserter, arrested and tried by court-martial. For encouraging or harboring deserters or for obstructing the draft, fines and imprisonments were imposed.

Though the method followed was unnecessarily laborious, the work had been so far completed that the first draft under the new law was made in July, 1863.

[19]In a supplemental conscription act of July 4, 1864, this provision for exemption by the payment of commutation money was dropped: *U. S. Stat. at Large,* XIII, 379.

Hundreds of enrolling officers collected the names, which were corrected and amplified by consulting polling lists, assessment books, pay-rolls, and the like. These names were turned over to the headquarters of the enrollment bureaus, which then proceeded to the work of reducing the lists to those actually subject to call, eliminating all who were disqualified, or were entitled to exemption. The number of men called for at the time of each draft was apportioned among the States according to population, and in filling these quotas credit was given for volunteers.

A considerable interval was usually allowed between the time of the call and the final date for completing the quota, and during this interval volunteering was actively stimulated with the object of supplying the required number without compulsion if possible. One community vied with another to make the best showing, and this swelling of the number of volunteers was one of the important indirect effects of the draft. Everywhere throughout the country local political units incurred heavy debts in order to pay bounties for volunteers and thus reduce the number of men to be drafted.[20] In the State of New Jersey there were more than one hundred laws passed at one session of the legislature authorizing various districts to incur obligations for this purpose, and laws of a similar sort were passed in other States.[21] Incidentally this bounty sys-

[20]The bounty problem, together with other matters pertaining to conscription, was ably and wittily presented by Fred A. Shannon in a paper entitled "Conscription and the Bounty Problem," read at the meeting of the American Historical Association at Ann Arbor, Michigan, December, 1925.

[21]31 *N. J. Law Reps.* 193, Booth *vs.* Town of Woodbury, 32 Conn. 118; Speer *vs.* School Directors . . . of Blairsville, 50 Pa. St. Reps. 150; Taylor *vs.* Thompson *et al.*, 42 Ill. 9; Ferguson *vs.* Landram, 64 Ky. 548; *Laws of Delaware*, 1861-65, Ch. 462; *Local and Private Acts of Ky.*, 1865., Chs. 610, 648.

tem proved to be most unfortunate, because the mercenary motive was hardly the proper incentive for volunteering and the resources of the people were drained for an unessential expenditure. The system raised the price of substitutes, and also encouraged the vile practice of deserting to obtain bounties on re-enlistment. Enlistment was actually retarded to a certain extent by the bounty system; for in those districts where the bounties were low, enlistments would fall off, and in any case where there seemed a prospect of an increase in the amount of the bounty, men who were enlisting for that motive would wait till they could command a higher price.

When the time came for drafting, the names of all eligibles were placed on cards and then drawn from a wheel by blindfolded officers, this part of the procedure being conducted in as public a manner as possible. Men thus drafted were given notice, and a period of time was allowed during which they could establish exemption, provide substitutes or pay commutation money. Those who did not escape by any of these methods would be served with a notice from the provost marshal directing them to appear at a specified rendezvous at a certain time. It was at this point that military control over the men began.

The difficult conditions under which the Conscription Act was administered are matters of familiar history. In many districts, where passion had been aroused to a high pitch by the war, and where disloyalty was loudly proclaimed in the newspapers, it was hard to get officers to face the personal dangers which threatened any who were connected with the draft. To prevent the reenforcement of the armies great numbers of disaffected citizens paid the commutation money or adopted less justifiable methods of evasion, such as misrepresenting their age, feigning sickness, pretending imbecility, or departing for Canada. Firms existed for the purpose of establishing physical or mental disability, an experienced attorney and an "elastic" country doctor being all that was needed to supply the required affidavits. Plots of secret societies and outspoken opposition on the part of "peace advocates" and other disaffected men proved extremely irritating to the Government and offered continual temptation to the use of despotic measures. As to actual mob violence, this was not particularly alarming in itself; since it was always strictly local, and broke down on the first appearance of troops. It was only where such violence coincided with a sympathetic attitude on the part of the civil authorities that the situation boded serious trouble. In the case of the draft riot in New York in July, 1863, the most alarming feature in the situation was not the overpowering of the police and the provost marshal's guard by the mob.[22] It was rather the friendly attitude of Governor Seymour toward the rioters and his declaration that he would use his influence to have the draft suspended. Elsewhere, as in Indiana, Ohio, and Wisconsin,[23] forcible

[22]For the draft riot in New York, see Nicolay and Hay, *Lincoln*, VII, 32-57; Rhodes, *History of the United States*, IV, 320 *et seq.*; Horace Greeley, *American Conflict*, II, 501 *et seq.*

[23]The correspondence of Governor Morton (among the State archives at Indianapolis) and the life of Morton by W. D. Foulke contain important information concerning military affairs in Indiana. The best published source on this subject is W. H. H. Terrell, *Report of the Adjutant General of Indiana*. Similar information for Wisconsin is to be found among the governors' letter books, preserved by the Wisconsin Historical Society at Madison. The facts in Druecker *vs.* Salomon, 21 Wis. 628, reveal circumstances connected with draft riots. Concerning disturbances in Ohio, see *O. R.*, Ser. I, Vol. 23, pt. 1, pp. 395-397. There was trouble in various other States. Halleck addressed Grant concerning the withdrawal of troops from the field to cope with resistance to the draft in disaffected districts. (Halleck to Grant, Aug. 11, 1864, *O. R.*, Ser. I, Vol. 42, pt. 2, p. 111.) Grant replied opposing such a use of his forces. (*Ibid.*, p. 193.)

resistance to the draft found similar approval on the part of the local authorities, and Federal troops had to be sent to the scenes of trouble in order to clear the atmosphere. All of these conditions need to be borne in mind in studying the legal aspects of the draft, for sometimes the antagonistic attitude of certain State judges toward the Conscription Act was merely a part of the many-sided campaign of obstruction which this measure encountered in regions where the Union cause or the Lincoln administration was unpopular.[24]

IV

As was naturally to be expected, conscription produced many legal perplexities. Satisfactory judicial precedents were lacking and many unforeseen problems of interpretation arose. The President's wide discretionary power under the acts was contested; *habeas corpus* proceedings were interposed to release drafted men; the right to employ the militia in suppressing draft troubles was controverted; the liability of aliens was debated; and the constitutionality of the conscription acts was in many quarters disputed. Often the cases under this head touched other questions than the draft, such as military control over civilians, conflicts of State and Federal authority, the nature of the war powers, and the legality of executive procedure during the war.

On the subject of executive discretion most of the controversy centered around the act of 1862, which, as we have seen, left many important details of execution to the President and the State governors. The regulations which the War Department issued upon the authority of the President, in accordance with the

---

[24]For a comprehensive official account of the enforcement of the Conscription Act, see historical report of the Operations of the Enrollment Branch, Provost Marshal General's Bureau, Washington, D. C., Mar. 17, 1866: *O. R.*, Ser. III, Vol. 5, pp. 712 *et seq.*

act, named the quotas of the States and called upon the governors to fill these quotas either according to State law or by following a specified method contained in the regulations. According to this method, enrollment lists were to be filed with the sheriffs, and the governors of the States were to appoint commissioners for the counties, whose duty it was to hear proofs of exemption, grant excuses, conduct the draft, and accept substitutes; while provost marshals in the States, appointed by the War Department on nomination of the governors, were to put down disturbances, enforce attendance at rendezvous, keep the men in custody and perform similar functions.[25]

The validity of these orders under the President's authority, involving that of the governors' acts in accordance therewith, was in various cases presented for judicial determination. It was argued in a Wisconsin case that, in view of the division of our Government into three branches, the creation of such a large field of executive discretion in a matter of such high importance as conscription amounted to a delegation of legislative power to the President, and that for this reason the Militia Act of 1862 was unconstitutional. The State court held otherwise and pointed to the distinction between "those important subjects which must be entirely regulated by the legislature itself, and those of less interest in which a general provision may be made and power given to those who are to act under such general provision to fill up detail."

When the militia were once called forth [said the court], it was a matter of no vital importance how they should be detached and drafted. Congress indicated an intention of

[25]General Orders, War Department, Nos. 94, 99, Aug. 4 and Aug. 9, 1862: *O. R.*, Ser. III, Vol. 2, pp. 291, 333-335.

adopting the State laws upon the subject, as far as they were applicable. When they were not applicable, or none existed, the President was authorized to make proper rules and regulations for enrolling the militia and drafting them. And this no more partakes of legislative power than that discretionary authority intrusted to every department of the Government in a variety of cases. This practice of giving discretionary power to other departments or agencies who were intrusted with the duty of carrying into effect some general provisions of law, had its origin at the adoption of the Constitution, and in the action of the first Congress under it. . . . It was undoubtedly in strict conformity to the views entertained by the great statesmen of that day.[26]

In order to appreciate the extent and meaning of the court's doctrine in this case, one must remember that the act of 1862 not only failed to cover details but it did not even specifically provide for a draft. The act referred to "enrolling" and "calling forth" the militia; but the drafting, or the use of compulsion, was deducible from the law only by inference. Nor can one find in the Militia Act of 1795, of which the act of 1862 was an amendment, any provision for a "draft" of the militia. The Federal statutes contained, in 1862, no specific provision for a draft. Notwithstanding this, Federal drafts were conducted in various States in that year.[27] Even where the draft of this year was conducted upon State authority, this was done under the President's order. It is therefore apparent that the first draft for the raising of Federal troops ever conducted in our history under the Constitution was a presidential

[26] *In re* Griner, 16 Wis. 447, 458.

[27] For an account of the draft of November, 1862, in Wisconsin, which occasioned serious trouble, see *Sen. Mis. Doc. No. 71*, 38 Cong., 1 sess. (This draft was made not in pursuance of State law, but under regulations issued by the War Department.)

draft. It was instituted by rules and regulations which the President promulgated through the War Department upon authority derived only inferentially from an act of Congress. This was a truly remarkable extension of executive power in a democratic state, and the legality of the draft of 1862 was a matter of grave question in the minds of many thoughtful men.

The same question of executive discretion under the draft law came up in a later Wisconsin case—that of *Druecker* vs. *Salomon*,[28] the specific point at issue being the governor's power to make arrests to suppress a draft riot. Again the discretionary power of the President was upheld. The well-known cases of *Martin* vs. *Mott*[29] and *Luther* vs. *Borden*[30] were cited to illustrate the discretionary authority lodged with the executive and to show that the President is the exclusive judge of the existence of an insurrection and of the necessity of calling out the militia. A distinction was drawn between discretionary and ministerial acts. In the case of the former, the determination on the part of the executive is final. Such a power is to be exercised only by the executive and there is no chance for judicial examination or review. In the latter the executive is limited to a given line of conduct and must not misuse his authority. In the case in hand, the governor's order for the arrest was within the proper field of executive discretion, the governor being clothed with the discretionary power of the President *pro hac vice*. On this ground the court held that the governor's acts must be regarded in a certain sense as the acts of the President, adding that, though such power was "dangerous to liberty," it was "absolutely necessary to every free government."

[28] 21 Wis. 628.
[29] 12 Wheaton 19.
[30] 7 How. 1.

In McCall's case, which arose in a Federal district court in Pennsylvania, the delegation of the regulating power to the President in matters touching the draft was sustained; and the President's right to act through the Secretary of War, governors, and commissioners was also upheld. The court said:

> Of course, Congress cannot constitutionally delegate to the President legislative powers. But it may in conferring powers constitutionally exercisable by him prescribe . . . special rules of their administration; or may authorize him to make the rules. . . . When . . . Congress, in conferring a power . . . not only omits to prescribe regulations of its exercise, but, as in the present case, expressly authorizes him to make them, he may, . . . consistently with the legislative purpose declared, make any such regulations . . . as Congress might have specially prescribed.[31]

V

Conscription necessarily involved custody over drafted men not in active military service, and this proved a troublesome issue which frequently found its way into the courts in various forms. If there appeared any defect in the military claim to any person held by the provost marshal, injunction or *habeas corpus* proceedings were likely to be instituted to obtain that person's discharge; and in this way the legality of this military custody was subjected to judicial inquiry. The issue became seriously complicated in cases where proceedings for discharge were brought in the State courts, for this would result in holding Federal officers accountable to State tribunals. Though such jurisdiction on the part of State courts was defeated, it was vigorously claimed, and presented an irritating source of friction. Usually and regularly, however, proceedings looking to release from custody were brought in the lower Fed-

[31] 15 Fed. Cas. 1230.

eral courts, and they commonly arose from *habeas corpus* petitions.[32] It may be said that provost marshals everywhere had to defend before the civil tribunals their control over men whom they claimed to hold under the draft, and that the Federal courts were at all times open to petitioners who felt they had a case justifying discharge.

The fundamental fact of the provost marshal's custody and of the Federal court's jurisdiction in the matter of release was treated in the case of Daniel Irons, which arose in the circuit court of the northern district of New York in September, 1863.[33] In this case the court held that a drafted person remains in the custody of the provost marshal from the time of his report for duty till the time of his discharge, and that a Federal court may decree the discharge through *habeas corpus* proceedings. The exact time when the military custody began was the hour at which the drafted man was required to report to the provost marshal as indicated in the notice sent to him, and this control could be legally exercised whether the man actually appeared or not. Thus military control as a legal fact was independent of actual possession of the men involved.

It was claimed that under the act of 1862 a drafted militiaman had the option to appear at rendezvous or pay a fine. The courts denied this claim, however, and the President's orders which gave provost marshals the power to force attendance at rendezvous were upheld.[34]

It sometimes happened that State governors were re-

---

[32]When examining the files and dockets of the Federal district court at Cleveland, Ohio, the writer found numerous *habeas corpus* hearings in the war years by means of which men under military authority were released. Many of these were minors who enlisted without their parents' consent.

[33]13 Fed. Cas. 98.

[34]Case, 2 Wendt's Pittsburgh Reports 402.

quested to release men who had been taken under the conscription law. When Governor Morton of Indiana received such a request from the wife of a drafted man he informed her that soldiers in the service of the United States were beyond the control of the governor, and that the Secretary of War alone could discharge them.[35] His statement would have been more accurate if he had said that the matter of discharge lay with the War Department or with the Federal courts.

It followed as a necessary corollary of the military control over drafted men that those who failed to report became deserters. This uncomfortable status applying to men never mustered into the service aroused widespread opposition, but the legal principle was perfectly clear and was supported by incontestable precedents. So early an opinion as that of Justice Bushrod Washington in the case of *Houston* vs. *Moore*, heard by the Supreme Court in 1820, authoritatively disposed of the question by declaring men to be in military service from the time of rendezvous.[36]

In the act of 1863 this question was not left to judicial interpretation, but the law specified that any drafted person failing to respond to notice was to be deemed a deserter, and sent to the nearest military post for trial and punishment. This harsh, though logical,

---

[35]Letter of Governor Morton to a lady in Blackford County, November 26, 1864: Morton Correspondence, MSS., Indiana State Library.

[36]This was a case brought up for review from the Pennsylvania Supreme Court to the Supreme Court of the United States, and it involved the constitutionality of a Pennsylvania law providing that a State court-martial could discipline militia delinquents when called into Federal service. While admitting that a State legislature could not fix penalties against militiamen when Congress had acted for this purpose, the court held that power could be conferred by State law upon State courts-martial to enforce Federal law upon delinquents in the militia. The delinquency in this case consisted in failure to join the militia at the time and place of rendezvous. (18 U. S. 1.)

provision proved a source of considerable difficulty, and in some cases arguments which went so far as to deny the constitutionality of the Conscription Act seem to have been prompted by a desire to save drafted boys from the penalties of "desertion."

In one of the prominent cases a State judge denied that Congress had the right to have provost marshals treat freemen as deserters directly after serving notice upon them. To bring the militia into "actual service," he argued, there must be obedience to the call and some act of organization, mustering, rendezvous or marching done in pursuance of the national appeal. As a practical matter it is hard to see how conscription could have been made effective on any such basis; for, if these limitations had been observed, the filling up of the army would have rested upon a process quite as voluntary as that of enlistment, and the only compulsion permitted by the National Government would have been such as applies equally to enlisted and drafted men. It is significant that the judge who argued so was opposed to national conscription *in toto* and could see no way by which such conscription could be legally accomplished.[37]

VI

Another source of difficulty was the use of the militia for suppressing draft troubles. There were various communities in which the provisions of the draft could be executed only by the use of force. Troops were needed not only to put down riots but to protect officers engaged in conducting the enrollment, drawing the names, serving notices and guarding men on their way to and from rendezvous. The National Government was fre-

[37]This was the case of Kneedler *vs.* Lane, 45 Pa. 238.

quently called upon to supply these troops; but Union commanders strenuously opposed withdrawing forces from the field for this purpose, and State governors were expected to do all in their power to maintain the orderly operation of the draft without asking for Federal assistance. As a consequence the State militia was called upon for this disagreeable duty. An example of this occurred in connection with the draft disturbances in Ozaukee County, Wisconsin, in December, 1862, where a mob attacked the commissioner with guns, clubs, and stones so that intervention by the State militia became necessary. A militia captain complained of such service, but the Wisconsin governor took the ground that the militiamen were liable for such duty and should respond where needed.[38]

VII

The inevitable question of exemption because of conscientious scruples arose, as it is sure to do in all cases where compulsory military service is adopted. In the Militia Act of 1862 there was no clause covering the subject and the granting of such exemption seems to have been left largely to the discretion of the State governors through whom, as we have seen, the law was enforced. The working rule in Indiana, as drafted by Governor Morton and approved by the War Department, was that no sweeping exemption on this ground should be permitted, but that ministers in actual charge of pastoral duties should be excused from service.[39]

---

[38]Governor Salomon to Lincoln, Dec. 1, 1862; Same to Commander of Ozaukee Guards, Jan. 17, 1863; Governors' Correspondence, MSS., Wisconsin State Historical Library.

[39]Governor Morton to Secretary Stanton, August 30, 1862: Morton Correspondence (MSS., Indiana State Library.) By agreement between the Indiana Friends and Governor Morton, a plan was devised in

The law of 1863 enumerated exhaustively the conditions of exemption, but made no provision for the conscientious objector. Not even ministers were exempt. The result was that Quakers and others whose beliefs forbade warlike effort of any sort were placed in a very difficult position.

There is evidence of real suffering on the part of some who rigidly adhered to their conscientious scruples. A most remarkable case was that of one Pringle,[40] a Vermont Quaker whose piety was so deep and whose objections to war so pronounced that when he was drafted in the summer of 1863 he not only flatly refused to violate the Scriptures by serving himself, but was too conscientious to hire a substitute, thus tempting a fellow being to sin. Neither would he pay commutation money.[41] It was a case of Pringle versus the United States. He was hustled by force into a car with other conscripts and carried to a camp of rendezvous near Boston. Being assigned to fatigue duty, he refused, and stood his ground like a martyr. No amount of bullying or argument could shake him, since in fact he stood ready to die rather than conform to military discipline. In consequence of this remarkable stand he was thrust into the guardhouse along with vile and desperate men. An attempt to induce him to be trans-

---

accordance with which many Quakers paid the sum of $200 each for exemption in 1862, but this was found to be without authority of law, and the money was refunded. (Foulke, *Life of Oliver P. Morton*, I, 199.)

[40]Cyrus G. Pringle, *Record of a Quaker Conscience* (N. Y. Macmillan, 1918); "The United States *versus* Pringle," *Atlantic Monthly*, Vol. 111, pp. 145-162 (Feb., 1913).

[41]Quaker principles during the war were interpreted by the official bodies of that denomination as opposed to the payment of commutation money. Many individual Quakers, however, adopted this plan of avoiding service and were leniently treated by their brethren. (R. M. Jones, *Later Periods of Quakerism*, II, 729-730.)

ferred to hospital service and later to the work of the bureau for colored refugees in the South was without avail. He would not "purchase life at the cost of peace of soul."

When the conscripts were carried to Alexandria, Virginia, to be equipped, Pringle refused to receive a gun. In the hurried excitement of equipping a regiment his arguments were wasted on the petty officers to whom they were directed, and the equipment, including the gun, was forcibly buckled on him. He was gagged for refusal to clean his gun; but, in general, this inflexible, serene Quaker was not seriously mistreated by the officers who had to deal with him. Finally the problem was referred to Lincoln himself, who disposed of the matter by directing that the man be sent home.[42] So Pringle won his case.

The trials of such as Pringle finally claimed the attention of Congress and the question of modifying the law in their favor was debated in January, 1864.[43] It developed in the debate that the clergy had made no strenuous objection to their lack of exemption. There had been some petitions for the relief of ministers from military service, but this represented only a small fraction of the clergy of the country. On the other hand, many of the clergy had expressed gratitude to Congress for requiring them to perform military duty, and had congratulated themselves on this recognition of their manhood. The suggestion to exempt ministers struck a snag in the Senate when it was shown that in the wealthy

[42]Lincoln's sympathy for the Quakers was often shown, and his letter to Mrs. Gurney, widow of a distinguished Quaker minister, is a classic. (Nicolay and Hay, *Lincoln,* VI, 326 *et seq.*; R. M. Jones, *Later Periods of Quakerism,* II, 736; F. G. Cartland, *Southern Heroes, or the Friends in War Time,* 137.)

[43]*Cong. Globe,* 38 Cong., 1 sess., pp. 204 *et seq.*

Amana Society (numerous in Erie County, New York) every member was a minister![44]

As the lawmakers sought some consistent basis on which to offer relief to conscientious objectors, the more serious phases of the question appeared. While piteous stories were told of the sufferings of this class of people—stories of moral heroism among humble men—yet, as Senator Anthony of Rhode Island pointed out, not one efficient soldier had been added to the army by the impressment of men conscientiously scrupulous against bearing arms.[45] Something, he said, should be conceded to a class of people that had consistently opposed slavery and had not been slaveholders even in slaveholding States.

The importance of such considerations was conceded, and an act was passed, February 24, 1864, which afforded a qualified exemption on religious grounds.[46] Members of religious denominations whose articles of faith opposed the bearing of arms were to be considered "non-combatants" when "drafted into the military service," and were to be assigned to duty in hospitals, or in the care of freedmen, or they were to pay $300 for the benefit of sick and wounded soldiers. Satisfactory evidence was required showing conduct consistent with their declaration of scruples. This half-way measure was accepted as a well-meant concession by Congress, in spite of the fact that the alternative of non-combatant service already existed in practice as a matter of executive policy, and had been made available in a number of instances.[47]

---

[44]*Ibid.*, p. 207.

[45]*Ibid.*, p. 204.

[46]*U. S. Stat. at Large*, XIII, 9, sec. 17.

[47]An excellent study of both Northern and Southern conscientious objectors is to be found in *The Treatment of Conscientious Objectors during the Civil War*, by Gertrude Ady, an unpublished master's dis-

VIII

A still more difficult question of exemption presented itself in the case of foreigners. It was generally conceded that the doctrine of inalienable allegiance was dead, and that expatriation was a recognized right. This principle, however, merely meant that those former aliens whose change of allegiance had been completed, and who were therefore citizens of the United States, were liable to military service. This did not go far enough. There were many thousands of foreign settlers in the country who were to all intents and purposes Americans, having adopted the new land as their permanent home. These men had lived for years under the protection of our laws, and many of them had exercised political rights. Some of the newer States of the West made their laws particularly liberal in order to attract immigrants, and had admitted unnaturalized aliens to the voting privilege. In view of these facts it was very natural that the question of claiming the service of these foreign inhabitants should be raised. To raise the question, however, was to present both constitutional and international difficulties. The question whether non-citizens could be drafted into the army was a serious constitutional problem, and it was also a grave issue of international law as to whether one nation may impress for military duty the subjects of other nations residing within its borders.

It was in Wisconsin that this question appeared in

---

sertation prepared at the University of Illinois in 1922. Some of the books dealing with this subject are Rufus M. Jones, *Later Periods of Quakerism;* Ethan Foster, *Conscript Quakers;* Pringle, *The Record of a Quaker Conscience* (Macmillan, 1918); *Memoir and Correspondence of Eliza P. Gurney;* Edward N. Wright, *Conscientious Objectors in the Civil War;* Margaret E. Hirst, *The Quakers in Peace and War.*

its most acute form. The laws of that State permitted alien declarants to vote after one year's residence, and there had been a flood of German immigration into the State during the fifties. The foreign element of the State was so large that the exemption of those who were unnaturalized would have made it a real hardship for the State to raise its quota estimated on the basis of general population. The draft of 1862 was conducted in Wisconsin in accordance with Federal executive regulations under the militia law which has already been discussed,[48] and with regard to the Germans a mass of correspondence passed between the governor and Secretary Seward at Washington.

The first decision of policy in this matter was therefore made by the Secretary of State.[49] Having given particular attention to the Wisconsin correspondence, and having sent a special messenger to confer with Governor Salomon, he announced in November, 1862, that all who had voted in the State should be held liable to the draft, regardless of alienage, and that doubtful cases should be referred to the Department of State, not that of War. Investigations were conducted for the State Department by local draft commissioners, and election records were searched for this purpose. On the other side the various consuls (e.g., the Consul of Württemberg at Milwaukee) also took part in these investigations. Since the consuls had been fully advised as to the necessity of making a declaration regarding voting, it was considered a "safe presumption" that the applicant had voted in those cases where there was

---

[48]See above, pp. 252-253.

[49]The governors' letter books in the Wisconsin State Historical Library at Madison (especially from November, 1862, to January, 1863) and the "domestic letters" of the Department of State at Washington form the chief basis for this part of the discussion.

no statement bearing on that point. As the governor stated, there was also a strong presumption that aliens of more than six years' residence had voted, and the consuls so understood it. In all of the cases investigated, the application for exemption on the ground of alienage was denied where it was found that the applicant had exercised the franchise.

Up to March, 1863, there had been no legislation by Congress covering the case of foreigners, but the Conscription Act passed at that time was made to include "persons of foreign birth who shall have declared . . . their intention to become citizens."[50] Doubts were expressed at the time as to the wisdom as well as the constitutionality of this provision.[51] The opponents of the measure argued that the United States has no right to compel aliens who have taken the preliminary oath to do military service, but that this right of compulsion applies only to citizens. Though they admitted the right of expatriation, they pointed out that the transfer of allegiance was not completed until the final oath had been taken. The United States could not, for instance, require an alien declarant to serve in war against his home country, and the right assumed in this provision of the law amounted to that.

That our Government should have made the declaration of intention to become an American citizen the basis for forcing aliens into military service seems the more remarkable when one examines the legal effect of such declaration. So far as the privileges or rights of nationality are concerned, this legal effect is *nil.* It has been often held in our courts that "mere declaration of intention" does not confer citizenship. Such a

---

[50] *U. S. Stat. at Large,* XII, 731, sec. 1.

[51] For the debates on this subject, see *Cong. Globe,* 37 Cong., 3 sess., pp. 992, 1001, 1384; 38 Cong., 1 sess., pp. 228 *et seq.*

declaration, for instance, does not entitle a man to a passport; and it has no international value in the event of the declarant returning to his native country. In other words this preliminary oath of declaration confers none of the rights of American citizenship; and yet in the Conscription Act it was made the basis of imposing the heaviest obligation of citizenship—namely, military service.[52]

The best justification for the provision, perhaps, was that some of the States conferred the voting privilege upon those who had made the declaration, and that such persons had become "State citizens." There was at this time, of course, no constitutional definition of United States citizenship; and the whole matter was in considerable confusion, owing to the principle announced in the Dred Scott case that citizenship in a State did not involve, in the full sense, citizenship in the United States.

Yet, in spite of the fact that the constitutional definition of United States citizenship had not been introduced, such citizenship was a distinct reality. In such things as the issuance of passports and the protection of our nationals abroad, citizenship in the United States was as real before the adoption of the Fourteenth Amendment as afterward. So far as former aliens were concerned, the case was covered entirely by the uniform naturalization laws of Congress, and this phase of the question was in no way affected by State action. In its proper meaning the phrase "State citizenship" related to matters within the competence of State governments, certainly not to such a matter as the naturalization of aliens, in which international complications were sure to arise. One could hardly appeal to this "State citizenship," then, in justification of the national law

[52]Moore, *Digest of International Law,* III, 336, 338, 343.

which imposed military service upon unnaturalized foreigners.

Having once adopted the principle that aliens could be liable to the draft, Congress took a further step in application of the principle. By the act of February 24, 1864, voting was made an absolute basis for military liability.[53] According to this act, no foreigner was to be exempt "who [had] at any time assumed the rights of a citizen by voting" at any State, Federal, or territorial election. The fact of voting was to be conclusive against any claim for exemption on the basis of alienage, and the same was true with regard to office-holding.

This provision, as we have already seen, had originated with Secretary Seward, and had long existed as a matter of executive regulation. Here again the peculiar dual system characteristic of the American Government was manifest in the fact that the exercise of a right conferred by State law was made the basis of a Federal obligation.

IX

Were the conscription laws of the Civil War "constitutional"? It is now, of course, generally conceded that Congress has the power of conscription, but in the sixties this power was emphatically disputed.[54] As the laws

[53] *U. S. Stat. at Large*, XIII, 9, sec. 18.

[54] In 1863 the famous editor of the New York *Tribune* wrote to Secretary of War Stanton: "It is folly to close our eyes to the signs of the times. The people have been educated to the idea of individual sovereignty, & the principle of conscription is repugnant to their feelings & cannot be carried out except at great peril to the free States. . . . The entire system must be changed. . . . Drafting is an anomaly in a free State; it oppresses the masses. Like imprisonment for debt . . . it must and will be reformed out of our system of political economy." (Horace Greeley to Stanton, June 12, 1863: Stanton Papers, No. 52634.)

were never tested as to constitutionality before the Supreme Court, the question must be discussed on the basis of prevailing legal opinion.

In 1814 James Monroe, Secretary of War, presented to Congress a plan for increasing the army involving compulsory enrollment. Touching the constitutional question he said:

> The idea that the United States cannot raise a regular army in any other mode than by accepting the voluntary service of individuals is believed to be repugnant to the uniform construction of all grants of power. . . . An unqualified grant of power gives the means necessary to carry it into effect. . . . The commonwealth has a right to the service of all its citizens, or rather the citizens . . . have a right collectively and individually to the service of each other to repel any danger which may be menaced. The manner in which this service is to be apportioned among the citizens, and rendered by them, are objects of legislation. . . . The power of the United States over the *militia* has been limited, and for raising regular *armies* granted without limitation.[55]

In a paper that was not published during his lifetime, Lincoln elaborated his views on the subject.[56] He wrote:

> They tell us the law is unconstitutional. It is the first instance, I believe, in which the power of Congress to do a thing has ever been questioned in a case when the power is given by the Constitution in express terms. Whether a power can be implied when it is not expressed has often been the subject of controversy; but this is the first case in which the degree of effrontery has been ventured upon, of denying a power which is plainly and distinctly written down in the Constitution. . . . The case simply is, the Constitution provides that the Congress shall have power to raise and support

[55] *Niles' Weekly Register*, VII, 138-139.

[56] Nicolay and Hay, *Lincoln*, VII, 49-57.

armies; and by this act the Congress has exercised the power to raise and support armies. This is the whole of it. . . . The Constitution gives Congress the power, but it does not prescribe the mode or expressly declare who shall prescribe it. In such case Congress must prescribe the mode, or relinquish the power. There is no alternative. . . . If the Constitution had prescribed a mode, Congress could and must follow that mode; but, as it is, the mode necessarily goes to Congress, with the power expressly given. The power is given fully, completely, unconditionally. It is not a power to raise armies if State authorities consent, nor if the men to compose the armies are entirely willing; but it is a power to raise and support armies . . . without an "if."

These views indicate the convictions of the administration, while the passage of the act by substantial majorities in both houses shows the preponderance of legislative opinion in its favor.[57] That Congress gave particular attention to the matter of constitutionality is shown by the debates and by the unusual preamble, in which the "duty" of the Government "under the Constitution" is mentioned.

For judicial interpretation on the point of constitutionality we must turn to the decisions of State courts; and, instead of following these decisions case by case, it will be better for our purpose to review the principal arguments on both sides.[58]

---

[57]In the House the vote on the Conscription Act was 115 yeas and 49 nays. (*Cong. Globe*, 37 Cong., 3 sess., p. 1293.) The yeas and nays were not taken on the final passage of the bill in the Senate, but the sentiment of the upper house may be judged by the vote on the motion of Senator Bayard of Delaware "to postpone indefinitely the consideration of the bill." This motion was defeated by a vote of 11 to 35. (*Ibid.*, p. 1389.)

[58]For the cases whose arguments are summarized in the following paragraphs, see Ferguson *vs.* Landram, 64 Ky. 548; Druecker *vs.* Salomon, 21 Wis. 628; The Conscription Cases, 9 Wright (Pa.) 238; *In re* Griner, 16 Wis. 447; Kneedler *vs.* Lane, 45 Pa. 238. The cita-

The opponents of conscription usually adopted the State-rights, strict-constructionist line of argument and made much of the distinction between the *militia* and the *army*. The militia, they argued, is a State institution. Congress is limited to calling it out and providing its discipline when in "actual service" of the United States. The extent to which the conscription law interferes with this State institution by bringing State militiamen and State officers within the draft, amounts to a breach of the Constitution. The Fathers never contemplated giving to Congress so sweeping a power as conscription, knowing, as they did, the arbitrary abuse to which this might lead; and if they had so contemplated, they would have introduced some check upon the power. They meant to guard against a war of conquest. By limiting Congress to voluntary enlistment they made it certain that no war could be fought that was not a people's war. If Congress had this power of conscription, then it could raise troops by compulsion in time of peace, and this is wholly inconsistent with the well-known jealousy of standing armies which obtained at the time the Constitution was adopted. If Congress may compel military service, then it may compel people to lend money—it may take their horses, their lands, their ships, their homes! Where will you stop? During the War of 1812 conscription was defeated. But that was a foreign war. The present con-

---

tions contained in these decisions offer a sufficient guide to the legal literature on the subject. In some of the Southern States there were notable decisions concerning the constitutionality of conscription, the legal principles involved being the same as those at the North. See, for instance, *Ex parte* Hill, 38 Ala. 429; Barber *vs.* Irwin, 34 Ga. 27; *Ex parte* Coupland, 26 Tex. 386; Jeffers *vs.* Fair, 33 Ga. 369. For ex-President Buchanan's views in support of the constitutionality of the conscription law, see *Works of James Buchanan*, ed. by J. B. Moore, XI, 341.

flict, however, is but an insurrection, or rebellion. For insurrections and rebellions a specified method is provided in the Constitution—namely, the calling out of the State militia. To establish a draft in order to "suppress insurrection" is a dangerous innovation without constitutional warrant. In time of rebellion the Government should not imitate the rebels by violating the Constitution, but should stick to the fundamental law, so as not to dishearten the friends of constitutional order.

It was also urged that the Conscription Act was unconstitutional in that it subjected the citizen to martial law and overthrew fundamental guarantees intended to protect individual rights. Only when "in actual service," it was urged, can State militiamen be subjected to military discipline prescribed by Congress. To treat men as military deserters because they do not respond to the draft is to deny the right of trial by jury and to deprive them of various kindred guarantees.

In spite of these objections the national power was upheld by a strong preponderance of judicial opinion. That this is a government of limited powers was conceded; but, in language reminiscent of Hamilton, Marshall, and Webster, it was argued that the general government is supreme in those activities for which it was created, and that such powers as are granted may be exercised to an unlimited extent. The power to "declare war" and to "raise armies" are given without qualification as to means, and conscription is a "necessary and proper" means to "carry into effect" these powers. As to the intention of the "Fathers," history shows that the Constitution was created to correct one of the most flagrant defects of the old Articles of Confederation under which Congress was given power to declare war, but was powerless to conduct a war on its own authority, since it could only *request* troops from the States. It was to avoid this embarrassment that the general government was given an independent power to "raise . . . armies."

The army and the militia are distinct and separate, and the authority of Congress over the army is superior to the authority of the States over the militia. Ordinarily, there is no conflict between these two institutions and they may exist peaceably side by side; but in times of great emergency, when they do conflict, a local and subordinate power must always bow to a general power granted for vital purposes. Service in the State militia does not exhaust the liabilities of citizenship, and Congress is not deterred from calling a State militiaman into the army. It is true that the will of the people should be the controlling factor in these matters; but the people, through their representatives in Congress, must have the power to lay the burdens of national defense equally upon the willing and the unwilling. Abuse is to be avoided not by withholding this essential power, but by so shaping the general structure of the Government as to make it responsive to the popular will. In every free government the citizen must surrender some portion of his absolute right for the general good. The power of conscription must lie somewhere; and it can only lie with the National Government, which has the power of war and peace and the control of foreign relations, as well as the power of raising armies. The conscription law does not violate the clauses which guarantee jury trial and prohibit unreasonable seizures and searches. The drafted soldier is under military discipline, and the Constitution gives him no more protection against court-martial proceedings if he fails to report for duty than it gives a deserter from the army.

In the large sense, of course, it may be said that

the conscription law did stand the test of constitutionality. The law of 1863 was not challenged as to constitutionality before the Supreme Court. If this had happened it is unlikely that a Court which sustained the war power in the *Prize Cases*, and which withheld disapproval of the military trial of Vallandigham, would have taken the drastic wartime step of invalidating the national law for the raising of the army. Chief Justice Taney, however, would have done so. In fact he was, so to speak, loaded for the purpose.[59] Judicial doctrine as to compulsory military service has now been definitely settled in the *Selective Draft Law Cases* in which the validity of the Selective Service Act of 1917 was upheld. In delivering the opinion of the court in these cases Chief Justice White characterised the contention of the opposition as simply a denial to Congress of the power to raise armies which the Constitution gives and an assailing of the wisdom of the framers in conferring authority on Congress and not leaving it with the States. The army power he held to be in no way controlled by State functions concerning the militia, and he referred to the strengthening of the principle of national conscription by the Fourteenth Amendment which "broadened the national scope of the Government under the Constitution by causing citizenship of the United States to be paramount and dominant instead of being subordinate and derivative, . . ." In 1918, when this opinion of a unanimous court was announced, the country was much more willing to receive it than in Civil War times.[60]

---

[59]Taney actually prepared an opinion declaring the conscription act unconstitutional. It was, of course, undelivered, and remained for many years unpublished and virtually unknown. See P. G. Auchampaugh, *Tyler's Quar. Hist. and Geneal. Mag.*, XVIII, 72-87 (Oct. 1936).

[60]Selective Draft Law Cases (Arver *vs.* U. S., etc.), 245 U. S. 366.

CHAPTER XII

THE POLICY OF CONFISCATION

I

One of the questionable war measures adopted by both sides in the Civil War was the confiscation of the property of individuals adhering to the enemy.[1] Two laws for the forfeiture of enemy property were passed by the Confederate Congress, and the Government of the United States retaliated with two confiscation acts. Thus both belligerents carried the effects of war over into the field of civil life, and punished non-combatants with legal processes of doubtful validity.

By a Confederate statute of May 21, 1861, debts due to Northerners were confiscated; and a further act of August 30, 1861, sequestered the property of "aliens,"

[1]The basis for Chapters XII, XIII, and XIV is the writer's study entitled "The Confiscation of Property during the Civil War," a doctoral thesis presented to the University of Chicago in 1911. Only a minor part of the thesis was printed. The writer has published two articles on this subject: "Some Legal Aspects of the Confiscation Acts of the Civil War," *Am. Hist. Rev.*, XVIII, 79-96, and "Captured and Abandoned Property during the Civil War," *ibid.*, XIX, 65-79.

by which was meant those adhering to the Union.[2] In passing the act of August 6, 1861,[3] the United States Congress began its confiscation policy with a measure of limited scope directed only against property devoted to hostile use. Condemnation of such property was to take place in the district or circuit courts of the United States. The district attorney might institute proceedings; or any person might file an information with the attorney, in which latter case half the proceeds went to the informer.[4] Though this measure was eclipsed by the more comprehensive act of July 17, 1862, it remained law during the war.

The Federal confiscation law of 1862 differed both in degree and in kind from that of 1861; for it was a punitive measure directed against persons, taking their property by way of penalty, and it embraced in its terms all those who adhered to the "rebellion." The law was under consideration during the whole of the long session of the Thirty-Seventh Congress, and an amazing volume of oratory was poured forth in its discussion. Each member of House and Senate, it seemed, had a confiscation speech in his pocket; and so numerous were the orations on this subject that many members had to be content with "leave to print" their remarks in the appendix of the *Congressional Globe*, with the privilege of distributing printed copies to their constituents. The spirit animating the radicals who urged

---

[2]For the Confederate confiscation acts, see *Stat. at Large, Provis'l Gov't of C. S. A.*, 201; *O. R.*, Ser. IV, Vol. 1, p. 586; McPherson, *Political History of the Rebellion*, 205; Moore, *Rebellion Record*, IV, P. 7, VI, Diary of Events, 13; XII, Doc. 3 and Doc. 34; J. W. Draper, *Civil War in America*, I, 537; J. C. Schwab, *The Confederate States of America, A Financial and Industrial History of the South during the Civil War*, 110 *et seq.*

[3]*U. S. Stat. at Large*, XII, 319.

[4]A later portion of the act related to slaves used in hostilities against the United States. (*Infra*, p. 357.)

confiscation was expressed by Senator Morrill who declared that "clemency on the lips of an American Senator to the malignant enemy of the Republic is cruelty to its friends."[5] There was much extreme talk about punishing "rebels," crippling the financial resources of the Confederacy, and increasing Federal revenue; but on constitutional and legal matters there was little clear reasoning. To raise such points as the war power of Congress, the status of the "rebels," the legal character of the Civil War, the restrictions of the attainder clause of the Constitution, or the belligerent rights as against the municipal power of Congress, was to reveal a deplorable confusion of logic, and a jarring of opinions even among those who voted together. United in their notion as to the principal result sought, the supporters of confiscation, it would seem, had as many different views regarding the constitutional justification of their measure as there were individual speakers.

To the opponents of confiscation, who were chiefly border-State men and Democrats, such an extreme measure seemed a shocking thing. "Such a sweeping proposition," said Senator Carlile, "so unjust and cruel a measure, one better calculated to continue the war forever and exhaust the whole country, never has been in the history of the world, and I predict never will be again, proposed to any legislative assembly representing a civilized community."[6] "The sure and certain effect of this bill," said Senator Browning, "would be to make peace and reunion an impossible thing."[7] He argued that a majority of those acting against the Union were constrained by circumstances beyond their control; and he was in favor of measures that would win back his

[5] *Cong. Globe*, 37 Cong., 2 sess., p. 1074.
[6] *Ibid.*, p. 1157.
[7] *Ibid.*, p. 1137.

"brethren of the South" rather than fill them with despair. He further argued that the bill violated the attainder clause of the Constitution, and that measures should be taken against slavery as the sole cause of the war rather than indiscriminately against all property. Finally, after long months of debate during which each house was considering its own bill, conflicting purposes were adjusted by a conference committee of the Senate and House; and a measure was thus evolved which passed the two branches of Congress.[8]

As we have already seen, the law thus passed was at once a treason act and a confiscation act. The first four sections, relating to the crimes of treason and rebellion and prescribing punishments, have been treated in a previous chapter.[9] Under sections 5 and 6 the property of certain designated classes of "rebels" was made subject to forfeiture. A distinction was made between two main groups. The property of all officers of the Confederate Government whether civil, military, or naval, was declared seizable at once without qualification. Other persons in any part of the United States who were supporting the "rebellion" were to be warned by proclamation and given sixty days in which to return to their allegiance; if they failed to do so, their property was to be confiscated. Proceedings against suspected property were to be instituted in the Federal district or territorial courts, and the method of trial was to conform as nearly as might be to that of revenue or admiralty cases. If found to belong to a person who had engaged in the "rebellion," or who had given it aid and comfort, the goods were to be condemned "as enemies' property" and to become the property of the

---

[8] *U. S. Stat at Large*, XII, 589.

[9] Chapter IV.

United States.[10] The proceeds were to be paid into the treasury of the United States and applied to the support of the armies. Three sections referring to slaves do not concern us here. By section 13 the President was authorized to pardon those engaging in the rebellion.[11]

It is a fact of considerable interest that the second confiscation bill barely escaped the presidential veto.[12] Lincoln had never been enthusiastic for confiscation and he objected to several features of the proposed measure. He therefore prepared a rather elaborate veto message.[13] His strongest objection was that the title to real

[10]The "second Confiscation Act" covered three subjects: (1) the punishment of "treason" and "rebellion," sections 1 to 4; (2) confiscation of property, sections 5 to 8; and (3) emancipation of slaves, sections 9 to 12. Section 13 related to pardon and section 14 to the courts' power to carry the act into effect. A careful study shows that these three parts of the act were by no means closely articulated. For instance, the act nowhere attached any confiscation or forfeiture to a conviction for treason or rebellion. The penalty for treason was declared to be either death or a composite penalty of fine, imprisonment, emancipation of slaves and disqualification from office holding. Confiscation was provided not as a part of a criminal sentence against the person, but as a separate and distinct action *in rem* against "enemies'" (not traitors') property. Forfeiture did not begin with an indictment but with a libel of information as in revenue or admiralty cases. Furthermore, as we shall note later, the process prescribed for confiscating property was inapplicable to the case of slaves (e.g., the condemned property was to be "sold"); and the act was altogether hazy as to the method by which the liberation of slaves was to be accomplished. See *infra*, Chapter XV, and note the interesting remarks of Henry Winter Davis of Maryland in the *Congressional Globe*, 38 Cong., 1 sess., p. 214.

[11]In the Reconstruction period, when many eccentric things were done, Congress repealed this section (Act of Jan. 21, 1867, *U. S. Stat. at Large*, XIV, 377); but neither the repeal nor the original section affected the pardoning power of the President, which is derived not from Congress but from the Constitution.

[12]One of Lincoln's most valued friends, Senator Browning of Illinois, advised the President to veto the confiscation bill as unconstitutional and as an offense to the border States. (MS. Diary of Orville H. Browning, July 14, 1862.)

[13]Notwithstanding the fact that he signed the bill, Lincoln transmitted his veto message to Congress. (*Senate Journal*, July 17, 1862, pp. 872-874; Nicolay and Hay, *Works*, VII, 280-286.)

estate was to be forever extinguished. "For the causes of treason," he pointed out, "and the ingredients of treason not amounting to the full crime," the bill declared forfeitures extending beyond the lives of the guilty parties. This feature of the bill the President regarded as a violation of the attainder clause of the Constitution. The President's next objection showed an equally keen insight into legal points. He argued that by proceedings *in rem* the act would forfeit property "without a conviction of the supposed criminal, or a personal hearing given him in any proceeding." The act was punitive, yet the proceedings were all against the property, as in admiralty cases. This was unsatisfactory to the President, who felt that the owners should have a personal hearing.

When it was known in Congress that the President intended to veto the bill, a rather unusual proceeding was resorted to. A joint resolution, "explanatory" of the original measure, was rushed through both houses, declaring that the law was not to be construed as applying to acts done prior to its passage, nor as working "a forfeiture of the real estate of the offender beyond his natural life."[14] Although this left an important part of his objections untouched—i.e., as to the condemnation of property without allowing a personal hearing to the supposed criminal—Lincoln approved the measure in its modified form; and on the last day of the session, July 17, 1862, he signed the act and the explanatory resolution "as . . . substantially one."

II

These widely different measures of confiscation were put into operation side by side, and remained so dur-

[14] *U. S. Stat. at Large*, XII, 627.

ing the war. Though the act of 1862 was far more sweeping and drastic than that of 1861, yet it did not entirely supersede the earlier law; and prosecutions in a given case might be instituted under either act, or under both.[15] By the terms of each of the statutes the forfeiture of property was made a strictly judicial process, enforced through the Federal courts under the direction of the Attorney General and the district attorneys. The Senate substitute bill had contemplated a special board of commissioners to enforce confiscation, but this plan, which would have provided personnel and administrative machinery intended particularly for the seizure of property, was not followed.

In beginning suit, a libel of information, analogous to that directed against smuggled goods, would be filed by the district attorney. A monition or public advertisement would then be issued by the marshal, summoning the owner to appear in court and establish his loyalty. If the owner appeared to answer the libel, a hearing of both sides would usually follow, though there were cases where the owner was not permitted any hearing. Where the owner did not appear, an *ex parte* hearing was conducted. In case of condemnation, the marshal would be directed to sell the property at public auction, turning the proceeds, after payment of costs, into the public treasury.

The methods by which the Government obtained information concerning confiscable property were various.[16] Written depositions were sometimes taken by United States commissioners, but much of the information came from less regular and reliable sources. A citi-

[15]In the Wiley case (27 Fed. Cas. 337) the libel was under the act of 1861 and the proofs under that of 1862.

[16]The instances here cited are selected from data found in the corespondence of the Attorney General's office.

zen of Philadelphia, to take a typical instance, volunteers information concerning "a million dollars invested in the North by citizens of Charleston, S. C.," with the suggestion that this property is "probably confiscable," and that further particulars will be gladly given. Or, again, letters are received from citizens in Illinois and Wisconsin, alleging that the Hon. J. C. Breckinridge of Kentucky, the late Vice President, has considerable lands in those States, against which the Government should proceed. A district attorney in Minnesota proposes a trip to New Bern, N. C., for which he requests a Government pass that he may obtain evidence against several persons of high rank who own valuable property in Minnesota. The Union authorities intercept a letter written by a "rebel" prisoner in Washington to his uncle in Germany, and discover that this "rebel" owns considerable property in Memphis, Tennessee, then in the Union lines. A dispatch is received by the United States consul at St. Petersburg regarding "rebel" property in New Orleans, and the information is transmitted by Secretary of State Seward to Attorney General Bates. These scattered instances suggest how various were the sources, and how indirect the routes by which information came into the hands of the Government for purposes of confiscation. Sometimes useful clues would be secured in this irregular way, but no legal action could be safely begun without a laborious search for such records of ownership and such proof of disloyalty as would afford a definite basis for prosecution.

It was under great difficulties that the law officers performed their unwelcome duty of enforcing the confiscation laws. Confused by perplexing legal questions, the district attorneys received little help from the Attorney General, who invariably "declined to advise the law officers . . . as to what constitutes a proper case for action under the law."[17] The local officers, thus left to their own responsibility, naturally hesitated to begin suit; and this difficulty was augmented by the lack of provision for defraying the expense of preparing suit in cases where the Government should fail to obtain judgment. The very correctness and completeness of judicial procedure was an obstacle in a strenuous time when things had to be done quickly and when a dilatory execution would defeat the whole purpose of the law. It was natural under the circumstances for an impatient general or provost marshal to take the law into his own hands and thus become involved in a dispute with the judiciary. These vigorous men regarded confiscation as a war measure, and proceeded to carry it out as such.[18] It was on the whole fortunate that so formidable a power, and one that might have been so easily abused, had been carefully guarded by Congress.

In determining the authority of the court in any given case of confiscation, the leading factor was the location

---

[17]Acting Attorney General T. J. Coffee to R. I. Milton, U. S. Commissioner, Albany, N. Y., Sept. 2, 1861: Attorney General's Letter Books. (A series of such letters was issued to district attorneys and marshals during the same month. The one cited is merely typical.)

[18]Instances of military efforts to enforce confiscations were numerous. When a provost marshal at St. Louis seized securities owned by a suspected "rebel," his action was denounced by the acting Attorney General as "unjustifiable, absurd, illegal, and null." (Acting Attorney General Coffee to Acting Secretary of War Scott, Nov. 12, 1861, Attorney General's Letter Books.) An attempt by the military governor of the District of Columbia to seize the furniture of John A. Campbell led to a miniature state of war between court officers attempting to execute a writ of replevin to restore the property and a military force of six men who guarded it. (*House Ex. Doc. No. 44*, 37 Cong., 3 sess.) Determined attempts were made by General Wallace in Maryland and General Butler in Louisiana to carry out the confiscation acts, and the naval authorities also made extensive seizures in their river expeditions. (*O. R.*, Ser. III, Vol. 4, pp. 407 *et seq.*, Ser. I, Vol. 15, pp. 571 *et seq.*; Ser. I, Vol. 34, pt. 1, p. 213; Mrs. Alexander's Cotton, 2 Wall. 404-408; *Cong. Globe*, 37 Cong., 3 sess., pp. 1431 *et seq.*)

of the property. Jurisdiction, in other words, depended on *situs*. The court could proceed against only such property as lay within the bounds of its district. A district court in New York, for instance, could not acquire jurisdiction over the stock of an Illinois corporation.[19] Actual confiscation was therefore limited to those districts where Federal courts were in operation; and naturally the greater amount of the property seized during the war was located in the North, though owned by "rebels."

Actual seizure or "arrest" of the property was necessary in order to begin suit, but minor irregularities in the marshal's action were not construed as fatal defects. Since manual seizure was impossible in the case of intangible property, a sort of "stoppage at the source" was adopted. The court ignored the paper evidence of the property in the hands of the owner, and proceeded by means of attachments upon those from whom the obligation was due. A promissory note would be "seized" by notifying the signer, possession of the note itself being unnecessary. Where the property consisted of commercial stock, seizure meant serving notice upon the corporation. In the case of a debt owed by an individual, process was served upon the debtor, subjecting him to the order of the court with regard to the debt. A debt owed by a city could be seized by serving notice upon the proper officer of the City. For the seizure of a deposit due by a Northern to a Southern bank, an attachment upon the deposit with notification to one of the officers of the Southern bank was sufficient.[20]

---

[19] U. S. *vs.* 1756 Shares of Stock, 27 Fed. Cas. 337.

[20] Concerning procedure in confiscation cases, see Tyler *vs.* Defrees, 78 U. S. 331; Instructions of Attorney General Bates to district attorneys, *Ann. Cyc.*, 1863, p. 219; Bragg *vs.* Lorio, 4 Fed. Cas. 2; Miller *vs.* U. S., 78 U. S. 268.

In developing a procedure for the trial of confiscation cases, the courts were confronted with the fact that forfeiture is ordinarily a proceeding *in rem* and that admiralty procedure was indicated in both of the acts, while at the same time the punitive character of the second Confiscation Act seemed to call for those features of criminal procedure that are intended as safeguards for the accused. Strict conformity to admiralty rules was given up and the advantages of a common law remedy were extended to the defendant. Judgments of lower courts were sometimes overruled by the Supreme Court on the ground that the proceedings had been erroneously conducted on the admiralty instead of the common law side of the court.[21] The main resemblance to admiralty practice lay in the detailed process of instituting suit—i.e., the filing of the libel, the seizure by the marshal, the publication of the monition, and the summoning of the owner—and in the *ex parte* hearing in case of default.

---

[21]The chief reason for insisting on the common law remedy was to preserve the right of trial by jury. It was therefore held that, in cases where either party should demand it, issues of fact should be so tried. This point was definitely expressed in the case of United States *vs.* Athens Armory: "This court [*i.e.*, the Supreme Court] cannot undertake to say that the national legislature in passing this statute [the act of 1862] contemplated the expansion of the jurisdiction of the admiralty so far beyond what was understood and intended by it at the time of the formation of the Constitution, as to withdraw from the suitor, in a seizure like this, the right of a trial by jury, and to transfer the determination of the cause to the breast of a single judge." (24 Fed. Cas. 881.) This preservation of a common law remedy was demanded not only on the grounds of general justice but also as a compliance with that clause of the Judiciary Act of 1789 which provided that practice in the district courts in connection with forfeitures should be such as to save to suitors in all cases the right to a common law remedy, where the common law is competent to give it. (*U. S. Stat. at Large,* I, 76; The Case of Moses Taylor, 71 U. S. 411. See also: Union Ins. Co. *vs.* U. S., 6 Wall. 759; Armstrong's Foundry, 6 Wall. 767; U. S. *vs.* Hart, 6 Wall. 770, 773 n., Morris' Cotton, 8 Wall. 507.)

III

When the actual effects of forfeiture came to be determined in the courts, there were various problems that had to be settled. A matter of considerable dispute, for instance, was the question as to the duration of the forfeiture under the act of 1862. Though Congress had taken pains to be explicit on this point, passing an explanatory resolution which limited the forfeiture to the offender's lifetime, there still remained some doubt as to whether decrees of confiscation involved surrender of the full title or of merely a life interest.[22] This difficulty was met by the Supreme Court in the case of *Bigelow* vs. *Forrest*, in which it was decided that a decree of condemnation and order of sale under the second Confiscation Act conveyed only a "right to the property . . . terminating with the life of the person for whose act it had been seized."[23] No title could therefore be conferred which would outlast the life of the original offender.

As to forfeitures under the act of 1861, their effect was held to be absolute, permitting no recovery of the property by the owner's heirs.[24] The reasoning of the Su-

---

[22]A Federal judge in Virginia held that the absolute forfeiture of real estate was in keeping with the intention of the Constitution and the statute. Congress did not mean, he declared, that the "traitor" should merely surrender a life interest, but rather that the forfeiture must be perfected during his life. As for the joint resolution, he interpreted it as merely intended to keep the legislation within the constitutional rights of Congress which permit no attainder of treason that shall work corruption of blood or forfeiture *except during* the life of the person attainted. In his mind the words "except during" applied to the specific legal act by which the forfeiture was accomplished, rather than to its duration. (Opinion of Judge Underwood in the Hugh Latham case: *Ann. Cyc.*, 1863, p. 221.)

[23]9 Wall. 339.

[24]Kirk *vs.* Lynd, 106 U. S. 315.

preme Court in this connection emphasized the difference in the nature of the two acts. Whereas proceedings under the act of 1862 were directed against the owner because the statute declared his acts to be crimes, the proceedings under the act of 1861 were directed merely against the property. Nothing was said about treason in the earlier act; therefore the principles of attainder would not apply. Condemnations under this act were based upon the hostile use of the property, and were regarded as analogous to the condemnation of goods for smuggling. This interpretation was held to require the whole title to be surrendered.

Since under the second Confiscation Act the forfeiture terminated with the offender's life, a further question arose as to his "reversionary right." A deed to the life estate in a piece of realty obtained at a confiscation sale would not carry a title in fee to the property, since the heirs of the "rebel" owner would have a future interest which would take effect upon his death. Such a situation affords an example of a "reversion" which has been defined as the estate left in a party after he has conveyed away less than a fee. This naturally involves a "reversionary tenant"—i.e., a holder of the future rights which revert when the user's interest terminates.

It is well understood in realty law that such a reversionary right in property is marketable, and may be transferred. The question arose frequently whether, after confiscation had been completed, the dispossessed "rebel" could still consider himself as the holder and possible conveyer of that remaining share in the estate which subsisted after the life interest had been transferred. It is clear that if he could convey this expectant right the penalty of forfeiture would be much less severe.

In dealing with this phase of confiscation the Supreme

Court reversed its own position. The provision limiting the duration of the forfeiture was at first interpreted as an advantage to the heirs alone; and it was held in *Wallach* vs. *Van Riswick*[25] that the offender had no power to dispose of the future title of his property. This ruling was softened after the war by an opinion to the effect that the disability to dispose of the permanent title was removed by pardon; and finally, the court criticized its own opinion in the Wallach case and held that the offender, by covenant of warranty, could convey a permanent future assurance of title which would hold good against the claims of his heirs.[26]

IV

To what extent were the confiscation acts enforced, and how much property was confiscated? The answer to this question seems paradoxical; for the courts handled a considerable volume of business under the head of confiscation, and yet the results were insignificant. As there were hundreds of treason indictments but no punishments, so there were many confiscation cases, but only a small amount of property confiscated.[27] One must take

---

[25] 92 U. S. 202.

[26] Avengo *vs.* Schmidt, 113 U. S. 293; Shields *vs.* Schiff, 124 U. S. 351; Ill. Cent. R. R. *vs.* Bosworth, 133 U. S. 92; Jenkins *vs.* Collard, 145 U. S. 552.

[27] Of the eighty-three cases of confiscation shown on the dockets of the Federal district court in Indianapolis from September, 1862, to May, 1865, forty-four resulted in forfeiture. The property was miscellaneous in character, including considerable movable and intangible property besides real estate. From these forfeitures the United States derived the meager sum of $5,737. In the District of Columbia from May, 1863, when condemnations began, to September, 1865, the number of cases docketed was fifty-two, and the number of forfeitures twenty-seven. The total proceeds amounted to $33,265. These data were derived from the Federal court records at Indianapolis and Washington, from which elaborate notes were taken by the writer.

Amounts Deposited in the United States Treasury as Net Proceeds of the Confiscation of Property under the Act of July 17, 1862

District	Amount deposited in U. S. Treasury	Amount paid to Assistant U. S. Treasurer subject to order of court
New York	$19,614.84	....
Delaware	347.73	....
District of Columbia	....	$33,265.48*
West Virginia	11,000.00	....
Kentucky	7,305.17	....
East Tennessee	242.21	....
East Missouri	1,411.30	....
Southern Ohio	4,853.57	....
Louisiana	67,972.18	....
Indiana	5,737.99	....
Michigan	4,000.15	....
Arkansas	7,195.53	....
Total	$129,680.67	$33,265.48

*The money for the District of Columbia cases never passed to the credit of the United States, and was ultimately restored to the owners by order of the court.

account of the cases "dismissed," "appealed," "settled without suit," or in which the judgment was for the owner; and even in the case of forfeitures the proceeds turned into the treasury were no adequate measure of the sums involved. The costs attached to the filing and publication of the libel, and the fees charged by district attorneys, clerks and marshals, substantially reduced the balance remaining to the United States.[28]

[28]In one of the District of Columbia cases the marshal's return of sale showed that the property yielded $3600, but the fees of the district attorney, marshal and clerk, together with incidental expenses, amounted to $664, leaving a balance of $2936. The district attorney alone received $340 in this case. A similar return in Indiana showed proceeds of $202, and the costs were exactly equivalent to the proceeds. (U. S. District Court Files, Washington and Indianapolis.)

The table on page 289 indicates in condensed form the results of forfeitures under the confiscation statute of 1862 as reported by the Solicitor of the Treasury in 1867.[29] There are certain omissions in this report. None of the Virginia confiscations are reported, though the records show 1149 cases at Richmond, Alexandria, and Norfolk. A controversy existed regarding the Virginia forfeitures owing to the dishonesty of the clerk whose default to the United States treasury amounted to $110,000, while the proceeds he turned in amounted to $23,000.[30] In addition, there were many forfeitures in Kansas but no proceeds turned in.[31] Moreover, in some districts which do not appear in the Solicitor's report, because they yielded no proceeds, there was considerable activity in the application of the confiscation laws. Even in such sparsely settled regions as New Mexico[32] and Nevada,[33] which were hardly more than mining camps, the disturbance due to attempted confiscations required considerable attention from the Washington authorities. Cases under the first Confiscation Act are also omitted;

---

[29]*Sen. Doc. No. 58*, 40 Cong., 2 sess.

[30]Though the clerk received $93,937 as proceeds from the Richmond cases and $39,334 from those at Norfolk, his only return to the United States treasury was for $23,000. (U. S. treasury warrant No. 410, June 30, 1864.) There are numerous unpublished papers concerning the Virginia confiscations in the "Cotton and Captured Property Record" of the Treasury Department.

[31]The correspondence of the Attorney General's office with the Federal district attorney in Kansas shows that the attempts made at Washington to obtain satisfactory reports of the Kansas confiscation cases were unsuccessful. (Letter Book C [1863], Attorney General's Office, p. 185.) Irregularities in this connection were commented upon by the Supreme Court in Osborn *vs.* U. S. (91 U. S. 474.)

[32]Correspondence regarding seizures in New Mexico may be found in the Attorney General's files under the following dates: Sept. 27, 1862; Jan. 1, 1863; Mar. 28, 1863; Aug. 9, 1863. A considerable controversy arose over the seizure of the mines of Sylvester Mowry in this territory.

[33]Report of T. D. Edwards, District Attorney for Nevada: Attorney General's Papers, June 24, 1864.

but these were much less numerous than those under the later and more sweeping act, and, being closely analogous to the seizure of contraband property, they were distinct in principle from the main body of confiscations. If we make allowances for these omissions we find that approximately $300,000 can be accounted for as proceeds from confiscation sales.[34]

When all has been said, however, it is clear that there was not a sufficiently diligent and systematic enforcement of the acts to produce any marked effect other than a feeling of irritation and injury on the part of a few despoiled owners.[35] Confident predictions of the supporters of confiscation as to the material weakening of the enemy's resources were doomed to disappointment. Financially, then, confiscation was a failure, while the other purpose of the act, that of punishing "rebels," was unequally and unjustly accomplished. No practical object in the prosecution of the war was achieved by

[34]The sum to be added from Virginia would include the amount of the clerk's default (nearly $110,000), together with the amount which he paid into the treasury ($23,000), this latter amount not having been counted in the Solicitor's report. The amount of $30,000 may be allowed for the Kansas cases.

[35]In addition to seizures under the confiscation acts, forfeitures of property were effected by various other methods during the Civil War. Large amounts of cotton were taken under the Captured and Abandoned Property Act, and much real estate in the South was forfeited for failure to pay the Federal direct tax. (These matters are discussed below, in Chapter XIV.) Military captures were governed by the laws of war which protected private property and denounced pillage. The following rule was included in the instructions issued to regulate the conduct of the Union armies in the field: "Private property, unless forfeited by crimes or by offenses of the owner, can be seized only by way of military necessity for the support or other benefit of the Army or of the United States." The owner was to be given receipts so that he might at a future time obtain indemnity. (*O. R.*, Ser. III, Vol. 3, pp. 148 *et seq.*, 152, 686.) Property was condemned for violation of the non-intercourse regulations; and the property of the Confederate Government, on this continent and in Europe, was appropriated wherever possible. No formal confiscation was necessary for such property. (U. S. *vs.* Tract of Land, 28 Fed. Cas. 203.)

appropriating the private property of a few unoffending noncombatants. The whole experience pertaining to the Civil War confiscations was such as to condemn the policy of promoting war by extreme punitive measures for the coercion of individuals.

CHAPTER XIII

THE RIGHT OF CONFISCATION

I. Position of the Supreme Court regarding the belligerent right of confiscation
II. Views of authorities on international law
III. Opinions of American jurists
IV. Special case of the confiscation of debts
V. The "rebel's" standing in court
VI. Constitutionality of the Confiscation Acts

We turn now to some of the broader questions of right and justice which the confiscation policy involved. Opinion on this subject was most diverse at the very time when the cases were most numerous, and when, therefore, the pressure upon the judicial authorities was heaviest. The final settlement of these mooted questions did not occur until after the war; in some cases so long afterward that the issue was practically dead, and little benefit could be derived from the decisions as guides to the lower tribunals. When during the war we find doubt on such fundamental points as the constitutionality of the law itself, and the question as to whether a supposed "rebel" could be heard in his own defense, we need no longer wonder that judicial action in these cases was so often unsatisfactory. If in addition we remember that during the war both Congress and the courts did their work under heavy pressure, and sometimes in haste and confusion, we can better understand such miscarriages of justice as the confiscation acts produced.

I

When we come to consider the right of a belligerent under international law to confiscate enemy's property, we are confronted with a difference of opinion among authorities, and a divergence between the abstract legal rule and the actual modern practice of leading nations. While the confiscation policy was under discussion both sides appealed to the law of nations in support of their contentions. As is usual in such controversies, much would have been gained if the direct issue had been clearly stated and kept in mind. Freed from its entanglements, the question amounts to this: Has a belligerent in a public war the right under the law of nations to confiscate private property within its jurisdiction belonging to individuals among the enemy? In its actual discussion, however, the issue was confused; and it is necessary to take account of the misapprehensions and inaccuracies as well as the reasonable differences of opinion among the legislators in order to assess the confiscation debates at their true value.

Throughout the discussion there was commonly a failure to discriminate between a general confiscation of property within the jurisdiction of the confiscating government, and the treatment accorded by advancing armies to private property found within the limits of military occupation.[1] Opponents of confiscation errone-

[1]The argument of Garret Davis of Kentucky in the Senate illustrates this erroneous use of authorities. Speaking on the Senate bill, he quoted Wheaton as follows: "Private property on land is exempt from confiscation with the exception of such as may become booty in special cases . . . and of military contributions. This exemption extends even to an absolute . . . conquest of the enemy's country." It is plain that Wheaton here referred to military seizure. (*Cong. Globe*, April 22, 1862, 37 Cong., 2 sess., p. 1759; Wheaton, *International Law* [Boyd's 3d ed.], 467.)

ously appealed to the general rule exempting private property on land from the sort of capture which similar property must suffer at sea, and the substantial merits of their main case were thus obscured by irrelevant arguments. The exemption of private property on land is a principle governing armies in their operations. The illegality of military capture on land analogous to prizes at sea was so obvious and so well recognized that it would hardly require continual reaffirmation. This sort of capture was altogether distinct from forfeitures under the confiscation acts, by which the Government attacked through its courts such enemy property as might be available within its limits.[2] It is this general forfeiture by judicial process which should be borne in mind while discussing the belligerent right of confiscation as applied during the Civil War.

The Supreme Court in the leading confiscation case, *Miller* vs. *United States*, construed the acts as the exercise of a war power, not as a municipal regulation.[3] Without arguing the points of law involved, the court plainly rested the authorization for the acts upon the law of nations. On this broad basis confiscation was sustained as "an undoubted belligerent right." Stress was laid upon the use of the expression "enemies' property"[4] in the act of 1862. The fact that the earlier sections of the act referred to treason and rebellion was not under-

---

[2]This citation of the rule against military captures as if it applied to forfeitures under the Federal confiscation acts occurs also in Dunning, *Essays on the Civil War and Reconstruction, and Related Topics*, 31-32.

[3]11 Wall. 268.

[4]The court thus treated the condemnation of "enemies'" property as a matter quite different from the infliction of a criminal penalty of confiscation upon "rebels." It is difficult to discover the "intention of the legislators" on this point. Those who passed the act did not all intend the same thing, and some were not even aware of the distinction.

stood by the court as removing the legislation from the category of regular belligerent measures. The conflict was held to be as truly a public war as if waged between two independent nations, and those engaged in it were therefore public enemies.

Were we concerned merely with finding the authoritative American doctrine regarding the belligerent right of confiscation, we would need to go no further than the Miller decision; since it stands as the pronouncement of the highest tribunal in the country. We should not overlook the fact, however, that the decision rested upon a presumption which has caused much controversy and honest difference of opinion. The question was a fair one whether the right of confiscation could be clearly supported on the basis of the law of nations, and this was a point of larger importance and greater difficulty than would be indicated by the off-hand assertion of the court that Congress was exercising "an undoubted belligerent right." Our courts have regularly accepted international law as a "part of our law";[5] and while a law of Congress would hardly be ruled out on the ground that it violated international law, care is usually taken to consider as carefully as possible the rules of international law whenever they bear upon a given case, and even to interpret laws in the light of these rules.[6] It will therefore aid our historical appreciation of the confiscation policy if we view it side by side with the legal principles which had been developing in Continental countries and in America on the subject.

---

[5]It is the developed and advanced principles of international law that have become a part of our law. In Ware *vs.* Hylton, 3 Dallas 281, Justice Wilson said: "When the United States declared their independence, they were bound to receive the law of nations in its modern state of purity and refinement." See also Hilton *vs.* Guyot, 159 U. S. 163, and The Paquette *Habana*, 175 U. S. 700.

[6]Chief Justice Marshall in *The Charming Betsy*, 2 Cranch 118.

II

The chief Continental writers on international law whose opinion would carry weight in America were, perhaps, Grotius, Vattel, Bynkershoek, Burlamaqui, Rutherford, and Pufendorf. Grotius, the pioneer authority in the field of modern international law, could, of course, be cited in support of many extreme measures of warfare which advanced usage has discarded. Drawing his views from a wide range of ancient and medieval sources, he allows to a belligerent very extensive powers over the persons and property of the enemy. In that section of his *De Jure Belli* which deals with the treatment of enemy property on land, Grotius dwells chiefly upon rights of conquest, distribution of spoils and booty, and the relative share of individuals and governments in goods obtained by military seizure. In his closest approach to the subject of confiscation as understood in the Civil War, he remarks, without any indication of approval, that enemy goods found among us at the outbreak of war" become usually the property of the persons in possession, not of the State, thus taking for granted the right of appropriation. He then refers without comment to a startling passage in the old Roman jurist Tryphonius, declaring that persons found in a foreign country become, on the sudden outbreak of war, the slaves of those among whom they are found. Referring to the existing variety of regulations in different nations, he points out that in some countries it may "be introduced as a rule of law for the whole of an enemy's goods found there to be confiscated." We may quote Grotius, then, as authority for the belligerent right of confiscation, but in so doing we must remember that the tone of his work is often that of reluctant statement of unregenerate practice.[7]

Vattel threw the force of his great influence upon the side of the milder practice and insisted that, as a matter of public faith, it was the duty of a sovereign declaring war to protect both the persons and property of enemy subjects within his dominions. He wrote:

> War now being carried on with so much moderation and indulgence, safeguards are allowed to houses and lands possessed by foreigners in an enemy's country. For the same reason he who declares war does not confiscate the immovable goods possessed in his country by his enemy's subjects. In permitting them to purchase and possess those goods he has in this respect admitted them into the number of his subjects. But the income may be sequestered, for hindering the remittance of it to the enemy's country.[8]

Bynkershoek stated in its bald severity the extreme view of the rights of a belligerent over the enemy. He said: "Since it is a condition of war that enemies, by every right, may be plundered and seized upon, it is reasonable that whatever effects of the enemy are found with us who are his enemy, should change their master and be confiscated, or go into the treasury."[9]

Burlamaqui treated of military and naval captures and did not make clear his position as to confiscation proper. In his view large powers over the goods of an enemy were conferred by the laws of war. His mixture of legal rules with "natural right" philosophy, and his loose statement of principles, render him valueless as a

---

[7]Grotius, *De Jure Belli ac Pacis*, Lib. III, Cap. vi, sec. xiii.

[8]Vattel, *Laws of Nations* (Luke White ed., Dublin, 1792), Bk. III, sec. 76.

[9]Bynkershoek, *Quaestiones Juris Publici* (1737), Lib. I, Cap. 7, p. 175.

serious authority, but he was nevertheless quoted in support of the right of confiscation.[10]

In Rutherford we find no direct treatment of the subject. He discussed the taking of property as an equivalent for damages and expenses, or to bring the other nation "to do what is right," and such a seizure in his view implied an obligation to return the goods when satisfaction had been given for the injury done. His general attitude resembles that of Burlamaqui.[11]

Pufendorf confined his remarks on the treatment of private property in war to the subject of captures, on which his opinions were humane and conservative, derived as they were from the natural right philosophers, from Grotius, and from modern history. What he said on the subject of booty, captures, and the levy of contributions upon inhabitants of territory in hostile occupation should not have been cited as applying to the question of general confiscation at all; but he was nevertheless so quoted, as for instance by Justice Story, dissenting, in *Brown* vs. *United States*.[12]

A study of these earlier writers fails to reveal any noticeable preponderance of legal opinion on the side of confiscation as a belligerent right. Vattel and Pufendorf favored the more humane practice; Burlamaqui and Rutherford did not deal with confiscation in the broader sense; Grotius stated the extreme right of the belligerent over the enemy's property without indicating approval; and Bynkershoek was almost alone in referring to confiscation as a "reasonable" practice. To derive from

[10]Burlamaqui, *Principles of Natural and Political Science* (Nugent trans., Boston, 1792), 375 *et seq.;* Cited by Story (dissenting) in Brown *vs.* U. S., 8 Cranch 143, and by Chase in Ware *vs.* Hylton, 3 Dallas 226.

[11]Rutherford, *Institutes of Natural Law* (2nd. Amer. ed., 1832), Ch. ix, *passim.*

[12]Pufendorf, *Droit de la Nature et des Gens,* Lib. VIII, Ch. v. sec. xvii *et seq.;* Story's dissenting opinion in Brown *vs.* U. S., 8 Cranch 143.

these writers any substantial authority for the form of confiscation adopted during the Civil War requires, to say the least, a rather sympathetic editing.

III

Turning now to the views of American jurists, we find a convenient starting point in the case of *Ware* vs. *Hylton*, argued before the Supreme Court in 1796.[13] The matter at issue was the right of Virginia, on the authority of a State law of sequestration passed during the Revolution, to seize debts due to British subjects and prevent their recovery after the war. The case is of interest because it called forth expressions by prominent American lawyers concerning the belligerent right of confiscation. John Marshall, arguing for Virginia's claim, regarded it as unquestioned "that independent nations have in general the right of confiscation."[14] In the same case Justice Chase declared that every nation at war with another is authorized "by the general and strict law of nations, to seize and confiscate all movable property of its enemy (of any kind or nature whatsoever) wherever found, whether within its territory or not."[15]

But perhaps the most important early American decision on confiscation was that in *Brown* vs. *United States*,[16] rendered by Chief Justice Marshall in 1814, and taken by many as the most authoritative interpretation of the American law on the subject down to the time of the Civil War. A British cargo had been seized at the outbreak of the War of 1812, and Marshall treated the controversy as one relating to the general class of "British property found on land at the commencement

[13] 3 Dallas 199.
[14] *Ibid.*, p. 210.
[15] *Ibid.*, p. 226.
[16] 8 Cranch 110.

of hostilities." Basing his rather sweeping conclusion upon the *ex parte* citation of authorities submitted by the counsel for the appellant, Marshall wrote: "It may be considered as the opinion of all who have written on the *jus belli* that war gives the right to confiscate but does not itself confiscate the property of the enemy." A special act, so the court held, was necessary to authorize seizures; and, since no such act had been passed relating to the War of 1812, the property was released. This release of the property, it should be noted, takes from the case such force as it might have had if a specific act of confiscation had been sustained. Justice Story went further than Marshall and maintained in his dissenting opinion that the right of confiscation vested at once in the executive without express statutory provision. Both Marshall and Story were positive as to the abstract right; but when one traces the authorities which these men quoted, he is likely to find treatments of capture, or booty, or the levy of contributions —topics quite distinct from confiscation.

Certain recognized treatise writers touched upon the subject of confiscation. Chancellor Kent, whose *Commentaries on American Law* first appeared in 1826, based his treatment of the question upon the Brown decision which he considered as definitely settling the point for the United States "in favor of the sterner rule," but qualified his statement by referring to modern authority and practice which was contrary to the "right."[17]

Wheaton, on the other hand, directing his attention to the practice of modern nations rather than to strict legal rules, reached the opinion that "property of the enemy found within the territory of the belligerent State, or debts due to his subjects by the government or indi-

[17]James Kent, *Commentaries on American Law* (11th ed.), I, 66-67.

viduals at the commencement of hostilities, are not liable to be seized and confiscated as prizes of war." He added, however, that the rule is "not inflexible"; that it depends largely upon treaty stipulations; and that "like other precepts of morality, of humanity, and even of wisdom, it is addressed to the judgment of the sovereign—it is a guide which he follows or abandons at his will; and although it cannot be disregarded by him without obloquy, yet it may be disregarded."[18]

Taking Wheaton's interpretation, then, the Federal Congress, in adopting the confiscation policy at the time of the Civil War, was setting aside a "not inflexible" rule of humane usage as a retaliatory measure against the Confederate Government which had sequestered Northern debts and property; while, according to the views of Marshall, Story, and Kent, it was acting in harmony with its strict legal rights as a belligerent power.[19]

---

[18]Henry Wheaton, *Elements of International Law* (Lawrence's 6th ed., Boston, 1855), Part iv, Ch. i, p. 369.

[19]It may not be amiss to observe the light in which confiscation has been regarded by later authorities. F. H. Geffcken, in his edition of the treatise by the Berlin professor, Heffter, strongly denounces confiscation, though Heffter himself supported the practice. Hall incorrectly refers to the Confederate Act of Sequestration of August, 1861, as the only instance of confiscation since Napoleon, thus ignoring the Federal confiscation acts. He characterizes confiscation as a "dying right" which he hopes "will never again be put in force." Lawrence follows Hall, repeating his error as to the Confederacy furnishing the only instance of confiscation since Napoleon, and denounces the practice with even more emphasis. He says: "We may join the great majority of Continental publicists in the assertion that the International Law of our own time does not permit the confiscation of the private property of enemy subjects found on the land territory of the State at the outbreak of war." Woolsey states the American rule that enemy private property is confiscable by strict legal right, but expresses the hope that the national legislature will "never consent to disgrace the country by an act of that kind." During the first World War the property of persons residing in Germany and of interned aliens in this country was taken over by the Alien Property Custodian of the United States under the authority of the Trading with the Enemy Act. This

IV

There is a particular phase of confiscation which is quite distinct in principle from other kinds of forfeiture—namely, the confiscation of debts. Both the Confederate sequestration law, and the Federal Confiscation Act of 1862 applied to debts, the difference between the two measures being partly a matter of enforcement, and partly one of emphasis in the statutes themselves. The language of the Confederate statute and the machinery devised for its enforcement indicated an intention to apply the law chiefly to intangible forms of property, and debts due from citizens in the South to Northern creditors formed a large portion of the property contemplated for seizure. In the Federal law, however, the seizure of debts, though authorized by the broad wording of the statute, was but incidental. Southern planters were financially dependent upon Northern brokers and bankers, through whom they made purchases and realized in advance upon the income from their crops marketed abroad. The balance of indebtedness was consequently unfavorable to the South. According to Schwab, the most careful estimate of the outstanding indebted-

has been treated as temporary custody rather than as confiscation. The joint resolution of July, 1921, declaring peace with Germany, provided that all such property should be retained by the United States until satisfactory action should be taken by the German government concerning American claims, and the latest report of the Custodian shows that the major portion of this property has been returned. In commenting on this subject, J. W. Garner writes with disapproval of the practice of confiscation. (Heffter, *Le Droit International de l' Europe* [Geffcken ed., trans. by Bergson], 310, editor's note: W. E. Hall, *International Law* [7th ed., Oxford, 1917], pp. 462-464; T. J. Lawrence, *Principles of International Law* [7th ed.], pp. 402-404; Theodore D. Woolsey, *Introduction to the Study of International Law* [5th ed., N. Y., 1879], p. 203; Arthur G. Hays, *Enemy Property in America* [Albany, 1923], pp. 52, 54, 68, 174; J. W. Garner, *International Law and the World War*, I, 104-105.)

ness of the South to the North in 1861 placed the amount at forty million dollars. Though the amount actually sequestered did not exceed $380,000 in gold, yet the potential effects of the law were very great.[20] It is not suggested, of course, that one section was any more blameworthy than the other in the adoption of this policy, for both sides were using the same weapon.

Confiscation of debts is even harder to defend as a belligerent right than the seizure of tangible property. Even so early a writer as Vattel pointed out that "in regard to the advantage and safety of commerce, all the sovereigns of Europe have departed from this rigor." Seizure of debts would, according to Vattel, be so injurious to public faith as to affect very seriously the freedom and security of international business relations.[21]

In *Brown* vs. *United States*, Story thus stated what he regarded as the principle prevailing in 1814: "On a review of the authorities I am entirely satisfied that, by the rigor of the law of nations and of the common law, the sovereign of a nation may lawfully confiscate the debts of his enemy, during war or by way of reprisal; and . . . I think this opinion fully confirmed by the judgment of the Supreme Court in *Ware* vs. *Hylton*, . . . where the doctrine was explicitly asserted by some of the judges, reluctantly admitted by others, and denied by none."[22] Story's interpretation of the opinions in *Ware* vs. *Hylton* overlooks the fact that Justices Patterson and Wilson argued against the reputableness of the practice, while Cushing did not touch the question.

[20] J. C. Schwab, *The Confederate States of America*, III, 120. On the South's financial indebtedness to the North one should consult also, but with caution, T. P. Kettel, *Southern Wealth and Northern Profits* (N. Y., 1861), and *DeBow's Review*, XX, 744; XXI, 308; XXII, 623; XXIII, 225.

[21] Vattel, *op. cit.*, III, 5, 77.

[22] 8 Cranch 142.

Only Chase and Iredell gave their full support to the right. The following was Judge Patterson's comment: "The truth is that the confiscation of debts is at once unjust and impolitic; it destroys confidence, violates good faith, and injures the interests of commerce; it is . . . in most cases impracticable."[23] The odium attaching to the seizure of debts was well stated in 1814 by Davis, arguing for the appellant in *Brown* vs. *United States*: "It seems to be now perfectly settled by the modern law and practice of nations that debts are never to be confiscated; that it has become a disgraceful act in any government that does it; that these debts are suspended, and the right to recover them necessarily taken away by the war; but that upon the return of peace, the debts are revived, and the right to recover them perfectly restored."[24]

Even as far back as Magna Carta, debts and property of foreign merchants in England were protected at the outbreak of war in return for reciprocal guarantees from other countries,[25] while the commercial ascendancy of England in modern times has inclined her toward the policy of leaving enemies' debts untouched. The disastrous consequences of the failure of an attempted sequestration of debts, such as that undertaken by Napoleon against England, might have served as a signal for caution; for in the settlement concluded at Paris in May, 1814, indemnity was exacted for the French confiscation of English debts.[26] Even in the case of the confiscations

[23] 3 Dallas 254.

[24] 8 Cranch 118.

[25] *Magna Carta*, Cap. 41. G. B. Adams and H. Morse Stephens, *Select Documents of English Constitutional History*, 47. For a commentary on this subject, see Kent, *Commentaries* (11th ed.), I, 66.

[26] For the satisfaction of these debts France assumed an annuity of 3,000,000 francs, representing a capital of 60,000,000 francs. (Additional Articles between France and Great Britain to the Treaty of Paris,

by the American States during the Revolution, and in spite of American success, the final adjustment of the matter involved the payment by the United States Government of a round sum for the satisfaction of British creditors. In 1796 the Supreme Court of the United States decreed that a British debt confiscated by Virginia during the Revolution should be recovered in British sterling with interest computed from July 7, 1782, the date of the preliminary treaty between Great Britain and the United States.[27] Jay's treaty had previously provided for the final adjustment of these debts by a commission; and after a temporary suspension of the commission a settlement of the matter was finally made in January, 1802, requiring the payment of $2,664,000 by the United States Government.[28]

Perhaps the best indication of the practical necessity of exempting debts from seizure is to be found in the well-established practice among modern nations of exchanging treaty guarantees that in event of war debts will not be sequestered. In Jay's treaty of 1794 the clause providing for such exemption was more than a stipulation; it was a declaration of principle. After providing against the sequestration of private debts, the treaty proceeded as follows: "it being unjust and impolitic that debts and engagements, contracted and made by individuals having confidence in each other and in their respective governments, should ever be destroyed or impaired by national authority on account of national differences and discontents."[29]

May 30, 1814, Art. 4; Convention between Great Britain and France, April 25, 1818. For these treaties, see Hertslet, *Map of Europe by Treaty*, I, 21-22, 551.)

[27]Ware *vs.* Hylton, 3 Dallas 199.

[28]John Bassett Moore, *History and Digest of International Arbitrations*, I, 298; *U. S. Stat. at Large*, II, 192.

[29]Article X of the Jay Treaty: *U. S. Stat. at Large*, VIII, 122.

V

One of the graver questions which arose in the execution of the confiscation policy was as to the "standing in court" that should be conceded to the owner of confiscable property. Since confiscation grew out of the crime of rebellion, as defined in the act of 1862, it would appear that at least a quasi-criminal character pertained to confiscation proceedings. Recognition of this quasi-criminal character would require that the suspected rebel should be brought into court and given a hearing, and that the guarantees of the Fifth and Sixth Amendments of the Constitution should be extended to him. This was more than a matter of form, for to exclude the principles of criminal procedure and to treat the cases purely as actions against property, would entail a denial of fundamental rights.

The Supreme Court refused in general to treat confiscation as a criminal proceeding. A rather serious irregularity in the wording of the libel in a Louisiana case—an irregularity which would have ruled out an indictment in a criminal action—was not held by the court to be a substantial defect. In stating the opinion of the court, Justice Strong declared that the proceedings were "in no sense criminal proceedings," and were "not governed by the rules that prevail in respect to indictments or criminal informations."[30] The only subject of inquiry, in the opinion of the court, was the liability of the property to confiscation; and persons were referred to only to identify the property.[31]

---

[30]The Confiscation Cases, 87 U. S. 104-105. Three of the justices dissented to this opinion.

[31]Justice Field, dissenting in Tyler *vs*. Defrees (78 U. S. 331), contended that confiscation was essentially a criminal proceeding. President Lincoln also held this view. *Supra*, p. 280.

This problem of the true character of confiscation proceedings was, in one of its aspects, merely a phase of the larger question of rebel status as distinguished from belligerent status, and went to the very root of the legal nature of the Civil War. As we have noted in a previous chapter, the flexible rule of double status, including both that of a "rebel" and of a public belligerent, was adopted, and was announced by the Supreme Court in the *Prize Cases* as well as in other decisions. The Confiscation (or Treason) Act of 1862 was, in accordance with this rule, interpreted as an exercise of both sovereign and belligerent rights.

In *Miller* vs. *United States* the Supreme Court drew a careful distinction between the first four sections of the act "which look to the punishment of individual crime, and which were therefore enacted in virtue of the sovereign power," and the subsequent sections (including confiscation) "which have in view a public war, and which direct the seizure of property of those who were in fact enemies, for the support of the armies of the country."[32]

It will be readily seen that the question of rebel status, and the related question as to whether confiscation should be enforced as a criminal proceeding, had a real practical importance. One of the common difficulties in the enforcement of the confiscation acts was to decide whether, in seizing the property of persons adhering to the "rebellion," opportunity should be given for the supposed "rebel" to appear in court and plead his cause. On the one hand stood the principle that an enemy has no standing in court; while on the other hand, by the very nature of the proceeding, judgment must rest upon a determination of the fact as to whether or not the party was actually engaged in the rebellion, a

[32] 78 U. S. 308.

point on which the owner could claim a right to be heard.

The practice during the war on this matter was uncertain and frequently detrimental to the owner's interest. In the district court for the eastern district of Virginia a general rule was prescribed which disallowed a hearing in the case of persons supporting the rebellion.[33] In a case tried before Judge Betts of the southern district of New York in November, 1863,[34] the defendant, a resident of Alabama, duly filed an answer to the allegations set forth in the libel against his property; but the judge ordered this answer to be stricken from the files on the ground that the defendant was an alien enemy, and hence had no *persona standi* in a court of the United States.[35] The only point which Judge Betts regarded as at all relevant was that the claimant, Leroy M. Wiley, resided in Eufaula, in the State of Alabama. "The court," he declared, "must take judicial notice that Alabama is an insurrectionary State, having been at the commencement of this suit, and yet continuing, in a condition of rebellion and actual hostility against the United States. That condition constitutes all the inhabitants of that State alien enemies of this country." On this ground alone Wiley was excluded from court and his property condemned. Circuit Justice Nelson of New York, in reviewing the action of Judge Betts, declared that, even though the claimant's status as an alien enemy might be admitted, he should have been allowed to plead and contest the charges made in the libel, since a similar privilege had been extended to owners in prize cases.

In criticizing Judge Betts's position a contemporary

[33]Semple *vs.* U. S., 21 Fed. Cas. 1072.

[34]*Ann. Cyc.*, 1863, p. 220.

[35]Jecker *vs.* Montgomery, 18 How. 112, and cases therein cited.

writer pointed out that, if Betts's doctrine was correct, "the mere fact of Mr. Wiley's residence in a Southern insurrectionary State precludes him from appearing and contesting the allegations of the libel that he has rendered active aid to the rebellion. . . . Under such a practice every dollar of property owned by Southern citizens in the North, no matter how loyal, need only be seized under an allegation of disloyal practices; and as the accused cannot be heard to deny that allegation (and if he remains silent no proof of it is required), the whole matter is very summarily disposed of."[36]

This question whether a "rebel" should have a hearing in a Federal court on the issue of the condemnation of his property, waited until after the war for its settlement by the Supreme Court. The case was that of *McVeigh* vs. *United States*, a prominent confiscation case which resembled that in which Judge Betts had given his radical decision. A libel of information had been filed in the eastern Virginia district to reach certain real and personal property of McVeigh, who was charged with having engaged in armed rebellion. McVeigh appeared by counsel, interposed a claim to the property, and filed an answer to the information. By motion of the district attorney, however, the appearance, answer, and claim were stricken from the files for the reason that the respondent was a "resident of the city of Richmond, within the Confederate lines, and a rebel." The property was condemned and ordered to be sold.

When this case reached the Supreme Court the judgment was reversed, and the action of the district attorney unanimously condemned.[37] The court held that

---

[36] *Ann. Cyc.*, 1863, pp. 220-221.

[37] 78 U. S. 259 (1870). See also Windsor *vs.* McVeigh, 93 U. S. 274.

McVeigh's alleged criminality lay at the foundation of the proceeding, and that the questions of his guilt and ownership were therefore fundamental in the case. The order to strike the claim and answer from the files on the ground that McVeigh was a "rebel" amounted to a prejudgment of the very point in question without a hearing. The court below in issuing this order had acted on the theory that no enemy of the United States could have standing in its courts, but the higher tribunal refused to allow such an application of this principle. The Supreme Court was thus committed to the proposition that a suspected "rebel" should not be denied the right to a hearing in connection with the seizure of his property. Had this conclusion been pronounced early enough to produce uniformity of practice in the lower courts during the war, the advantage of the McVeigh decision would have been greater.

This allowance of a hearing to the rebel *if he should appear* did not, however, prevent adverse judgment in case of default. In the nature of the case, it frequently happened that the owner was absent, supposedly participating in the "rebellion." Not only was it an impossibility in most instances for him to appear before a distant Federal court and defend his property; it was frequently difficult for him even to receive notice of the libel, since the method of notification was the publication of a monition in a local newspaper which commonly would not reach the absent owner. The concession that an owner might "appear" by his agent was an advantage, but it did not by any means satisfy the needs of all the cases.

The statutes were not explicit as to whether judgments should be rendered on default, and it became a nice question of interpretation as to whether such judgments were valid. The fact, however, that proceedings were *in rem*, with general conformity to admiralty procedure, justified the presumption that in case of the owner's failure to make appearance, the court should enter a decree of condemnation without hearing. It was usually taken for granted that this was the intention of the law. Finally, in *Miller* vs. *United States*, it was laid down that in case of default judgment should be entered against the property. The certification of the default in due form was to be regarded as establishing all the facts averred in the information as in the case of confession or actual conviction upon evidence. It was not even necessary, said the court, to conduct an *ex parte* hearing after the default.[38]

VI

The question of the constitutionality of the confiscation acts is a composite rather than a simple problem. In preceding pages various legal controversies have been considered as distinct issues pertaining to the application and interpretation of the confiscation laws; but from a different point of view some of these questions may be looked upon in their relationship to the constitutionality of this legislation. No decision was had on this subject of constitutionality during the war; and when finally in 1871 the matter was made a direct issue before the Supreme Court in the Miller case, much of the way had been cleared by earlier decisions. The primary question of the nature of the Civil War had been fully treated in the *Prize Cases*,[39] where the court had defined the conflict as one of sufficient magnitude to give the United States all the powers which might be exercised in the case of a foreign war, while at the same

[38] 78 U. S. 301-303.

[39] *Supra*, pp. 52 *et seq.*

time the rights of the United States as a sovereign over the "insurrectionary" districts were upheld.

On the basis of these previous decisions the court proceeded to analyze the confiscation acts and declare their validity.[40] The action was brought under both confiscation acts to forfeit certain shares of stock in Michigan alleged to be the property of Samuel Miller, a Virginia "rebel." The most important problems before the court under the head of constitutionality were: first, to decide under what category to place confiscation—i.e., whether to regard it as the exercise of war power, or as a municipal regulation; and second, to deal with the objection that the acts involved a violation of the Fifth and Sixth Amendments which guarantee impartial trial and property rights. As to the first of these problems, the court laid down the doctrine that the confiscation acts were passed not as a municipal regulation, but as a war measure. With a tone of certainty which, as we have seen, the authorities hardly warranted, the court declared that "this is and always has been an undoubted belligerent right." Congress had, said the court, "full power to provide for the seizure and confiscation of any property which the enemy or adherents of the enemy could use for the purpose of maintaining the war against the government."[41] The act of 1861, and the fifth, sixth, and seventh sections of the act of 1862, were therefore construed as the enforcement of belligerent rights which Congress amply possessed during the Civil War. This portion of the court's decision was far from convincing;

---

[40] Miller *vs.* U. S., 78 U. S. 268.

[41] A Federal district judge in New York, dealing with the question of German property in America during the first World War, said in 1923 (in an unreported decision): ". . . Congress has not as yet committed itself to a confiscation of enemy property, and the rules of international law have been against it for two centuries." (Stoehr *vs.* Miller, U. S. Dist. Ct., so. dist., N. Y., Jan. 22, 1923; A. G. Hays, *op. cit.*, p. 174.)

for, aside from the fact that the belligerent right of confiscation was a matter of some doubt, it was ably maintained that the whole tone of the second Confiscation Act marked it as a measure to punish "rebels," that confiscation was the penalty for rebellion, and that the forfeitures were directed against persons for their crimes, not primarily against property as a sinew of war.

Having placed the confiscation acts within the category of war measures, the court found little difficulty in dealing with the objection that the acts constituted a violation of the Fifth and Sixth Amendments. The relevant provisions in these amendments are that no person shall be deprived of his property without due process of law, and that in all criminal prosecutions the accused shall enjoy the right to a speedy and public trial by an impartial jury of the State and district wherein the crime shall have been committed. The acts, as we have above noted, permitted judgment by default without a jury trial, in a distant State, without a personal hearing, and without a determination of the facts as to the guilt of the owner. One of the essential features of the Miller case was that the defendant, a citizen of Virginia, had disregarded the notice, and the Federal court in Michigan had entered a decree by default. It was admitted by the Supreme Court that if the purpose of the acts had been to punish offenses against the sovereignty of the United States—i.e., if they had been statutes against crimes under the municipal power of Congress— there would have been force in the objection that Congress had disregarded its constitutional restrictions. Since, however, the acts were passed in exercise of the war powers, they were held to be unaffected by the limitations of the Fifth and Sixth Amendments.

Three of the justices—Field, Clifford, and Davis—dissented from this opinion. Their grounds of disagreement were that the forfeitures in question were punitive in their nature, being based on the municipal, not the war power of Congress; that condemnations must depend upon the personal guilt of the owner; and that therefor a judgement based on mere default in such cases would amount to denial of "due process of law."

These contentions of the dissenting judges not only agree exactly with one of the important points in Lincoln's objections, but they harmonize with the position of the Supreme Court itself when dealing with the problem whether a "rebel" should have a hearing. We noticed in connection with the McVeigh case that the court insisted upon the necessity of allowing a hearing to the owner in case he appeared in court.[42] The dissenting judges were merely applying the same broad principle to the case of default, and were mindful of the fact that in a criminal proceeding judgments by default are not permitted. As Justice Field remarked in *Tyler* vs. *Defrees*, "The authority to render the decree is in express terms made conditional upon a particular fact being found. . . . As the record . . . shows that no hearing was had, and no finding was made, the decree of forfeiture . . . appears to me to be an act of judicial usurpation."[43]

To the thoughtful student this view of the minority judges seems but a natural protest against an extreme doctrine. The dissenting position appears still stronger when it is remembered that the majority judges admitted the incompetence of Congress to allow judgments such as the confiscation acts permitted on the basis of municipal law, and that the "war power" theory was the convenient door of escape from this constitutional difficulty.

---

[42]McVeigh *vs.* U. S., 78 U. S. 259.

[43]Dissenting opinion of Justice Field. Tyler *vs.* Defrees, 78 U. S. 354.

CHAPTER XIV

RESTORATION OF CAPTURED AND CONFISCATED PROPERTY

I. Virtual confiscation in connection with the direct tax
II. Captured and abandoned property
III. Executive policy concerning confiscation after the war
IV. Effect of pardon upon the restoration of confiscated property
V. Restoration of captured and abandoned property

How far was the process of confiscation undone by restorations which followed the war? It must be answered that the restoration of property actually taken under confiscation proceedings was only partial. This was primarily a matter of judicial interpretation, not of executive clemency; and the courts chose to adopt a rather technical and complicated reasoning which was hardly in keeping with the broad policy of amnesty pursued by the executive. But before we turn to a consideration of the administration's attitude toward the confiscation acts after the war, and the judicial effect of pardon upon confiscated property, it is necessary to include within our study certain forms of seizure which practically amounted to confiscation, though carried out under legal forms quite different from those of the confiscation acts. In the collection of the direct tax in the "insurrectionary" districts a kind of forfeiture was practiced which departed so far from the principles of the usual tax sale and involved such discriminations against disloyal owners that it amounted to confiscation. The Captured Property Act, under which millions of dollars' worth of cotton and other property in the South was taken over by treasury officials who followed in the wake of the Union armies, differed only in method, and not at all in principle, from confiscation proper. Having noted these forms of virtual confiscation, we will then be in a better position to treat the subject of restorations as a whole.

I

The remarkable seizures under the direct tax levy were based upon the act of June 7, 1862, "for the collection of direct taxes in insurrectionary districts within the United States."[1] An earlier statute, providing for a direct tax to obtain war revenue, had apportioned quotas among all the States, including those in insurrection.[2] It was now enacted that in those States or districts where the tax quotas could not be peaceably collected, special tax commissioners should be appointed by the President; and that as soon as the military authority of the United States could be established, these commissioners should make assessments "upon all the lands and lots of ground" situated in the insurrectionary territory. This assessment was to be based upon the real estate valuation in force in 1861. A penalty of fifty per cent of the tax proper was added; and, upon default of the owners to pay the tax and penalty, the land was to be "forfeited to the United States," and the commissioners were to conduct public "tax sales," selling to the highest bidder, or bidding in the property for the Government. The tax-sale certificate of the commissioners was to be suffi-

[1] *U. S. Stat. at Large*, XII, 422. For an amendment passed on February 6, 1863, see *ibid.*, p. 640.

[2] *Ibid.*, pp. 294 *et seq.*

cient to convey a title in fee simple to the land, free from all encumbrances.[3]

Commissioners were appointed in accordance with this unusual statute for each of the insurrectionary States. It was impossible, at first, for the act to be enforced uniformly throughout the South, for it was only in those districts where the Union forces maintained a foothold that these so-called tax sales could be conducted. Collections continued until 1866, however, and the reports on this subject show a very considerable amount of money taken from the South in the enforcement of the various provisions touching this direct tax. Taking the one State of South Carolina, we find that, in addition to $222,000 paid as tax, sales of land brought in approximately $370,000, and lands were "bid in by the commissioners for the United States" to the value of $300,000. These amounts totaled $892,000, although South Carolina's quota was only $363,000. The tax obtained from all the "insurrectionary States" was about $2,300,000 and the forfeitures amounted to approximately $2,400,000. The total of the amounts apportioned to these States was $5,100,000; and, since a very large allowance must be made for undervaluation of lands obtained by the Government,[4] it would probably be more accurate

[3]*Ibid.*, p. 423, sec. 4. After the war there was considerable trouble because of the action of State courts in evicting purchasers of lands sold under Federal authority for non-payment of the direct tax. (*Sen. Doc. No. 98*, 41 Cong., 2 sess.)

[4]In the case of Tennessee, the lands bid in for the United States were valued at $309,000, but this was based upon the assessment of 1860, and subsequent improvement brought the value to a figure in excess of $1,000,000. (Report of internal revenue bureau: *Cong. Globe*, 42 Cong., 2 sess., p. 3387.) In McKee *vs.* U. S. (164 U. S. 292) the Supreme Court said: "The fact is well known . . . that . . . the amounts of such sales [for failure to pay the direct tax in the South] were frequently and generally very much less than the real value of the property sold." General David Hunter strongly disapproved of

to say that the States of the South overpaid the tax than to speak of any deficiency in the supplying of their "quotas."[5]

The Union Government could hardly have devised a measure more odious to the people of the South. The levy of a Federal tax directly upon particular plots of ground in regions dominated by the State-rights doctrine was particularly distasteful; and the use of a method not adopted in the North made the partiality of the measure the more apparent. The tax collector of the enemy's Government was thus brought into immediate relations with helpless citizens of those portions of the South which fell into Union possession, and this naturally awakened deep resentment. Objection was made that in view of the added penalty of fifty per cent, required only in the "insurrectionary" States, the tax was not proportionately levied, and was therefore unconstitutional. In dealing with this objection the Supreme Court held that the penalty was no part of the tax, but was a fine "for default of voluntary payment in due time." The validity of the tax under the Constitution was therefore upheld.[6]

Seizures under this act differed from ordinary tax sales. A valuable estate would be sold to pay a trifling

---

these tax sales in the South. In 1863 he wrote to Stanton of the "glaring impolicy" of such sales; the insufficient publicity; the lack of general competition; the encouragement afforded to speculators who obtained lands for a low price and received high prices for such land as was used by the Government; the driving off of the inhabitants; and the never-ending litigation that would follow. (Hunter to Stanton, February 11, 1863; Stanton Papers, X, 52253.)

[5]A statistical report of 1872 concerning the direct tax collections and forfeitures in the South is to be found in the *Cong. Globe*, 42 Cong., 2 sess., p. 3387. President Cleveland stated to Congress in 1889 that about $2,300,000 was credited to the "insurrectionary States," but obviously this did not include the amounts of the forfeitures. (*Senate Journal*, Mar. 2, 1889, 50 Cong., 2 sess., p. 503.)

[6]De Treville *vs.* Small, 98 U. S. 527 (Oct., 1878).

tax; and the surplus, over and above the amount of the tax, instead of being paid to the owner, as in the usual tax sale, was turned into the Federal treasury. The customary privilege of redemption which belongs to a dispossessed owner whose property has gone to pay a tax was conditioned upon the taking of an oath to support the Constitution of the United States.

Whatever this sort of proceeding might be called, it is clear that its effect was confiscation. In fact, since in these forfeitures a title in fee simple was acquired, the effect was greater than in the case of the Confiscation Act of 1862 under which only a life interest was taken. In some cases commissioners required owners to pay the tax in person, which was often an impossibility. The question was significantly raised whether these extraordinary discriminations were consistent with the Constitution, and whether such a form of procedure could be called "due process of law." Even granting that the Federal Government's sovereignty would justify the levying of a tax upon Southerners during the "rebellion," it is difficult to see how these sweeping forfeitures can be defended on the basis of "tax sales."

The most notable instance of seizure under the direct tax legislation was the case of the famous Arlington estate in Virginia, belonging to General Robert E. Lee. A tax amounting to $92.07 was levied upon this estate; and in September, 1863, the whole property was sold for its non-payment.[7] The tax commissioners "bid in" part of the estate for the Federal Government at $26,800. (The "bidding in" meant that the United States ob-

---

[7]In case of non-payment of the tax the law provided as follows: ". . . the . . . . commissioners shall be authorized . . . to bid off [the land] for the United States at a sum not exceeding two-thirds of the assessed value thereof, unless some person shall bid a larger sum." (Amendment of Feb. 6, 1863: *U. S. Stat. at Large*, XII, 640.)

tained title to the property and this valuation was placed upon it.) For other portions of the estate there were various other purchasers. The grounds acquired by the Government were made into a national cemetery for the graves of Union soldiers.

After the death of Mrs. Robert E. Lee, her son, G. W. P. C. Lee, claiming to have valid title to Arlington, petitioned Congress to vote compensation to him in return for which he would yield all his rights in the property and avoid litigation for its recovery.[8] He based his claim on the ground that the sale of the property by the commissioners amounted to confiscation, and could not be held valid. The extraordinary measures adopted to enforce the tax were, he argued, unconstitutional. Instead of the sale of only so much of the property as was necessary to pay the tax with interest and penalties, the whole estate was forfeited to the United States and sold. In this case the amount of the tax had actually been offered by Mrs. Lee through her agent; but the commissioners had refused to accept such payment, and the petitioner declared that this refusal rendered the whole proceeding void. Further, it was argued that the United States could not in justice secure more than a life interest, and that the national legislature could not acquire jurisdiction over this estate without the consent of Virginia. This petition was referred to the Committee on Judiciary, and was not heard of further.[9]

The next phase of the case was a suit brought in the United States Circuit Court in Alexandria, Virginia, and later appealed to the Supreme Court, in which the title of the United States under the tax-sale certificate was contested. The decision in the case of *United States* vs.

---

[8]*Sen. Misc. Doc. No. 96*, 43 Cong., 1 sess.

[9]*Cong. Record*, 43 Cong., 1 sess., p. 2812.

Lee is long and technical.[10] The lower court had declared Lee's title valid, and this decision was affirmed. The arguments of the court, however, did not attack the validity of this general class of tax sales; it was rather the conduct of these particular commissioners which was denounced. In spite of the principle that the United States cannot be sued without its consent, it was held that action could properly be brought because of the acts of persons who as agents of the United States might have interfered in an unwarranted way with individual property rights. The action of the commissioners in this case, in ruling that the owners must pay the tax in person, was held to be faulty; and where the amount of the tax had been tendered through an agent and refused, it was held that no proceedings could be legally conducted which assumed the owner's voluntary default. Any tax-sale certificate secured under such regulations was therefore held to be invalid.

In view of this decision an appropriation became necessary in order to establish the title of the United States to the Arlington cemetery. The matter was finally settled by the payment of $150,000 as compensation to the Lee heirs, in return for which a release of all claims against the property was obtained.[11]

Although various attempts were made to secure legislation adjusting the many inequalities which resulted from the direct tax of the Civil War, nothing was done until March 2, 1891, when an act was passed providing for a reimbursement of the amounts collected from the States under the direct tax act of August 5, 1861.[12] Payments in restoration of the tax were to be made to the gov-

[10] 106 U. S. 196.

[11] *U. S. Stat. at Large*, XXII, 584; *Cong. Record*, 47 Cong., 2 sess., pp. 584, 2680, 3661.

[12] *U. S. Stat. at Large*, XXVI, 822.

ernors; and where collections had been made by the United States from citizens or inhabitants "either directly or by sale of property," the sums paid to the governors were to be held in trust for the benefit of such citizens. Individual restitution to cure forfeitures was provided by special clauses concerning two parishes in South Carolina where unusual hardships had been suffered, and by a general provision that sums received into the treasury "from the sale of lands bid in for taxes in any State . . . in excess of the tax assessed thereon" should be paid to the owners or heirs.[13] Jurisdiction was given to the Court of Claims over cases arising under these provisions for restitution, and its decisions were fairly liberal; but the Government admittedly restored less than it took,[14] and at best such tardy restoration could only partially undo the effect of the original forfeitures.[15]

II

In the Captured Property Act we find virtual confiscation in a still different form. As the Federal armies advanced, it was to be expected that they would make captures of large amounts of private property, especially cotton, and would leave in their train estates and mis-

---

[13]In these two South Carolina parishes a difficulty arose because there was a general failure to pay the tax, and a large quantity of land was bid in for the Government and later *sold to the former owners* for amounts greatly in excess of the sums at which the property had been bid in. One lot bid in at $100 was resold to the owner for $2600. (*House Doc. No. 101*, 45 Cong., 3 sess.)

[14]In McKee *vs.* United States the Supreme Court stated that Congress did not intend by the act of March 2, 1891, to restore the whole value of the property sold for taxes. (164 U. S. 294.)

[15]For cases in which the Supreme Court construed this act of restoration, see 164 U. S.: 287, 294, 373. For similar decisions of the Court of Claims see 29 Ct. Cls. Reps. 231, 236; 30 *ibid.*, p. 346; 31 *ibid.*, p. 245.

cellaneous property abandoned by the owners. Much of this property would be of such a nature that the military authorities could not dispose of it; and unless some action were taken it would be left without ownership. To meet this situation Congress passed, March 3, 1863, the act relating to "captured and abandoned property."[16] Property of a non-warlike character seized by the military authorities was regarded as "captured," while the term "abandoned" was held to apply to property "whose owner shall be voluntarily absent and engaged in aiding or encouraging the rebellion."[17] General military captures of private property were of course not contemplated; but an exception was made of cotton because of its peculiar commercial importance,[18] and because a large share of all the cotton of the South was in reality public movable property, since it had been acquired in one way or another by the Confederate Government.[19] The Union authorities, therefore, seized all the cotton they could lay hands on; but the other movable property taken under the Captured Property Act was negligible in amount. Treasury agents were to be sent throughout the South to take over the property, forwarding it to places of sale in the loyal States, the proceeds being turned into the national treasury.

This act was essentially an exercise of the "belligerent right of confiscation" in a form different from that of the confiscation acts, and applying to property which the latter could not reach. The competence belonged to Congress, according to the Supreme Court, to provide for the forfeiture of the property of *all persons* within

---

[16]*U. S. Stat. at Large*, XII, 820.

[17]*Sen. Doc. No. 22*, 40 Cong., 2 sess.; U. S. *vs.* Padelford, 9 Wall. 531.

[18]Mrs. Alexander's Cotton, 2 Wall. 404; Whitfield *vs.* U. S., 92 U. S. 165.

[19]*House Exec. Doc. No. 97*, 39 Cong., 2 sess.

the Confederacy, loyal as well as disloyal, on the principle that all inhabitants of enemy territory are enemies.[20] This, however, would have been an extreme measure, and the restoration of the property of loyal citizens was therefore provided for in the act. In so doing, Congress renounced a part of its strict belligerent rights as the Supreme Court understood them.

The Treasury Department proceeded vigorously in carrying out the provisions of this law, and an elaborate machinery for collecting and marketing captured property was soon developed.[21] This machinery included "supervising agents," "local agents," "agency aids," and customs officials designated for this work, while over all there was a "general agent" connected with the treasury office in Washington.

This army of treasury officials which was thus set upon the trail of captured property in the South did not find their chase a holiday pastime. Though within the Union lines, they were in the enemy's country; and they found that its inhabitants had either deserted or were hostile to the removal of property. Cases of personal injury to the officials were frequent enough to render the work highly dangerous. Marks and other evidences of the character and ownership of cotton were often destroyed; and cotton was hauled to the woods or swamps and concealed in advance of the agent's arrival, or in cases where this was impossible it was frequently burned. Agents of the Confederate Government were at the same time abroad through the South collecting cotton; and this complicated the work of the Union officials, while it increased the tendency to evasion on the part of owners. Naturally much of the cotton

[20] Mrs. Alexander's Cotton, 2 Wall. 404, 419.

[21] A mass of unpublished material in the archives of the Treasury Department constitutes the chief source for this portion of the study.

collected was in unfit condition and in need of overhauling or rebaling before being put on the market. Above this difficulty there still remained the danger of secret raids upon the government depots, resulting in the theft or demolition of the cotton, or perhaps the substitution of an inferior grade for that contained in the government stores. Sales were required to be conducted in the loyal States, but a serious obstacle to this plan was the lack of sufficient means of transportation. Quartermasters were chiefly concerned with supplying the armies, and their coöperation with treasury officials for the removal of captured property was half-hearted.

The system was, as might have been expected, productive of fraud. Inducements were offered to private individuals for collecting cotton and this led to many irregular seizures. Residents sometimes represented themselves as agents and simply robbed under this pretended authority, while some of the agents themselves committed outrages through blunder or dishonesty. False reports might be submitted, and immediate supervision could be evaded by the pretext of direct orders from Washington to dispose of the cotton in some other way than through the office of the next superior agent.

Considering these difficulties, the Captured Property Act was quite extensively enforced; for we find that by May, 1868, the gross sales amounted to about thirty million dollars, while the net proceeds were about twenty-five million. Of the property thus taken, over ninety-five per cent was cotton.

The control of deserted houses and plantations was one of the important problems involved in the execution of the Captured Property Act. If the owner was absent aiding the "insurrection," his property was legally regarded as "abandoned" and was given over to the jurisdiction of the Treasury Department. No attempt was made to disturb the title to this deserted property, which was merely held under the temporary control of the Union officials, ready to be returned to loyal owners after the war in the event of their loyalty being proved, or possibly to be confiscated if owned by a "rebel."

As illustrated by the case of Louisiana, the machinery for administering these abandoned estates involved a "plantation bureau" at New Orleans in charge of a "superintendent of plantations," under whom was placed a corps of agents and inspectors whose function it was to keep the central office in touch with the large number of lessees and occupants to whom the estates were leased or granted. Rents and proceeds derived from this period of temporary control were appropriated by the Government and placed in the captured property "fund."[22]

The wartime disturbance of ordinary conditions of life was nowhere more strikingly revealed than in this system of operating deserted plantations. Neglect of improvements, dilapidation of buildings, and deterioration due to inexperienced farming were everywhere evident. The lessee's interest extended only to the harvesting of the immediate crop, and this object was furthered in disregard of the permanent up-keep of the property. Several plantations might at times be in control of one individual or firm and this led to the transfer and indiscriminate mixture of movable property which should have been localized in particular estates. The Negroes, suddenly shifted to a free status and a

---

[22]These statements are based on the treasury archives which include lists of plantations administered under the Treasury Department, plantation inventories, plantation bureau records, inspectors' reports, and other like material.

system of lax discipline, became unruly and faithless to contract. Offers of higher wages or easier work would easily seduce them from one plantation to another and such a departure of laborers might occasion the loss of a whole crop. These difficulties were enhanced by the military authorities, who caused constant annoyance by deporting mules without compensation, issuing rations to idle Negroes, and enrolling "hands" as "contraband" troops. Sometimes a plantation was occupied for months as a camp or recruiting station, making cultivation impossible.

It is clear that the essential policy embodied in the Captured Property Act was one of confiscation. The Government based its claim to the proceeds of "captured" property, and the revenue from "abandoned" property, upon the owner's disloyalty. It should be noted, however, that seizures under the act did not involve final condemnation, since the statute itself contemplated relief to all "loyal" claimants who would, within two years after the close of the war, prove their right before the Court of Claims. In addition, the President's proclamations of unconditional pardon and general amnesty finally removed all distinction between "loyal" and "disloyal" owners, and required the restoration, so far as practicable, of all forfeited property rights. The post-war executive policy, and the pronouncements of the courts regarding the intricate legal phases of restoration, require careful consideration; and these matters now claim our attention.

III

There appears to have been no definite executive policy concerning confiscation after the war. Attorney General Speed's first instructions to district attorneys in May, 1865, directed the discontinuance of confiscation proceedings; but these orders were later revoked, and the Government's attorneys were instructed not only to press cases then pending, but to begin new prosecutions. "Undoubtedly you have authority to proceed in all cases where property is confiscated by reason of the acts of its owner done since July 17, 1862," wrote the acting Attorney General to the district attorney at Providence in September, 1865. "The suppression of the rebellion does not stop the execution of the Confiscation Act."[23]

In Virginia particularly many new confiscation cases were instituted in 1865. In the order of President Johnson regarding the establishment of Federal authority in Virginia after the close of the war, we find the following: "The Attorney General will instruct the proper officials to libel and bring to judgment, confiscation and sale, property subject to confiscation, and enforce the administration of justice within said State."[24] In accordance with this order, Speed issued a special instruction to the district attorney in Virginia, calling upon him to "enforce confiscation," and this intention of the Government was also brought to the notice of Judge Underwood of the Federal district court.[25] Hundreds of new cases were docketed during the summer of 1865, the three chief centers being Alexandria, Norfolk, and Richmond. Over one hundred farms and town sites in and around Norfolk were actually condemned, put on sale, and the larger part of them sold at this time.[26] Loud and numerous were the complaints

---

[23]Attorney General's Letter Books.

[24]Executive Order, May 9, 1865: *O. R.*, Ser. III, Vol. 5, p. 14.

[25]Speed to Chandler, May 13, 1865; Speed to U. S. Marshal Underwood, May 13, 1865: Attorney General's Letter Books.

[26]Chicago *Tribune*, Oct. 2, 1865, p. 1, and Nov. 17, 1865, p. 1. The writer has found in the Federal court records at Richmond about four hundred confiscation cases initiated after the close of the war.

that the people of Virginia were unnecessarily vexed, and that private ends were served in the execution of the Confiscation Act.

It was not long, however, before a decided reversal of policy was to be observed in the matter of confiscation. In contradiction of the earlier instruction which emanated from his office, the Attorney General wrote in June, 1866, concerning the second Confiscation Act: "I think it was a war measure and expired with the war." Seizures in Virginia had been halted in September, 1865, and in December Speed wrote concerning the "confiscation docket" in Florida that it was not the wish of the Government to persecute by confiscation those who were obedient to law, but rather persons known to be contumacious or rebellious. "Impressing you with the idea that the Government not only desires to be magnanimous, but can afford to be so," he said to the district attorney, "I instruct you to dismiss confiscation proceedings at your discretion or to continue to try, always saving costs so far as you can."[27]

In these instructions it will be noticed that the selection of a few flagrant cases rather than a general prosecution of the confiscation law seemed to be the administration's policy, as in the matter of treason at this time. It may be added that poverty was a factor which in part determined the Government's attitude. A rather surprising instruction which calls to mind Johnson's discrimination against men of wealth in issuing pardons, appeared in Attorney General Speed's comment on a New York case in which application had been made for the dismissal of confiscation proceedings. "If Mrs. G——is now a loyal woman and

---

[27]This material is derived from the Attorney General's papers and letter books.

in need," he said, "it might help her application. On the other hand, if she is still a rebel and rich, I do not think that the Government should let go its hold upon her property."

This renewed execution of the confiscation acts after the war naturally occasions surprise and may seem difficult to account for. Viewed from any standpoint the acts of confiscation were war measures and virtually, though not legally, the war ended when Lee's and Johnston's armies surrendered in April, 1865. Why, then, should the practical close of the war serve as the occasion for an intensified enforcement of war measures?

The answer is not far to seek, and is to be found in those same circumstances which, for a time, produced increased activity in the bringing of treason indictments. One of the purposes of these penal statutes was the punishment of Southern "rebels" (or perhaps, the more conspicuous leaders among them) and it was not until the close of the war that this intention could be realized. The imprisonment of Davis and others prominent in the Confederacy shows that such a purpose was, for a time, seriously entertained. Furthermore, the thousands of prosecutions and damage suits brought against Union men by returned Confederates, and the more or less extensive persecution of loyal men in the South, produced a strong sentiment for retaliation. It was the inevitable aftermath of civil war. Besides, the vindictive reconstructionists were clamoring for severe measures, and their influence could not be ignored by the administration.

It should always be remembered, however, that this renewed zeal for punishing "rebellion" spent itself before the object was really attained. By the bringing of indictments and the filing of libels against property the courts were crowded with cases; but actual confiscation was rare, just as executions for treason were unknown. The disposition to press confiscation proceedings as an after-war punishment was, in fact, only a passing phase. Beginning with September, 1865, the Government halted proceedings by various special instructions to district attorneys; and from this time on the cases were continued or suspended until they were finally dismissed in 1866 and 1867. Though the administration preferred, for a year or two, to retain confiscation as a potential weapon and to begin proceedings in many individual cases, its policy usually stopped short of the actual condemnation of property; and zealous efforts to accomplish such condemnation were frequently restrained by the authorities at Washington.

IV

In considering the restoration of property after the war, the distinction between the various kinds of forfeiture must be noted. Where property was taken under the confiscation acts a full judicial process had always been completed, culminating in a decree of condemnation and a sale conferring title upon a new purchaser, while the proceeds went to the Federal treasury. Seizures under the Captured Property Act, however, did not, as we have seen, involve a conclusive transfer of title, but rather a conditional acquisition by the Government, subject to possible restoration where loyalty could be proved. These two kinds of seizures involved radical differences, both as to principle and method, when the question of restoration presented itself; and they will therefore require separate treatment.

In all cases of restoration, the primary consideration was the effect of pardon. Both of the confiscation acts were silent on the subject of restoration, but when the executive department announced its policy of pardon the effect of this action upon forfeited property rights inevitably presented itself. The first pardon proclamation of President Lincoln,[28] and the first three of President Johnson,[29] contained various conditions, one of which was the stipulation that confiscated property should not be returned; but finally a proclamation of December 25, 1868, declared an unconditional pardon for all, without the requirement of an oath, and without any reservation whatsoever.[30] The layman might hastily conclude that this unqualified pardon would require the restitution of property where it had been confiscated; but the legal effect of pardon[31] in cases of this sort was a matter of judicial interpretation and hence outside of executive authority, while the principles of law which were invoked in its decision transcended ordinary intelligence.

As regards the act of 1861, the Supreme Court, in the case of *Armstrong's Foundry* (decided in 1867),[32] held that the statute regarded the owner's consent to the hostile use of the property as an offense for which

---

[28] Lincoln's proclamation of pardon, Dec. 8, 1863: *U. S. Stat. at Large,* XIII, 737.

[29] Johnson's pardon proclamations, May 29, 1865; Sept. 7, 1867; July 7, 1868: *U. S. Stat. at Large,* XIII, 758; XV, 700, 702. In these general proclamations of pardon, rights of property were restored "except as to any property of which any person may have been legally divested under the laws of the United States." President Johnson was liberal in the granting of individual pardons. The list issued on July 19, 1867, included 3600 names and that of December 4, 1867, 6400 names. (*House Exec. Doc. No. 32,* 40 Cong., 1 sess.; *ibid., No. 16,* 40 Cong., 2 sess.) These special pardons, however, did not restore confiscated property.

[30] *U. S. Stat. at Large,* XV, 712.

[31] The subject of pardon under the administrations of Lincoln and Johnson is discussed by J. T. Dorris in a doctoral dissertation entitled "Pardon and Amnesty during the Civil War and Reconstruction," submitted to the University of Illinois in 1926.

[32] 6 Wall. 766.

confiscation was the penalty; hence, pardon would restore to the claimant that portion of the proceeds which went to the Government. As to the informer's share, no opinion was expressed.

A different line of interpretation was followed in the case of the second Confiscation Act, for here the court declared that not even universal amnesty could restore lost property rights. The court argued that this act was passed in exercise of belligerent rights, not for the punishment of treason; and that the pardon of the "traitor" could not relieve him of the forfeiture.[33] It was further held that property which had been sold to a purchaser in good faith and for value could not be interfered with, and that proceeds deposited in the treasury were beyond the reach of judicial action, since Congress alone has power to reappropriate money conveyed into the treasury.[34] The well-known practice by which Congress regularly does appropriate money to cover financial judgments against the United States seems not to have been given its due weight.

The judicial interpretation of the two acts is something of a puzzle, for it does not appear that any broad underlying principles were consistently adhered to. The inconsistency appears especially when we compare the decisions concerning restoration as the result of pardon with the earlier decisions as to the extent and duration of the forfeiture. In the case of the act of 1861 the whole title in fee was held to be surrendered on the ground that the proceeding was merely against the property;[35] but, when the question of restoration came up, the punitive nature of the act was recognized in the

---

[33]Semmes *vs.* U. S., 91 U. S. 27.

[34]Knote *vs.* U. S., 95 U. S. 149; Wallach *vs.* Van Riswick, 92 U. S. 202; Osborn *vs.* U. S., 91 U. S. 474.

[35]Kirk *vs.* Lynd, 106 U. S. 315; *supra*, pp. 286-287.

decision that the pardoned owner was entitled to that share of the proceeds which went to the Government. In seizures under the act of 1862, the court allowed only the life interest to be forfeited,[36] thus at least partly recognizing the confiscation as a penalty for a criminal offense; but no recovery was allowed by reason of pardon, on the ground that the taking of the property was not in the nature of a punishment, but was a weapon of belligerency.

Another inconsistency, upon which the expressions of the Supreme Court throw little light, has to do with the restitution of proceeds deposited in the national treasury. Such restitution was allowed in the case of *Armstrong's Foundry*,[37] nothing being said about the exclusive right of Congress to control the appropriation of money; but in *Knote* vs. *United States*,[38] one of the prominent cases concerning the second Confiscation Act, this exclusive function of Congress was made one of the chief grounds for refusing restoration.

In the case of confiscations completed by judicial process, then, restoration was possible as a result of pardon only where the property had been condemned under the act of 1861, and then only the Government's share of the proceeds was returned. Considering the comparatively small number of condemnations under the earlier act, it is evident that this class of restorations was insignificant.

V

For seizures under the Captured Property Act, the procedure regarding restoration was quite different from

[36]Bigelow *vs.* Forrest, 9 Wall. 339; *supra*, p. 286.
[37]6 Wall. 766.
[38]95 U. S. 149.

that which we have just considered. Though much of the work of restoration was done by the Treasury Department, and also by the Freedmen's Bureau (which was forced to part with the greater portion of the property once under its control and was thus disappointed in its prospect of making allotments to freedmen), these releases were but incidental; and the primary agency for determining these restorations was the Court of Claims. By the original act relating to captured and abandoned property the Court of Claims was designated as the tribunal before which claims for the restoration of property should be preferred;[39] and by a further enactment of July 27, 1868, the remedy thus given was declared to be exclusive, precluding the claimant from "suit at common law, or any other mode of redress whatever."[40] Upon proof of ownership *and loyalty*, the claimant was to be entitled to the residue of the proceeds of his property after deducting necessary expenses for sale and other incidental matters.

In dealing with these cases the Court of Claims followed, not too rigidly, certain rules of its own making. It required the claimant to show that he was the owner of the property claimed and that he had never given aid or comfort to the "rebellion." The Government was not to be loaded with the burden of proving disloyalty. Voluntary residence in an insurrectionary district was taken as *prima facie* evidence of a rebellious character; and this must be rebutted by satisfactory testimony covering the whole period of the war, and showing that no act of sympathy to the Confederate movement had been willingly performed.[41]

[39] *U. S. Stat. at Large*, XII, 820, sec. 3.

[40] *Ibid.*, XV, 243, sec. 3.

[41] For typical decisions of the Court of Claims on this subject, see Ct. of Cls. Reps. as follows: III, 19, 177, 218, 240, 390; IV, 337; V, 412, 586, 706.

The Court of Claims thus became the tribunal for judging the facts as to the conduct of thousands of professed Unionists in the South; and its hearings assumed somewhat the character of a judgment-day proceeding, where, after the deeds of all had been laid bare, the faithful were rewarded and the rebellious turned away. The voluminous testimony which the court examined constitutes a significant body of material revealing in detail the conduct of "loyal" Southerners; and for the historian who takes up the study of the Civil War loyalists it will have a value similar to that of the papers of the New York royal commission for the study of the corresponding topic in the Revolutionary War.[42]

Men and women of Union sympathies, as this testimony shows, were scattered in considerable numbers throughout the South. Surrounded as they were by a repressing and persecuting majority, they naturally found it difficult to express their loyalty in any active, organized form. They had to be content, therefore, with a negative attitude, a sort of "passive resistance," refusing to take any voluntary measures against the Government at Washington, and performing individual acts of friendship to the Federal troops. We find them resisting the Confederate draft, carrying provisions and medicine to Union soldiers, contributing to funds for the welfare of the blue-coats, attending the boys in the hospitals, and in other ways befriending the Union cause.

This "loyalty," which meant treason from the Confederate standpoint, naturally incurred local persecution; and the Unionist of the South moved constantly in an atmosphere of scorn and prejudice, continually

[42]C. H. Van Tyne, *The Loyalists in the American Revolution.*

disturbed by threats of personal violence. Furthermore, he was often compelled against his will to give support to the Southern cause. It was an exceptional Unionist indeed who was not pressed into the conscript lines, compelled to subscribe to a Confederate loan, or forced to labor on intrenchments; and in addition to all this, he must pay taxes into the "rebel" treasury. Children even caught up the feud, and the refusal of one daring youth to give up the Stars and Stripes for the neighbor boys to spit upon resulted in a severe laceration, and later a fatal blow from a brickbat.

In conducting these suits, the Court of Claims found its docket well crowded. The total amount paid out in judgments in such cases up to February, 1888, was reported as $9,864,300.[43] When we remember that the sum involved in each case was usually small, and that these figures represent only the claims which were allowed, we can form an idea of the vast amount of this litigation which the court handled.

The central point of law touching these claims was the effect of pardon and amnesty upon the rights of claimants for property seized during the war. Were disloyal owners permanently divested of their property by that proviso which required proof that the owner had "never given any aid or comfort to the . . . rebellion,"[44] or could the consequences of disloyalty be avoided by the President's proclamation of pardon and amnesty, and the owner's acceptance of the oath of allegiance? This question was presented in the case of *United States* vs. *Klein*, appealed from the Court of Claims to the Supreme Court.[45] The most liberal view

[43] *Treasury Department Circular*, Jan. 9, 1900, No. 4. For a list of judgments by the Court of Claims from 1863 to 1867, see *House Misc. Doc. No. 50*, 40 Cong., 1 sess., pp. 2-9.

[44] Sec. 3 of the Captured Property Act: *U. S. Stat. at Large*, XII, 820.

[45] 13 Wall. 128.

was sustained. In main substance the opinion was that Congress had intended to restore property not only to loyal owners, but to those who had been hostile and might later become loyal; that after the proclamation of general amnesty the restoration of property to all *bona fide* owners claiming under the Captured Property Act became the duty of the Government; and that such restoration became the "absolute right of the persons pardoned," the Government having constituted itself the trustee, not only for claimants protected by the original act, but for all who might later be recognized as entitled to their property. "Pardon and restoration of political. rights," declared the court, "were in return for the oath and its fulfillment. To refuse it would be a breach of faith not less cruel and astounding than to abandon the freed people whom the executive had promised to maintain in their freedom."

After this decision of the Supreme Court, therefore, all claimants who had been dispossessed through the operation of the Captured Property Act were, regardless of original loyalty, entitled to restoration. There was, however, another proviso in the act which more seriously affected the claimant's prospect of recovery. Suit for recovery must be brought, according to the law, within two years "after the suppression of the rebellion."[46] The President's proclamation of August 20, 1866, in which for the first time the entire suppression of the rebellion throughout the country was declared, was taken by the court as marking the legal termination of the war.[47] Unfortunately for the claimants, the decision in the Klein case did not come until 1871, so that those who could not claim original loyalty first

[46] *U. S. Stat. at Large*, XII, 820, sec. 3.
[47] U. S. *vs*. Anderson, 9 Wall. 56.

learned of the restoring effect of pardon too late for a claim to be allowed, supposing that the two-year limitation should be insisted upon. Agitation was begun to obtain relief for those claimants who, under the former requirement of loyalty, had allowed the two-year limitation to lapse without taking advantage of their right to plead before the Court of Claims. Various bills to revive the right of such claimants have been presented to Congress, and the House Committee on Judiciary has at various times reported favorably on such legislation; but the proposed bills and committee reports have been lost in the general oblivion of the congressional calendar.[48]

As to abandoned estates, restoration moved much more swiftly. The chief agency for this purpose was the Bureau of Refugees, Freedmen and Abandoned Lands. This institution was created by Congress, March 3, 1865, to provide protection and support for emancipated Negroes; and abandoned real property, as well as certain other property, was entrusted to its administration.[49] Estates which had been administered on a lease system by treasury agents were placed in charge of the bureau, with the intention that deserted lands should be allotted in small holdings to individual freedmen. Some land was actually assigned in South Carolina and Georgia, but in general the bureau either used its land for colonies of freedmen or continued the lease system until, by President Johnson's order, it was instructed in August, 1865, to return the property of all who had been pardoned. As Commissioner Howard's reports show, the uncertainty of tenure over the bu-

---

[48]The bill introduced on April 30, 1921, by Mr. Overstreet is typical. *H. R. 5592*, 67 Cong., 1 sess. See also *House Reports* as follows: 51 Cong., 1 sess., No. 784; 52 Cong., 1 sess., No. 1377.

[49]*U. S. Stat. at Large*, XIII, 507.

reau's holdings defeated the plan of allotments to freedmen; and the occupation of these estates was only temporary. The bureau restored 15,452 acres of land seized under the second Confiscation Act, 14,652 acres received as abandoned and allotted to freedmen, and 400,000 acres of abandoned property which had never been allotted. Thus the total restorations amounted to 430,104 acres.[50]

Taking the subject of restoration as a whole, it may be said that the policy pursued by Congress and the courts left much to be desired. In particular, the failure to allow the restoration of property taken under the second Confiscation Act, and the inaction which has allowed a minor proviso in the Captured Property Act, regarding a mere time limitation for the filing of a claim, to defeat a recognized right of recovery, are sources of disappointment. Though the general notion as to the number of dispossessed owners is doubtless exaggerated, yet one cannot but wish that the general oblivion which has removed former disabilities from those who adhered to the Southern cause, could have brought restoration for every case of confiscated or captured property.

---

[50] *Autiobiography of Oliver O. Howard*, II, Ch. xlix; *House Exec. Docs.*, 39 Cong., 1 sess., Nos. 11, 70, 99.

CHAPTER XV

STEPS TOWARD EMANCIPATION

I. The belligerent right of emancipation: The war power of Congress over slavery
II. How the war forced the question of emancipation upon the government: Policy with regard to military emancipation and the return of fugitive slaves
III. Emancipation in relation to confiscation
IV. Liberation of slave-soldiers: Other emancipating measures of Congress
V. Lincoln's plan of gradual abolition by State action with Federal compensation

We shall consider in this and the following chapter not the general bearings of the oft-discussed subject of emancipation as a matter of policy, but rather those questions of governmental power and authority which the subject involves. Our first inquiry will concern itself with the problem of the war power over slavery. The authority which the National Government was led to assume by the compulsion of circumstances in opposition to an avowed policy of non-interference will then be examined and this will be found to involve tentative steps toward emancipation, as in the confiscation acts. Our attention will then turn to Lincoln's earnestly advocated proposal for gradual abolition by State action with Federal compensation to slave owners. An analysis of the executive proclamation of freedom will follow, after which we will note those conflicts of authority which were characteristic of that transitional stage when the question of slavery, though dealt with piecemeal by various national measures, was still within the domain of State jurisdiction. Finally, our attention will be directed to the constitutional amendment which was adopted as the only way out of the uncertainty and confusion touching slavery which the war bequeathed.

I

It was a generally accepted axiom of American constitutional law in 1861 that slavery was a domestic institution of the States, and that as a State institution it was outside Federal jurisdiction. When the Civil War came, however, it was widely believed that the Government acquired a power in this field which in peace times it did not have. This extraordinary authority to strike at slavery during the great national emergency is what we mean by the "war power over slavery." Some there were who justified this war power by claiming the "belligerent right" of emancipating an enemy's slaves—a right which they held to be within the laws of war—while others maintained that the question was domestic, not international, and that control over local affairs normally lying within State jurisdiction could be assumed by the National Government as an enlarged municipal power growing out of insurrection and civil war.

Prior to the Civil War the American tendency had been to deny the right of liberating an enemy's slaves as coming within the recognized laws and usages of modern warfare. This was a natural attitude for the principal slaveholding country in the world where the domestic slaveholding interest inevitably affected international policy. Lord Dunmore's proclamation decreeing freedom to the slaves of Virginia "rebels" was a familiar theme for denunciatory comment by the patriots of the Revolution; and the activity of the British commanders in deporting American slaves at the close of the Revolutionary War occasioned a wordy controversy between the United States and England. But perhaps the chief instance which came to mind when the subject was broached was the action of the British in enticing slaves from American masters during the War of 1812 and in carrying them off in alleged violation of the Treaty of Ghent.[1] It will be worth our while to observe how this situation drew from John Quincy Adams, our Secretary of State, an emphatic protest and a vigorous denial of the belligerent right of emancipation. Thus the New England statesman who has been credited with originating the policy which took form in Lincoln's Emancipation Proclamation was, strangely enough, the author of the most weighty utterances opposing the war power over slavery.

In 1814 Cochrane, the British Admiral, issued a proclamation which referred to the desire of "many persons now resident in the United States . . . to withdraw therefrom, with a view of entering his Majesty's service, or of being received as free settlers in some of his Majesty's Colonies." The proclamation continued in these words:

> This is therefore to give notice
>
> That all those who may be disposed to emigrate from the United States will, with their families, be received on board his Majesty's . . . vessels of war, or at the military posts that may be established upon or near the coast of the United States where they will have the choice of either entering into his Majesty's sea or land forces, or of being sent free settlers

[1] J. B. Moore, *Digest of International Arbitrations*, I, 350 *et seq.*

to the British possessions in North America, or the West Indies, where they will meet with all due encouragement.[2]

The main purpose and effect of this proclamation was to entice slaves from American masters and liberate them. In the Treaty of Ghent the restoration of such slaves along with other "private property" was stipulated; but, in spite of the treaty, slaves were carried away in the process of British evacuation. Since the precise meaning of the treaty provision was a matter of disagreement between the two nations, the question was referred to arbitration by the Emperor of Russia; and it is in the dispatches pertaining to this arbitration that Adams' most significant statements are found. He sent a carefully worded instruction on this subject to Henry Middleton[3] in 1820, which contained the following passage:

The distinction in the language of the Article [i.e., the first article of the treaty of Ghent], as strong as words can make it, between public property . . . and private property including slaves is this. Public property by the Laws of War is liable to be taken, and applied by the captor to his own use. Private property on shore by the same Laws of War is protected from capture, and ought not to be taken at all.

. . .

With the exception of maritime captures, private property in captured places is by the usages of civilized nations respected. . . . The British nation as well as the United States consider slaves as property . . . ; millions of such slaves are held as property in the British Dominions and they are recognized as such by the terms of the Article.

---

[2] *Ibid.*, I, 350.
[3] U. S. Minister at St. Petersburg.

Mr. Adams then referred to Cochrane's proclamation and continued as follows:

It is not openly addressed to slaves, nor does it avow its real object. From the use of the phraseology which it adopts, the inference is conclusive that the real object was such as the Admiral did not choose to avow, and the only supposable motive for the disguise is the consciousness that it was not conformable to the established usages of war among civilized nations. The wrong was in the proclamation. *Admiral Cochrane had no lawful authority to give freedom to the slaves belonging to the citizens of the United States.*[4] *The recognition of them by Great Britain, in the treaty, as property, is a complete disclaimer of the right to destroy that property by making them free.*[5]

Writing again to Middleton on the same subject, on November 6, 1820, Mr. Adams said:

In the statement of the British ground of argument . . . , they have broadly asserted the right of emancipating slaves—private property—as a legitimate right of war. This is utterly incomprehensible on the part of a nation whose subjects hold slaves by millions, and who in this very Treaty recognize them as private property. No such right is acknowledged as a Law of War by writers who admit *any* limitation. The right of putting to death all prisoners in cold blood and without special cause might as well be pretended to be a Law of War, or the right to use poisoned weapons, or to assassinate. I think the Emperor will not recognize the right of emancipation as legitimate warfare, and am persuaded you will present

---

[4]The italics are in the original.

[5]Letter of instruction by John Quincy Adams to Henry Middleton, United States Minister at St. Petersburg, July 5, 1820: *U. S. Ministers' Instructions* (MSS., Dept. of State), Vol. 9, pp. 18 *et seq.* In W. C. Ford's edition of the *Writings of John Quincy Adams* (VII, 46-52) this letter is printed in part, but the whole section concerning the carrying away of slaves is omitted.

the argument against it, in all its force, and yet without prolixity.[6]

The American contention was borne out in the settlement of this matter; and, since this was the chief instance in which the belligerent right of emancipation was discussed as it affected the United States, it is correct to think of Adams' statements as expressing the official American doctrine on the subject up to the time of the Civil War. It may be added that the British in this controversy did not seek to justify emancipation under the laws of war, but merely argued for a narrow construction of the wording of the treaty as to the slaves which were to be restored, and that the decision of the arbitrator was restricted to a question of grammar.

In spite of this official statement of Adams, the belligerent right of emancipation as a matter of international law was frequently asserted during the Civil War, as for instance by Representative Sedgwick of New York, who said in debate: "The law of nations clearly sanctions the emancipation of the enemy's slaves by military force and authority. It is an understood and received doctrine."[7] Disagreement as to what the "laws of war" permit is a common thing, and it is not remarkable that many who considered emancipation an expedient measure justified it on this ground.[8]

---

[6] *U. S. Ministers' Instructions* (MSS., Dept. of State), Vol. 9, p. 57; W. C. Ford, *Writings of J. Q. Adams*, VII, 83. An interesting commentary on this whole subject is to be found in Henry Wheaton, *Elements of International Law* (ed. by W. B. Lawrence, Boston, 1863), p. 495, note 167, p. 611, note 189.

[7] *Cong. Globe*, Jan. 30, 1863, 37 Cong., 3 sess., p. 629.

[8] A careful reading of Vattel, Wheaton and Halleck, who were perhaps the three authorities on international law most frequently cited at the time of the Civil War, fails to reveal any sanction of the belligerent right of emancipation. None of the three gives any specific

There were, however, other grounds, besides the "laws of war," on which the war power over slavery was asserted. It was urged that Congress had the power to legislate against slavery in States engaged in insurrection. Whiting, Solicitor of the War Department, declared: "Whenever, in the judgment of Congress, the 'common defense' and 'public welfare,' in time of war, require the removal of the condition of slavery, it is within the scope of its constitutional authority to pass laws for that purpose."[9] American constitutional lawyers do not, in general, cite the phraseology of the preamble as equivalent to a grant of power to Congress; but it must be remembered that much of the argument of the time was of this broad, inclusive nature. Whiting continued by declaring that the treaty-making power may abolish slavery. "A clause in any treaty abolishing slavery would, *ipso facto*, become the supreme law of the land, and there is no power whatever that could interfere with or prevent its operation."[10] By this reasoning, the Government may do any unconstitutional thing, so long as it embodies such action in a treaty!

In his further discussion of the subject Whiting asserted that Congress could abolish slavery in the States under the law of eminent domain (taking property for a public use or purpose);[11] and that Congress could

---

treatment of the subject, but they all emphasize the respect paid to private property. (Vattel, *The Law of Nations*, ed. by J. Chitty [Philadelphia, T. and J. W. Johnson, 1844], 364-370; Henry Wheaton, *Elements of International Law*, ed. by W. B. Lawrence [Boston, 1863], p. 597; H. W. Halleck, *International Law* [New York, 1861], p. 456.)

[9]W. Whiting, *War Powers under the Constitution* (Boston, 1871), 28.

[10]*Ibid.*, p. 135.

[11]*Ibid.*, Ch. i. To base emancipation upon the right of eminent domain would require compensation for the slaves so taken. The committee on war claims of the House of Representatives declared in 1874 that emancipation was "not a taking for public use," and they held that no basis for compensation existed on this ground. (*House Report No. 262*, 43 Cong., 1 sess., p. 53, n. 109.)

emancipate to secure "domestic tranquillity," to "suppress insurrection," or to maintain a "republican form of government." The fugitive slave clause he regarded as a prohibition upon the States; and, since there was a prohibition upon Congress in connection with the slave trade, the omission of any prohibition regarding slavery itself convinced him that the framers designed that Congress should control slavery.

"Laws passed for that purpose," he said, "in good faith, against belligerent subjects, not being within any express prohibition of the Constitution, cannot lawfully be declared void by any department of government."[12] Such a statement, of course, ignores the whole fundamental principle of delegated powers. The powers of Congress depend not upon absence of prohibition, but upon either express or implied grant. Such defective reasoning, however, runs through the whole of Whiting's treatment of the subject.

In the debates concerning the slavery question the constitutional arguments of the Congressmen and Senators varied according to the policies which they urged. Some radicals, like Thaddeus Stevens, proposed to take the action whether constitutional or not; while others, like Trumbull, asserted that the Constitution conferred this as well as every other power "necessary for the suppression of the rebellion."[13] Still others adopted Sumner's formula of "State suicide" and declared that the States, by seceding, had forfeited their Statehood and reverted to a territorial status under national control. This State-suicide principle of Sumner, it should be noted, offered no basis for nation-wide action against slavery, but only for abolition within the seceded States.

Of course to those who considered that war gave

[12]Whiting, *War Powers*, 132. [13]*Ann. Cyc.*, 1862, p. 282.

the right to do illegal things, constitutional difficulties concerning slavery offered no embarrassment. Quoting the maxim "*inter arma silent leges*," they could say with Sumner: " . . . the Constitution itself is only a higher law; nor can it claim to speak in time of war, . . . more than any other law."[14]

Conservatives in Congress in denying the war power of Congress over slavery usually based their objections on the well understood principle that the Constitution made slavery within the States a State matter. Speaking of the emancipating features of the confiscation bill of 1862, Senator Garret Davis of Kentucky said: "Congress has neither the expressly delegated nor implied power to liberate these slaves." "On the pretext of invoking assistance to execute an express power, Congress cannot assume a greater and more extensive one, particularly one so formidable as to enable it . . . to break down the great principle of our complicated system—that all the internal affairs of the States are exclusively under their own governments."[15] In like vein Senator Carlile of Virginia said: "The slaves are to be emancipated in violation of the Constitution. . . . The want of power in Congress to interfere with slavery in the States where it exists has always heretofore been admitted; the most ultra abolitionists admit that Congress cannot interfere with slavery in the States, and because this is so, they denounce the Constitution as a covenant with death and a league with hell."[16]

It is of interest to notice that the war did not swerve President Lincoln from the view that he had previously expressed (in the debate with Douglas and elsewhere) that Congress had no constitutional power to overthrow

[14]*Cong. Globe*, Jan. 27, 1862, 37 Cong., 2 sess., p. 2964.
[15]*Ibid.*, p. 1762.
[16]*Ann. Cyc.*, 1862, p. 355.

slavery in the States.[17] In his public pronouncement concerning the Wade-Davis bill of 1864, of which he disapproved because of its drastic process of "reconstruction," Lincoln said: "I am . . . unprepared . . . to declare a constitutional competency in Congress to abolish slavery in [the] States."[18] He added that he hoped the object would be achieved by constitutional amendment.[19]

II

We must now examine some of the earlier measures of interference with slavery which the war situation produced. In the first stages of the war the administration was committed to the policy of non-interference in this field.[20] Lincoln's disclaimer of any intention to interfere with slavery in the States, previously made on various occasions, was repeated in the inaugural address of 1861.[21]

---

[17]In conversation with Senator Browning of Illinois, Lincoln expressed his conviction that Congress had no power over slavery in the States. Diary of Orville H. Browning, July 1, 1862.

[18]Section 12 of the Wade-Davis reconstruction bill, which passed Congress in July, 1864, but was not signed by the President, provided for the emancipation of the slaves of the "rebel" States, and their posterity, (*Cong. Globe*, 38 Cong., 1 sess., p. 3449.) For Lincoln's view, see his "proclamation" concerning the Wade-Davis bill, July 8, 1864: Nicolay and Hay, *Works*, X, 153.

[19]Further questions closely related to the belligerent right of emancipation are discussed below, pp. 373-378.

[20]As an indication of Lincoln's conservatism concerning slavery early in the war it is of interest to notice that before he issued his Emancipation Proclamation he expressed the view that so much of slavery as should remain after the war would be in the same state as before the war. Diary of Orville H. Browning, July 1, 1862.

[21]Lincoln's views regarding slavery cannot be dealt with at length here. He was not an "abolitionist." He did not favor the repeal of the fugitive slave law; he did not oppose the admission of slave States, for he felt that the States should make such constitutions as their people might see fit; he did not, as senatorial candidate in 1858, "stand pledged" to abolition of the slave trade between the States. He did

Congress uttered a similar disclaimer when it adopted, almost without dissent, the Crittenden resolution of July 22, 1861, which declared that "this war is not waged . . . in any spirit of oppression, or for any purpose of conquest or subjugation, or . . . of overthrowing or interfering with the rights or established institutions of [the][22] States, but to defend and maintain the supremacy of the Constitution, and to preserve the Union with all the . . . rights of the several States unimpaired."[23]

The scope of this book does not include a discussion of the reasons why this policy of non-interference was abandoned for one of active emancipation. There were enough factors which contributed to this result without supposing any lack of good faith on the part of the Government. It is sufficient to recall that Congress, and to a certain extent the executive, became increasingly radical under the influence of the "war

not consider that Congress had any right to interfere with slavery in the States where it existed. He thought Congress had the right to abolish slavery in the District of Columbia, but he favored such abolution only if gradual and accompanied by compensation as well as a referendum to obtain an expression of the sentiment of the people. He regarded slavery as an evil; but considered that, as it was in process of extinction, it was sufficient to look forward to its peaceable disappearance. A careful reading of all of Lincoln's utterances on the subject shows that his "house-divided-against-itself" speech cannot fairly be interpreted as a threat of interference with slavery in the South. When it came to *extending* slavery, Lincoln felt that this should be resisted; and he considered it the right and duty of Congress to prohibit slavery in the territories. The Dred Scott dictum that Congress had no such right he refused to accept; and he looked forward to the time when the reverse of this doctrine would be approved by the Supreme Court itself. Such were, in the main, Lincoln's views at the time when he became President. ("The Lincoln-Douglas Debates" [*Illinois Historical Collections*, Vol. III], *passim*, especially pp. 150-152; Nicolay and Hay, *Works*, Vols. III, IV, V, especially III, 273 *et seq.*)

[22]The wording in the resolution is "those States," referring to the States in "insurrection."

[23]*Cong. Globe*, July 22, 1861, 37 Con.g, 1 sess., p. 222.

mind"; that the purpose of the war widened as the months of desperate fighting passed;[24] that the foreign situation seemed to call for a more definite declaration concerning slavery; and that, in order to deal with various practical phases of the slavery problem as they came up, the Government found itself forced either to take some steps toward emancipation or to become both its own enemy and an active promoter of slavery. Lincoln's references to non-interference with slavery in his first inaugural are not to be interpreted as a prediction of governmental policy in the event of civil war, but as a pledge offered in the hope of keeping the slave States in the Union. It is not the part of statesmanship to adhere stubbornly to a given policy after all chances for its success have been lost; and as far as President Lincoln was concerned the policy of non-interference was at least given a fair trial during the first year and a half of the war. When the Emancipation Proclamation of September 22, 1862, indicated that this former policy was abandoned, there was not only a hundred-day warning given, but there was also the pledge of Federal pecuniary aid to any State that should adopt emancipation by its own laws.[25]

---

[24]Lincoln's view as to the inevitable alteration of policy because of war was expressed in the following words: "In the annual message last December, I thought fit to say, 'The Union must be preserved; and hence all indispensable means must be employed'. I said this, not hastily, but deliberately. War has been made, and continues to be, an indispensable means. A practical reacknowledgment of the national authority would render war unnecessary, and it would at once cease. If, however, resistance continues, the war must also continue; and it is impossible to forsee all the incidents which may attend and all the ruin which may follow it. Such as may seem indispensable, or may obviously promise great efficiency toward ending the struggle, must, and will, come." (Message of March 6, 1862: Nicolay and Hay, *Lincoln*, V, 209.) See also Randall, *Lincoln the President*, II, 126-203.

[25]"There was more than a year and a half of trial to suppress the rebellion before the proclamation issued; the last one hundred days of

The President acted with decision when it was a matter of overruling generals who exceeded their military authority by taking the question of emancipation into their hands. When, on August 30, 1861, General Frémont declared the confiscation of the property "of all persons in the State of Missouri who shall take up arms against the United States, or who shall be directly proven to have taken an active part with their enemies in the field," and declared their slaves free, President Lincoln ordered that the proclamation be so modified as to conform to the Confiscation Act of 1861, which applied only to slaves and other property put to hostile use.[26]

Similarly, when General Hunter in May, 1862, declared that "slavery and martial law in a free country are altogether incompatible," and added that "the persons in . . . Georgia, Florida, and South Carolina heretofore held as slaves are therefore declared forever free," the President gave public notice that the order was unauthorized and void.[27] Both Frémont's and Hunter's orders were in essence political; for, instead of dealing with any specific military problem concerning slaves, they proclaimed a comprehensive and sweeping policy of emancipation far beyond any immediate military necessity.

When it came, however, to the question of returning fugitive slaves who found their way within the Union lines, quite a different problem was presented. Just after General Benjamin F. Butler assumed control at

---

which passed under an explicit notice that it was coming." (Lincoln, August 26, 1863, to Union men at Springfield, Illinois. Quoted in Rhodes, *History of the United States*, IV, 410. And see also Lincoln's letter to McClernand, Jan. 8, 1863: Nicolay and Hay, *Works*, VIII, 181.)

[26] *Ibid.*, VI, 353.

[27] *Ibid.*, VII, 171.

Fortress Monroe, there came within his lines three slaves, the property of Colonel Mallory, in command of the Confederate force in that region. Because he needed workmen and because he was "credibly informed that the negroes in this neighborhood are employed in the erection of batteries and other works by the rebels, which it would be nearly or quite impossible to construct without their labor," Butler decided to hold them and employ their services. In an interview under flag of truce with Major Carey of the Virginia troops, Butler stated his position as follows:

> . . . he [Major Carey] desired to know if I did not feel myself bound by my constitutional obligations to deliver up fugitives under the Fugitive Slave Act. To this I replied that the Fugitive Slave Act did not affect a foreign country, which Virginia claimed to be, and that she must reckon it one of the infelicities of her position that, in so far at least, she was taken at her word.[28]

It was in these words that General Butler reported the matter to General Scott at Washington, and in this report he said nothing about having referred to the Negroes as "contraband of war." Both Butler and Major Carey, however, have testified that this phrase was used by Butler in the interview. Referring to this famous phrase in later years, Butler said: "as a lawyer I was never very proud of it, but as an executive officer I was very much comforted with it as a means of doing my duty."[29]

The problem involved here was not that of "contra-

---

[28]*Private and Official Correspondence of General Benjamin F. Butler*, I, 104.

[29]John Hay refused to credit Butler with authorship of the word "contraband" as applied to Negroes in hostile service, but Butler, replying vigorously in his autobiography, said: "If he had put the question

band" in the strict sense, but the problem of dealing with fugitive slaves, belonging to "rebel" owners, and finding their way into the Union lines. In the early part of the war, some of the generals adopted Butler's course; while others, as for instance Halleck in Missouri and General Williams in Louisiana, refused to receive such fugitives into their lines.[30] The matter was finally settled by Congress. On March 13, 1862, Congress enacted an "additional article of war" prohibiting persons in the military or naval service "from employing any of the forces . . . for the purpose of returning fugitives from service or labor, who may have escaped."[31] A further step was taken on July 17, 1862, when Congress enacted that no slave escaping into any State from another State should be delivered up except for crime, unless to a loyal owner. Slaves of "rebel" owners coming into the Union lines were by this act declared free.[32]

This fugitive slave question offers an excellent example of the manner in which the unavoidable incidents of a war over a vastly extended front with a slaveholding power inevitably forced upon the Government the question of emancipation. As to the operation of the Federal fugitive slave law, it is sufficient to say that the state of war made that law inapplicable as between the United States and the Confederate

---

to me I should have answered: 'A poor thing, sir, but my own'. If he had inquired of Major Carey, that gentleman would have answered that 'contraband' was the ground upon which I refused to release Mallory's slaves." To confirm this, Butler produced a letter from Major Carey written in 1891. (*Butler's Book* [Autobiography and Personal Reminiscences of Major General Benj. F. Butler], Ch. vi; Nicolay and Hay, *Lincoln*, IV, Ch. xxii.)

[30] *Ann. Cyc.*, 1862, p. 754.

[31] *U. S. Stat. at Large*, XII, 354.

[32] *Ibid.*, p. 589.

States; while loyal slave owners within such Union States as Kentucky and Missouri were permitted to recover their slaves until late in the war, when the fugitive slave acts were repealed.[33]

III

Another form in which the emancipation question presented itself was in connection with the subject of confiscation. The first Confiscation Act, passed on August 6, 1861, provided that "whenever . . . any person claimed to be held to labor or service . . . shall be required or permitted . . . to take up arms against the United States or . . . to work . . . in any military or naval service whatsoever against the Government and lawful authority of the United States, . . . the person to whom such labor or service is claimed to be due shall forfeit his claim to such labor."[34] It is perhaps a just criticism of this act to say that it should not have gone so far as it did without going farther. The act did not specifically say that such slaves should be free, though this was the plain inference; and no provision was made for carrying into effect the forfeiture of this particular class of property. The act as it related to slaves was of little practical importance,[35] yet it should be noted as one of the earlier steps which pointed toward a fuller policy of emancipation.

The emancipating feature of the second Confiscation

---

[33]The act of June 28, 1864, declared that the fugitive slave acts of 1793 and 1850 "are hereby repealed." (*Ibid.*, XIII, 200.)

[34]*Ibid.*, XII, 319.

[35]Senator Trumbull, on March 29, 1864, said of the first Confiscation Act: "That act . . . has not been executed. So far as I am advised not a single slave has been set at liberty under it." (*Cong. Globe*, 38 Cong., 1 sess., p. 1313.)

Act, that of July 17, 1862, must now be examined. This was, primarily, a treason act and a confiscation act. The provisions concerning slaves must be considered in relation to all the other provisions. The law provided that any one thereafter committing treason should "suffer death, and all his slaves, if any, [should] be declared and made free"; or, at the discretion of the court, imprisonment and fine might be imposed instead of death, in which case also the slaves were to be made free, and the fine was to be levied on the property, excluding slaves. In its later sections the law imposed confiscation upon all persons engaged in or aiding the rebellion, and provided in some detail for the condemnation of property by proceedings *in rem* in the Federal district courts, as well as for its sale and the depositing of the proceeds in the treasury. Then, in section nine, the following provision was added:

> *And be it further enacted*, That all slaves of persons who shall hereafter be engaged in rebellion against the Government of the United States, or who shall in any way give aid or comfort thereto, escaping from such persons and taking refuge within the lines of the army; and all slaves captured from such persons or deserted by them and coming into the control of the Government of the United States; and all slaves of such persons found on or being within any place occupied by rebel forces and afterwards occupied by the forces of the United States, shall be deemed captives of war, and shall be forever free of their servitude, and not again held as slaves.[36]

An examination of the whole act shows that the emancipation of slaves is provided for separately from the confiscation of property; and the distinction between the confiscating and the emancipating features of the act is important. The act does not confiscate slaves

[36] *U. S. Stat. at Large*, XII, 589-592.

as property. The earlier sections (which provide in detail for the condemnation in the Federal courts of all the estate and property, money, stocks, credits, and effects of the offender, for its sale and the disposition of the proceeds) make no reference to slaves, and the provision regarding the "sale" of the "property" would be inapplicable to slaves, when freed.

It is therefore a puzzling question as to how, in the intention of Congress, this Confiscation Act was to be used as a measure of emancipation. There are no provisions whatever for making this emancipation effective. It was not an act of general emancipation, but one declaring freedom in such a way that certain facts would have to be shown in regard to any individual slaves who should claim freedom under it—especially the fact of ownership by a particular person and of the rebellious character of that person. To determine such facts would be essentially a judicial function; and it has been held by the Supreme Court that forfeiture of property under the laws of Congress is a question whose decision belongs to the courts.[37] If it had been seriously contemplated that the courts were actually to enforce the emancipating features of the act, something would presumably have been said regarding procedure; for, as to the confiscation of property, the procedure was carefully specified.[38] It was provided that proceedings *in rem* were to be brought, with conformity, as nearly as possible, to admiralty actions. Certainly in such an unfamiliar field as this a definite provision as to procedure was to be expected. Section fourteen of the act, it is true, declared that "the courts . . . shall have full power to institute proceedings, make orders and

[37]Gelston *vs.* Hoyt, 3 Wheaton 246, Slocum *vs.* Mayberry, 2 Wheaton 3.

[38]*Supra*, p. 285.

decrees, issue process, and do all things necessary to carry this act into effect," but this provision seems to apply to the clauses relating to confiscation, for the act did not even say that the courts had any functions whatever as regards slaves. It is a general rule, of course, that where a right is guaranteed by Federal law, the Federal courts are available to a suitor claiming such a right;[39] and it might be said that a slave could bring a civil action in a Federal court to obtain freedom, or possibly, to obtain damages for illegal detention in servitude, citing the Confiscation Act as justification for such a suit; but, to mention only a few of the difficulties involved here, this would have put an onerous and expensive burden upon the slave; it would have involved one-sided suits in which, under the existing circumstances, the masters would not have been heard; the number of such suits would have exceeded the capacity of the courts; and such civil actions would have ignored the punitive features of a law which imposed emancipation as a penalty for supporting the "rebellion."

No court may seize anything beyond its reach nor determine anything outside its jurisdiction. If the courts were to have enforced the emancipating clause of the act, the following steps would have been necessary:

1. The courts would have had to develop a procedure for the purpose, under the doubtful authority of the fourteenth section. We have already noted the difficulties which this would have involved.

2. Physical possession of the slaves would have had to be acquired. The law said that all slaves of "rebels" taking refuge within the military lines, and by certain

[39]"The judicial power shall extend to all Cases . . . arising under this Constitution, the Laws of the United States," etc. (*Constitution of the United States*, Art. III, sec. 2). See also the Judiciary Act of 1789, *U. S. Stat. at Large*, I, 85-86.

other means coming within military possession, were to be deemed "captives of war" and to be "forever free." The rather eccentric phrase "captives of war" in this connection emphasized the fact that control of those slaves was to be obtained through military action, though that was not the case concerning confiscable property. It is evident, however, that the actual freeing of the slaves by military authority was not intended; and that the determination of rebel ownership and the issuing of decrees of freedom were in the nature of judicial, rather than military, functions. Yet the law did not say that the military authorities should turn the slaves over to the courts. What should be done with them was left in doubt. It is true that the Emancipation Proclamation of September 22, 1862, enjoined upon the military officers the enforcement of the emancipating clause of the second Confiscation Act; but this injunction was unaccompanied by specific instructions as to how the clause was to be enforced, or as to the many puzzling questions that would arise in seeking to apply both the confiscation law and the proclamation. In response to an inquiry by General Schofield, Judge Advocate General Holt gave the opinion that military protection should be given to slaves designated as free by the confiscation law of 1862, and that "certificates" of freedom be issued to such slaves;[40] but this policy advised by a law officer of the War Department does not seem to have been put into practical effect. Neither the military authorities nor the courts had any clear understanding as to how they were to carry out the confiscation law in its relation to the liberation of slaves.

3. In the third place, the courts would have had to

---

[40] *O. R.*, Ser. III, Vol. 3, p. 525; Ser. II, Vol. 6, p. 209.

make good their jurisdiction in dealing with the slaves. As to confiscable property, it was held that jurisdiction depended upon *situs*—i.e., only such property as was found within the boundaries of a particular district court's jurisdiction could be seized and condemned by that court. Senator Trumbull pointed out that his Confiscation Act did not itself divest title to property, and that judicial action against the property[41] located in loyal States within reach of the Federal courts (while the "rebels" themselves were out of such reach) was necessary in order to complete the confiscation.[42] Under such limitations, the use of the courts under the Confiscation Act for emancipating slaves would have been impracticable.

4. Having developed a procedure, obtained the slaves, and established jurisdiction, the courts would have had to determine the essential facts. Had they done this in thc manner that was adopted regarding confiscable property, this determination of facts (as to ownership of the slave and the "rebel" character of the owner) would have been performed in the owner's absence and, as was the practice in some cases, without giving even his agent a hearing; for a "rebel," it was said, has no *persona standi* in a Federal court.[43]

5. Finally, the courts would have had to issue some decree of emancipation for particularly designated

---

[41]Proceedings for confiscation were *in rem* against the property, not *in personam* against the offender. Yet the offender's guilt was the basis of the confiscation. The Supreme Court's decision that a "rebel" should not be denied "standing in court" in an action concerning his property came after the war, too late to affect the forfeitures; and even this decision did not overcome the difficulty involved in condemning the property on default when the owner, as was usual, did not try to appear. All this has been treated elsewhere. (*Supra*, pp., 307-312.)

[42]*Cong. Globe*, 37 Cong., 2 sess., p. 1571.

[43]*Supra*, p. 310.

slaves. Some document suitable for legal record would have been necessary, divesting the title, as a realty deed conveying a piece of land or a decree of condemnation and sale in the case of forfeited goods. Since the act itself did not divest the title, the need of such a decree is evident. It appears that the United States courts did not consider such decrees of liberation proper; and there is no instance, within the writer's knowledge, of any such decree having been issued. In fact there is no evidence of the actual enforcement of the emancipating clause of the act.[44]

On close analysis, therefore, it is hard to see by what process any particular slaves could have legally established that freedom which the second Confiscation Act "declared." The emancipating clause of the act is an example of loose legislation which is the more remarkable in view of the voluminous debates which every phase of this closely contested bill called forth in both houses.

IV

Simultaneously with the second Confiscation Act Congress passed another law which involved emancipation. This was the measure which conferred freedom upon slave-soldiers. The Militia Act of July 17, 1862, provided that when any slave belonging to an enemy of the United States should render military service, he should be forever thereafter free; and his mother, wife, and children (unless belonging to loyal owners) should be free.[45] It would seem that this act really added

---

[44]Lincoln said concerning the second Confiscation Act: "I cannot learn that that law has caused a single slave to come over to us." (Sept. 13, 1862: Nicolay and Hay, *Works*, VIII, 30.)

[45]Section 13 of the act calling forth the militia: *U. S. Stat. at Large*, XII, 599.

nothing to the emancipating clause of the Confiscation Act, which declared all such slaves free on the ground of "rebel" ownership, except that an additional reason for this freedom was now found in military service; and, as military service is a matter of record, it would be a useful basis of establishing freedom in the legal sense, in case the war should close without any more comprehensive measure of liberation. It was rather surprising that this law did not at the same time provide similar freedom for slave-soldiers owned by loyal masters, with compensation to such masters,[46] for it was widely recognized that no Negro who had served under the colors should be reënslaved.

It will thus be seen that before the issuance of the Emancipation Proclamation in September, 1862, Congress had provided manumission by various measures, the provisions of which to a certain extent overlapped. The liberation of slaves of "rebel" ownership coming within the Union lines, the liberation of slaves belonging to "rebels" under the Confiscation Act of July, 1862, and the emancipation of slave-soldiers of "rebel" ownership—all this had been provided for by Congress before the President issued his famous edict. For these reasons the comment has sometimes been made that the freeing of slaves during the war was accomplished by Congress rather than by the President.

These measures of Congress struck at slavery as a State institution. But Congress did not stop here. In the national field also, where its normal jurisdiction applied (unless one should accept the Dred Scott

[46]This defect was cured in the act of February 24, 1864, amending the "act for enrolling and calling out the national forces." The twenty-fourth section provided freedom for drafted slaves belonging to loyal owners, with bounties to the owners. Compensation was also made available for loyal owners of colored volunteers, and such volunteers were made free. (*U. S. Stat. at Large*, XIII, 11.)

"dictum" to the contrary) Congress acted in the interest of freedom. Slavery in the District of Columbia was abolished, with compensation to loyal owners, on April 16, 1862; and emancipation in the territories (but without compensation) was provided by act of June 19, of the same year.[47]

V

Our attention must now turn to that form of emancipation which Lincoln favored in preference to any other because it came nearest to satisfying his sense of what was statesmanlike, equitable, and legally sound. This was gradual emancipation by voluntary action of the States with Federal coöperation and compensation. In recommending, on March 6, 1862,[48] that Congress should pass a resolution pledging financial aid for this purpose, the President pointed out that the matter was one of perfectly free choice with the States; and that his proposition involved "no claim of a right by Federal authority to interfere with slavery within State limits, referring, as it does, the absolute control of the subject . . . to the State and its people." Lincoln was too good a lawyer to ignore the constitutional limitations as to the power of Congress over slavery in the States, and the legal importance of the vested rights of slave owners which called for compensation. On

---

[47] *U. S. Stat. at Large,* XII, 376, 432, 538, 665. In an able analysis of the Dred Scott case, E. S. Corwin has shown that Taney's denial of congressional power to prohibit slavery in the territories was not an "obiter dictum," but a canvassing afresh of the question of jurisdiction. He points out, however, the irrelevancy of Taney's argument in invoking the doctrine of "vested rights" in the interpretation of the "due process" clause, and thus denouncing the Missouri Compromise as a violation of the Fifth Amendment. (*Am. Hist. Rev.*, XVII, 52-69.)

[48] *Cong. Globe,* 37 Cong., 2 sess., p. 1102.

April 10, 1862, Congress passed the following resolution,[49] in the identical form proposed by the President.

> *Be it resolved* . . . That the United States ought to co-operate with any State which may adopt gradual abolishment of slavery, giving to such State pecuniary aid, to be used by such State in its discretion, to compensate for the inconveniences, public and private, produced by such a change of system.

This joint resolution was directed primarily to the border States, but it offered pecuniary assistance to any State that should abolish slavery. An unfavorable reply to the proposal was made by a congressional delegation from the border States,[50] and the scheme was never carried out. It came very near, however, to being put to a practical test in Missouri. Even before that State had passed an emancipation law, both houses of Congress passed bills giving actual financial aid to the State for the purpose of emancipation. The bills disagreed in form, and time was lacking in the short session ending in March, 1863, to perfect and pass the same bill through the two houses; but the affirmative action of both houses on the actual appropriation of money is significant of the serious purpose of Congress to fulfill the Federal side of the proposal.[51]

Five months after the initiation of the scheme for compensated abolition, the executive proclamation of emancipation, which we will consider on a later page,

---

[49] *Ibid.*, Appendix, p. 420.

[50] *Ann. Cyc.*, 1862, p. 722.

[51] In the House bill Federal bonds to the amount of ten million dollars were provided. The Senate bill provided bonds up to twenty million dollars; but, if emancipation should not be effected before July 4, 1865, the amount to be delivered was to be only ten million. (*Cong. Globe*, Jan. 6, 1863, 37 Cong., 3 sess., p. 209; *Senate Journal*, Feb. 12, 1863, p. 243.)

was issued (September 22, 1862). The proclamation, however, did not apply in the border States, nor universally within the Confederate States; and its issuance by no means indicated an abandonment of the scheme for State abolition with Federal compensation. In the September proclamation the President specifically declared his intention to "recommend the adoption of a practical measure tendering pecuniary aid" to loyal slave States voluntarily adopting immediate or gradual abolishment. The compensation scheme was his idea of the proper method for the permanent eradication of slavery, while the proclamation was a measure of partial application whose legal effect after the war he regarded as doubtful.

As a side light on the President's policy of making compensation to slave owners, it is interesting to study a general order concerning the military use of property and slaves in the Southern States, which he issued on the very day when the Emancipation Proclamation was broached in Cabinet meeting (July 22, 1862). He ordered that property be used where necessary for military purposes, but that "none shall be destroyed in wantonness or malice." He further directed "that . . . commanders employ . . . so many persons of African descent as can be advantageously used for military or naval purposes, giving them reasonable wages for their labor," and ordered "that, as to both property and persons of African descent, accounts shall be kept . . . as a basis upon which compensation can be made in proper cases." This order was written in Lincoln's handwriting and was issued as a general order by the War Department.[52] It is of interest as showing how the President, while occupied with the subject of emancipa-

[52]Stanton Papers, VIII, No. 51769; *O. R.*, Ser. III, Vol. 2, p. 397; Nicolay and Hay, *Works*, VII, 287.

tion by proclamation, was at the same time mindful of the property rights of slave owners.

In his annual message of December 1, 1862, Lincoln presented at some length a detailed project for compensated emancipation which he wished to have adopted as articles amendatory of the Constitution. These proposed amendments provided for the delivery of United States bonds to every State which should abolish slavery before the year 1900. All slaves made free by the chances of war were to be forever free, but loyal owners of such slaves were to be compensated. The President, in this message, argued elaborately and eloquently for the adoption of his scheme.[53]

An examination of this able message reveals much concerning the legal phases of emancipation as viewed by the President. He treated the subject of the liberation of slaves as one still to be decided, showing that he did not regard thc Emancipation Proclamation as a settlement or solution of the question in the large sense. State action was still to be relied upon for the legal accomplishment of emancipation; and this was in harmony with the statement which the President is reported to have made in his interview with the border-State delegation on March 10, 1862, "that emancipation was a subject exclusively under the control of the States, and must be adopted or rejected by each for itself; that he did not claim, nor had this Government any right to coerce them for that purpose."[54]

The message shows further that he considered compensation the correct procedure; and believed that such compensation by the Federal Government, the expense of which would be borne by the whole country, was

[53]Nicolay and Hay, *Works*, VIII, 93-131.

[54]McPherson, *Political History of the Rebellion*, 210 *et seq.*

equitable. He would set constitutional discussions at rest by writing his plan of liberation (even to the amount and interest rate of the bonds and the terms of their delivery) into the fundamental law. Yet, though he was proceeding by constitutional amendment, his method was not to emancipate by purely national action; for the matter was still to be left to the States and would apply only in those States which should choose to coöperate. It was to be voluntary emancipation by the States with compensation by the nation. For even so much national action as was involved in "coöperation" with States desiring to give freedom to their slaves, Lincoln favored the adoption of a constitutional amendment, though this financial "coöperation" is the sort of thing that Congress nowadays regards as a part of an ordinary day's work.

We need not, of course, conclude that the President, in his own mind, doubted the constitutionality of the proposal for compensated emancipation; though, as we have seen, he did doubt the constitutional power of Congress to impose liberation upon a State. He said in communicating his original proposal to the border-State delegation that his proposition, since it merely contemplated cooperation with States which should voluntarily act, involved no constitutional difficulty.[55] In his December message he made no reference to any defect in the constitutional power of Congress to act as he proposed. The plain inference is, not that the President considered an amendment necessary to legalize his project; but that he wished the scruples of those who did think so satisfied, and also that he wished so grave and important a matter to be dealt with by a solemn, fundamental, act.

---

[55]Nicolay and Hay, *Works*, VII, 125-126.

Since this project for State abolition with Federal aid was never adopted, we need not dwell further upon the many interesting questions which it presented. Perhaps its chief interest is to be found in the light it throws upon Lincoln's lawyerlike caution in dealing with the slavery question as a matter of permanent law.

All these cautious legal considerations in Lincoln's mind and this circumspection in his official acts should not be regarded as dimming his intense conviction as to the moral wrong and shameful social abuse of slavery. To review his works is to find emphatic and numerous expressions of this conviction. Space is lacking for a full showing of these statements, but a few typical ones may be noted here. In 1854: "This declared indifference . . . for the spread of slavery, I cannot but hate. I hate it because of the monstrous injustice of slavery itself. I hate it because it. . . enables the enemies of free institutions . . . to taunt us as hypocrites . . . ." In 1855: "I hate to see the poor creatures hunted down and caught . . . ." In 1859: "Never forget that we have before us this whole matter of the right or wrong of slavery in this Union . . . ." In 1864: "I am naturally antislavery. If slavery is not wrong, nothing is wrong. I cannot remember when I did not so think and feel . . . ."[56] These sentiments were among the deep fundamentals of Lincoln's liberal thought.

---

[56]For these statements see Nicolay and Hay, *Works*, II, 205, 282; V, 122; X, 65. For a full and useful compilation of Lincoln's many utterances on slavery (with references), see Archer H. Shaw, ed., *Lincoln Encyclopedia*, 298-339.

CHAPTER XVI

EMANCIPATION COMPLETED

I. Legal basis of the Emancipation Proclamation
II. Effect and validity of the proclamation
III. Legal confusion arising where Federal laws of emancipation encountered slave codes in loyal States
IV. Action of the border States concerning slavery
V. The anti-slavery amendment: Controversy concerning such use of the "amending power"
VI. Legality of the process by which the Thirteenth Amendment was ratified
VII. Considerations concerning the lack of compensation to slaveholders

I

Our attention will be directed in this chapter to the public measures by which the eradication of slavery in this country was actually accomplished. President Lincoln issued a preliminary proclamation of emancipation on September 22, 1862, from which we may quote the following words:

> I, Abraham Lincoln, President of the United States . . . , and Commander-in-Chief of the army and navy thereof, do hereby proclaim . . . that hereafter, as heretofore, the war will be prosecuted for the object of practically restoring the constitutional relation between the United States and each of the States. . . . [In the next paragraph the President states that he will again recommend to Congress the adoption of a practical measure giving pecuniary aid to States not in rebellion which may abolish slavery.]
>
> That on the first day of January [1863], all persons held as slaves within any State, or designated part of a State, the

people whereof shall then be in rebellion against the United States, shall be then, thenceforward, and forever free; and the Executive Government of the United States, including the military and naval authority thereof, will recognize and maintain the freedom of such persons, and will do no act . . . to repress such persons . . . in any efforts they may make for their actual freedom. [The proclamation then quotes the act of Congress prohibiting the use of the military forces to return fugitive slaves, and the emancipating clauses of the second Confiscation Act, and enjoins the armed forces of the United States to obey and enforce these enactments.]

And the Executive will in due time recommend that all [loyal] citizens . . . shall (upon the restoration of the constitutional relation between the United States and their respective States and people, if that relation shall have been suspended or disturbed) be compensated for all losses by acts of the United States, including the loss of slaves.[1]

One hundred days later, on January 1, 1863, the definitive proclamation was issued. Beginning with a preamble referring to the earlier proclamation of warning, the President continued:[2]

Now therefore I . . . by virtue of the power in me vested as Commander-in-Chief of the Army and Navy . . . in time of actual armed rebellion . . . , and as a fit and necessary war measure for suppressing said rebellion, do . . . order and designate . . . the following [as rebellious districts], to-wit:

Arkansas, Texas, Louisiana [except certain designated parishes], Mississippi, Alabama, Florida, Georgia, South Carolina, North Carolina, and Virginia [except "West Virginia" and certain other designated portions].[3]

---

[1]Nicolay and Hay, *Works,* VIII, 36-41.

[2]*Ibid.*, pp. 161-164.

[3]The excepted portions of Virginia, besides "the forty-eight counties designated as West Virginia" (for which the process of separate statehood had not yet been completed), were "the counties of Berkeley, Accomac, Northampton, Elizabeth City, York, Princess Anne, and Norfolk, including the cities of Norfolk and Portsmouth." It should be noted that Tennessee was omitted from the proclamation.

And . . . I do order and declare that all persons held as slaves within said designated States and parts of States are, and henceforward shall be, free; and that the Executive Government of the United States, including the military and naval authorities thereof, will recognize and maintain the freedom of said persons.

[The President then enjoins orderly conduct upon freedmen and offers to receive them into the armed service for garrison and naval duty.]

And upon this act, sincerely believed to be an act of justice, warranted by the Constitution upon military necessity, I invoke the considerate judgment of mankind, and the gracious favor of Almighty God.

An extensive controversy was waged as to the legal basis for this "edict" of freedom. It was urged in opposition that slavery was a State affair;[4] that the only source of power for the Federal Government was the Constitution, and that under it the Government had no authority over slavery within the States; that preserving the Constitution, not breaking it, was the purpose of the war; that under international law private property on land was exempt from seizure; that emancipation was especially discredited as a belligerent right; that it amounted to the taking of property without "due process of law"; and that such action in the form of a proclamation was a mere usurpation of power on the part of the executive.

On the affirmative side it was admitted that the right of emancipation was not specifically granted by the Constitution; but it was urged that that instrument authorizes the Government to wage war, and thus to

[4]Lincoln admitted this as a rule applying in peace times, and in time of war as a limitation upon Congress, but not upon the executive. Rigid consistency would, perhaps, have required him to veto certain emancipating measures of Congress which, nevertheless, he signed.

exert war powers against an enemy. International law, so the argument ran, is at all times an available part of our Government's legal resources; and in time of war the "usages of war" which are a part of international law must always be included among the legitimate sources of governmental authority. During the Civil War belligerent rights were declared by the Supreme Court to belong to the United States in its dealings with the secessionist power; and all the inhabitants of the States in "insurrection" were, in the eyes of the law, "enemies." The seizure of an enemy's property is a right as well as a necessary result of war, it was argued; and, if necessary for military purposes, such property may be destroyed. Those humane considerations which, in modern times, modify the right of seizure and limit it to such property as is useful in the prosecution of war are not to be ignored; but emancipation is a humane measure, striking at a kind of "property" which modern nations have ceased to recognize; and the military importance of slavery to the enemy constitutes it a legitimate target against which the right over enemy property may be exerted. As to the President's exercise of the power by proclamation, that was held to be justified by the general rule that the President's powers as commander-in-chief include belligerent rights derived from the usages of war, as, for example, the authority to proclaim a blockade of the enemy's coast. The proclaiming of such a blockade, it was urged, though not specifically authorized by the Constitution, is generally conceded to be within the President's war power; and emancipation was claimed as an analogous right.

The right to free an enemy's slaves, it was also argued, is embraced within the law of military occupation. In support of this view it was a common thing to quote certain well-known statements of John Quincy Adams regarding slavery and "martial law."[5] We need not pause here to comment on the lack of harmony between these later views of Adams as an anti-slavery leader and the earlier arguments which as Secretary of State he urged against the belligerent right of emancipation. Whether he regarded these seemingly opposite views as consistent, or whether he had changed his mind, is a matter that need not detain us; but during the Civil War he was cited as a convincing authority by both the supporters and the opponents of military emancipation. In 1842 Adams argued that an invaded country has all its laws swept away and is subjected to martial law. When two hostile armies are set in martial array, the commanders of both, he declared, have the power to emancipate all the slaves in the invaded territory. Citing an instance of military abolition of slavery in South America, he observed, "It was abolished by . . . military command . . . and its abolition continues to be law to this day. It was abolished by the laws of war, and not by municipal enactments."[6] Military authority, said Adams, takes the place of municipal institutions, slavery among the rest. "From the instant

---

[5]C. F. Adams, "John Quincy Adams and Martial Law," Mass. Hist. Soc. Proceedings, second series, XV (1901-1902), 436-478.

[6]*Ibid.*, p. 442. It appears that Adams was in error in his use of South American examples. He evidently referred to the action of Bolivar in 1816 in proclaiming freedom to slaves in certain parts of Venezuela which was at that time united with Colombia. This action, however, was but partial, and it did not put an end to slavery in that country; for Bolivar himself requested the Venezuelan Congress to abolish slavery in later years, and Codazzi, the geographer, calculated that there were 49,000 slaves in Venezuela in 1839. Effectual abolition of slavery did not come in Venezuela until 1854, nor in New Granada (Colombia) until 1851. Thus when Adams spoke in 1842 of abolition by military authority in South America, slavery actually existed in those countries to which he was referring. (M. Landaeta Rosales, *La Libertad de los Esclavos en Venezuela;* W. S. Robertson, *History of the Latin American Nations*, 366, 409.)

your slave State becomes a theater of war, servile, civil or foreign, the war powers of Congress extend to interference with slavery in every way."

An examination of the context and the historical setting of these utterances, which were made in debate in the House of Representatives in 1837 and 1842, shows that Mr. Adams was contending primarily at this time for the right of those opposed to slavery to present petitions to Congress; that he objected to the extreme wording of a proposed resolution to the effect that Congress had no power to interfere "in any way" with the subject of slavery; and that, in justifying interference with slavery in time of war, he seems to have had in mind a situation in which the people of the free States would be called upon to aid in putting down servile insurrection in the South, thus giving their lives and money for the purpose, as he said, of keeping the blacks in slavery. Under these circumstances, he would consider the freeing of the slaves by military power justified; but such a situation differed materially from that which really existed during the Civil War. It should be added that, in using the expression "martial law," he intended to refer to the law of military occupation, though his statements as Secretary of State, in 1820, certainly excluded manumission of slaves as a right of a military occupant.

Some of the arguments justifying the proclamation showed considerable flexibility of interpretation. It was argued, for instance, that the Constitution did not recognize slaves at all, considering the Negro in the South on the same basis as the apprentice.[7] It was also said

---

[7]It was argued in the report of the American Freedmen's Inquiry Commission, in May, 1864, that, in the section referring to the apportionment of Representatives and direct taxes, the words "other persons" were used in contrast to "free persons" precisely in the same

that property in slaves was a debt, similar to "the debt an artisan might contract, if he gave . . . his promissory note for so many months' labor."[8] It was then added that the emancipation of slaves was merely the confiscation of debts! Such champions of the President's power also argued that if, as Commander-in-Chief, he should violate the rules of war concerning the property of non-combatants, it would be "an offense, not against the Constitution, but against international law." "The legality of his acts" in that case might be "called in question, not their constitutionality."[9]

In considering the grounds on which Lincoln himself justified the proclamation, we must remember that he really favored emancipation by State action with Federal compensation to the owners, but realized that there was no prospect of this proposal being adopted by the seceded States. We must remember, also, that prior to the issuance of the proclamation he had been "prompt and emphatic in denouncing any interference by the general Government with the subject."[10] On various occasions he declared his conviction that Congress (even during the war) had no legal power to strike at slavery in the States. He thought, however, that the executive had powers which Congress did not have.

He based his proclamation solely upon the "war power." He issued it "by virtue of the power in me vested as Commander-in-Chief of the Army and Navy

---

sense that the phrase "those bound to service for a term of years" was so used. It was then stated that the Constitution did not recognize the Negro as a slave any more than the apprentice. (*O. R.*, Ser. III, Vol. 4, pp. 345-346.)

[8] *Ibid.*, p. 349.

[9] *Ibid.*, p. 352.

[10] *Diary of Gideon Welles*, I, 70-71. (July 13, 1862.) Welles adds: "This was, I think, the sentiment of every member of the Cabinet, all of whom, including the President, considered it [slavery] a local, domestic question."

. . . and as a fit and necessary war measure." He characterized it as an act "warranted by the Constitution *upon military necessity*."[11] "As Commander-in-Chief," he once said, rather loosely, "I suppose I have a right to take any measure which may best subdue the enemy."[12] Again he said, "I think the Constitution invests its Commander-in-Chief with the law of war in time of war," and he added that the law of war gives the right to take property "whenever taking it helps us or hurts the enemy."[13] In fact, he considered military necessity the only just basis for the proclamation,[14] and he even justified it on the ground that the war at times necessitated things that were normally "unconstitutional." "I felt that measures otherwise unconstitutional," he said, "might become lawful by becoming indispensable to the preservation of the Constitution through the preservation of the nation."[15] In these extracts we have the gist of Lincoln's views on the subject. It is perhaps sufficient to say that he considered liberation of the enemy's slaves an appropriate and necessary military measure coming within the laws of war.

II

Having observed the basis upon which the proclamation rested, we must now inquire as to its legal effect and validity. In this connection the limitations within the proclamation itself should be carefully noted. Those

---

[11]The words in italics were, as Rhodes points out, inserted by Lincoln in a passage suggested by Chase. (Rhodes, *History of the United States*, IV, 213, n.)

[12]Nicolay and Hay, *Works*, VIII, 32.

[13]*Ibid.*, IX, 98.

[14]"The . . . proclamation has no constitutional or legal justification, except as a military measure," said Lincoln. (*Ibid.*, IX, 109.)

[15]*Ibid.*, X, 66.

portions of Confederate territory which were within the control of the military forces of the Union were, in general, excepted from the terms of the proclamation. These exceptions were made, as President Lincoln said, because "military necessity" did not require the application of the proclamation in these regions.[16] Largely for this reason, the proclamation has been frequently described as a measure having little or no effect. "Immediate practical effect it has none," said the New York *World*, "the slaves remaining in . . . the same condition as before." "So long . . . as the present political and military status continues, the freedom declared by this proclamation is a dormant, not an actual freedom. . . . The proclamation is issued as a war measure. . . . But that cannot be a *means* of military success which presupposes this same military success as the condition of its existence."[17] "We show our sympathy with slavery," Seward is reported to have said, "by emancipating slaves where we cannot reach them, and holding them in bondage where we can set them free."[18] "The proclamation applied only to States and parts of States under rebel control. It did not emancipate any slaves within the emancipator's reach," is the comment of Horace White.[19] The British statesman, Earl Russell, wrote on January 17, 1863: "The Proclamation of the President of the United States . . . appears to be of a very strange nature. It professes to emancipate all slaves in places where the United States authorities cannot exercise any jurisdiction . . . but it does not decree emancipation . . . in any States, or parts of States, occupied by fed-

[16]*Ibid.*, IX, 109.

[17]Editorial, New York *World*, Jan. 3, 1863.

[18]Don Piatt, *Memoirs of Men Who Saved the Union*, 150. (Cited in Horace White, *Life of Lyman Trumbull*, 222.)

[19]Horace White, *Life of Lyman Trumbull*, 222.

eral troops . . . and where, therefore, emancipation . . . might have been carried into effect. . . . The proclamation . . . makes slavery at once legal and illegal. . . . There seems to be no declaration of a principle adverse to slavery in this proclamation. It is a measure of war, and a measure of war of a very questionable kind."[20]

The Emancipation Proclamation is commonly regarded as a measure which marked a distinct change in the purpose of the war, so that from the time of its issuance the war was pursued with the object of overthrowing slavery. There is truth in this view, and one does note after the proclamation an increasing determination on the part of the Government to conduct the conflict as a war against slavery; but if the seceded States had done all that Lincoln asked and returned to the Union in response to his preliminary proclamation of September, 1862, there was nothing in the proclamation to prevent the war from ending with slavery still preserved. Preservation of slavery in non-rebellious regions seemed to be implied in the proclamation. Russell made a true observation when he said that Lincoln's proclamation contained "no declaration of a principle adverse to slavery."

Comments by Lincoln's critics on the futility of the proclamation were common enough; but we read with wonder the following language of Lincoln himself, uttered after the proclamation had been presented in Cabinet and decided upon as a policy of the administration: "What good would a proclamation of emancipation from me do?" was the President's question to a church delegation. "I do not want to issue a document that the whole world will see must necessarily be inoperative,

---

[20]Note of Russell to Lyons, January 17, 1863: Henry Wheaton, *Elements of International Law*, ed. by W. B. Lawrence (Boston, 1863), supplement, p. 37.

like the Pope's bull against the comet. Would my word free the slaves, when I cannot even enforce the Constitution in the rebel States? Is there a single court, or magistrate, or individual that would be influenced by it there?"[21]

Of course the history of the war amply proves that, as a practical measure, the proclamation was more than a "bull against the comet." One needs only to read soldiers' reminiscences to learn how the Negroes hailed the proclamation as their liberation from generations of bondage, how they flocked to the armies in embarrassing numbers, how thousands of them accompanied Sherman to the sea.[22] The records of the war give ample evidence of the actual carrying out of the proclamation. As a way of weakening the enemy, slaves were encouraged to come within the Union lines and their treatment was a matter receiving careful thought. Thousands were used as soldiers; many were put to labor for wages, either for the Government or for loyal employers; the women, children, and infirm became wards of the nation. Camps for freed Negroes were established as a temporary expedient; and, to cope with the larger aspects of the new problem, the generals organized specially created departments of Negro affairs, which undertook the manifold activities that later fell to the Freedmen's Bureau.[23] It is instructive to read on this subject the comprehensive orders of General Butler issued in December, 1863.[24] He detailed one of his colonels as a "general superintendent of Negro affairs," with headquarters at Fortress Monroe, and under him were ap-

---

[21]Nicolay and Hay, *Works*, VIII, 30.

[22]Rhodes, *History of United States*, V, 26; J. M. Schofield, *Forty-six Years in the Army*, Ch. xix.

[23]*O. R.*, Ser. III, Vol. 3, pp. 686, 917-918.

[24]*Ibid.*, pp. 1139-1144.

pointed various district superintendents and local superintendents, with duties extending over parts of Virginia and North Carolina. These officers were to decide what Negroes were free by the proclamation; take a Negro census; supervise contracts with white employers so as to prevent fraud; keep accounts of lands allotted to colored tenants; coöperate with persons coming to teach the freedmen; and, in general, to deal with the whole problem of the liberated slaves. Later the War Department took up the Negro problem in a comprehensive way; and, in 1865, Congress created for this purpose, before the war ended, the Freedmen's Bureau.[25] It is true that, in general throughout the Confederacy, the slaves remained quiet and loyal to their Southern masters;[26] but it is also true that, where Federal armies advanced, thousands came within Union control. The practical effect of the proclamation, then, can hardly be disputed.

Its legal effect is a different matter.[27] Slavery existed on the basis of law; and if it were to be permanently abolished, this would have to be done by some process of law. Just what would have been the status of slavery if there had been no anti-slavery amendment, is a difficult question. While insisting that the freedom declared in his proclamation was irrevocable,[28] Lincoln had

[25]The Freedmen's Bureau was created by act of March 3, 1865: *U. S. Stat. at Large*, XIII, 507.

[26]Concerning the absence of servile insurrection as a result of the Emancipation Proclamation, see Rhodes, *History of the United States*, V, 460-461.

[27]There was an obscure case at St. Louis early in 1863 which involved the legality and applicability of the Emancipation Proclamation. A Negro slave, escaped from Arkansas (to which the proclamation applied), was convicted of grand larceny. The judge decided that the proclamation made him free, and that he should be imprisoned in the penitentiary as a "free criminal," whereas a slave would have been punished with lashes on the bare back. (New York *World*, Feb. 6, 1863.)

[28]Rhodes *History of the United States*, V, 58, 59; Nicolay and Hay, *Works*, VIII, 182; IX, 249; XI, 31.

doubts as to the manner in which the courts would treat his edict. He thought that it was a war measure and would be inoperative at the close of the war, but he was not sure.[29] His attitude toward the Thirteenth Amendment showed how conscious he was of legal deficiencies in the proclamation,[30] and these doubts were reflected in Congress where proposals to incorporate the proclamation into Federal law were presented by supporters of the administration.[31]

One of the ablest lawyers of that day put the matter thus: "That an army may free the slaves of an enemy is a settled right of law. . . . But if any man fears or hopes that the proclamation did as a matter of law by its own force, alter the legal status of one slave in America . . . he builds his fears or hopes on the sand.

---

[29]Nicolay and Hay, *Lincoln*, X, 123.

[30]The proclamation, said Lincoln, "falls short of what the amendment will be. . . . A question might be raised whether the proclamation was legally valid. It might be urged that it only aided those that came into our lines, and that it was inoperative as to those who did not give themselves up; or that it would have no effect upon the children of slaves born hereafter; in fact it would be urged that it did not meet the evil. But this amendment is a king's cure-all for all evils. It winds the whole thing up." (Nicolay and Hay, *Works*, X, 353.)

[31]Various acts were proposed in Congress to give effect to the Emancipation Proclamation. Representative Arnold of Illinois introduced a bill "for . . . carrying into more complete and immediate execution" the President's proclamation. It "prohibited" the reënslaving of any person declared free by the proclamation, but imposed no penalty. When the Wade-Davis bill was under consideration, Sumner moved an amendment providing that the proclamation "is hereby adopted and enacted as a statute of the United States and as a rule for the government of the military and naval forces thereof." (A sort of additional "article of war.") "I wish to see emancipation in the rebel States," said Sumner, "placed under the guarantee of an act of Congress. I do not wish to see it left to float on a presidential proclamation." Neither of these measures was adopted, but they gave a certain satisfaction to such opponents of emancipation as Saulsbury of Delaware, who remarked that he had not so soon expected the President's friends to make open confession that his acts were illegal. (*Cong. Globe*, 38 Cong., 1 sess., pp. 20, 3460.)

It is a military act and not a decree of a legislator. It has no legal effect by its own force on the status of the slave. . . . If you sustain the war you must expect to see the war work out emancipation."[32] And Secretary Welles of the Navy wrote in 1863: "What is to be the ultimate effect of the Proclamation, and what will be the exact status of the slaves . . . were the States now to resume their position, I am not prepared to say. The courts would adjudicate the questions; there would be legislative action in Congress and in the States also." He added, however, that no slave who had left a "rebel" master and come within the Union lines, or who had served under the flag, could ever again be forced into involuntary servitude.[33]

Hare, a reliable authority on constitutional law, is somewhat more positive as to the permanent effect of

---

[32]Speech of R. H. Dana, Jr., at Providence, R. I.: New York *Tribune*, April 13, 1865. In his annotations of Wheaton's treatise on international law, Mr. Dana discussed the legal force and significance of the Emancipation Proclamation. He said: "Although the language of the proclamation is general, and in the present tense, as if giving a legal *status* of freedom, from its date, to all slaves in the designated States, still . . . it would seem that, being a military measure by a commander-in-chief who had no general legislative authority over regions . . . not in his possession, it could not operate further than as a military order. From that time, all slaves coming under the control of the forces of the United States in the manner recognized by the law of belligerent occupation, were to be free. If this is the correct view, . . . it became therefore a question of fact, as to each slave and each region of the country, whether the forces of the Union had such possession as to give effect to the proclamation." Dana added that the President could have no legislative functions "which could operate, by a mere declaration of his will, in places out of his belligerent control," but went on to say that "all the designated districts did at last come under the military occupation of the armies of the Union, in such sense as to effect the emancipation of all slaves in the strictest view of the law of belligerent occupation, and the system of slavery has since been abolished . . . by an amendment to the Constitution." (Henry Wheaton, *Elements of International Law*, ed. by R. H. Dana, Jr. [Boston, 1866], 441, n.)

[33]*Diary of Gideon Welles*, I, 415. (Aug. 22, 1863.)

the proclamation. It was, he said, a mere command which could effect no change till executed by the hand of war; "but if carried into execution it might, like other acts *jure belli*, work a change that would survive on the return of peace."[34] Admitting the right of emancipation as coming within the *jus belli*, one could say that the liberated slave would be as secure in his altered status as contraband property, if seized, would be in its new ownership. This would apply only to those slaves actually liberated by the incidents of war.

Taken at its best, however, the proclamation, with its partial application, was not a comprehensive solution of the slavery problem; and, in spite of this striking use of national authority, the slavery question, from 1863 to 1865, still remained, in large part, a State matter.

III

Thus there came, in the fast moving development of public policy during the Civil War, an awkward, transitional stage when the laws concerning slavery were half State, half national. Especially between 1863 and 1865, the main question as to the legal existence of slavery within a State rested with the State itself, while at the same time there were various acts on the statute-books of the nation which seriously interfered with the institution. Though slavery still existed within the border States, yet many (in some cases a great majority) of the actual "slaves" of these States might be free by Federal law. Among those thus made free were slave-soldiers and their families, slaves belonging to "rebels," and slave refugees from the States in "rebellion." Control of Negroes in general was a matter of State jurisdiction; yet

[34] J. I. C. Hare, *American Constitutional Law*, II, 945-946.

such control might easily be carried to the point of conflict with national authority, as for instance in a case where the wife of a slave-soldier, seeking employment at wages as a free woman, might find herself confronted with the State law prohibiting slaves from running at large, and forbidding the hiring or harboring of fugitives from labor. Such conflicts were, in fact, numerous.

Furthermore, though certain classes of slaves had become "free" by national law, they were *free Negroes*; and the laws defining their status as freemen were State laws, for the Fourteenth Amendment giving civil rights to the colored race had not yet been passed. Free Negroes in the border States did not have the privileges of whites. In Kentucky, Maryland, and Delaware, the immigration of free Negroes was forbidden, and those within the States were under special disabilities. Vagrant free Negroes, for instance, could be sold as slaves for one year in Maryland; and such Negroes were under definite restrictions as to the holding of assemblages, being forbidden to congregate in camp meetings without white supervision. The laws of these States[35] hedged in the legal process of emancipation with various restrictions, requiring written record of manumission, by deed or will.[36] Consequently, the Federal laws broadly conferring "freedom" upon whole classes of Negroes without any provision for the legal proving of such freedom by particular individuals, introduced an unfamiliar method of liberation (if it could be called a "method") which would be difficult to administer in a State still endeavoring to conserve slavery.

---

[35] *The Maryland Code*, 1860, Art. 66; *Revised Statutes of Kentucky*, 1860, pp. 359 *et seq.*; *Revised Statutes of Delaware*, 1852, Ch. 52.

[36] By Kentucky law, slaves could be emancipated only on condition of being removed from the State; and no deed or will of emancipation could confer absolute freedom until such removal should have been effected. (*Revised Statutes of Kentucky*, 1860, Ch. 93, Art. ix.)

This legal confusion was sure to produce serious conflict in case an aggressive attempt to protect the freedmen on the part of the Federal authorities should be met by a determination to assert State rights. Such a situation existed in Kentucky in 1865. Various judges in that State decided that the Federal law giving freedom to the families of slave-soldiers was unconstitutional;[37] and white employers hiring such persons were prosecuted in the State courts for the offense of harboring slaves. General J. M. Palmer of the Federal army, who remained within the State after the war because of the disturbed condition of affairs, took the emphatic position that slavery had "ceased to exist in Kentucky," and used his military power to make the freedom of the colored people effective. Palmer argued that 165,000 of the slaves of Kentucky were free as Federal soldiers, as the close kinsmen of soldiers, or as belonging to "rebels." He then asked, Why may not the remaining 65,000 also be free, though the mode of their emancipation has not been pointed out? Some States, he said, once had laws against witchcraft but not necessarily witches. "They have laws in Kentucky in reference to slavery, but in my judgment no slaves." "The whole slave system of Kentucky," he asserted, "is subverted and overthrown, and . . . in point of law and fact [it] controls no one."

Finding the passage of the Ohio River blocked and other travel closed to Negroes whether free or slave, and desiring to avert pestilence and relieve labor shortage, Palmer ordered his provost marshals to issue passes to unemployed Negroes, and ordered ferry boats, steamboats, and railroads to transport them. This was done as an emergency measure, and no attempt was made to investigate the question of freedom. "The free," he

[37]Statement of General J. M. Palmer: Chicago *Tribune*, Oct. 27, 1865, p. 1.

said, "had a right to demand from me that protection which . . . slave laws denied them. If, in separating the free from the slaves, the discriminations were not always accurate, it was the fault of those who made the separation necessary."[38]

The resistance of the State authorities to General Palmer's course was defiant and widespread.[39] Owners advertised the departure of their slaves, and employers though in need of labor refused to hire the "fugitives." Many suits and prosecutions in the State courts resulted: damage suits to recover the value of escaped slaves; criminal actions against officers "giving passes to Negroes not their own property"; actions for false imprisonment brought by State officials who were arrested for expelling Negroes from railroad cars; indictments for illegally harboring runaway slaves, and the like. Many individuals brought actions against General Palmer, and in the case of *The Commonwealth of Kentucky* versus *John M. Palmer*[40] it was held by the highest court in the State that the Federal Government had no constitutional power to abolish slavery by military force in Kentucky, and that the general was guilty of felony. It was only by the Thirteenth Amendment that this deadlock on the slavery question within the State was terminated.

IV

Except Kentucky and Delaware, every one of the border slaveholding States abolished slavery by State action before the Thirteenth Amendment went into

---

[38]Letter of J. M. Palmer to Secretary Stanton, October 2, 1865: Chicago *Tribune*, Oct. 17, 1865, p. 3; Stanton Papers, Oct. 2, 1865.

[39]Frankfort (Ky.) *Commonwealth*, September 9, 1865; *Personal Memoirs of J. M. Palmer*, 243-247; 264-266.

[40]2 Bush 570.

effect. In West Virginia a clause providing gradual emancipation was inserted in the first constitution of the newly formed State in 1863, to fulfill one of the requirements of its admission into the Union.[41] By constitutional amendment slavery was immediately abolished in Tennessee in February, 1865; and that portion of the old constitution which prohibited the legislature from emancipating slaves without the owners' consent was abrogated.[42] In Maryland abolition was effected by an ordinary law which merely "repealed" the slave code of the State concerning Negroes, such code being originally but the enactment of the legislature.[43] A still different method was adopted in Missouri, where the institution was abolished by ordinance passed by a State convention. This occurred on January 11, 1865, a month before the legislature ratified the Thirteenth Amendment.[44]

In Delaware, which contained in 1865 about 20,000 free Negroes with less than one-tenth as many slaves, one finds a remarkable tenacity in clinging to an institution that was crumbling on every side. The legislature condemned the Emancipation Proclamation "as a flagrant attempt to exercise absolute power under the pretense

---

[41]Constitution of West Virginia (1863), Art. XI, sec. 7; *U. S. Stat. at Large*, XII, 633.

[42]The inconveniences of what we have called the "transitional" phase of emancipation are illustrated by the message of Governor W. G. Brownlow of Tennessee, April 4, 1865, in which he objected to Tennessee being overrun with emancipated slaves from other States, and suggested a "separate territory" where they could permanently settle. (*Acts of the State of Tennessee*, 1865, p. 5. For abolition by the convention in Tennessee, see *ibid.*, ix-xiii.)

[43]Section 82 of the code concerning Negroes, making it possible to recover against free Negroes breaking labor contracts, was not repealed. (*The Maryland code*, 1860, Art. 66; *Laws of Maryland*, 1865, p. 306.)

[44]E. M. Violette, *A History of Missouri* (1918), Ch. xix; *General Statutes of Missouri*, 1866, p. 46; H. A. Trexler, *Slavery in Missouri, 1804-1865*, pp. 239-240.

of military necessity," and refused to ratify the Thirteenth Amendment taking occasion to express their "unqualified disapproval" thereof. Governor Cannon's advice that Delaware pass an emancipation law was not followed.[45]

The action of Delaware and Kentucky emphasized the fact that the war closed with slavery still a matter of State law, though seriously interfered with by national authority. The ultimate disposition of the slavery issue was, as Gideon Welles said, "one of the most delicate and important problems . . . that had ever devolved on those who administered the government"; for while the progress of events demanded the complete abolition of slavery, it was necessary, at least as to those commonwealths which did not secede, to show respect for State rights. Welles thought that the only way out "was for the border States to pass emancipation laws";[46] but, for a problem which had become so definitely a national issue as had the slavery question by 1865, an amendment to the Federal Constitution was considered both more appropriate and more effective.

V

We find the legal necessity for a constitutional amendment abolishing slavery well expressed by Senator Trumbull of Illinois, who reported the Thirteenth Amendment from the Committee on the Judiciary. Reviewing the various acts by which Congress had dealt piecemeal with the slavery question, he declared that these were ineffectual for the destruction of slavery, while the force

[45] *Maryland Documents*, 1864, p. 25; *Delaware House Journal*, 1865, pp. 11, 148, 153; *Delaware Senate Journal*, 1865, pp. 126, 128; *Laws of Delaware*, 1861-1865, p. 684.

[46] *Diary of Gideon Welles*, I, 403. (Aug. 13, 1863.)

and effect of the President's proclamation were matters of controversy. The opponents of the proclamation, Trumbull said, declared "that it was issued without competent authority, and . . . cannot effect the emancipation of a single slave." Moreover, the proclamation excepted from its provisions "almost half the slave States."[47]

Some more effectual way of getting rid of slavery, he said, must be found. As to the suggestion that Congress pass such a law, Trumbull pointed out that the inability of Congress to interfere with slavery in the States had long been an "admitted axiom" in peace times and that the war power conferred no such right. Constitutional amendment he found to be "the only effectual way of ridding the country of slavery . . . so that it cannot be resuscitated." "This amendment adopted," he said, "not only does slavery cease, but it can never be reëstablished by State authority, or in any other way than by again amending the Constitution." He therefore proposed the submission to the States of the following amendment:

Article XIII

Sec. 1. Neither slavery nor involuntary servitude, except as a punishment for crime whereof the party shall have been duly convicted, shall exist within the United States, or any place subject to their jurisdiction.

Sec. 2. Congress shall have power to enforce this article by appropriate legislation.

This amendment was the first example of the use of the amending process to accomplish a specific reform on a nation-wide scale, outside what may be called, in a narrow sense, the strictly constitutional function, which

[47] *Cong. Globe*, 38 Cong., 1 sess., p. 1314.

is to declare what the government shall be, how it shall be formed in its various branches, and how far its authority shall extend. The first ten amendments, establishing fundamental limitations upon the Federal power; the Eleventh, limiting the jurisdiction of the Federal courts; and the Twelfth, perfecting the process of choosing the President, had all dealt with matters of a truly constitutional, as distinct from a legislative, character. To many minds, therefore, the Thirteenth Amendment represented a new use of the "amending power." In the congressional debates upon the resolution of proposal, not only the expediency and wisdom of such an amendment, but also its "constitutionality" was elaborately discussed.

That process which Trumbull advocated to silence all legal doubts was thus assailed as being itself invalid. The abolition of slavery, it was said, was outside the scope of the Constitution altogether. Slavery was a domestic institution, lying wholly within the field of State jurisdiction, an institution which did not exist by virtue of the Federal compact, but had its roots far back in colonial times. With such an institution the Federal Government had nothing to do, except, indeed, to "protect" it in the particular ways specified by the Constitution itself. If such an omnipotent power be granted, it could be used "to blot out of existence any State in this Union." It was not to be supposed that the "Fathers" would have entered into the Federal agreement if it had been suggested that in the future the rights of property or the relation of master and slave within the States would be invaded.

Being asked whether it was not competent for the framers originally to have prohibited slavery by constitutional provision, an opponent of the amendment answered: Yes, all the States in *making* the Constitution could have done this; but it does not follow that what the original parties to the agreement could have done by unanimous action can now be effected by three-fourths of the States and imposed upon the dissenting ones. Regarding the Constitution as being in the nature of a contract, such action would be in fraud of the original agreement, being contrary to the purposes that all had in view when the agreement was made. It would be similar to a case where various parties unanimously form a contract for given purposes and then three-fourths of the parties, having in view a matter beyond the original agreement, turn and say to the dissenting fourth: "We will bind you because you have entered in." Such action, it was urged, would be regarded as fraud by the courts.[48]

As Congressman Pendleton of Ohio expressed it, "neither three-fourths of the States, nor all the States save one, can abolish slavery in that dissenting State; because it lies within the domain reserved entirely to each State for itself, and upon it the other States cannot enter."[49] "The Constitution," declared Pruyn of New York, "would never have been ratified had it been supposed by the States that, under the power to amend, their reserved rights might one by one be swept away. This is the first time in our history in which an attempt of this kind has been made, and should it be successful it will . . . be an alarming invasion of the principles of the Constitution." The matter, he added, should be left with the States, or there should be passed "a supplementary article to the Constitution, not as an amendment,

---

[48]Speech of Senator Saulsbury: *Cong. Globe,* 38 Cong., 1 sess., p. 1441. This passage in Senator Saulsbury's speech is paraphrased, not directly quoted, above.

[49]*Ann. Cyc.*, 1865, p. 207.

but as the grant of a new power based on the consent *of all the States, as the Constitution itself is.*"[50]

Pruyn's idea was that where so fundamental a change is involved, something more than an amendment is necessary. He therefore introduced the suggestion of "a supplementary article" which would have the assent of all the States, as did the "Constitution itself." He thought of a mere amendment as something different from the Constitution. The idea of such a distinction is natural enough, and it is indeed hard in our ordinary thought to exalt a constitutional amendment to the height of one of the great articles of the original Constitution. It may be natural also for those in the minority to feel a certain resentment against an instrument of government which was agreed to as a whole by every State entering the Union,[51] and yet which allows an amendment to be made by only three-fourths of the States and two-thirds of Congress.

Yet political scientists would recognize no such distinction. Aside from the restriction concerning the "equal suffrage"[52] of the States in the Senate, the Constitution, since 1808, has contained no unamendable part, and it designates no field of legislation that may not be reached by the amending power. An amendment prop-

[50] *Cong. Globe,* 38 Cong., 2 sess., p. 154. The italics are in the original.

[51] When each State entered the Union, it accepted the whole Constitution at the time of entering.

[52] Even the provision regarding equal representation of the States in the Senate is not, in the strictest sense, "unamendable." The constitutional requirement is not that this feature of the government shall remain unchanged, but that the consent of a State is necessary before that State's equal suffrage in the upper house can be denied. (*Constitution of the United States,* Art. V.) Furthermore, it has been argued that no constitution should contain unamendable parts, and that a provision declaring a certain part "unamendable" is not binding, since the constitution-making power is one of full and unrestrained sovereignty. (J. A. Woodburn, *The American Republic,* 209-210; J. W. Burgess, *The Civil War and the Constitution,* I, 134.)

erly made becomes "valid, to all intents and purposes, as part of this Constitution," having as much force as any other article. There is no valid distinction between "the Constitution itself" and the amendments. The Constitution at any given time includes all up to the latest amendments, and excludes portions that have not survived the amending process. We should think not of "the Constitution *and its amendments*," but of "the Constitution *as amended*." This is especially true when we reflect that certain of the amendments supplant or construe portions of the original document.[43]

Those who, in the discussion we have just noted, argued against any amendment that would fundamentally alter the "Constitution itself," had in mind, primarily, the reserved power principle, and denied that, by the "amending power," the "general government" would have a right to do away with the reserved rights of the States. There is a confusion of thought here, for there is no "amending power" belonging to the Federal Government. When an amendment is adopted it is done not by the "general government," but by the supreme sovereign power of the nation—i.e., the people—acting through State legislatures or State conventions. Even the reserved power principle (which, by the way, is expressed in the Tenth Amendment) is within the amending power of the people.

This amending power, it may be noted, is equivalent to the constitution-making power and is wholly above the authority of the Federal Government. An alternative method of amending the Constitution is permitted in which Congress has practically no participation; for

[53]The Eleventh Amendment is not so much an alteration of the Constitution as it is a rule of construction. It would have been unnecessary if the original Constitution had not been given an interpretation which many regarded as unreasonable even though a literal application of the words of the Constitution seemed to justify it.

an amendment may be proposed by a convention which Congress is required to call upon the application of the legislatures of two-thirds of the States, and it then becomes valid when ratified by legislatures or conventions in three-fourths of the States.[54] The function of Congress in such a case would be merely to issue the call for the convention (which would be obligatory) and to propose one of two possible modes of ratification. It will thus be seen that the Federal Government not only lacks the "amending power," but it does not even possess the exclusive right to initiate an amendment.

VI

The contention, therefore, that the question of slavery constituted subject matter beyond the reach of constitutional amendment, while supported by very ingenious arguments, will hardly bear analysis. But there was another ground on which the validity of the anti-slavery article was attacked. It was urged that the method of adoption prescribed by the Constitution was not complied with, in that the valid ratification of three-fourths of all the States was not in fact obtained.

It is significant that Trumbull himself, the author of the amendment, expressed doubts as to whether the Constitution could be legally amended during the Civil War. When, in 1863, an amendment suggested by another Senator was under discussion, he raised the question whether the United States had "authority in enough of the States of this Union to obtain the expression of their opinion as to whether they would consent to a change or not."[55] When he presented the Thirteenth Amendment, however, in March, 1864, the probabilities for obtaining a legal ratification seemed stronger.

---

[54]*Constitution of the United States,* Art. V.
[55]*Cong. Globe,* January 29, 1863, 37 Cong., 3 sess., p. 592.

His calculations were based upon the acceptance of the amendment by three-fourths of all the States, including those which had seceded, but which for this purpose, he considered "States of the Union."

The following table gives the complete showing as to the status and the ratifying action of all the States.

TABLE SHOWING STATES AT THE TIME OF THE ADOPTION OF THE THIRTEENTH AMENDMENT, DECEMBER 18, 1865

NOTE. Italics indicate those States whose ratifications were counted in Seward's proclamation of December 18, 1865, declaring the amendment in force.

Free States of the Union			Slave States of the Union	States of the Former Confederacy	
Cal.	*Md.*	*Ohio*	Del.	*Ark.*	*La.*
Conn.	*Mich.*	Ore.	Ky.	*Tenn.*	Miss.
Ill.	*Minn.*	*Pa.*		*N. C.*	*Ala.*
Ind.	*Mo.*	*R. I.*		*Va.**	*Ga.*
Ia.	*N. H.*	*Vt.*		Tex.	*S. C.*
Kas.	N. J.	*W. Va.*		Fla.	
Me.	*N. Y.*	*Wis.*			
Mass.	*Nev.*				
		Total, 23	Total, 2	Total, 11	
Total of all the States, 36.					

*The United States Government recognized the "restored government" of Virginia; and that State was, rather fictitiously, represented in the Federal Congress in the early part of the war. It was not, however, considered to be in the Union in 1865.

In December, 1865, when the amendment went into force, the thirty-six States came within the following classification: slave States of the former Confederacy, 11; free States of the Union, 23; slave States of the Union, 2 (Delaware and Kentucky). As Delaware and Kentucky refused to ratify, it would be necessary to have the favorable action of at least four of the States once belonging to the Confederacy in addition to all the free States to make up the full three-fourths. As a matter of fact, while action in four of the free States was still being awaited, Secretary Seward, counting the ratifications of eight of the former Confederate States, in addition to that of 19 of the free States, proclaimed, on December 18, 1865, that the amendment was in force.[56]

As to the justice of submitting an amendment at a time when the Southern States were in no position to consider it, and "imposing it upon one-fourth which had not ratified it," the friends of the amendment pointed out that all the States in entering the Union had agreed to abide by such amendments as three-fourths should make; that the Southern States could not plead disability to vote, since no one was denying them the opportunity to return to the Union and express themselves on the question; and that all States not voting for the amendment were in fact counted as being against it, inasmuch as no action at all was equivalent to negative action.[57]

The question as to the validity of the amendment at the time of Seward's proclamation of adoption hinges upon the competency of the States formerly within the Confederacy to pass valid resolutions of ratification. In a letter to the Senate, on December 18, 1865, President Johnson explained that all the seceded States except Florida and Texas had reorganized their governments and were "yielding obedience to the laws and Government of the United States."[58] He then enumerated

---

[56]Constitution of the United States, as amended to January 1, 1923, (Annotated): *Sen. Doc. No. 96*, 67 Cong., 2 sess., p. 28. See also George Ticknor Curtis, *Constitutional History of the United States*, II, 653-654.

[57]Argument of Senator Harlan: *Cong. Globe*, 38 Cong., 1 sess., p. 1437.

[58]*Ann. Cyc.*, 1866, p. 131.

those which had ratified the Thirteenth Amendment. If these ratifications were to be accepted, it must be on the ground that competent governments existed within the States in question at the time of ratification. It is matter of familiar history that the governments in these States were of a provisional character, created by conventions which had assembled in compliance with Johnson's generous plan of reconstruction, and that the radicals of Congress, rather unfortunately, took the matter out of Johnson's hands and refused recognition to these reorganized governments.

Without pursuing to the limit all the legal phases of a question which, after all, contains many matters of idle speculation, it may suffice to notice the various ingredients that must be included in any argument which would maintain that the Thirteenth Amendment was valid as declared by Seward's proclamation. Such an argument affirms the following points:

1. All the States, including those which seceded, should be reckoned in the total, three-fourths of which must ratify.

2. The ratifying action of the eight seceded States was competent and legal.

3. The Secretary of State's proclamation, declaring that the amendment was in force on December 18, 1865, was valid. (No resolution by Congress, for instance, was necessary.)

4. The subsequent refusal of Congress to recognize "Johnson's reorganized States" did not invalidate the amendment.

It is of course a well-known fact that, at the moment when the amendment was proclaimed as ratified by the votes of various States of the former Confederacy, there were many radicals in Congress declaring that there were no such States in existence.[59] The plan of such radicals as to the amendment was to leave the "rebel" States out of the count in estimating the total, three-fourths of which would be necessary to declare the amendment in force.[60] Such a plan had, perhaps, more of consistency than that which Congress actually adopted —that is, "quietly assenting"[61] to Seward's proclamation which assumed that most of the seceded States were back in the Union, and then denying to such States representation in Congress and otherwise holding them out of the Union for a period of years.[62] Inconsistencies and legal fictions offered no obstacle in that period when, for instance, Virginia was permitted representation in the Senate while kept out of the electoral College, and a

---

[59]Concerning these radicals Edward Bates thus wrote: " . . . in debate in H of R old Thad. [Stevens] amidst other ravings declared that '*The State of Tennessee is not known to this House or to Congress!*' A very ignorant House it would seem—ignorant alike of the Constitution & of Geography. . . . And in the Senate Mr. Howard of Michigan refused to 'recognize them as States' ! ! And so it seems that they are not *States in the Union*, yet they can enact a Constitution for the United States! Are these men mad?" (MS. Diary of Edward Bates, Dec. 12 and Dec. 21, 1865.)

[60]Strangely enough, Nicolay and Hay speak of the Thirteenth Amendment as having been "ratified by 21 out of the 26 States." (Nicolay and Hay, *Works*, X, 352, n.)

[61]Rhodes, *History of the United States*, V, 554; Blaine, *Twenty Years of Congress*, II, 140.

[62]Two weeks before Seward's proclamation of December 18, 1865, Senator Sumner proposed a joint resolution declaring that sundry States "by reason of rebellion were without legislatures," and that it belonged to Congress to determine when the process of constitutional amendment is complete. The question of counting State resolutions of ratification was, in his opinion, bound up with the problem of reconstruction, which rested with Congress. On these premises his resolution declared "that the amendment abolishing slavery has become and is a part of the Constitution of the United States." This eccentric resolution (by which Congress would have assumed a merely ministerial function belonging to the Secretary of State) was not passed. (*Cong. Globe*, Dec. 4, 1865, 39 Cong., 1 sess., p. 2.)

Vice-President was declared elected from a State which was excluded from the electoral count.[63]

As to the main question in the case of the Thirteenth Amendment, enough States ultimately ratified it to remove all doubts as to its validity; and, historically, this validity has dated from Seward's proclamation of December 18, 1865.[64]

VII

Emancipation was thus effected in the United States without any compensation to the slaveholders. It may be pertinent to recall in this connection that the English Parliament, in passing the emancipation act of 1833,[65] granted the amount of £20,000,000 as compensation for what was regarded as the "destruction" of slave property. In addition to the value of the slaves themselves, it was explained in Parliament that other matters should be considered, such as the value of the land which was principally maintained by slave labor, and the prospective value of children to be born. As a matter of fact, the actual amount of compensation granted was hit upon in a sort of dicker with the West Indian proprie-

[63]In February, 1865, Congress declared that Tennessee was not entitled to representation in the electoral college which chose the President and Vice-President. In this election Andrew Johnson, a citizen of Tennessee, was elected Vice-President. (*Cong. Globe*, 38 Cong., 2 sess., appendix, p. 159.)

[64]In construing the Thirteenth Amendment the courts have held that slavery and involuntary servitude in general (not merely in the case of Negroes) is prohibited; that laws establishing peonage are unconstitutional; that a law merely recognizing a distinction between the races is not invalid; that it is unconstitutional for Congress to prohibit such a distinction in public conveyances; that all within the jurisdiction of the National Government, as well as within the States, are covered by the amendment; and that the Selective Service Act of 1917 did not establish involuntary servitude. Some of these decisions have been modified. *Sen. Doc. No. 96*, 67 Cong., 2 sess., pp. 621-623.

[65][British] *Annual Register*, 1833, pp. 197 *et seq.*

tors; but the fundamental fact is that the English Government considered that in abolishing slavery there were property interests involved which demanded compensation.

As we have seen, Lincoln thought so too; and Congress accepted the principle of compensation in a resolution pledging pecuniary aid to those States which should liberate their slaves. An interesting question arises as to whether this pledge of support, made in 1862, was binding or applicable in 1865 when nation-wide emancipation was accomplished. Those border States which adopted emancipation prior to the ratification of the Thirteenth Amendment certainly believed that they were entitled to compensation from the Federal Government, in spite of the rejection of the proposal by their own representatives. As Governor Swann of Maryland pointed out in January, 1865, "the first and only authorized response of the people of Maryland to the offer of Congress was the abolition of slavery in accordance with the terms of the resolution."[66] And Bradford, the outgoing Governor, in referring to the President's recommendation concerning pecuniary aid and the joint resolution of Congress on the subject, declared: "If there can be any meaning in the language quoted, it expressed a promise to that effect, and if any State can conscientiously claim a fulfillment of that promise, Maryland can."[67]

The Maryland legislature in February, 1865, created a committee to go to Washington and confer with the President to see whether influence might be brought to bear to induce Congress to give aid to the State. In taking this action the legislature, in a series of *whereas* clauses, put it on record that the offer of aid had been

[66] *House Journal and Documents, Maryland*, 1865, Document C.
[67] *Ibid.*, Document A.

used to induce voters to support abolition in the State, and that the people of Maryland, "acting under" the President's recommendation and the offer of Congress, had in fact abolished slavery.[68]

If Maryland should claim such compensation, Missouri could make a similar claim, while even in Kentucky, where the abolition of slavery was resisted to the last, the possibility of compensation seems to have been envisaged; for that State, in 1866, passed a law to obtain and preserve evidence as to slave property of which the citizens of the State had been deprived.[69]

After the war, however, the matter of compensation for emancipated slaves was given little thought. President Lincoln, as late as February of 1865, still favored compensation, even to the States of the South at the close of the war; but, even if he had lived, it is doubtful whether this object could have been accomplished.[70] The joint resolution of Congress expressing a willingness in 1862 to coöperate with any State that would free its slaves, represents simply a stage in the rapidly developing policy regarding abolition. It was perhaps not felt that the offer should hold good indefinitely, since a cer-

---

[68] *Journal of the Proceedings of the House of Delegates*, Maryland, 1865, pp. 190, 336.

[69] "Whereas the people of Kentucky . . . by proclamations, military orders, and the Thirteenth Amendment to the Federal Constitution, [had] been deprived of their slave property without compensation" etc., it was enacted that persons so deprived should offer proof before the county courts, and the records were to be filed. ("Act to preserve evidence of claims to slave property in Kentucky," February 17, 1866: *Laws of Ky.*, 1865-1866, p. 64.)

[70] At the Hampton Roads Conference Lincoln is reported to have said that he "would be willing to be taxed to remunerate the Southern people for their slaves"; that "he believed the people of the North were as responsible for slavery as the people of the South"; and that he would be in favor "of the Government paying a fair indemnity for the loss to the owners." (Nicolay and Hay, *Lincoln*, X, 124.) The President's statements are thus reported by Alexander H. Stephens, one of the Southern commissioners at the conference.

tain amount of promptness on the part of the States was desired in order to influence the outcome of the war. At a time when Lincoln was laboring hard to put the scheme into practical effect, the border-State Congressmen and Senators contributed their part to the burial of the project.

In 1865 the question of abolition had acquired a different horizon; for a new policy, namely, abolition by constitutional amendment, had been put forth. The amendment was a mandate to the National Government, not an act of that government; and it was very different from State action, for which alone compensation had been promised. Under these circumstances, the obligation, if such existed, toward those few States whose independent abolition of slavery occurred just before the adoption of the nation-wide amendment, was lost sight of. Had slavery been abolished in time of peace, it is not unlikely that compensation might have been provided, for the arguments and precedents favoring such compensation were sound; but the war mind of 1865 gave little heed to the property rights of slaveholders.[71]

[71]The Fourteenth Amendment of the Constitution provides that "neither the United States nor any State shall assume or pay . . . any claim for the loss or emancipation of any slave."

CHAPTER XVII

STATE AND FEDERAL RELATIONS DURING THE CIVIL WAR

I

"It is a fact of our national history that the Civil War put the separate States definitely and irrevocably in subordination to the central government."—H. G. PEARSON, *Life of John A. Andrew*, II, 122.

This quotation exemplifies a point of view which is quite general among historians. It is customary to emphasize the "presidential dictatorship" and the excessive tendency toward centralization of power at Washington as fundamental facts in treating the history of the Civil War. So much has been said concerning this nationalizing tendency that the other side of the actual situation obtaining during the war has been obscured. It is not generally realized how far the National Government did act by and through the States.

Taking the war as a whole, one does find a certain gathering-in of governmental activities by the Federal authorities. But early in the war—in general until the spring of 1863—things were done, or attempted to be done, "by States." In the field of finance, we have the "direct tax" for which quotas were levied upon the States; and the actual raising of the tax was to be accomplished by the States after the fashion of Revolutionary days. Even in the vitally important domain of military affairs, the expanding of the army was primarily "by States," as seen in the Militia Act of 1862, and in the drafts made during that year.

The national administration, especially in the early part of the war, showed a scrupulous regard for State functions, this attitude being carried even to the point of hampering the Government. On the other side, the States were jealous of retaining important activities; and their action frequently encroached upon Federal jurisdiction, as in the case of State trespass suits or *habeas corpus* proceedings instituted against Federal officers.

It was far from true that the Government at Washington deliberately used the war as an opportunity to increase its power. Lincoln's Cabinet contained men who stoutly upheld State rights; and Lincoln himself, both because of his clear perception of constitutional questions and because of his anxiety to avoid offending border-State sentiment, showed a wholesome regard for the proper authority of the States. What happened was rather that, as the war progressed, more and more responsibility was gradually and reluctantly assumed by the Federal Government because of the necessities arising out of State jealousy and administrative deadlock. The nationalizing laws of the Civil War period, such as the Conscription Act and the act creating the system of national banks, begin with the year 1863. It was not until State action had proved a failure following two years of actual practice—sometimes because of enthusiasm for the war, and sometimes because of opposition to it—that the National Government was drawn into the performance of functions without which the national cause would have failed. While recognizing the fact of nationalization as an incident of the war, we should avoid the mistake of attributing this to a persistent and deliberate purpose.

II

One of the strange anomalies of the war was Kentucky's attempted policy of neutrality. Without reciting the details of this interesting episode it will be sufficient to recall that a majority of the people of Kentucky were probably friendly to the States of the Confederacy, and, while devoted to the Union, were yet believers in the principle of State sovereignty and the right of secession. Had a convention been called in January, 1861, as Governor Magoffin desired, the State would probably have seceded. When Lincoln issued his call for troops on April 15, 1861, the Governor sent an emphatic refusal; and, shortly after, the policy of neutrality was set forth in a resolution passed by the State senate which declared that Kentucky would neither sever connection with the National Government nor take up arms for either party, but would "arm herself for the one purpose of preserving tranquillity and peace within her own borders."[1]

It is outside the scope of this book to examine the purposes or conditions which prompted this neutral attitude. Sometimes it has been denounced as an anti-Union measure, while again it has been referred to as a "trick" by which the Union men saved the day in Kentucky at a time when no other device could have pre-

[1] *Ky. House Jour.*, May 24, 1861, p. 182; *Ky . Sen. Jour.*, May 24, 1861, pp. 143-144; W. P. Shortridge, in *Miss. Vall. Hist. Rev.*, Mar., 1923; A. C. Quisenberry, in Ky. State Hist. Soc. *Register*, XV, 9 (Jan., 1917); W. D. Foulke, *Life of Oliver P. Morton*, I, Ch. xi; Nicolay and Hay, *Lincoln*, IV, Ch. xii; E. Merton Coulter, *Civil War . . . in Ky.*, 35-124.

vented secession. It is undoubtedly true that good Union men supported the neutrality policy, and it has even been contended that Lincoln was its originator. The national administration showed a disposition to respect this neutral position, at least up to a certain point, but the plan quickly broke down because of its utterly impracticable character.

What concerns us more particularly here is to note the legal implications that are wrapped up in this neutral attitude. Does not the power of declaring neutrality presuppose independence? Does it not involve the war-making power? But the power of making war is one of the functions which the States renounced and gave over to the National Government by the plain terms of the Constitution. For the purpose of making war the nation is a unit. This does not mean that State action is dictated from above so much as that for federal purposes the *people* act, not by States, but through the National Government which they create and control. War is a federal function *par excellence.* It may be practicable that certain things be done by States, but war-making is not one of them. A war in which only a portion of the nation takes part, or in which some States go to war while others are "neutral," is wholly inconsistent with the peculiar federal system as provided by the American Constitution.

As Lincoln showed, this so-called "neutrality" would really amount to taking sides. It would be disunion completed, this erecting of an impassable wall of separation between the Unionist and the secessionist forces—yet not quite impassable, "for under the guise of neutrality it would tie the hands of Union men and freely pass supplies from among them to the insurrectionists, which it could not do as an open enemy. . . . It would do for the disuinionists that which . . . they most desire—feed them well, and give them disunion without a struggle of their own."[2]

It is only fair to say that many who promoted the policy of neutrality thought differently, and conceived of their measure as tending toward peace, mediation, and ultimate reunion without a serious war; and there is much to be said for the patriotic purpose which inspired their course. When the matter is regarded as a problem of constitutional interpretation, however, many difficulties appear. Our States are not independent, separate nations. They are parts of a union; and, in their character as such, certain obligations and limitations are incurred, one of which is that the power of war (which includes the power of neutrality) has been intrusted to the central government. To insist upon separate State action which would keep one of the States "neutral" in a war to preserve the Union is to go the whole way with the theory of secession. There is no such middle ground as the action of Kentucky would presuppose.

Analogous to the case of Kentucky's "neutrality" is the action of Maryland authorities in seeking to obstruct the passage of Federal troops over the territory of the State. In these matters of sovereignty which belonged to the United States, the Federal authority must be, as Marshall showed, supreme. When the States perform their rightful functions, they should be unmolested; and it is equally true that the Federal government must not be impeded by State interference when it acts within its proper domain. Interference in the movement of the nation's armies would be as truly unwarranted as obstructing the nation's business by means of State taxation, which was so convincingly denounced by John Marshall. The language which he employed in dis-

[2]Nicolay and Hay, *Works*, VI, 307.

allowing the tax imposed by Maryland upon the United States Bank[3] could be used with equal force in dealing with the contemplated attempt by the same State to stop the national forces on a mission that was vital to the preservation of the nation.

III

The most numerous as well as the most serious problems of adjustment between the Federal and State governments arose in the sphere of military affairs.[4] The militia is at once a national and a State institution. In its main features, the division of function touching the militia was about as follows during the Civil War: Congress defined what constituted the enrolled militia, provided the armament, prescribed the drill and tactical organization, and had the power of discipline (i.e., the punishing of offenses by courts-martial) over such part of the militia as was actually employed in Federal service. The State governments recruited and raised the force and paid the expenses thereof while in State

---

[3]M'Culloch *vs.* Md., 4 Wheaton 316.

[4]The activities of Robert Dale Owen as "State Agent for Indiana" early in the Civil War illustrate the manner in which the States assumed control of military matters. Acting for Governor Morton, he was energetic in purchasing rifles, sabers and revolvers; shipping arms from New York to Fortress Monroe as well as to Indianapolis; procuring greatcoats, blankets and equipment for the soldiers; visiting various Indiana regiments in the field; making contracts for which the Federal Government paid; and doing many things which transcended the bounds of State functions. On one occasion he wrote to Morton: "I fear that if you trust wholly to the Government to send you what more guns we may need, you will be likely to get trash. I hear very poor accounts of the purchases made by the Government agent in Europe." (Owen to Morton, Dec. 2, 1861.) One of the objects for which Owen exerted himself was to have "the Arsenal" at Indianapolis continued when the interests of the Federal Government seemed to require its discontinuance. (Morton Correspondence, [State Archives of Indiana, Indianapolis], *passim.*)

service. The State governor appointed the officers, and was the commander-in-chief of the militia as a State institution. The control of the militia while in State service rested with the States. It was by State authority that the militia was drilled, governed, and commanded. Though the drill was *prescribed* by Congress, it was conducted by the State, and the discipline was normally under State authority.[5]

An important national power regarding the militia has always been that of calling it into Federal service. When so called out, the militia largely loses its character as a State institution. It is under Federal discipline, and is subject to the orders of the President as Commander-in-Chief. Here is an example, then, where State-appointed officers are commanded by the President. Moreover, the President is the judge of his own powers in this respect. It is within the President's discretion to determine not alone the occasion for calling the militia into national service, but also the strength and composition of the State quotas. The President's power of issuing regulations as to the manner of calling out the militia embraces a vast sweep of authority, and in another chapter we have noted that this was even extended during the Civil War to include the power of conscription.[6]

In the years 1861 and 1862 it may be truly said that the nation's forces were largely raised, and even to a certain extent equipped, paid and transported, by State action. President Lincoln's proclamation of April 15, 1861, was a calling forth of "the militia of the several States."[7] Of course, the States raised these troops. Aside from this and other occasions when the militia was

[5]Federal and State functions concerning the militia are discussed in G. B. Davis, *Military Law*, Ch. v. And see *supra*, pp. 241-242.

[6]*Supra*, pp. 245-247, 252-255

[7]*U. S. Stat. at Large*, XII, 1258

called, the only other methods employed for raising national forces during the first two years of the war were the slight increase of the regular army and the recruiting of large numbers of "U. S. Volunteers." As to the "volunteers," which constituted the bulk of the Union army, State action was of great importance. The governors of the States commonly directed the recruiting of the volunteer regiments (though they did not have the exclusive power of doing so), and the governors commissioned the staff, field, and company officers thereof.[8] By the President's regulations, which were intended to carry out the purposes of the Militia Act of 1862, much power was given to the governors, who were in effect made the enforcing agents in executing this Federal measure. Under these regulations it was made the duty of the governors to carry out the details of the draft as prescribed by the War Department at Washington.[9]

It will aid us to appreciate what the State governments did in providing Federal troops if we remember that at the beginning of July, 1861, when the first war Congress assembled, the Union forces exclusive of the regular army numbered about 260,000 men.[10] These men, partly militia and partly United States volunteers,

---

[8]*Ibid.*, XII, 269; Pearson, *Life of J. A. Andrew*, I, Ch. viii. State action in the selection of officers for the United States Volunteers did not end with the appointment of the regimental officers by the governor; for in the appointment of the generals the President recognized a sort of "right of nomination" on the part of the Congressmen and Senators from the State. Senator Browning of Illinois made the following note in his diary which illustrates this fact: "Went to Trumbull's rooms to meet the Ill. delegation and agree upon Brig. Gen'ls for our State. I was for Prentiss, McClernand, Payne, Richardson, Palmer, Grant, and Stokes." (MS. Diary of Orville H. Browning, July 27, 1861.)

[9]*Supra*, pp. 252-253.

[10]The Secretary of War reported the three months' militia as 80,000 and the United States volunteers as 188,000. (Report of the Sec. of War, July 1, 1861. *Sen. Ex. Doc. No. 1*, 37 Cong., 1 sess., p. 21.)

were recruited and brought together through the agency of the State governments. In the case of the volunteers, some regiments were even raised in advance of a Federal call.

A study of the activities of such governors as Morton[11] of Indiana and Andrew of Massachusetts[12] reveals the vast importance of the functions which devolved upon the State executives in the early part of the war.[13] Andrew at Boston and Morton at Indianapolis were war ministers as truly as Cameron at Washington. In fact they far outran the lagging efforts of Cameron, and their excellent work was hampered by the manner in which the War Department dampened recruiting ardor or delayed in accepting the regiments offered.[14]

---

[11]W. H. H. Terrell, *Report of the Adjutant-General of Ind.*, Vol. I, *passim;* Foulke, *Life of Oliver P. Morton.*

[12]H. G. Pearson, *Life of John A. Andrew.*

[13]On July 12, 1861, Senator Browning of Illinois, after visiting the encampment of Rhode Island volunteers at Washington, wrote ". . . the whole [is] apparently under the direction of Governor Sprague of Rhode Island who is with them in camp." (MS. Diary of Orville H. Browning.) Early in 1862 Governor Tod of Ohio wrote to Stanton asking four questions: (1) What control had the governor over State troops, in camp or in the field, after they had been mustered into the service of the United States? (2) What were his duties in the procuring or issuing of military supplies? (3) Would the Federal government refund to the State "*all* the money expended directly and indirectly in the raising, equipping, sustaining and mustering of the troops?" (4) What control did the governor have over military prisoners sent to the State for safe keeping? The fact that such a letter could be written by a governor to the Secretary of War nine months after the firing at Sumter, shows both the extent of the governor's activities and the indefiniteness of the relationships involved. (Tod to Stanton, Jan. 28, 1862: Stanton Papers, II, No. 50513.)

[14]While Yates in Illinois was working energetically to raise United States regiments, expecting that the Government would accept all that were raised, Cameron sent word to him: "Let me earnestly recommend to you . . . to call for no more than twelve regiments, of which six only are to serve for three years or during the war, and if more are already called for, to reduce the number by discharge." (*Report of the Adjutant-General of Ill.*, I, 11, I. O. Foster, "Relation of Illinois to the Federal Government during the Civil War" [MS. disserta-

When orders from Washington failed to arrive, Andrew went ahead in the absence of orders. To a great extent he, and other governors of his stamp, bore the immediate burden of the emergency. Andrew directed the recruiting of the early Massachusetts regiments, the appointment of the officers, the examination and equipment of the troops, the chartering of steamers and railroads for their transportation, and the raising of emergency funds by which the first bills were paid. For a time, since Massachusetts had prematurely sent forward four thousand men, the State had to *maintain them in the field*, in a quasi-hostile territory four hundred and fifty miles distant. In all this rush of patriotic activity there was no time to quibble about authority, and men assumed responsibility in full confidence that their actions would later receive ratification and support.

Unfortunately, but inevitably, confusion and friction arose between State and Federal authority in these military matters. Instances of such lack of adjustment were very numerous, but we must be content to note a few examples. Governor Andrew, for instance, sought to place a contract for building a monitor for Massachusetts; but the Navy and Ordnance officers loudly protested on the ground that the United States needed all the ironclads and heavy cannon that the country was producing. The governor then labored hard to have an ironclad detailed to protect Boston harbor; but Lincoln replied that the alarm was baseless and that if each State on the seaboard were seized with a similar panic and the Government attempted to satisfy them all, the result would be such a diversion of our resources from the

tion, University of Illinois].) Governor Morton insisted upon furnishing six regiments though the call was for four. (Foulke, *Morton*, I, 128.) Cameron accepted only three of the ten regiments offered by Ohio, and a similar situation existed with regard to Massachusetts and other States. (Pearson, *Andrew*, I, 224, 225.)

main object of attacking the enemy that we might as well give up the war.[15]

The differences between General Benjamin F. Butler and Governor Andrew concerning the recruiting of United States volunteers developed a heated controversy and produced a veritable deadlock between the State and Federal governments which was only relieved by the timely resignation of the Secretary of War.[16] The incident grew out of the plan, legalized by Congress, by which the State governors raised regiments of United States volunteers and commissioned the officers. But not infrequently the President conflicted with this power by authorizing individuals to raise volunteers. General Butler, urging that there ought to be no discrimination against loyal Democrats, and alleging that the Massachusetts governor would not commission political opponents, obtained an order under the authority of the President, authorizing him to raise six regiments in the New England States. According to this order, Butler was to "fit out and prepare such troops as he [might] judge fit" for a contemplated expedition down the eastern shore of Maryland and Virginia to Cape Charles. When Secretary Cameron wired the New England governors to give their approval to this scheme, Andrew refused consent. The wavering War Secretary then issued an order that the regiments should be recruited under the authority of the governors.

Deadlock resulted when Andrew refused to commission Butler's list of officers; and, by pressure, Butler brought about the issuance of a remarkable order from Washington creating the "Department of New England" and placing six States under his own command for the purpose of recruiting these regiments. Com-

---

[15]Pearson, *Andrew*, II, 128-130. [16]*Ibid.*, C. viii.

missions for Butler's officers were announced by the President, but Andrew proceeded to show how inadequate and incomplete this list was. In this state of affairs Cameron resigned, the new Secretary, Stanton, came to Andrew's support, and the disputed points concerning these regiments were satisfactorily adjusted. The "Department of New England" was abolished and the Butler-Andrew quarrel was closed. The incident is mentioned not for its own sake, but because such details of maladjustment must always be remembered in any discussion of State and Federal relations during the war.

Other similar clashes of authority must be passed over with bare mention.[17] Early in the war the States were allowed to buy arms, and the competition of State purchasing agents in this country and abroad forced up the price of arms more than one hundred per cent. Where Federal commanders found it necessary to declare martial law in the loyal States, the governors strenuously objected; and sometimes the State authorities brought about the arrest of Federal officers. After State forces had been placed in the field, governors sometimes urged that important generals be recalled on leave of absence to conduct recruiting within the States. The curse of politics was added to official friction when a Northern governor, being refused guns and troops for service within his State, attributed this attitude of the Federal Government to the influence of politicians who would be glad to discredit him before the President. Or again, in the exercise of the vast appointing power of the governor, which included the appointment of

[17]Administrative relations between the States and the Federal Government during the Civil War are discussed in W. B. Weeden, *War Government, Federal and State, 1861-1865.* An intensive study of such problems for one State is to be found in I. O. Foster, "The Relation of the State of Illinois to the Federal Government during the Civil War," a doctoral thesis prepared at the University of Illinois in 1925.

Federal military officers, the taint of politics was either present or its presence was charged by the opposite party. Knowing Lincoln's desire to be fair to both sides malcontents would appeal to the President over the head of the governor, and unfortunate misunderstandings would result.

Though the country was far from approaching the condition of "a nation in arms" which obtained during the World Wars, yet local military activity was so thoroughly interwoven with the national cause that a clear-cut separation of State and Federal forces was impossible. This was illustrated by the curious "agreement" between President Lincoln and Governor Gamble of Missouri whereby the governor, in commissioning the commander of the Missouri State militia acting as home guards, was to select an officer who was also to be placed by the President in command of the Department of the West.[18] We find another example showing the interrelation of the State militia and the Federal forces in connection with the "Pennsylvania Reserve Corps" raised for home protection in 1861, but later incorporated into the Federal army by special act of Congress. This arrangement resulted in difficulties as to the filling of vacancies among the officers, and necessitated elaborate adjustments relative to Federal compensation for this use of State troops.[19]

In his annual report to Congress, December 1, 1861, the Secretary of War wrote concerning the selection of officers for the United States volunteer regiments:

> At present each Governor selects and appoints the officers for the troops furnished by his State, and complaint is not

[18]Nicolay and Hay, *Lincoln*, V. 96-97.

[19]Letter of General Meade to General S. S. Williams, October 20, 1862: *Messages of Governor A. G. Curtin Relative to the Reserve Corps, Pennsylvania Volunteers* (Harrisburg, 1863).

infrequently made that, when vacancies occur in the field, men of inferior qualifications are placed in command over those in the ranks who are their superiors in military experience and capacity. The advancement of merit should be the leading principle in all promotions, and the volunteer soldier should be given to understand that preferment will be the sure reward of intelligence, fidelity, and distinguished service.[20]

But the mention of examples to illustrate this overlapping of Federal and State authority in the field of military affairs must not be prolonged to a wearisome length.[21] If the full story of this phase of the war were told it would show that far more was left to State action than is commonly supposed, and that, as the war progressed, military control was of necessity absorbed by the National Government. There was an essential disharmony between the State and the national viewpoints, and the paramount needs of the nation inevitably asserted themselves, so that Governor Andrew,

---

[20] *Sen. Exec. Doc. No. 1*, 37 Cong., 2 sess., p. 9. The policy of permitting governors to commission officers for the volunteer regiments was adopted, as General Upton says, partly to meet State-rights objections. Many of the Senators and Representatives, he says, "held that the volunteers were militia, or State troops, whose officers under the Constitution could only be appointed by the Executive of the States." (Upton, *Military Policy of the United States*, 259.) It should be further noted that early in the war the doubtful expedient of having the men of the United States volunteer regiments elect their own officers was tried. The act of July 22, 1861, for the raising of volunteer forces, provided that for the filling of vacancies the men of each company should vote for officers as high as captain, while vacancies above the rank of captain were to be filled by the votes of the commissioned officers. (*U. S. Stat. at Large*, XII, 270.) This provision of law, said General Upton, incorporated the "worst vice known in the military system of any of the States," for it "tempted every ambitious officer and soldier to play the demagogue." (Upton, *op, cit.*, p. 260.) On August 6, 1861, this section was repealed. (*U. S. Stat. at Large*, XII, 318.)

[21] The whole subject of State and Federal relations as to military matters during the Civil War is ably discussed by Fred A. Shannon in "State Rights and the Union Army," (*Miss. Vall. Hist. Rev.*, XII, 51-71), and in *The Organization and Administration of the Union Army, 1861-65.*

for instance, from having been virtually "war minister" in 1861 became (as he said) after March, 1863, in respect to the raising of troops, merely "an official in Stanton's huge department."[22]

IV

It has sometimes been said that the governors are the President's "subordinates" in bringing the militia into Federal service. It has also been suggested that the governors of Virginia, North Carolina, Kentucky, Tennessee, Missouri and Arkansas (the border-State governors who refused Lincoln's call for troops and otherwise defied the Government), made themselves "subject to United States court-martial," and "ought to have been arrested, tried, and condemned by a military tribunal."[23] Such a suggestion as this raises the whole question of national obligations and liabilities of the State executives.

Two distinct questions are here involved: First, may the governor of a State be properly considered a "subordinate" of the President? Second, if the governor fails to perform his national duty or defies the National Government, is there any Federal power of discipline or punishment that may be exercised over him?

In considering the first of these questions it may be noted that the President, in calling the militia into Federal service, habitually makes his proclamation, or executive order, enforceable through the State governors. Furthermore it has been held that a requisition by the President upon a State governor for militia is in legal intendment an order.[24] The President has the right to

---

[22]Pearson, *Andrew*, II, 122.

[23]Burgess, *The Civil War and the Constitution*, I, 175.

[24]*U. S. Supreme Court Reps.* (5 Law. Ed., Rose's Notes) p. 1016; Houston *vs.* Moore, 5 Wheaton 1.

designate the governor as the officer by whom the militia is to be called forth, and it is also within the power of Congress to pass a law enforceable through State governors.

But in such instances it would be a misuse of terms to speak of the governor as the "subordinate" of the President. The President does not order the governors to do so and so. The order is *upon* the citizens, *through* the governors. The dignity of the governors as the highest executive officers of the States is respected by the President, who calls upon them to do certain things but does not presume to order them. It is a relation of comity rather than one of superior and inferior.

It has been urged that since the President is Commander-in-Chief of the national militia, while the governors are commanders-in-chief of the State militia, therefore the governors are the "subordinates" of the President. But such is not the case. At any given time, the militia is either in the service of the State or in the Federal service. It is in one or the other of these services. If in the State service, the governor is the commander; if in Federal service, the President is commander. There are blunders enough in the constitutional and statutory provisions regarding the militia, but here is one that was happily avoided. The militia is not at the same time under the command of the governors and of the President.

Turning to the second question above propounded, we may now inquire whether there is any legal recourse available to the National Government for compelling a State governor to do his Federal duty. That a governor has Federal duties is, of course, clear. It is a Federal duty for a governor to remand a criminal fleeing into his State from one of the other States. The Federal statute of 1793 reads: "it shall be the duty of the executive authority of the State . . . to cause the fugitive to be delivered."[25]

But it is another matter when one talks of compelling the governor to perform this duty. This very subject was covered by the Supreme Court of the United States in 1860 in the case of *Kentucky* vs. *Dennison.* Chief Justice Taney, speaking of the act for the rendition of criminals, said:[26]

> The act does not provide any means to compel the execution of this duty, nor inflict any punishment for neglect or refusal on the part of the Executive of the State; nor is there any . . . provision in the Constitution which arms the Government of the United States with this power. . . . It is true that Congress may authorize a particular State officer to perform a particular duty. . . . But if the Governor of Ohio refuses to discharge this duty, there is no power delegated to the General Government, either through the Judicial Department or any other department, to use any coercive means to compel him.

Even within the State, judicial action may not restrain nor coerce the governor in the performance of executive acts.[27] It is inaccurate to speak of a governor being liable, for failure to perform official acts, to a United States court-martial or to any other form of Federal coercion.

There is, indeed, an indefiniteness in American law concerning the relation of the President to the State governors, so that when their functions unexpectedly converge or overlap it is usually necessary to fall back upon some improvised *modus vivendi* of coöperation.

Our law and our body of legal doctrine are full enough

---

[25]Act of Feb. 12, 1793. *U. S. Stat. at Large*, I, 302.

[26]Kentucky *vs.* Dennison, 65 U. S. 66, 107 *et seq.*

[27]In some States, governors are placed under the operation of judicial writs as to purely ministerial acts. (*Ruling Case Law*, XII, 1009.)

in matters touching the relation of the State and nation in the legislative sphere, and this is also true in the judicial sphere. Where Federal and State laws conflict, the Federal law supersedes that of the State; and in case a State court issues a decision repugnant to Federal law, that decision may be set aside by a Federal court. But in executive matters, where the governor acts in a field in which the President and his Cabinet also act, the national executive does not undertake to "set aside," or to direct, the action of the State executive. Normally, of course, the President and his Cabinet do not act over the same subject matter as the governors, but they were constantly doing so during the Civil War, and this overlapping produced many strange situations and led to numerous irregutarities.[28]

Nor is it merely a question of "compelling" a recalcitrant State governor to do his Federal duty. It is more often a question of honest difference of opinion as to what that duty is. So long as the Federal executive and the State executive move in separate channels, all is well; but when their courses converge, difficulty develops, not as a rule because one side defies the other, but rather because the definition of the respective duties involved is not sufficiently clear.[29]

---

[28]A governor may not, independently, exercise the war power. Where a State governor arrested "rebel" sympathizers and announced that they would be confined until certain Union prisoners should be released, his action, in the opinion of the Judge Advocate General, transcended the police power of the State and amounted to an assumption of the war power. It was therefore held illegal. (*Digest of the Opinions of the Judge Advocates General* [Revised ed., 1901], p. 695.)

[29]For general treatments of the powers of the governor, see: J. A. Fairlie, "The State Governor," *Mich. Law. Rev.*, X, Nos. 5 and 6; Finley and Sanderson, *The American Executive*, J. M. Mathews, *American State Government.*

V

A significant chapter of Civil War history is that which concerns the financial relations between the States and the National Government. In this field, as in the military sphere, State action for national purposes was frequent, usually leading to the result that the nation finally had to pay, after having suffered from the inefficiency of State performance.

The direct tax law of August 5, 1861, named the quotas that each State should pay, even including those within the Confederacy.[30] The apportionment of the quotas, as required by the Constitution, was according to population, which every expert in public finance knows to be an unsound basis for taxation. Wealth, not numbers, is the proper criterion. Federal machinery was provided for levying upon real estate and collecting directly from individual citizens within the States, but such Federal machinery was to be employed only in those States which neglected to raise their specified quotas by their own officers and in their own way.

This tax ultimately yielded a revenue of approximately seventeen million dollars, of which $2,300,000 was reported as having been contributed by the Southern States.[31] Long after the war, in 1891, Congress passed a bill reimbursing the States for the amounts which they had paid under this tax.[32] The general impression that the South had not borne its due share in this taxation—an impression which the facts do not

---

[30] *Supra*, p. 317.

[31] Message of President Cleveland, March 2, 1889: *Senate Journal*, 50 Cong., 2 sess., p. 503.

[32] *U. S. Stat. at Large*, XXVI, 822.

bear out—appeared to be the principal reason for the reimbursing measure.[33]

A similar bill had been passed in 1889 but was vetoed by President Cleveland for excellent reasons. He urged that the reimbursement constituted a bald gratuity unjustified by the mere existence of a treasury surplus; that such an expenditure was not for a legitimate public purpose, and was unconstitutional; that the people should not be familiarized with the spectacle of their Government repenting the collection of taxes and restoring them; and that if a distribution to the original payers were attempted, many fraudulent claims and bitter contests would result.[34] This unfortunate experience with the "direct tax" has done much to discredit the whole plan of raising a Federal tax by means of State quotas, and the method has never been used since the Civil War. It may now, in fact, be regarded as obsolete.

A curious use of the State taxing power is to be seen in those laws which levied taxes upon all the citizens in order to raise a fund for the benefit of drafted men. Sometimes revenue obtained in this manner was used to pay commutation money, thus permitting the drafted men to avoid service; sometimes substitutes were paid for, while again the men who preferred to serve would be paid the equivalent of the substitute price. Several of the Northern States had such laws and as a rule they were upheld by the State courts, though they occasioned grave constitutional discussions.

In justifying such acts it was argued that the States share with Congress the power to raise armies and may therefore legislate on the subject; that every citizen is

[33]This prevailing view ignores the extensive forfeitures by means of land sales in the South for non-payment of the tax. See *supra*, pp. 318-319.

[34]*Senate Journal*, 50 Cong., 2 sess., pp. 501-507.

equally obligated to perform military service; that this equal obligation justifies a tax upon all to relieve the few who are drafted; that State action to provide commutation money was merely a compliance with the $300 clause of the Conscription Act; and that it was in the public interest to retain for the community the economically superior services of the drafted men, permitting inferior substitutes to take their places in the army![35]

It remained for the Supreme Court of Kentucky to issue the clearest statement denouncing the unconstitutionality of this sort of legislation. A citizens' committee in a Kentucky county had borrowed over $100,000 on the credit of the county to be used for the relief of about two hundred drafted men, either as direct payments or to purchase substitutes. A law of the State was then passed authorizing the issuing of bonds and the levying of a tax by the county court to repay the sum borrowed. In the State Supreme Court this and other similar acts of the legislature were declared unconstitutional.

The court held that Congress has the exclusive power to raise and support armies, and it was pointed out that the States may not tax for an exclusively national purpose. Whatever might be the great moral obligation of every citizen to bear arms, the specific obligation rested upon the drafted men only; and a tax to relieve them would be for a private, not a public, purpose. The constitutional taxing power of the State legislature, it was held, did not cover such an assessment.[36]

We have already observed the extensive military activities of the State governments in the early part of

---

[35]For a citation of decisions dealing with laws of this sort, see *supra*, p. 249, n. 21.

[36]Ferguson *vs.* Landram, 64 Ky. 548.

the war. Naturally these activities had their effect upon the financial relations of the States to the nation. The States demanded reimbursement from the national treasury for their expenditures, and it was promptly granted. The special session of 1861 witnessed the enactment of three measures dealing with this subject.

1. In the army appropriation bill of July 17, 1861, the item of $10,000,000 was set aside "to refund to the States expenses incurred on account of volunteers called into the field."[37]

2. An act of July 27, 1861, without carrying any definite appropriation, directed in general terms that payments be made to the States to cover the cost of "enrolling, subsisting, clothing, supplying, arming, equiping [*sic*], paying and transporting its troops."[38]

3. A third law appropriated $2,000,000 to be spent under the discretion of the President in supplying arms and other aid to loyal citizens of States in which rebellion existed or was threatened.[39]

The statute just mentioned was put to an extraordinary use in Indiana. Owing to the Democratic plan to pass a measure that would wrest the control of the militia from the hands of the governor, the Republican minority absented themselves from the legislature. As a result the State government was left without the tax laws and appropriations necessary to carry on its business. When the matter was presented in person to Secretary Stanton in Washington, and he was told that Lincoln knew of no law by which aid could be extended, Stanton is said to have replied, "By God, I will find a law." The law providing the appropriation to cover expenses of supplying arms to loyal citizens

---

[37] *U. S. Stat. at Large*, XII, 264. [38] *Ibid.*, p. 276.

[39] Act. of July 31, 1861: *Ibid.*, p. 283.

in States threatened with rebellion was therefore stretched to cover an order issued by President Lincoln advancing $250,000 to Morton, who was held accountable for the sum. Of the sum thus advanced, $160,000 was used to pay interest on the State debt. In effect the transaction was an advance from the national treasury, without specific congressional appropriation, for the purpose of tiding a State over a serious financial crisis.[40]

This general policy of compensating the States for their war expenditures was further pursued from year to year until the resulting aftermath of war claims presented a problem of bewildering magnitude. The general law of July 27, 1861, was looked upon as a pledge to which the Government was committed, and Congress kept on appropriating money to carry out the act until in 1871 it was repealed; but even after the repeal, unexpended balances were reappropriated and fresh appropriations for the same object were passed. Over forty-two million dollars had been refunded to the States by 1880, while there still remained nearly nine millions unpaid.[41]

In describing the formidable problems involved in making these reimbursements, the Examiner of State Claims wrote in 1880: ". . . it would probably be beyond the power of the judges . . . of the Court of Claims . . . to memorize or collate the administrative rulings or precedents that underlie the departmental actions touching allowances . . . on these claims."[42] The debates which have occurred whenever these claims have been presented in Congress give evidence of the State jealousies involved. When, for instance, the

[40] Foulke, *Morton*, I, Ch. xxii; Stampp, *Indiana Politics*, 176-185.
[41] *Sen. Exec. Doc. No. 74*, 46 Cong., 2 sess., p. 199.
[42] *Ibid.*, p. 6.

claim of Pennsylvania was presented for a special reimbursement to cover expenses incurred in calling out the militia at the time of Lee's invasion in 1863, Representative Fernando Wood moved to insert "New York," Representative Rogers, "New Jersey," and the claims of other States were then presented.[43] Though similar repayments had been made to the States in previous wars, yet neither sound political science nor actual experience would seem to justify the practice of allowing the States to perform national functions and then look to the nation for reimbursement.

VI

We may conclude this study of State and Federal relations by noting those jurisdictional conflicts which arose when attempts were made to hold Federal officers answerable to the State courts. Such attempts were frequent. We have noted in another chapter that in many cases officers of the Federal Government were subjected to criminal prosecutions or to lawsuits within the States because of acts performed in their official capacity.[44] The answer of the Federal Government, as we have seen, was to provide in the Indemnity Act that the President's orders should serve as a complete defense in such cases, and to require the removal of such actions to the Federal courts, whose jurisdiction was in this way greatly expanded at the expense of the States.

But other forms of coercion or restraint were resorted to by the State judges. The writ of *habeas corpus* was frequently used for the purpose of releasing men held

[43] *Cong. Globe*, April 23, 1864, 38 Cong., 1 sess., p. 1793.
[44] *Supra*, Chapter IX.

in military custody by officers who were enforcing the Federal conscription law, or to free citizens subjected to military arrest.[45] At times the use of the writ by the State judges was based upon an assumption of concurrent jurisdiction. The argument *ab inconvenienti* was advanced, and it was contended that the State judge might be applied to in preference to the Federal judge on the ground of greater accessibility.[46] Or again it was urged that since the *habeas corpus* privilege had been suspended in the Federal courts the State tribunals offered the citizen's only recourse for enjoying this high privilege, and the writ could therefore be directed even against Federal officers, the assumption being that the Federal judge would be willing to grant the writ, but was restrained by the President's action from making effective the privilege involved.

More often, however, the situation presented itself as a clash of authority, and the instances of this use of the State judicial power may commonly be traced to a sentiment adverse to some phase of Federal policy. Where opposition to conscription was strong, local judicial relief would be sought on the ground that the individual in question was not liable to military service, or on the broader ground that the conscription law itself was unconstitutional. In the one case the State judge would be asked to assume the function of preventing a Federal official from misusing his powers under the law, denying to the Federal officer the authority, under executive regulations, to determine the liability of particular individuals, and making such

[45] 45 Pa., 238, esp. 301 *et seq.;* Opinion of William Whiting, Solicitor of the War Department: *O. R.*, Ser. III, Vol. 3, p. 460.

[46] *Ex Parte* Hill, 38 Ala. 429; *ibid.*, 458 These Alabama cases present a precise parallel between the law of the United States and that of the Confederate States on this subject.

officer answerable for his conduct to the State judges. In the other case the State court would be exercising its right to apply the Federal Constitution as superior to a Federal statute. This right the State court undoubtedly has, and it is even a duty, made so by that clause which declares the national Constitution to be binding upon State judges, who are under oath to uphold it. The error involved was not in claiming this right, but in adopting an unwarranted method of procedure in exercising it. The authority to issue a decision denying the constitutionality of a Federal law does not justify a State judge in the use of a method which amounts to controlling a Federal officer and preventing the discharge of his functions.

The leading decision on this subject is that of the Supreme Court of the United States in *Ableman* vs. *Booth*, announced by Chief Justice Taney in 1858.[47] A State court in Wisconsin had issued a writ of *habeas corpus* for the release of a prisoner held by a Federal commissioner operating under the Fugitive Slave Act of 1850. The Chief Justice showed that the judges and courts of Wisconsin had no basis for the power thus assumed. He said:

> If the judicial power exercised in this instance has been reserved to the States, no offense against the laws of the United States can be punished by their own courts without the permission and according to the judgment of the courts of the State in which the party happens to be imprisoned; for, if the Supreme Court of Wisconsin possessed [this authority] their supervising and controlling power would embrace the whole criminal code of the United States.[48]

After referring to the supremacy of "this Constitution,

[47] 62 U. S. (21 How.) 506 [48] *Ibid.*, p. 515.

and the laws made in pursuance thereof," the Chief Justice continued:

> But the supremacy thus conferred . . . could not peacefully be maintained, unless it was clothed with judicial power equally paramount in authority to carry it into execution; for if left to the courts of justice of the several States, conflicting decisions would unavoidably take place, and the local tribunals could hardly be expected to be always free from . . . local influences. . . . It was essential therefore, . . . that [the United States Government] should have the power of establishing courts of justice, altogether independent of State power, to carry into effect its own laws.[49]

So convincing was this decision that it held in spite of attempts to explain away its meaning or to show that it was not applicable to the wartime situation. Thus Federal supremacy in Federal matters was not seriously impaired and in general it may be said that these jurisdictional controversies served as annoyances and embarrassments rather than actual obstructions. The usual result of incidents of this nature was that the officer subjected to the writ refused to obey its mandate, as he could well afford to do with the whole government back of him. A general instruction was issued to provost marshals directing them in such cases to make known to the State judges that their prisoners were held under the authority of the United States. They were further instructed to refuse obedience to State judicial mandate, and to resist the execution of process if such resistance should become necessary.[50]

That the issue here involved went to the very heart of the question as to the constitutional division of jurisdiction between the State and the nation is evident.

---

[49] *Ibid.*, p. 518. See also Tarble's Case, 13 Wall. 397.

[50] *O. R.*, Ser. III, Vol. 3, pp. 460-461, 818.

The decisions on the subject read like commentaries on the fundamental doctrine of our constitutional law and are replete with citations drawn from the *Federalist*, Marshall, Story, Kent and other sources that rank among our legal classics. Had the Federal Government yielded on the points involved it might as well have abdicated its powers.

When a close study is made of relations between the loyal States and the National Government, some familiar generalizations may have to be revised as to the degree of centralization involved. By the end of the war the importance of State governments had receded, but during much of the conflict a remarkable amount of the nation's business—even the military business—was left to the States. Excess of authority on the part of zealous governors, interference and strong protest by such as Seymour, irregularity, friction, maladjustment, and in the end the payment of the bills out of the national purse—these are the facts which the war history reveals. When in 1863 nationalizing laws came to be passed, their object was the efficient performance of truly national functions after trial and error had proved State performance to be unsatisfactory. The National Government did not extend its power by the assumption of State functions so much as by taking to itself the conduct of its own affairs. Nationalizing measures were for national objects, intended to overcome undue decentralization.[51]

---

[51]Among recent books dealing with the subject matter of this chapter, see William B. Hesseltine, *Lincoln and the War Governors*, Kenneth M. Stampp, *Indiana Politics during the Civil War*.

CHAPTER XVIII

THE PARTITION OF VIRGINIA

I. Long-standing differences between eastern and western Virginia
II. Unionist movement in the western counties: Reorganization of the government of Virginia
III. The launching of the "restored government"
IV. Steps taken for the formation of the new State: The "Wheeling ordinance" of August 20, 1861
V. Action of the Federal Government toward the new State movement: The West Virginia bill in Congress
VI. Attitude of Lincoln and his Cabinet toward the West Virginia bill: Admission of the new State
VII. Later career of the "restored government": Attempts to obtain representation of "Virginia" in the Congress at Washington
VIII. Attitude of Virginia and of the Supreme Court in the controversy between Virginia and West Virginia concerning certain disputed counties
IX. General considerations concerning the process by which the new commonwealth was created

The upheaval in State affairs which characterized the war for the Union left all the States save one intact. The confusing spectacle of rival State governments appeared in various border commonwealths where Unionist and secessionist forces were about evenly divided, and it might have been supposed that the forces of disruption which the war unleashed would cause the formation of various new political units; but it was only in Virginia that the disintegrating process left a permanent effect. For our purpose the partition of

Virginia will be treated, not as a matter of State development, but as a phase of our constitutional history. Our particular interest will be to inquire into the effect of domestic war upon the constitutional process of State-making.

I

It has not been proved to the satisfaction of the writer that the exigencies of the Civil War alone furnished an adequate motive for the permanent disruption of the Old Dominion. Had the purpose been merely to safeguard the Union interest in Virginia during the period of the war, it is reasonable to suppose that some method short of making a new commonwealth could have been found. It is true that citizens in western Virginia who supported the Federal Government found themselves confronted with a condition of affairs which approached anarchy and hence stood in need of a government other than that at Richmond to which they could look for protection; but a Unionist government for Virginia was established to meet this need, and, as it was extended to all the districts in which Unionists could hope for substantial support, one may well ask whether the Federal cause required that a separate State be formed. Certain it is that many strong Union men did not desire separation. Because of various grievances and sectional differences, however, talk of separation had long been in the air, and the great activity of the separationists, whether they constituted a majority or not, enabled them to effect their purpose as a war measure.[1]

[1]On the formation of West Virginia the older books should be used with caution. Granville D. Hall's *Rending of Virginia* is an uncritical vindication of the new State movement and the same may be said of William P. Willey, *An Inside View of the Formation of the State*

The divergences between the eastern and western portions of the State have often been pointed out. The physiography of the counties beyond the Blue Ridge was quite distinct from that of the valley, piedmont and tide-water sections, so that the western counties looked toward the Ohio into which their rivers poured, while in the east the flow of commerce and the general outlook was toward the Atlantic. Social and religious differences divided the Scotch-Irish and German elements in the northwest from the English in the lower counties.[2] Slaves were few in those portions of the State which bordered upon Ohio and Pennsyl-

---

of West Virginia, and of Granville Parker, *The Formation of the State of West Virginia*. In Virgil A. Lewis, *History of West Virginia*, the whole movement is treated, but this is done from the point of view of the separationists. The same author has brought together a useful collection of documents under the title *How West Virginia was Made*. One finds a typical justification of the measures taken for the erection of the new State in the historical account that opens the reports of cases before the State supreme court (1 W. Va. 5-81), and useful contemporary articles are found in *Appleton's Annual Cyclopedia*, especially for 1861 and 1863. The principal newspaper to be consulted is the Wheeling *Intelligencer*. On August 24, 1902, this newspaper published a "souvenir edition" celebrating its fiftieth anniversary; and in this issue the part which the newspaper played in the formation of the State was set forth. Among the recent studies one may mention C. H. Ambler, *Sectionalism in Virginia from 1776 to 1861*, and H. J. Eckenrode, *Political History of Virginia during the Reconstruction*. Of primary importance is James C. McGregor, *The Disruption of Virginia*, McGregor's book has the merit of presenting the subject afresh in a scholarly manner from a study of the sources without the bias that inevitably appears in the pages of West Virginia writers. *The Semicentennial History of West Virginia*, by James Morton Callahan, is especially useful for the bibliography on pp. 284-293. Unique interest attaches to the Pierpoint papers, a large mass of unpublished material in the Virginia archives at Richmond. The present writer made extensive use of these manuscripts in the preparation of this chapter; and, so far as his knowledge goes, they had not previously been examined for such a purpose. Further studies by Maude F. Callahan, William Baird, and J. A. C. Chandler are noted in the bibliography at the end of this book. And see titles by Ambler below, p. 476, n. 73.

[2]For a discussion of the differences between the eastern and western portions, see C. H. Ambler, *Sectionalism in Virginia*.

vania, and it was only in the east that the institution was of economic and social importance.[3]

Grievances accumulated as the years passed and the westerners became increasingly resentful at what they considered the contemptuous neglect of the east, in whose hands rested actual control of State affairs. The main grievances were the mixed basis of representation by which slave property as well as free population was taken into account in apportioning delegates; the disproportion between the number of those entitled to vote and those upon whom the burdens of taxation and militia service fell; the limitation of the suffrage to freeholders; the restriction of internal improvements to the east; the *viva voce* vote, and the limited taxation of slave property as compared with the full taxation of the real estate and business interests of the west. When the constitution of 1830 was framed, it was felt to be so partial to the "eastern aristocrats" that every voting delegate from the west opposed it; and when submitted to the people it was condemned in the west by an impressive majority. In 1850-51 a genuine effort at compromise resulted in constitutional changes favorable to the west, and a more conciliatory spirit was manifest in the decade preceding the Civil War; but with the opening of that conflict the fires of sectionalism were rekindled and the Unionists seized the reins of leadership in the western counties while the secessionists obtained control in the east.

---

[3]Under date of October, 1861, the auditor of the "restored State" of Virginia gave the following figures regarding the population of the proposed State of "Kanawha": white, 273,737; free colored, 1110; slaves, 6810. (*Journal of the Senate* [of "restored Virginia"], regular session, Wheeling, commencing Dec. 2, 1861, p. 28.)

II

When the Richmond convention secretly passed the ordinance of secession on April 17, 1861, there was brought home to each fireside and each community the momentous question of hazarding life and fortune upon the new cause or of resting these precious stakes upon the old Union to which allegiance had been due. A true understanding of the Unionist movement in western Virginia is to be obtained, not by reading ordinances, appeals, proclamations, and resolutions, but by studying the manner in which the people of the western counties viewed the hard realities of their exposed position when confronted with actual war. At every step in the progress of the movement one must take account of the turbulence and confusion of the times, the intimidation practiced by both sides, the powerful social sanctions as well as the physical violence brought to bear against those who resisted the dominant element in the locality; the administering of oaths under military pressure; the use of force at the polls; the many irregularities in the choice of delegates and in the conduct of elections; the hurried flight to Kentucky or Ohio of those who found life intolerable at home; and the military activity which accompanied the agitation of political issues.[4] It was a time of domestic strife and even of revolution—a time in which the greatest turbulence was seen at the border, where Unionists and secessionists were intermingled. The bitterness of these times is now happily forgotten, but it aids our historical appreciation of such a subject as the creation of West Virginia to remember that the various steps

---

[4]On all these conditions the Pierpoint Papers (MSS., Virginia State Library) throw a flood of light.

leading to the formation of this new commonwealth were taken in the excitement of conflict and war, rather than in that calm deliberation which is needful for the process of State-making.

Organized resistance in the western counties was quickly developed by active Unionist leaders. In the various localities Union mass meetings were held in which the "heresy" of secession was denounced and defiance of the Richmond Government was voiced. A mass meeting at Clarksburg issued on April 22, 1861, a call for a convention of delegates from the northwestern counties; and this convention assembled on May 13 at Wheeling, where Unionist and separationist agitation centered. This "first Wheeling Convention" contained delegates from only twenty-six of the fifty counties that were later included in West Virginia.[5] Delegates to this convention were chosen in various mass meetings with little formality, and there was no real system of representation. The delegation from each county depended upon the number that happened to be chosen or the number that wished to attend rather than upon any authorized basis of apportionment. "More than one third of the . . . delegates," says McGregor, "were from the district immediately around Wheeling" and "the farther the county was . . . from Wheeling, the fewer the delegates."[6]

This improvised "May Convention" denounced the Virginia ordinance of secession and the agreement with the Confederacy; urged the citizens to condemn the ordinance by popular vote; and called upon the people

[5]For a map of these counties, see J. M. Callahan, *Semi-centennial History of West Virginia*, p. 150. The counties are listed in 1 W. Va. 47. It is there stated that the "committee on credentials reported duly accredited delegates from twenty-six counties."

[6]McGregor, *Disruption of Virginia*, 193.

to elect loyal men as representatives in Congress and members of the legislature. In the event of the ratification of the ordinance of secession, the convention recommended that the counties "disposed to coöperate" send delegates to a "general convention" to meet on June 11 "to devise such measures . . . as the safety and welfare of the people may demand." Citing the political axiom that "government is founded on the consent of the governed," the convention called upon the "proper authorities of Virginia" to permit a peaceful and lawful separation of the Unionist counties from the rest of the State.[7]

It should be noted that this "May Convention" was quite without regular authority to take action either for Virginia or for the northwestern portion thereof. The June convention in its address to the people of northwestern Virginia confessed the irregular character of the earlier convention, saying: "It was literally a mass convention, and from the irregular manner of the appointment of its delegates, was not calculated for the dispatch of business."[8] Its chief act was to lay the track for the later convention whose measures were to extend to the fundamental alteration of the government.

Before adjournment, the first Wheeling convention appointed a "central committee" of nine members to act as an emergency executive body to organize the Unionist movement. One of the chief functions of this committee was to prepare plans for the more important convention that was to meet in June.

In the interval between the first and second Wheeling conventions, the people of Virginia, on May 23, voted

---

[7] *West Virginia Legislative Handbook*, 1916, pp. 261-263. (This book is cited because of the convenient form in which various sources are assembled.)

[8] *Ibid.*, p. 275.

on the ordinance of secession, and a decisive majority of the votes in the northwestern portion were cast against the ratification of that ordinance.[9]

Such, in brief, were the preliminaries of that "June convention" in Wheeling whose action was of such decisive importance in the movement for separate statehood. As this convention launched the movement for the formation of the "loyal" government of Virginia, and also the new State movement, the process by which it was made up deserves attention; though this is a subject on which the various historical accounts throw little light. The "Central Committee of the Union Convention of Western Virginia," which we have above mentioned, functioned as a sort of junta for promoting the whole movement, taking counsel from many Unionists in and out of Virginia as to the most feasible plans to be pursued, corresponding with leading men in the various counties, and preparing in advance a program to be laid before the coming convention. In various counties, "committees of safety" (reminiscent of the patriot committees of the American Revolution) were appointed, usually by some sort of mass meeting. If, in any county, a few men were actively interested in the movement that was being engineered at Wheeling, they could with little difficulty hold a mass meeting and obtain election as members of the local committee of safety. The delegates to the June convention were chosen in various ways, sometimes by mass meeting, sometimes by the county committee, sometimes apparently by self-appointment. There was no popular

[9]West Virginia writers have stated that 40,000 out of the 42,000 votes cast in the northwestern counties were against secession (1 W. Va. 55), but the vote for all of Virginia as announced by Governor Letcher was 125,950 to 20,373. As McGregor shows, however, doubt was cast on the correctness of the returns as given out by Letcher. (McGregor, *Disruption of Virginia*, 180.)

election in the true sense.[10] In one instance the Wheeling committee wrote to a prominent man in Charleston, stating that the people of western Virginia were looking to their old leaders for counsel, and urging his "attendance as a member of the convention to be held on the 11th inst."[11] There was no reference to any election as a delegate. The whole process of preparing for this Wheeling convention was such as to promote the selection of men actively interested in what the convention was expected to do—i.e., lay plans for a separate State—rather than to obtain a general representation of all shades of opinion.[12] To determine the number of counties "represented" would involve

---

[10]A Union man thus wrote to Pierpoint from Wayne County: "Now it is well known that had not the people of Buffalo Shoals taken the stand [for the Union] that they did, no Delegate would have been sent to Wheeling from this county. Cabell county was not represented because there were no Northern men to inform the people, I mean such as dared to act. Now an election cannot be held in this county until it is subdued by soldiers, many rebels swearing they will die first rather than submit." (John Adams to F. H. Pierpoint, Buffalo Shoals, July 20, 1861: Pierpoint Papers.)

[11]Letter from the office of the Central Committee, Wheeling, July 1, 1861, to George W. Summers, Charleston: Pierpoint Papers.

[12]The activity of county committees of Unionists in organizing the June convention is illustrated by the following letter: "We the County Committee of Cabell County do certify that Edward D. Wright and B. D. McGinnis have been duly appointed Delegates to represent this County in the Union Convention of Western Virginia to be held on the 11th of June, 1861. [Signed] J. C. Plybun, C. G. Stephenson, Isaiah Ray, S. Hatton, J. Graham, Committee." The following letter illustrates the mass meeting method of organization: "At a meeting of a number of citizens of Loudoun County, Virginia, for the purpose of electing delegates to a convention at Wheeling to form a provisional government for the State of Virginia, [it was] Resolved *first,* that the chairman appoint a committee of five, when the following names were announced by the chair: George Townsend, T. J. McGaha, Isaiah Virts, Conrad Darr, Daniel Fry; *second,* that delegates to the convention be elected, when the following gentlemen were unanimously elected: W. F. Mercer, D. T. Bond, Thos. B. March, John B. Dutton. On motion, the meeting adjourned. B. Kabrich, Pres., T. J. McGaha, Sec. June 23, 1861." (Pierpoint Papers.)

THE PARTITION OF VIRGINIA

Data as to county lines based upon Lloyd's Official Map of Virginia as of 1861.

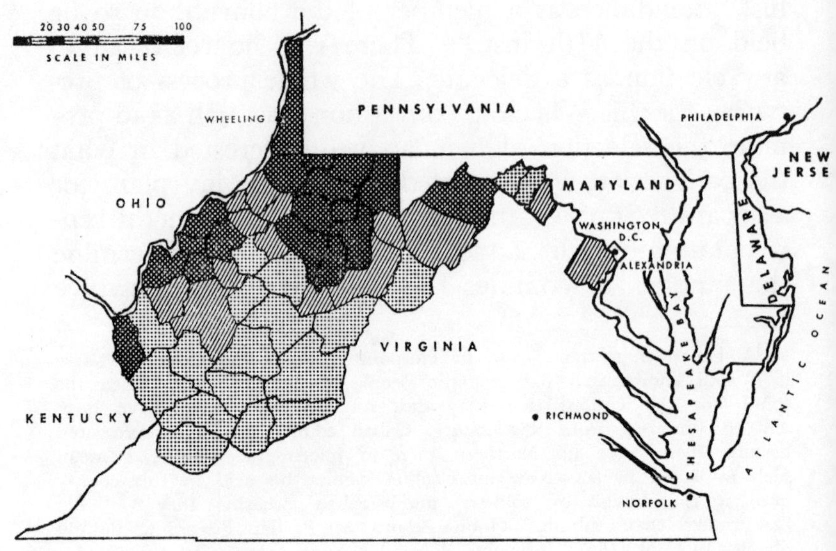

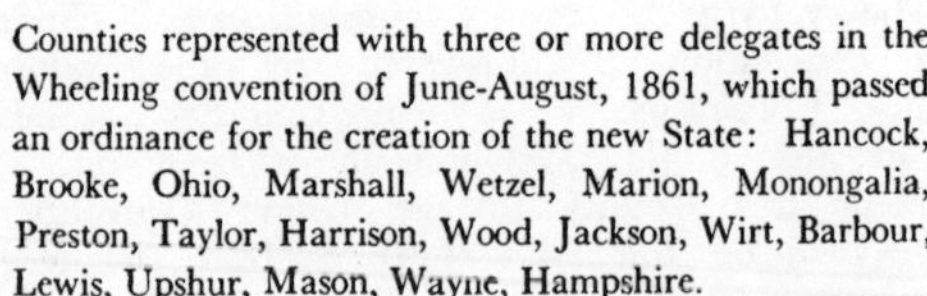

Counties represented with three or more delegates in the Wheeling convention of June-August, 1861, which passed an ordinance for the creation of the new State: Hancock, Brooke, Ohio, Marshall, Wetzel, Marion, Monongalia, Preston, Taylor, Harrison, Wood, Jackson, Wirt, Barbour, Lewis, Upshur, Mason, Wayne, Hampshire.

Counties represented in this convention with two delegates or less: Tyler, Pleasants, Ritchie, Doddridge, Roane, Gilmer, Tucker, Randolph, Putnam, Kanawha, Webster, Hardy, Jefferson, Alexandria, Fairfax.

Counties unrepresented in this convention but nevertheless included in the new State: Cabell, Calhoun, Braxton, Clay, Nicholas, Boone, Logan, Wyoming, Mercer, McDowell, Pocahontas, Fayette, Raleigh, Greenbrier, Monroe, Pendleton, Morgan, Berkeley.

discussion as to what constituted representation,[13] but even if we accept the convention's own statement that the number of counties represented was thirty-four,[14] this was but slightly more than two-thirds of the forty-eight counties constituting West Virginia at the time of admission, while the major portion of Virginia, adhering as it did to the Confederacy, was of course unrepresented. It is evident, therefore, not merely that this June convention was revolutionary, but that, considered as a revolutionary body, it was in no sense representative of the State of Virginia for which it presumed to act.

Assuming functions appropriate only to a Virginian constitutional convention, this body of men from the west, meeting at Wheeling on June 11, passed an "ordinance for the reorganization of the State govern-

[13]In July, 1863, Senator Carlile, of "restored Virginia," informed the United States Senate that the June convention at Wheeling did not fairly represent even the people of western Virginia. This is well brought out in McGregor, *op. cit.*, pp. 294-295.

[14]"The number of counties actually represented is thirty-four. . . . Several of the delegates escaped from their counties at the risk of their lives, while others are still detained at home by force or menace against them or their families and property." (Address of the Second Convention, Wheeling, June 25, 1861: *West Virginia Legislative Handbook*, 1916, pp. 275-276.) By glancing at the map on the opposite page, the reader will have a graphic representation of the importance of the panhandle and its vicinity in the new-State movement. It was from the counties near Pennsylvania and Ohio that the active separationists came; while in contrast to this, a continuous group of counties covering about half the area of the new State had no participation in the convention which passed the "Wheeling ordinance," but were in spite of this fact included in West Virginia as ultimately defined. The people had no opportunity, county by county, to determine whether they would adhere to Virginia or join the new commonwealth; but their fate was determined by the whole vote cast within the boundaries indicated by the convention. McGregor states that this plan was adopted to avoid "certain rejection in at least two thirds of the counties." (*Disruption of Virginia*, pp. 235-236.) In general those opposed to separation did not vote, and this was particularly true of secessionists. (The list of delegates used in preparing the accompanying map is found in Lewis, *How West Virginia Was Made*, pp. 79-81.)

ment." By this ordinance it was provided that a temporary government, consisting of governor, lieutenant governor, attorney general and council of five, should be appointed by the convention itself; while a permanent government was to be created by requiring an oath of loyalty of all State, county, town and city officials, members of the legislature, judges, officers of militia, and officers and privates of volunteer companies not mustered into the service of the United States. The oath was as follows:

> I solemnly swear (or affirm) that I will support the Constitution of the United States, and the laws made in pursuance thereof, as the supreme law of the land, anything in the constitution and laws of the State of Virginia or in the ordinances of the [secession] convention at Richmond . . . to the contrary notwithstanding; and that I will uphold and defend the government of Virginia as vindicated and restored by the convention which assembled at Wheeling on the eleventh day of June, eighteen hundred and sixty-one.

Where the oath was refused by any elective officer, his office was to be declared vacant and special elections were to be held to fill the vacancy. Appointive offices were to be filled at once by the governor.[15]

It is to be seen that by this ordinance a form of government was devised which, while drawing its support exclusively from the Unionist element of the State, claimed to be the only legitimate government of Virginia. The legal fiction thus created was of vital importance in the whole movement for the creation of the new commonwealth.

---

[15] *West Virginia Legislative Handbook*, 1916, pp. 268-269. There was no popular ratification of the far-reaching acts of this June convention.

III

If space sufficed, it would be of interest to observe the steps taken to launch the "restored government" of Virginia on the basis of the paper plan drawn up by the second Wheeling convention. Extraordinary conditions of turbulence and uncertainty, which at times verged upon anarchy, confronted the Wheeling governor, Francis H. Pierpoint, chosen by the convention. The approximate collapse of civil government left the country open to bandits and guerrillas, and a kind of terrorism characterized the coercive methods practiced by both sides. A Methodist preacher of Boone County wrote that the disunion party was too strong for the Unionists of "that Reagon." "All the Judges, Lawyers, Shureffs . . . Clarks, Meranchents, politions slave holders and drunkerds," he said, "out number us Considerable; . . . they have bin forming Compneys and taking men and women and swaring them into the Suthern Confedsy and not to give infermation or feed eney union men and even swaring little boys to give them infermation."[16] He added that his own home had been entered by armed men and that his life was "thertened by the Rebbles." A citizen of Weston wrote the governor that the rebels in Roane and Calhoun had come over in mass on the Kanawha River and were entering the houses of Unionists, stripping them of household goods, even cutting up bed cord, leading off the horses, and creating general confusion.[17] From Ironton, Ohio, came a letter describing conditions in Cabell, Wayne and adjoining counties where, according

[16]Robert Hager to "Govener Piarepoint E. S. Q.," Gallipolis, Ohio, July 30, 1861: Pierpoint Papers.

[17]H. H. Withers to Governor Pierpoint, Weston, Va., Nov. 9, 1861: *ibid.* (Pierpoint was the governor's own wartime spelling.)

to the informant, there was no civil authority, no law, no protection to the persons and property of either loyal or disloyal citizens. All, he said, was anarchy and confusion.[18]

Reports from many other localities, crowding in upon the Pierpoint administration, told the same story. A "county committee" sent word from Ritchie Court House, that, while home guards were being formed and a Union organization was being effected in the county, there were "no mails" and the committee was out of touch with events. Citizens of Fairfax County asked that steps be taken to give relief from the "present condition of anarchy" under which they suffered. Four hundred citizens of Gilmer County, deploring the turbulent conditions confronting them, with "certain reckless individuals lurking in the woods and brush, shooting at the soldiers, citizens, etc., annoying and endangering the lives and property of all law-abiding citizens," signed a paper pledging to each other "our lives, our fortunes and our sacred honor," and resolving that they would exert themselves as citizens to maintain social order and bring offenders to justice. A somewhat illiterate citizen of Cabell County referred to the deplorable condition into which the people of that region were thrown by depredations and outrages committed by armed bands that were ravaging the entire country for fifty miles distant, and appealed for protection from these "gorrilla" companies. A large number of citizens of Sistersville in Tyler County petitioned for like protection, reporting that they could no longer look for protection to the civil authorities. Pleasants County was reported to be of "questionable loyalty," and one of its inhabitants wrote that it was

---

[18] A. McCullough to Pierpoint, Ironton, O., Aug. 7, 1861: *ibid.*

"difficult to tell who among us is a real friend of the government." Governor Pierpoint's brother, Larkin Pierpoint, wrote from Ritchie Court House asking "Dear Brother Frank" whether he had better go with a volunteer company that was being formed for the Union service, saying that he was ready to fight and wanted to do his duty "if I know what it is."

Bandits frequently took advantage of this weakness of civil government, and for protection against these, as well as to resist the secessionists, "home guards" were organized as a sort of impromptu military force; and various "battles" were fought in a kind of neighborhood war that the military historians do not record. In all this violence and confusion there was a tendency to doubt each man's loyalty until proved; rumor magnified the actual turbulence which in reality was bad enough; and honest men doubted which way duty led.[19]

To administer oaths and hold elections for the "restored government" of Virginia under such conditions was a difficult task. Many refused the Wheeling oath, being uncertain as to whether the government would be recognized as valid, and doubting its ability to establish and defend itself as the successor of the old government of Virginia.[20] There is much significance in the letter of one Joseph Applegate of Wellsburg who

---

[19]These details are taken, *passim*, from the Pierpoint manuscripts in the Virginia State Library.

[20]The Richmond legislature passed various measures against the "usurped government" under Pierpoint, and many felt anxious as to consequences in case of Confederate success. (*Acts of the Gen. Assembly of Va.* [Called Session, 1862, Richmond], p. 11; *ibid.* [Adjourned Session, 1863], p. 88.) A citizen of Wellsburg wrote to Governor Pierpoint that he was not prepared to take the Wheeling oath. "Your government has not been recognized," he said, "neither have you shown an ability to establish and defend the government or the people thereof as against the old government." (O. W. Langfitt to Pierpoint, July 8, 1861: Pierpoint Papers.)

wrote to the Wheeling governor: "I resign the commission I received of you . . . to swear the officers of the county of Brooke on account of reasons known already to you."[21] Where possible, advantage was taken of Federal military aid; and one of Pierpoint's advisers urged that the oath be pressed in the presence of the army, for "should it be removed," he said, "officeholders may refuse to take the oath, hold on, and rebel against your authority."[22]

To round out the organization of the Wheeling government with suitable officials in the various counties was therefore a serious undertaking. The very conditions under which elections were held to fill the offices of those refusing the Wheeling oath were such as to deprive secessionists of a ballot, since no secessionist could qualify for office holding, and naturally the elections were regarded as purely Unionist affairs. Secessionists, therefore, did not ordinarily vote at all; and where possible they actively obstructed the elections, regarding them as illegal. The presence of troops was frequently necessary for the holding of elections (which in many of the counties were conducted in but a part of the voting places), and it was often difficult to find a sufficient number of Union men who were capable of discharging the duties of the various offices. In some cases Unionist officers when elected found themselves unable to enforce the laws or collect the taxes.

Special interest attaches to the legislative branch of this "restored government." By the Wheeling ordinance of June 19, the legislature of Virginia was made to consist of all members chosen on May 23 who would take the test oath, together with additional members specially chosen to take the places of those who re-

[21]Letter of Joseph Applegate, June 22, 1861: Pierpoint Papers.
[22]J. S. Carlile to Pierpoint, June 26, 1861: *ibid.*

fused the oath. When the first legislature of the "restored government" met in special session on July 1, 1861, under call of Governor Pierpoint, only twelve days had elapsed since the passage of the ordinance creating the new government. Obviously this was insufficient for the completion of the various steps necessary for the fulfillment of that ordinance—i.e., the administering of the oath; the submission of evidence of refusal to take the oath; the issuing of writs vacating the offices of non-jurors and providing special elections to fill the vacancies; due publication of such coming elections for the information of persons entitled to vote; the appointing of special commissioners of election in those counties in which the sheriffs refused to comply with the ordinance; the actual holding of the elections in the different precincts; the counting of the votes; the assembling of the returns; and the preparation of certificates showing who were elected.

When one looks closely into the personnel of the "restored legislature," the first fact to claim notice is that, in large part, the membership of the June convention and that of the "restored" legislature were identical. The May convention had "recommended" that those senators and delegates elected to the general assembly on May 23 "who concur[red] in the views of this convention" should have seats in the coming June convention. Thus men who had been chosen as members of a legislature which under the old Virginia constitution must meet in Richmond and contain representatives from the whole State, became members of a convention which reorganized Virginia's government, putting it under the control of a minor part of the State; and then the same men served in the new legislature that was constituted by their own act of reorganization.

Theoretically, according to the method of the reorganizers, there should have been in the "restored" legislature loyal members from every county in the State, or at least enough loyal members to constitute a quorum. Little is said in the various histories of West Virginia as to the actual membership of this reorganized legislature, but light on this subject may be obtained from the rather inaccessible journals of the various sessions. The journal of the House of Delegates for the extra session of July, 1861, reveals, on the fifteenth day of the session, a membership consisting of twenty-nine delegates, representing thirty counties, while the total number of counties in Virginia at that time was 149 and the constitutional membership of the lower house was 152.[23] Only two members had traveled farther than two hundred miles to attend the session; and all the members except these two were from the western portion of the State. The report of the committee on privileges and elections was given quite loosely. It merely listed the men "claiming seats as delegates," noted that the committee "believed" the said delegates to be "duly elected and entitled to their seats," and then admitted that members from only seventeen counties had presented regular certificates of election. The only action taken on this report on membership was to lay it on the table.[24] The journal of the Senate for this session listed only eight names as members, though the Virginia Senate should have numbered fifty.[25]

---

[23] *Journal of the House of Delegates of Virginia* (Extra Session beginning July 1, 1861, Wheeling), 47 *et seq.*

[24] *Ibid.*, pp. 47-48.

[25] *Journal of the Senate of Virginia* (Extra Session commencing July 1, 1861, Wheeling), 25.

IV

The "reorganized" legislature did not deal at once with the question of forming a new State, leaving this matter for the time to the convention which had closed its session on June 25, 1861, adjourning to meet on August 6. The measure of chief importance taken by the legislature in its special session of July, 1861, was the election of Waitman T. Willey and John S. Carlile as United States Senators from Virginia to take the seats of James M. Mason and R. M. T. Hunter whose places had been vacated.[26]

On reassembling, the convention passed on August 20 the "Wheeling ordinance," which provided as follows:[27]

> *Whereas* it is represented to be the desire of the people inhabiting the counties hereinafter mentioned to be separated from this commonwealth, and be erected into a separate State, and admitted into the union of States, and become a member of the government of the United States:
>
> The people of Virginia, by their delegates assembled in convention at Wheeling, do ordain that a new State, to be called the State of Kanawha, be formed and erected. . . . [The boundaries of the proposed State were then indicated and the counties enumerated.]

The ordinance further provided for an election, to be held on the 24th of October within the boundaries of the proposed State, in which the people should vote for or against the new State, and should also choose delegates to a constitutional convention. When the

[26] *Journal of the House of Delegates of Virginia* (Extra Session commencing July 1, 1861, Wheeling), 32; *Journal of the Senate* (same session), 24.

[27] *West Virginia Legislative Handbook*, 1916, pp. 280-283.

election was held, 18,408 votes were announced as having been cast for the new State and 781 against it.[28]

The next step was the framing of a constitution for the new commonwealth. The delegates chosen in October met at Wheeling on November 26 and by February 18 they had completed an instrument of government, dropping the picturesque name "Kanawha" and substituting "West Virginia." On April 3 the people of the region proposed for the new State voted on the constitution, the votes for ratification numbering 18,862 to 514 for rejection.[29]

It was at this stage of the proceedings that the "restored legislature" gave its consent to the formation of the new State. This was done by an act passed on May 13, 1862.[30]

That clause of the Constitution of the United States which forbids the erection of a new State within the jurisdiction of an existing State without the consent of the legislature of such State was thus technically or nominally complied with; but the "Virginia legislature" which gave this consent consisted of about thirty-five members in the lower house and ten in the upper house,

---

[28]This was the vote officially announced. McGregor analyzes it and advances the view that it does not represent the sentiment of the people of western Virginia. (McGregor, *op. cit.*, p. 255.)

[29]Virgil A. Lewis, *How West Virginia Was Made*, 321. Senator Carlile, referring to the process of constitution-making for the new State, pointed out that in one county of about 800 voters there were only 76 votes for the delegate to the constitutional convention. In another, about 400 out of 1200 votes were cast. The popular vote on the constitution, he showed, numbered only about 19,000 as compared to a normal vote of 47,000. (*Cong. Globe*, 37 Cong., 2 sess., pp. 3313-14, and 37 Cong., 3 sess., p. 54.) McGregor points out that the records of the constitutional convention for the new State were not printed because "the discussion had revealed so plainly the opposition of the people of West Virginia both to the North and to the new State that the publication of the debates might interfere with the admission of the State." (McGregor, *op. cit.*, ix.)

[30]*Acts of the Gen. Assembly* (Extra Sess., Wheeling, May, 1862), Ch. I.

while the full membership according to the Virginia constitution should have been one hundred fifty-two delegates and fifty senators. With the exception of the "eastern shore" and two counties opposite Washington, the constituencies represented in this legislature were entirely limited to the counties of the northwest. Even in the northwest many counties were without representation, while two-thirds of the State—i.e., Confederate Virginia—was entirely unrepresented. To say that in this way "Virginia" gave her consent, is to deal in theory and fiction and to overlook realities.

V

The Federal Government was naturally called upon to recognize and assist the Unionist government under Pierpoint. At the very outset President Lincoln gave assurance of his support and the War Department recognized the Wheeling government as entitled to an appropriation from the Federal treasury under the act of July 31, 1861, by which financial assistance was to be extended for the protection of loyal citizens in States which had seceded.[31] That President Lincoln's encouraging attitude toward Pierpoint at this stage did not necessarily involve approval of the separate State movement is shown by the President's comparison of Pierpoint's case with that of Johnson in eastern Ten-

---

[31]Sec. of War Cameron to Daniel Lamb, Oct. 30, 1861: Pierpoint Papers. While claiming Federal benefits, the Wheeling government declined to assume Virginia's quota of the Federal direct tax of 1861 on the ground that the collection of the tax "when three-fourths of the white population, and nearly all the free Negroes and slaves, are beyond our reach, would be not only unjust, but impossible." (*Journal of the Senate of Virginia* [Regular Session, Wheeling, December 2, 1861], pp. 48, 49.)

nessee and of Gamble in Missouri to whom similar Federal assistance had been extended.[32]

When Carlile and Willey, with credentials from Wheeling, applied in the United States Senate for admission as senators from Virginia, conservative men objected, urging that the real government of Virginia was at Richmond, not Wheeling, and that on July 9, when certificates of election of these men were issued, no vacancy existed, since Hunter and Mason were not expelled until July 12. The general attitude of the Senate, however, was that they "should not stick in the bark as to dates," and that any hesitancy in grasping the hands of those whose hearts were for the Union would be unworthy of the hour. A vote to refer the credentials of these Senators to the Committee on the Judiciary failed, and the Senators were admitted on July 13, 1861.[33]

When the "West Virginia bill" (for the admission of the new State into the Union) was discussed in Congress, considerable opposition to the project was developed.[34] The invalidity of the Pierpoint government

[32]Daniel Lamb to Pierpoint, Sept. 19, 1861: Pierpoint Papers.

[33]*Cong. Globe*, July 13, 1861, 37 Cong., 1 sess., p. 109. W. F. Mercer, Union candidate of Loudoun County for the Virginia legislature, wrote to Pierpoint that he claimed election in spite of the fact that his opponent received one hundred more votes than he did, and added: "If we are ruled down to strict parliamentary law, we will be left without representation; but if the policy of the Senate of the United States in the case of Messrs. Carlile and Willey obtains, there will be no difficulty in the case." (Mercer to Pierpoint, Nov. 26, 1861: Pierpoint Papers.)

[34]Representative Joseph Segar of Virginia opposed the new State bill because of its weakening effect upon the "restored government." "As the matter now stands," he said, "we have a loyal government for the whole of Virginia. . . . But pass this new State bill and we have a government only for the northwest portion. All the rest is left to rebellion or revolution, or, what is worse, no law at all. . . . I am unwilling to give up West Virginia to a separate organization, because it is a Union nucleus around which a great Union mass will ultimately gather." (*Cong. Globe*, Dec. 10, 1862, 37 Cong., 3 sess., p. 55.)

was stressed and it was urged that the administration was obtaining too much advantage by the creation of four senators (two each for Virginia and West Virginia) together with fifteen electoral votes for Virginia and six or eight for West Virginia. It was felt that the temptation to repeat the process in other seceded States might prove too strong to be resisted. Crittenden of Kentucky refused to accept the view that old Virginia no longer existed, asserting that the close of the rebellion would restore the State to the Union and that it should be returned whole, not divided. Those forming the State, he said, were the same as those consenting to its erection. "It is the party applying for admission consenting to the admission. That is the whole of it."[35] Crittenden's remarks deserve attention because of his dignity, border-state importance, and devotion to the Union.

Those favoring the bill urged that, as the government of Virginia had lapsed because of the illegal action of the authorities at Richmond, the loyal people of western Virginia were justified in taking possession of the government; but as a rule those who spoke for the new State dealt in practical considerations rather than in constitutional arguments. One of the frankest statements was that of Thaddeus Stevens. He made it clear that he was not deluded by the idea that the State was being admitted in pursuance of the Constitution. The argument of constitutionality he considered a "forced argument to justify a premeditated act." The

[35]*Cong. Globe*, Dec. 9, 1862, 37 Cong., 3 sess., p. 47. Crittenden, of course, was using the pro-Union argument. Expecting the restoration of the Union, he said: "Look to the future. . . . If Virginia were to-morrow to lay down . . . arms . . . and ask to be admitted . . . to be part of us, . . . what could you say to her if you had created a new State out of her territory?"

majority of the people of Virginia constituted the State of Virginia even though the individuals thereof had committed "treason." Though secession was treason, it was, so far as the State corporation was concerned, a valid act and governed the State. We may admit West Virginia, he said, not as a constitutional measure, but "under our absolute power which the laws of war give us in the circumstances in which we are placed. I shall vote for this bill," he said, "upon that theory, and upon that alone; for I will not stultify myself by supposing that we have any warrant in the Constitution for this proceeding."[36]

When the bill came to a vote, there were 23 yeas and 17 nays in the Senate,[37] Senator Carlile (one of the Senators from restored Virginia) voting in the negative. In the House the vote stood 96 to 55.[38]

VI

When the West Virginia bill was presented to President Lincoln he was placed in a painful dilemma. The thought of disrupting the Old Dominion caused him much distress, but it was represented to him that the vetoing of the bill would discourage the Union movement in western Virginia and seriously antagonize the Congress. The President called the members of his

---

[36] *Ibid.*, p. 50.

[37] Among the active promoters of the bill in the Senate were Wade of Ohio, Collamer of Vermont and Willey of "Virginia." Border-State senators such as Bayard and Saulsbury of Delaware, Powell and Davis of Kentucky, and Kennedy of Maryland, and conservatives such as Browning of Illinois, opposed the measure. Sumner opposed the bill because his amendment providing immediate emancipation failed and he objected to a "new slave State." Trumbull voted nay for the same reason and also because he thought the new State would weaken the existing Unionist government in Virginia. For the vote, see *Cong. Globe*, 37 Cong., 2 sess., p. 3320.

[38] *Cong. Globe*, 37 Cong., 3 sess., p. 59.

Cabinet into consultation on the subject; and, at the suggestion of Attorney General Bates,[39] written opinions from every Cabinet secretary were requested. Each member read his opinion aloud in full council and gave it to the President. The President then read the paper which he had prepared on the subject.

The legality and expediency of this important measure of state were thoroughly discussed in these papers. Seward, Chase and Stanton favored the separation. Seward argued that the United States could not recognize secession and must recognize loyalty. The "restored government," he held, was "incontestably the State of Virginia."[40]

Chase contended that in case of insurrection the loyal element must be taken to constitute the State, that the denial of powers of government to this loyal element on the ground that men clothed with official responsibility had joined in rebellion against their country would be absurd, that the legislature which gave its consent to the formation of the new State "was the true and only lawful legislature of the State of Virginia," and that nothing was wanting to make the proceeding constitutional. Referring to the fear lest the case of West Virginia would form a precedent, thus involving "the necessity of admitting other States under the consent of extemporized legislatures assuming to act for whole States though really representing no important part of their territory," he said that such apprehensions were groundless, since no parallel case existed. This portion of his remarks seemed to hint that such a precedent would have been considered undesirable.[41]

---

[39]Bates to Stanbery, St. Louis, Aug. 3, 1867: Attorney General's papers.

[40]Nicolay and Hay, *Lincoln*, VI, 300-301.

[41]*Ibid.*, pp. 301-303.

Stanton briefly stated his reasons for holding that the West Virginia bill was constitutional. "The Constitution," he said, "expressly authorizes a new State to be formed . . . within the jurisdiction of another State.[42] The act of Congress is in pursuance of that authority. The measure is sanctioned by the legislature of the State within whose jurisdiction the new State is formed. . . . I have been unable to perceive any point on which the act . . . conflicts with the Constitution."

The negative side was maintained by Welles, Blair, and Bates. Welles could not close his eyes to the fact that the organization claiming to be the State of Virginia was nothing more than a provisional government, and that it was "composed almost entirely of . . . loyal citizens . . . beyond the mountains." While admitting that a temporary recognition of this government might be proper, yet, he said, "When . . . this loyal fragment goes farther, and . . . proceeds . . . to erect a new State within the jurisdiction of the State of Virginia, the question arises whether this proceeding is regular, right, and, in honest faith, conformable to . . . the Constitution."[43] Turning to his diary, we find the question answered in the following words: "The requirements of the Constitution are not complied with, as they in good faith should be, by Virginia, by the proposed new State, nor by the United States."[44]

Blair characterized the argument that Virginia had given her consent as "confessedly merely technical." "It is well known," he said, "that the elections by which the movement [for separation] has been made did not take place in more than a third of the counties of the State." He considered the dismemberment highly ir-

[42]Stanton Papers, X, No. 52066.

[43]Nicolay and Hay, *Lincoln*, VI, 304-306.

[44]*Diary of Gideon Welles*, I, 191. (Dec. 4, 1862.)

regular and "unjust to the loyal people in the greater part of the State, who [were] held in subjection by rebel armies" and whose consent was not obtained.[45]

Special importance attaches to the opinion of Edward Bates because it was the official opinion of the Attorney General and because its analysis of the legal points involved was much more elaborate than that of any other Cabinet minister.[46] Bates contended that States must exist before they can be admitted into the Union. Congress, he said, has no power to *make* States, for a free American State can be made only by its own people. The duty of the United States toward the faithful element in Virginia, as he saw it, was to restore Virginia to the Union as she was before the insurrection. The restored government was merely a provisional government intended as a patriot nucleus. No real "legislature of Virginia," according to his view, had consented to the separation.

Such was Bates's official opinion. His unofficial and confidential statements on the subject were more emphatic. He wrote in his diary of "a few reckless Radicals, who manage those helpless puppets (the *straw* Governor, & Legislature of Virginia) as a gamester manages his marked cards," and added: "I have warned one member of W. V. of the fate preparing for his misbegotten, abortive State. These Jacobins, as soon as they get, by the Alexandria juggle, an anti-slavery Constitution for Virginia, will discover that West Virginia was created without authority—and then, having no further use for the political bantling, will knock the blocks from under, and let it slide. For, already, they begin to be jealous of the double representation in the Senate."

---

[45]Nicolay and Hay, *Lincoln*, VI, 306-308.
[46]*Opins. Attys. Gen.*, X, 426-435.

Again Bates wrote that the West Virginia bill was precipitately passed with "the most glaring blunders" because its sponsors feared discussion and dreaded "any revival among the M. C.s of a sense of justice and decency."[47]

There is evidence that President Lincoln disapproved of the disruption of the State,[48] but his objections were overborne by the conviction that the admission of West Virginia was necessary because of its effect upon the outcome of the war. No legal consideration, he said in his written opinion, is ever given to those who do not choose to vote, and in this case those who did not vote were not merely neglectful of their rights, but in rebellion against the Government. "Can this government stand," he asked, "if it counts those against it the equals of those who maintain loyalty?" If so, then he thought that their treason enhanced the constitutional value of the disloyal. "Without braving these absurd conclusions," he said, "we cannot deny that the body which consents to the admission of West Virginia is the Legislature of Virginia." He added that more would be gained than lost by admitting the new State; and, with this practical consideration uppermost in his mind, he signed the bill.[49]

Since the constitution of the new State had not dealt with slavery in a manner satisfactory to Congress, the bill as passed provided that the people of West Vir-

---

[47]MS. Diary of Edward Bates, Dec. 15, 1864; Oct. 12, 1865.

[48]Senator Browning of Illinois, a close friend of Lincoln, referred in his diary to Lincoln's "distress" at the West Virginia bill; and this statement as to the President's attitude is confirmed by Gideon Welles. (MS. Diary of Orville H. Browning, Dec. 15, 1862; *Diary of Gideon Welles*, I, 191.) Senator Willey wrote to Pierpoint: "We have great fears that the President will veto the new State bill.." (W. T. Willey to Pierpoint, Washington, Dec. 17, 1862: Pierpoint Papers.)

[49]Lincoln's opinion is given in full in Nicolay and Hay, *Lincoln*, VI, 309-311.

ginia should vote upon a gradual emancipation clause to be inserted in the State constitution; and the ratification of this clause was made a condition of the admission of the State. All of the conditions having been met, President Lincoln, on April 20, 1863, issued a proclamation declaring West Virginia to be admitted into the Union.[50] As this proclamation was to take effect in sixty days, the legal birthday of West Virginia was June 20, 1863.

VII

When the new State government was launched at Wheeling, the "restored government" transferred its capital to Alexandria, situated in a protected position across the Potomac from Washington. From 1863 to the end of the war, this straw government controlled hardly more than the cities and environs of Alexandria and Norfolk, together with that exposed peninsula consisting of the counties of Northampton and Accomac, known as the "eastern shore." The chief *raison d'être* of this government (which had drawn its support almost entirely from the west) had been to give the consent of Virginia to the erection of the new State; but after this purpose had been accomplished, it bravely maintained the legal fiction that it was still the government of Virginia.

With a new capital and a new official family, Mr. Pierpoint addressed himself to the task of "reorganizing" those few districts in the eastern portion of the State in which his influence could be felt. Offices here were declared vacant because of disloyalty; vacancies were filled by appointment or special election; and mem-

[50] *U. S. Stat. at Large,* XIII, 731.

bers of Congress were sent from congressional districts within the domain of the restored State.

One of the important acts of the Alexandria government was the making of a new constitution for Virginia. This was done by a constitutional convention of fifteen delegates which met at Alexandria in February, 1864. By the new constitution slavery was abolished; loyalty to the "restored government" and the United States was required; and Confederate office holders were disfranchised.[51]

Never was the vitality of a legal fiction better illustrated than by this attenuated government which, despite the lack of funds, buildings, troops, territory and all the material evidences of political power, stoutly defended its paper existence. It was a government whose legislature had no capitol building in which to meet, whose courts did not function, whose prisoners and insane patients had to be sent to Ohio or Pennsylvania, and whose governor, after four months in Alexandria, was still unable to obtain a dwelling for himself and family. Pierpoint's status was not well understood and in the letters which he received there is an amusing variety of titles. He was variously addressed as "Governor of Loyal Virginia," "Governor of East Virginia," "Military Governor of Eastern Virginia," "the Govverner of west virginey," and "Governor of new Virginia." To cheer a governor with so tenuous a hold on office, Governor Boreman of West Virginia wrote encouraging letters, dispelling the fear that Pierpoint would be liable because of illegal acts; urging that the process of creating West Virginia would never be declared void as Pierpoint suspected; assuring him

[51]Eckenrode, *Political History of Virginia during the Reconstruction*, 19-22.

that his West Virginia friends appreciated his difficulties and would stand by him; commending Lincoln in whom the Alexandria governor seems to have lost confidence; and, when Grant was advancing on Richmond, hailing the capture of that city as an event that would give Pierpoint "something to do, which is better than being comparatively idle."[52]

That this Alexandria government was but the logical continuation of the "restored government of Virginia" at Wheeling hardly admits of doubt; and yet there was a marked change in the attitude of the Federal Congress toward the Virginia Unionists after the removal from Wheeling to Alexandria. Though "Virginia" was represented in the Thirty-seventh Congress (from 1861 to 1863), the State was not represented at all in the lower house of the Thirty-eighth Congress (1863-1865); and in the two succeeding Congresses the State was not represented in either house. It was not until 1869 that the long and painful process of reconstruction in Virginia had proceeded to the point where representation in Congress was again permitted; and then the restoration was accomplished by a method quite independent of the "restored State" movement.

The efforts of the Unionists of Virginia to obtain representation in Congress during the war present a curious study. Since the Confederate occupation of the major part of the State prevented Unionists from voting in their own counties, the Wheeling convention, in August, 1861, authorized "loyal citizens" to vote for members of Congress anywhere within their congressional districts;[53] and a section of the old Virginia code was found by which, in the absence of regular commis-

---

[52] Pierpoint Papers. (Pierpoint was never governor of West Virginia.)

[53] *West Virginia Legislative Handbook*, 1916, p. 280.

sioners of election (who were required by law to be appointed by the county court), any two freeholders might conduct an election.[54] In accordance with these provisions, there were various so-called congressional elections in Virginia during the war, in which a few precincts out of whole congressional districts would participate, and Congress would then be asked to seat the successful candidates on the ground that loyal minorities should not be denied representation because of the rebellious attitude of majorities. Of those who obtained seats from Virginia in the Thirty-seventh Congress, only two—Joseph E. Segar and Lewis McKenzie—represented constituencies in the eastern part of the State. Three members—Brown, Blair, and Whaley—represented that part which became West Virginia. Segar's claim to represent the "eastern shore" and the vicinity of Norfolk was long contested, and he was once rejected; but, after another election had been held which was more to the liking of his Washington colleagues, he was seated.[55]

For the Alexandria district there were contesting claims by Upton and Beach;[56] and, after both of these

---

[54] *Virginia Code of 1860*, Ch. vii, par. 11.

[55] Segar's first claim was based upon twenty-five votes at Hampton, Elizabeth City County, on October 24, 1861. There was no poll elsewhere in the district. After the rejection of this claim another election was held (in three of the seventeen counties composing the district) in which he received 559 of the 1018 votes cast. On this election he was seated on May 6, 1862. (*House Misc. Docs.*, Nos. 5 and 29, 37 Cong., 2 sess.; *Biographical Congressional Directory* [*Sen. Doc. No. 56*, 61 Cong., 2 sess.], p. 224.)

[56] The Richmond secession convention prohibited the election of members of the United States Congress. Owing to this action and also because of threats of violence, polls were not opened at the regular date, May 23, 1861. In a few precincts, however, voters sent in irregular returns in favor of Upton. Beach claimed to have been chosen at a special election held in October, 1861, on the authority of an ordinance passed by the Wheeling convention; but this election was

had been rejected, McKenzie was finally seated when but a few days of the session remained. Since the votes for Segar and McKenzie were but fragmentary, it appears that Congress was at this time recognizing the right of loyal minorities in the State to representation.

But this principle was not recognized in the Thirty-eighth Congress. Though there were various claimants for seats from Virginia in that Congress, the House of Representatives rejected them all and left the State without representation. Segar protested against this as a great injustice. He reminded the House that in 1862 he had been seated when he had received only 559 votes out of a total of 1018, and could not understand why he should be rejected in 1864 when he received 1300 out of 1667 votes. The House, he declared, did not customarily inquire whether or why certain voters were absent from the polls, but based their decisions upon a majority of the votes actually cast, disregarding absentees. The four counties which had voted for him were paying Federal taxes and he claimed that they were entitled to Federal representation. Virginia, he insisted, was a State, and the Alexandria government was a real government. Its weakness, he pleaded, should be its protection; and it should be preserved as a Union nucleus with a view to restoring the whole State around it as a center.[57] Another speaker, Chandler, pointed out that Virginia had furnished 25,000 Union troops and was entitled to Union recognition.[58]

The House, however, proceeded on the principle that Representatives should not be seated from a fragment

---

valid only on the theory that there had been no election in May. The House solved the puzzle by rejecting both claims. (*House Misc. Doc. No. 26*, 37 Cong., 2 sess.; *Sen. Doc. No. 56*, 61 Cong., 2 sess., p. 224.)

[57] *Congl Globe*, May 17, 1864, 38 Cong., 1 sess., pp. 2313 *et seq.*

[58] *Ibid.*, p. 2321.

of a district when a free election in the whole district had been prevented by reason of "rebel" control.[59] It was on this basis that Virginia was denied representation in Congress after 1863. If such a rule had been acted upon during the two preceding years, no representatives would have been seated from the eastern part of the State. Moreover, this principle of free election, if recognized in the first two years of the war, would have defeated the whole process by which West Virginia was created.

The later attitude of Congress, by which representation was denied to the State over which Pierpoint claimed to rule, accentuated the irregularity of the whole West Virginia movement. The "restored government" was recognized by Congress as competent to act for all of Virginia in the matter of consenting to the division of the State; but when this division had been accomplished, and despite the advance of Union arms, none of the territory over which this same government claimed authority was considered to be sufficiently reclaimed to be entitled to representation in Congress. The further rejection of this "restored State" as the instrument for bringing Virginia back into the Union after the war suggests that its chief function was to provide a nominal compliance with that requirement of the Federal Constitution that no State shall be disrupted without its consent.[60]

After this rude handling by the Washington Congress, the experiment of trying to maintain a fictitious

---

[59] *Ibid.*, pp. 2311, 2323.

[60] On April 4, 1867, Pierpoint was removed by Federal authority and H. H. Wells was made military governor. The reconstruction of the State is well described in H. J. Eckenrode, *Political History of Virginia during the Reconstruction.* Eckenrode commends Pierpoint's conciliatory policy after the war, but shows that this policy was overthrown by the radical Republicans who seized control.

government for Virginia encountered further obstacles at Norfolk where it met the formidable and contentious opposition of General B. F. Butler. Assuming control of the United States forces at Norfolk in November, 1863, Butler found himself in occupation of a region over which jurisdiction was claimed by the government at Alexandria under Pierpoint. The general denounced this government as useless, spurious and even disloyal, and took measures to withdraw the city of Norfolk from its control. At the time of the election of municipal officers he used his military authority to cause the people to vote whether or not they wished the city government to be maintained. With "singular unanimity," he said, "the qualified voters of Norfolk . . . decided against the further existence of civil government."[61]

Butler then ordered the suspension of civil government in Norfolk,[62] and the city was subjected to military rule, with Butler in supreme charge. The city judge, Edward K. Snead, was brought before Butler and a serio-comic examination was conducted in which Butler took occasion to argue elaborately against the validity of the "restored government" of Virginia, saying that if there were forty governors of Virginia, "they must not set themselves up against my authority in Norfolk," while Snead called attention to the fact that the President could revoke any illegal military orders of Butler. The examination concluded as follows:

Butler: I have determined that you cannot disobey my military orders. Do you propose to do so?

Snead: Yes, Sir.[63]

---

[61]The vote as reported by Butler was 330 to 16: *Private and Official Correspondence of B. F. Butler*, IV, 580.

[62]*Ibid.*, p. 589.

[63]*Ibid.*, p. 574.

Butler then issued an order imprisoning Judge Snead, and justice within the city was thenceforward administered by Butler's military courts. Police matters were placed under the provost marshal; the superintendent of prison labor took charge of the streets; schools (both white and colored) were placed under a military commission; taxes and appropriations were controlled by the military commandant; and such matters as fire protection, street lighting and harbor control were put under military administration.[64] In brief, as Butler said, the city was under martial law, and civil affairs were subjected to military control.

Attorney General Bates entered the lists as a champion of the civil government of Virginia, and in a letter to the President he denounced Butler's "arbitrary orders." He deplored the dangerous anomaly of a military officer ordering an election by the people on any subject; denounced the absurdity of appealing to popular vote on the question whether the laws should prevail or martial law be established; sharply censured an election in which the military authorities fixed the qualification of voters, counted the ballots, and declared the vote; and finally called upon the President to revoke these military orders.[65] Lincoln then interfered to prevent a proposed election which Butler was planning to conduct on the eastern shore, and shortly after this Butler was removed from his Virginia command.[66] In this Pierpoint-Butler controversy and on other occasions Lincoln

---

[64]*Ibid.*, p. 589.

[65]Bates to President Lincoln, July 11, 1864: Attorney General's letter books. This letter is also found in the Bates manuscripts at the Jefferson Memorial Library, St. Louis.

[66]The Pierpoint Papers include considerable material concerning the controversy between Pierpoint and Butler. The subject is briefly treated in Nicolay and Hay, *Lincoln*, IX, Ch. xix.

showed some intention of recognizing the legitimacy of the "restored government." In April, 1865, however, he proposed that the Richmond legislature be recognized as the agency for restoring Virginia to the Union.[67]

VIII

After the war Virginia acquiesced in the separation, and the decisions of her own judiciary conceded the legality both of the new State and of the "restored government" of Virginia. The United States Supreme Court never found it necessary, therefore, to deal with any direct challenge of the constitutionality of the process of separation. In connection with the boundary controversy, however, certain significant legal matters were presented to that court. Virginia laid claim to Jefferson and Berkeley counties on the ground that a vote of the people (required as to these counties by the new State's constitution and the "restored government's" act of consent) had not in a sufficient sense been taken, and also because the restored State had withdrawn its consent as to these counties before the transaction was consummated.[68] The Supreme Court declared the certificate of the Governor of Virginia, reporting a vote of the counties in favor of the transfer, to be conclusive upon the court; and on this ground the claim of West Virginia to the disputed counties was sustained.[69]

In the absence of any decision on the main question of the creation of the new State, this controversy over the boundary may be studied not so much for what was decided as for what was assumed to be already settled.

---

[67]H. G. Connor, *John Archibald Campbell*, 177-178.

[68]The question of the disputed counties is treated in Eckenrode, *op cit.*, pp. 15-17.

[69]Va. *vs.* W. Va., 78 U. S. 39 (December, 1870).

Virginia brought the suit, referring in her complaint to the boundary controversy "between the Commonwealth and the State of West Virginia." In her bill of complaint and the argument of her counsel no reference was made to the illegality of the process by which the new State was formed and various statutes of the "restored government" were cited in such terms as to admit the competency of that government to act for Virginia in regard to the division of the State. The counsel for the old State referred to the Alexandria government as the "Commonwealth of Virginia," and their contention was not that this "restored government" lacked authority to act for Virginia, but that as to the disputed counties the acts of that government were mere proposals which never became operative.

Turning to the opinion of the Supreme Court we find that the validity of West Virginia's legal existence was assumed without question. The case was considered to be within the court's jurisdiction as a boundary controversy between two States; the acts of "Virginia" consenting to the division were cited as competent; and the court affirmed the existence of "a valid agreement between the two States consented to by Congress, which agreement made the accession of these counties dependent upon the result of a popular vote in favor of that proposition." This valid agreement, which the court cited because of its bearing upon the transfer of the two disputed counties, had as its main significance the consent of the old State to the formation of the new one. As a part of its reasoning concerning the validity of this contract between the States, the court pointed out that Congress had approved the contract, citing for this purpose the act admitting West Virginia. In sum, this case, with its decision in favor of West Virginia, amounts to an admission by the old State and an affirmation by the

Supreme Court that the proceedings concerning the partition of Virginia were valid. The whole controversy as to which one of the States possessed the two counties would obviously have been without significance if this validity had not been conceded.

IX

It is not the writer's purpose to attempt to state the "verdict of history" (if such a thing exists) as to the process of dividing Virginia. A new State was brought into the Union with full rights, and when once this was done it was too late to reconsider the legality of the process by which the new commonwealth was created. Not every historic wrong is capable of being righted by subsequent measures; and any undoing of the process of partition after the war was out of the question. The only thing to do then was to accept the separation as an accomplished fact, and Virginia loyally adjusted herself to this changed situation.

Some questioning, however, may be allowed to the student of American constitutional history, who can hardly fail to be impressed by the orderliness and the aptitude for governmental processes which have characterized the American people. It is a legal-minded people which has given to the world the constitutional convention and has taken great care in new emergencies to proceed correctly and in harmony with sound principles in ordering its political life. It has the oldest government in the world based upon a written constitution and its respect for this fundamental instrument has been profound and lasting. Did the methods used in bringing West Virginia into being measure up to the standards that the American people have raised and in general adhered to?

When West Virginia writers deal with this question, they usually shift the emphasis to the need for a government to which Unionists in Virginia—chiefly in the western part—could look for protection. In organized society, it was argued, the citizen's duty of allegiance and the government's obligation to afford protection are reciprocal. Only rightful governments which truly protect the citizen are entitled to allegiance, and only loyal citizens are entitled to governmental protection. When State officers, as Governor Pierpoint expressed it, forswear their allegiance to the Federal Constitution, "turn traitors" and seek to subject the people to a foreign government, their offices become vacant. Bereft of governmental protection by a convulsion in the body politic, the Unionists of Virginia in 1861, said he, proceeded "in the mode common in a republican government in organizing a State by a convention representing the loyal people of the State, to appoint the necessary agencies for carrying on the government under the existing Constitution and laws of the State for the protection of the people."[70] Though the "restored government" so created represented less than a majority of the people of the State, yet, according to the governor's argument, it was the only rightful government; since rebels have no rights under a government against which they rebel, and a majority by turning rebels cannot deprive the loyal of their rights. Though there are occasions, said Pierpoint, when the people have a "right to rebel," yet this is like the right of justifiable homicide in self-defense, and is to be exercised only when every other method of redress fails. But there was in fact, said he, no such situation justifying secession in 1861.

---

[70]Message of Governor Pierpoint, Dec. 7, 1863: *Journal of House of Delegates of Virginia* (sess. of 1863-64, Alexandria), p. 12.

This argument, it will be noted, touches only upon the need for a Unionist State government in Virginia and does not answer the question as to the necessity for a new State. These are distinct questions. If the need for a State government to protect the west in its loyalty to the Union were the chief consideration, then why could not the "restored government" which governed the western counties from 1861 to 1863 have been continued throughout the war, increasing its domain of jurisdiction as the armies advanced and constituting a nucleus around which Virginia might have been brought back whole into the Union? If, then, the demand for a new State was normal and permanent (and not simply a matter connected with the issues of the war), the separate commonwealth could have been founded after the war in a peaceable, deliberate manner without undue Federal intervention and with every opportunity for Virginia as a whole to act, both upon the main question whether a new State should be created and also upon subsidiary questions (such as the apportionment of the debt, and the fixing of the boundary) in which important interests of the old commonwealth were involved.

The irregular method by which the new State was formed, and the adoption of a mere fiction as a basis for claiming fulfillment of a constitutional provision, had various unfortunate effects. It substituted a kind of sophistry to excuse the non-fulfillment of a solemn legal obligation, and it presented an example of a measure which even its supporters did not wish to be emulated elsewhere or used as a precedent. Those who argued for the new State were careful to insist that the case of western Virginia was *sui generis*, and that no other instance would arise in which a similar proceeding would be undertaken. But if the method of forming this new State were correct and justifiable, why should it not have been extended? If the hopeful new-state movement for eastern Tennessee, which ended in preliminaries, had been vigorously promoted, the use of the same methods could hardly have been consistently denied.

Those who base the justification for the new State upon the Unionists' need for a State government should explain why the Federal cause required two governments, one at Wheeling and the other at Alexandria. The Unionist government for Virginia as a whole—i.e., the Pierpoint government—was greatly weakened by the new State movement, and to this extent it might be said that the cause of loyalty to the Federal Union was injured; for the government which, until June of 1863, wielded real power in Wheeling, was left stranded and subjected to derision as a "straw government" in Alexandria.

Nor is the case adequately covered by presenting grievances and sectional considerations showing the wisdom of dividing the commonwealth; for the question is not merely the need for a new State, but the justification of the irregular process by which the new State was formed. The difference between an irregular and a normal process of dividing a State is shown by comparing the case of West Virginia with that of Maine. The Massachusetts legislature carefully guarded the process by which the district of Maine was to be erected into a new State, providing that there must be a majority of at least 1500 in favor of separation on the part of the people of the district, and specifying how delegates should be elected to a constitutional convention, how application should be made to obtain the consent of Congress for the creation of the new State, how the constitution was to be voted upon in the towns, and how it was to take effect if adopted by a majority of the voters, while otherwise the constitution of Massachusetts should remain in force, "that no period of anarchy may happen to the people of the said proposed State." The transfer of cases to the courts of the new State was provided for; and various important conditions were stipulated as a part of the old State's act of consent, such as the retention by Massachusetts of half the unappropriated lands within the new State and the making of needful arrangements concerning Bowdoin College and the Indians. These terms were to be incorporated into the new State's constitution and were to be subject to modification or annulment by agreement of the legislatures of both States, but by no other power or body whatsoever.[71]

In contrast to this careful safeguarding of the interests of Massachusetts, Virginia had no way of protecting her interests as to details, no opportunity to stipulate appropriate conditions as to the separation. In at least two respects—as to the boundary and as to the State debt—Virginia suffered because of this failure to establish adequate guarantees at the time of separation. As to the boundary, it was the west alone which determined which counties should go into the new State, and in the case of Jefferson and Berkeley counties (which were not included in the new State at the time President Lincoln proclaimed its existence in April, 1863), it was claimed that no considerable part of the polls had been opened and no adequate vote ever held on the question of joining West Virginia. Had the process of separation been normal and the method of voting in each locality carefully prescribed by a legislature truly representative of Virginia, this difficulty could have been avoided.

On the question of the debt, Virginia suffered severely; for the new State neglected for more than fifty years to assume its equitable portion, forcing the old State to resort to a long and painful litigation before the United

[71]Act of June 19, 1819: *Gen. Laws of Mass.*, 1819, Ch. clxi.

States Supreme Court in order to overcome an obstructive attitude on the part of the younger commonwealth which at times verged upon defiance.[72] It seems clear that if Virginia had in reality been consulted on the matter of separation, a better solution could have been found for the apportionment of this financial burden.[73]

---

[72]Elsewhere the writer has discussed the complicated question of the Virginia debt. (*Pol. Sci. Quar.*, Dec., 1915, XXX, 553-577.) West Virginia's portion of the debt as fixed by a decree of the United States Supreme Court was finally paid and a satisfaction of judgment was filed on March 1, 1920. For recent decisions on the debt question the following citations may be noted: 209 U. S. 514; 220 U. S. 1; 222 U. S. 17; 231 U. S. 59; 234 U. S. 117; 238 U. S. 202; 241 U. S. 531; 246 U. S. 565.

[73]On the whole problem of the partition of Virginia one should consult, besides the titles mentioned, *West Virginia, the Mountain State*, by Charles H. Ambler, and *Francis H. Pierpont: Union War Governor of Virginia and Father of West Virginia*, by the same author. (The spelling "Pierpont" was adopted later in life.) Papers submitted by the cabinet in response to Lincoln's request for their opinions on the West Virginia matter are found in the R. T. Lincoln Collection, Libr. of Cong., nos. 20387, 20438-20593 *passim.* On the abortive new-state movement in eastern Tennessee, see James W. Patton, *Unionism and Reconstruction in Tennessee, 1860-1869.*

CHAPTER XIX

THE RELATION OF THE GOVERNMENT TO THE PRESS

I. Freedom of the press in American law
II. Lack of censorship during the Civil War: Military control of telegraphic communication
III. Activities of newspapers during the war: Continual revelation of military information
IV. Military measures available against correspondents and editors
V. The "suppression" of newspapers
VI. Exclusion from the mails and other civil measures of control
VII. The arrest of editors
VIII. General comment on problems of press control during the war

I

One of the difficult problems of government under President Lincoln was that of dealing with a disloyal and remarkably active press during the progress of a desperate war. The Government was tempted almost beyond endurance to the adoption of drastic measures of repression, but was all the time confronted with the peculiar safeguards which in our democratic Constitution surround the expression of popular sentiment.[1]

[1]The author has found but little interference with freedom of speech (as distinguished from freedom of the press) during the Civil War. As there were no judicial prosecutions because of oral utterances against the Government, the main features of this subject are included within the discussion of arbitrary arrests and the trial of civilians by military commissions. For these subjects, see Chapters VII and VIII. The Vallandigham case is the one conspicuous instance of inter-

The whole tenor of American law, it must be remembered, is opposed to the forcing or suppression of opinion. An untrammeled forum for public expression is one of the cardinal ideals of American political liberty, and by the First Amendment of our Constitution Congress is prohibited from making any law "abridging the freedom of speech or of the press." The controversy over the Sedition Act of 1798 illustrated in a striking manner the vitality of the principle embodied in this amendment. Enacted during the régime of reactionary Federalism which prevailed during the presidency of John Adams, the law was so framed as to offer a weapon against the administration's political opponents. It declared the penalty of fine and imprisonment against any person who should "write, print, utter, or publish . . . any false, scandalous and malicious writing . . . against the government of the United States, or either house of the Congress . . . or the President . . . with intent to defame [them] or to bring them . . . into contempt or disrepute." Writings calculated to excite hatred against the President or Congress, or to stir up sedition or unlawful combinations, were placed under a like prohibition.[2]

This law, it may be noted, was by no means as arbitrary as those measures of repression by which the press and the public forum have been throttled in European monarchies. For, in the first place, the act was a law of

---

ference with freedom of speech during the war, and the arrest of this agitator was made without express authority from the President who commuted the sentence of the military commission from imprisonment to banishment. When Vallandigham returned to the United States via Canada, the Confederate authorities having sped his departure from their midst, he was allowed to go unmolested, though delivering violent speeches. The mere expression of disloyal sentiments was not ordinarily regarded as grounds for military arrest. For the Vallandigham case, see *supra*, pp. 176-179.

[2] *U. S. Stat. at Large*, I, 596.

Congress, not an imperial ukase or edict; it was enforceable through the regular courts with all of the safeguards which that implies; falsity and malice were made essential attributes in the crime,[3] so that there could be no conviction for the printing of a true statement (or even of a false one with innocent motives); and finally, the protection of jury trial was afforded to the accused. The offensive features of this law were not those which pertained to the method of conviction and punishment, but rather to the description of the crime. The law was repugnant primarily because it made criminal the uttering of certain writings directed against the Government.

One of the prominent cases under this act was that of Matthew Lyon, a Vermont editor who was found guilty of seditious writing and of having published a libel against John Adams. He was sentenced in October, 1798, to an imprisonment of four months, and a fine of one thousand dollars and costs.[4] In general, however, there was but slight enforcement of the law. The significant day, March 3, 1801, which historians regard as the end of the Federalist régime, was named in the act itself as the date of its termination; and it was therefore unnecessary for the Jeffersonian party, coming into power on the following day, to repeal the statute. Though the constitutionality of this law was never tested before the Supreme Court, yet there has always been a certain discredit attaching to a measure which contributed so largely to

[3]The wording was "false, scandalous *and* [not *or*] malicious."

[4]U. S. Circuit Court, Vermont, Oct. 9, 1798: Wharton, *State Trials*, 333; 15 Fed. Cas. 1183. Another victim of the Sedition Act was Thomas Cooper, who was imprisoned for a time at Philadelphia and who later made some amusing efforts to obtain a prosecution of Hamilton, stanch Federalist that he was, for alleged violation of the act in connection with a letter in which Hamilton attacked the President. For an interesting discussion of this subject, with annotations supplying information on the enforcement of the Sedition Act, see the article by Dumas Malone in the *Am. Hist. Rev.*, XXIX, 76-81.

the downfall of the administration and the party which enacted it. The later viewpoint with regard to the act is shown in the report of the Judiciary Committee of the House of Representatives in 1832 which denounced the law as unconstitutional[5] (in which opinion most constitutional lawyers would now concur) and recommended relief to the Lyon heirs. The relief was granted in 1840 when Congress refunded the fine, thus registering its disapproval of such legislation.[6]

When the Civil War opened there were no laws on our statute-books which were at the same time laws against the press and laws to punish crimes against the Government; nor were any such laws passed at any time during the war, in spite of far greater provocation than that which confronted the administration of President Adams. There was the law against conspiracy, the Treason Act of 1862, and the law which severely punished any one who resisted the draft or counseled resistance; but these measures were not, in fact, effective for the punishment of journalistic disloyalty.

Editors and proprietors of papers were, indeed, legally responsible for what their sheets contained, but this responsibility was by no means peculiar to editors and publishers of newspapers, being derived merely from the general law of libel, which applies alike to all. But the laws applying to libel take into view only personal injury, as for instance by the defamation of character, and do not recognize the injury to the public interest which is involved in the defamation or undermining of a gov-

[5]The problem of the constitutionality of a Federal sedition act, in its bearing on the reserved-power principle, the treason clauses, and the First Amendment, is discussed in Chafee, *Freedom of Speech*, 199-207.

[6]*House Rep. No. 218*, 22 Cong., 1 sess.; Act of July 4, 1840: *U. S. Stat. at Large*, VI, 802.

ernment. Seditious libel, as found in England,[7] is unknown in this country, and libel here is conceived as merely an offense against the person defamed. For such an offense, a newspaper proprietor or editor is liable precisely as any other person would be.

Furthermore, prosecutions or civil actions for libel are within the province of the State judiciary, and are therefore inappropriate as instruments for vindicating the Federal Government against abuse. Even such laws as we now have in the United States requiring the registration of the owners, managers, and editors of publications were not in existence during the Civil War, and it was an easy matter to conceal the actual ownership of a newspaper. When all of these legal limitations are taken into account, the difficulties encountered by the Lincoln Government in dealing with journalistic offenses may be better appreciated.

II

A striking fact concerning the subject of journalistic activity during the Civil War was the lack of any real censorship. There were, it is true, some efforts to establish a telegraphic censorship. In April, 1861, the Government took exclusive control of the telegraph lines radiating from Washington; and the function of censoring the dispatches sent over the wires from the national

[7]A British statute of December 30, 1819, dealt with "blasphemous . . . or . . . seditious libel, tending to bring into Hatred or Contempt the Person of His Majesty," etc. (60 Geo. III, & 1 Geo. IV, Cap. viii.) Concerning earlier English law on the subject of sedition, see Chafee, *Freedom of Speech*, 21 *et seq.* The Americans, says Chafee, detested the English law of sedition, which was a "product of the view that the government was master" while Americans believed that the Government was servant, and one of the purposes of the First Amendment was to get rid of the English crime of sedition. Chafee shows that attempts shortly after 1800 to revive common law prosecutions for seditious libel in this country were a complete failure. (*Ibid.*, pp. 30-31.)

capital was at different times under the charge of the Treasury, the State, and the War Departments. Operating under instructions from the Cabinet officer in whose department he was placed, the censor excluded communications giving military information, and also those which were deemed to convey too much news concerning the activities of the Government. Reports of delicate diplomatic questions, criticisms of Cabinet members, comments giving the mere opinion of correspondents, advance information of contemplated measures, and stories injurious to the reputation of officers, were denied the wires.

A sort of "*entente cordiale*" between the Government and the newspaper correspondents was attempted. In a conference of the press representatives with General McClellan in August, 1861, a "treaty of peace and amity" (as Russell of the London *Times* called it) was drawn up. It was agreed that the editors were to abstain from printing anything which could give aid or comfort to the enemy, and a like caution was to be observed by the correspondents. In return, the Government was to give the press adequate facilities for obtaining and transmitting suitable intelligence, especially touching military engagements. Thus a *modus vivendi* was to be inaugurated which would do away with the necessity of any censorship. For various reasons, however, the scheme broke down. Editors differed from the Government as to what was proper to print; many papers refused to limit themselves by any such pledge; and the intense rivalry of newspapers proved more powerful than the restraints of any voluntary agreement.

After nearly a year of experimentation, an administrative policy of telegraphic control was evolved. Beginning with February 2, 1862, it was ordered that the President, by virtue of congressional authorization, would establish military supervision of all telegraph lines in the United States, the censoring function being lodged with the War Department. All telegraphic communications concerning military matters not authorized by the Secretary of War, or the commanding general of the district, were forbidden; no further facilities for receiving information by telegraph or transporting their papers by railroad were to be extended to journals violating the order; and for the general supervision of telegraphic business a special officer was appointed with the title of Assistant Secretary of War and General Manager of Military Telegraphs. In the sifting of news the American Telegraph Company coöperated with the Government, requiring oaths of loyalty and secrecy from employees and allowing no access to the messages or the operating rooms except to those duly authorized by the Government telegraph manager. No unofficial messages conveying military information were transmitted by wire; and news-writers were forced to bring in their war stories in person, to employ a messenger, or to use the mails. As a further precaution communications were sent in code, and the cipher operator constituted at all times an important medium between officers.[8]

This governmental supervision of the telegraph was but a feeble measure of news control. In the early days of the censorship, when the suppression of messages was limited to Washington, "contraband" intelligence might be transmitted through the telegraph offices of Baltimore, Philadelphia, or New York. Information of a highly confidential nature might be suppressed in Washington and then sent over the wires from other points. Even after the control of the telegraph became general,

[8]*House Rep. No. 64*, 37 Cong., 2 sess.; *O. R.*, Ser. II, Vol. 2 p. 40; Ser. III, Vol. 1, pp. 324, 394-395; Nicolay and Hay, *Lincoln*, V, 141; Russell, *My Diary, North and South*, Aug. 5, 1861; July 10, 1861.

messages could be freely sent by mail, and this became the regular method by which reporters at the front conveyed their "copy." Throughout the war unauthorized news items continually found their way into print through numerous unsealed channels. Even the process of communication between the generals in the field and the War Department was by no means water-tight, and news trickled out through mysterious "leaks." As for a really effective censorship, which would deal in a comprehensive way with the general problem of publicity, it was not even attempted.

III

This laxity of press control coincided with a period of remarkable activity in journalistic enterprise.[9] For covering the campaigns of the war the great metropolitan dailies developed elaborate organizations and expended huge sums. Newspaper correspondents were everywhere. Many of them had official positions as government clerks, army nurses, or signal officers, and were thus advantageously placed for obtaining news. They attached themselves to generals' headquarters, dined at officers' mess, had the use of army horses and wagons, were supplied with government passes enabling them to witness battles and pass freely through the armies, sailed on admirals' flagships, took passage on army trains or government steamers, and were at times even employed for the conveyance of confidential dispatches.

The typical correspondent's first thought was for his newspaper, and his chief concern was to scent the kind of "copy" that his readers demanded. The possibility that such "copy" might reveal military secrets, defame a

[9]The author has treated the newspaper during the Civil War in the *Amer. Hist. Rev.*, XXIII, 303-323.

general, or undermine public confidence in the Government's conduct of the war, was usually considered of secondary importance. Such generals as Grant and Sherman, who kept their counsel and avoided reporters, were written down; while inferior men gained brilliant repute by means of favors given at Government expense to correspondents. The "special's" story had to be written at all events, and if reliable news was wanting,[10] the account would be made up from guesswork, off-hand prophecy, camp gossip, or the indiscreet utterances of some disgruntled subordinate officer. Certain men, as a matter of policy, must be played up as heroes, while others were denounced, and always the partisan flavor of the reporter's paper was preserved.

The continual revelation of military information by the newspapers of the Civil War period seems a shocking thing in contrast to the elaborate restrictions that have been imposed for safeguarding military secrecy during later wars. Plans of campaign, movements of troops, the location and strength of military units—all such information was regularly published to the world. An account of Grant's movements, selected at random from the New York *Daily News*, gives the course of march of a cavalry division, refers to reënforcements from Meade, and proclaims the assembling of Generals Grant, Meade, and Butler at Burnside's headquarters. This is but typical of the sort of detailed information

---

[10]The following example will illustrate the unreliable nature of some of the wartime news. The New York *Tribune*, on September 5, 1861, contained this statement: "The report of the death of Jefferson Davis is confirmed by information which appears trustworthy." There followed a brief account of Davis' life. On September 7th the *Tribune* said, in commenting on the favorable attitude toward Davis taken by Governor Magoffin of Kentucky: "But Davis is dead actually and Magoffin is so politically." (New York *Tribune*, Sept. 5. 1861, p. 4; Sept. 7, 1861, p. 4.)

which the papers constantly supplied. At the time, Lee did not know that Burnside was still with Grant.[11]

A copy of the Chicago *Times* in September, 1863, which promptly reached the headquarters of the Confederate general, Braxton Bragg, contained the following account of the movements of the Federal army:[12]

> Crittenden's Corps moved eastward to feel the strength of the enemy, with the intention of crossing the mountains to the north and east of Chattanooga, crossing the Tennessee river at a ford some thirty miles above Chattanooga. This crossing safely effected, Crittenden will swing into the rear of Chattanooga, and if possible take the place. The intention is to strike that point offensively at the same time that Burnside attacks Buckner at Knoxville. This will at once prevent Buckner from receiving any reënforcements, and also if not captured greatly endanger his retreat, for it will be impossible to retreat toward Bragg. Meanwhile, if Crittenden succeeds well in his efforts upon Chattanooga . . . , Thomas and McCook will move rapidly upon Rome, Georgia. . . . It is . . . believed that Bragg will not resist at Rome. . . . Rosecrans will, if possible, whip Bragg in detail, disperse his forces, and then attack Johnston alone, for united the two rebel armies would certainly outnumber ours.

Many instances of the same sort could be mentioned. The location of Grant's guns secretly placed against Vicksburg in 1863 was published; his proposed concentration upon City Point in July, 1864, was revealed; Sherman's objectives in his Georgia march and the disposition of his various corps were proclaimed; full details concerning the land and sea expedition against Wilmington, N. C., in December, 1864, were supplied.

---

[11]New York *Daily News*, July 2, 1864; *Lee's Confidential Dispatches to Davis*, 272.

[12]*O. R.*, Ser. I, Vol. 30, pt. 4, p. 600.

Northern papers practically functioned as Confederate spies in Union camps, for copies of these journals were easily obtained by Southern generals. General Lee, with a practiced eye for detecting military information, regularly scanned the enemy's papers; and his confidential dispatches to President Davis show that he gained many bits of valuable information concerning the army of the Potomac at times when the Union generals were quite mystified as to his own forces.[13]

In addition to this revelation of military information, it must be remembered that numerous powerful newspapers of the North were openly hostile to the Government in their editorial utterances, and pursued their enmity toward the administration to the point of encouraging disloyalty. Early in 1863, for instance, the New York *World* thus spoke of Lincoln's policy of emancipation:

> We have doubtless surfeited our readers with specimens of the turgid, ranting and senseless predictions of the emancipationists; but nauseous and disgusting as is the dose, we must insist on repeating it in still larger measure. Nothing is more important than that the people should understand the claims to statesmanship of their actual rulers. It is by this miserable balderdash that the country is governed. The administration shines, like the moon, by reflected light. It borrows its ideas and its policy so far as it has any, from these crazy radicals. . . . By surrendering itself to their wild and reckless guidance it is ruining the country; and it is important that the people should see, even at the expense of a good deal of disgust and loathing, what has been substituted in the public counsels for statesmanlike sagacity and far-seeing wisdom.[14]

---

[13] *Am. Hist. Rev.*, as above cited.

[14] The editorial continued by giving extracts from Greeley's *Tribune* concerning emancipation. (New York *World*, Feb. 7, 1863.)

Yet the *World* was not one of the extreme anti-war or peace-at-any-price sheets, but a great, respectable newspaper which professed loyalty to the Union cause.

In its editorial pages the Chicago *Times* continually flayed the President in a tone which suggested personal malice. At the time of Lincoln's second inauguration, on March 4, 1865, the *Times* spoke as follows:[15]

> The inaugural addresses of the past presidents of the United States are among the best of our state papers. . . . Contrast with these the inaugural address of Abraham Lincoln delivered in the City of Washington on Saturday and printed in these columns this morning! "What a fall was there, my countrymen." Was there ever such a coming out of the little end of the horn? Was ever a nation, once great, so belittled? Is such another descent of record in the history of any people? We had looked for something thoroughly Lincolnian, but we did not foresee a thing so much more Lincolnian than anything that has gone before it. We did not conceive it possible that even Mr. Lincoln could produce a paper so slipshod, so loose-jointed, so puerile, not alone in literary construction, but in its ideas, its sentiments, its grasp. . . . By the side of it, mediocrity is superb.

The following comment which appeared in the Baltimore *Exchange* suggests strong sympathy with the cause of disunion:[16]

> The war of the South is the war of the people, supported by the people. The war of the North is the war of a party, attempted to be carried on by political schemers, independently of the people, on the credit of a divided country, and on the . . . faith of an old Union—which has in reality ceased to exist.

Though selections of this sort could be extended almost indefinitely, one more must suffice. When the President

[15]Editorial, Chicago *Times*, Mar. 6, 1865.
[16]Baltimore *Exchange*, July 10, 1861.

in the summer of 1864 issued a call for an additional 500,000 men, the Indianapolis *Sentinel* thus appealed to its readers:[17]

> We ask the plain, sober, thinking people of Indiana to reflect seriously upon the present condition of public affairs. What confidence can be placed in the capacity and integrity of the men who are administering the government when the events of the past three years are reviewed? Notwithstanding the assurance given from time to time . . . that each [call] was to be the last, and that no more would be necessary for the suppression of the rebellion, at this late day the President issues a call for five hundred thousand more men! . . . Can we arrive at any other conclusion . . . than that the "best government on earth" will be destroyed if the present party rule is perpetuated?

One can easily imagine the effect of such language upon that public morale which is so essential for the support of armies in the field; and yet the above extracts are not examples of the worst utterances that may be found in the newspapers of the time, but rather of the daily tone of many powerful journals. They are representative of the sort of injurious journalism which the administration regularly tolerated, while instances of governmental repression directed against newspapers were but the exception.

IV

Having noted those forms of newspaper activity which hurt the Government, we may now inquire as to the measures adopted for controlling these abuses. In the first place it should be noted that correspondents accompanying the armies had the status of civilian camp-followers and were within the range of military jurisdiction,

[17]Editorial, *Daily State Sentinel* (Indianapolis), July 28, 1864.

being subject to punishment by court-martial for violation of any part of the military code. In particular, the 57th Article of War fitted their case. This provided that any one "convicted of holding correspondence with, or giving intelligence to, the enemy, either directly or indirectly," should suffer death, or such other punishment as a court-martial should decree.[18]

As against news writers this section of the military code was rarely, if ever, applied. General Sherman, who was constantly urging vigorous measures against offending correspondents, initiated a case against a reporter who wrote accounts of the Union operations at Vicksburg; but conviction failed because of the court's ruling that the identical communication must be proved to have gone to the enemy, and such evidence was not at hand.[19] This part of the military law, however, was often referred to in army orders and offered a military means of news control. A general order of the War Department was issued amplifying this "article" by declaring that all correspondence, verbal or in writing, printing or telegraphing, concerning military operations or movements on land or water, or regarding troops, camps, arsenals, intrenchments, or military affairs within the several military districts, by which intelligence might be given to the enemy, without the sanction of the general in command, was prohibited; and that violators would be proceeded against under the 57th Article of War.[20]

An instance of military justice directed against an editor is to be found in the case of Edmund J. Ellis, editor and proprietor of the *Boone County Standard* of

[18] *U. S. Stat. at Large*, II, 366.

[19] General W. T. Sherman to John Sherman, dated "Camp before Vicksburg," Feb. 12, 1863: *The Sherman Letters*, ed. by Rachel S. Thorndike, 190.

[20] *O. R.*, Ser. III, Vol 1, p. 390.

Columbia, Missouri. Because of certain articles which appeared in his paper, Ellis was arraigned before a military commission in February, 1862, charged with "the publication of information for the benefit of the enemy and encouraging resistance to the Government and laws of the United States." Ellis' plea denied the jurisdiction of a military commission over his case, declaring that the matters charged were "wholly and exclusively of civil cognizance." He was nevertheless found guilty and banished from Missouri during the war, while the press, type and equipment of his newspaper were confiscated.[21]

As in all wars, intercourse with the enemy was interdicted, except under flags of truce or on the basis of special executive permits. In the opinion of the Judge Advocate General, this prohibition made illegal a system of correspondence maintained between Northern and Southern papers by means of publications entitled "personals." It was always within the power of a general to exclude reporters from his lines, and in a number of cases this measure was applied. The exclusion of particular men, while others were admitted, was sometimes accomplished by requiring passes which could be denied to hostile journalists or those who disregarded regulations.

A very extreme measure which was threatened but, it would seem, never actually applied, was to treat reporters as spies. Sherman, for instance, announced at one time that all correspondents accompanying his expedition should be so treated, declaring that they were spies because their publications reached the enemy, giving minute information concerning his forces.[22] This threat does not appear to have been enforced in any actual in-

[21] *Ibid.*, Ser. II, Vol. 1, pp. 453-457.

[22] *The Sherman Letters*, ed. by Rachel S. Thorndike, 187.

stance. Unless the informer could be shown to be in the employ of the enemy, the term spy would be inappropriate, while in any case the 57th Article of War was a sufficient weapon without raising the question as to whether the offender was a "spy" or not. Though, in general, military control over correspondents may have been possible under existing rules, it was not, in fact, made effective. The ingenuity and persistence of newspaper men were difficult to deal with; and, as we have seen, publication of military information continued on an extensive scale throughout the war.

V

Where the activities of a newspaper produced too grave a menace, it sometimes happened that the newspaper itself was "suppressed," which usually meant that by military action its publication was temporarily suspended. Cases in which this drastic method of press control was applied were fairly numerous, although it is also true that throughout the war the most flagrant disloyalty was suffered to continue in many prominent papers. Among the newspapers subjected for a time to military "suppression"[23] were the Chicago *Times*, the New York *World*, the New York *Journal of Commerce*, the Dayton (O.) *Empire*, the Louisville (Ky.) *Courier*, the New Orleans *Crescent*, the *South* of Baltimore, the *Maryland News Sheet* of Baltimore, the *Baltimore Gazette*, the *Daily Baltimore Republican*, the Baltimore *Bulletin*, the Philadelphia *Evening Journal*, the New

[23]The *Bee*, the *Delta*, and the *Crescent* of New Orleans were suppressed by General B. F. Butler, and the *Daily Times* and the *Banner* of Nashville were suppressed by Governor Andrew Johnson. (*Private and Official Correspondence of B. F. Butler*, I, 476; Hall, *Andrew Johnson, Military Governor of Tennessee*, 43.)

Orleans *Advocate*, the New Orleans *Courier*, the Baltimore *Transcript*, the Thibodaux (La.) *Sentinel*, the Cambridge (Md.) *Democrat*, the Wheeling *Register*, the Memphis *News*, the Baltimore *Loyalist*, and the Louisville *True Presbyterian*.[24]

A detailed examination of the circumstances of these various suppressions is impossible here, but the two most striking instances, those of the Chicago *Times* and the New York *World*, may be discussed with some fullness.

The suppression of the Chicago *Times* was an incident closely bound up with the agitation concerning Vallandigham. As the latter's arrest for a disloyal speech was an instance of military action unprompted by the Washington administration, so also the seizure of the paper was a measure taken on the initiative of General Burnside. Because of comments severely attacking the administration and expressing sympathy for Vallandigham, General Burnside, on June 1, 1863, issued "General Order No. 84," which contained the following paragraph: "On account of the repeated expression of disloyal and incendiary sentiments, the publication of the newspaper known as the Chicago *Times* is hereby suppressed." Brigadier General Ammen, commanding the district of Illinois, was charged with the execution of this order, and under his authority Captain Putnam, in command at Camp Douglas, Chicago, warned the management that the paper must not be issued on the morning of the 3rd, under penalty of military seizure.[25]

A civil remedy for restraining the military authorities

[24]For the suppression of newspapers the principal source is the *Official Records*. The general index and the volume indexes cite the papers on which information is to be found See also *Ann. Cyc.*, 1864, pp. 393-394; *Check List of American Newspapers*, Library of Congress, 81 *et seq.*

[25]*Ann. Cyc.*, 1863, pp. 423 *et seq.*; *O. R.*, Ser. I, Vol. 23, pt. 2, p. 381.

was now attempted. Upon application of the publishers, Judge Drummond of the Federal circuit court issued a writ of injunction temporarily restraining Captain Putnam from any interference with the publication of the paper until the question of granting a permanent injunction could be heard in open court. This judicial order was disregarded; and in the early morning of the 3rd the office was seized, and the publication of that morning's issue prevented. There were no further proceedings on the injunction.

Agitation ran high in the city and various citizens' meetings were hastily called. Resolutions of protest adopted by a mass meeting held in the courthouse square on the evening of the 3rd, were matched by resolutions of approval passed on the following night by the "loyal citizens of Chicago." To these latter the idea of suppressing the *Times* was not new; for nearly a year before Governor Yates had reported that the immediate suppression of the paper was the "urgent and almost unanimous demand" of the "loyal citizens" of the city, and that unless this action were taken he feared that the people would take the matter into their own hands.[26]

The action of President Lincoln concerning the suppression of the *Times* was taken with deliberation after a careful balancing of motives. According to Secretary Welles, the President and every member of the Cabinet regretted Burnside's act.[27] On the day the order was issued Stanton directed a letter to Burnside expressing the President's disapproval of the action of General Hascall who had interfered in various ways with certain newspapers in Indiana. He advised Burnside that the dissatisfaction within his department would only be in-

---

[26]Yates to Stanton, Aug. 7, 1862: *O. R.*, Ser. III, Vol. 2, p. 316.
[27]*Diary of Gideon Welles*, I, 321.

creased "by the presence of an indiscreet military officer who will . . . produce irritation by assuming military powers not essential to the preservation of the public peace."[28] Having written thus, Stanton added the following significant postscript after word of the order concerning the *Times* had been received:

Since writing the above letter the President has been informed that you have suppressed the publication or circulation of the Chicago *Times* in your department.[29] He directs me to say that in his judgment it would be better for you to take an early occasion to revoke that order. The irritation produced by such acts is in his opinion likely to do more harm than the publication would do. The Government approves of your motives and desires to give you cordial and efficient support. But while military movements are left to your judgment, upon administrative questions such as the arrest of civilians and the suppression of newspapers not requiring immediate action the President desires to be previously consulted.[30]

Had this word from Washington, tactfully advising Burnside to revoke his own order, been transmitted by telegraph instead of by mail, it is possible that the *Times* might never have been actually suppressed. Certainly it would never have been if that general had consulted Washington first. As to overruling Burnside, that was a course which the President was reluctant to take, since he dreaded the weakening of the military authority. On the 4th of June, however, a Cabinet meeting having intervened, this step was taken.[31] The revocation of

---

[28]*O. R.*, Ser. II, Vol. 5, p. 723.

[29]This doubtless refers to Burnside's "General Order number 84" above mentioned. The publication of the *Times* was suppressed and the circulation of the New York *World* within the department was prohibited.

[30]*O. R.*, Ser. II, Vol. 5, p. 724.

[31]*Ibid.*, Ser. III, Vol. 3, p. 252.

Burnside's order was communicated by telegram through Secretary Stanton, and the publication of the paper was resumed.[32]

The case of the New York *World* presents some interesting differences from that of the Chicago *Times*; for, unlike Burnside, General Dix at New York acted reluctantly under a specific presidential order. Moreover, in the New York case the legal methods of resistance attempted in the city and State differed widely from those taken in Chicago. The *World*, in the issue of May 18, 1864, published a bogus proclamation of President Lincoln, gloomily recalling recent disasters, setting a day for public humiliation and prayer, and calling for 400,000 men. On the day of the publication of this forged document, the following order of the President was obtained through the action of Secretary of War Stanton and sent to General Dix, who was in command at New York:[33]

Whereas, there has been wickedly and traitorously . . . published this morning, in the New York *World* and the New York *Journal of Commerce* . . . a false and spurious proclamation purported to be signed by the President . . . which . . . is of a treasonable nature designed to give aid and comfort to the enemies of the United States . . . you are therefore commanded forthwith to arrest and imprison . . . the editors, proprietors and publishers of the aforesaid newspapers, and all such persons as, after public notice has been given of the falsehood of said publication, print and publish the same with

[32]On June 3 certain prominent citizens decided to request the suspension of Burnside's order. Senator Lyman Trumbull and Representative I. N. Arnold transmitted this request, with their approval, to Lincoln by wire. Lincoln himself stated that this dispatch strongly influenced him in favor of revoking the order. (*O. R.*, Ser. I, Vol. 23, pt. 2, p. 385; Nicolay and Hay, *Works*, X, 108; White, *Life of Trumbull* 206-209.)

[33]New York *World*, July 11, 1864. Though Lincoln signed this order, it appears to have been drafted in the War Department.

intent to give aid and comfort to the enemy; and you will hold the persons so arrested in close custody until they can be brought to trial before a military commission for their offense. You will also take possession by military force, of the printing establishments of the New York *World* and *Journal of Commerce*, and hold the same until further orders, and prohibit any further publication thereof.

This order was dated "Executive Mansion, Washington, D. C., May 18, 1864," and it was signed by Abraham Lincoln, President, and countersigned by William H. Seward, Secretary of State. General Dix reluctantly executed the order to the extent of taking into custody some of the men connected with the management of the papers, seizing the newspaper offices, and holding them under military guard. On the third day the men were released and the suspension discontinued.

Owing to the determined intervention of Governor Seymour of New York, an important issue concerning freedom of the press became complicated by the interjection of a conflict between State and Federal jurisdiction. The governor caused the incident to be brought to the attention of the local grand jury, but this body found no indictment against the general and his subordinate officers. Instead, they passed a formal resolution declaring it inexpedient to examine into the matter. The governor then sent a letter to A. Oakley Hall, district attorney of the County of New York, directing him to prosecute the officers concerned before a city magistrate. As a result, warrants were issued for the arrest of General Dix and his subordinates as criminal violators of law, on the charge of "kidnaping," and "inciting to riot." Though there was no actual physical arrest, the State claimed a technical arrest, since the general and the other defendants gave a verbal recognizance which was accepted as adequate security for their further appearance. The case, of course, came directly under the fourth section of the Indemnity Act, which has been described in a previous chapter, since the seizures and arrests had been made in obedience to a specific order of the President.

In due course the case of *The People* vs. *John A. Dix and Others* came up for trial before City Judge A. D. Russell.[34] Though an obscure case in the sense that it never went higher than the municipal court, it was elaborately argued by distinguished counsel and it involved legal principles of great importance. In their endeavor to sustain the rather eccentric charge of kidnaping and inciting to riot, the prosecution reviewed the testimony showing that a Mr. Halleck of the *World* had been taken into custody against his will, and that, as an incident of the arrest, crowds assembled and a turbulent condition resulted. New York, it was argued, was not under martial law; the ordinary courts were in full control of the city; and it was a usurpation to hold citizens outside the sphere of military operations amenable to military power. As to the order of the President, that itself was illegal, and no lawful right could be conferred by it. Nor could the Indemnity Act of March 3, 1863, interposing the President's orders as a defense in suits against governmental officers, avail in such a case, for it was unconstitutional.

The counsel for the defense answered that since the grand jury had considered the case, and had failed to indict, the law was fully vindicated. It was argued that a state of war existed over the whole country, not merely in the field of actual operations; that the war power resided in the Federal, not the State government; that the Supreme Court had declared the President to be

[34]New York *World*, Aug. 8, 1864.

clothed with the war power; and that Congress by the Habeas Corpus Act of 1863 had authorized imprisonment without recourse to the usual channels of law. It was further urged that no criminal intent had been established on the part of the defendants, and that the case did not come within the legal definition of kidnaping.

The prosecution was concluded by a harmless decision of Judge Russell, affirming the unconstitutionality of the Indemnity Act and decreeing that General Dix and those associated with him in the execution of the President's order should be held "subject to the action of the grand jury of the city and county."

Concerning the main principle of journalistic freedom in war time, the Dix case settled nothing; but the whole incident has a certain historical importance as a prominent example of newspaper suppression. As Secretary Welles tells us, the President assumed full responsibility for the suspension,[35] and yet the arbitrary character of the order can hardly be disputed. The presidential order recited as a fact that the false proclamation had been "wickedly and traitorously" published; yet this treasonable intent was not asserted even by General Dix, and in the trial the counsel for the defense commended the general's action in releasing the men on "discovering them to be innocent." The order was a hasty one, based upon mere suspicion of wrongful intent, and the administration itself felt that the action was ill-advised.

VI

Besides the "suppression" of obnoxious journals, various other measures were taken in dealing with the newspaper problem. In some cases a single edition of a paper

[35] *Diary of Gideon Welles*, II, 67. (July 5, 1864.)

was seized. Or again, the circulation of a paper within a given area would be prohibited. The circulation and sale of the Cincinnati *Enquirer* and Chicago *Times* were temporarily prohibited by General Palmer within the Department of Kentucky;[36] and General Burnside took similar action, excluding the New York *World* from the Department of the Ohio. Such action was not the exclusion of objectionable matter in military areas and for military purposes, but rather the withholding of papers from whole districts in the North on the ground of disloyalty, and was intended as a partial measure for press control. Even in New Haven, Connecticut, for instance, the circulation of the New York *Daily News* was prohibited.[37]

Action by the postal authorities was naturally invoked to check the distribution of offensive papers. The usual method was exclusion of specified journals from the mails.[38] It does not appear that any postal espionage (as such) existed, though the State and War departments did undoubtedly at various times detain and open letters in search of treasonable correspondence. Intercourse with the enemy was of course prohibited, and there were no postal facilities between the seceded States and the North. Naturally the Post Office Department coöperated with the military authorities in the prevention of such intercourse.[39]

In some cases the Postmaster General in denying the mails to certain papers merely carried out orders originating with the Secretary of State or the Secretary of War, but at other times he assumed the function of determining what papers should be excluded. When Post-

---

[36] *O. R.*, Ser. I, Vol. 49, pt. 2, pp. 55, 139.
[37] *Ibid.*, Ser. II, Vol. 2, p. 54.
[38] *Ibid.*, Ser. I, Vol. 50, pt. 1, p. 896.
[39] *Ibid.*, Ser. II, Vol. 2, pp. 12-13, 1054.

master General Blair, in the latter part of 1861, excluded certain papers condemned as disloyal by the Federal grand jury at New York, the question of his right to do so was raised in the House of Representatives, which instructed its Judiciary Committee to "inquire . . . by what authority of Constitution and law, if any, the Postmaster General undertakes to decide what newspapers may and what shall not be transmitted through the mails of the United States."[40]

An elaborate reply was sent by the Postmaster General in which the power to exclude matter from the mails was fully reviewed.[41] Starting with the doctrine that freedom of the press, but not license, is guaranteed, Blair declared that while his department claimed no power to suppress treasonable publications, it could not be called upon to give them circulation. "It could not and would not interfere with the freedom secured by law, but it could and did obstruct the dissemination of that license which was without the pale of the Constitution and law." Blair then quoted Justice Story's view that the First Amendment was not intended "to secure to every citizen an absolute right to speak, or write, or print whatsoever he might please," but that it merely guaranteed the right of the citizen to utter his opinions without any prior restraint[42] so long as he did no injury to another man's person, property, or reputation, and caused no disturbance of the public peace or subversion of the Government. The history of the exclusion of certain matter from the mails during Jackson's administration was reviewed; and it was pointed out that the right of the

[40] *House Journal*, Dec. 1, 1862, p. 7.

[41] *House Misc. Doc. No. 16*, 37 Cong., 3 sess., Jan. 20, 1863.

[42] Chafee shows that the constitutional guarantee of freedom of speech and of the press means much more than absence of prior restraint. (*Freedom of Speech*, Ch. 1.)

Postmaster General to know the contents of newspapers and to refuse to deliver such as would stir up murder or insurrection, was upheld at the time, and was later sustained by an opinion of Attorney General Holt. In this opinion the Attorney General had said: "On the whole it seems clear to me that a deputy postmaster . . . is not required by law to become knowingly the enforced agent or instrument of enemies of the public peace, to disseminate, in their behalf, . . . printed matter the design and tendency of which are to promote insurrection."

While disclaiming any disposition to exclude matter merely because it was obnoxious to some special interest, Blair did insist that a course of precedents had existed in his department for twenty-five years, "known to Congress, not annulled or restrained by act of Congress, in accordance with which newspapers and other printed matter, decided by postal officers to be insurrectionary, or treasonable, or in any degree inciting to treason or insurrection, have been excluded from the mails and post offices of the United States solely by the authority of the executive administration." With this policy the Judiciary Committee concurred, and the investigation was carried no further.[43]

VII

One of the measures occasionally used was the arbitrary arrest of offending editors. When, for instance, a marshal of one of the Federal district courts in New York wrote to Secretary Seward early in the war describing a certain paper as a secession sheet and asking what should

---

[43]Concerning measures taken by the postal authorities, see further: *O. R.*, Ser. II, Vol. 2, pp. 70, 82, 162, 179, 283, 495, 496, 501 940; N. Y. *World*, Aug. 2, 8, 15 and 18, 1864; *Sen. Exec. Doc. No. 19*, 37 Cong., 3 sess.; *Diary of Gideon Welles*, index under "Mails."

be done, Seward directed the marshal to arrest the editor and send him to Fort Lafayette.[44] Here was an example of a military imprisonment to be executed by an officer of a civil court upon the order of a minister of foreign affairs! After the War Department took over the matter of arrests, the policy toward journalists remained much the same. Secretary Stanton, in February, 1862, sent an order to officers in various important cities in these terms: "All newspaper editors and publishers have been forbidden to publish any intelligence received by telegraph or otherwise respecting military operations by the United States forces. Please see . . . that this order is observed. If violated, . . . seize the whole edition and give notice to this department, that arrests may be ordered."[45] Though the military information constantly appearing in the papers leads us to conclude that this order was not generally enforced, yet it shows that the administration regarded the military arrest of Northern editors as a legitimate measure for the control of journalistic abuses.

The exercise of this form of newspaper control, however, was usually unfortunate. The more prominent the editor, the greater was the newspaper's gain in prestige in the eyes of its readers and sympathizers because of the martyr's pose which the editor invariably assumed. When, for example, F. Key Howard, editor of the Baltimore *Exchange*, was arrested and confined in Fort Lafayette and elsewhere, he sent a vigorous letter to the Secretary of War demanding instant and unconditional release.[46] He stood his ground heroically and demanded, not pardon, but vindication. He refused to appear before

---

[44] *O. R.*, Ser. II, Vol. 2, pp. 66, 68. The order was subsequently countermanded.

[45] *Ibid.*, p. 246.

[46] *Ibid.*, pp. 783-786.

an "irresponsible tribunal," and would not seal his lips to obtain discharge. The paper continued publication for a time while its editor and proprietor were in prison, and the net result was simply to afford this journal a more conspicuous rostrum from which to hurl its anathemas against the Government. On the morrow of Howard's arrest the *Exchange* declared in an indignant editorial that the unrestricted right of the press to discuss and condemn the war policy of the Government is identical with the freedom of the people to do the same thing,[47] and thus the trumpet blasts for journalistic freedom were added to the general chorus of anti-war sentiment. After an imprisonment of several months, Howard and his associate Glenn were released.[48]

In general it may be said that where editors or proprietors of papers were confined as "prisoners of state," this action was taken because the authorities had some reason to suppose them disloyal and that after short periods of confinement they were released just as arbitrarily as they were arrested. In its legal aspects this phase of the subject differs not at all from the general question of arbitrary arrest and imprisonment which we have previously discussed.

Action of the civil courts for dealing with newspaper abuses (by prosecutions for obstructing the draft, conspiracy, and the like) yielded no results. Grand juries did occasionally bring indictments against editors, but no case of this sort was carried through to conviction. For resisting the draft, John Mullaly, editor and proprietor of the *Metropolitan Record*, New York, was prosecuted under the act of February 29, 1864, but he was discharged on the ground that the draft had not

---

[47]Editorial, Baltimore *Exchange*, Sept. 13, 1861.

[48]*O. R.*, Ser. II, Vol. 2, pp. 778, 786, 793, 795.

gone into actual operation at the time when his utterances were printed.[49] In announcing his opinion, United States Commissioner Osborn upheld the right of citizens to criticize governmental measures. As we have observed elsewhere, a variety of conditions operated to inhibit effective prosecutions for disloyalty, and these conditions applied with particular force in the case of newspapers.

VIII

In seeking a just interpretation of the question of press control during the Civil War, one must balance the immediate and practical considerations, of which the executive branch must be ever watchful, with the constitutional and legal phases of the subject. When powerful papers were upsetting strategy by the revelation of military secrets, discrediting the Government, defaming the generals, weakening the morale of soldier and citizen, uttering disloyal sentiments, fomenting jealous antagonism among officers, and clamoring for a peace which would have meant the consummation of disunion, even the most patient administration charged with the preservation of the Union by war, would have been tempted to the use of vigorous measures of suppression. Yet in face of this strong provocation there stood the citizen's fundamental right of a free press. Though for every wrong there should be some remedy, it seemed that our Constitution and laws lacked a specific legal remedy for journalistic wrongs against the Government. The urgings of the war mind and the demands of military men tended to pull the Government in the direction of arbitrary measures, while that deeper sense of regard for law was at the same time operating as a powerful restraining

[49] New York *World*, Aug. 29, 1864.

force. In a Cabinet containing both Lincoln and Stanton, the conflict of these opposite tendencies must necessarily have been intense. Such a struggle always occurs in war time, and the conditions peculiar to the war for the Union intensified the struggle to an unusual degree. At times, when the public danger seemed really threatened, or the provocation became too great, acts of questionable legality such as the suppression of papers or the arrest of editors were resorted to. Opinions will differ as to whether such acts were justifiable, and support will be found by skillful advocates for either view. Great public questions are more than legal questions, and those will be found who justify the act while admitting the illegality.

Those military measures of control which were well within the military code and were taken for military objects, would occasion the least condemnation. The subjection of news-writers accompanying the army to military discipline, the denial of confidential information to correspondents, the censoring of their dispatches at headquarters for military objects, the punishment by court-martial of such correspondents as conveyed useful intelligence to the enemy—such measures as these could hardly be questioned on the ground of illegality. That part of the military code which severely prohibits communication with the enemy is, like the rest of the code, an act of Congress passed in accordance with the constitutional right of that body to "make rules for the government . . . of the land and naval forces," and this code has never been seriously regarded as inconsistent with the First Amendment. The striking fact about this part of the military code is that it was used so little and that journalists were dealt with so leniently. In no case was the extreme penalty, death, enforced against a correspondent for giving intelligence to the enemy, though many did so; and the trial of these men by court-martial was, as we have seen, extremely rare. Usually their punishment was merely exclusion from the lines of a military command.

The larger question of the war power over the press, however, is not concerned with measures coming within the military code, but rather with the extension of military rule into the sphere appropriate to the civil law. The most plausible justification for the summary suppression of a newspaper directed to the legal merits of the question, would seem to be the doctrine that under martial law military rule temporarily supplants the ordinary law; but the establishment of martial law in peaceful districts remote from actual military operations is to say the least a questionable practice, and the leading instances of newspaper suppression occurred where no martial law had been proclaimed. Though the Supreme Court has issued no opinion which covers specifically this question of newspaper suppression as a war measure, yet the underlying principle of the Milligan case,[50] discountenancing the extension of military jurisdiction into regions within the control of the civil authorities, would seem to apply to the military seizure of a newspaper as well as to the military trial of a citizen. Cases such as those of the New York *World* and the Chicago *Times*, which we have considered in this chapter, though somewhat relieved by the prompt restoration of the papers and the release of those imprisoned, will doubtless be remembered as unfortunate instances of the exercise of military power in a sphere where the supremacy of the civil authorities should have been conceded.

It would be a mistake, however, to dwell upon the various instances of suppression without balancing them

---

[50]*Supra*, pp. 179-183.

against the far greater number of instances in which the temptation to drastic action was resisted. Despite particular occasions of harsh treatment, the prevailing policy was one of tolerance and leniency. As we have already observed, no true newspaper censorship existed during the war. The military control of the telegraph and the quite ineffective supervision of correspondents' dispatches had none of the characteristics of a real censorship. It is a significant fact that the word "censorship" does not occur in the index to the Government documents for the Civil War period, nor in the index of the *Congressional Globe*, nor in the general index of the *Official Records* of the war. Despite great provocation there was no Espionage Act and no Sedition Act during the Lincoln administration.[51] During a time when disloyalty was widespread and defiant, the anti-Lincoln and anti-Union organs were, as a rule, left undisturbed; and the continuous stream of abuse which the opposition papers emitted was in itself a standing evidence of the fact that liberty of the press, even to the point of license, did exist.

Lincoln's view as to the appropriate course to be taken toward newspapers was expressed as follows in a letter to General Schofield: "You will only arrest individuals and suppress assemblies or newspapers when they may be working palpable injury to the military in your charge, and in no other case will you interfere with the expression of opinion in any form or allow it to be interfered with violently by others. In this you have a discretion to exercise with great caution, calmness and forbearance."[52]

---

[51] "We fought the Civil War with the enemy at our gates and powerful secret societies in our midst without an Espionage Act." (Chafee, *Freedom of Speech*, 116.) Chafee goes on to comment upon Lincoln's caution with regard to freedom of the press.

[52] Nicolay and Hay *Works*, IX, 148.

In applying this policy of forbearance the President was compelled to disappoint many zealously loyal citizens who, while their sons were fighting for the Union, could not bear to see disloyal editors remain unmolested in furnishing a form of aid to the enemy which was more potent than rifles. Such feelings prompted many mass meetings and caused many letters and petitions to be sent to Washington urging that the publication of "Copperhead" papers be prohibited. Often popular indignation vented itself in mob action against obnoxious papers, resulting in the destruction of the newspaper offices, attacks or worrying threats directed against editors, and similar disturbances.[53] Under such conditions military seizure might be a protection to the newspaper as well as a means of preserving the public peace.

Where this popular opinion was operative, however, the Government could well afford to refrain from drastic measures. Ignoring the papers, allowing them to "strut their uneasy hour and be forgotten" (as President Wilson expressed it),[54] was often the most effective course, espe-

---

[53]A mob at Chester, Illinois, destroyed the office of the *Picket Guard* in July, 1864. The Bridgeport (Conn.) *Farmer* was attacked by a mob of five hundred and its office demolished because it "favored the rights of the South." In complaining of a disloyal editor, Charles Fishback of Indianapolis wrote as follows to Seward: "The people are getting tired of sending their sons to fight the rebels while such as this editor, more mischievous by far than if armed with muskets, are allowed to furnish aid and comfort to the enemy unmolested." In Ohio the *Gazette* and *Citizen* at St. Clairsville, the *Gazette* at Bellefontaine, the *Iron Valley Express* published at Jackson Court House, the Dayton *Empire*, the Marion *Mirror*, the Columbus *Crisis*, the Lancaster *Eagle*, the Starke County *Democrat*, the Wauseon *Democrat*, and the *Mahoning Sentinel* (of Youngstown) were affected by mob disturbances. These are but a few of many instances that could be mentioned to indicate the intensity of popular feeling against journals that were regarded as disloyal. (Cairo [Ill.] *Daily Democrat*, July 30, 1864; *O. R.*, Ser. II, Vol. 2, pp. 377, 806; *Ann. Cyc.*, 1864, p. 393; New York *Tribune*, (Aug. 24, 1861, p. 4.)

[54]Speech of President Wilson before Congress, Dec. 4, 1917.

cially in the case of those journals whose very abusiveness caused them to forfeit public respect. Where, on the other hand, there existed a solid basis of popular sympathy for a newspaper, oppressive action would but strengthen this sentiment and weaken the administration. It is the old story of the inability of government to coerce or supplant opinion.

CHAPTER XX

SUMMARY AND CONCLUSION

I. American and English attitude toward the rule of law
II. Lincoln's interpretation and application of the war power
III. Lack of legal precision during the Civil War: Conflicting theories as to its nature
IV. Absence of effective checks by Congress and the Supreme Court
V. Mitigating factors: General appraisal of Lincoln's government
VI. Bearing of Civil War issues upon later constitutional history: Parallel problems under Wilson

Specific problems have been the burden of the preceding pages; but as one takes a broad view of the constitutional aspects of the Civil War there are certain outstanding considerations which emerge from the details and which, in turn, illuminate the details themselves. Brief comment on some of these considerations may serve as a conclusion to our study.

I

Though no one expects government in war time to be normal, yet in studying any government it is useful to have in mind some norm or standard in comparison with which it may be judged. One finds such a norm in the principle of the "rule of law" which has been made familiar to English and American readers through Professor Dicey's *Law of the Constitution*. It will be worth while to recall what this principle involves in order to have it in view while commenting on governmental practice under Lincoln's presidency. In England, as Professor Dicey shows, the "rule of law" means that every man's legal rights or liabilities are almost invariably determined by the ordinary courts; that executive officers have a more limited discretion and less arbitrary power than in other European countries; and that no man is above the law, but all are amenable to the jurisdiction of the ordinary tribunals, officers being personally liable for wrongs done, even though in an official capacity. He adds that personal rights in England do not derive from a constitution but inherently exist.[1]

American political philosophy is in accord with this principle. Our ideal, it has been said, is a "government of laws, not of men." Law is above government: government is under law. Martial law, while sometimes used in this country, is viewed with distrust and is regarded as abnormal. We think of it as the setting aside of law, not as its fulfillment. The military power we believe to be subordinate to the civil; and even amid serious disturbances we have preferred to rely upon civil procedure. There is in this country a deplorable disregard for law as it restrains individuals; but this is entirely consistent with that other disposition to subject our rulers to legal restraints. Our respect for the Supreme Court is typical of our attitude in this matter.

Nor is it conformable to American political philosophy to hold that during war legal restraints are to be ignored. The maxim "necessity knows no law" appears to the American legal genius as a half-truth rather than a fundamental or central principle. Too often the maxim is a mere excuse. Unrestrained military power even in war is repugnant to the American mind. Inter-

[1] A. V. Dicey, *Introduction to the Law of the Constitution*, Ch. iv.

national law (which includes the "laws of civilized warfare"), treaty obligations, and at least a proximate preservation of civil rights (not ignoring those of an enemy population under military occupation) are factors which should restrain any warring government. The view that prevails in America is that even amid arms the laws hold; and one of the great doctrines of the Supreme Court, as announced in the Milligan case, is that the Constitution is not suspended during war.

This conception of a reign of law is, of course, but an ideal. We believe that the settled, permanent will of the whole community, as expressed in fundamental law, is a great stabilizing force; and in the ordering of our political life we believe that every effort should be made to give superior force to our mature, sober judgment as against the designs of our rulers.

The ideal is never realized, but such is the manner of ideals. Though in a sense we always live under a government of men, yet the rule of law as a standard has its definite value none the less.

II

When the Government under Lincoln is set over against this standard, its irregular and extra-legal characteristics become conspicuous. It is indeed a striking fact that Lincoln, who stands forth in popular conception as a great democrat, the exponent of liberty and of government by the people, was driven by circumstances to the use of more arbitrary power than perhaps any other President has seized. Probably no President has carried the power of proclamation and executive order (independently of Congress) so far as did Lincoln. It would not be easy to state what Lincoln conceived to be the limit of his powers. He carried his executive authority to the extent of freeing the slaves by proclamation, setting up a whole scheme of state-making for the purpose of reconstruction, suspending the *habeas corpus* privilege, proclaiming martial law, enlarging the army and navy beyond the limits fixed by existing law, and spending public money without congressional appropriation. Some of his important measures were taken under the consciousness that they belonged within the domain of Congress. The national legislature was merely permitted to ratify these measures, or else to adopt the futile alternative of refusing consent to an accomplished fact. We have seen how the first national use of conscription, in connection with the Militia Act of 1862, was an instance of presidential legislation. We have also noted the exercise of judicial functions by Lincoln or those acting under his authority, in regions under martial law, in Southern territory under Union occupation, in the application of military justice, in the performance of quasi-judicial functions by executive departments, and in the creation of "special war courts" such as the "provisional court of Louisiana." It thus appears that the President, while greatly enlarging his executive powers, seized also legislative and judicial functions as well.

Lincoln's view of the war power is significant. He believed that rights of war were vested in the President, and that as President he had extraordinary legal resources which Congress lacked. For example, he promulgated the "laws of war" to regulate the conduct of the armies; and in vetoing the Wade-Davis bill of 1864 he questioned the constitutional competency of Congress to abolish slavery in the States at a time when his own edict of emancipation had been in force for eighteen months. Lincoln tended to the view that in war the Constitution restrains Congress more than it restrains the President. Yet the view of the Supreme Court was that Congress may exercise belligerent powers and that in the use of these powers over the enemy the restraints of the Constitution do not apply.[2] Lincoln's view, under pressure of severe circumstance, led naturally to that course which has been referred to as his "dictatorship"; and, as illustrated in the *Prize Cases*, it produced uncertainty as to the legality of the war. Though the validity of Lincoln's acts was sustained by a majority of the court—which could hardly have decided otherwise on so vital a political question—yet four dissenting judges held that the President's action alone was not sufficient to institute a legal state of war. Lincoln's plea in defense, to the effect that his acts within the legislative domain could be legalized by congressional ratification, could hardly be accepted as consistent with the constitutional separation of powers; and this whole phase of the President's conduct illustrates not so much a permanently acceptable principle, but rather Lincoln's ability to retain popular confidence while doing irregular things. It should be added that Lincoln excelled in human reasonableness, and that his character included not only a readiness to act in an emergency, but also a high regard for the rule of law.

III

In all this extension of governmental power there was a noticeable lack of legal precision. A tendency toward irregularity may be observed as a characteristic of the

[2]Miller *vs.* U. S., 78 U. S. 268. This should be distinguished from the doctrine of the Milligan case that as to the nation's own citizens the restraints of the Constitution do apply in war; but the difficulty of preserving such a distinction during the Civil War, with its double theory as to the status of those adhering to the Confederacy, is obvious.

period, in military and civil administration, in legislation, and in legal interpretation. Congress did its work loosely and various of its laws were never carried out; while others produced bewilderment in the officers who sought to apply them. The Southern States were taxed as if part of the United States; yet the property out of which such tax must be paid was declared confiscable as belonging to enemies. The Unionist government of Virginia was considered competent to authorize the disruption of the State; but later this same government (removed from Wheeling to Alexandria) was denied representation in Congress and rejected as the instrument of reconstruction. Eight States of the former Confederacy, after assisting in ratifying the anti-slavery amendment of the Constitution, were treated as outside the Union. Legal interpretation in the 'sixties often smacked of sophistry—so much so that to many men an open confession of unconstitutionality appeared preferable to the labored reasoning that was all too common. Much of the legal inconsistency arose from confusion as to what the war was, whether it was extramural or within the family. Was the Government facing something like a magnified Whiskey Insurrection, or was it dealing with war in the international sense? Confronted with this dilemma, the Supreme Court adopted the convenient and practical solution of accepting both alternatives.[3]

The conflict was defined as both a public war and a rebellion, with the result that in Southern territory the United States claimed both belligerent and municipal powers. Many bootless and mystifying discussions resulted from this acceptance of two inconsistent viewpoints.

---

[3]*Supra*, Chapter III.

Yet there was nothing more natural than that these two opposite theories of the war should both be adopted. As to the insurrectionary theory, its adoption resulted from the Government's unwillingness to accept disunion as justified and to give up Federal sovereignty in the South; while the recognition of the struggle as a public war arose from the practical necessity of dealing with a nation in arms as a regular belligerent. The existence side by side of two opposing legal principles is understandable if we remember that the insurrectionary theory was not in fact applied as against Southern leaders and their adherents. They were not held personally liable as insurrectionists as were the leaders of the Whiskey Insurrection; instead, the Confederacy was in practice treated as a government with belligerent powers.

IV

If we were to ask how far our usual constitutional checks operated during the Civil War to prevent an extreme use of power, we would find that neither Congress nor the Supreme Court exercised any very effective restraint upon the President. Congress specifically approved the President's course between April and July, 1861; and, as to the *habeas corpus* question, after two years' delay, Congress passed an ambiguous law which was at the same time interpreted as approving and disapproving the doctrine that the President has the suspending power. The net effect, however, was to support the President; and immunity from prosecution was granted to officers who committed wrongs during the suspension.[4] It is true that the Habeas Corpus Act of 1863 directed the release of prisoners unless indicted in

[4] *Supra*, Chapter IX.

the courts. This was equivalent to saying that the President's suspension of the privilege, which was authorized by this act, was to be effective in any judicial district only until a grand jury should meet. On paper this law radically altered the whole system regarding political prisoners, making arbitrary imprisonment illegal after grand juries had examined the prisoners' cases. The significant fact, however, is that the law was ineffective. It did not, in fact, put an end to extra-legal imprisonments; nor did it succeed in shifting the control of punishments from executive and military hands to judicial hands.

As to the courts, a careful study will show that they did not function in such a way as to control the emergency. In dealing with disloyal practices the courts played a passive rather than an active rôle. They dealt in a hesitating way with cases that were brought to them; but the President, through the Attorney General and the district attorneys, controlled the prosecutions, and where it appeared that treason indictments were being pushed toward conviction, the administration at Washington showed actual embarrassment at the Government's success. Its way of dealing with dangerous citizens was not by prosecution in the courts, but by arbitrary imprisonment, followed by arbitrary release. The terrors of the old treason law proving unsuitable to the emergency, its penalty was softened; but even the softened penalty was not enforced. There is a striking contrast between the great number of arbitrary arrests and the almost negligible amount of completed judicial action for treason, conspiracy, and obstructing the draft. It was widely argued that the courts could not deal with the emergency, and that this inability justified an extraordinary extension of military power.

The Supreme Court of the United States did not, during the war, exert any serious check upon either Congress or the President. In the *Prize Cases* the court approved Lincoln's acts in the early months of the war. Such an extreme measure as confiscation was upheld by the court, though its validity, both in the international and the constitutional sense, was seriously questioned. It was not the Supreme Court, but Chief Justice Taney, hearing the Merryman petition in chambers, who denounced the President's suspension of the *habeas corpus* privilege. After the war, it is true, the court, in the Milligan case, declared a military régime illegal in regions remote from the theater of war; but while the war was in progress the court had declined to interfere with the action of a military commission in a similar case, that of Vallandigham. On the whole it appears that, while extreme measures were being taken, neither Congress nor the courts exerted any effective restraint. Instead of the "rule of law" prevailing, as Dicey defined it, men were imprisoned outside the law and independently of the courts; and governmental officers were given a privileged place above the law and made immune from penalties for wrongs committed.

V

This is one side of the picture. There is, however, another side; and we must note certain factors which at least partly redeemed the situation. The greatest factor, perhaps, was the legal-mindedness of the American people; and a very great factor was Lincoln himself. His humane sympathy, his humor, his lawyerlike caution, his common sense, his fairness toward opponents, his dislike of arbitrary rule, his willingness to take the people into his confidence and to set forth patiently the reasons for unusual measures—all these elements of his character operated to modify and soften the acts of overzealous subordinates and to lessen the effect of harsh measures upon individuals. He was criticized for leniency as often as for severity. Though there were arbitrary arrests under Lincoln, there was no thoroughgoing arbitrary government. The Government smarted under great abuse without passing either an Espionage Act or a Sedition Law. Freedom of speech was preserved to the point of permitting the most disloyal utterances. While a book could be written on the suppression of certain newspapers, the military control of the telegraph, the seizure of particular editions, the withholding of papers from the mails, and the arrest of editors, yet in a broad view of the whole situation such measures appear so far from typical that they sink into comparative insignificance. There was no real censorship, and in the broad sense the press was unhampered though engaging in activities distinctly harmful to the Government. As to Lincoln's attitude in this matter, it should be remembered that in general he advised non-interference with the press, and that he applied this policy prominently in the case of the Chicago *Times*.

To suppose that Lincoln's suspension of the *habeas corpus* privilege set aside all law would be erroneous. The suspension was indeed a serious matter; but men were simply arrested on suspicion, detained for a while, and then released. The whole effect of their treatment was milder than if they had been punished through the ordinary processes of justice. As to the military trial of civilians, it should be noticed that the typical use of the military commission was legitimate; for these commissions were commonly used to try citizens in military areas for military crimes. Where citizens in proximity to the Union army were engaged in sniping or bushwhacking, in bridge burning or the destruction of railroad or telegraph lines, they were tried, as they should have been, by military commission; and this has occasioned little comment, though there were hundreds of cases. The prominence of the cases of Vallandigham and Milligan should not obscure the larger fact that these cases were exceptional: in other words, the military trial of citizens for non-military offenses in peaceful areas was far from typical. It was thus a rare use of the military commission that was declared illegal in the Milligan case.

Legally, the Civil War stands out as an eccentric period, a time when constitutional restraints did not fully operate and when the "rule of law" largely broke down. It was a period when opposite and conflicting situations coexisted, when specious arguments and legal fictions were put forth to excuse extraordinary measures. It was a period during which the line was blurred between executive, legislative, and judicial functions; between State and Federal powers; and between military and civil procedures. International law as well as constitutional interpretation was stretched. The powers grasped by Lincoln caused him to be denounced as a "dictator." Yet civil liberties were not annihilated and no thoroughgoing dictatorship was established. There was nothing like a Napoleonic *coup d'état*. No undue advantage was taken of the emergency to force arbitrary rule upon the country or to promote personal ends. A comparison with European examples shows that Lincoln's government lacked many of the earmarks of dictatorial rule.[5] His administration did not, as in some dictatorships, employ criminal violence to destroy its

[5] The author has attempted to deal with this subject in the *So. Atl. Quar.*, XXVIII, 236-252 (July 1929).

opponents and perpetuate its power. It is significant that Lincoln half expected to be defeated in 1864. The people were free to defeat him, if they chose, at the polls. The Constitution, while stretched, was not subverted. The measures taken were recognized by the people as exceptional; and they were no more exceptional than the emergency for which they were used. Looking beyond the period called "reconstruction," the net effect, as Lincoln had said, was not to give the nation a taste for extreme rule any more than a patient, because of the use of emetics during illness, acquires a taste for them in normal life. In a legal study of the war the two most significant facts are perhaps these: the wide extent of the war powers; and, in contrast to that, the manner in which the men in authority were nevertheless controlled by the American people's sense of constitutional government.

VI

The bearing of Civil War decisions and policies upon later constitutional history lies outside the scope of this book: hence comment on this final subject must be narrowly confined and limited to bare suggestion. Constitutionally and otherwise, secession has been a dead issue since the war; for the South, while cherishing the achievements of its sons and daughters in the "lost cause," has loyally accepted the decision of battle. Our ability to maintain on these shores a continental nation which is also a union of States has been demonstrated. After the war ended, and the new wounds of reconstruction had begun to heal, the nation resumed its normal constitutional course. In other words, the war did not result in any overturning of constitutional government. A new federalism has now arisen which involves not only a vast extension of national functions,[6] but a species of State and Federal "coöperation" through which the authorities at Washington have found a new governmental resource by partnership with the States in agricultural education, road building, social security, etc. It is curious to note that this was partly foreshadowed in Lincoln's plan for State emancipation with Federal compensation, and that Lincoln proposed for the purpose a constitutional amendment.[7] Among the unforeseen legal results of the war is the discovery of unexpected possibilities in the Fourteenth Amendment which in judicial interpretation has been expanded far beyond its original purpose.[8]

Discussion of the Government under Lincoln leads naturally to a comparison with that of Wilson. Since, however, an adequate treatment of issues arising during later wars is excluded by the title and purpose of

---

[6]The amendments which followed the Civil War, the liberal interpretation of the interstate commerce clause, and the notable expansion of Federal functions in the machine age (very largely with Supreme Court support) amply illustrate this tendency. That the tendency has had its ups and downs is shown, for instance, by the Court's setting aside of certain acts of Congress to check the evil of child labor, but the broad movement to control child labor on the Federal level has nevertheless succeeded, as have other socially minded movements associated with the "welfare state." The old vocabulary as to State and Federal powers has been largely discarded, and there has developed a new kind of control which is neither strictly State nor national, but regional, and which operates through interstate agreements permitted by Congress. Such permission is contemplated in the Constitution.

[7]*Supra*, Chapter XV, sec. v.

[8]It is not within the scope of this book to treat the judicial interpretation of the Fourteenth Amendment. Passed to confer civil rights upon the Negro and to protect him against State action that might impair his rights, the amendment came to be used as a powerful instrument to restrain the States in the regulation of corporations. The subject is well summarized in C. A. Beard, *Contemporary American History, 1877-1913*, Ch. iii. For the later interpretation of the Thirteenth Amendment, see *supra*, p. 401 n.

this book, we must be content with noting the recurrence of certain former problems in the Wilson period, and that briefly. The obvious emphasis upon the greater magnitude of the first World War over the War of the States is somewhat misleading; for, taking the country over, the forces at the front in the Civil War were comparable to those of the United States in World War I, while the human cost of the Civil War was greater. Since one was a domestic struggle while the other was waged across three thousand miles of ocean, and since one was of more than twice the duration of the other, comparison at many points is futile. The vastly greater complexity of "modern war" is seen particularly in material matters; and the great expansion of governmental powers under Wilson was most conspicuous on the economic side. World War I introduced the conception of "economic mobilization" which extended to undreamed dimensions and involved governmental control over all essential material factors. Under Wilson the President's powers over food, fuel, railroads, shipping, industries, trade, agriculture, and finance, were enormously expanded; yet as to executive powers assumed independently of Congress, it still appears that Lincoln went farther than any President. Wilson never assumed, independently, such power as is illustrated in Lincoln's Proclamation of Emancipation or his suspension of the *habeas corpus* privilege. Most of Wilson's powers, in fact, were derived from congressional authorization;[9] while Lincoln's most conspicuous acts were without legislative authority. The extent to which President Wilson's orders affected the machinery of government finds no parallel under Lincoln; but constitutionally one of the significant developments in each

---

[9] C. A. Berdahl, *War Powers of the Executive in the United States.*

of these war periods is the great expansion of executive authority.[10]

On the question of disloyalty a comparison of the Lincoln and Wilson administrations shows a striking similarity of "problems," and an equally striking contrast as to measures.[11] Lincoln's sweeping assumption of control over the arrest, detention, and release of "political prisoners" involved neither the enforcement of statutes passed by Congress, nor prosecution in the courts. These matters were handled under Lincoln with irregularity, confusion, and scant organization. Under Wilson, on the other hand, the arsenal of legislation was full and the organization elaborate. The Attorney General's office under Bates in 1864 comprised eight persons and had not yet been raised to the dignity of a department. It took no significant part in dealing with disloyalty. The yearly sum for salaries was $18,264.[12] Gregory's Department in 1918 had a salary expenditure

[10] For Wilson's Government there are many competent books and articles. The following references may be noted: A. E. McKinley, *Collected Materials for the Study of the War* (2d ed., Philadelphia, 1918); F. L. Paxson, "The American War Government, 1917-1918," *Am. Hist. Rev.*, XXVI, 54-76; *Economic Mobilization in the United States for the War of 1917* (Monograph No. 2, Historical Branch, General Staff, 1918); C. A. Berdahl, *War Powers of the Executive in the United States* (Univ. of Ill. Studies in the Social Sciences, Vol. IX); *Preliminary Economic Studies of the War*, edited by David Kinley (a series of volumes published by the Carnegie Endowment for International Peace); *Handbook of Economic Agencies for the War of 1917* (Monograph No. 3, Historical Branch, General Staff, 1919). The Government documents and periodical literature on the subject are of great volume, while the unpublished archives in Washington are of staggering proportions. For the Supreme Court adjudication of constitutional points connected with the World War, see articles by Thomas Reed Powell, in *Mich. Law Rev.*, XIX, XX, XXI, *passim*. The Department of Justice issued during the war a large number of bulletins under the title "Interpretation of War Statutes."

[11] W. A. Dunning, "Disloyalty in Two Wars," *Am. Hist. Rev.*, XXIV, 625-630.

[12] Payroll for Sept., 1864: Attorney General's papers.

of $530,000, and had built up a huge central organization with an elaborate field force. The secret-service division of the Department was five times as large in 1918 as in 1916. Besides its regular employees, the Department commanded the service of 250,000 citizen volunteers. It was said in 1918 that "never in its history has the country been so thoroughly policed as at the present time."[13] Naturally this highly developed department assumed a dominant rôle in dealing with disloyal practices.

Such practices were, during the Wilson era, handled in the courts and in pursuance of law, not by any suspension of the *habeas corpus* privilege. In April, 1917, the legal weapons for matters of disloyalty included little more than the treason statutes,[14] the various conspiracy statutes,[15] and the old law of 1798 concerning alien enemies.[16] The Government was unable to obtain any conviction under the treason statutes;[17] and the conspiracy law likewise proved inadequate, thus presenting an interesting parallel to the situation under Lincoln. For dealing with alien enemy activities, as the Attorney General stated, the statute of 1798 did provide an effective instrument. Whatever defects existed were soon remedied by Congress, which provided an ample basis for dealing with disloyalty through the Espionage Act,[18] the Selective Service Act,[19] and especially the so-called "Sedition Law," which was passed in 1918 as an amend-

[13] *Report of the Attorney General*, 1918, pp. 14-15.

[14] I.e., the treason laws of 1790 and 1862. *Revised Statutes of the U. S.*, secs. 5331-5334.

[15] *Ibid.*, sec. 5336.

[16] *Ibid.*, sec. 4067.

[17] *Report of the Attorney General*, 1918, pp. 41-42.

[18] *U. S. Stat. at Large*, XL, 217.

[19] Under the Selective Service Act of May 18, 1917, any person inducing another to evade military service was made punishable. (*Ibid.*, 76, sec. 6.)

ment to the Espionage Act.[20] Heavy penalties were imposed by this measure upon any one inciting disloyalty or mutiny (or attempting to do so); abusing the Government; uttering contempt of the form of government; or promoting the enemy's cause. It is beyond the scope of this book to treat of the enforcement of these statutes: suffice it to note that they were actively enforced, and that the suppression of disloyalty was thus accomplished within the law and through the civil courts, rather than by extra-legal means.[21] As to those who were caught in the machinery, they were more severely punished than were the political prisoners under Lincoln.

The social psychology of war time had, of course, much to do with these acts and these prosecutions; for in the high-pitched spirit of the national mind, any hint of anti-war sentiment brought scorn and suspicion. The Government, of course, had this situation as well as disloyalty to cope with; and one of the results of the systematic and lawful program of prosecution was to suppress the officious activities of self-appointed committees, and to discourage "extra-legal measures of intimidation and punishment." In this respect, a problem arose which was similar to that of Lincoln's administration.[22] It was claimed by Wilson's Department of Justice that domestic lawlessness and "privately organized neighborhood committees" resulted in less harm than in previous wars.[23]

Prosecutions under the Espionage Act and its 1918

---

[20]Act of May 16, 1918: *ibid.*, p. 553.

[21]Other statutes, of course, bore upon disloyalty, such as the Threats-against-the-President Act, the Trading-with-the-Enemy Act, the Sabotage Law, and the act concerning the naturalization of alien enemies. (*U. S. Stat. at Large*, XXXIX, 919; XL, 411, 533, 542.)

[22]Violent attacks by Unionists upon newspapers that were regarded as disloyal have been noted above (p. 509).

[23]*Report of Attorney General*, 1918, p. 23.

amendment covered oral and published utterances, and the problem of the disloyal brought into view the whole question of freedom of speech and of the press.[24] While under Lincoln such utterances were either ignored or dealt with by the executive after the manner of martial law—e.g., by the military suspension of a newspaper—during World War I they were dealt with in a punitive way by the enforcement of statutes, the punishments resulting from conviction in the courts after jury trial.[25] It is Chafee's view that "the Espionage Act prosecutions break with a great tradition in English and American law."[26] "Almost all the convictions," he says, "have been for expressions of opinion about the merits and conduct of the war."[27]

As to conscription, there was more of contrast than of parallel; for the prompt, economical, and efficient draft of 1917 bore no resemblance to that of the Civil War with its costly machinery, its scandals of bounty-jumping, its substitutes and commutation money, its inefficient enforcement, and its stigmatizing of the conscript. In one matter, that of the conscientious objector,

---

[24]The question of news control involves, of course, much more than a discussion of the Espionage Act, but that discussion cannot be undertaken here. See Chafee, *Freedom of Speech*, and Lucy M. Salmon, *The Newspaper and Authority*. The exclusion of matter by the postal authorities operated during the Wilson era on lines somewhat similar to those of the Civil War, but with larger statutory power. See *supra*, Chapter XIX,, sec. vi, and compare Chafee, *op. cit.*, pp. 106 *et seq.* To treat the Committee on Public Information here would obviously involve too great a digression; but it may be noted in passing that this committee depended largely upon voluntary coöperation by the press, and that under Wilson such voluntary coöperation was successfully developed in many other fields, as for instance in food control. Such coöperation was tried under Lincoln as to newspapers, but it broke down. (*Am. Hist. Rev.*, XXIII, 305.)

[25]Chafee, however, has pointed out that in times of popular panic jury trial proves illusory as a protection in matters involving freedom of speech. (Zechariah Chafee, *Freedom of Speech*, 76-80.)

[26]*Ibid.*, p. 116.

[27]*Ibid.*, p. 57.

there was a close parallel; for in each case the option of non-combatant service was offered to those whose religious scruples against war were genuine.[28]

Lack of space requires the omission of comparisons concerning such matters as the treatment of enemy property,[29] State and Federal relations,[30] pardon and amnesty, and the like; nor is there room to comment upon congressional attempts to assume the President's power.[31] We must conclude by noting one more parallel, and that the most striking of all—the parallel between Lincoln's statement of the larger meaning of the war in 1861 and that of Wilson in 1917. Wilson, in his war message and at other times, spoke of democracy as being at stake in the World War. Referring to the issue of disunion, Lincoln said: "And this issue embraces more than the fate of these United States. It presents to the whole family of man the question whether a constitutional republic, or democracy—a government of the people by the same people—can or cannot maintain its territorial integrity against its own domestic foes. . . . It forces us to ask, Is there in all republics this inherent and fatal weakness?"[32] Though under different circumstances

[28]In this respect section 4 of the Selective Service Act of 1917 resembled section 17 of the Act of February 24, 1864: *U. S. Stat. at Large*, XIII, 9; XL, 78.

[29]It is contended that the original non-confiscatory purposes of the Enemy Trade Act of 1917 were partly abandoned in certain amendments which authorized "a modified form of confiscation consisting of a forced sale of German interests to American citizens only," and which legalized the acquisition of German-owned patents. Carl Zollman, in *Mich. Law Rev.*, XXI, 277-289. For the act and its amendments, see *U. S. Stat. at Large*, XL, 411, 459, 1020.

[30]For a discussion of State espionage acts during the World War, in their constitutional bearings and in their relation to the Federal Government, see Chafee, *op. cit.*, pp. 110 *et seq.*

[31]For a comparison of congressional attempts under Lincoln and under Wilson to "set up an extra-legal executive agency," see W. E. Dodd, *Woodrow Wilson and his Work*, 253 *et seq.*

[32]Richardson, *Messages . . . of the Presidents*, VI, 23. (The same conception reappeared as the central theme in the Gettysburg Address.)

and in different senses, Lincoln and Wilson struck the same note. Both considered that democracy was in the balance; and both were sustained amid bitter struggles by the belief that they were contending for political principles of world-wide importance.

The period of "World War II"[33] lies outside the bounds of this volume. Problems of Congress, Court, and President in the years of Franklin Roosevelt and later, have their own focus and orientation. Current American constitutional issues—social and economic undertakings, expansion of the FBI, unprecedented prosecutions for treason, sedition trials, vast problems of enemy occupation, incalculable perils of the atomic age, the international trial of war criminals, antisubversive measures, new programs for civil rights—such developments in our own day require elaborate and searching discussion in their own setting. Through all these mutations of the machine age and of world conditions there are some things that remain. The profound reverence still paid to the memory of Lincoln, and the perpetuation of the Wilson concept through the United Nations, stand as evidence that the democratic faith in what Wilson called the "organized opinion of mankind," in spite of heartbreaking and disastrous setbacks, still has vitality.

---

[33]The conflict that began in 1914 was not called "World War I" at the time. World conflicts had raged in the period of Napoleon and before. The name "World War II" for the conflict that began with the Nazi attack upon Poland in 1939 was unfortunately chosen; the designation "Axis War" would have served better. And nomenclature fits in too easily with world catastrophe in predictions of that colossal stupidity, "World War III."

BIBLIOGRAPHY

Source Collections

AMES, HERMAN V., *State Documents on Federal Relations* (1789-1861). New York, 1907.

[Appleton's] *American Annual Cyclopedia.* 42 vols. New York, 1862-1903. A valuable yearbook, containing much source material. Briefly cited as "*Ann. Cyc.*"

JOHNSON, ALLEN (ed.), *Readings in American Constitutional History, 1776-1876.* Boston, 1912. A source book to illustrate the "history of American polity."

MCPHERSON, EDWARD, *The Political History of the United States during the Great Rebellion.* New York, 1864. A varied collection of documents by the clerk of the House of Representatives.

MOORE, FRANK, *The Rebellion Record: A Diary of American Events with Documents, Narratives, Illustrative Incidents, Poetry, etc.* 12 vols. including supplement, New York, 1861-1868.

MOORE, JOHN BASSETT, *Digest of International Law as Embodied . . . in Documents . . . of the United States.* House Doc. No. 551, 56 Cong., 2 sess. 8 vols. 1906.

Public Documents

Congressional Documents. This voluminous series is issued under the following titles for each session of Congress: *House Executive Documents, House Miscellaneous Documents, House Reports, Senate Executive Documents, Senate Miscellaneous Documents, Senate Reports.* Benjamin F. Poore's *Descriptive Catalogue of Government Publications, 1774-1881,* is the indispensable guide to these documents.

Congressional Globe.

House Journal. Appears in the series of Congressional Documents, one volume being issued for each session of the House of Representatives.

RICHARDSON, J. D., *Messages and Papers of the Presidents.* Published as a Government document (House Misc. Doc. No. 210, 53 Cong., 2 sess.) and also separately.

Reports of Executive Departments. The yearly reports of the War Department and certain reports of the Treasury Department are of value for the subject of this book.

Senate Journal. Issued for each session of the Senate in the series of Congressional Documents.

Statutes at Large of the United States of America. Contains all the laws assembled in the order of their passage, and includes also presidential proclamations and treaties.

Statutes at Large of the Provisional Government of the Confederate States of America, February, 1861 to February, 1862. Includes Confederate Constitution. Richmond, 1864.

TERRELL, W. H. H., *Report of the Adjutant-General of the State of Indiana.* 8 vols. Indianapolis, 1865-1869. A valuable history of Indiana's participation in the Civil War, with full statistics. The first volume is especially useful. Similar reports of other States throw much light on State and Federal relations.

War of the Rebellion: Official Records of the Union and Confederate Armies. In four series, 128 vols. 1880-1901. Besides military matter, this indispensable collection contains a vast amount of material on political, administrative and constitutional problems. Cited as "*O.R.*"

War of the Rebellion: Official Records of the Union and Confederate Navies.

State Publications

It is not feasible to give a list of State publications bearing upon the subject of this book, but most of the useful records are included in the following general designations: codes or revised statutes, in which are included the constitutions; session laws; legislative journals, including as a rule the governors' messages; State "documents," comprising miscellaneous reports from various executive officers; reports of the adjutants general (especially useful on State and Federal relations and on problems connected with conscription); handbooks or bluebooks (giving statistical information, official directories, etc.); court reports. (For Illinois, for instance, the series known as "Illinois Reports" comprises decisions of the Illinois Supreme Court.)

Legal Opinions, Decisions, Etc.

Digest of the Opinions of the Judge Advocates General.

Federal Cases. Comprises decisions of the circuit and district courts of the United States. Rich in historical interest.

Opinions of the Attorneys General of the United States. 1791-. Wash., 1852-.

United States Court of Claims Reports.

United States Reports. Decisions of the U. S. Supreme Court. Comprises all the cases included in the older series which is named after reporters, such as Dallas, Cranch, Wheaton, Peters, Howard, Black, and Wallace.

[NOTE. Many cases of importance are to be found in the English reports.]

Legal Authorities

BATY, THOMAS, and MORGAN, J. H., *War: Its Conduct and Legal Results.* London, 1915. Discusses the exercise of war powers in England during the first year of the World War.

BINNEY, HORACE, *The Privilege of the Writ of Habeas Corpus under the Constitution.* Philadelphia, 1862-1865. There are three parts of this treatise, issued at separate times. These well-known war pamphlets show much learning and the argument is forceful.

BIRKHIMER, WILLIAM E., *Military Government and Martial Law.* Second ed., rev. Kansas City, Mo., 1904. Deals with martial law and military occupation, drawing largely from Civil War experience.

BLACKSTONE, WILLIAM, *Commentaries on the Laws of England.* In four books. First edition published at Oxford, 1765-1769. Among the editions of Blackstone are those by Cooley, Kerr, William C. Jones, Archbold, and Chitty. Cooley's comments are especially illuminating.

BURLAMAQUI, J. J., *Principles of Natural and Political Science.* Nugent trans., Boston, 1792.

BYNKERSHOEK, C. VAN, *Quaestiones Juris Publici.* 1737.

The Constitution of the United States, as amended to January 1, 1923 (Annotated). Sen. Doc. No. 96, 67 Cong., 2 sess. A useful guide to the constitutional law of the United States.

CHAFEE, ZECHARIAH, JR., *Freedom of Speech.* New York, 1920. Traces American law on control of speech and press in a most thorough manner, and treats judicial construction of the First Amendment. Deals chiefly with practice during the Wilson era. Contains bibliography and valuable appendices.

CURTIS, GEORGE TICKNOR, *Constitutional History of the United States from their Declaration of Independence to the Close of their Civil War*. 2 vols. New York, 1889-1896. This work is valuable for the subjects which it treats, but it does not even attempt a discussion of constitutional problems arising during the Civil War.

DANA, R. H., JR., *Enemies' Territory and Alien Enemies*. Boston, Cambridge, 1864. Rare and out of print. Interprets the Supreme Court's decision in the *Prize Cases*.

DAVIS, GEORGE B., *A Treatise on the Military Law of the United States*. 3d ed. rev., N. Y., 1913. A standard treatise. Author was Judge Advocate General of the United States.

DICEY, ALBERT VENN, *Introduction to the Study of the Law of the* (English) *Constitution*. 7th ed., London, 1908. First edition published in 1885 under the title "Lectures introductory to the Study of the Law of the Constitution." The English conception of the "rule of law" is presented in Chapter IV.

FINLASON, WILLIAM F., *A Review of the Authorities as to the Repression of Riot or Rebellion, with Special Reference to Criminal or Civil Liability*. London, 1868.

——, *A Treatise on Martial Law, as allowed by the Law of England, in Time of Rebellion, etc*. London, 1866.

FINLEY, JOHN H., *The American Executive and Executive Methods*. New York, 1908.

GROTIUS, HUGO, *De Jure Belli ac Pacis*. First published in 1625. Seventy-five editions have been listed by Professor Reeves of the University of Michigan. *New York Times Book Review*, April 12, 1925, p. 24.

HALL, W. E., *A Treatise on International Law*. 7th ed., Oxford, 1917.

HARE, J. I. C., *American Constitutional Law*. 2 vols., paged continuously. 1st ed., Boston, 1889.

HAYS, ARTHUR GARFIELD, *Enemy Property in America*. Albany, New York, 1923. A useful commentary on the Trading-with-the-Enemy Act, with a digest of reported and unreported cases.

HUGHES, CHARLES E., *War Powers under the Constitution*. Sen. Doc. No. 105, 65, Cong., 1 sess., 1917. An address covering fourteen pages delivered before the American Bar Association at Saratoga, New York, September, 1917. Upholds a wide extension of the war powers with historical argument and elaborate citations.

KENT, JAMES, *Commentaries on American Law*. 2 vols. 14th ed., Boston, 1896. (First published, 1826-1830.)

LALOR, JOHN J., *Cyclopedia of Political Science . . . and the Political History of the United States.* 3 vols. New York, 1904. First published 1881. Especially valuable for the articles by Alexander Johnston.

MCLAUGHLIN, A. C., and HART, A. B., *Cyclopedia of American Government.* 3 vols. New York, 1913.

The Military Laws of the United States. Prepared under the direction of Elihu Root, Secretary of War, by Brig. Gen. George B. Davis, Judge Advocate General, with supplement. Wash., Government Printing Office, 1911.

PARKER, JOEL, *Habeas Corpus and Martial Law.* Cambridge, Mass., 1861. The author, a professor in the Harvard Law School, answers Taney's opinion in the Merryman case and argues in favor of instituting martial law in war time in the vicinity of an army.

—— *Three Powers of Government.* New York, 1869.

PUFENDORF, SAMUEL VON, *De Jure Naturae et Gentium.* A ponderous study of ancient and medieval usage, with which is interwoven seventeenth century doctrines of natural right philosophy. First published in 1672.

VATTEL, E. DE, *Law of Nations, or principles of the law of nature applied to the conduct and affairs of nations and sovereigns.* Luke White, ed., Dublin, 1792. Though basing much of his reasoning upon the "law of nature," Vattel relied extensively on modern international usage.

WHEATON, HENRY, *Elements of International Law.* This important treatise was quoted as the chief American authority at the time of the Civil War. It was first published in 1836. The sixth edition by Lawrence appeared in Boston in 1855, and the eighth edition by R. H. Dana, Jr., was published in Cambridge in 1866. Dana's annotations are extensive and have unique value with reference to Civil War practice, especially in regard to the treatment of enemy property. The later Boyd edition (London, 1889) should also be noted.

WILLOUGHBY, W. W., *Constitutional Law of the United States.* 2 vols. New York, 1910.

WILSON, WOODROW, *Constitutional Government in the United States.* New York, 1911.

Biographical Works

MOWBRY, DUANE, "Letters of Edward Bates and the Blairs, Frank P. (Sr. and Jr.), and Montgomery, from the private papers and correspondence of Senator James R. Doolittle of Wisconsin." *Mo. Hist. Rev.*, XI, 123-146.

BLAINE, JAMES G., *Twenty Years of Congress.* 2 vols. Norwich, Conn., 1884. Colored by the author's Northern sympathies, but valuable in its analysis of congressional problems and its pointed characterizations of public men.

The Works of James Buchanan, Comprising His Speeches, State Papers, and Private Correspondence. Collected and edited by John Bassett Moore. 12 vols. Philadelphia & London, 1911. The eleventh volume touches upon many questions arising during the Civil War. Clear reasoning and loyalty to the Union pervade these letters.

BUTLER, GENERAL BENJAMIN F., *Butler's Book.* Boston, 1892. Gives B. F. Butler's opinion of B. F. Butler.

PARTON, JAMES, *General Butler at New Orleans.* Boston, 1892. Parton closely consulted Butler concerning the material for this book which was written, with Butler's approval, during the war. In a letter to Parton, Butler insisted that only the impartial truth be told. The book is in general eulogistic.

MARSHALL, JESSIE AMES, ed., *Private and Official Correspondence of General Benjamin F. Butler.* 5 vols., privately issued, 1917. A rich and extensive collection edited by Butler's granddaughter.

——, *Papers of John A. Campbell, 1861-1865.* Southern Hist. Soc. Papers, n. s., IV, 3-81.

CONNOR, HENRY G., *John Archibald Campbell, Associate Justice of the United States Supreme Court, 1853-1861.* Boston, 1920. Treats the informal negotiations with the Confederate commissioners in March and April, 1861, the Hampton Roads Conference, and Lincoln's visit to Richmond in 1865.

HARRIS, WILMER C., *Public Life of Zachariah Chandler, 1851-1875.* Mich. Hist'l Com., 1918. An account of a Northern "fire eater" in Congress.

Diary and Correspondence of Salmon P. Chase. Am. Hist. Ass. An. Rep., 1902, Vol. II. The portion of the diary here printed covers the period from July 21 to October 12, 1862. Of special interest are the letters from George S. Denison, charged with treasury duties in Louisiana.

DANA, CHARLES A., *Recollections of the Civil War.* New York, 1898.

CRAVEN, JOHN J., *Prison Life of Jefferson Davis*. New York, 1905. Based on a daily record kept by the chief medical officer at Fortress Monroe.

DAVIS, VARINA, *Jefferson Davis, ex-President of the Confederate States of America: A Memoir by His Wife*. New York, 1890. Frequently reproduces Davis' own words.

GORDON, ARMISTEAD C., *Jefferson Davis*. New York, 1918. Devotes a chapter to Davis' imprisonment and trial.

Jefferson Davis, Constitutionalist, His Letters, Papers, and Speeches. Collected and edited by Dunbar Rowland. 10 vols. Miss. Dept. of Archives and History. Jackson, Miss., 1923. The most important work in print for a study of Davis' career. (Briefly cited as Rowland, *Davis*.)

Letters of John Hay and Extracts from His Diary. 3 vols. Printed but not published, 1908. Selected by Henry Adams; edited by Mrs. Hay. Only the initials of proper names are printed.

Autobiography of Oliver Otis Howard. 2 vols. New York, 1907.

From the Autobiography of Hershel V. Johnson, 1856-1867. Am. Hist. Rev., XXX, 311-336. Significant because of Johnson's opposition to secession and because of his career as Confederate States senator. Contributed to the *Review* by Professor Percy Scott Flippin.

FREEMAN, DOUGLAS SOUTHALL (ed.), *Lee's Dispatches*. New York, 1915. Unpublished letters of General Lee to President Davis, 1862-1865. A valuable collection of confidential dispatches.

NICOLAY, JOHN G., and HAY, JOHN (eds.), *Complete Works of Abraham Lincoln*. Gettysburg ed., 12 vols. New York, 1905. Cited as "Nicolay and Hay, *Works*." Far from complete.

NICOLAY, JOHN G., and HAY, JOHN, *Abraham Lincoln: A History*. An elaborate account by Lincoln's private secretaries who not unnaturally uphold the war President's position in every controversy. 10 vols., 1890. Cited as "Nicolay and Hay, *Lincoln*."

Uncollected Letters of Abraham Lincoln. Now first brought together by Gilbert A. Tracy; with an introduction by Ida M. Tarbell, Boston and New York, 1917.

TARBELL, IDA M., *The Life of Abraham Lincoln*. 2 vols. New York, 1909. Particularly useful because of the appendix to Vol. II, which contains hundreds of otherwise unpublished Lincoln papers.

Notes of Colonel W. G. Moore, Private Secretary to President Johnson, 1866-1868. *Am. Hist. Rev.*, XIX, 98-132.

FOULKE, W. D., *Life of Oliver P. Morton.* 2 vols. Indianapolis, 1899. A full, but not exhaustive, biography of Indiana's war governor. Concerning the administration of military matters it adds little to Terrell's reports as adjutant general.

Personal Recollections of John M. Palmer. Cincinnati, 1901.

Letter of Governor [Francis H.] *Pierpoint to . . . the President . . . on . . . Abuse of Military Power in the Command of General Butler in Virginia and North Carolina.* Washington, 1864.

RUSSELL, WILLIAM HOWARD, *My Diary, North and South.* New York, 1863. Brilliant and often caustic observations by the correspondent of the London *Times.*

SEWARD, FREDERICK WILLIAM, *Reminiscences of a War-time Statesman and Diplomat, 1830-1915.* The author was Assistant Secretary of State under Lincoln, Johnson, and Hayes.

The Works of William Henry Seward. Ed. by George E. Baker. 5 vols. Boston, 1887-1890. Fifth volume also appears as "The Diplomatic History of the War for the Union."

BANCROFT, FREDERIC, *The Life of William H. Seward.* 2 vols. New York, 1900.

SHERMAN, JOHN, *Recollections of Forty Years.* Chicago, 1895. Covers Sherman's career as Representative and Senator from Ohio, and as Secretary of the Treasury.

THORNDIKE, RACHEL S. (ed.), *The Sherman Letters: Correspondence between General Sherman and Senator Sherman from 1837 to 1891.* New York, 1894.

HOWE, M. A. DEWOLFE (ed.), *Home Letters of General Sherman.* New York, 1909.

Memoirs of General W. T. Sherman. New York, 2 vols., 1875.

STEPHENS, ALEXANDER H., *A Constitutional View of the War between the States.* 2 vols. Philadelphia, 1868-1870. Ably presents the Southern constitutional viewpoint. Includes autobiographical material.

——, *The Reviewers Reviewed: A Supplement to the "War between the States."* New York, 1872.

Recollections of Alexander H. Stephens: His Diary Kept When a Prisoner at Fort Warren, Boston Harbor, 1865; Giving Incidents and Reflections of His Prison Life, etc. Ed., with a biographical study by Myrta L. Avary. New York, 1910.

WOODBURN, JAMES ALBERT, *The Life of Thaddeus Stevens*, Indianapolis, 1913.

STEINER, BERNARD C., *Life of Roger Brooke Taney, Chief Justice of the United States Supreme Court.* Baltimore, 1922.

WHITE, HORACE, *Life of Lyman Trumbull.* Boston & New York, 1913. Throws light on the *habeas corpus* question, confiscation, the suppression of the Chicago *Times*, and the Thirteenth Amendment.

Diary of Gideon Welles, Secretary of the Navy under Lincoln and Johnson. Edited, with introduction, by John T. Morse, Jr. 3 vols. Boston and New York, 1911. A record of primary importance for the history of the Lincoln administration. Mr. Howard K. Beale has pointed out (*Am. Hist. Rev.*, XXX, 547-552) that Welles made numerous emendations in his diary—"probably thousands" of them—prior to publication, and that the Diary as printed cannot be regarded as a strictly contemporaneous record. It would be a mistake, however, to conclude that the Diary has been discredited as an historical source. It is merely that the printed edition does not show the deletions and emendations, most of which were unimportant. For all portions of the Diary used in this book the author has consulted the original manuscript in the Library of Congress.

General Accounts

CHADWICK, F. E., *Causes of the Civil War.* (The American Nation: A History, ed. by A. B. Hart, Vol. 19.) New York, 1905.

CHANNING, EDWARD, *History of the United States*, Vol. VI: The War for Southern Independence. New York, 1925.

DAVIS, JEFFERSON, *The Rise and Fall of the Confederate Government.* 2 vols. New York, 1881.

DRAPER, JOHN W., *The Civil War in America.* New York, 1867. Uncritical and lacking in documentation.

DUNNING, WILLIAM A., *Essays on the Civil War and Reconstruction and Related Topics.* New York, 1898. An excellent discussion of legal problems arising out of the war and their relation to the American constitutional system. Emphasis is placed upon reconstruction and only a brief treatment of Civil War problems is given.

—, *Reconstruction, Political and Economic.* (American Nation: A History, Vol. 22.)

HOSMER, J. K., *The Appeal to Arms.* (American Nation: A History, Vol. 20)

—, *Outcome of the Civil War.* (American Nation: A History, Vol. 21.)

OBERHOLTZER, ELLIS PAXSON, *A History of the United States Since the Civil War.* 3 vols., New York, 1917.

RHODES, JAMES FORD, *History of the United States from the Compromise of 1850 to the Final Restoration of Home Rule at the South in 1877.* 7 vols. New York, 1893-1906. The most thorough general history of the Civil War that has been written.

——, *History of the Civil War, 1861-1865.* New York, 1917. A fresh work on a smaller scale.

SCHWAB, JOHN C., *The Confederate States of America, A Financial and Industrial History of the South during the Civil War.* New York, 1901.

WARREN, CHARLES, *The Supreme Court in United States History.* 3 vols. Boston, 1922. Richly supplied with material drawn from contemporary sources. The third volume treats of the Civil War period.

Monographs and Special Studies

BERDAHL, CLARENCE A., *War Powers of the Executive in the United States.* Univ. of Ill. Studies in the Soc. Sciences, Vol. IX, Nos. 1 and 2. Urbana, Ill., 1921. Especially useful in its analysis of the President's civil powers in war time.

BROOKS, ROBERT P., *Conscription in the Confederate States of America, 1862-1865.* Bull. of the Univ. of Ga., Vol. XVII, No. 4. Athens, Ga., 1917.

BRUMMER, SIDNEY DAVID, *Political History of New York State during the Period of the Civil War.* Columbia Univ. Studies in Hist., etc., Vol. XXXIX, No. 2, New York, 1911.

CALLAHAN, JAMES M., *Semi-Centennial History of West Virginia.* Pub. by W. Va. Semi-Centennial Commission, 1913. Contains a useful bibliography, pp. 284-293.

CHAMBRUN, CHARLES A. DE P., marquis de, *The Executive Power in the United States.* Lancaster, Pa., 1874. Ch. X deals with the executive power under Lincoln.

COLE, A. C., *The Era of the Civil War, 1848-1870.* (Centennial Hist. of Ill., Vol. III.) Springfield, Ill., 1919. A scholarly account, well grounded in source material.

DAVIS, WILLIAM W., *The Civil War and Reconstruction in Florida.* Columbia Univ. Studies in Hist., etc., Vol. LIII, No. 131. New York, 1913. An elaborate and useful monograph, dispassionately written.

ECKENRODE, HAMILTON J., *The Political History of Virginia during the Reconstruction.* Johns Hopkins Univ. Studies in Hist. and Pol. Sci., Ser. XXII, Nos. 6, 7, 8. Baltimore, 1904. Chs. I and II are especially valuable for a study of the "restored government" of Virginia and its relations with the Government at Washington.

FICKLEN, JOHN ROSE, *History of Reconstruction in Louisiana* (through 1868). Johns Hopkins Univ. Studies in Hist. and Pol. Sci., Ser. XXVIII, No. 1. Baltimore, 1910. This study was cut short by Professor Ficklen's untimely death and the volume was edited by Professor Pierce Butler.

HALL, CLIFTON R., *Andrew Johnson, Military Governor of Tennessee.* Princeton Univ. Press, 1916. A scholarly dissertation based upon the sources, including the Johnson papers in the Library of Congress.

HALL, GRANVILLE D., *The Rending of Virginia.* Chicago, 1902. Written from the West Virginia viewpoint. The writer reported the proceedings of the Constitutional Convention of West Virginia of 1861 to the Wheeling *Intelligencer.*

HIRST, MARGARET E., *The Quakers in Peace and War: An Account of Their Peace Principles and Practice.* Introduction by Rufus M. Jones. New York, 1923. An exhaustive, scholarly treatment of Quaker opposition to war and military training in England, the United States and abroad.

LEWIS, VIRGIL A., *History of West Virginia.* Philadelphia, 1889.

——, *How West Virginia was Made.* Charleston, W. Va., 1909. A sourcebook.

LONN, ELLA, *Reconstruction in Louisiana.* New York, 1918. This excellent study begins with 1869, supplementing the work of Professor Ficklen.

MCGREGOR, JAMES C., *The Disruption of Virginia.* New York, 1922. An able monograph in the light of which many oft-stated views, particularly as to the extent of popular support for the new State movement, have had to be revised.

MARSHALL, JOHN A., *The American Bastile: A History of Illegal Arrests and Imprisonments during the Civil War.* Philadelphia, 1869. A compilation prepared by the historian of the Association of Prisoners of State. Made up of the experiences of prisoners. Adds little to the *Official Records*, except abuse.

MOORE, ALBERT B., *Conscription and Conflict in the Confederacy.* New York, 1924. Ch. VIII, "The Courts and Conscription," gives judicial opinion of Confederate conscription and throws indirect light upon the Federal conscription law.

PARKER, GRANVILLE, *The Formation of the State of West Virginia.* Wellsburg, W. Va., 1875.

PLUM, WILLIAM R., *The Military Telegraph during the Civil War in the United States.* Chicago, 1882.

RANDALL, JAMES G., *The Confiscation of Property during the Civil War.* Indianapolis, Henkel-Randall Printing Co. (formerly the Mutual Printing Co.), 1913. A dissertation for the University of Chicago, much condensed in publication.

SCOTT, EBEN GREENOUGH, *Reconstruction during the Civil War in the United States of America.* Boston and New York, 1895. Devoted largely to constitutional history and a discussion of the legal relation of the States to the Union.

SELLERY, GEORGE CLARK, *Lincoln's Suspension of Habeas Corpus as Viewed by Congress.* Bulletin of the Univ. of Wisconsin, Hist. Ser., Vol. I, No. 3, pp. 213-286. Traces the development of legislative action concerning the writ.

TREXLER, HARRISON ANTHONY, *Slavery in Missouri, 1804-1865.* Baltimore, 1914. A Johns Hopkins dissertation, largely based on unpublished sources.

UPTON, EMORY, Brevet Major General, U. S. Army, *The Military Policy of the United States.* Washington, Gov't. Ptg. Office, 1911. An elaborate, scholarly study which devotes much space to the Civil War, reviewing executive and legislative measures to meet the emergency, treating the President's war powers, and criticizing in detail the inefficiency which characterized the military policy of that period.

WEEDEN, W. B., *War Government, Federal and State.* Boston, 1906. Deals with certain phases of administration during the Civil War, showing that government in State and nation was badly muddled and that the public business was inefficiently and wastefully handled.

WHITE, HOWARD, *Executive Influence in Determining Military Policy in the United States.* Univ. of Ill. Studies in Soc. Sciences, Vol. XII, No. 1. Urbana, Ill., 1924.

WHITING, WILLIAM, *War Powers under the Constitution of the United States.* Boston, 1871. Written first as war pamphlets and later republished in many editions. Shows more legal learning than judgment, and seeks to justify everything which the Government did. Author was Solicitor for the War Department at the time of the Civil War. As a study of constitutional problems of the Civil War this volume, in spite of its faults, has value, particularly because of its many references, and the documents which it incorporates.

WILLEY, WILLIAM P., *An Inside View of the Formation of West Virginia.* Wheeling, 1901. An uncritical work written from the viewpoint of the separationists. Contains character sketches of prominent West Virginians.

Articles in Periodicals

ADAMS, CHARLES FRANCIS, "John Quincy Adams and Martial Law," *Mass. Hist. Soc. Proc.*, 2d Ser., XV, 436-478 (1902). Emphasizes Adams' support of emancipation as a possible military measure and credits him with originating the Emancipation Proclamation.

BALLANTINE, "Unconstitutional Claims of Military Authority." *Yale Law Jour.*, Jan., 1915.

DOUGLAS, CLARENCE D., "Conscription and the Writ of Habeas Corpus during the Civil War." *Historical Papers*, published by Trinity College Historical Society, Durham, N. C., Ser. XIV, 1923.

DUNNING, WILLIAM A., "Disloyalty in Two Wars." *Am. Hist. Rev.*, XXIV, 625-630.

FISHER, S. G., "Suspension of Habeas Corpus during the War of the Rebellion." *Pol. Sci. Quar.*, III, 454-488.

HAGAN, HORACE H., "United States *vs.* Jefferson Davis," *Sewanee Review*, XXV, 220-225 (April, 1917).

HALL, JAMES PARKER, "Freedom of Speech in War Time." *Columbia Law Rev.*, XXI, 526-537.

HART, A. B., "Constitutional Questions of the Civil War." McLaughlin and Hart, *Cyclopedia of American Government*, I, 288.

HOLDSWORTH, W. S., "Martial Law Historically Considered." *Law Quart. Rev.*, XVIII, 117-132.

J. H. A., "Martial Law." *American Law Register*, o. s. IX, 498-511. (May, 1861.)

NICHOLS, ROY F., "The United States *vs.* Jefferson Davis." *Am. Hist. Rev.*, XXXI, 266-284.

OAKES, JAMES, "Lessons from the Civil War Conscription Acts." *Ill. Law Rev.*, XI, 77-97.

PEABODY, JUDGE C. A., "The United States Provisional Court for Louisiana, 1862-1865." *Amer. Hist. Ass. Ann. Rep.*, 1892, pp. 197-210.

POLLOCK, FREDERICK, "What is Martial Law?" *Law Quart. Rev.*, XVIII, 152-158.

"The Provisional Judiciary of Louisiana." *Amer. Law Reg.*, n.s., IV, 257-269 (Mar., 1865).

RANDALL, JAMES G., "Some Legal Aspects of the Confiscation Acts of the Civil War." *Am. Hist. Rev.*, XVIII, 79-96.

——, "Captured and Abandoned Property during the Civil War." *Am. Hist. Rev.*, XIX, 65-79.

——, "The Virginia Debt Controversy." *Pol. Sci. Quar.*, XXX, 553-577.

——, "The Newspaper Problem in Its Bearing upon Military Secrecy during the Civil War." *Am. Hist. Rev.*, XXIII, 303-323.

——, "The Indemnity Act of 1863: A Study in the Wartime Immunity of Governmental Officers." *Mich. Law Rev.*, XX, 589-613.

——, "The Rule of Law under the Lincoln Administration." Paper read at the meeting of the American Historical Association, December, 1925.

RICHARDS, H. EARLE, "Martial Law." *Law Quart. Rev.*, XVIII, 133-142.

SHANNON, FRED A., "State Rights and the Union Army." *Miss. Vall. Hist. Rev.*, XII, 51-71.

——, "Conscription and the Bounty Problem." Paper read at the meeting of the American Historical Association, December, 1925.

——, "The Mercenary Factor in the Creation of the Union Army." *Miss. Vall. Hist. Rev.*, XII, 523-549.

WATSON, D. K., "The Trial of Jefferson Davis: An Interesting Constitutional Question." *Yale Law Jour.*, XXIV, 669-676.

Newspapers

It is impracticable to give a list of newspapers for the Civil War period. The writer's above-mentioned article in the *American Historical Review* (XXIII, 303-323) sets forth some of the conditions under which the papers of the time were published and suggests certain precautions which the historian should observe in their use. In a legal study the daily journals must often be consulted as the only published source of certain otherwise unreported judicial decisions. One finds in the New York *Tribune* for December, 1864, for instance, and also in the *Times*, elaborate reports of the Opdyke-Weed libel suit; and one must turn to the daily papers for reports of the prosecution of General Dix for his action in suppressing the New York *World* in 1864. Much of the material for a study of the formation of West Virginia is to be found in the pages of the Wheeling *Intelligencer*. Among the metropolitan dailies the

Tribune, *World*, *Times*, *Daily News*, and *Herald* of New York, and the Chicago *Tribune* deserve special mention. One must make allowance for anti-Lincoln bias in reading the Chicago *Times* and the same may be said of the New York *Daily News*, the New York *World*, and, to a certain extent, the New York *Herald*. The eccentricities of Greeley are evident in the New York *Tribune*. Specific instances in which newspaper sources have been used for statements incorporated into the text of this book are indicated in the footnotes. Representative lists of newspapers are given in the following guides: *A Check List of Newspapers in the Library of Congress* (Washington, 1901); *Checklist of Newspapers and Official Gazettes in the New York Public Library* (New York, 1915); *A List of Newspapers in the Yale University Library* (New Haven, 1916); Frank W. Scott, *Newspapers and Periodicals of Illinois, 1814-1879* (*Illinois Historical Collections*, Vol. VI).

Archives and Manuscripts

To a large extent the material for this book has been sought in unpublished sources, and in the following pages the more important groups of such sources are indicated. An introduction to the archives of the Federal Government is given in C. H. Van Tyne and W. G. Leland, *Guide to the Archives of the Government of the United States in Washington* (2d ed., Washington, 1907). A very complete report by the Librarian of Congress on Federal archives outside of Washington is given in *House Document 1443*, 62d Congress, 3d session (1913). The most important guide to manuscripts is the *Handbook of Manuscripts in the Library of Congress* (Washington, 1918). As new manuscripts are acquired by the Library of Congress they are listed in the *American Historical Review*.

Archives of the Treasury Department, Washington. Especially for the subject of confiscation these archives are of great value. The mass of material concerning captured property, the records touching Confederate sequestration, the papers concerning the "cotton loan" and other transactions of the Confederate treasury, and the more general collection of Confederate archives (partly captured and partly purchased), are among the historical material in these records.

Attorney General's Papers. MSS. formerly in the Library of Congress, Washington. Information concerning the Attorney General's office is to be found in James S. Easby Smith, *The Department of Justice: Its History and Functions* (Wash., 1904) and in the following documents: *Sen. Rep. 507*, 50 Cong., 1 sess.; *Sen. Ex. Doc. 109*, 47 Cong., 1 sess. The Department of Justice was not created until 1870 and the personnel of the Attorney General's office at the time of the Civil War was inadequate for its heavy duties, as there were only eight persons on the entire staff of the office in 1862, including four clerks and a messenger. The papers of historical interest for the Civil War period are the incoming letters (which are a mere jumble with no sort of arrangement), the letter books, giving fair copies of outgoing letters, and beautifully written copies of instructions to district attorneys. By a laborious examination of the great mass of incoming papers the writer has found many things of historical interest, especially communications from district attorneys over the country regarding conditions attending the enforcement of war statutes.

Archives of the State Department, Washington. Inasmuch as the Secretary of State had charge of arbitrary arrests in 1861, the archives of the State Department are of value for this subject. Lists of political prisoners arrested early in the war are to be found among the Department's records, but these have been published in the *Official Records*. The "domestic letters" cover many subjects such as the liability of aliens under the Conscription Act, arrests of foreigners, instructions to Federal officials regarding the disregard of the writ of *habeas corpus*, pretended foreign citizenship of Confederate agents, and requests to the Post Office Department regarding the interception of letters of suspected persons.

United States District and Circuit Court Records. The records of the United States circuit and district courts are for the most part well preserved, except where some accident has caused their destruction, as in the case of the Chicago fire of 1871. In the docket books the arrangement is chronological and a brief indication of the proceedings under each case is given, but for the full record one must turn to the papers filed under the various cases. The importance of these records for unreported cases is obvious, but it should be added that the most significant actions have been reported in the set known as *Federal Cases*.

Records of the United States Supreme Court. Since the published reports of the Supreme Court include only cases brought to trial, one must consult the original docket for information regarding such a case as that of Jefferson Davis, in which a decree of the Supreme Court was sought but not obtained, owing to the dismissal of the case. A useful compilation known as "Records and Briefs of the United States Supreme Court" is found in the Law Division of the Library of Congress. In this compilation one may obtain full printed records (which often exceed a thousand pages for a single case), briefs of counsel, reports of special masters, and like material.

State Archives. The archives of the State governments for the period of the Civil War are of uneven quality. In Ohio, Pennsylvania, Illinois and elsewhere, the governors' correspondence is not available. The writer was unable, for instance, to satisfy his curiosity as to what became of the papers of Governor Curtin of Pennsylvania. The correspondence of Governor Morton of Indiana may be consulted in the State Library at Indianapolis and certain papers of Governor Salomon of Wisconsin are deposited in the library of the State Historical Society at Madison. The executive papers at Richmond, Virginia, are of interest. While not attempting the impossible task of searching all the State archival material, the writer examined enough to afford an insight into typical problems of State administration in their relation to the National Government.

Bates Diary. The rather full diary of Attorney General Bates is not a systematic journal, but rather a series of occasional jottings, with notes, clippings, pasted-in letters, and miscellaneous material. Bates resisted certain extraordinary measures of military control and in general took a conservative attitude, emphasizing civil rights as against governmental encroachment. For access to this diary in manuscript the author is indebted to Miss Helen Nicolay of Washington. For the published diary see below under Howard K. Beale, p. 550.

Bates Papers. Some of Bates' papers are to be found in the Jefferson Memorial Library at St. Louis.

Diary of Orville H. Browning. A voluminous journal by Senator Browning of Illinois, successor of Douglas, devoted friend of Lincoln, and Secretary of the Interior under Johnson. With minor gaps the record is continuous from 1850 to 1881, and it is very full for the years of the Civil War when Browning held a uniquely intimate and confidential relation with the President. As a man of conservative views, Browning differed with Lincoln on various measures in the latter part of the war, but he always retained the President's confidence and friendship. The diary throws much light on the personnel and activities of the war Congresses. An interesting account of the diary, with significant extracts, is to be found in a pamphlet entitled "The Diary of Orville H. Browning: A New Source for Lincoln's Presidency," by Professor Theodore Calvin Pease of the University of Illinois (University of Chicago Press, 1924). See *The Diary of Orville Hickman Browning*, ed. by T. C. Pease and J. G. Randall, *Illinois Historical Collections*, XX, XXII, 1925-1933.

Johnson Papers. MSS. in the Library of Congress, Washington. This important collection comprises 179 bound volumes covering the period from 1831 to 1891. It is of importance not only for Johnson's presidency, but for the period of his service as military governor of Tennessee.

Pierpoint Papers. MSS. in the Virginia State Library, Richmond. There are thirty-three boxes in this interesting collection of archives of the "restored government" of Virginia. The papers are rich in local color, revealing many details that have never appeared in print, and are of importance for a study of the West Virginia movement. Besides a great number of letters to and from Governor Pierpoint, the collection includes election returns (revealing the irregular character of Unionist elections in Virginia), signed oaths of allegiance to the United States, and reports of executive officials.

Stanton Papers. MSS. in the Library of Congress, Washington. Original letters of Lincoln, Chase, Grant, Seward, Curtin, Bates, Greeley and many other prominent men are found in this voluminous collection. Though military matters claim chief attention, a great variety of subjects is covered. The collection comprises thirty-six volumes of manuscripts.

Trumbull Manuscripts. Library of Congress, Washington. An extensive collection comprising seventy-seven volumes of private correspondence from 1855 to 1872. The papers are most numerous for the year 1861. They include many interesting letters from Trumbull's Illinois constituents concerning public measures with which he was particularly associated, such as the second Confiscation Act and the Habeas Corpus Act. There are many papers giving expressions of sentiment concerning the slavery question. Photo-duplicates of the more important papers are available in the Illinois Historical Survey, Urbana Illinois.

Welles Papers. MSS. in the Library of Congress, Washington. This collection includes miscellaneous letters, Welles' official letter books as Secretary of the Navy, manuscripts of magazine articles, the original manuscript of the Welles Diary, clippings, and scrap books.

SUPPLEMENTAL BIBLIOGRAPHY

This supplemental list includes a selection of works since 1926, when the original edition of the present book appeared. There is no effort here to give "a Lincoln bibliography." For that purpose, see *Lincoln Bibliography* by Jay Monaghan for books down to 1939; more recent titles will be found in the files of the *Abraham Lincoln Quarterly*, published by the Abraham Lincoln Association of Springfield, Illinois. That association is now far advanced in its important project of publishing a complete and scholarly edition of Lincoln's works. The early filling of that need will be a welcome boon to Lincoln students. Since the present book does not attempt to treat the Lincoln administration in general (nor Lincoln the lawyer, Lincoln and politics, etc.), there are many titles found in Monaghan that do not appear here. Works mentioned below are not separated into categories, but consolidated into one list alphabetically arranged by authors' surnames.

The list here given is supplemental in two senses. Obviously it should include, for the period since 1926, studies bearing upon problems of the Lincoln administration—e.g., David M. Silver's history of the Supreme Court during the Civil War, Samuel Klaus's book on the Milligan case, and the work of Frank Freidel concerning Lieber and General Orders No. 100. In addition, it has been thought best, in the light of present student interest, to take some account of the considerable literature devoted to problems arising out of World War II. Questions that arose under Lincoln have their later counterparts. Though they are so different in their complexity and dimensions as to be different in kind, these later developments present interesting comparisons, and one may better study them by recurrence to principles long recognized. One may look from the Lincoln period to recent experience, and back once more to the Lincoln situation. This is especially true as to the governing of occupied territory, and the effort (or hope) to assist a conquered enemy toward self rule. It is recognized that this recent material cannot be covered with any claim to completeness, but only by representative titles.

AGNEW, THEODORE L., JR., "The Peace Movement in Illinois, 1864: A Re-interpretation." Master's dissertation (manuscript), Univ. of Ill., 1938.

AMBLER, CHARLES H., *Francis H. Pierpont: Union War Governor of Virginia and Father of West Virginia*. Chapel Hill, 1937.

——, *West Virginia, the Mountain State*. New York, 1940.

ANGLE, PAUL M., *A Shelf of Lincoln Books: A Critical Bibliography of Lincolniana*. New Brunswick, 1946. Evaluated guide to the basic works. Highly useful in the bewildering mass of Lincoln titles.

AUCHAMPAUGH, PHILIP G., "A Great Justice on State and Federal Power." *Tyler's Quar. Hist. and Geneal. Mag.*, XVIII, 72-78 (1936). Gives Taney's unpublished and undelivered opinion that the conscription act of 1863 was unconstitutional.

BAKER, LA FAYETTE C., *Secret Service*. Washington, 1898. The author, head of Stanton's secret police, has been described as "a veritable Fouché." (Thomas D. McCormick, in *Dic. of Amer. Biog.*, I, 523.)

BARINGER, WILLIAM E., *A House Dividing: Lincoln as President Elect*. Springfield, Ill., 1945. Background of the war, problems as to compromise, making of the cabinet, etc.

BASLER, ROY P., ed., *Abraham Lincoln: His Speeches and Writings*. Cleveland and New York, 1946. Valuable for its considerable coverage; indispensable for its scholarly editing.

BEALE, HOWARD K., *The Diary of Edward Bates*, 1859-1866. Washington, 1933. Vol. IV of *Ann. Rep., Amer. Hist. Assoc.* for the year 1930. Prior to this publication the Bates diary was used in manuscript by the present writer, through the kindness of Miss Helen Nicolay.

——, "What Historians Have Said About the Causes of the Civil War." Included in *Theory and Practice in Historical Study*, ed. by C. A. Beard and others. New York, 1946.

BERDAHL, CLARENCE A., *Documents and Readings in American Government* (with J. M. Mathews). New York, 1928. Revised 1947.

BINKLEY, WILFRED ELLSWORTH, *The Powers of the President; Problems of American Democracy.* Garden City, N. Y., 1937.

BONHAM, MILLEDGE L., "New York and the Civil War." *History of the State of New York*, ed. by A. C. Flick, vol. VII. New York, 1933-1937.

BOUDIN, LOUIS B., *Government by Judiciary.* 2 vols. New York, 1932.

BRYSON, LYMAN, "Lincoln in Power." *Pol. Sci. Quar.*, LXI, 161-174 (1946).

BULLARD, F. LAURISTON, "Lincoln Pardons Conspirator on Plea of an English Statesman." *Amer. Bar Assoc. Jour.*, XXV, 215-220 (1939). Alfred Rubery, British youth convicted for engaging in privateering escapade, was pardoned by Lincoln as an act of friendship to John Bright.

——, "Lincoln and the Courts of the District of Columbia." *Ibid.*, XXIV, 117-120 (1938).

——, "Abraham Lincoln and the Statehood of Nevada." *Ibid.*, XXVI, 210-213, 313-317 (1940).

——, "Anna Ella Carroll and Her 'Modest' Claim." *Lincoln Herald*, L, 2-10 (Oct., 1948). Much has been claimed for Miss Carroll of Maryland—e.g., as to war powers—and some of the treatment has been fictional. Bullard's is the best historical appraisal.

BURGESS, JOHN W., *The Civil War and the Constitution, 1859-1865.* 2 vols. New York, 1901.

CARPENTER, A. H., "Military Government of Southern Territory, 1861-1865." *Ann. Rep., Amer. Hist. Assoc. for the Year 1900* (2 vols., Washington, 1901), I, 467-98.

CATTERALL, HELEN T., ed., *Judicial Cases Concerning American Slavery and the Negro.* 3 vols. Washington, 1926-1932.

CHAFEE, ZECHARIAH, Jr., *Free Speech in the United States.* Cambridge, Mass., 1941 and 1948.

COLBY, ELBRIDGE, "Occupation Under the Laws of War." *Columbia Law Rev.*, XXV, 904-922; XXVI, 146-170 (1925-1926).

COLE, ARTHUR C., "Lincoln and the American Tradition of Civil Liberty." *Jour. Ill. State Hist. Soc.*, XIX, 102-114 (1926).

—, "Lincoln's Election an Immediate Menace to Slavery in the States?" *Amer. Hist. Rev.*, XXXVI, 740-767 (1931). See also Hamilton, J. G. de R. This question was debated between Dr. Cole and Dr. Hamilton before the Miss. Vall. Hist. Assoc. at Chattanooga in 1930.

COMMAGER, HENRY STEELE, *Documents of American History*. New York, 1948. Contains the leading documents in American constitutional history. Valuable source book. Useful for bibliography.

CONNOR, SIDNEY, and FRIEDRICH, CARL J., eds. "Military Government." *Annals, Amer. Acad. Pol. and Soc. Sci.*, vol. 267 (1950). Entire issue devoted to military government. Covers all areas.

CORWIN, EDWARD SAMUEL, *The President, Office and Powers: History and Analysis of Practice and Opinion*. New York, 1940. 3rd ed., 1948.

—, *Liberty Against Government: The Rise, Flowering and Decline of a Famous Concept*. Baton Rouge, 1948.

COULTER, E. MERTON, *The Confederate States of America 1861-1865*. Baton Rouge, 1950. *A History of the South*, vol. VII. Questions under Lincoln involved problems for the South as well as for the North. The legal nature of the Civil War is well treated on pp. 60 ff. (See esp. 61 n.)

CRAVEN, AVERY, "The Civil War and the Democratic Process." *Abr. Lincoln Quar.*, IV, 269-292 (1947). The conflict involved "contradiction of the basic assumption . . . that men are endowed with reason . . .; that rational discussion of issues . . . [constitutes] a procedure by which [differing] groups . . . could live and work in unity. . . ."

—, *The Repressible Conflict*. Baton Rouge, 1939. Three lectures dealing with factors prior to April, 1861.

—, *The Coming of the Civil War*. New York, 1942. Refutes the over-familiar concept that the war was "inevitable."

CURRENT, RICHARD NELSON, *Old Thad Stevens: A Story of Ambition*. Madison, Wis., 1942. Informative on Lincoln's difficulties with Congress (e.g., in chap. xiii, "With Malice toward Lincoln.")

CUSHMAN, ROBERT EUGENE, *Leading Constitutional Decisions.* 7th ed., New York, 1940.

DAYTON, ARETAS, A., "Recruitment and Conscription in Illinois during the Civil War." Doctoral dissertation (manuscript), Univ. of Ill., 1940.

DENNETT, TYLER, ed., *Lincoln and the Civil War in the Diaries and Letters of John Hay.* New York, 1939.

DODD, WILLIAM E., "Abraham Lincoln and His Problem, 1861." *Research and Progress,* I, 106-110 (1935).

DORRIS, JONATHAN TRUMAN, "President Lincoln's Clemency." *Jour. Ill. State Hist. Soc.,* XX, 547-568 (1928).

—, "*Pardon and Amnesty during the Civil War and Reconstruction* (abstract of doctoral thesis, Univ. of Ill., 1929).

—, Pardoning the Leaders of the Confederacy." *Miss. Vall. Hist. Rev.,* XV, 3-21 (1928).

DOWELL, C. M., *Military Aid to the Civil Power.* Ft. Leavenworth, Kansas, 1925.

DUDLEY, HAROLD M., "The Election of 1864." *Miss. Vall. Hist. Rev.,* XVIII, 500-518 (1932).

DUMOND, DWIGHT L., "The Mississippi: Valley of Decision." *Ibid.,* XXXVI, 3-26 (1949). Deals forcefully with civil rights in relation to antislavery agitation.

—, *The Secession Movement; 1860-1861.* New York, 1931.

—, *Southern Editorials on Secession.* New York, 1931. Intro. treats the secession movement, with survey of Southern sentiment.

DYER, BRAINERD, "Francis Lieber and the American Civil War." *Huntington Libr. Quar.,* II, 449-65 (July 1939).

EDGERTON, HENRY W., "The Incidence of Judicial Control Over Congress." *Cornell Law Quar.,* XXII, 299-348 (1937). Excellent analysis of the practical effect of judicial supremacy. Complete survey by cases. Concludes that, if one thinks of the rights of human beings, there have been very few instances when the Supreme Court has restored such rights by overthrowing acts of Congress.

EISENSCHIML, OTTO, *Why Was Lincoln Murdered?* Boston, 1937. See chap. xxix for criticism of Stanton's methods during Lincoln's presidency.

FAIRMAN, CHARLES, *The Law of Martial Rule.* Chicago, 1931. 2nd., ed. 1943.

——, *Mr. Justice Miller and the Supreme Court, 1862-1900.* Cambridge, Mass., 1939.

FISCHER, LEROY HENRY, "Adam Gurowski and the Civil War: A Radical's Record." Doctoral dissertation (manuscript), Univ. of Ill., 1943. Excellent treatment of this irascible old radical and critic of Lincoln.

——, "Lincoln's Gadfly—Adam Gurowski." *Miss. Vall. Hist. Rev.*, XXXVI, 415-434.

FISH, CARL RUSSELL, *The American Civil War: An Interpretation.* New York, 1937. Edited by William Ernest Smith. Posthumously published work by a distinguished authority.

FRANKLIN, JOHN HOPE, *From Slavery to Freedom.* (New York, 1947.) Elaborate and scholarly study of Negro background and history. Chaps. xv and xvi deal with Civil War period.

FREIDEL, FRANK, *Francis Lieber, Nineteenth Century Liberal.* Baton Rouge, 1948. Important and scholarly biography, showing Lieber's political philosophy, work as publicist, constitutional views, and codification of the usages of war.

——, "General Orders 100 and Military Government." *Miss. Vall. Hist. Rev.*, XXXII, 541-556 (1946).

FRIEDRICH, CARL J., *American Experiences in Military Government,* World War II. New York, 1948.

——, See also Connor, Sidney.

FULLER, GRACE HADLEY, comp. *Military Government: A List of References* (Washington, 1944). Mimeographed list (122 titles) issued by Library of Congress, division of bibliography.

GABRIEL, RALPH H., "American Experience with Military Government." *Amer. Hist. Rev.*, XLIX, 634-637 (July, 1944).

GLENN, GARRARD, *The Army and the Law.* Revised by A. Arthur Schiller. New York, 1943.

GOBLE, GEORGE W., *The Design of Democracy.* (Norman, Okla., 1946). Stanchly upholding freedom of speech, the author writes (p. 109): "We should cultivate the habit of being reasonably certain of our facts before becoming a party to the circulation of stories which reflect upon the honesty or sincerity of persons engaged in political life." This is said apropos of attacks upon Washington, Lincoln, Wilson, and other leaders.

GRAY, WOOD, *The Peace Movement in the Old Northwest, 1860-1865; A Study in Defeatism.* Chicago, 1935.

——, *The Hidden Civil War: The Story of the Copperheads.* New York, 1942.

HAINES, CHARLES GROVE, *The Conflict over Judicial Powers in the United States to 1870.* New York, 1909.

——, *The American Doctrine of Judicial Supremacy.* 2d ed. Berkeley, 1932.

HAMILTON, J. G. DE ROULHAC, "Lincoln's Election an Immediate Menace to Slavery in the States?" *Amer. Hist. Rev.*, XXXVII, 700-711 (1932). See also Cole, Arthur C.

HARBISON, WINFRED A., "The Opposition to President Lincoln within the Republican Party." Doctoral dissertation (manuscript), Univ. of Ill., 1930.

——, See also Kelly, Alfred H.

——, "The Elections of 1862 as a Vote of Want of Confidence in President Lincoln." *Papers of Mich. Acad. of Science*, XIV, 499-513 (1931).

HARRINGTON, FRED HARVEY, *Fighting Politician: Major General N. P. Banks.* Philadelphia, 1948. Treats Lincoln's policy toward Louisiana.

HARRIS, ALFRED G., "Lincoln and the Question of Slavery in the District of Columbia." *Lincoln Herald*, vol. 52:2-16 (Feb., 1950). Deals largely with fugitive slaves. The second of a series of three articles. The first (*ibid.*, June, 1949) dealt with Lincoln's plan of emancipation while in Congress; the third will treat emancipation in the District.

HENDRICK, BURTON J., *Lincoln's War Cabinet*. Boston, 1946.

HESSELTINE, WILLIAM B., *Lincoln and the War Governors*. New York, 1948.

—, "Lincoln's War Governors." *Abr. Lincoln Quar.*, IV, 153-200 (1946).

—, *Civil War Prisons: A Study in War Psychology*. Columbus, Ohio, 1930.

—and WOLF, HAZEL C., "The Altoona Conference and the Emancipation Proclamation." *Pa. Mag. of Hist. and Biog.*, LXXI, 195-205 (1947). Conference of governors designed to assert their authority in the national government and to bring pressure upon Lincoln.

HOCKETT, HOMER C., *The Constitutional History of the United States*. 2 vols. New York, 1939.

HOFSTADTER, RICHARD. *The American Political Tradition and the Men Who Made It*. New York, 1948.

HOLBORN, HAJO, *American Military Government: Its Organization and Policies*. Infantry Journal Press, 1947.

HUBBART, HENRY CLYDE, *The Older Middle West 1840-1880*. New York, 1936. Important for Vallandigham, western protest, "democracy in convulsion," the draft, and like problems.

HUMBERT, W. H., *The Pardoning Power of the President*. Washington, 1941.

HURST, WILLARD, "Treason in the United States." *Harvard Law Rev.*, LVIII, 226-272; 395-444; 806-846 (1944-1945).

JONES, JOHN PAUL, JR., "Abraham Lincoln and the Newspaper Press during the Civil War." *Americana*, XXXV, 459-472 (1941).

KELLY, ALFRED H. and HARBISON, WINFRED A. *The American Constitution: Its Origins and Development*. New York, 1948. Excellent, up-to-date treatise for student use.

KIRKLAND, EDWARD CHASE, *The Peacemakers of 1864*. New York, 1927.

KLAUS, SAMUEL, ed., *The Milligan Case*. New York, 1929.

KLINGBERG, FRANK WYSOR, "James Buchanan and the Crisis of the Union." *Jour. So. Hist.*, IX, 455-474 (1943). Shows, among other things, the rôle of a President in influencing events.

——, "The Southern Claims Commission: A Postwar Agency in Operation." *Miss. Vall. Hist. Rev.*, XXXII, 195-214 (1945).

——, "The Case of the Minors: A Unionist Family within the Confederacy." *Jour. So. Hist.*, XIII, 27-45 (1947).

——, "Operation Reconstruction: A Report on Southern Unionist Planters." *N. C. Hist. Rev.*, XXV, 466-484 (1948).

——. (Note. A book by Dr. Klingberg, being a general study of the Southern Claims Commission, as yet unpublished, will throw new light, as do the above articles, on the subject of Unionism in the South. This commission examined the records of numerous Southerners who claimed wartime loyalty to the United States.)

KONVITZ, MILTON R., *The Constitution and Civil Rights.* New York, 1947. 254 pp.

LAWRENCE, ALEXANDER A., *James Moore Wayne: Southern Unionist.* Chapel Hill, 1943.

LIBRARY OF CONGRESS: *Provisions of Federal Law Held Unconstitutional by the Supreme Court of the United States.* Washington: Govt. Printing Office, 1936. Covers all the cases. Much more than a list or series of citations. Gives extracts from decisions, comments by authorities, etc.

——, "Constitutional Problems of Lincoln's Administration: Books and Articles Published Since 1926." Compiled by Donald H. Mugridge. Unpublished list of fifty-two titles. Gen. Ref. and Bibl. Div., Libr. of Cong., 1950. (This typewritten list was prepared at the request of the author.)

MCLAUGHLIN, ANDREW C., "Lincoln, the Constitution, and Democracy." *Abr. Lincoln Assoc. Papers*, 1936, 25-59.

——, *A Constitutional History of the United States.* New York, 1935.

MCMASTER, JOHN B., *History of the People of the United States During Lincoln's Administration.* New York, 1927.

MACARTNEY, CLARENCE EDWARD, *Lincoln and His Cabinet.* New York, 1931.

MALONE, DUMAS, "Jefferson and Lincoln." *Abr. Lincoln Quar.*, V. 327-347 (1949). Malone notes that Lincoln referred to Jefferson as "the most distinguished politician [public man] of our history."

MANGUM, CHARLES S., *The Legal Status of the Negro.* Chapel Hill, 1940.

MATHEWS, JOHN MABRY, *American Constitutional System.* New York, 1932. Revised 1940.

MEADE, ROBERT D., *Judah P. Benjamin: Confederate Statesman.* New York, 1943.

MEARNS, DAVID C., *The Lincoln Papers: The Story of the Collection with Selections to July 4, 1861.* 2 vols., paged as one. Garden City, N.Y., 1948. A selection from the vast and rich mass of documents in the R. T. Lincoln Collection, Library of Congress, opened on July 26, 1947. See intro. for scholarly history of the Collection.

MILTON, GEORGE FORT, *Abraham Lincoln and the Fifth Column.* New York, 1942.

——, *The Use of Presidential Power, 1789-1943.* Boston, 1944.

MITCHELL, STEWART, *Horatio Seymour of New York.* Cambridge, Mass., 1938.

MONAGHAN, JAY, *Lincoln Bibliography, 1839-1939.* 2 vols. Springfield, Ill., 1943-1945.

MUGRIDGE, DONALD H. See Library of Congress.

NEVINS, ALLAN, *Frémont, Pathmarker of the West.* New York, 1939. Supersedes earlier 2 vol. biography by Nevins. New study with additional material, remodeled narrative, and fresh appraisal.

——, *Ordeal of the Union.* 4 vols. New York, 1947-50. Projected multi-volume work. Comprehensive and readable history of the American people in the period of internal conflict.

NICHOLS, ROY FRANKLIN, *The Disruption of American Democracy.* New York, 1948. Traces factional strife before 1860, when, for the only time in American history, the decision at the presidential polls was not peaceably accepted.

NICOLAY, HELEN, *Lincoln's Secretary: A Biography of John G. Nicolay.* New York, 1949. Important for new material drawn from Nicolay's letters and papers.

——, "Lincoln's Cabinet." *Abr. Lincoln Quar.*, V., 255-292 (1949).

NYE, RUSSEL B., *Fettered Freedom: Civil Liberties and the Slavery Controversy, 1830-1860.* East Lansing, Mich., 1949. Treats in detail such subjects as petition, use of mails, academic freedom, freedom of the press, etc. Denial of elemental constitutional rights to antislavery men is a theme that runs through the book.

——, "Civil Liberties and the Antislavery Controversy." *Science and Society*, Spring, 1945.

The Occupation of Enemy Territory. A series of fourteen articles by Carl J. Friedrich, George Boas, and others. *Pub. Opinion Quar.*, Winter, 1943. The whole issue is devoted to this subject.

PARGELLIS, STANLEY, "Lincoln's Political Philosophy." *Abr. Lincoln Quar.*, III, 275-290 (1945).

PARKS, JOSEPH H., "A Confederate Trade Center Under Federal Occupation: Memphis, 1862 to 1865." *Jour. So. Hist.*, VII, 289-314 (1941).

PATTON, JAMES W., *Unionism and Reconstruction in Tennessee, 1860-1869.* Chapel Hill, 1934.

PIERSON, WILLIAM W., JR., "The [Congressional] Committee on the Conduct of the Civil War." *Amer. Hist. Rev.*, XXIII, 550-576 (1918).

POLLARD, JAMES E., *The Presidents and the Press.* New York, 1947. For Lincoln, see pp. 312-396.

POMEROY, EARL S., "Lincoln, the Thirteenth Amendment, and the Admission of Nevada." *Pac. Hist. Rev.*, XII, 362-368 (1943).

POST, CHARLES GORDON, *The Supreme Court and Political Questions.* Johns Hopkins Univ. Studies . . ., LIV, no. 4. Baltimore, 1936.

POTTER, DAVID M., *Lincoln and His Party in the Secession Crisis.* New Haven, Conn., 1942.

PRATT, HARRY E., "David Davis, 1815-1886." Doctor's dissertation (manuscript), Univ. of Ill., 1930.

——, "The Repudiation of Lincoln's War Policy in 1862—Stuart-Swett Congressional Campaign." *Jour. Ill. State Hist. Soc.*, XXIV, 129-140 (1931).

PRITCHETT, C. HERMAN, *The Roosevelt Court: A Study in Judicial Politics and Values, 1937-1947.* New York, 1948. Useful for present-day parallels of Lincoln's problems. Treats constitutional fundamentals, dissent, "compulsion of the beaten track" as against "law in the making," civil rights, military tribunals, martial law, etc Includes constitutional cases of World War II, such as those of Cramer, Haupt, Viereck, and Yamashita.

RAMSDELL, CHARLES W., "Lincoln and Fort Sumter." *Jour. So. Hist.*, III, 259-288 (1937).

RANDALL, J. G., "The 'Rule of Law' under the Lincoln Administration." *Hist. Outlook*, XVII, 272-278 (1926).

——, "Lincoln in the Role of Dictator." *So. Atl. Quar.*, XXVIII, 236-252 (1929). Shows the inappropriateness of the term "dictator" as applied to Lincoln.

——, "The Interrelation of Social and Constitutional History." *Amer. Hist. Rev.*, XXXV, 1-13 (1929).

——, "Lincoln's Task and Wilson's." *So. Atl. Quar.*, XXIX, 349-368 (1930).

——, *The Civil War and Reconstruction.* Boston, 1937.

——, "The Civil War Restudied." *Jour. So. Hist.*, VI, 439-457 (1940)

——, "When War Came in 1861." *Abr. Lincoln Quar.*, I, 3-42 (1940).

——, "The Unpopular Mr. Lincoln." *Ibid.*, II, 255-280 (1943).

——, "Civil and Military Relationships under Lincoln." *Pa. Mag. of Hist. and Biog.*, July, 1945.

——, *Lincoln the President: Springfield to Gettysburg.* 2 vols. New York 1945. Further volumes in preparation.

——, *Lincoln and the South.* Baton Rouge, 1946.

——, *Lincoln The Liberal Statesman.* New York, 1947.

RANKIN, ROBERT S., *When Civil Law Fails: Martial Law and its Legal Basis in the United States.* Durham, N. C., 1939.

REED, H. CLAY, "Lincoln's Compensated Emancipation Plan and its Relations to Delaware." *Delaware Notes*, Ser. 7, 27-78 (Univ. of Del., 1931).

ROBINSON, WILLIAM M., JR., *The Confederate Privateers*. New Haven, 1928.

——, *Justice in Grey: A History of the Judicial System of the Confederate States of America*. Cambridge, Mass., 1941. Interesting contrasts and parallels to the judicial system of the United States. (The Confederacy had no Supreme Court. Robinson explains why this was so.)

——, "The Confederate District Courts in Admiralty." *So. Atl. Quar.*, XXIX, 190-199 (1930).

ROSKE, RALPH JOSEPH, "The Post Civil War Career of Lyman Trumbull." Doctoral dissertation (manuscript), Univ. of Ill., 1949. Trumbull was important in relation to confiscation, the thirteenth amendment, rights of freedmen, impeachment, etc. Shows the sequel of problems arising under Lincoln and continuing under Johnson.

RUSS, WILLIAM A., JR., "The Struggle Between President Lincoln and Congress over Disfranchisement of Rebels." (Part I), *Susquehanna Univ. Stud.*, March, 1947.

SANDBURG, CARL, *Abraham Lincoln: The War Years*. 4 vols. New York, 1939.

SCHILLER, A. ARTHUR, *Military Law and Defense Legislation*. St. Paul, 1941.

SEITZ, DON C., *Lincoln The Politician*. New York, 1931.

SELLERS, JAMES L., "James R. Doolittle." *Wisconsin Mag. of Hist.*, XVII, XVIII, 3-84.

SHANNON, FRED ALBERT, *The Organization and Administration of the Union Army, 1861-1865*. 2 vols. Cleveland, 1928.

SHAW, ARCHER H., ed. *The Lincoln Encyclopedia: The Spoken and Written Words of A. Lincoln*. New York, 1950. Valuable for Lincoln's utterances arranged by key-words. Unreliable as to authenticity; contains spurious passages. See H. E. Pratt, in *Lincoln Herald*, Feb. 1950, 55-56.

SHUGG, ROGER W., *Origins of Class Struggle in Louisiana: a Social History of White Farmers and Laborers During Slavery and After, 1840-1875.* Baton Rouge, 1939.

SILVER, DAVID MAYER, "The Supreme Court during the Civil War." Doctoral dissertation (manuscript), Univ. of Ill., 1940. To be developed and prepared for publication by Dr. Silver, now at Butler University.

SMITH, CHARLES W., *Roger B. Taney, Jacksonian Jurist.* Chapel Hill, N. C., 1936.

SMITH, DONNAL V., *Chase and Civil War Politics.* Ohio Hist. Coll., vol. II. Columbus, 1931.

SMITH, EDWARD CONRAD, *The Borderland in the Civil War.* New York, 1927. Treats "restoration" of Virginia, the Copperheads, etc.

SMITH, GEORGE WINSTON, "Carpetbag Imperialism in Florida 1862-1868." *Fla. Hist. Quar.* Pt. I, XXVII, 99-130 (1948). Pt. II, XXVII, 260-299 (1949).

SMITH, PAUL S., "First Use of the Term 'Copperhead.'" *Amer. Hist. Rev.*, XXXII, 799-800 (1927).

SMITH, WILLIAM ERNEST, *The Francis Preston Blair Family in Politics.* 2 vols. New York, 1933.

SPAIGHT, J. M., *War Rights on Land* (London, 1911).

SQUIRES, J. DUANE, "Some Enduring Achievements of the Lincoln Administration, 1861-1865." *Abr. Lincoln Quar.*, V, 191-211 (1948).

STAMPP, KENNETH M., "Lincoln and the Strategy of Defense in the Crisis of 1861." *Jour. So. Hist.*, XI, 297-323 (1945).

——, *Indiana Politics During the Civil War.* Indianapolis, 1949.

——, *And the War Came: The North in the Secession Crisis.* Baton Rouge, 1950.

SWISHER, CARL B., *Roger B. Taney.* New York, 1935.

——, *American Constitutional Development.* Boston, 1943.

——, *Stephen J. Field, Craftsman of the Law.* Wash., D. C., 1930.

TILLEY, JOHN SHIPLEY, *Lincoln Takes Command.* Chapel Hill, N. C. 1941. Severely anti-Lincoln.

U. S. General Staff, *Rules of Land Warfare*, War Department Doc. 467. Washington, 1914.

U. S. War Department, *Field Manual 27-10*, *Rules of Land Warfare.* Washington, 1940.

WALL, A. J., *A Sketch of the Life of Horatio Seymour, 1810-1886.* New York, 1929.

WARREN, CHARLES, *The Making of the Constitution.* Boston, 1928. Throws light on intention of framers.

WILEY, BELL I., *Southern Negroes, 1861-1865.* New Haven, 1938.

WILLIAMS, T. HARRY, *Lincoln and the Radicals.* Madison, Wis., 1941.

——, "The Committee on the Conduct of the War." *Jour. Amer. Mil. Hist. Inst.*, III, 139-156 (1939). Critical study of this "investigating" committee.

WOLDMAN, ALBERT A., *Lawyer Lincoln.* Boston, 1936.

WRIGHT, EDWARD N., *Conscientious Objectors in the Civil War.* Philadelphia, 1931.

ZANE, JOHN MAXCY, "Lincoln the Constitutional Lawyer." *Abr. Lincoln Assoc. Papers*, 1932, 27-108.

ZINK, HAROLD, *American Military Government in Germany.* New York, 1947.

——, "A Political Scientist Looks at Military Government in the European Theater of Operations." *Amer. Pol. Sci. Rev.*, XL, 1097-1112 (1946).

ZORNOW, WILLIAM, "Treason as a Campaign Issue in the Reelection of Lincoln." *Abr. Lincoln Quar.*, V, 348-363 (1949).

INDEX